In anthropology as much as in popular imagination, kings are figures of fascination and intrigue, heroes or tyrants in ways presidents and prime ministers can never be. This collection of essays by two of the world's most distinguished anthropologists—David Graeber and Marshall Sahlins—explores what kingship actually is, historically and anthropologically. As they show, kings are symbols for more than just sovereignty: indeed, the study of kingship offers a unique window into fundamental dilemmas concerning the very nature of power, meaning, and the human condition.

Reflecting on issues such as temporality, alterity, and utopia—not to mention the divine, the strange, the numinous, and the bestial—Graeber and Sahlins explore the role of kings as they have existed around the world, from the BaKongo to the Aztec to the Shilluk and beyond. Richly delivered with the wit and sharp analysis characteristic of Graeber and Sahlins, this book opens up new avenues for the anthropological study of this fascinating and ubiquitous political figure.

* * *

If you deem that anthropology is neither a form of pompous navel-gazing, nor an exercise in making preposterous generalizations out of sketchy personal experiences, this book is for you. With impeccable scholarship, conceptual imagination, and wit, David Graeber and Marshall Sahlins think anew, and within a broad comparative scope, an ancient and illustrious question: why and how can a single man come to rule over the many as the embodiment or the delegate of a god? Such a question, they show, can only be answered by shifting towards an analysis where human, non-human, and meta-human persons are treated on the same ontological level as parts of a hierarchical cosmic polity. A golden spike in the coffin of eurocentrism, sociocentrism and anthropocentrism!

Philippe Descola (Collège de France), author of *Beyond nature and culture*

The wealth and volume of the ethnographic data analyzed in this book is dizzying. The authors allow us to venture along a variety of paths, ranging from the well-established kingdoms of Africa and Asia to the apparently egalitarian societies of Papua New Guinea and the Americas, revealing the astonishing dispersal of the "stranger king" model. The

authors' decisive step was to reject, on a strictly ethnographic basis, the commonplace analytic division made between cosmology and politics. It is in the ritual sphere, where spirits of diverse kinds meet with humans, that the diverse forms of state originate. A relationship that shows spiritual life, even in societies marked by egalitarianism, to be a domain impregnated with the same relations of hierarchy, control and subjection that characterize the kingdoms of this world. A work that will make history for sure.

Aparecida Vilaça (Museu Nacional/Universidade Federal do Rio de Janeiro), author of *Praying and preying: Christianity in indigenous Amazonia*

Two of the world's leading anthropologists combine their "complementary observations" to offer the most productively disruptive work on kingship since Hocart. The lost world they exhume is a continual affront to contemporary theory: a world where superstructure determines base and sociology recapitulates cosmology (kings are gods imitating men, not the reverse); where connection, competition, and imitation (of galactic hegemons, for example) are the reality and the monadic society a fiction. At the same time, their paleohistory of sovereignty points the way toward a deeper understanding of our contemporary moment, where sovereignty has become "popular" and we are ruled by kleptocrats and buffoon kings.

Sheldon Pollock (Columbia University), author of *The language of the gods in the world of men*

Graeber and Sahlins' *On kings*—a dialogue, not a union—takes Divine Kingship from its burial ground in the classics and puts it deep into enduring concerns about the brutality of political processes over the long haul of human history, ancient and current in ever new forms. In case studies of sovereign rulers conceived as gods, demons, nurslings, ancestral guests, and populist heroes—ultimate strangers—Graeber and Sahlins invite us to reconsider the nature of tyranny from inside the tiger's many mouths and to ask how we might, for once, refuse the king his long customary seat at the table.

Gillian Feeley-Harnik (University of Michigan), author of *The Lord's table: The meaning of food in early Judaism and Christianity*

ON KINGS

Hau
BOOKS

www.haubooks.com

ON KINGS

David Graeber and Marshall Sahlins

Hau Books
Chicago

Cover, Frontispiece of Thomas Hobbes' *Leviathan*, by Abraham Bosse, with creative input from Thomas Hobbes, 1651, with a sketch from *Arctic Researches and Life Among the Esquimaux: Being the Narrative of an Expedition in Search of Sir John Franklin in the Years 1860, 1861, and 1862* by Charles Francis Hall (circa 1865).

Cover and layout design: Sheehan Moore

Typesetting: Prepress Plus (www.prepressplus.in)

ISBN: 978-0-9861325-0-6
LCCN: 2017951344

Hau Books
Chicago Distribution Center
11030 S. Langley
Chicago, IL 60628
www.haubooks.com

Hau Books is printed, marketed, and distributed by The University of Chicago Press.
www.press.uchicago.edu

Table of Contents

Analytical table of contents

Preface

This book is more of a conjunction than a collaboration of its two authors. The several studies on kingship and kingly politics assembled here were originally conceived and written separately by one or the other—for conferences or on other occasions—and were then elaborated with these common purposes in mind. Accordingly, the effect is a set of complementary observations on kingship rather than a cumulative and sustained argument. The closest thing to the latter is the Introduction, where we gather the observations on various aspects of kingship featured in the several individual studies. It almost goes without saying that the overall result is a work "on kings," but not all about kings: it does not pretend to deal with kingship in all its structural dimensions and historical manifestations. Except where otherwise indicated, our observations on kingship concern its so-called "traditional," premodern, or archaic forms—which are, however, its most common, indeed archetypal, forms.

Of the seven essays comprising the book, all but two are published here for the first time. The exceptions are Marshall Sahlins' "The original political society" (chapter 1, published simultaneously with this book in *HAU: Journal of Ethnographic Theory* 7 [2], 2017: 91–128) and David Graeber's "The divine kingship of the Shilluk: On violence, utopia, and the human condition" (chapter 2, original: *HAU: Journal of Ethnographic Theory* 1 [1], 2011: 1–62). "The original political society" is based on the Inaugural Arthur M. Hocart Lecture at SOAS, University of London, April 29, 2016). Chapter 3 by Sahlins, "The atemporal dimensions of history: In the old Kongo kingdom, for example," was developed from a paper in the conference on *The varieties of historical experience* at the University of Chicago (April 2014); chapter 4 by Sahlins, "The stranger-kingship of the Mexica," was a plenary lecture at the Fiftieth Anniversary Celebration of the Museo Nacional de Antropología, Mexico (October 2014); chapter 5 by Graeber, "People as nursemaids of the king: notes on monarchs as children, women's uprisings, and the return of the ancestral dead in central Madagascar," was written for this volume but appeared in abbreviated form as "Le peuple, nurse du roi: notes sur les monarques enfants dans le centre de Madagascar," in *Madagascar, d'une crise l'autre: ruptures et continuité*, edited by Mireille Razafindrakoto, François Roubaud, and Jean-Michel Wachsberger (Paris: ORSTOM, 2017, pp. 120–44); chapter 6 by Sahlins, "Cultural politics of core–periphery relations," was developed from the keynote lecture of a conference on Cultural imperialism and soft power at the University of Chicago Center, Beijing (December 2016); and chapter 7 by Graeber, "Notes on the politics of divine kingship: Or, elements for an archaeology of sovereignty," was written for this volume and has not been published elsewhere in any form.

* * *

D. G.: I would like to thank all those who thought with, argued with, helped, or generally put up with me during the period in question, but since I can't fit in all their names, I would like to draw special attention to (in alphabetical order) Neil Aptaker, the late Roy Bhaskar, Sophie Carapetian, Rebecca Coles, Boris T. Corovic, Ayca Cubukcu, Giovanni da Col, Ewa Domaradzka, Magdalen Drummond, Gillian Feeley-Harnik, Stephan Feuchtwang, Livia Filotico, Charlie Gilmore, Stephanie Grohmann, Andrej Grubacic, Havin Guneser, Keith Hart, Rebecca Hudson, Insa Koch, Zeynep Kurban, Erica Lagalisse, Mark Lamont, Nhu Le, Lauren Leve, Rona Lorimer, Sharifa Syed Ahmad Mayang, Christina Moon, Dyan Neary, Yancey Orr, Mathijs Pelkman, Elif Sarican, Alpa Shah, John Summers, Marine Temersohn, Terence Turner, David Wengrow, Hylton White, and Heather Williams. Finally, of course, to my teacher and mentor, Marshall Sahlins. There was a widespread rumor in Chicago that I was "unteachable." I like to think this volume demonstrates that this was not the case.

M. S.: For intellectual aid and comfort in relation to the composition of one or more of my essays, I would like to thank (in alphabetical order) Mauro Alameida, Ralph Austen, Robert Brightman, Manuela Carneiro da Cunha,

Giovanni da Col, Cécile Fromont, Bruce Lincoln, Alan Rumsey, Gregory Schrempp, Alan Strathern, Dame Marilyn Strathern, and Eduardo Viveiros de Castro. Special thanks also to my research assistants, Jonathan Doherty, Sean Dowdy, and Rob Jennings. And gratitude for aid in presentations of relevant lectures or conference papers goes to the following: in Mexico, Antonio Soborit and Leopoldo Trejo Barrientos; in Chicago, Stephan Palmie, Richard Rosengarten, and Charles Stewart; in London, Giovanni da Col, Fabio Gygi, and Edward Simpson; and in Beijing, Judith Farquhar, and Bruce Lincoln. I should acknowledge in advance the patience of readers—or beg their indulgence—for the recurrent expositions of aspects of stranger-kingship and galactic polities. It is not only that these lectures or essays were written on different occasions for different audiences, but that discussions of these same phenomena were necessary for the arguments in each of them. Finally, special thanks to David Graeber: David was a student of mine; I supervised his thesis at the University of Chicago. Since then it has been difficult to say who is the student and who the teacher.

D. G. (London), M. S. (Chicago)
August 2017

Theses on kingship

David Graeber and Marshall Sahlins

STRUCTURES

Kingship in general

Kingship is one of the most enduring forms of human governance. While we cannot know its precise historical origins in time and space, it is attested during virtually all eras on all continents, and for most of human history the tendency was for it to become more common, not less.

What's more, once established, kings appear remarkably difficult to get rid of. It took extraordinary legal acrobatics to be able to execute Charles I and Louis XVI; simply killing a royal family, as with the tsars, leaves one (apparently forever) burdened with substitute tsars; and even today, it seems no coincidence the only regimes almost completely untroubled by the Arab Spring revolts of 2011 were those with longstanding monarchies. Even when kings are deposed, the legal and political framework of monarchy tends to live on, as evidenced in the fact that all modern states are founded on the curious and contradictory principle of "popular sovereignty," that the power once held by kings still exists, just now displaced onto an entity called "the people."

One unanticipated side-effect of the collapse of European colonial empires has been that this notion of sovereignty has become the basis of constitutional orders everywhere—the only partial exceptions being a few places, like Nepal or Saudi Arabia, which had monarchies of their own already.

It follows that any theory of political life that does not take account of this, or that treats kingship as some sort of marginal, exceptional, or secondary phenomenon, is not a very good theory.

In this volume, then, we propose some elements for a theory of kingship. The arguments set out from territory we have both explored already: in the one case, in the classic essays on the stranger-king; in the other, in the divine kingship of the Shilluk. The collection focuses particularly on what has been called "divine" or "sacred" kingship, but with the understanding that a thorough examination of its common features can reveal the deep structures underlying monarchy, and hence politics, everywhere.

What follows are a series of general propositions inspired by the findings of the essays collected in this book. Certain entries, perhaps, lean more toward the perspective of one author than the other, but we believe the dialogic tension to be fertile, and that the resulting propositions may suggest important new directions for research.

The cosmic polity

Human societies are hierarchically encompassed—typically above, below, and on earth—in a cosmic polity populated by beings of human attributes and metahuman powers who govern the people's fate. In the form of gods, ancestors, ghosts, demons, species-masters, and the animistic beings embodied in the creatures and features of nature, these metapersons are endowed with far-reaching powers of human life and death, which, together with their control of the conditions of the cosmos, make them the all-round arbiters of human welfare and illfare. Even many loosely structured hunting and gathering peoples are thus subordinated to beings on the order of gods ruling over great territorial domains and the whole of the human population. There are kingly beings in heaven even where there are no chiefs on earth.

It follows that the state of nature has the nature of the state. Given the governance of human society by metaperson authorities with ultimate life-and-death powers, something quite like the state is a universal human condition.

It also follows that kings are imitations of gods rather than gods of kings—the conventional supposition that divinity is a reflex of society notwithstanding. In the course of human history, royal power has been derivative of and dependent on divine power. Indeed, no less in stateless societies than in major kingdoms, the human authorities emulate the ruling cosmic powers—if in a reduced form. Shamans have the miraculous powers of spirits, with whom, moreover, they interact. Initiated elders or clan leaders act the god, perhaps in masked form, in presiding over human and natural growth. Chiefs are greeted and treated in the same ways as gods. Kings control nature itself. What usually passes for the divinization of human rulers is better described historically as the humanization of the god.

As a corollary, there are no secular authorities: human power is spiritual power—however pragmatically it is achieved. Authority over others may be acquired by superior force, inherited office, material generosity, or other means; but the power to do or be so is itself deemed that of ancestors, gods, or other external metapersons who are the sources of human vitality and mortality. In this cultural framework, a privileged relation to the metapersonal rulers of the human fate is the raison d'être of earthly social power. Moreover, as demonstrated in worldly accomplishments, this access to metahuman powers may have subjugation effects on people beyond those directly affected by the acts of the persons of authority. It's "charisma"—in the original, god-infused sense.

In this god-infused sense, Shilluk say the king is Juok (the god), but Juok is not the king. The divinity of the king is a kind of intersubjective animism. As a modality of the One over Many, divinity itself can be understood as the personified head of a class of things that are thus so many instances/instantiations of the godhead—which is also to say that as a partible person, the god is immanent in the creatures and features of his or her realm. Hawaiians speak of symbolically relevant plants, animals, and persons as so many "bodies" (*kino lau*) of the god: in which sense Captain Cook was famously the god Lono, but Lono was not Captain Cook. Such intersubjective animism is not all that rare: shamans are possessed by their familiars and victims by their witches. Idolatry and kinship are likewise forms of a broad metaphysics of intersubjective being.

Compared with the kind of cosmic polities that exist among foragers and many others, mortal kingship represents a limit on state power. There is simply no way that any mortal human, whatever his pretensions, whatever the social apparatus at his disposal could ever really wield as much power as a god. And most kings, despite the absolute nature of their claims, never seriously make the attempt.

For half of humanity, though, the creation of mortal kingship represents a major blow: because kings are, in virtually every known case, archetypically male. Nowadays, scholars are used to writing off Paleolithic or Neolithic representations of powerful female figures as mere "mythological" representations, of no political significance, but in the cosmic polities which then existed, this could not have been the case. If so, fixing divine political power in the male head of a royal household was a blow for patriarchy in two ways: not only was the primary human manifestation of divine power now masculine, but the main purpose of the ideal household is producing powerful men.

The precise historical trajectory by which divine powers—sovereignty properly speaking—devolved from metahuman beings to actual human beings, if it can ever be reconstructed, will be likely to take many unexpected turns. For instance: we know of societies (in aboriginal California, or Tierra del Fuego) where arbitrary orders are given only during rituals in which human beings impersonate gods, but those who give the orders are not the gods, but clowns, who appear to represent divine power in its essence; in related societies (e.g., the Kwakiutl), this develops into clown-police who hold sway during an entire ritual season; then, in yet others, into more straightforward seasonal police. In such cases, sovereignty is contained in time: outside the specific ritual or seasonal context, decentralization ensues, and those vested with sovereign powers during the ritual season are no different from, and have no more say than, anybody else. Sacred kingship, in contrast, would appear to be largely a means of containing sovereign power in space. The king, it is almost always asserted, has total power over the lives and possessions of his subjects; but only when he is physically present. As a result, an endless variety of strategies are employed to limit the king's freedom of motion. Yet there is at the same time a mutually constitutive relation between the king's containment and his power: the very taboos that constrain him are also what render him a transcendent metabeing.

Stranger-king formations

Stranger-kingdoms are the dominant form of premodern state the world around, perhaps the original form. The kings who rule them are foreign by ancestry and identity. The dynasty typically originates with a heroic prince from a greater outside realm: near or distant, legendary or contemporary, celestial or terrestrial. Alternatively, native rulers assume the identity and sovereignty of exalted kings from elsewhere and thus become foreigners—as in the Indic kingdoms of Southeast Asia—rather than foreigners becoming native rulers. The polity is in any case dual: divided between rulers who are foreign by nature—perpetually so, as a necessary condition of their authority—and the underlying autochthonous people, who are the "owners" of the country. The dual constitution is constantly reproduced in narrative and ritual, even as it is continuously enacted in the differential functions, talents, and powers of the ruling aristocracy and the native people.

The kingdom is neither an endogenous formation nor does it develop in isolation: it is a function of the relationships of a hierarchically ordered, intersocietal historical field. The superiority of the ruling aristocracy was not engendered by the process of state formation so much as the state was engendered by the a priori superiority of an aristocracy from elsewhere—endowed by nature with a certain *libido dominandi*. The ruling class precedes and makes a subject class.

On his way to the kingdom, the dynastic founder is notorious for exploits of incest, fratricide, patricide, or other crimes against kinship and common morality; he may also be famous for defeating dangerous natural or human foes. The hero manifests a nature above, beyond, and greater than the people he is destined to rule—hence his power to do so. However inhibited or sublimated in the established kingdom, the monstrous and violent nature of the king remains an essential condition of his sovereignty. Indeed, as a sign of the metahuman sources of royal power, force, notably as demonstrated in victory, can function politically as a positive means of attraction as well as a physical means of domination.

For all the transgressive violence of the founder, however, his kingdom is often peacefully established. Conquest is overrated as the source of "state formation." Given their own circumstances—including the internal and external conflicts of the historical field—the indigenous people often have their own reasons for demanding a "king to lead us and to go out before us and fight our battles"

(1 Samuel 8:20). Even in the case of major kingdoms, such as Benin or the Mexica, the initiative may indeed come from the indigenous people, who solicit a prince from a powerful outside realm. Some of what passes for "conquest" in tradition or the scholarly literature consists of usurpation of the previous regime rather than violence against the native population.

While there is frequently no tradition of conquest, there is invariably a tradition of contract: notably in the form of a marriage between the stranger-prince and a marked woman of the indigenous people—most often, a daughter of the native leader. Sovereignty is embodied and transmitted in the native woman, who constitutes the bond between the foreign intruders and the local people. The offspring of the original union—often celebrated as the traditional founder-hero of the dynasty—thereby combines and encompasses in his own person the essential native and foreign components of the kingdom. Father of the country in one respect, as witness also his polygynous and sexual accomplishments, the king is in another the child-chief of the indigenous people, who comprise his maternal ancestry.

Even where there is conquest, by virtue of the original contract it is reciprocal: the mutual encompassment of the autochthonous people by the stranger-king and of the king by the autochthonous people. The installation rites of the king typically recreate the domestication of the unruly stranger: he dies, is reborn, and nurtured and brought to maturity at the hands of native leaders. His wild or violent nature is not so much eliminated as it is sublimated and in principle used for the general benefit: internally as the sanction of justice and order, and externally in the defense of the realm against natural and human enemies. But even as the king is domesticated, the people are civilized. The kingship is a civilizing mission. The advent of the stranger-king is often said to raise the native people from a rudimentary state by bringing them such things as agriculture, cattle, tools and weapons, metals—even fire and cooking, thus a transformation from nature to culture (in the Lévi-Straussian sense). As has been said of African societies, it is not civilized to be without a king.

As allegorized in the original union, the synthesis of the foreign and autochthonous powers—male and female, celestial and terrestrial, violent and peaceful, mobile and rooted, stranger and native, etc.—establishes a cosmic system of social viability. In a common configuration, the autochthonous people's access to the spiritual sources of the earth's fertility is potentiated by king's conveyance of fecundating forces, such as the rain and sun that make the earth bear fruit. Each incomplete in themselves, the native people and foreign rulers together make a viable totality—which is what helps the kingdom to endure, whatever the tensions of their ethnic-cum-class differences.

Although they have surrendered the rule to the foreign king, the native people retain a certain residual sovereignty. By virtue of their unique relation to the powers of the earth, the descendants of the erstwhile native rulers are the chief priests of the new regime. Their control of the succession of the king, including the royal installation rituals, is the warrant of the foreign-derived ruler's legitimacy. In the same vein, the native leaders characteristically have temporal powers as councilors of the stranger-king, sometimes providing his so-called "prime minister." To a significant extent, the principle that the sovereignty of the king is delegated by the people, to whom it belongs by origin and by right, is embedded in stranger-king formations, hence widely known before and apart from its early modern European expressions.

Notwithstanding the superiority and perpetual foreign ethnicity of the ruling aristocracy, they are often not dominant linguistically or culturally, but are assimilated in these respects by the indigenous population. Correlatively, the identity of the kingdom is usually that of the native people.

European colonization is often in significant aspects a late historical form of indigenous stranger-kingship traditions: Captain Cook, Rajah Brooke, and Hernando Cortés, for example.

KINGSHIP POLITICS

In general

Political struggle over the power of the king generally takes the form of a battle between two principles: divine kingship and sacred kingship. In practice, divine kingship is the essence of sovereignty: it is the ability to act as if one were a god; to step outside the confines of the human, and return to rain favor, or destruction, with arbitrariness and impunity. Such power may be accompanied by the theory that the king by doing so demonstrates he is an actual embodiment of some already-existing metahuman being. But it may not be; it could as easily be that by acting in this way, the king himself becomes a metahuman being. Japanese shoguns (a few anyway), Roman emperors, or Ganda *kabaka* could all become gods in their own right. To be "sacred," in contrast, is to be set apart, hedged about by customs and taboos; the restrictions surrounding sacralized kings—"not to touch the earth, not to see the sun" in Frazer's famous dictum— are ways not only of recognizing the presence of unaccountable divine power, but also, crucially, of confining, controlling, and limiting it. One could see these two principles as refractions of different moments of the stranger-king narra- tive: the first, of the terrible power of the king on his arrival; the second, his encompassment and defeat by his subjects. But in this larger sense, both are always present simultaneously.

All the classic issues of divine kingship, then—the royal displays of arbitrary power, the king as scapegoat, regicide (by duel or sacrifice), the use of royal ef- figies, the oracular role of dead monarchs—can best be understood as different moves in a continual chess game played between king and people, in which the king and his partisans attempt to increase the divinity of the king, and the pop- ular factions attempt to increase his sacralization. Stranger-kingship provides the deep structural foundations for a vernacular politics in which representatives of humanity (often literally) did battle with their gods, and sometimes prevailed.

The chief weapon in the hands of those who oppose the expansion of royal power might be termed "adverse sacralization"—to recognize the metahuman status of the monarch, to "keep the king divine" (Richards 1968), requires an elaborate apparatus which renders him, effectively, an abstraction, by hiding, containing, or effacing those aspects of his being that are seen as embodying his mortal nature. Kings become invisible, immaterial, sealed off from contact with their subjects or with the stuff and substance of the world—and hence, often, confined to their palaces, unable to exercise arbitrary power (or often any power) in any effective way.

Royal regicide is just the ultimate form of adverse sacralization.

When popular forces win, the result can thus take the form of Frazerian sacred kingship, or the reduction of the monarch to ceremonial figurehead, like the latter-day Zhou emperor or present-day queen of England.

When kings definitively win (e.g., by allying with a newly emerging civil or military bureaucracy), a different range of conflicts ensue, largely, between the living and the dead. Having overcome boundaries in space, kings will regularly attempt to similarly overcome boundaries in time, and translate their metahuman status into some form of genuine immortality. Insofar as they are successful, they create a series of dilemmas for their successors, whose legitimacy is derived from their ancestry, but who at the same time are necessarily placed in a position of rivalry with them.

Anthropologists have long remarked on the phenomenon of sinking status. Over time, the progressive distancing of cadet persons and branches from the main line of succession is an endemic source of strife in royal lineages, often leading to fratricidal violence—especially among paternal half-siblings, each backed by their own maternal kinsmen (cf. Geertz and Geertz 1975). The succession chances of the junior princes of each generation become increasingly remote, unless they seize by force and guile the kingship to which they have diminishing claim by right. Beside the violence of an interregnum, the effect is often a centrifugal dispersion of royals—those who withdraw or are defeated—into the outer reaches of the kingdom or even beyond, where they may take power in a lesser realm of their own. This is a major source of stranger-king formation and of regional configurations of core–periphery relations (galactic polities). It may also play a role in the formation of so-called "empires."

This problem is complicated even further by a central contradiction between two forms of sinking status: horizontal and vertical. On the one hand, each collateral line that breaks off from the dynastic core descends ever lower in status as new ones are constantly produced, unless some radical means of self-promotion succeed in at least temporarily reversing their decline. On the other hand, the central line itself is usually seen as declining steadily in status, as the current ruler becomes ever more distant from the founding hero, god, or stranger-king. As a result, the branch of the royal line identified with the highest-ranking ancestor (the oldest) is also the lowest-ranking branch of the royal line.

The inevitability of sinking status over time leads to the dilemma of how to manage the royal dead. Deceased members of the dynasty are likely to be present in political life through shrines, mummies, relics, tombs, or even palaces; to communicate their will and perspectives through mediums, oracles, or similar means. The paradox of horizontal and vertical sinking status—that older ances-tors rank higher for the same reason their descendants rank lower—becomes all the more acute the more active the role of the dead in contemporary politics becomes. This role can be very active indeed: Inca royal mummies continued to own the same palace, lands, and retinues of retainers they had possessed in life, forcing each new ruler to conquer new territories to support his own court. In all such systems, if things were left to their own devices for too long, living kings would be crowded out and overwhelmed by legions of the dead. So the dead had to be controlled, limited, contained—even purged. Like living kings, they had to be rendered more sacred, more bounded by restrictions that were restrictive of their power—even if those restrictions were ultimately constitutive of that power.

It is a general sociological principle that the more ancestors are seen as funda-mentally different sorts of being from present-day mortals, the more they are likely to be seen as a source of power; the more similar, the more they are seen as rivals and sources of constraint. The memory of a totemic killer whale ances-tor, or witchetty grub, is in no sense an imposition on the living; by contrast, the memory of a man remembered and venerated by his many descendants is very much a rival for any descendant whose life project is to achieve exactly the same thing. Only so many ancestors can become famous. Still, there is always a balance here: if ancestors are entirely effaced, their descendants lose all status; if they have too much power, they are seen as stifling those same descendants' self-realization. The result is often another variant of the politics of ritual subterfuge so typical of dealing with life-giving gods: they must be contained, driven off, or even destroyed, all in the ostensible name of honoring them.

Ordinary mortals may or may not face this problem (it all depends on how they see themselves in time and history), but kings, whose legitimacy is based at least in part on descent from other kings, must always face it. To flee one's domain and become a stranger-king elsewhere is in fact one way to escape the choke-hold of the dead, but a stranger king's descendants will begin to have the same problem, and it will only get worse as time goes on.

Much of the more extravagant behavior of the rulers of powerful kingdoms or "early states" can be seen as attempts to escape this chokehold, that is, as modes of competition with the dead. One might attempt to efface the dead, or become the dead, but this is rarely entirely effective. One might enter into direct competition in the creation of timeless monuments, in conquest, or in the ritual sacrifice of ever greater numbers of subjects in attempts to manifest ever greater arbitrary sovereign power. One might even—this is sometimes done—attempt to reverse the direction of history entirely, and invent a myth of progress. All of these expedients create new problems.

The ordinary balance of power between king and people is often maintained through intense emotional engagements: love, hatred, or some combination of the two. These often take the form of paradoxical inversions of what would normally be expected to be the result of those emotions: Shilluk or Swazi kings took on divine status at the moment people united in hatred against them; the nurturant love of Merina toward infantilized rulers might alternate between indulgence for acts that might otherwise be seen as atrocities, and harsh chastisement when they were seen as overstepping bounds.

The perfection of the king, his court, palace, capital, or immediate surroundings, is not precisely a model of the universe; it is a model of the universe restored to a state of abstract Platonic perfection, one which it lacks in ordinary experience. Perhaps it once had this state. Perhaps it is felt it someday will again. The newly founded royal city, a projection of a single human vision imposed on the material world, can thus be seen as the prototype for all future utopias: an attempt to impose an image of perfection not just onto the physical world but also into the lives of those mortal humans who actually lived in it. Ultimately, of course, this is impossible. Humans cannot be reduced to Platonic ideals, and the fundamental quandaries of human life, revolving as they do particularly around reproduction and death, cannot be legislated away; such states of transcendent perfection can perhaps be attained in moments of ritual performance, but no one can live in such a moment for their entire life, or even any substantial part of it. Some royal capitals try to exclude birth, infirmity, and (natural) death from the royal settlement entirely. Going that far is unusual. But something along these lines always happens. At the very least, royal courts will be marked by elaborate codes of etiquette which require that even everyday social interaction be governed by the pretense that such things do not exist. These codes set standards of comportment that are then realized at ever greater degrees of imperfection the further one travels (socially or physically) from the royal court.

In this way, where prophets foretell the total future resolution of the contradictions and dilemmas of the human condition, kings embody their partial present-day resolution.

The arbitrariness of stranger-kings is, however paradoxically, the key to their ability to establish themselves as avatars of justice. The ability to seize or destroy anything, even if only very occasionally deployed, is structurally similar to the ownership of everything; it is an undifferentiated relation between the monarch and everyone and everything else. This indifference is also impartiality, since such an absolute monarch has—in principle at least—no particular interest which might bias his judgment in disputes between his subjects. They are all the same to him. For this reason, kings will always claim some kind of absolute despotic power, even if everyone is aware such claims mean next to nothing in practice—since otherwise, they would not be kings. At the same time, the all-encompassing nature of such claims renders the very power of the king potentially subversive of existing social arrangements. While kings will, generally, represent themselves as embodiments and bastions of all existing hierarchies and structures of authority (e.g., by insisting that he is "Father of his People," the monarch above all confirms the authority of actual fathers over their wives, children, and dependents), the ultimately undifferentiated nature of their power also meant all subjects were, ultimately, the same—that is, equal. As the Scottish Enlightenment philosopher Henry Home (Lord Kames) was perhaps first to point out, the difference between absolute despotism, where all are equal except for one man, and absolute democracy, is simply one man. There is thus a deep structural affinity between the contemporary notion that all citizens are "equal before the law" and the monarchical principle that they are equal as potential victims of purely arbitrary royal depredation.

In political life, this tension can take many forms. Commoners may appeal to the king against his "evil councilors." Kings or emperors may frame themselves as popular champions against the interests of the aristocracy. Alternately, everyone, regardless of status, can unify against the king.

As a result, even when kings are gone—even when they are deposed by popular uprisings—they are likely to linger in ghostly form, precisely as such a unifying principle. Royal spirit mediumship in much of Africa and Madagascar, and the modern notion of "popular sovereignty," are both contemporary examples of this principle.

Core–periphery relations (galactic polities)

Centrifugal dissemination of influential political, ritual, and material forms from central kingdoms often evokes a centripetal attraction and movement of peoples from the hinterlands. Peripheral societies have been rendered subordinate culturally while still independent politically. It is probably a law of political science that all great kingdoms were marginal once. Originally oriented to a powerful center from the peripheries, they succeed by some advantage—as in trade or warfare—in replacing their erstwhile superiors.

Indeed, in these core–periphery configurations centered on dominant kingdoms, there are endemic impulses of "upward nobility" at every level of the intersocietal hierarchy. The apical kingdoms themselves are competitively counterposed in a larger geopolitical field, which they seek to dominate by universalizing their own claims to power. On one hand, they engage in what is variously described in these pages as "utopian politics" or "the real-politics of the marvelous" by tracing their origins to world-historical heroes (such as Alexander the Great), legendary god-kings (such as Quetzalcoatl), fabled cities (such as Troy or Mecca), ancient or contemporary world powers (such as the Roman or Chinese empires), and/or great gods (such as Shiva). On the other hand, they demonstrate their universality by acquiring—through tribute, trade, or pillage—and domesticating the wild, animistic powers ensouled in the exotic objects of the barbaric hinterlands.

In a famous ethnographic case reported by Edmund Leach (1954), chiefs of the Kachin hill tribe of Burma have been known to "become Shan": that is, to ally with and adopt the lifestyle of Shan princes. For their part, Shan princes take on the political and ritual trappings of Burmese or Chinese kings—some of which may also filter up to the hill peoples. This phenomenon of "galactic mimesis," in which lesser chiefs assume the political forms of their proximate superiors, is a prevalent dynamic of core–periphery systems, impelled by competition within and between political entities throughout the intersocietal hierarchy. The competition takes one of two common forms. In a process of "complementary schismogenesis," individuals contending for leadership in a given community, or communities competing for power within a larger galactic field, attempt to trump their local adversaries by affiliating with a superior chief; they scale up their own status to a higher register of the regional hierarchy. Or conversely, in a process of "antagonistic acculturation," a lesser group may attempt to resist the encroachment of a neighboring power by adopting the latter's own political apparatus and thus effect a stand-off—the way the Vietnamese long claimed their own mandate of heaven as a "southern empire" on equal basis with the Chinese "northern empire." Note that in any case the elements of high political status, including kingship, are disseminated by a mimetic process through the region and on the initiative of the less powerful peoples.

Taken together with acculturative influences radiating outward from core kingdoms, galactic mimesis has the effect of creating hybrid societies whose political and cosmological forms are largely not of their own devising and indeed surpass any possible "determination by the economic basis." Given the pervasiveness of core–periphery relations the world around, even in parts of the "tribal zone," this kind of hybridity or uneven development is more often the norm of sociocultural order than the exception. The "superstructure" exceeds the "infrastructure."

THE POLITICAL ECONOMICS OF TRADITIONAL KINGSHIP

Kingship proprietary schemes are complex. On one hand, the country is divided into local properties, of which the ancestors of the inhabitants, or the indigenous spirits with whom the ancestors have made a pact, are the "true owners"—and the decisive agents of the area's fertility. Correlatively, the local subject population, who have ritual access to these metaperson authorities through their initiated elders or priestly leaders, are themselves deemed the "owners," the "earth," the "land," or some such designation of their founder rights to the country relative to the ruling aristocracy—especially in stranger-kingdoms, where the latter are foreign by origin and ethnic identity. Although possessory in relation to the rulers, the local people's rights are only usufructuary in relation to the spiritual inhabitants, whose ultimate ownership must be duly acknowledged by the current occupants. (Notice that these relations between the local people and the autochthonous spirits are themselves analogous to the larger structure of the stranger-kingdom.) On the other hand, the ruling aristocracy and the king—who by tradition may have been poor and landless originally except as they were granted land by the native people—may also be "owners"; but here in the sense of lordship over large landed estates and their inhabitants, giving them tributary rights to a portion of product and manpower generated by the underlying population. Whereas the subject people's relation to the process is productive, by virtue of their control of the primary means, the rulers' relation to the process is extractive, by virtue of their domination of the producing people. As the East African Nyoro people put it: "The Mukama [the king] rules the people; the clans rule the land" (Beattie 1971: 167).

Accordingly, the kingdom economy has a dual structure, marked by fundamental differences between the *oikos* economics of the underlying population and the specifically political economics of the palace and aristocracy, undertaken with an eye toward the material subsidization of their power. Devoted rather to a customary livelihood, the primary sector is organized by the kinship and community relations of the subject people. The ruling class is principally concerned with the finished product of the people's work in goods and manpower, on which it takes a toll that helps fund an elite sphere of wealth accumulation, oriented particularly to the political finalities of strengthening and extending its sphere of domination. Labor in this sphere is organized by corvée, slave, and/or client relations. Beside support of an imposing palace establishment, it is notably employed in the accumulation of riches from extramural sources by means of raid, trade, and/or tribute. Employed, then, in conspicuous consumption, monumental construction, and strategic redistribution—and possibly in further military exploits—this wealth has subjugating effects, both directly, as benefiting some, and indirectly, as impressing others. Moreover, the material success of the king is the sign of his access to the divine sources of earthly prosperity, thereby doubling the political effects of his wealth by the demonstration of his godly powers.

Kingship is a political economy of social subjugation rather than material coercion. Kingly power does not work on proprietary control of the subject people's means of existence so much as on the beneficial or awe-inspiring effects of royal largess, display, and prosperity. The objective of the political economy is the increase in the number and loyalty of subjects—as distinct from capitalist enterprise, which aims at the increase of capital wealth. To paraphrase a Marxian formula, the essential project of kingship economics is P–W–P′—where the political command of people gives an accumulation of wealth that yields a greater command of people—by contrast to the classic capitalist formula, W–P–W′—where the proprietary control of productive wealth (capital) gives the control of people (labor) in the aim of increasing productive wealth.

One might justly say that "spirits own the means of production," were it not that in the form of plants, animals, significant artifacts, and even land, and the natural forces of growth, these so-called "spirits," and more properly called "metapersons," *are* the means of production. Having their own dispositions and intentions, they are indeed *their own persons*, and, together with divinities, ancestors, and other such metaperson powers, they are known to be responsible for the success or failure of human work. Accordingly, the "means of production" characteristically includes ritual, especially sacrificial ritual, as an essential part of work—as in the famous Tikopian "work of the gods."

It also follows that the political benefits of material success—the rewards in status and influence—go to the shamans, priests, elders, lineage heads, big-men, chiefs, or kings, who have by ascription or achievement priority of access to these metahuman sources of human prosperity—but not necessarily, or only to a lesser extent, to the hunters, gardeners, or others who did the work. The alienation of the worker from his product was a general condition long before its notoriety in capitalism. So far as the social credit goes instead to the reigning politicoreligious authorities, political power may thus have an "economic basis"—although the "economic basis" is not economic.

Also by the way, cannibalism is a widespread condition, even among many societies that profess to abhor it. Cannibalism is a predicament of the animistic hunter or gardener, who must live by consuming animals or plants which (who) are essentially persons themselves. Hence the taboos and other ritual respects accorded to these species and their metaperson masters—again as a necessary condition of "production."

ON SHOPWORN CONCEPTS THAT HAVE OUTLIVED THEIR USEFULNESS

"Cultural relativism," properly understood, has not outlived its usefulness. What is useless is the vulgar sense of relativism to the effect that the values of any society are as good as, if not better than, the values of any other, including our own. Properly understood, cultural relativism is an anthropological technique for understanding cultural differences, not a charitable way of granting moral absolution. It consists of the provisional suspension of our own moral judgments or valuations of other people's practices in order to place them as positional values in the cultural and historical contexts that gave rise to them. The issue is what these practices mean, how they came about, and what their effects are for the people concerned, not what they are or are worth in our terms.

In this same relativist regard, the local people's ontological scheme, their sense of what there is, must likewise be considered in itself and for itself, and not be distorted by analytic concepts that substitute our certainties of "reality" for theirs. Take the category of "myth," for example. In standard English, to label a statement as "myth" means it's not true. Hence in speaking of other people's "myths," we characteristically assert that what they know as sacred truth, and upon which they predicate their existence, is fictional and unbelievable—for us. Having thus debunked the constitutional basis of their society—as in the ethnological oxymoron "mythical charter"—we are given liberty to write it off as essentially unreal for them too: an epiphenomenal mystification of their actual sociopolitical practice. What is then typically left to the scientific project is a more or less feckless search for the "kernel of historical truth" in a narrative riven with irrelevant fantasy—in this way ignoring that the concepts thus devalued are the true history at issue. For taken in that veridical capacity by the people concerned, the so-called "myth" is truly organizing their historical action.

"Life, after all, is as much an imitation of art as the reverse." So commented Victor Turner (1957: 153) in regard to the way Central African Ndembu villagers applied principles from the traditions of Lunda kingship they had learned as children to their current social relations. Or again, this is how important political leaders likewise inform and structure their own public actions by the relations encoded in dynastic epics. The past is not simply prologue, but, as Turner says, it is "paradigm." Historical causes in the mode of traditions have no temporal or physical proximity to their effects: they are inserted into the situation, but they are not of it. Embedding the present in terms of a remembered past, this kind of culturally instituted temporality is a fundamental mode of history-making, from the omnipresent Dreamtime of Australian Aboriginals to the state politics of Kongo kings. But then, what actually happens in a given situation is always constituted by cultural significations that transcend the parameters of the happening itself: Bobby Thomson didn't simply hit the ball over the left-field fence, he won the pennant. The better part of history is atemporal and cultural: not "what actually happened," but what it is that happened.

This does not mean that just because Nuer now insist they are all descended from a man named "Nuer" who lived ten generations ago, we must ignore documentary evidence of the existence of Nuer before 1750. It does mean that if we do not care what being Nuer means to Nuer, then or now, we have no business speaking about "Nuer" at all.

Shopworn economic concepts

"Things," for example. The Cartesian distinction of *res cogitans* and *res extensa*, subjects and objects, is not a good description of ontological schemes largely constituted on grounds of human attributes or personhood. As already repeatedly noted, in the societies at issue in this work the features of the environment with which people are significantly engaged, and even important productive artifacts of their own making, have the inner and essential qualities of human persons. The conventional anthropological concept of "the psychic unity of humanity" has to be extended to the subjectively infused universe for many or most of these societies. It was a distinctive Judeo-Christian conceit that the world was made of nothing, that spirit or subjectivity was not immanent in it—and for Adam's eating an apple humans would be condemned to wearing themselves to death working on obdurate matter, thorns, and thistles. For most of the world, economic praxis has necessarily entailed intersubjective relations with the beings on which (with whom) people work and which (who) decide the outcome. The plants that the Achuar women of Amazonia nurture are their children, even as the success of their efforts is due to the goddess of cultivation. Here it is not simply that human skills are a necessary but not sufficient cause of the successful outcome, but that human skills are the signs of divinely endowed powers. Our own parochial economic science of a Cartesian world notwithstanding, in this respect there are no simple "things:" the so-called "objects" of people's interest have their own desires.

Likewise "production": the notion of a heroic individual working creatively on inert matter, thereby transforming it into a useful existence by his own effort according to his own plan, does not describe an intersubjective praxis in which metaperson-alters are the primary agents of the process (Descola 2013: 321ff.).

It is more accurate to say that people *receive* the fruits of their efforts from these sources than that that they *create* them (e.g., Harrison 1990: 47ff.). The forces that make gardens grow, animals available, women fertile, pots come out intact from the kiln and implements from the forge—forces variously hypostasized as *mana, semangat, hasina, nawalak, orenda,* etc.—are not of human origin. Conventional notions of the supposed functional effects of the relations of production on the larger relations of society are nonstarters in regard to the many societies so ontologically constituted.

Our notion of "production" is itself the secularization of a theological concept, but it derives from a very specific theology, in which an all-powerful God creates the universe *ex nihilio* (Descola 2013: 321ff.)—an idea which is maintained in our cosmology in multiple ways even after God has been ostensibly taken out of the picture. But consider the hunter, forager, or fisher. Does she "produce" anything? At what point does a trapped fish or uprooted tuber stop being a "natural" phenomenon and start being a "social product"? We are speaking of acts of transformation, attack, propitiation, care, killing, disarticulation, and reshaping. But the same is ultimately true of making automobiles. It's only if one imagines the factory as a black box, the way a man who doesn't know very much about the full course of pregnancy might imagine a woman's womb as "producing" (etymologically, "pushing out") something fully formed through one great burst of "labor," that it's possible to say "production" is the true basis of human life.

Shopworn concepts of sociocultural order

As implied in the preceding discussion—and amplified in the body of this work—several conceptual dichotomies of broad application in the human sciences are not receivable for the societies under consideration here, inasmuch as these binaries are not substantially differentiated, opposed, or otherwise ontologically pertinent. Typically, they are inappropriate ethnocentric projections onto culturally distinct others. But the peoples concerned do not distinguish:

- "Humans" from "spirits." So-called "spirits" (metapersons) have the essential qualities of persons.
- "Material" from "spiritual." They are largely and fundamentally alike on the common ground of humanity.
- "Supernatural" from "natural." Populated and activated by embodied persons, there is no subjectless "natural" world: a fortiori, no transcendent realm of "spirit."

- Hence, "this world" from an "otherworld." Metaperson-others are in people's everyday—and in dreams, every night—experience. People are known to communicate with so-called "spirits" and have customary social relationships with them, including sex and marriage.

There are no egalitarian human societies. Even hunters are ordered and dominated by a host of metaperson powers-that-be, whose rule is punitively backed by severe sanctions. The earthly people are dependent and subordinate components of a cosmic polity. They well know and fear higher authority—and sometimes they defy it. Society both with and against the state is virtually a human universal.

This does not mean the famous egalitarian ethos of so many hunting societies, and not just them, is an illusion. Just as assertions of the absolute power of the sovereign are also, tacitly, assertions of the absolute equality of his subjects (at least in relation to him), so assertions of metahuman power are also ipso facto ways of asserting that mortal humans are—in all the most important ways—the same. The difference is that a flesh-and-blood Sun King needs an apparatus of rule (which almost invariably becomes the primary object of hatred of his subjects); if the actual sun is king, well, human beings are pretty much all equal compared to the sun. The first ideals of political equality— especially, the refusal to give and take orders between adults, so well documented among many societies with particularly terrifying cosmic powers—are themselves an effect of the cosmic polity such men and women inhabit. This no less makes them pioneers of human freedom.

Note the disproportions in structure and power between the cosmic polity governing the human community—including divine beings with ultimate life-and-death powers over the people—and the organization of the human society itself. In both morphology and potency there is no equivalence between the human social order and the cosmic authors of its fate. Great gods on whom human life depends are known to peoples in the Arctic, the New Guinea Highlands, and Amazonia: as was said earlier, there are kings in heaven where there are not even chiefs on earth. Neither do kings on earth have the hegemonic scope and powers of the gods they imitate. This structural disproportion is one reason (among others) that the common human science of the "supernatural realm" as a discursive ideological reflex of the people's sociopolitical order, being designed to functionally support it whether by mystification or replication, is a theoretical practice as seriously flawed as it is habitually repeated. Durkheim notwithstanding.

Human societies of all kinds are never alone in another sense. Engaged in regional fields with societies of cultural others, they are largely formed in respect of one another. As noted above, even apart from imperial systems or galactic polities centered in dominant kingdoms, core–periphery relations are known in the "tribal zone"—as in the classic "culture areas" of the Native Americas, with their respective "cultural climaxes" (Kroeber 1947)—such that the structures and practices of any given society are predicated on those of other societies. Besides diffusion and acculturation by domination, a variety of other intercultural dynamics may be in play: including complementary schismogenesis, whereby interacting peoples take contrary cultural forms, whether in the mode of competition or interdependence; or the aforementioned galactic mimesis, whereby peripheral peoples take on the cosmopolitical forms of hierarchical superiors. The scandal is that while human societies are thus never alone, the human sciences have long pretended that they are. With few exceptions, such as recent world system and globalization theories, all our major paradigms of cultural order and change imagine that societies are self-fashioning monads—autonomous and sui generis. Durkheimian sociology is not the only one. Likewise, Malinowskian functionalism; the structural functionalism of Radcliffe-Brown; the Marxism of base and superstructure; evolutionism from Herbert Spencer to Leslie White and Julian Steward; Benedictian patterns of culture; even poststructuralist discourses and subjectivities: they all suppose that the forms and relations they are explicating are situated within a solitary sociocultural order and that the articulations and dynamics of that order are the critical matters at issue. The concept of culture has been unfortunately tied to a politics of nationalism since Johann Gottfried von Herder and his followers formulated it in that context.

And so, finally, we pass to that intellectual fetish whose worship today transcends even that of "the nation"—that is, its twin companion, "the state." Asking whether a kingdom is a state or not rarely tells you very much at all about its politics or constitution. Surely we have learned all there is to learn from the endless theorizing on "the origins of the state" or "the process of state formation" that so dominated theoretical debates of the twentieth century. In retrospect, we may well discover that "the state" that consumed so much of our attention never existed at all, or was, at best, a fortuitous confluence of elements of entirely heterogeneous origins (sovereignty, administration, a competitive political field, etc.) that came together in certain times and places, but that, nowadays, are very much in the process of once again drifting apart.

CHAPTER I

The original political society

MARSHALL SAHLINS

I am a Cartesian—a Hocartesian. I want to follow Hocart's lead in freeing oneself from anthropological conventions by adhering to indigenous traditions. "How can we make any progress in the understanding of cultures, ancient or modern," he said, "if we persist in dividing what people join, and in joining what they keep apart?" ([1952] 1970: 23). This essay is an extended commentary on the Hocartesian meditation encapsulated in *Kings and councillors* by "the straightforward equivalence, king = god" ([1936] 1970: 74). I mean to capitalize on the more or less explicit temporality entailed in the anthropological master's exegesis of this equivalence, as when he variously speaks of the king as the vehicle, abode, substitute, repository, or representative of the god (Hocart 1933, [1936] 1970, [1950] 1968). The clear implication is that gods precede the kings who effectively replicate them—which is not exactly the common social science tradition of cosmology as the reflex of sociology. Consider time's arrow in statements such as: "So present was this divine and celestial character to the Polynesian mind that they called the chiefs *lani*, heaven, and the same word *marae* is used of a temple and a chief's grave" (Hocart [1927] 1969: 11). Kings are human imitations of gods, rather than gods of kings.

That was the dominant view in Christendom for a long time before the modern celestialization of sovereignty as an ideological expression of the real-political order. From Augustine's notion of the Earthly City as an imperfect form of the Heavenly City to Carl Schmitt's assertion that the significant concepts of the modern state are "secularized theological concepts" ([1922] 2005: 36), human government was commonly considered to be modeled on the kingdom of God. Based on his own view of the ritual character of kingship, however, Hocart's thesis was more far-reaching culturally and historically: that human societies were engaged in cosmic systems of governmentality even before they instituted anything like a political state of their own. From the preface of *Kings and councillors*:

> The machinery of government was blocked out in society long before the appearance of government as we now understand it. In other words, the functions now discharged by king, prime minister, treasury, public works, are not the original ones; they may account for the present form of these institutions, but not for their original appearance. They were originally part, not of a system of government, but of an organization to promote life, fertility, prosperity by transferring life from objects abounding in it to objects dependent on it. ([1952] 1970: 3)

In effect, Hocart speaks here of a cosmic polity, hierarchically encompassing human society, since the life-giving means of people's existence were supplied by "supernatural" beings of extraordinary powers: a polity thus governed by so-called "spirits"—though they had human dispositions, often took human bodily forms, and were present within human experience.

The present essay is a follow-up. The project is to take the Cartesian thesis beyond kingship to its logical and anthropological extreme. Even the so-called "egalitarian" or "acephalous" societies, including hunters such as the Inuit or Australian Aboriginals, are in structure and practice cosmic polities, ordered and governed by divinities, the dead, species-masters, and other such metapersons endowed with life-and-death powers over the human population. There are kingly beings in heaven where there are no chiefs on earth. Hobbes notwithstanding, the state of nature is already something of a political state. It follows that, taken in its social totality and cultural reality, something like the state is the general condition of humankind. It is usually called "religion."

FOR EXAMPLE: CHEWONG AND INUIT

Let me begin with a problem in ethnographic perspective that typically leads to a cultural mismatch between the ancestral legacy of the anthropologist and her or his indigenous interlocutors. I know this is a problem, since for a long time I lived with the same contradiction I now see in Signe Howell's excellent study of the Chewong of the Malaysian interior. Although Chewong society is described as classically "egalitarian," it is in practice coercively ruled by a host of cosmic authorities, themselves of human character and metahuman powers. The Chewong are a few hundred people organized largely by kinship and subsisting largely by hunting. But they are hardly on their own. They are set within and dependent upon a greater animistic universe comprised of the persons of animals, plants, and natural features, complemented by a great variety of demonic figures, and presided over by several inclusive deities. Though we conventionally call such creatures "spirits," Chewong respectfully regard them as "people" (*beri*)—indeed, "people like us" or "our people" (Howell 1985: 171). The obvious problem of perspective consists in the venerable anthropological disposition to banish the so-called "supernatural" to the epiphenomenal limbo of the "ideological," the "imaginary," or some such background of discursive insignificance by comparison to the hard realities of social action. Thus dividing what the people join, we are unable to make the conceptual leap—the reversal of the structural *gestalt*—implied in Howell's keen observation that "the human social world is intrinsically part of a wider world in which boundaries between society and cosmos are non-existent" (2012: 139). "There is no meaningful separation," she says, "between what one may term nature and culture or, indeed, between society and cosmos" (ibid.: 135).

So while, on one hand, Howell characterizes the Chewong as having "no social or political hierarchy" or "leaders of any kind," on the other, she describes a human community encompassed and dominated by potent metapersons with powers to impose rules and render justice that would be the envy of kings. "Cosmic rules," Howell calls them, I reckon both for their scope and for their origins. The metahuman persons who mandate these rules visit illness or other misfortune, not excluding penalty of death, on Chewong who transgress them. "I can think of no act that is rule neutral," Howell writes; taken together, "they refer not just to selected social domains or activities, but to the performance of regular living itself" (ibid.: 140). Yet though they live by the rules, Chewong have no part in their enforcement, which is the exclusive function of "whatever spirit or non-human personage is activated by the disregard of a particular rule" (ibid.: 139). Something like a rule of law sustained by a monopoly of force. Among hunters.

When Signe Howell first visited the Chewong in 1977, she found them obsessively concerned with a tragedy that happened not long before. Three people had been killed and two injured for violating a weighty taboo on laughing at animals: a prohibition that applied to all forest creatures, the breach of which would potentially implicate all Chewong people. The victims had ridiculed some millipedes that entered their lean-to; and that night a terrific thunderstorm uprooted a large tree, which fell upon them. Here it deserves notice that while the Chewong profess to abhor cannibalism, like animist hunters generally, they nevertheless subsist on "people like us," their animal prey. Likewise similar to other hunters, they manage the contradiction by the ritual respects they accord wild animals: in this case, by the prohibition on ridiculing forest creatures—which also, by positioning the animals outside familiar human relations, apparently erases the cannibal implications from overt consciousness (cf. Valeri 2000: 143). Since the forest animals are not really like us, we can beat the cannibal rap.

The severe punishments for disrespecting forest creatures originated with certain immortals of the Above and the Below: the male Thunder God, Tanko, and the female Original Snake, whose abode is the primordial sea under the earth—and who is most responsible for maintaining rules of this type. There were never any humans the likes of Tanko and the Original Snake among Chewong themselves: no such human powers, whatever the conventional wisdom says about divinity as the mirror image of society. Tanko lives in the sky, whence the thunder he unleashes on taboo-violators is aptly said to be the sound of him laughing at the human predicament. His thunderbolts are also known to punish incest, causing severe joint pain and, if the behavior persists, death. On his frequent visits to earth, he indulges in contrasting sexual behavior—relations with distantly rather than closely related women—and with beneficial rather than fatal results: for without his sexual exploits there could be no Chewong people. Tanko descends to have intercourse with all human and animal females, which is what makes them fertile. Menstrual blood represents the birth of children he has sired, children unseen and unknown to their mothers, as they ascend to the heavens to live with their father. The semen of human males, however, is unable to procreate children until Tanko has copulated with the women concerned, which is to say until they have menstruated—from which it follows empirically that the god was indeed the condition of possibility of human reproduction.

The Original Snake is sometimes identified as the sky-wife of Tanko, a culture heroine who gave Chewong fire, tobacco, and night; but in her more usual form of a huge snake dwelling in chthonian waters, she is especially known for her malevolent powers. Knocking down trees and houses, her breath creates the destructive winds that punish people who violate the ordinances on the treatment of animals. She may also be provoked into moving while in the subterranean sea, causing an upwelling of waters that drowns the offenders—upon which she swallows them body and soul.[1] Not that the Original Snake is the only man-eater among the myriad indwelling and free-ranging metahumans whom Chewong encounter, more often for worse than for better. Without replicating the extraordinary catalogue compiled by Howell (1989), suffice it for present purposes to indicate the range: from female familiars who marry the human individuals for whom they serve as spirit guides; through various kinds of ghosts especially dangerous to small children and the creatures upon whose good will fruits bear in season; to the twenty-seven subtypes of harmful beings who were once human, and of whom Chewong say, "They want to eat us" (ibid.: 105). If there is indeed no boundary between the cosmos and the *socius*, then it's not exactly what some would call a "simple society," let alone an egalitarian one.

I hasten to reply to the obvious objection that the potent deities of the Chewong reflect a long history of relationships with coastal Malay states by noting that basically similar cosmologies are found among basically similar societies situated far from such influences. For an initial example the Central Inuit; thereafter, Highland New Guineans, Australian Aboriginals, native Amazonians, and other "egalitarian" peoples likewise dominated by metaperson-others who vastly outnumber them.

Of the Inuit in general it is said that a person "should never push himself ahead of others or show the slightest ambition to control other people" (Oosten 1976: 16), and in particular of the Netsilik of the Central Canadian Arctic that "there were no lineages or clans, no institutionalized chiefs or formal government" (Balikci 1970: xv). On the other hand, of the same Netsilik, Knud Rasmussen (1931: 224) wrote:

---

1.   One is reminded of the great Rainbow Serpent of Australian Aboriginals, as also by the Original Snake's relation to the celestial god Tanko, thus making a pair like the male sky deity and the autochthonous serpent of Australian traditions (see below on Magalim of the Central New Guinea Min peoples and Ungud of the Kimberleys, Western Australia).

The powers that rule the earth and all the animals, and the lives of mankind are the great spirits who live on the sea, on land, out in space, and in the Land of the Sky. These are many, and many kinds of spirits, but there are only three really great and really independent ones, and they are Nuliajuk, Narssuk, and Tatqeq. These three are looked upon as directly practicing spirits, and the most powerful of them all is Nuliajuk, the mother of animals and mistress both of the sea and the land. At all times she makes mankind feel how she vigilantly and mercilessly takes care that all souls, both animals and humankind, are shown the respect the ancient rules of life demand.

Ruling their respective domains—Nuliajuk or Sedna, the sea and the land; Tatqeq, the Moon Man, the heavens; and Narssuk or Sila, the meteorological forces of the air—these three "great spirits" were widely known under various names from East Greenland to the Siberian Arctic—which affords some confidence in their antiquity and indigeneity. While always complementary in territorial scope, they varied in salience in different regions: the Moon Man generally dominant in the Bering Strait and Sila in Greenland; whereas Sedna, as Franz Boas wrote, was "the supreme deity of the Central Eskimos," holding "supreme sway over the destinies of mankind" (1901: 119).[2]

The Central Inuit and Sedna in particular will be the focus here: "The stern goddess of fate among the Eskimos," as Rasmussen (1930: 123) characterized her. In command of the animal sources of food, light, warmth, and clothing that made an Inuit existence possible, Sedna played "by far the most important part in everyday life" (ibid.: 62). She was effectively superior to Sila and the Moon, who often functioned as her agents, "to see that her will is obeyed" (ibid.: 63). Accordingly, in his ethnography of the Iglulik, Rasmussen describes a divine pantheon of anthropomorphic power ruling a human society that was itself innocent of institutional authority. So whenever any transgression of Sedna's rules or taboos associated with hunting occurs,

the spirit of the sea intervenes. The moon spirit helps her to see the rules of life are daily observed, and comes hurrying down to earth to punish any instance of

---

2.   On the distribution and respective powers of these great spirits among Inuit and Siberian peoples, see the general summaries in Weyer (1932), Oosten (1976), Hodgkins (1977), and Merkur (1991). On the dominance of Sedna among the Central Inuit, see in particular Weyer (1932: 355–56).

neglect. And both sea spirit and moon spirit employ Sila to execute all punishments in any way connected with the weather. (Rasmussen 1930: 63; cf. 78)

Scholars perennially agonize over whether to consider the likes of Sedna as "gods." Too often some promising candidate is rejected for failing to closely match our own ideas of the Deity: an act of religious intolerance, as Daniel Merkur observed (1991: 37–48), with the effect of promulgating the Judeo-Christian dogma that there is only one True God. But, "Why not call them gods?"; for it happens that Hocart thus posed the question in regard to a close analogue of Sedna among Winnebago people, a certain "immaterial being in control of animal species" ([1936] 1970: 149; cf. Radin 1914). More than just species-masters, however, Sedna, Sila, and the Moon had the divine attributes of immortality and universality. All three were erstwhile humans who achieved their high stations by breaking with their earthly kinship relations, in the event setting themselves apart from and over the population in general. Various versions of Sedna's origin depict her as an orphan, as mutilated in sacrifice by her father, and/or as responsible for his death; the Moon Man's divine career featured matricide and incest with his sister; Sila left the earth when his parents, who were giants, were killed by humans. Much of this is what Luc de Heusch (1962) identified as "the exploit" in traditions of stranger-kingship: the crimes of the dynastic founder against the people's kinship order, by which he at once surpasses it and acquires the solitude necessary to rule the society as a whole, free from any partisan affiliation (see chapters 3 and 4). And while on the matter of kingship, there is this: as the ruling powers of earth, sea, air, and sky, all of the Inuit deities, in breaking from kinship, thereby become territorial overlords. Transcending kinship, they achieve a kind of territorial sovereignty. The passage "from kinship to territory" was an accomplished fact long before it was reorganized as the classic formula of state formation. This is not only to say that the origins of kingship and the state are discursively or spiritually prefigured in Inuit communities, but since, like Chewong, "the human social world is intrinsically part of a wider world in which boundaries between society and cosmos are non-existent," this encompassing cosmic polity is actually inscribed in practice.

Like the Chewong, the Inuit could pass for the model of a (so-called) "simple society" were they not actually and practically integrated in a (so-called) "complex society" of cosmic proportions. In the territories of the gods dwelt a numerous population of metahuman subjects, both of the animistic kind of persons indwelling in places, objects, and animals; and disembodied free souls, as of ghosts or demons. "The invisible rulers of every object are the most remarkable beings next to Sedna," Boas wrote: "Everything has its *inua* (owner)" ([1888] 1961: 591).[3] All across the Arctic from Greenland to Siberia, people know and contend with these *inua* (pl. *inuat*), a term that means "person of" the noun that precedes it. Or "its man," as Waldemar Bogoras translates the Chukchee cognate, and which clearly implies that "a human life-spirit is supposed to live within the object" (1904–9: 27–29). (Could Plato have imagined the perspectival response of Chukchee to the allegory of the shadows on the wall of the cave? "Even the shadows on the wall," they say, "constitute definite tribes and have their own country where they live in huts and subsist by hunting" [ibid: 281].) Note the repeated report of dominion over the thing by its person—"everything has its owner." Just so, as indwelling masters of their own domains, the gods themselves were superior *inuat*, endowed with something akin to proprietary rights over their territories and the various persons thereof. J. G. Oosten explains: "An *inua* was an anthropomorphic spirit that was usually connected to an object, place, or animal as its spiritual owner or double. The *inuat* of the sea, the moon, and the air could be considered spiritual owners of their respective territories" (1976: 27). Correlatively, greater spirits such as Sedna, mother of sea animals, had parental relations to the creatures of their realm, thus adding the implied godly powers of creation and protection to those of possession and dominion. Taken in connection with complementary powers of destruction, here is a preliminary conclusion that will be worth further exploration: socially and categorically, divinity is a high-order form of animism.

That's how it works in Boas' description of Sedna's reaction to the violation of her taboos on hunting sea animals. By a well-known tradition, the sea animals originated from Sedna's severed fingers; hence, a certain mutuality of being connected her to her animal children. For its part, the hunted seal in Boas' account is endowed with greater powers than ordinary humans. It can sense that the hunter has had contact with a corpse by the vapor of blood or death he emits, breaking a taboo on hunting while in such condition. The revulsion of the animal is thereupon communicated to Sedna, who in the normal course

---

3.   The distinction between "indwelling" and "free souls" (such as ghosts) is adopted from Merkur (1991). Reports of the ubiquity of the former among Inuit have been recurrent at least since the eighteenth century. Thus, from East Greenland in 1771: "The Greenlanders believe that all things are souled, and also that the smallest implement possesses its soul. Thus an arrow, a boot, a shoe sole or a key, a drill, has each for itself a soul" (Glann, in Weyer 1932: 300).

would withdraw the seals to her house under the sea, or perhaps dispatch Sila on punishing blizzards, thus making hunting impossible and exposing the entire human community to starvation. Note that in many anthropological treatments of animism, inasmuch as they are reduced to individualistic or phenomenological reflections on the relations between humans and animals, these interactions are characterized as reciprocal, egalitarian, or horizontal; whereas often in social practice they are at least three-part relations, involving also the master-person of the species concerned, in which case they are hierarchical—with the offending person in the client position. Or rather, the entire Inuit community is thereby put in a subordinate position, since sanction also falls on the fellows of the transgressor; and as the effect is likewise generalized to all the seals, the event thus engages a large and diverse social totality presided over by the ruling goddess.[4]

In the same vein, the many and intricate taboos shaping Inuit social and material life entail submission to the metaperson-others who sanction them, whether these prohibitions are systematically honored or for whatever reason violated. Of course, submission to the powers is evident in punishments for transgressions. But the same is doubly implied when the proscriptive rule is followed, for, more than an act of respect, to honor a taboo has essential elements of sacrifice, involving the renunciation of some normal practice or social good in favor of the higher power who authorizes it (cf. Leach 1976; Valeri 2000). In this regard, the existence of the Inuit, in ways rather like the Chewong, was organized by an elaborate set of "rules of life," as Rasmussen deemed them, regulating all kinds of behavior of all kinds of persons. For even as the main taboos concerned the hunt, the disposition of game, and practices associated with menstruation, childbirth, and treatment of the dead, the enjoined behaviors could range from how one made the first cut of snow in building an igloo, to whether a pregnant woman could go outside with her mittens on—never (Rasmussen 1930: 170). Rasmussen's major work on the "intellectual culture" of the Iglulik includes a catalogue of thirty-one closely written pages of such injunctions (ibid.: 169–204). As, for example:

- The marrow bones of an animal killed by a first-born son are never to be eaten with a knife, but must be crushed with stones (ibid.: 179).

---

4.   In a comparative discussion of species-masters in lowland South America, Carlos Fausto (2012: 29) notes that the topic has been relatively neglected by ethnographers, "due to a widespread view of the South American lowlands as a realm of equality and symmetry."

- A man suffering want through ill success in hunting must, when coming to another village and sitting down to eat, never eat with a woman he has not seen before (ibid.: 182).
- Persons hunting seal from a snow hut on ice may not work with soapstone (ibid.: 184).
- Young girls present in a house when a seal is being cut up must take off their *kamiks* and remain barefooted as long as the work is in progress (ibid.: 185).
- If a woman is unfaithful to her husband while he is out hunting walrus, especially on drift ice, the man will dislocate his hip and have severe pains in the sinuses (ibid.: 186).
- If a woman sees a whale she must point to it with her middle finger (ibid.: 187).
- Widows are never allowed to pluck birds (ibid.: 196).
- A woman whose child has died must never drink water from melted ice, only from melted snow (ibid.: 198).

Commented Boas in this connection: "It is certainly difficult to find out the innumerable regulations connected with the religious ideas and customs of the Eskimo. The difficulty is even greater in regard to customs which refer to birth, sickness and death" ([1888] 1961: 201–2).

The greater number of these "rules of life" were considerations accorded to Sedna. When they were respected, the sea goddess became the source of human welfare, providing animals to the hunter. But when they were violated, Sedna or the powers under her aegis inflicted all manners of misfortune upon the Inuit, ranging from sicknesses and accidents to starvation and death. Punishments rained upon the just and the unjust alike: they might afflict not only the offender but also his or her associates, perhaps the entire community, though these others could be innocent or even unaware of the offense. As it is sometimes said that Sedna is also the mother of humankind, that is why she is especially dangerous to women and children, hence the numerous taboos relating to menstruation, childbirth, and the newborn. But the more general and pertinent motivation would be that she is the mother of animals, hence the principle involved in her animosity to women is an eye-for-an-eye in response to the murder of her own children (cf. Gardner 1987; Hamayon 1996). Again, everything follows from the animist predicament that people survive by killing others like themselves. As explained to Rasmussen:

> All the creatures we have to kill and eat, all those we have to strike down and destroy to make clothes for ourselves, have souls like we have, souls which do not perish with the body, and which therefore must be propitiated lest they should revenge themselves on us for taking away their souls. (1930: 56)

Among Netsilik, Iglulik, Baffin Islanders, and other Central Inuit, the disembodied souls of the dead, both of persons and of animals, were an omnipresent menace to the health and welfare of the living. "All the countless spirits of evil are all around, striving to bring sickness and death, bad weather, and failure in hunting" (Boas [1888] 1961: 602; cf. Rasmussen 1931: 239; Balikci 1970: 200–1). In principle, it was the persons and animals whose deaths were not properly respected ritually who thereupon haunted the living. But in this regard, Rasmussen confirms what one may well have surmised from the extent and intricacy of the "rules of life," namely that the gods often act in ways mysterious to the people:

> There are never any definite rules for anything, for it may also happen that a deceased person may in some mysterious manner attack surviving relatives or friends he loves, even when they have done nothing wrong. . . . Human beings are thus helpless in the face of all the dangers and uncanny things that happen in connection with death and the dead. (1930: 108)

> There is hardly a single human being who has kept the rules of life according to the laws laid down by the wisdom of the ancients. (1930: 58)

In a way, the reign of the metaperson powers-that-be was classically hegemonic, which helps explain the seeming conflict between the common travelers' reports of the Inuits' good humor and their sense that "human beings were powerless in the grasp of a mighty fate" (ibid.: 32)—"we don't believe, we fear" (ibid.: 55). The ambivalence, I suggest, represents different aspects of the same situation of the people in relation to the metaperson powers-that-be. What remains unambiguous and invariant is that for all their own "loosely structured" condition, they are systematically ordered as the dependent subjects of a cosmic system of social domination. Hobbes spoke of the state of nature as all that time in which "men lived without a common power to keep them all in awe." Yet in Rasmussen's accounts of the Inuit, a people who might otherwise be said to approximate that natural state, "mankind is held in awe"—given the fear of hunger and sickness inflicted by the powers governing them (1931: 124).[5] If this accounts for the people's anxieties, it also helps explain the reports of their stoic, composed, often congenial disposition. This happier subjectivity is not simply seasonal, not simply due to the fact that times are good in terms of hunting and food supply, for that in itself would be because the people have been observant of Sedna's rules, and accordingly she makes the animals available. There is a certain comfort and assurance that comes from the people's compliance with the higher authorities that govern their fortunes—or if you will, their compliance with the "dominant ideology" (cf. Robbins 2004: 212). In the upshot, it's almost as if these polar inhabitants were bipolar—except that, beside the fear and composure that came from their respect of the god, on occasion they also knew how to oppose and defy her.

More precisely, if great shamans could on occasion force the god to desist from harming the people, it was by means of countervailing metapersons in their service: familiar spirits they possessed or who possessed them. Thus empowered, the shaman could fight or even kill Sedna, to make her liberate the game (upon her revival) in a time of famine (Weyer 1932: 359; Merkur 1991: 112). More often, the dangerous journeys shamans undertake to Sedna's undersea home culminate in some manhandling of her with a view to soothing her anger by combing the sins of humans out of her tangled hair. Alternatively, Sedna was hunted like a seal from a hole in the ice in winter: she was hauled up from below by a noose and while in the shaman's power told to release the animals; or she was conjured to rise by song and then harpooned to the same effect.

The last, the attack on the god, was the dramatic moment of an important autumnal festival of the Netsilik, designed to put an end to this tempestuous season and ensure good weather for the coming winter. Again it was not just the stormy weather with its accompaniment of shifting and cracking ice that was the issue, but the "countless evil spirits" that were so manifesting themselves, including the dead knocking wildly at the huts "and woe to the unhappy person they can lay hold of" (Boas [1888] 1961: 603). Ruling all and the worst of them was Sedna, or so one may judge from the fact that when she was ritually

---

5. Like the Chukchee shaman who told Bogoras:

    We are surrounded by enemies. Spirits always walk about with gaping mouths. We are always cringing, and distributing gifts on all sides, asking protection of one, giving ransom to another, and unable to obtain anything whatever gratuitously. (1904–9: 298)

hunted and harpooned, the evil metahuman host were all driven away. Sedna dives below and in a desperate struggle manages to free herself, leaving her badly wounded, greatly angry, and in a mood to seize and carry off her human tormenters. That could result in another attack on her, however, for if a rescuing shaman is unable to otherwise induce her to release the victim, he may have to thrash her into doing so (Rasmussen 1930: 100). Although the shamans' powers to thus oppose the god are not exactly their own, may one not surmise—as David Graeber develops at length in chapter 7 in this volume—there is here a germ of a human political society: that is, ruling humans qua metapersons themselves?

A word on terminology. Hereafter, I use "*inua*" as a general technical term for all animistic forms of indwelling persons, whether of creatures or things— and whether the reference is singular or plural. I use "metaperson" preferably and "metahuman" alternately for all those beings usually called "spirits": including gods, ghosts, ancestors, demons, *inua*, and so on. Aside from direct quotations, "spirit" will appear only as a last resort of style or legibility, and usually then in quotation marks—for reasons to which I now turn, by way of the life story of Takunaqu, an Iglulik woman:

> One day I remember a party of children out at play, and wanted to run out at once and play with them. But my father, who understood hidden things, perceived that I was playing with the souls of my dead brothers and sisters. He was afraid this might be dangerous, and therefore called upon his helping spirits and asked them about it. Through his helping spirits, my father learned . . . there was . . . something in my soul of that which had brought about the death of my brothers and sisters. For this reason, the dead were often about me, and I did not distinguish between the spirits of the dead and real live people. (Rasmussen 1930: 24)

WHY CALL THEM SPIRITS?

Sometime before Hocart was asking, "Why not call them gods?" Andrew Lang in effect asked of gods, "Why call them spirits?" Just because we have been taught our god is a spirit, he argued, that is no reason to believe "the earliest men" thought of their gods that way ([1898] 1968: 202). Of course, I cannot speak here of "the earliest men"—all those suggestive allusions to the state of nature notwithstanding—but only of some modern peoples off the beaten track of state systems and their religions. For the Inuit, the Chewong, and similar others, Lang would have a point: our native distinction between spirits and human beings, together with the corollary oppositions between natural and supernatural and spiritual and material, for these peoples do not apply. Neither, then, do they radically differentiate an "other world" from this one. Interacting with other souls in "a spiritual world consisting of a number of personal forces," as J. G. Oosten observed, "the Inuit themselves are spiritual beings" (1976: 29). Fair enough, although given the personal character of those forces, it is more logical to call spirits "people" than to call people "spirits." But in either case, and notwithstanding our own received distinctions, at ethnographic issue here is the straightforward equivalence, spirits = people.

The recent theoretical interest in the animist concepts of indigenous peoples of lowland South America, northern North America, Siberia, and Southeast Asia has provided broad documentation of this monist ontology of a personalized universe. Kaj Århem offers a succinct summary:

> As opposed to naturalism, which assumes a foundational dichotomy between objective nature and subjective culture, animism posits an intersubjective and personalized universe in which the Cartesian split between person and thing is dissolved and rendered spurious. In the animist cosmos, animals and plants, beings and things may all appear as intentional subjects and persons, capable of will, intention, and agency. The primacy of physical causation is replaced by intentional causation and social agency. (2016: 3)

It only needs be added that given the constraints of this "animist cosmos" on the human population, the effect is a certain "cosmo-politics" in Eduardo Viveiros de Castro's sense of the term (2015). Indeed, the politics at issue here involves much more than animist *inua*, for it equally characterizes people's relations to gods, disembodied souls of the dead, lineage ancestors, species-masters, demons, and other such intentional subjects: a large array of metapersons setting the terms and conditions of human existence. Taken in its unity, hierarchy, and totality, this is a *cosmic polity*. As Déborah Danowski and Viveiros de Castro (2017: 68–69) very recently put the matter (just as this article was going to press):

> What we would call "natural world," or "world" for short, is for Amazonian peoples a multiplicity of intricately connected multiplicities. Animals and other

spirits are conceived as so many kinds of "'people" or "societies," that is, as *po-litical entities*. . . . Amerindians think that there are many more societies (and therefore, also humans) between heaven and earth than are dreamt of in our philosophy and anthropology. What we call "environment" is for them a society of societies, an international arena, a *cosmopoliteia*. There is, therefore, no abso-lute difference in status between society and environment, as if the first were the "subject" and the second the "object." Every object is another subject and is more than one.

In what follows I offer some selected ethnographic reports of the coexistence of humans with such metapersonal powers in the same "intersubjective and per-sonalized universe"—just by way of illustration. But let me say here, and try to demonstrate in the rest of the essay, the implications are world-historical: for if these metaperson-others have the same nature as, and are in the same experien-tial reality with, humans, while exerting life-and-death powers over them, then they are the dominant figures in what we habitually call "politics" and "econom-ics" in all the societies so constituted. In the event, we will require a different anthropological science than the familiar one that separates the human world into ontologically distinct ideas, social relations, and things, and then seeks to discount the former as a dependent function of one of the latter two—as if our differentiated notions of things and social relations were not symbolically con-stituted in the first place.

Not to separate, then, what peoples of the New Guinea Highlands join: surrounded and outnumbered above, below, and on earth by ghosts, clan ances-tors, demons, earthquake people, sky people, and the many *inua* of the wild, the Mbowamb spend their lives "completely under the spell and in the company of spirits. . . . The spirits rule the life of men. . . . There is simply no profane field of life where they don't find themselves surrounded by a supernatural force" (Vicedom and Tischner (1943–48, 2: 680–81). Yet if the "other world" is thus omnipresent around Mt. Hagen, it is not then an "other world." These people, we are told, "do not distinguish between the purely material and purely spiritual aspects of life" (ibid.: 592). Nor would they have occasion to do so if, as is re-ported of Mae Enga, they conducted lives in constant intersubjective relations with the so-called "spirits." "Much of [Enga] behavior remains inexplicable to anyone ignorant of the pervasive belief in ghosts," reports Mervyn Meggitt. "Not a day passes but someone refers publicly to the actions of ghosts" (1965: 109–10). Or as a missionary-ethnographer recounts:

For the Central Enga the natural world is alive and endowed with invisible power. To be seen otherwise would leave unexplained numerous events. The falling
tree, the lingering illness, the killing frost, the haunting dream—all confirm the
belief in a relationship between the physical world and the powers of earth, sky,
and underworld. (Brennan1977: 11–12; cf. Feachem 1973)

Such metapersonal powers are palpably present in what is actually happening
to people, their fortunes good and bad. Hence Fredrik Barth's own experience
among Baktaman in the Western Highlands: "The striking feature is . . . how
empirical the spirits are, how they appear as very concrete observable objects in
the world rather than ways of talking about the world" (1975: 129, emphasis
in original). Supporting Barth's observation from his own work among nearby
Mianmin people, Don Gardner adds that "spirits of one kind or another are a
basic feature of daily life. Events construed as involving 'supernatural' beings are
commonly reported and discussed" (1987: 161).[6]

Mutatis mutandis, in the Amazonian forest, Eduardo Viveiros de Castro
comes to a similar appreciation of the gods and dead as immanently present
for Araweté. Listening to the nocturnal songs of shamans summoning these
metaperson-others to the village, the ethnographer

came to perceive the presence of the gods, as the reality or source of examples, in
every minute routine action. Most important, it was through these that I could
discover the participation of the dead in the world of the living. (1992: 13–14)

The presence of *maï* ['gods'] in daily life is astonishing: for each and every purpose, they are cited as models of action, paradigms of body ornamentation,
standards for interpreting events, and sources of news . . . . (1992: 74–75)[7]

The general condition of the cohabitation of humans and their metaperson-
al-alters in one "real world" is their psychic unity: their mutual and reciprocal

---

6.   Peter Lawrence and Meggitt speak of a general Melanesian "view of the cosmos
       (both its empirical and non-empirical parts) as a unitary physical realm with few, if
       any, transcendental attributes" (1965: 8).

7.   Yet the Araweté are no more mystical in such regards than is the ethnographer.
       The affective tone of their life, Viveiros de Castro notes, does not involve what we
       consider religiosity: demonstrations of reverence, devaluation of human existence,
       and so forth. They are familiar with their gods.

status as anthropopsychic subjects. The venerable anthropological premise of "the psychic unity of mankind"has to be more generously understood. For as Viveiros de Castro says, "There is no way to distinguish between humans and what we call spirits" (ibid.: 64). In effect, the so-called "spirits" are so many heterogeneous species of the genus *Homo:* "Human beings proper (*bide*) are a species within a multiplicity of other species of human beings who form their own societies" (ibid.: 55).[8] As is well known, the statement would hold for many peoples throughout lowland South America. Of the Achuar, Philippe Descola writes that they do not know the "supernatural as a level of reality separate from nature," inasmuch as the human condition is common to "all nature's beings. . . . Humans, and most plants, animals, and meteors are persons (*aents*) with a soul (*wakan*) and individual life" (1996: 93).

In speaking of the "own societies" of the metaperson-others as known to Araweté, Viveiros de Castro alludes to the "perspectivism" that his writings have done much to make normal anthropological science. Well documented from Siberia as well as Amazonia, the phenomenon offers a privileged instance of the coparticipation of humans with gods, ghosts, animal-persons, and others in the same complex society. In consequence of differences in their perceptual apparatus, both people and animals live unseen to each other in their own communities as fully human beings, bodily and culturally; even as each appears to the other as animal prey or predators. In this connection, the common ethnographic observation that because the nonhuman persons are as such generally invisible, they must inhabit a different, "spiritual" reality, is a cultural *non sequitur* for Araweté and other perspectivists. In Lockean terms the differences are only secondary qualities: due to perception—because of the different bodily means thereof—rather than to the thing thus perceived. In practice, moreover, the *socius* includes a variety of metapersonal communities: not only those of the animal *inua,* but also the villages of the gods, the dead, and perhaps others, all of them likewise cultural replicas of human communities. Accordingly, the human groups are engaged in a sociological complexity that defies the normal anthropological characterizations of their simplicity. A lot of social intercourse goes on between humans and the metahuman persons with whom they share the earth, as well as with those who people the heavens and the

---

8. Or else, like the various animals known to Naskapi of the Canadian Northeast, these other persons "constitute races and tribes among which the human is included" (Speck 1977: 30).

underworld. Apart from shamans, even ordinary humans may travel to lands of the metaperson-others, as conversely the latter may appear among people in human form. Human and nonhuman persons are often known to intermarry or negotiate the exchange of wealth—when they are not reciprocally eating one another.

SOCIAL RELATIONS OF PEOPLE AND METAPERSON-OTHERS

> A woman sits in a corner of the house, whispering to a dead relative; a man addresses a clump of trees. . . . When an illness or misfortune occurs, a father or neighbor will break knotted strips of cordyline leaf, talking to the spirits to find out which one is causing trouble and why. (Keesing 1982: 33)

This passage is one of many that exemplify how Roger Keesing makes good on the introductory promise of his fine monograph on the Kwaio people of Malaita (Solomon Islands): namely, "to describe Kwaio religion in a way that captures the phenomenological reality of a world where one's group includes the living and the dead, where conversations with spirits and signs of their presence and acts are part of everyday life" (ibid.: 2–3; cf. 33, 112–13). Likewise, the human world of the Lalakai of New Britain is "also a world of spirits. Human beings are in frequent contact with non-human others, and there is always the possibility of encountering them at any time" (Valentine 1965: 194). Yet beyond such conversations or passing encounters with metaperson-others, from many parts come reports of humans entering into customary social relations with them.

Inuit know of many people who visited villages of animal-persons, even married and lived long among them, some only later and by accident discovering their hosts were animal *inua* rather than Inuit humans (Oosten 1976: 27). A personal favorite is the Caribou Man of the northern Algonkians. In one of many similar versions, Caribou Man was a human stranger who was seduced by a caribou doe, went on to live with and have sons by her, and became the ruler of the herd (Speck 1977). French-Canadian trappers were not off the mark in dubbing Caribou Man "*le roi des caribou*," as the story rehearses the archetypal stranger-king traditions of dynastic origin, down to the mediating role played by the native woman and her foundational marriage to the youthful outsider (see chapter 3 in this volume). Besides the hierogamic experiences of Chewong women and the marriage of the gods with dead Araweté women, there are many permutations of such interspecies unions: some patrilocal and some matrilocal, some enduring and some ended by divorce due to home-sickness. A Kaluli man of the New Guinea Southern Highlands may marry a woman of the invisible world, relates Edward Schiefflin (2005: 97); when the man has a child by her, he can leave his body in his sleep and visit her world. Reciprocally, people from that world may enter his body and through his mouth converse with the people present. Then there was the Mianmin man of the Western Highlands who, beside his human wife, formed a polygynous arrangement with a dead woman from a different descent group. The dead wife lived in a nearby mountain, but she gardened on her husband's land and bore him a son (Gardner 1987: 164).

Don Gardner also tells of the time that the Ulap clan of the Mianmin saved themselves from their Ivik enemies by virtue of a marital alliance with their own dead. The lvik clan people were bent on revenge for the death of many of their kinsmen at Ulap hands. Sometime before, the big-man of the Ulap and his counterpart among their dead, who lived inside the mountain on which the Ulap were settled, exchanged sisters in marriage. When the big-man of the dead heard the Ivik were threatening his living brother-in-law, he proposed that the two Ulap groups exchange the pigs they had been raising for each other and hold a joint feast. In the course of the festivities, the ancestral people became visible to the Ulap villagers, who were in turn rendered invisible to the Ivik. So when the Ivik enemies came, they could not find the Ulap, although three times they attacked the places where they distinctly heard them singing. Throughout the Western Mianmin area, this account, Garner assures us, has the status of a historical narrative.

We need not conclude that relations between humans and their metaperson counterparts are everywhere and normally so sympathetic. On the contrary, they are often hostile and to the people's disadvantage, especially as the predicament noted earlier of the Inuit is broadly applicable: the animals and plants on which humans subsist are essentially human themselves. Although some anthropolo-gists have been known to debate whether cannibalism even existed, it is hardly a rare condition—even among peoples who profess not to practice it themselves. As already noticed, in many societies known to anthropology, especially those where hunting is a mainstay, the people and their prey are involved in a system of mutual cannibalism. For even as the people kill and consume "people like us," these metaperson-alters retaliate more or less in kind, as eating away human flesh by disease or starvation.

All over the Siberian forest, for instance,

> Humans eat the meat of game animals in the same way that animal spirits feed on human flesh and blood. This is the reason why sickness (experienced as a loss of vitality) and death in the [human] community as a whole are understood as a just payment for its successful hunting both in the past and the future. (Hamayon 1996: 79)

Married to the sister or daughter of the "game-giving spirit," an elk or reindeer, his brother-in-law the Siberian shaman thus enters an affinal exchange system of flesh—the meat of animals compensated by the withering of people—on behalf of the human community. Thus here again: "Being similar to the human soul in essence and on a par with hunters in alliance and exchange partners, spirits are not transcendent" (ibid.: 80). It is, to reprise Århem's expression above, "an intersubjective and personalized universe."

METAPERSON POWERS-THAT-BE

The metahuman beings with whom people interact socially are often hierarchically structured, as where gods such as Sedna and species-masters such as Caribou Man encompass and protect the individual *inua* in their purview. These hierarchies are organized on two principles which in the end come down to the same thing: the proprietary notion of the higher being as the "owner"—and usually also the parent—of his or her lesser persons; and the platonic or classificatory notion of "the One over Many," whereby the "owner" is the personified form of the class of which the lesser persons are particular instances. One can find both concepts in Viveiros de Castro's discussion of the Araweté term for metahuman masters, *nã*:

> The term connotes ideas such as leadership, control, responsibility, and ownership of some resource or domain. The *nã* is always a human or anthropomorphic being. But other ideas are involved as well. The *nã* of something is someone who has this substance in abundance. Above all, the *nã* is defined by something of

which it is the master. In this last connotation, he is at the same time "the representative of" and the "represented by" that something. (1992: 345)[9]

Although, in a spasm of relativism, Pascal famously said that a shift of a few degrees of latitude will bring about a total change in juridical principles, you can go from the Amazon forests or the New Guinea Highlands to the Arctic Circle and Tierra del Fuego and find the same ethnographic descriptions of greater metapersons as the "owners"-cum-"mothers" or "fathers" of the individual metapersonal beings in their domain. Urapmin say "that people get into trouble because 'everything has a father,' using father (*alap*) in the sense of owner. . . . In dealing with nature then, the Urapmin are constantly faced with the fact that the spirits hold competing claims to many of the resources people use" (Robbins 1995: 214–15). (Parenthetically, this is not the first indication we have that the "spirits" own the means of production, an issue to which we will return.) Among Hageners, the Stratherns relate, all wild objects and creatures are "owned" by "spirits," and can be referred to as their "pigs," just as people hold domestic pigs (1968: 190). "Masters of nature," to whom trees and many other things "belong," these *kor wakl* spirits are "sworn enemies of mankind" because people tend to consume foods under their protection without proper sacrifices. "The people are terribly afraid of them" (Vicedom and Tischner 1943–48, 2: 608, 659).

In the Siberian Arctic, large natural domains such as forests, rivers, and lakes had their "special owners," as Waldemar Bogoras calls them. The forest-master familiar to Russo-Yukaghir had "absolute power" over the animals there; he could give them away as presents, lose them at cards, or round them up and cause them to depart the country (Bogoras 1904–9 285). Not unusual either is the compounded hierarchy of metahuman owners, composed of several levels of *inua*-figures: as among Tupí-Guaraní peoples such as Tenetehara and Tapirapé, where species-masters are included in the domains of forest-masters, who in turn belong to the godly "owners" of the social territory. Similarly for Achuar, the individual animal *inua* are both subsumed by "game mothers"—who "are seen as exercising the same kind of control over game that mothers exercise over their children and domestic animals"—and also magnified forms of the

9. These species- and place-masters are known the length and breadth of the Western Hemisphere. For good examples see Wagley ([1947] 1983) on Tapirapé, Wagley and Galvao ([1949] 1969) on Tenetahara, Huxley (1956) on Urubu, and Hallowell (1960) on Ojibwa. As noted, the great Inuit god-*inua* are also represented as "owners" of their domains.

species—who, as *primus inter pares*, watch over the fate of the others. The latter
especially are the social interlocutors of the Achuar hunter, but he must also
come to respectful terms with the former (Descola 1996: 257–60). The chain of
command in these hierarchical orders of metaperson "owners" is not necessarily
respected in pursuing game or administering punishments to offending hunters,
but it is quite a bureaucracy.

As I say (and so have others), this sense of belonging to a more inclusive
power can be read as membership in the class of which the "owner" is the personified representative—that is, a logical and theological modality of the One
over Many. The ordering principle is philosophical realism with an anthropomorphic twist, where a named metaperson-owner is the type of which the several lesser beings are tokens. In a broad survey of the concept in the South
American lowlands, Carlos Fausto (2012) uses such pertinent descriptions of
the species-master as "a plural singularity" and "a singular image of a collectivity." Anthropologists will recognize classic studies to the effect: Godfrey Lienhardt (1961) on the totems or species-beings who subsumed the forms of the
same kind; and Edward Evans-Pritchard (1956) on the Nuer "God" (Kwoth),
manifested in a diminishing series of avatars. (Parenthetically, as species-masters are more widely distributed in the world than totems proper, the latter may
be understood as a development of the former under the special influence of
descent groups or other segmentary formations.) In his own well-known wan-
dering minstrel tour of animism—rather like the present article, composed of
ethnographic shreds and patches—E. B. Tylor conceived a similar passage from
"species-deities" to "higher deities" by way of Auguste Comte on the "abstraction" thus entailed and Charles de Brosses on the species archetype as a Platonic
Ideal (1903: 241–46).[10]

---

10. This classificatory logic is evident in Hermann Strauss' reports on the subsumption
    of the various Sky People of the Mbowamb into "He, himself, the Above." As the
    beings who "planted" the clan communities, together with their foods and customs,
    the Sky People are "owners" of the earthly people, but generally they remain at a
    distance and are involved only in times of collective disaster or need. Exceptionally,
    however, Strauss cites a number of Mbowamb interlocutors assigning responsibility
    to "The Above" for both individual and community misfortunes.

    If many men are killed in battle, they say "He himself, the Ogla [Above], gave
    away their heads." . . . When a great number of children die, the Mbowamb say,
    "He himself, the Above, is taking all our children up above." If a couple remain
    childless, everyone says "Their *kona* [land] lies fallow, the Above himself, as the
    root-stock man (i.e., owner) is giving them nothing." ([1962] 1990: 38–39)

That divinity originates as a kind of animism of higher taxonomic order is not a bad (Platonic) idea. Consider this notice of Sedna: "In popular religious thought, the Sea Mother is an indweller. She indwells in the sea and all of its animals. She is immanent in the calm of the sea, in the capes and shoals where the waters are treacherous, and in the sea animals and fish" (Merkur 1991: 136). Analogously, for the Aboriginal peoples of Northwest Australia, the cult of their great Rainbow Serpent, Ungud, could be epitomized as *inua* all the way down. A bisexual snake identified with the Milky Way, the autochthonous Ungud made the world. Les Hiatt summarized the process:

> Natural species came into existence when Ungud dreamed itself into new vari-
> ous shapes. In the same way Ungud created clones of itself as *wonjina* [local
> versions of Dreamtime ancestors], and dispatched them in various places,
> particularly waterholes. The *wonjina* in turn generated the human spirits that
> enter women and become babies. . . . Ungud is thus an archetype of life itself.
> (1996: 113)

In his informative account of the local Ungarinyin people, Helmut Petri specifies that the numerous *wonjina* were transformed into "individual Ungud serpents," such that "Ungud appeared in the Aborigines' view at one time as an individual entity, at another time as a multiplicity of individual beings" ([1954] 2011: 108). This included the spirit children whom the *wonjina* deposited in the waterholes: they were given by Ungud. Hence the One over Many, down to individual human beings, for each person thus had an "Ungud part" (see also Lommel [1952] 1997).

It only needs to be added, from Nancy Munn's revelatory study of analogous phenomena among Walbiri, that in participating intersubjectively in an object world created by and out of the Dreamtime ancestors, human beings experiencing "intimations of themselves" are always already experiencing "intimations of others": those Dreamtime heroes "who are superordinate to them and precede them in time" (1986: 75). Accordingly, violation of any part of the country is "a violation of the essence of moral law" (ibid.: 68). While clearly different from other societies considered here, these no less "egalitarian" Australian Aborigines are thus no less hierarchical. "It's not our idea," Pintupi people told Fred Myers in regard to the customs and morality established in perpetuity by the Dreamtime ancestors. "It's a big Law. We have to sit down beside that Law like all the dead people who went before us" (Myers 1986: 58).

THE COSMIC POLITY

By way of integration of themes presented heretofore, there follows a sketch of the cosmic polities of the Mountain Ok-speaking Min peoples of New Guinea.[11]

There was no visible or proximate political state in the center of New Guinea, the region of the Fly and Sepik River headwaters traditionally inhabited by the Mountain Ok or Min peoples. All the same, the Telefolmin, Urapmin, Feramin, Tifalmin, Mianmin, and others could be fairly described as governed by metahuman powers whose authority over otherwise politically fragmented peoples was exercised through obligatory rules effectively backed by punitive force. The Hocartesian question might well be, "Why not call it a state?" Or else, if this cosmic polity were unlike a state in that the controlling powers largely outnumbered the civil society of humans, their regime could be all the more dominating. Experientially, the people live in a condition of subjugation to a host of metaperson powers-that-be, whose numerous rules of order are enforced by the highest authorities, often through the offices of the lesser personages in their aegis.

Among the Central Min peoples, where this regime achieved its most integrated form, it was dominated by the cosmocratic duo of Afek, mother of humans and taro, and the serpentine Magalim, who preceded her as the autochthonous father of the numerous creatures of the wild (Jorgensen 1980, 1990a, 1998). Parents of all, Afek and Magalim were themselves children of none. The beginnings of their respective reigns were marked by violent breaches of kinship relations, giving them the independence that was the condition of their universality. Afek was notorious for committing incest with her brother, whom she later killed (and revived). Magalim was born of himself by intervening in the sexual intercourse of a human couple. Emerging as a serpent, he was subsequently rejected by his would-be mother, swallowed his foster-father, and killed his father's brothers. Magalim has been likened to the Rainbow Serpent

---

11. I am especially indebted to Dan Jorgensen for his unstinting, generous, and informative replies to my many questions about the ethnography of the Telefolmin and of Min peoples in general. His knowledge and interpretations of this material, as of anthropology more broadly, are extraordinary—though, of course, I take responsibility if I have misconstrued the information he provided. I have also relied heavily on several of his writings, especially Jorgensen (1980, 1990a, 1990b, 1990c, 1996, 1998, 2002). Also most useful have been Barth (1975, 1987), Wheatcroft (1976), Brumbaugh (1987, 1990), and Robbins (1995, 1999, 2004).

figures of Aboriginal Australian traditions: among other resemblances, by his habitation of subterranean waters, from which he rises when irritated to cause destructive floods (Brumbaugh 1987). Afek adds to the analogy by her own resemblance to Australian Dreamtime ancestors, creating features of the landscape and endowing the customs of the human groups she gave rise to in the course of her travels. Thereafter Afek's presence would be mediated primarily by the human ancestors whose cult of fertility she established, whereas Magalim as indwelling "boss" of the land acted through the multifarious *inua* of its creatures and features. Although in effect they thus organized complementary domains— Afek the human sphere and Magalim its untamed environs—through their respective human and metahuman subjects each extended into the jurisdiction of the other—often there to do harm.[12]

Much of Min cultural order, including the taboos that sanction it, is the codification of the legendary doings of Afek in the mode of mandatory custom. "Since that time," Tifalmin people say, "men and women have known how to do things" (Wheatcroft 1976: 157–58). The precedents thus set by episodes in the epic of Afek's advent include the different social and sexual roles of men and women and the rituals and practices of menstruation, initiation, childbirth, and death. Indeed, death itself was initiated by Afek along with the westward journey of the deceased on the underground road to the land of the dead—whence in return come life-giving shell valuables, hence Afek is also the originator of wealth, exchange, and long-distance trade. Afek bore the taro plant that iconically distinguishes the Min people, making a complementary schismogenesis of it by destroying the swamps in the Telefolmin region, thereby marking the contrast to lowland sago peoples. Along her journey, she established the men's cult houses where the remains of the ancestors of each Min group and the associated initiation rituals would guarantee the growth of their youth and their taro. Afek's ritual progress culminated in the construction of her own great cult house, Telefolip, in the Telefolmin village of that name.

---

12. As a civilizer who carved a human cultural existence out of the wild, displacing its "nature spirits," Afek's story is similar to stranger-king traditions. A further similarity is her union or unions with local men (or a dog). Although the Min peoples are generally known as "Children of Afek," there are alternate local traditions of the autochthonous origins of certain groups from animal ancestors. The same sort of opposition between indigenous "owners" and the incoming rulers is in play in the domination of the area by the Telefolmin people, who arrived at their present location and achieved their superior positon by early military feats.

Afek's house became the ritual center of the Mountain Ok region, thus giving the Telefolmin people a certain precedence over the other Min groups. Rituals performed in connection with the Telefolip house radiated Afek's benefits in human and agricultural fertility widely among the other Min communities. If the house itself deteriorated, the growth of taro in the entire region would decline in tandem. The several Min groups of a few hundred people each were thus integrated in a common system of divine welfare centered on the Telefolip shrine. The overall effect was a core–periphery configuration of peoples in a tribal zone with the Telefolmin custodians of Afek's legacy at the center. As described by Dan Jorgensen (1996: 193): "The common linkage to Afek locates Mountain Ok cults in a regional tradition. Myths concerning Afek not only account for the features of a particular ritual system or aspects of local cosmology, but also place groups relative to one another in terms of descent from Afek (or a sibling)" (cf. Robbins 2004: 16–17). "A surprisingly ambitious ideology," comments Robert Brumbaugh, "because it does not link up with any economic or political control from the center" (1990: 73). Here is another instance where the superstructure exceeds the infrastructure. What does link up with the superiority of Telefolmin, as Brumbaugh also says, is Afek's continued presence:

> In Telefolmin religion, Afek remains present and accessible. Taro fertility is a visible sign of her power, just as her bones are the visible signs of her presence. . . . Thus the Falamin, when addressing the local ancestors in ritual, consider that they are heard by Afek as well. When stronger reassurances are needed, the local ancestor is bypassed, new personnel take charge of the ritual and Afek is invoked directly. Groups without access to bones of Afek—it seems that not all groups have them—are covered by Afek's promise to hear and respond when she is called upon for taro. (1990: 67)

But "Magalim always ruins Afek's work," Telefolmin say, breaking her "law" by deceiving men into killing their friends, seducing women, driving people mad, causing landslides and floods, and wrecking gardens (Jorgensen 1980: 360). Capricious and malicious, Magalim is oftimes (but not always) the enemy of people: a menace especially among the Central Min, where he is the father, owner, and thereby the common form in the persons of the animals, plants, rocks, rivers, cliffs, and so on, that inhabit and constitute the environment—where human persons hunt, garden, and otherwise traverse with disturbing effects. "All things of the bush are Magalim's children, *Magalim man*," Jorgensen was told.

"If you finish these things, Magalim is their father and he will repay you with sickness, or he will send bad dreams and you will die" (ibid.: 352).

The wild has its own hierarchy: at least three levels of Magalim-persons, encompassed by the archetypal All-Father serpent. Jorgensen notes that certain species-masters of distinct name "look after" marsupials and wild pigs, even as Magalim himself looks after snakes. But all are in turn encompassed in Magalim, as "All these names are just names. The true thing is Magalim" (ibid.). Likewise for Urapmin, Joel Robbins refers to intermediate species-masters controlling their particular animal-persons; these "owners" being in turn subsumed in the greater Magalim-Being. Certain "marsupial women" are guardians of the many marsupial kinds that people hunt and eat. Taking a fancy to a hunter, a marsupial woman may have sex with and marry him. Thereafter she comes to him in dreams to inform him about the whereabouts of game. But marsupial women have been known to become jealous of their husband's human wife, especially if the latter is too generous in sharing marsupials with her own relatives. Then the hunter has accidents in the bush or falls sick, or even dies if he does not leave his human spouse (Robbins 2004: 210).

In any case, where Magalim reigns, the principle holds that all particular *inua*, whether of living creatures or natural features, are also forms of him. The individual Magalim-persons who cause Feramin people trouble may be treated as acting on their own or as agents of Magalim All-Father. The people may say, "Tell your father to stop making thunderstorms—and not to send any earthquakes either" (Brumbaugh 1987: 26). Magalim, however, is not always causing trouble for Feramin. Without changing his notorious disposition, he may turn it on strangers, whom he is reputed to dislike, and thus become protector of the local people. Indeed, he defends Feramin tribal territory as a whole. The Feramin were divided into four autonomous communities ("parishes"); but Magalim's remains were in the care of a single elder, and when ritually invoked before battle, they made all Feramin warriors fierce and their arrows deadly. "Without subdivision by parishes," Brumbaugh writes, "the territory of Feramin as a whole is considered under the influence of Magalim, who watches over its borders and the well-being of the traditional occupants" (ibid.: 30).

Protector of the entire territory from an abode within it, a subterranean being who can cause earthquakes, Magalim is the indwelling *inua* of the land itself: "boss of the land," the people now say. Indeed, if all the creatures and prominent natural haunts of the wild are so many aliases of Magalim, as Jorgensen puts it, it is because he is "identified with the earth and its power." "Everything depends on Magalim," Jorgensen was often told, including Afek and all her people who "sit on the top of the ground" (1998: 104). Kinship to territory: the self-born Magalim, slayer of his foster-kin, becomes god of the land.

Hence add gardeners to the tragic predicament of the animist hunters. The Urapmin, according to Robbins, are constantly aware they are surrounded by "nature spirits" (*motobil*) who are original "owners" of almost all the resources they use (2004: 209–10). Consequently, "every act of hunting or gardening causes some risk," even on non-taboo grounds, should it disturb the metaperson-owners—who would thereupon punish the person responsible "for failure to observe their version of the laws" (ibid.: 211). Interesting that New Guineans and Australian Aborigines, although without any native juridical institutions as such, have been quick to adapt the European term "law" to their own practices of social order. In other contexts, Robbins speaks of "the law of the ancestors," apparently referring to the numerous taboos based on traditions of Afek that organize human social relationships. The Urapmin term here translated as "law"—*awem* (adj.), *aweim* (n.)—maps a moral domain of prohibitions based "on kinds of authority that transcend those produced *simply* by the actions and agreements of men" (ibid.: 211). Otherwise said, these laws are "sacredly grounded prohibitions aimed at shaping the realm of human freedom" (ibid.: 184). Given the range of social relationships and practices established by Afek, it follows that the laws were "complex" and "left everyone laboring under the burdens of at least some taboo all the time" (ibid.: 210–11). Although Urapmin boast of having been the most taboo-ridden of all Min people, it could not have been by much. Among others, the Tifalmin knew taboos that were likewise "very powerful . . . sustaining and interpenetrating many other normative and ethical aspects of everyday life" (Wheatcroft 1976: 170). This could be true virtually by definition, inasmuch as by following Afek's precedents, the entire population would be ordered by taboos marking the social differences between men and women and initiatory or age-grade statuses. Negative rules predicate positive structures—and at the same time uphold them.[13]

In Telefolmin, Urapmin, and probably elsewhere, violations of Afek's taboos were as a rule punished occultly, without Afek's explicit intervention. On the other hand, in Tifalmin the metaperson-powers of both the village and the bush were actively engaged in sanctioning the many taboos of "everyday

---

13. I am indebted to Dan Jorgensen for this point: which, as he observes, derives from observations of Lévi-Strauss.

life." Often punishments emanated from the prominent ancestors whose remains were enshrined in Afek's cult house. Alternatively, they were inflicted by the "vast congresses" of thinking and sentient animal "ghosts" (*sinik*), *inua* who struck down people with disease or ruined their gardens. The last suggests that even people who adhere to Afek's food taboos may thereby suffer the vengeance of the species-masters—that is, for killing and eating the latter's children. As Don Gardner observed for Mianmin, since every animal has its "mother" or "father," human mothers and children become vulnerable to an equivalent payback for what was done to the species-parent's child. And among the Central Min, where the parent is an All-Father like Magalim, the threat is apparently constant as well as general in proportion. Brumbaugh writes of Magalim:

> All smells connected with women and children bring danger from Magalim. He may make women pregnant, eat an unborn child and leave one of his own, or come unseen between a couple having intercourse in the bush to give his child instead; it will then be a contest between the power of the man and the power of Magalim that determines the future of the child. (Brumbaugh 1987: 27)

It follows that to the extent people are socially objectified in terms of the wild foods they could or could not eat, they are in double jeopardy of suffering harm: whether magically or indirectly from Afek, mother of humans, for eating wrongly; or from the mother or father of the animal for eating it at all. Here again are "cosmic rules" of human order, enforced throughout the social territory by metaperson authorities to whom it all "belongs."

DETERMINATION BY THE RELIGIOUS BASIS

Of the South American lowland people, the Piaroa, Joanna Overing writes:

> Today, Masters of land and water own the domains of water and jungle . . . both of whom acquired their control over these habitats at the end of mythical time. These two spirits guard their respective domains, protect them, make fertile their inhabitants, and punish those who endanger their life forces. They also cooperate as guardians of garden food. The relevant point is obviously that the inhabitants of land and water are not owned by man. (1983–84: 341)

Since, as a general rule, the peoples under discussion have only secondary or usu-fructuary rights to the resources "owned" by metaperson-others, it follows that their relations of production entail submission to these other "people like us." In conventional terms, it could justifiably be said that the spirits own the means of production—were it not that the "spirits" so-called are real-life metapersons who in effect *are* the primary means-cum-agents of production. Fundamental resources—plants, animals, celestial and terrestrial features, and so on—are con-stituted as intentional subjects, even as many useful tools are "person-artifacts."[14] Marked thus by an intersubjective praxis, this is an "economy" without "things" as such. Not only are metahuman persons ensouled in the primary resources, they thereby govern the outcome of the productive process. As intentional be-ings in their own right, they are the arbiters of the success or failure of hu-man efforts. For theirs are the life-forces—which may be hypostatized as *mana*, *hasina*, *wakan*, *semengat*, *orenda*, *nawalak*, or the like—that make people's gar-dens grow, their pigs flourish, and game animals become visible and available to them. Some decades ago, Jonathan Friedman and Michael Rowlands put the matter generally for "tribal" peoples: "Economic activity in this system can only be understood as a relation between producers and the supernatural. This is because wealth and prosperity are seen as directly controlled by supernatural spirits" (1978: 207).

Of course we are speaking of the people's own notions of what there is and how it comes to be: a culturally informed reality they share with metaperson-others to whom they are subjected and indebted for life and livelihood. When faced with the assurance of Kwaio people that their prosperity is "a result of ancestral support," Roger Keesing refrains from the temptation "to say that the sacred ancestral processes are a mystification of the real physical world," for, "in a world where the ancestors are participants in and controlling forces of life, this conveys insights only at the cost of subjective realities" (1982: 80). But why, then, "subjective realities"? If the ancestors participate in and control the people's everyday existence—if they are "empirical," as Fredrik Barth might say—the demystification would shortchange the "objective" realities.[15] Not to

---

14. "In the Amerindian case . . . the possession of objects must be seen as a particular case of the ownership relation between subjects, and the thing-artefact as a particular case of the person-artefact" (Fausto 2012: 33).

15. Later in the same monograph, Keesing attempts to recuperate these "political insights" in favor of the conventional view that the spiritual powers are an ideological reflex of the Kwaio big-man system. But aside from the fact that the Kwaio spirit-world

worry, however: in due course, with a few pertinent ethnographic notices in hand, I consider what scholarly good or harm would come from crediting such "determination by the religious basis."

It is not as if the producing people had no responsibility for the economic outcome—even apart from their own knowledge and skill. The Inuit shaman explains that: "No bears have come in their season because there is no ice; and there is no ice because there is too much wind; and there is too much wind because we mortals have offended the powers" (Weyer 1932: 241). Even so, something then can be done. Around the world, the common recourse for this dependence on the metaperson agents of people's prosperity is to pay them an appropriate tribute, as in sacrifice. Sacrifice becomes a fundamental relation of production—in the manner of taxation that secures benefits from the powers-that-be. As Marcel Mauss once put it, since spirits "are the real owners of the goods and things of this world," it is with them that exchange is most necessary ([1925] 2016: 79). A Tifalmin man tells how it works:

> When we bring secretly hunted marsupial species into the *anawok* [men's cult house] during ceremonies, we tell the *amkumiit* [ancestral relics] and the pig bones [of feasts gone by], "you must take care of us and make our pigs grow fat and plentiful, and our taro immense." As soon as we told them this, shortly afterwards we see the results in our gardens. They do just what we petitioned. (Wheatcroft 1976: 392)

For all this hubris, however, the Tifalmin are not really in control. Edmund Leach notably remarked of such sacrifices that the appearance of gift and reciprocity notwithstanding, the gods don't need gifts from the people. They could easily kill the animals themselves. What the gods require are "signs of submission" (Leach 1976: 82–93). What the gods and the ancestors have, and peoples such as the Tifalmin seek, is the life-force that makes gardens, animals, and people grow. The metahuman powers must therefore be propitiated, solicited, compensated, or otherwise respected and appeased—sometimes even tricked—as a necessary condition of human economic practice. Or as Hocart had it, based on his own ethnographic experience: "There is no religion in Fiji, only a system that in Europe has been split into religion and business." He knew that in Fijian, the

---

is much more complex morphologically than Kwaio society, there are no Kwaio big-men with the life-and-death powers even of their ancestral predecessors.

same word (*cakacaka*) refers indiscriminately to "work"—as in the gardens—or to "ritual"—as in the gardens.

So why call it "production"? How can we thus credit human agency if the humans are not responsible for the outcome: if it is the ancestors according to their own inclinations who make the taro grow; or if it is *Sila Inua*, the Air, and the bears themselves who make hunting successful? In a golden few pages of his recent work *Beyond nature and culture* (2013), Philippe Descola argues persuasively that our own common average native notion of "production" fails to adequately describe human praxis in a metahuman cosmos. Where even animals and plants are thinking things, the appropriate anthropology should be Hocartesian rather than Cartesian. Rather than a subject–object relation in which a heroic individual imposes form upon inert matter, making it come-to-be according to his or her own plan, at issue here are intersubjective relations between humans and the metaperson-others whose dispositions will be decisive for the material result. Descola can conclude from his Amazonian experience that it is "meaningless" to talk of "agricultural production" in a society where the process is enacted as interspecies kinship:

> Achuar women do not "produce" the plants that they cultivate: they have a personal relationship with them, speaking to each one so as to touch its soul and thereby win it over; and they nurture its growth and help it to survive the perils of life, just as a mother helps her children. (2013: 324)

Not to forget the mistress and mother of cultivated plants, Nankui, described by Descola elsewhere (1996: 192ff.): the goddess whose presence in the garden is the source of its abundance—unless she is offended and causes some catastrophic destruction. Hence the necessity for "direct, harmonious, and constant contact with Nankui," as is successfully practiced by women who qualify as *anentin*, a term applied to persons with the occult knowledge and ritual skills to develop fruitful relations with the goddess.

The way Simon Harrison describes the agricultural process for Manambu of the Middle Sepik (New Guinea), people do not *create* the crops, they *receive* them from their ancestral sources. "What could pass for 'production,'" he writes, "are the spells by which the totemic ancestors are called from their villages by clan magicians to make yams abundant, fish increase, and crocodiles available for hunting" (1990: 47). For "yams are not created by gardening," but, like all cultivated and wild foods, "they came into the phenomenal world by being 'released' from the mythical villages by means of ritual" (ibid.: 63). Note that this is a *political* economy, or, more exactly, a cosmopolitical economy, inasmuch as the human credit for the harvest goes to those who gained access to the ancestors by means of their secret knowledge—rather than the gardener who knew the right soils for yams. Of course, one may accurately say that, here as elsewhere, human technical skills, climatic conditions, and photosynthesis are responsible for the material outcome, for what actually happened; but also here as elsewhere, the decisive cultural issue, from which such specific political effects follow, is, rather, *what it is that happened*—namely, the clan magicians summoned the yams from the ancestral villages. Such is the human reality, the premises on which the people are acting—which are also the beginnings of anthropological wisdom.

Further ethnographic notices of the spiritual nature of the material basis are easy to come by. I close with a final one that has the added advantage of addressing the issue, raised in Harrison's work, of human power in a cosmic polity. The site will be Melpa and their neighbors of the Hagen region. Here a variety of metahuman beings—Sky People deities (including their collective personification in "Himself, the Above"); "Great Spirits" of the major cults; the human dead, both recently deceased kin and clan ancestors; and the numerous "nature spirits" or *inua*-owners of the wild—are the agents of human welfare:

> In trade and economic affairs . . . in campaigns of war or at great festivals, any success is seen as the result of the help of benevolent spirits. . . . Benevolent spirits are said to "plant our fields for us" and to "make our pigs big and fat." . . . They are said to "raise the pigs." (Strauss [1962] 1990: 148)

The functions of these metaperson-kinds are largely redundant; many are competent to promote or endanger the well-being of the people. It will be sufficient to focus on a few critical modes of life and death from the metapersons—with a view also to their constitution of human, big-man power.

Whereas the Sky People originally "sent down" humans and their means of existence, it is the recent dead and clan ancestors who are most intimately and continuously responsible for the health and wealth of their descendants—though for punishing people they usually enlist the ill-intentioned *inua* of the wild. As recipients of frequent sacrifices, the recent dead protect their kin from accidents, illness, and ill fortune. "They will 'make the fields and vegetable gardens for us . . . raise pigs for us, go ahead of us on journeys and trading trips, grant us large numbers of children . . . stay at our side in every way" (ibid.: 272). So likewise, on a larger scale, as when a meeting house is built for them, will the clan spirits "make our fields bring forth . . . our pigs multiply, protect our wives, children, and pigs from plagues and illness, keep sorcery and evil spirits at bay" (ibid.: 279). But if the gardens are planted without proper sacrifices, "the owner-spirit digs up the fruits and eats them" (Vicedom and Tischner 1943–48, 2: 677). By contrast to this constant attention, the Great Spirits of the collective cults are ceremonially celebrated only at intervals of years. On these occasions, the large number of pigs sacrificed testifies to the deities' exceptional ability to multiply things themselves by promoting the people's growth, fertility, and wealth. In such respects both the dead and the cult deities are particularly useful to big-men and would-be big-men, that is, as the critical sources of their human power:

> We rich people [i.e., big-men] live and sacrifice to the Kor Nganap [Female Great Spirit]; this enables us to make many *moka* [pig-exchange festivals]. Through this spirit we become rich, create many children who remain healthy and alive, and stay ourselves healthy. Our gardens bear much fruit. All this the Kor Nganap does, and that is why we sacrifice to it. (Vicedom and Tischner 1943–48, 2: 794)

The Stratherns relate that when a big-man goes on a journey to solicit valuables, he asks his clan-ancestors to come sit on his eyelids and induce his trading partner to part with his valuables. Big-men are also helped by the ghosts of close relatives, who may be enlisted by partaking of the pig backbone cooked especially for them. The same ancestors and ghosts are with the big-man in the ceremonial ground when he makes the prestations that underwrite his fame and status (Strathern and Strathern 1968: 192).

In another text, Andrew Strathern notes that traditional Hagen big-men had "a multitude of sacred and magical appurtenances which played an important part, from the people's own perspective, in giving them the very access to wealth on which their power depended" (1993: 147). Strathern here addresses a range of leadership forms in a variety of Highland New Guinea societies— including Baruya, Duna, Simbari Anga, Kuskusmin, and Maring, as well as Melpa—to show that the "ritual sources of power" amount to a Melanesian *Realpolitik*: the condition of possibility of human authority, as regards both the practices by which it is achieved and the reason it is believed. All the same, we need not completely abandon historical materialism and put Hegel right-side up again, for in these big-man orders one may still speak of economic determinism—provided that the determinism is not economic.

TO CONCLUDE

To conclude: we need something like a Copernican Revolution in the sciences of society and culture. I mean a shift in perspective from human society as the center of a universe onto which it projects its own forms—that is to say, from the received Durkheimian, Marxist, and structural-functionalist conventions—to the ethnographic realities of people's dependence on the encompassing meta-person-others who rule earthly order, welfare, and existence. For Durkheim, God was an expression of the power of society: people felt they were constrained by some power, but they knew not whence it came. But if what has been said here has any cogency, it is better to say that God is an expression of the lack of power of society. Finitude is the universal human predicament: people do not control the essential conditions of their existence. I have made this unoriginal and banal argument too many times, but if I can just say it once more: if people really controlled their own lives, they would not die, or fall sick. Nor do they govern the weather and other external forces on which their welfare depends. The life-force that makes plants and animals grow or women bear children is not their doing. And if they reify it—as *mana*, *semengat*, or the like—and attribute it to external authorities otherwise like themselves, this is not altogether a false consciousness, though it may be an unhappy one. Vitality and mortality do come from elsewhere, from forces beyond human society, even as they evidently take some interest in our existence. They must be, as Chewong say, "people like us."

But so far as the relation between the cosmic authorities and the human social order goes, in both morphology and potency there is no equivalence between them. As I have tried to show, especially by egalitarian and chiefless societies, neither in structure nor in practice do they match the powers above and around them. Among these societies there are no human authorities the likes of Sedna, Sila, Ungud, the Original Snake, Afek, Magalim, Nankui, or the New Guinea Sky People.[16] What Viveiros de Castro says in this regard to the Araweté and

---

16. Of the Huli equivalent of Hagener Sky People, R. M. Glasse writes: "Dama are gods—extremely powerful beings who control the course of nature and interfere in

Tupi Guarani peoples generally can be widely duplicated among the classically "acephalous" societies:

> How to account for the coexistence of, on one hand, a "loosely structured" organization (few social categories, absence of global segmentation, weak institutionalization of interpersonal relations, lack of differentiation between public and domestic spheres) with, on the other hand, an extensive taxonomy of the spirit world . . . an active presence of that world in daily life, and a thoroughly vertical "gothic" orientation of thought . . . ? Societies such as the Araweté reveal how utterly trivial any attempts are to establish functional consistencies or forced correspondences between morphology and cosmology or between institution and representation. (1992: 2–3)

Even apart from the numerous malevolent, shape-shifting beings with superhuman powers of afflicting people with all kinds of suffering, Viveiros de Castro describes a society of immortal gods in heaven without equal on earth, who make people's foods and devour their souls, who are capable of elevating the sky and resurrecting the dead, gods who are "extraordinary, splendid but also dreadful, weird—in a word, awesome" (ibid.: 69).[17]

But they do have shamans, precisely of similar powers (ibid.: 64)—as do many other such societies. Even where there are no chiefs, there are often some human authorities: big-men, great-men, guardian magicians, warriors, elders. Yet, given the basis of their authority, these personages are so many exceptions that prove the rule of domination by metaperson powers-that-be; for, like Inuit shamans or Hagen big-men, their own ability to command others is conveyed by their service to or enlistment of just such metaperson-others. Indeed, as Vicedom and Tischner write of Hageners: "Any manifestation of power in people or things is ascribed to supernatural or hidden power," whether in the form

---

the affairs of men." Notably, one Datagaliwabe, "a unique spirit whose sole concern is punishing breaches of kinship rules" (1965: 27)—including lying, stealing, adultery, murder, incest, violations of exogamic rules and of ritual taboos—inflicts sickness, accidents, death or wounding in war (ibid.: 37).

17. For a similar structure of divinity in a non-Tupi setting, see Jon Christopher Crocker (1983: 37 *et passim*) on the *bope* spirits of the Bororo. In both cases, by conveying to the gods their rightful share of certain foods, the people will be blessed with fertility and natural plenty.

of good harvests, many children, success in trade, or a respected position in the community (1943–48, 1: 43).

In insightful discussions of the Piaroa of the Orinoco region, Joanna Overing (1983–84, 1989) notes that human life-giving powers were not their own, but were magically transmitted to individuals from the gods by tribal leaders. By means of powerful chants, the *ruwang*, the tribal leader, was uniquely able to travel to the lands of the gods, whence he brought the forces for productivity enclosed within "beads of life" and placed them in the people of his community. Overing points out that this is no political economy in the sense that tribal leaders control the labor of others. But as they absorbed more divine powers than others, they were responsible for building the community: "Without the work of the *ruwang*, the community could not be created, and because of his greater creative power, he was also the most productive member of the community" (1989: 172).

In such cultural-ontological regimes, where every variety of human social success is thus attributed to metapersonal powers, there are no purely secular authorities. Roger Keesing relates of an ambitious young Kwaio man that he is well on his way to big-manship, as evidenced by his staggering command of genealogies, his encyclopedic knowledge of traditions of the ancestors and their feuds, his distinction as a singer of epic chants, and his acquisition of magical powers. Accordingly, he is "not only acquiring an intellectual command of his culture, but powerful instruments for pursuing secular ambitions as a feast-giver" (Keesing 1982: 208). Or for an Australian Aboriginal example: Helmut Petri concludes that the reason certain Ungarinyin "medicine men" and elders are leading and influential men of their communities is that they "are regarded as people in whom primeval times are especially alive, in whom the great heroes and culture-bringers are repeated and who maintain an inner link between mythical past and present" ([1954] 2011: 69). Not that those who so possess or are favored by divine powers are necessarily placed beyond the control of their fellows, for popular pressures may be put on them to use such powers beneficently. Here is where the famous "egalitarianism" of these peoples becomes relevant. Tony Swain (1993: 52) notes that the native Australian elders' shared being with the land entails the obligation to make it abound with life—a duty the people will hold them to. Swain is careful to insist that the leaders' access to ritual positions amounts to a certain control of "the means of production," hence that this is not the kind of communalistic, nonhierarchical society "imagined by early Marxists." But then, ordinary people, without direct access to metapersonal sources of fertility, "can and do order ritual custodians to 'work' to make them food: 'You mak'em father—I want to eat.'" All of which brings us back to the issue of mystification.

Earlier, I warned against too quickly writing off the human dependence on gods, ancestors, ghosts, or even seal-persons as so much mistaken fantasy. Well, nobody nowadays is going to attribute these notions to a "primitive mentality." And from all that has been said here, it cannot be claimed these beliefs in "spirits" amount to an ideological chimera perpetrated by the ruling class in the interest of maintaining their power—that is, on the Voltairean principle of "There is no God, but don't tell the servants." Here we do have gods, but no ruling class. And what we also distinctively find in these societies is the coexistence in the same social reality of humans with metahumans who have life-giving and death-dealing powers over them. The implications, as I say, look to be world-historical. As is true of big-men or shamans, access to the metaperson authorities on behalf of others is the fundamental political value in all human societies so organized. Access on one's own behalf is usually sorcery, but to bestow the life-powers of the god on others is to be a god among men. Human political power is the usurpation of divine power. This is also to say that claims to divine power, as manifest in ways varying from the successful hunter sharing food or the shaman curing illness, to the African king bringing rain, have been the raison d'être of political power throughout the greater part of human history. Including chiefdoms such as Kwakiutl, where,

> The chiefs are the assemblers, the concentrators, and the managers of supernatural powers. . . . The human chiefs go out to alien realms and deal with alien beings to accumulate *nawalak* [generic life-giving power], and to concentrate it in the ceremonial house. When they have become centers of *nawalak* the salmon come to them. The power to draw salmon is equated with the power to draw people. The power to attract derives from *nawalak* and demonstrates its possession. (Goldman 1975: 198–99)

It was not military power or economic prowess as such that generated the dominance of the Abelam people over the various other Sepik communities of New Guinea eager to adopt Abelam cultural forms; rather it was the "supernatural power" that their successes signified. "Effectiveness in warfare and skill in growing yams, particularly the phallic long yams," Anthony Forge (1990: 162) explains, "were in local terms merely the material manifestations of a more fundamental Abelam domination, that of power conceived essentially in magical and ritual terms." What enabled the Abelam yams to grow larger, their gardens to be more productive, and their occupation of land once held by others was their "superior access to supernatural power." Accordingly, the political-cum-cultural reach of the Abelam extended beyond their actual grasp. Beyond any real-political or material constraints, the Abelam were admired and feared for their superior access to cosmic power in all its forms, and notably for its "concrete expression" in rituals, buildings, and a great array of objects, decorations, and aesthetic styles. Abelam culture was thus carried abroad by its demonstrable command of greater force than its own (ibid: 163ff.).

Southeast Asian "tribals" and peasants are well known for sacrificial "feasts of merit" in which the display and/or distribution of livestock, foods, and ritual valuables such as porcelain jars and imported textiles is the making of local authorities. But it is not so much the economic benefits to the population at large that constitute this authority—as if the people were rendered dependent on the sponsor of the sacrificial feast for their own means of existence—as it is the privileged dependence of the feast-giver on the metahuman sources of people's prosperity. As Kaj Århem comments in regard to the "ritual wealth" thus expended:

> Such ritual wealth is regarded as objectivized spirit power—an indication that the owner is blessed and protected by personal spirits. Spirit possession manifests itself in good health and a large family. The blessings of the spirits are gained by proper conduct—keeping the precepts of the cosmologically underpinned social and moral order—and, above all, by continuously hosting animal sacrifices, the so-called "feasts of merit." Wealth, sacrifice, and spiritual blessing are thus linked in an endless, positive feedback circuit. The implied reification of spiritual potency in the form of wealth and worldly power—its acquisition and accumulation as well as its loss—is central to Southeast Asian cosmology and politics. (2016: 20)

Economic prowess is a metaphysical power.[18] Then again, there are other well-known ways, from the magical to the military, of demonstrating such metahuman potency. Even in the matter of kingship, the royal authority may have little or nothing to do with the accumulation and disposition of riches. In certain African stranger-kingships described elsewhere (see chapter 5 in this volume),

---

18. Geertz (1980) was right to speak of a Balinese "theatre state." So were those who criticized him for underplaying its material dimension.

power essentially rested on the ritual functions of ensuring the population's prosperity: the authority to do so being dependent on descent from exalted foreign
sources, complemented usually by traditions of the dynastic founder's exploits as
a hunter and warrior in the wild. As Shilluk, Lovedu, and Alur demonstrate, in
more than one African realm such stranger-kings "rained" but did not govern.
For all the superior foreign origin of an Alur chiefly dynasty, its connection
to the ancient great kingdom of Nyoro-Kitara, the Alur ruler, reported Aidan
Southall, was revered by his indigenous subjects more for his power to stop war
than to make it; "and the sanction to his ritual authority, which is always up-
permost in people's minds, is his power to make or withhold rain rather than his
power to call in overwhelming force to crush an opponent" ([1956] 2004: 246):

> Rain (*koth*) stood for material well-being in general, and a chief's ability to dem-
> onstrate his control over it was a crucial test of his efficacy. The chief's control
> of rain and weather, together with his conduct of sacrifice and worship at the
> chiefdom shrines, stood for his general and ultimate responsibility in the minds
> of his subjects for both their material and moral well-being. ([1956] 2004: 239)

You will have noticed that I have come back full circle to Hocart's *Kings and
councillors*. Government in general and kingship in particular develop as the organization of ritual. As said earlier, we scholars of a more skeptical or positivist
bent are at liberty to demystify the apparent illusions of the Others. We can split
up their reality in order to make society autonomous, expose the gods as fantasy,
and reduce nature to things. To put it in Chicagoese, we may say we know better than them. But if we do, it becomes much harder to know them better. For
myself, I am a Hocartesian.

A final note in this personal vein. Written by one of a certain age, this pre-
tentious article has the air of a swan song. Similarly, for its concern with disap-
pearing or disappeared cultural forms, it is something of the Owl of Minerva
taking wing at dusk. Still, it does manage to kill those two birds with one stone.

CODA

Already copyedited, this text was on its way to the printer when by happy chance
I discovered that in 1946 Thorkild Jacobsen had formulated the concept of a "cosmic state" in reference to Mesopotamian polities of the third millennium BCE.

Jacobsen's discussion of a universal metapersonal regime in a city-state setting indeed anticipates many of the attributes of "The original political society" as presented here—most fundamentally his observation that "the universe as an organized whole was a society, a state" ([1946] 1977: 149). Ruled by divine authorities, human society was merely a subordinate part of this larger society, together with all the other phenomena-cum-subjects inhabiting the cosmos, from beasts and plants to stones and stars: all animate beings (*inua*) likewise endowed with personality and intentionality. Jacobsen depicts this hierarchically organized world in which personkind was the nature of things in a number of parallel passages. For example:

> Human society was to the Mesopotamian merely a part of the larger society of the universe. The Mesopotamian universe—because it did not consist of dead matter, because every stone, every tree, every conceivable thing in it was a being with a will and a character of its own—was likewise founded on authority: its members, too, willingly and automatically obeyed orders which made them act as they should act. . . . So the whole universe showed the influence of the essence peculiar to Anu [Sky, king and father of the gods]. ([1946] 1977: 139)

By Jacobsen's descriptions, this universal animism was classificatory—the personalities of elements of the same kind were instances of a master personality of the species; and the scheme was hierarchical at multiple levels—species forms were in turn inhabited by higher, divine forms, such that the world was governed through the indwelling being of cosmocratic gods in every existing thing. While the whole universe manifested the essence of Anu, the goddess Nidabe created and inhabited the useful reeds of the wetlands and by her presence made them flourish. "She was one with every reed in the sense that she penetrated as an animating and characterizing agent, but she did not lose her identity in that of the concrete phenomena and was not limited to any or all the existing reeds" (ibid.: 132). Note that this kind of philosophical realism, with the god as personification of the class of which individuals are participatory members, is a general logic of partibility or dividualism. The god is a partible person manifest in various other beings—like the "myriad bodies" (*kino lau*) of Hawaiian gods—and at the same time exists independently of them. By the same token (pun intended), the several members of a divine class are at once manifestations of the god and (in)dividuals in their own right and kind.

Following this classificatory logic, Jacobsen achieves a description of divine kingship in Mesopotamia of the kind known from classic anthropological accounts in which, for all that the king is a certain god, the god is not the king. Nyikang is Juok, but Juok is not Nyikang; Captain Cook is Lono, but Lono is not Captain Cook. Just so, the Mesopotamian king is Anu, but Anu is not the king. Indeed, given the partibilities involved, the Mesopotamian king in various capacities is also Enlil, Marduk, or any and all the great gods. (Interesting that Hocart [(1936) 1970: 88] recounted the analogous claim of an important Fijian chief who, after enumerating the great gods of the chiefdom, said, "These are all my names.") This type of intersubjective animism is by far the most common type of divine kingship: the king as human manifestation of the god, as an avatar of the god, rather than the human as the deity in his own person, such as the self-made Roman god, Augustus. Jacobsen also thus testifies to the principle that human authority is the appropriation of divine power. In the cult, the Mesopotamian king enacted the god and thereby controlled and acquired the god's potency. By a kind of usurpation, as it were, a man could "clothe himself with these powers, with the identity of the gods, and through his own actions, when thus identified, cause the powers to act as he would have them act" (Jacobsen [1946] 1977: 199).

For the rest, Jacobsen's text delivers on the usual ontological suspects of a metapersonal cosmos: no subject–object opposition, and, a fortiori, no differentiation of humans from nature—or can we not say: no culture–nature opposition? (Similar observations are made in the same volume by John A. Wilson [(1946) 1977] on ancient Egypt and H. and H. A. Frankfort [(1946) 1977] on ancient civilizations in general.) Given this universal subjectivity as a matter of common experience, neither did the ancient Mesopotamians know a transcendent, "supernatural" realm. "The Mesopotamian universe did not have 'different levels of reality'" (Jacobsen [1946] 1977: 149).

The ethnographic examples of "The original political society" were deliberately taken from so-called "egalitarian societies" situated far from any state system to avoid the possibility that the cosmic polities at issue had been diffused or otherwise transplanted from an already existing regime of ruling kings and high gods. However, comparing Jacobsen's account with peoples such as the Inuit and New Guinea highlanders, something of the reverse seems more likely: that the ancient civilizations inherited cosmological regimes of the kind long established in human societies. If so, the human state was the realization of a political order already prefigured in the cosmos: the state came from heaven to earth—rather than the gods from earth to heaven.

CHAPTER 2

The divine kingship of the Shilluk
On violence, utopia, and the human condition

DAVID GRAEBER

God kills us.

Malagasy proverb

"States," I once suggested, have a peculiar dual quality: they are always at the same time "forms of institutionalized raiding or extortion, and utopian projects" (Graeber 2004: 65). In this essay I'd like to put some flesh on this assertion by reexamining one of the most famous cases in the history of anthropology: the divine kingship of the Shilluk of the Nilotic Sudan.[1]

The Shilluk have been, since at least Sir James Frazer's time, the *locus classicus* for debates over the nature of divine kingship; however, the kingdom might seem an odd choice for an exploration of the nature of the state. The Shilluk kingdom was clearly not a state. The Shilluk *reth*, or king, lacked any sort of administration and had little way to enforce his will. Nonetheless, I think that one reason anthropologists, and others, have found the Shilluk case so compelling is

---

1.   These words were written six years ago, and reflection on cases like this has since inspired me to question whether the nature of the "state" is even the most useful thing to ask. But I thought it best to leave the argument largely as it stood in the original. I should note that "Shilluk" is an Arabization of the native term, *Collo* or *Chollo*. Most of the king's current subjects now use *Chollo* when writing in English. I have kept to the historical usage largely to avoid confusion.

not just because they seem to come so close to actually enacting Frazer's apparently whimsical fantasy about primordial god-kings who are ritually sacrificed when their term expired, but because they share an intuition that these apparently minimal, stripped-down versions of sovereign power can tell us something profound about the nature of power more generally, and hence, ultimately, states. It strikes me this is especially true of the aforementioned predatory and utopian elements, both of which can be seen here in embryonic form.

A proviso is in order. I am not saying this because I believe the Shilluk political system to be in any sense "primitive," or think that forms of sovereignty that were later to blossom into the modern state were only beginning to emerge here like some half-formed idea. That would be absurd. Anyone living, like the Shilluk, within a few days' journey of ancient centers of civilization like Egypt, Meroe, or Ethiopia was likely to be perfectly aware of what a centralized government was. It is even possible (we don't know) that Shilluk kings were distinctly more powerful in the past than they were when our records kick in in the eighteenth and nineteenth centuries. But one thing is clear from existing records: if the Shilluk were organized the way they were at that time, it is because those elements in Shilluk society that clearly would have liked to, and occasionally tried to, create something similar to surrounding states and empires had largely failed to convince the rest of the Shilluk population to go along with them. As a result, the Shilluk kingdom was a system of institutionalized raiding, and a utopian project, and very little else.

I am also aware that the word "utopian" might seem odd here; one might just as easily substitute "cosmological project." Royal palaces, royal cities, or royal courts almost invariably become microcosms, images of totality. The central place is imagined as a model of perfection, but at the same time, as a model of the universe; the kingdom, ideally, should be another reproduction of the same pattern on a larger level. I emphasize the word "ideally." Royal palaces and royal cities always fall slightly short of heaven; kingdoms as a whole never live up to the ideals of the royal court. This is one reason the term "utopia" seems appropriate. These are ideals that by definition can never be realized; after all, if the cosmos, and the kingdom, really could be brought into conformity with the ideal, there would be no excuse for the predatory violence.

Perhaps the most fascinating thing about the Shilluk material is that these two elements are so clearly seen as linked. Sovereignty—that which makes one a sovereign—is defined as the ability to carry out arbitrary violence with impunity. Royal subjects are equal in that they are all, equally, potential victims;

but the king too is a victim in suspense, and in myth as well as ritual, it is at the moments when the people gather together to destroy the king—or at least to express their hatred for him—that he is mysteriously transformed into an eternal, transcendental being. In a cosmological system where separation is seen as balanced antagonism, opposition literally as at least potential hostility, the king inhabits a kind of tiny paradise, set apart from birth, death, and sickness; set apart equally from ordinary human sociality; representing exactly this sort of imperfect ideal. Yet his ability to do so rests on a delicate balance of relations of opposition and barely contained aggression—between humans and gods, between king and people, between fractions of the royal family itself—that will, inevitably, destroy him.

All this will become more clear as I go on. Let me begin, though, with a very brief survey of theories of divine kingship and the place of the Shilluk in them. Then I will demonstrate how I think these pieces can be reassembled to create the elements for a genealogy of sovereignty.

THEORIES OF DIVINE KINSGHIP

The Shilluk first became famous, in Europe and America, through James Frazer's book *The golden bough*. They are so firmly identified with Frazer that most are unaware the Shilluk did not even appear in the book's first two editions (1890 and 1900). Originally, in fact, Frazer drew largely on classical literature in making an argument that all religion was to some degree derived from fertility cults centered on the figure of a dying god, and that the first kings, who embodied that god, were ritually sacrificed. This idea made an enormous impression on anthropology students of the time (and even more, perhaps, on artists and intellectuals), many of whom were to fan out across the world looking for traces of such institutions in the present day. The most successful was Charles Seligman, who discovered in the Shilluk kingdom an almost perfect example, in 1911 sending Frazer a description that he incorporated, almost verbatim, in the book's third edition (C. G. Seligman 1911; Frazer 1911a; Fraser 1990: 200–201).

One reason the Shilluk seemed to fit the bill so nicely was that Frazer had argued that divine kingship was originally a form of spirit possession. To find a king whose physical health was said to be tied to the fertility and prosperity of the kingdom, or even who was therefore said to be ritually killed when his powers begin to wane, was not difficult. There were endless examples in Africa and elsewhere. But for Frazer, divine kings were literally possessed by a god. Frazer also felt the notion that kings were possessed by the spirits of gods would necessarily lead to a practical problem: How does one pass this divine spirit from one mortal vessel to another? Clearly, he felt, this would demand some sort of ceremony. But death tends to be a random and unpredictable affair. How could one be sure the ceremony would be conducted at the moment of the king's death? Frazer concluded the only way was to arrange for the king's death to occur at an appropriate moment: either after a fixed term, or, at the very least, when his weakened condition meant death seemed to be approaching anyway. And the only way to do that was of course by killing him.

All this was precisely what the Shilluk did appear to do. The Shilluk king, or *reth*, was indeed said to embody a divine being—a god, or at least a demigod— in the person of Nyikang, the legendary founder of the Shilluk nation. Every king was Nyikang. The *reth* was not supposed to die a natural death. He might fall in battle with the nation's enemies. He might be killed in single combat after a rival prince demanded a duel, as they had a right to do, or be suffocated by his own wives or retainers if he was seen to be physically failing (a state which was indeed seen to lead to poor harvests or natural catastrophes). On his death, though, Seligman emphasized, Nyikang's spirit left him and entered a wooden effigy. Once a new *reth* was elected, the candidate had to raise an army and fight a mock battle against the effigy's army in which he was first defeated and cap- tured, then, having been possessed by the spirit of Nyikang, which passed from the effigy back into his body, emerged victorious again.

Frazer made the Shilluk famous, and their installation ritual has become one of the classic cases in anthropology—which in a way is rather odd, since the Shilluk are one of the few Nilotic peoples never to have been the subject of sustained anthropological fieldwork. Their notoreity is partly due to the fact that E. E. Evans-Pritchard chose the Shilluk as the case study with which to carry out his own ceremony of ritual regicide, directed at Frazer himself. In 1948, tak- ing advantage of new ethnographic material provided by local colonial officials who had received some anthropological training, Evans-Pritchard delivered the first Frazer lecture on the subject (1948)—a lecture essentially designed to deal the death-blow to Frazer's whole problematic. In it, he argued that there was no such thing as a divine king, that Shilluk kings were probably never ritually exe- cuted, and that the installation ritual was not really about transferring a soul, but about resolving the tension between the office of kingship (figured as Nyikang), which was set above everyone equally, and the particular individual who held it, with his very particular background, loyalties, and local support base:

> In my view kingship everywhere and at all times has been in some degree a sacred office. *Rex est mixta persona cum sacerdote.* This is because a king symbolizes a whole society and must not be identified with any part of it. He must be in the society and yet stand outside it and this is only possible if his office is raised to a mystical plane. It is the kingship, and not the king who is divine. (1948: 36)

The intricacies of Shilluk royal ceremonial, according to Evans-Pritchard, arose from "a contradiction between dogma and social facts" (ibid.: 38): these were a people sufficiently well organized to wish for a symbol of national unity, but not well organized enough to turn that symbol into an actual government.

Evans-Pritchard was always a bit coy about his theoretical influences, but it's hard not to detect here a distant echo the Renaissance doctrine of the "King's Two Bodies," that is, the "body politic," or eternal office of kingship (ultimately including the community of his subjects), and "body natural," which is the physical person of the individual king. This intellectual tradition was later to be the subject of comprehensive study by the German historian Ernst Kantorowicz (1957), whose student Ralph Giesey (1967), in turn, explored the way that during Renaissance English and French inauguration rituals, the relationship between the two bodies was acted out through royal effigies. Later anthropologists (Arens 1979, 1984; Schnepel 1988, 1995) recognized the similarity with Shilluk ritual and went on to explore the parallels (and differences) much more explicitly.

Evans-Pritchard's lecture opened the way to a whole series of debates, most famously over his claim that ritual king-killing was simply a matter of ideology, not something that ever really happened. The "Did Africans really kill their kings?" debate raged for years, ending, finally, with an accumulation of empirical evidence that forced a general recognition that at least in some cases—the Shilluk being included among them—yes, they did.

At the same time, some of Frazer's ideas were discovered to have been not been nearly so fanciful and irrelevant as Evans-Pritchard suggested. Since the 1980s, at least, there has, indeed, been something of a Frazerian revival.

No one has been more responsible for this revival than the Belgian anthropologist Luc de Heusch—who, ironically, began his intellectual journey (1962) by setting out from Evans-Pritchard's point that in order to rule, a king must "stand outside" society. Essentially he asked: What are the mechanisms through which a king is made into an outsider? In any number of African kingdoms, at least, this meant that at their installations, kings were expected to make some kind of dramatic gesture that marked a fundamental break with "the domestic order" and domestic morality. Usually this consisted of performing acts—murder, cannibalism, incest, the desecration of corpses—that would, had anyone else performed them, have been considered the most outrageous of crimes. Sometimes such "exploits" were acted out symbolically: pretending to lie next to one's sister or stepping over one's father's body when taking the throne. At others they were quite literal: kings actually would marry their sisters or massacre their close kin. Always, such acts marked the king as a kind of "sacred monster," a figure, effectively, outside of morality (de Heusch 1982a, 1982b, 2000).

Marshall Sahlins (1981b, 1983b, 2007, this volume) has taken all this much further, pointing out, for one thing, that the vast majority of kings, in all times and places, not only try to mark themselves as exterior to society, but actually claim to come from someplace other than the lands they govern—or at the very least to derive from ancestors who do. There is a sense almost everywhere that "society," however conceived, is not self-sufficient; that power, creative energy—life, even—ultimately comes from outside. On the other hand, raw power needs to be domesticated. In myth, this often leads to stories of wild, destructive young conquerors who arrive from far away, only to be eventually tamed on marriage to "daughters of the land." In rituals, it often leads to ceremonies in which the king is himself conquered by the people.

De Heusch's concern was different. He was mainly interested in how, in African installation rituals, kings are effectively "torn from the everyday kinship order to take on the heavy responsibility of guaranteeing the equilibrium of the universe" (1997: 321). Kings do not begin as outsiders; they are made to "stand outside society." But in contrast to Evans-Pritchard, de Heusch insisted this exteriority was not just a political imperative. Kings stand outside society not just so they can represent it to itself, but so that they can represent it before the powers of nature. This is why, as he repeatedly emphasized, it is possible to have exactly the same rituals and beliefs surrounding actual rulers, largely powerless kings like the Shilluk *reth*, and "kings" who do not even pretend to rule over anything at all, but are simply individuals with an "enhanced moral status," like the Dinka masters of the fishing spear.

In such matters, Frazer's observations did indeed prove useful, especially because he began to map out a typology. In "The dying god" (1911a), Frazer described how kings act as what de Heusch calls "fetish bodies": that is, as magical charms manufactured by the people, "a living person whose mystical capacity is closely tied to the integrity of his physical being" (2005a: 26).[2] And while Frazer might not have understood that such kings were, indeed, seen as having been created by the people, de Heusch insisted he was quite correct in holding that, having been so consecrated, their physical strength was tied to the prosperity of nature, and that's why they could not be allowed to grow sickly, frail, and old. But in a later volume, *The scapegoat* (1911c), Frazer discovered another aspect: the king who absorbs the nation's sin and pollution, and is thus destroyed as a way of disposing of collective evil. The two are obviously difficult to reconcile. Yet in a surprising number of cases (e.g., Quigley 2005) they seem to coexist.

It's the scapegoat aspect that has generated the most voluminous literature—largely because students of divine kingship soon connected it with René Girard's quasi-psychoanalytic "scapegoat theory" (Makarius 1970; Scubla 2002), one which was gaining increasing popularity in French intellectual circles from the 1970s on. Girard, famously, argued that the scapegoat mechanism is really the secret lying behind all myth, ritual, and religion and is, indeed, what allows the very possibility of human sociality itself. Girard's is one of those arguments that, even if so overstated it might seem self-evidently absurd, nonetheless never fails to find an audience because it managed to find a way of framing something we are taught to already suspect is true—that is, that society is always, everywhere founded on some kind of fundamental violence—in a way no one had ever thought to propose before. Girard does not seek to find the sources of that violence in some presocial nature, but quite the opposite. The story goes like this: We learn to desire by observing what others desire. Therefore we all want the same things. Therefore we are necessarily in competition. The only way humans can avoid thus plunging into a Hobbesian war of all against all is to

---

2.   I am summarizing, not assessing, theories at this point, so I will not enlarge on the fact that de Heusch seems to me to be working with a fundamentally mistaken idea of the nature of African fetishes, which are rarely embodiments of fertility but ordinarily embodiments of destructive forces (Graeber 2005). I think he is quite right and profoundly insightful when he argues that kings are often created by the same mechanisms as fetishes, as I have myself argued for Merina sovereigns (Graeber 1996a), mistaken when he goes on to claim that the key innovation here is that, unlike fetishes, the power of kings does not have to be constantly ritually maintained, as there are any number of counterexamples (e.g., Richards 1968) where it definitely does.

direct their mutual hostility outward onto a single object. This generally means selecting some arbitrary victim, who is first reviled as the cause of all their troubles and expelled from the community, most often by killing him. Once this happens, though, everything suddenly turns around: the former scapegoat is suddenly treated as an exalted being, even a god, because he is now the embodiment of society's ability to create itself by the very act of killing him. This mechanism, Girard argues, is the origin of all society and culture. The logic is, in classic Freudian style, circular: since we cannot face the reality, we are always denying it; therefore, it cannot possibly be disproved. Still, applying this model to the problem of divine kingship has interesting effects. Kings become, effectively, scapegoats in waiting (Muller 1980; Scubla 2003). Hence de Heusch's "exploits" are, for Girardians, actual crimes. They ensure that the king is, by definition, a criminal; hence it is always legitimate to execute him, should it come to that. His sacred *pneuma*, then, is anticipatory: the reflected glow of the role the king might ultimately play in embodying the unity the people will achieve in finally destroying him.

Over the course of the ensuing debate the idea that such kings embody gods was gradually abandoned. De Heusch rejected the expression "divine kingship" entirely. And kings actually taken to be living gods are in fact surprisingly rare: the Egyptian Pharaoh may well have been the only entirely unambiguous example (Frankfort 1948; cf. Brisch 2008).[3] Better, he argued, to speak of "sacred kingship." Sacred kings are legion. But de Heusch also emphasizes that sacred kings are not necessarily temporal rulers. They might be. But they might equally be utterly powerless. Different functions—the king as fetish, the king as scapegoat, the king as military commander or secular leader—can either be combined in the same figure or be distributed across many; in any one community, any given one of them may or may not exist (de Heusch 1997).

De Heusch's ultimate conclusion is that A. M. Hocart ([1927] 1969, 1933, [1936] 1970) was right: kingship was originally a ritual institution. Only later did it become something we would think of as political—that is, concerned with making decisions and enforcing them through the threat of force. As with any such statement, though, the obvious question is: What does "originally" mean here? Five thousand years ago when states first emerged in Egypt and Mesopotamia? And if so, why is that important? Or is the idea, instead, that whenever

---

3.   Though part of the problem in saying that a king is a god is that the definition of "god"—or even, for that matter "is"—is entirely ambiguous here.

states emerge, it is invariably from within ritual institutions? This seems highly unlikely to be true in every case. Or is de Heusch simply saying that it is possible to have kings with ritual responsibilities and no political power, but not the other way around? If so, it would appear to be a circular argument, since then it would only be those political figures who have ritual responsibilities whom the analyst is willing to dignify with the name of "king."

It seems to me that de Heusch's real accomplishment is to demonstrate that what we are used to thinking of as "government" (or, maybe better, "governance") is not a unitary phenomenon. Simon Simonse (2005: 72), for instance, observes that, really, all most Africans ask of their sacred kings is what most Europeans demand of their welfare states: health, prosperity, a certain level of life security, and protection from natural disasters.[4] He might have added: however, most do not feel it necessary or desirable to also grant them police powers in order to achieve this.

The question of governance, then, is not the same as the question of sovereignty. But what is sovereignty? Probably the most elegant definition is that recently proposed by Thomas Hansen and Finn Stepputat (2005, 2006): in its minimal sense, sovereignty is simply the recognition of the right to exercise violence with impunity. This is probably the reason why, as these same authors note, those arguing about the nature of sovereignty in the contemporary world—the breakdown of states, the multiplications of new forms of semicriminal sovereignty in the margins between them—rarely find the existing anthropological literature on sacred kingship particularly useful.[5]

---

4. Simonse's comment has a particularly piquant irony when one considers the current popularity of the notion of "biopower": the idea that modern states claim unique powers over life itself because they see themselves not just ruling over subjects, or citizens, but as administering the health and well-being of a biological population. Probably the question we should be asking is how it happened that there were governments that did *not* have such concerns. This must have had something to do with the peculiar role of the church in the European Middle Ages.

5. I am simplifying their argument. Sovereign power for Hansen and Stepputat is marked not only by impunity but also by a resultant transcendence—the "crucial marks of sovereign power" are "indivisibility, self-reference, and transcendence" (2005: 8), as well as a certain "excessive" quality. In many ways their argument, especially when it draws on that of Georges Bataille with his reflections on autonomy and violence, comes close to the one that I will be developing. But it is also exactly in this area that it deviates the most sharply, since Bataille's position is ultimately profoundly reactionary, reading authoritarian political institutions back into the very nature of human desire. I like to think my position is more hopeful.

It seems to me this need not be the case. The existing literature does contain elements from which a relevant analysis can be constructed. Any such analysis would have to begin with the notion of transcendence: that in order to become the constitutive principle of society, a sovereign has to stand outside it. I mean this is not quite in either Evans-Pritchard's or de Heusch's sense; what I am suggesting is that the various "exploits" or acts of transgression by which a king marks his break with ordinary morality are normally seen to make him not immoral, but a creature beyond morality. As such, he can be treated as the constituent principle of a system of justice or morality—since, logically, no creature capable of creating a system of justice can itself be already bound by the system it creates. Let me take a famous example here. When European visitors to the court of King Mutesa of the Ganda kingdom tried to impress him by presenting him with some new state-of-the-art rifle, he would often respond by trying to impress them with the absolute quality of his power: testing the rifle out by randomly picking off one or two of his subjects on the street. Ganda kings were notorious for arbitrary, even random, violence against their own subjects. This, however, did not prevent Mutesa from also being accepted as supreme judge and guardian of the state's system of justice. Instead, such random acts of violence confirmed in him in a status similar to that often (in much of Africa) attributed to God, who is seen simultaneously as an utterly random force throwing lightning and striking down mortals for no apparent reason, and as the very embodiment of justice and protector of the weak.

This, I would argue, is the aspect of African kingship which can legitimately be labeled "divine." Creatures like Mutesa transcend all ordinary limitations. Whether they were said to embody a god is not the issue.[6] The point is that they *act* like gods—or even God—and get away with it.

For all that European and American observers ordinarily professed horror at behavior like Mutesa's, this divine aspect of kingship is echoed in the modern nation-state. Walter Benjamin (1978) posed the dilemma quite nicely in his famous distinction between "law-making" and "law-maintaining" violence. Really it is exactly the same paradox, cast in the new language that became necessary once the power of kings ("sovereignty") had been transferred, at least

---

6.   The Ganda kingship, for example, was almost entirely secular. Not only are we not dealing with a "divine king," in the sense of one identified with supernatural beings, we are not even dealing with a particularly sacred one—except insofar as any king is, simply by virtue of hierarchical position, by definition sacred.

in principle, to an entity referred to as "the people"—even though the exact way in which "the people" were to exercise sovereignty was never clear. No constitutional order can constitute itself. We like to say that "no one is above the law," but if this were really true, laws would not exist to begin with: even the writers of the United States Constitution or founders of the French Republic were, after all, guilty of treason according to the legal regimes under which they had been born. The legitimacy of any legal order therefore ultimately rests on illegal acts—usually, acts of illegal violence. Whether one embraces the left solution (that "the people" periodically rise up to exercise their sovereignty through revolutions) or the right solution (that heads of state can exercise sovereignty in their ability to set the legal order aside by declaring exceptions or states of emergency), the paradox itself remains. In practical terms, it translates into a constant political dilemma: How does one distinguish "the people" from a mere unruly mob? How does one know if the hand suspending habeas corpus is that of a contemporary Lincoln or a contemporary Mussolini?

What I am proposing here is that this paradox has always been with us. Obviously, any thug or bandit who finds he can regularly get away with raping, killing, and plundering at random will not, simply by that fact, come to be seen as a power capable of constituting a moral order or national identity.[7] The overwhelming majority of those who find themselves with the power to do so, and willing to act on it, never think to make such claims—except perhaps among their immediate henchmen. The overwhelming majority of those who do try fail. Yet the potential is always there. Successful thugs do become sovereigns, even creators of new legal and moral systems. And genuine "sovereignty" does always carry with it the potential for arbitrary violence. This is true even in contemporary welfare states: apparently this is the one aspect that, despite liberal hopes, can never be completely reformed away. It is precisely in this that sovereigns resemble gods and that kingship can properly be called "divine."

This is not to say that Evans-Pritchard was wrong to say that kings are also always sacred. Rather, I think this perspective allows us to see that the mechanics of sacred kingship—turning the king into a fetish or a scapegoat—often operate (whatever their immediate intentions) as a means of controlling the obvious dangers of rulers who feel they can act like arbitrary, petulant gods. Sahlins' emphasis on the way stranger-kings must be domesticated,

---

7. Benjamin himself suggested that the popular fascination with the "great criminal" who "makes his own law" derives from precisely this recognition.

encompassed, and thus tamed by the people is a classic case in point. It is by such means that divine kings are rendered merely sacred. In the absence of a strong state apparatus, situations of power are often fluid and tenuous: the same act that at one point marks a monarch as a transcendent force beyond morality can, if the balance of forces shift, be reinterpreted as simple criminality. Thus can divine kings indeed be made into scapegoats. In this, at least, the Girardians are right.

There is every reason to believe this logic applies to the Shilluk king (or *reth*) of the eighteenth and nineteenth centuries as well. Consider the following two stories, preserved by the German missionary Dietrich Westermann (and bearing in mind that while there is no way to know if these incidents ever actually happened, it doesn't really matter, since the repetition of such stories constitutes the very stuff of politics):

Story 1: One day a man named Ogam was fishing with a member of the royal family named Nyadwai. He caught a choice fish and the prince demanded he turn it over, but he refused. Later, when his fellow villagers suggested this was unwise, he pointed out there were dozens of princes, and belittled Nyadwai: "who would ever elect him king?"

Some years later, he learned Nyadwai had indeed been elected king.

Sure enough he was summoned to court but the king's behavior appeared entirely forgiving. "The king gave him cattle; built him a village; he married a woman, and his village became large; he had many children."

Then one day, many years later, the King destroyed the village and killed them all. (Westermann 1912: 141)

Here, we have an example of a king trying to play god in every sense of the term. Such a king appears arbitrary, vindictive, all-powerful in an almost biblical sense. If one examines it in the context of Shilluk institutions, however, it begins to look rather different. Ordinarily, Shilluk kings did not even have the power to appoint or remove village chiefs. In the complete absence of any sort of administrative apparatus, their power was almost entirely personal: Nyadwai created and destroyed Ogam's village using his own personal resources, his own herd of cattle, his own personal band of retainers. If he had tried to exterminate the lineage of a real village chief, not one he had made up, he would likely have found himself in very serious trouble. What's more, a *reth*'s power in fact was almost entirely dependent on his physical presence.

Here's another story, about the death of that same bad king Nyadwai, here seen as having getting his commeupance for taking such high-handed behavior altogether too far:

Story 2: There was once a cruel king, who killed many of his subjects, "he even killed women." His subjects were terrified of him. One day, to demonstrate that his subjects were so afraid they would do anything he asked, he assembled the Shilluk chiefs and ordered them to wall him up inside a house with a young girl. Then he ordered them to let him out again. They didn't. So he died. (Westermann 1912: 175; cf. P. P. Howell n.d. SAD 69/2/57)[8]

The story might even serve as a story of the origin of ritual regicide, though it isn't explicitly presented as such, since this was precisely the way kings were said to have originally been put to death. They were walled in a hut with a young maiden.[9]

Stories like these help explain a peculiar confusion in the literature on Shilluk kingship. Nineteenth-century travelers, and many twentieth-century observers, insisted the *reth* was an absolute despot wielding complete and arbitrary power over his subjects. Others—most famously Evans-Pritchard (1948)—insisted that he was for most effective purposes a mere symbolic figurehead who "reigned but did not govern," and had almost no systematic way to impose his will on ordinary Shilluk. Both were right. As divine king, *reths* were expected to make displays of absolute, arbitrary violence, but the means they had at their disposal were extremely limited. Above all, they found themselves checked and stymied whenever they tried to transform those displays into anything more systematic. True, as elsewhere, these displays of arbitrariness were, however paradoxically, seen as closely tied to the *reth*'s ability to dispense justice: nineteenth-century *reths* could spend days on end hearing legal cases, even if, under ordinary circumstances, they were lacking in the means to enforce decisions and appear to have acted primarily as mediators.

---

8.   Though we should probably make note of the denouement, at least according to Westermann: they elected a new king, who promptly accused them of murder and killed them all. It's only Howell's notebook that gives his name.

9.   The custom was discontinued, it was said, when once the maiden died first, and the king complained so loudly about the stink that they agreed from then on to switch to suffocation (C. G. Seligman 1911: 222; C. G. Seligman and B. Z. Seligman 1932: 91–92; Westermann 1912: 136; Hofmayr 1925: 300).

Evans-Pritchard was writing in the 1940s, at a time when displays of arbitrary violence on the part of a *reth* would have been treated as crimes by colonial police, and when the royal office had become the focus of Shilluk national identity and resistance. So he had every reason to downplay such stories of brutality.[10] Indeed, in his lecture, they are simply ignored. Nonetheless, they are crucial; not only for the reasons already mentioned, but also because, under ordinary circumstances, the arbitrary violence of the king was central in constituting that very sense of national identity. To understand how this can be, though, we must turn to another part of Sudan during a more recent period during which the police have largely ceased to function.

The Shilluk as seen from Equatoria

Here let me turn to the work of Dutch anthropologist Simon Simonse on rainmakers among a belt of peoples (the Bari, Pari, Lulubo, Lotuho, Lokoya, et al.) in the furthest South Sudan. Rainmakers are important figures throughout the area, but their status varies considerably. Some have (at one time or another) managed to make themselves into powerful rulers; others remain marginal figures. All of them are liable to be held accountable in the event that (as often happens in the southern Sudan) rain does not fall. In fact, Simonse, and his colleague, Japanese anthropologist Eisei Kurimoto, are perhaps unique among anthropologists in being in the vicinity when these events actually happened.[11]

What Simonse describes (reviewing over two dozen case studies of historically documented king-killings) is a kind of tragic drama, in which the rainmaker and people come to gradually define themselves against each other. If

---

10. In a broader sense, he was doubtless aware that the colonial perception of Africa as a place of arbitrary violence and savagery had done much greater violence to Africans—that is, justified much worse atrocities—than any African king had ever done. This is the reason most contemporary Africanists also tend to avoid these stories. But it seems to me there's nothing to be gained by covering things up: especially since the actual arbitrary violence performed by most African kings was in fact negligible or even completely imaginary (what mattered were the stories), and even those who even came close to living up to Euro-American stereotypes, like Shaka or Mutesa, killed far fewer of their own subjects than most European kings during the period before they became figureheads.

11. If nothing else, one can say the question "Do they really kill their kings?" can now be said to be definitively resolved; though, at the same time, it is also clear that it is the least powerful of these figures who are the most likely to fall victim.

rains are delayed, the people, led by the chief warrior age grade, will petition the rainmaker, make gifts, rebuild his residence, or reinstate taxes or customs that have fallen into abeyance so as to win back his favor. If the rain continues not to fall, things become tense. The rainmaker is increasingly assumed to be withholding the rains, and perhaps unleashing other natural disasters, out of spite. The rainmaker will attempt stalling techniques (blaming others, sacrificial rituals, false confessions); if he is also a powerful ruler, the young men's age-set will begin to rally more and more constituencies against him to the point where, finally, he must either flee or confront a community entirely united against him. The methods of killing kings, Simonse notes, tend to take on the gruesome forms they do—beatings to death, burials alive—because these are ways in which everyone could be said to have been equally responsible. It is the community as a whole that must kill the king. Indeed, it only becomes a unified community—"the people," properly speaking—in doing so: since the creation and dispatching of rainmakers is about the only form of collective action in which everyone participates. All this is, perhaps, what a Girardian would predict, except that, far from being the solemn sacrificial rituals with willing victims that Girard imagines, king-killings more resembled lynch mobs, and rainmakers fought back with every means at their disposal. This was especially true if they held political power. Often one hears of a single lonely, armed rainmaker holding off an entire incensed population. During a famine between 1855 and 1859, for instance, one Bari king who had acquired a rifle (no one else had one) used it on three separate occasions to disperse crowds assembled to kill him. In 1860, one of his subjects told a French traveler:

> We asked Nyiggilo to give us rain. He made promises and demanded cattle as a payment. Despite his spells the rain did not come. So we got angry. Then Nyiggilo took his rifle and threatened to kill everybody. We had to leave him be. Last year the same thing happened for a third time: then we lost patience. We slit Nyiggilo's stomach open and threw him into the river: he will no longer make fun of us. (Simonse 1992: 204)

It is easy to see why rainmakers in this context might wish to acquire a monopoly on firearms, or to develop a loyal personal entourage. In fact, Simonse argues that, throughout the region, when state-like forms did emerge, it was typically when rainmakers, caught in an endless and very dangerous game of bluffing and brinksmanship with their constituents, successfully sought means to reinforce their position: by intermarrying with neighboring kings, allying themselves with foreign traders, establishing trade and craft monopolies, building up a permanent armed following, and so on—all in way of ensuring that, when things next came to a showdown, they would be more likely to survive (2005: 94–97).

In such polities, "the people," insofar as such an entity could be said to have existed, was seen essentially as the king's collective enemy. Simonse (1992: 193–95) records several striking instances of European explorers encountering kings in the region who urged them to open fire into crowds or to carry out raids against enemy villages, only to discover that the "enemies" in question were really their own subjects. In other words, kings often really would take on the role attributed to them in rain dramas: of spitefully unleashing arbitrary destruction on the people they were supposed to protect.

Simonse compares the opposition between king and people with the segmentary opposition between lineages or clans described by Evans-Pritchard among the Nuer (ibid.: 27–30), where each side exists only through defining itself against the other. This opposition too is necessarily expressed by at least the potential for violence. It might seem strange to propose a segmentary opposition between one person and everybody else, but if one returns to Evans-Pritchard's actual analysis of how the Nuer segmentary system works, it makes a certain degree of sense. Evans-Pritchard (1940) stressed that in a feud, when clan or lineage A sought to avenge itself on clan or lineage B, any member of lineage B was fair game. They were treated, for political purposes, as identical. In fact, this was Evans-Pritchard's definition of a "political" group—one whose members were treated as interchangeable in relation to outsiders.[12] If so, the arbitrary violence of divine kings—firing randomly into crowds, bringing down natural disasters—is the perfect concrete expression of what makes a people a people—an undifferentiated, therefore political, group. All of these peoples—Bari, Pari, Lolubo, etc.—became peoples only in relation to some particularly powerful rainmaker; and owing to the rise and fall of reputations, political boundaries were always in flux.

Simonse's analysis strikes me as important. True, in the end, he does appear to fall into a Girardian framework (this may well be unavoidable, considering the nature of his material), seeing scapegoat dramas as the primordial truth behind

---

12. So today, an American citizen might be so little regarded by her own government that she is kicked out of hospitals while seriously ill or left to starve on the street; if, however, she then goes on to be killed by the agent of a foreign government, an American has been killed and it will be considered cause for war.

all politics. So he can say that ritual king-killing of the Shilluk variety can be best seen a kind of compromise, an attempt to head off the constant, unstable drama between king and people by institutionalizing the practice,[13] while the state, with its monopoly on force, is an attempt to eliminate the drama entirely (Simonse 2005). Myself, I would prefer to see the kind of violence he describes not as some kind of revelation of the essential nature of society, but as a revelation of the essential nature of a certain form of political power with cosmic pretensions—one by no means inevitable, but which is very much still with us today.

Three propositions

The core of my argument in this essay boils down to three propositions. It might be best to lay them out at this point, before returning to the Shilluk material in more detail. The first I have already outlined; the second is broadly inspired by Marshall Sahlins; the third is my own extrapolation from Simonse:

1. *Divine kingship*, insofar as the term can be made meaningful, refers not to the identification of rulers with supernatural beings (a surprisingly rare phenomenon),[14] but to kings who make themselves the equivalent of gods—arbitrary, all-powerful beings beyond human morality—through the use of arbitrary violence. The institutions of sacred kingship, whatever their origins, have typically been used to head off or control the danger of such forms of power, from which a direct line can be traced to contemporary forms of sovereignty.

2. *Sacred kingship* can also be conceived as offering a kind of (tentative, imperfect) resolution for the elementary problematic of human existence proposed in creation narratives. It is in this sense that Pierre Clastres (1977) was right when he said that state authority must have emerged from prophets

---

13. It's also important to note here that, as Schnepel emphasizes (1991: 58), the Shilluk king was not himself a rainmaker; rather, he interceded on the part of his subjects with Nyikang, who was responsible for the rains.

14. As I mentioned earlier, the Egyptian Pharaoh is one of the few unambiguous examples. Another is the Nepali king. But the latter case makes clear that identification with a deity is not is in itself, necessarily, an indicator of divine kingship in my sense of the term. The Nepali king is identified with Vishnu, but this identification either originated or only came to be emphasized in the nineteenth century when the king lost most of his power to the prime ministers; it was, in fact, the token of what I've been calling sacred kingship, in which the king became too "set apart" from the world to actually govern.

rather than chiefs, from the desire to find a "land without evil" and undo death; it is in this sense, too, that it can be said that Christ (the Redeemer) was a king, or kings could so easily model themselves on Christ, despite his lack of martial qualities. Here, in embryo, can we observe what I have called the utopian element of the state.

3. *Violence*, and more specifically antagonism, plays a crucial role here. It is a peculiar quality of violence that it simplifies things, draws clear lines where otherwise one might see only complex and overlapping networks of human relationship. It is the particular quality of sovereign power that it defines its subjects as a single people. This is, in the case of kingdoms, actually prior to the friend/enemy distinction proposed by Carl Schmitt ([1922] 2005). Or, to be more specific, one's ability to constitute oneself as a single people in a potential relation of war with other peoples is premised on a prior but usually hidden state of war *between the sovereign and the people.*

The Shilluk case, then, seems to be especially revealing, not, as I say, because it represents some primordial form of monarchy, but because—in the attempt to build something like a state in the absence of any real administrative apparatus—these mechanisms are unusually transparent. I suspect the reality behind divine kingship is also unusually easy to make out here because of the particular nature of Nilotic cosmology, and, most notably, Nilotic conceptions of God, who manifests himself in mortal life almost exclusively through disaster. One consequence is a peculiar relation between the transcendent and utopian elements, where it is the hostility of the people that makes the king a transcendent being capable of offering a kind of resolution to the dilemmas of mortal life.[15]

A BRIEF OUTLINE OF SHILLUK HISTORY

The Shilluk are something of an anomaly among Nilotic people. Most Nilotes have long been seminomadic pastoralists, for whom agriculture was very much

---

15. Though, as we shall see in the last chapter, the scenario where kings vanish and become immortal gods at precisely the moment when their subjects betray or express hostility to them traces back at least to Semiramis, the mythic queen of Assyria, and is commonplace throughout East Africa. One theme of this volume—my own contributions to it anyway—is precisely the relation between antagonism and transcendence, which appears to be structural.

a secondary occupation. Famed for their fierce egalitarianism, their social life revolves largely around their herds. The Shilluk are not entirely different—like Nuer and Dinka, they tend to see their lives as revolving around cattle—but in practice they have, for the last several centuries at least, become far more sedentary, having been fortunate enough to find themselves a particularly fertile stretch of the White Nile that has allowed intensive cultivation of durra, a local grain. The result was a population of extraordinary density. By the early nineteenth century there were estimated to be around two hundred thousand Shilluk, living in some hundred settlements arranged so densely along the Nile that foreigners often described the 200 miles of the heart of Shilluk territory as if it consisted of one continuous village. Many remarked it appeared to be the most densely settled part of Africa outside of Egypt itself (Mercer 1971; Wall 1975).

"Fortunate," though, might seem an ill-chosen word here, since, owing to the density of population, a bad harvest could lead to devastating famine. One solution was theft. Lacking significant trade-goods, the Shilluk soon became notorious raiders, attacking camps and villages for hundreds of miles in all directions and hauling off cattle and grain and other spoils. By the seventeenth century, the 300-mile stretch of the Nile north of the Shilluk country, unsuitable for agriculture, was already known as their "raiding country," where small fleets of Shilluk canoes would prey on caravans and cattle camps. Raids were normally organized by settlement chiefs. The Shilluk *reth* appears to have been just one player in this predatory economy, effectively one bandit chief among many, and not even necessarily the most important, since while he received the largest share of booty, his base was in the south, closer to the pastoral Dinka rather than to the richer prey to the north (Mercer 1971: 416). Nonetheless, the *reth* acquired a great deal of cattle and used it to maintain a personal entourage of *Bang Reth*, or "king's men," who were his principal retainers, warriors, and henchmen.

Actually, it's not clear if there was a single figure called the "*reth*" at all in the early seventeenth century, or whether the royal genealogies that have come down to us just patched together a series of particularly prominent warriors.[16] The institutions of "divine kingship" that have made the Shilluk famous appear to have been created by the *reths* listed on most royal genealogies as number

---

16. Frost (1974: 187–88) suggests the institution might ultimately derive from military leaders referred to as *bany*, who, at least among the neighboring Dinka, also have rainmaking responsibilities.

nine and ten: Tokot (c. 1670–90), famous for his conquests among the Nuba and Dinka, and, even more, his son Tugo (c. 1690–1710), who lived at a time when Shilluk successes had been reversed and the heartland itself was under attack by the Dinka. Tugo is said to have been the first to create a permanent royal capital, at Fashoda,[17] and to create its shrines and famous rituals of installation (Ogot 1964; Mercer 1971; Frost 1974; Wall 1975; Schnepel 1990: 114). Ogot was the first to suggest that Tugo effectively invented the sacred kingship, fastening on the figure of Nyikang—probably at that time just the mythic ancestor of local chiefly lines—and transforming him into a legendary hero around which to rally a Shilluk nation that was, effectively, created by his doing so. Most contemporary historians have now come around to Ogot's position.

There is another way to look at these events. What happened might well be considered a gender revolution. In most Nilotic societies, matters of war (hence politics) are organized through male age-sets. By the time we have ethnographic information, Shilluk age-sets seem to have long since been marginalized (P. P. Howell 1941: 56–66).[18] Instead, political life had come to be organized around the *reth* in Fashoda, and Fashoda, in turn, was a city composed almost entirely of women.

How did this happen? We do not precisely know. But we do know that at the time Fashoda was founded, the status of women in politics was under open contestation. Tugo's reign appears to have been proceeded by that of a queen, Abudok, Tokot's sister.[19] According to one version of the story (Westermann

---

17. The name is an Arabization of its real name, Pachod. It is, incidentally, not the same as the "Fashoda" of the famous "Fashoda crisis" that almost brought war between Britain and France in 1898, since "Fashoda" in this case is—however confusingly— an Arabization of the name of a rather desultory mercantile town called Kodok outside Shilluk territory to the north.

18. Among the eastern Nilotic societies considered by Simonse, the chief warrior age-set was also responsible for representing the people against, and ultimately, if necessary, killing, the king. Among the Shilluk, this role seems to have been passed to royal women.

19. Actually, it is not entirely clear when Abudok ruled. Some genealogies leave her out entirely. Hofmayr places her before Tokot, and this has become the generally accepted version. Westermann (1912: 149–50) is ambiguous but appears to agree; however, his version also seems to make her the founder of Fashoda, which should place her closer to the time of Tugo, and elsewhere, in his list of kings (ibid.: 135), he places Abudok after Tokot. Crazzolara (1950: 136, n. 4) insists that she ruled after Tokot, as regent while Tugo was still a child. Howell's unpublished notes call

1912: 149–50), after Abudok had reigned for some years, the settlement chiefs informed her she would have to step down because they did not wish to be ruled by a woman; she responded by naming a young man in her care—Tugo—as her successor, and then, proceeded to the site of Fashoda with a bag of lily seeds to warn that henceforth the royal lineage would grow larger and larger until it engulfed the country entirely. This is usually interpreted as a spiteful prophecy, but it could just as easily be read as a story about the foundation of Fashoda itself (an act usually attributed to her former ward Tugo) and a sober assessment of the likely results of the institutions that developed there.

Later oral traditions (P. P. Howell n.d.: SAD 69/2/53–55) claim that Queen Abudok was responsible for "most of the Shilluk laws and customs" relating to the creation of *reths*.[20] Could it be that the entire institution of what came to be known as "divine kingship" was really her creation, a compromise worked out when she placed Tugo on the throne? We cannot know. But certainly the common wisdom of contemporary historians that these institutions were simply the brainchild of Tugo cannot be correct: it is very difficult to imagine a ruler who decided entirely on his own accord to deny himself the right to name his own successor, or to grant his own wives the right to have him executed. What emerged could only have been some a kind of political compromise, one that ensured no woman ever again attempted to take the highest office (none did) but otherwise, granted an extraordinary degree of power to royal women.

Here is a list, in fact, of such powers:

1. Where most African kings lived surrounded by a hierarchy of male officials, these were entirely absent from Fashoda. The *reth* lived surrounded only by his wives, who could number as many as a hundred, each with her own dwelling. No other men were allowed to set foot in the settlement after nightfall (Riad 1959: 197). Since members of the royal clan could not marry each other (this would be incest), these wives were uniformly commoners.

2. The king's senior wife seems to have acted as his chief minister, and had the power to hold court and decide legal cases in the *reth's* absence (Driberg

---

her Tokot's sister, who took over on his death, but hid the identity of his male offspring (she dressed them up as girls—P. P. Howell n.d.: SAD 69/2/54–55).

20. This from an unpublished manuscript in the Howell papers; the customs listed specifically center on rituals surrounding the "discovery" and creation of the effigies of Nyikang and Dak.

1932: 420). She was also responsible for recruiting and supervising secondary wives.

3. In the absence of any administrative apparatus, royal women also appear to
   have become the key intermediaries between Fashoda and other communities. Essentially they played all the roles that court officials would otherwise
   play.

   a. Royal wives who became pregnant returned in their sixth month to their
      natal villages, where their children were born and raised. They were, as the
      saying goes, "planted out" and allied themselves with a local commoner
      chief (Pumphrey 1941: 11), who became the patron of the young prince
      or princess. Those sons who were not eventually either elected to the
      throne or killed in internecine strife went on to found their own branches
      of the royal lineage, whose numbers, as Queen Abudok predicted, have
      tended to continually increase over the course of Shilluk history.

   b. Royal daughters remained in their mothers' villages. They were referred
      to as "Little Queen" and "their counsel sought on all matters of impor-
      tance" (Driberg 1932: 420). They were not supposed to marry or have
      children, but, in historical times at least, they became notorious for tak-
      ing lovers as they wished—then, if they became pregnant, demanding
      hefty payments in cattle from those same lovers to hush the matter up
      (P. P. Howell 1953b: 107–8).[21]

   c. Princesses might also be appointed as governors over local districts
      (Hofmayr 1925: 71; Jackson in Frost 1974: 133–34), particularly if their
      brothers became king.

4. Royal wives who had borne three children, and royal widows, would retire
   to their natal villages to become *bareth*, or guardians of royal shrines (C. G.
   Seligman and B. Z. Seligman 1932: 77–78). It was through these shrines
   that the "cult of Nyikang" was disseminated.[22]

5. While, as noted above, it was considered quite outrageous for a king to kill a
   woman, royal wives were expected to ultimately order the death of the king.

---

21. They, not the fathers, remained in control of the offspring of such unions. Colonial
    sources (C. G. Seligman 1911: 218; Howell 1953b: 107–8) insisted that in the past,
    princesses who bore children would be executed along with the child's father.

22. Another key medium for the spread of the cult of Nyikang appears to have
    been mediums loosely attached to the shrines, who had usually had no previous
    attachment to the court. According to Oyler (1918b: 288), these too were mainly
    women.

A *reth* was said to be put to death when his physical powers began to fade—purportedly, when his wives announced that he was no longer capable of satisfying them sexually (C. G. Seligman 1911: 222; P. P. Howell and Thomson 1946: 10). In some accounts (e.g., Westermann 1912: 136), the execution is carried out by the royal wives themselves.[23] One may argue about the degree to which this whole scenario is simply an ideological façade, but it clearly happened sometimes: Hofmayr, for instance, writes of one king's affection for his mother, "who had killed his father with a blow from a brass-ring" (1925: 127, in Frost 1974: 82).

I should emphasize here that Shilluk society was in no sense a matriarchy. While women held extraordinary power within the royal apparatus, that apparatus was not in itself particularly powerful. The fact that the queen could render judicial judgments, for instance, is less impressive when one knows royal judgments were not usually enforced. Governance of day-to-day affairs seems to have rested firmly in the hands of male settlement chiefs, who were also in charge of electing a new king when the old one died. Village women also elected their own leaders, but these were much less important.[24] Property passed in the male line. The *reth* himself continued to exercise predatory and sometimes brutal power through his personal retainers, occasionally raiding his own people as a mode of intervening in local politics. Nonetheless, that (divine, arbitrary) power seems to have been increasingly contained within a ritual apparatus where royal women played the central political role.

Insofar as royal power became more than a sporadic phenomenon, insofar as it came to embed itself in everyday life, it was, apparently, largely through the agency of the *bareth* and their network of royal shrines, spread throughout Shillukland. Here, though, the effects could hardly be overestimated. The figure of Nyikang, the mythic founder of the nation, came to dominate every aspect of ritual life—and to become the very ground of Shilluk social being. Where other Nilotic societies are famous for their theological speculation, and sacrifice—the

---

23. Charles and Brenda Seligman (1932: 91) say there were two versions of how this happens: in one, the wives strangle the king themselves; in the other, they lay a white cloth across his face and knees as he lies asleep in the afternoon to indicate their judgment to the male Ororo who actually kill him. They believed the latter to be older.

24. Oyler says they acted as "magistrates," but their jurisdiction was limited to disputes between women (1926: 65–66).

primary ritual—is there dedicated to God and cosmic spirits, here everything came to be centered on the "cult of Nyikang." This was true to such a degree that by the time Seligman was writing (1911; C. G. Seligman and B. Z. Seligman 1932), outside observers found it difficult to establish what Shilluk ideas about God or lineage ancestors even were. To give some sense of the "cult's" pervasiveness: while Nuer and Dinka who fell ill typically attributed their condition to attack by "air spirits," and sought cures from mediums possessed by such spirits, most Shilluk appear to have assumed they were being attacked by former kings—most often, Nyikang's aggressive son Dak—and sought the aid of mediums possessed by Nyikang himself (C. G. Seligman and B. Z. Seligman 1932: 101–2). While most ordinary Shilluk, as we shall see, assiduously avoided the affairs of living royalty, dead ones soon came to intervene in almost every aspect of their daily lives.

The obvious historical question is how long it took for this to happen. Here, information is simply unavailable. All we know is that the figure of Nyikang did gradually come to dominate every aspect of Shilluk life. The political situation in turn appears to have stabilized by 1700 and remained stable for at least a century. By the 1820s, however, the Ottoman state began attempting to establish its authority in the region, and this coincided with a sharp increase in the demand for ivory on the world market. Arab merchants and political refugees began to establish themselves in the north of the country. Nyidok (*reth* from 1845 to 1863) refused to receive official Ottoman envoys, but he kept up the Shilluk tradition of guaranteeing the safety of foreigners. Before long there were thousands of the latter, living in a cluster of communities around Kaka in the far north. *Reths* responded by creating new trade monopolies, imposing systematic taxes, and trying to create a royal monopoly on firearms.[25] They do not appear to have been entirely unsuccessful. Foreign visitors at the time certainly came away under the impression they had been dealing with a bona fide monarch, with at least an embryonic administration. At the same time, some also reported northerners openly complaining it would be better to live without a *reth* at all (Mercer 1971: 423–24).

The situation ended catastrophically. As the ivory trade was replaced by the slave trade, northern Shilluk increasingly signed up as auxiliaries in Arab raids

---

25. Already in the 1840s, foreign sources begin speaking of an annual tribute in cattle and grain, sometimes estimated at 10 percent (Frost 1974: 176). This seems, however, to have only been an early- to mid-nineteenth-century phenomenon.

on the Dinka; by 1861, a foreign freebooter named Mohammed Kheir thus managed to spark a civil war that allowed them to sack Fashoda and carry out devastating slave raids against the Shilluk heartland (Kapteijns and Spauding 1982: 43–46; Udal 1998: 474–82). There followed some forty years of almost continual warfare. The north battled the south; first the Ottoman regime, then the Mahdist regime in Khartoum, then finally the British intervened, trying to establish client governments; several *reths* were executed as rebels against one side or the other; Shilluk herds were decimated and the overall population fell by almost half. In 1899 British rule was established, Shilluk territory was restricted and those outside it were resettled, and the *reth* was reduced to the usual tax-collector and administer of local justice under a system of indirect colonial rule. At the same time, the royal installation ritual, which had fallen into abeyance during the civil wars, was revived and probably reinvented, and royal institutions, along with the figure of Nyikang, became, if anything, even more important as symbols of national identity—as, indeed, they remain to the present day.

Today, the position of the *reth* remains, but, like the Shilluk themselves, just barely. The tiny Shilluk kingdom is unfortunate enough to be located precisely on the front-lines of a civil war between largely Nuer and Dinka rebels and government-supported militias. Ordinary Shilluk have been victims of massacres, famines, massive out-migration, and forced assimilation, to the extent that at times some (e.g., Nyaba 2006) have argued there is a real danger of cultural or even physical extinction.

MYTHO-HISTORY

A word on Nilotic cosmologies

In order to understand the famous Shilluk installation rituals, we must first examine their mythic framework. This is somewhat difficult, since, as almost all early observers point out, their Shilluk informants—much unlike their Nuer and Dinka equivalents—were not much given to cosmological speculation. Instead, everything was transposed onto the level of historical epic. Still, in either case, it would appear the same themes were working themselves out, so it seems best to begin by looking at Nilotic cosmologies more generally.

Nilotic societies normally treat God as a force profoundly distant and removed from the human world. Divinity itself is rendered little or no cult, at least not directly. Instead Divinity is usually seen to be "refracted" through the cosmos, immanent particularly in storms, totemic spirits, numinous objects, or anything inexplicable and extraordinary. In one sense, then, God is everywhere. In another, he is profoundly absent. Creation stories almost invariably begin with a traumatic separation. Here is one typical, Dinka version.[26]

> Divinity (and the sky) and men (and the earth) were originally contiguous; the sky then lay just above the earth. They were connected by a rope. . . . By means of this rope men could clamber at will to Divinity. At this time there was no death. Divinity granted one grain of millet a day to the first man and woman, and thus satisfied their needs. They were forbidden to grow or pound more.
>
> The first human beings, usually called Garang and Abuk, living on earth had to take care when they were doing their little planting or pounding, lest a hoe or pestle should strike Divinity, but one day the woman "because she was greedy" (in this context any Dinka would view her "greed" indulgently) decided to plant (or pound) more than the permitted grain of millet. In order to do so she took one of the long-handled hoes (or pestles) which the Dinka now use. In raising this pole to pound or cultivate, she struck Divinity who withdrew, offended, to his present great distance from the earth, and sent a small blue bird (the colour of the sky) called *atoc* to sever the rope which had previously given men access to the sky and to him. Since that time the country has been "spoilt", for men have to labour for the food they need, and are often hungry. They can no longer as before freely reach Divinity, and they suffer sickness and death, which thus accompany their abrupt separation from Divinity. (Lienhardt 1961: 33–34)

In some versions, human reproduction and death are introduced simultaneously: the woman needs to pound more grain specifically because she bears children and needs to feed her growing family. Always, the story begins with the rupture of an original unity. Once, heaven and earth were right next to each other; humans could move back and forth between them. Or: there was a rope, or tree, or vine, or some other means of passage between the two. As a result, people lived without misery, work, or death. God gave us what we needed. Then the connection was destroyed.

---

26. One anomalous element has been eliminated: in this version, the cord ran parallel to the earth; in most, it is arranged vertically.

Stories like this can be termed "Hesiodic" because, like Hesiod's Prometheus story (or, for that matter, the story of the Garden of Eden), they begin with blissful dependency—humans being supplied whatever they need from a benevolent creator—to an unhappy autonomy, in which human beings eventually win for themselves everything they will need to grow and cook food, bear and raise children, and otherwise reproduce their own existence, but at a terrible cost. It does not take a lot of imagination to see these, first and foremost, as metaphors of birth; the loss of the blissful dependency of the womb, which the cutting of the cord, in the Nilotic versions, simply makes unusually explicit.

The problem is that once separation is introduced into the world, conjunction can only mean catastrophe. Now, when Divinity, as absolute, universal principle, manifests itself in worldly life, it can only take the form of floods, plagues, lightning, locusts, and other catastrophes. Natural disasters are, after all, indiscriminate; they affect everyone; thus, like the indiscriminate violence of divine kings, they can represent the principle of universality. But if God is the annihilation of difference, sacrifice—in Nilotic society the archetypal ritual—is its re-creation. The slaughter and division of an animal becomes a reenactment of the primal act of creation through separation; it becomes a way of expelling the divine element from some disastrous entanglement in human affairs by reestablishing everything in its proper sphere.[27] This was accomplished through violence: or to be more explicit, through killing, blood, heat, fire, and the division of flesh.

There is one way that Divinity enters the world that is not disastrous. This is rain. Rain—and water more generally—seen as a nurturant, essentially feminine principle, is often also treated as the only element through which humans can still experience some approximation of that primal unity. This is quite explicit in the southeastern societies studied by Simonse. The ancestors of rainmaking lines were often said to have emerged from rivers, only to be discovered by children minding cattle on the shore; in rituals, they re-created the vines that originally connected heaven and earth; they embody peace, coolness, fertilizing water (Simonse 1992: 409–11). Hence during important rainmaking rituals, communities must maintain a state of "peace" (*edwar*). Physical violence, drumming, shouting, drunkenness, dancing, are all forbidden; even animals sacrificed

---

27. So too, incidentally, with Vedic sacrifice, which reproduces the original creation of the world through the division of the body of a primordial being, or Greek sacrifice, which constantly re-created the divisions between gods, animals, and mortals. All these religious traditions appear to be historically related.

in rain ceremonies had to be smothered so no blood was spilled, and they had to be imagined to go to their deaths voluntarily, without resistance. The state was ended with a bloody sacrifice at the end of the agricultural season. *Edwar*, though, was simply an exaggerated version of the normal mode of peaceable, sociable comportment with the community—within human, social space—since even ordinarily, hot, bloody, violent activity was exiled to the surrounding wilderness. This was true of hunting and war, but it was also true of childbirth (the paradigm of traumatic separation): women in labor were expected to resort to the bush, and, like returning hunters or warriors, had to be purified from the blood spilled before returning to their communities (ibid.: 412–16).

The legend of Nyikang

The human condition, then, is one of irreparable loss and separation. We have gained the ability to grow our own food, but at the expense of hunger; we have discovered sex and reproduction, but at the cost of death. We are being punished, but our punishment seems utterly disproportionate to our crimes. This is another element stressed by Godfrey Lienhardt, and another way in which the Nilotic material resonates with the Abrahamic tradition. None of Lienhardt's informants claimed to understand why wishing to have a little more food was such a terrible crime. It is our fate as humans to have no real comprehension of our situation. If God is just, at the very least we do not understand in what way; if it all makes sense, we cannot grasp how. It's possible that, ultimately, there simply is no justice. When God is invoked, in Nilotic languages—including Shilluk—it is ordinarily as an exclamation, "Why, God?," above all when a loved one falls sick, with the assumption that no answer will be forthcoming.

Now, the Shilluk appear to be one of the few Nilotic peoples for whom such creation myths are not particularly important. The Shilluk past begins, instead, with a historical event: the exile of Nyikang from his original home. Still, one story is quite clearly a transposition of the other. Nyikang himself is the son of a king whose father descended from heaven.[28] His mother Nyakaya was a crocodile, or perhaps part-crocodile: she continues to be revered as a divinity inhabiting the Nile.[29] He is sometimes referred to as "child of the river."

---

28. In other versions, he traces back to a white or grey cow, created by God in the Nile.
29. Charles and Brenda Seligman (1932: 87–88) describe her as the embodiment of the totality of riverine creatures and phenomena, and notes that the priestesses who

Originally, Nyikang and his brother Duwat lived in a faraway land by a great lake or river in the south.

> They speak of it as the end of the earth, or some call it the head of the earth. . . . In that land death was not known. When a person became feeble through great age, he was thrown out in the cattle yard, or in the road near it, and the cows would trample him until he had been reduced to the size of an infant, and then he would grow to manhood again. (Oyler 1918a: 107)

Other versions gloss over this element—probably because the story that follows turns on a dispute over royal succession, and it is difficult to understand how this would come up if no one ever died. In some versions, the people are divided over whom to elect. In others, Nyikang is passed over in favor of his half-brother Duwat; he seizes some royal regalia and flees with his son Cal and a number of followers. Duwat follows in pursuit. In the end the two confront each other on either side of a great river. In some versions (Hofmayr 1925: 328), Duwat curses his brother to die, thus bringing death into the world. In others, he simply curses him never to return. Always, though, the confrontation ends when Duwat throws a digging stick at his brother and tells him he can use it to dig the graves of his followers. Nyikang accepts it, but defiantly, announces he will use it as an agricultural implement, to give life, and that his people will thus reproduce to overcome the ravages of death (ibid.; Oyler 1918a: 107–8; Westermann 1912: 167; Lienhardt 1979: 223; P. P. Howell n.d.: SAD 69/2/41–42).

Obviously, this is just another version of the creation story: the loss of a blissful deathless paradise where people were nonetheless permanently infantilized by their dependence on higher powers (in this version, arguing over succession to the kingship when the king in fact will never die). Even the digging stick reappears. This is a story of loss, but—as in so many versions of this myth—also a defiant declaration of independence. Nyikang's followers create a kind of autonomy by acquiring the means to reproduce their own life. Turning the symbol of death into an instrument of production is thus a perfect metaphor for what is happening.

---

maintain royal shrines also maintain her cult. Offerings to her are left on the banks of the Nile. She is also the goddess of birth. When river creatures act in unusual ways, they are assumed to be acting as her vehicle; when land ones do the same, they are assumed to be vehicles of Nyikang.

Nyikang's first sojourn is at a place called Turra, where he marries the daughter of the local ruler Dimo and has a son, the rambunctious and unruly Dak. Conflicts soon develop, and there are a series of magical battles between Nyikang and his father-in-law, which Nyikang always wins. Dak grows up to become a scourge of the community, attacking and pillaging at will. Finally, the entire community joins together to kill him. They decide they will sneak up on him while he's relaxing outside playing his harp. According to Riad's informant, "They were very afraid that Nyikang would avenge his son's death if only a few people murdered Dak, so they decided that all of them would spear him and his blood would be distributed upon all of them" (1959: 145). In other words, having been victims of arbitrary predatory violence, they adopt the same logic Simonse describes in the killing of sacred kings. "The people" as a whole must kill him. In this case, however, they do not succeed. Nyikang (or in some versions Dak) receives advance warning, and comes up with the idea of substituting an effigy made of a very light wood called *ambatch*, which he places in Dak's stead. The people come and one by one spear what they take to be the sleeping Dak. The next day, when the real, live Dak appears at what is supposed to be his own funeral, everyone panics and runs away (Westermann 1912: 159; Oyler 1918a: 109; Hofmayr 1925: 16; Crazzolara 1951: 123–27; P. P. Howell n.d.: SAD 69/2/47).

This is a crucial episode. While neither Nyikang nor Dak is, at this point, a king (they are both later to become kings), the story is clearly a reference to the logic described by Simonse: that both king and people come into being through the arbitrary violence of the former, and the final, unified retaliation of the latter. At the same time it introduces the theme of effigies. Nyikang and Dak are, indeed, immortalized by effigies made of *ambatch* wood, kept in a famous shrine called Akurwa, north of Fashoda. These play a central role in the installation of a new *reth*, and, since Evans-Pritchard at least, have been seen as representing the eternity of the royal office, as opposed to the ephemeral nature of any particular human embodiment. Here the first effigy is created literally as an attempt to cheat death. Even more, as we'll see, it seems to reflect a common theme whereby the people's anger and hostility—however paradoxically—becomes the immediate cause of the king's transcendence of mortal status.

To return to the story: Nyikang, Dak, and their small band of followers decide the time has come to move on and seek more amenable pastures. They have various adventures along the way. During their travels, Dak serves as Nyikang's advance guard and general, often getting himself in scrapes from which Nyikang then has to rescue him. The most famous is his battle with the Sun, in which Nyikang again confirms his aquatic character. Dak is the first to pick a fight with the Sun, and at first, he and his father's followers are scorched by the Sun's terrible heat, forcing Nyikang to revive many by sprinkling water over them. In the end Nyikang manages to best the enemy by using water-soaked reeds to slash—and thus "burn"—the legs of the Sun, who is thereby forced to retreat (Westermann 1912: 161, 166; Oyler 1918a: 113–14; Hofmayr 1925: 18, 55; see Lienhardt 1952: 149; Schnepel 1988: 448). Finally, he enters Shillukland, settles his followers, brings over existing inhabitants, even—in many stories—discovering humans masquerading as animals and revealing their true nature, and turning them into Shilluk clans.

The latter is actually a curious element in the story. Godfrey Lienhardt (1952) insisted that, unlike Nuer or Dinka heroes, who, as ancestors, created their people as the fruit of their loins, Nyikang creates the Shilluk as an "intellectual" project. He discovers, transforms, gives names, grants roles and privileges, establishes boundaries, gathers together a diverse group of unrelated people and animals, and renders them equal parts of a single social order. This is true, though putting it this way rather downplays the fact that he does so through right of conquest: that is, that he appears amidst a population of strangers who have never done anything to hurt him and threatens to kill them if they do not do his will.[30] It is not as if this sort of behavior was considered acceptable conduct by ordinary people under ordinary circumstances. In most stories, the figure of Nyikang is saved from too close an association with unprovoked aggression by effectively being redoubled. He plays the largely intellectual role, solving problems, wielding magic, devising rules and status, while the sheer arbitrary violence is largely pushed off onto his son and alter ego, Dak. In the Shilluk heartland, especially, Nyikang is always described as "finding" people who fell from the skies or were living in the country or fishing in the river, and

---

30. I will return to this point later. Of course, one could argue that this sort of behavior was considered legitimate in dealing with strangers: Shilluk were notorious raiders, and were in the eighteenth and nineteenth centuries apparently not above acts of treachery when dealing with Arabs or other foreigners in the "raiding country"—for instance, offering to ferry caravans across the Nile and then attacking, robbing, or even massacring them. (At the same time, foreigners who entered Shillukland itself were treated with scrupulous courtesy and guaranteed the safety of their persons and property.) Still, as we will see, ordinary Shilluk tended to rankle most of all at attempts to turn predatory violence into systematic power, which is exactly what Nyikang was doing here.

assigning them a place and a ritual task (to help build the some house or shrine, to herd Nyikang's sacred cattle, to supply the king with certain delicacies, etc.). Only in the case of people who transform themselves into animals—fish, turtles, fireflies, et al.—does he usually have to call in Dak, to net or spear or otherwise defeat them, whereon they ordinarily turn back into human beings and submit themselves. Submission is what renders people Shilluk (the actual word, *Chollo*, merely means subjects of the *reth*).[31] Though in a larger sense, intellectual understanding and physical conquest are conflated here; the stories of shape-shifters are paradigmatic: one can only tell what they really are by successfully defeating, even skewering them—by literally pinning them down.

For all this, Nyikang's conquest of Shillukland, however, remains curiously unfinished. The myths specify that he managed to subdue the southern half of the country, up to about where the capital is now. After this things stalled, as the people, tired of war, begin to murmur and, increasingly, openly protest Nyikang's leadership. Finally, at a feast held at the village of Akurwa (what is later to become his temple in Fashoda), Nyikang chides his followers, instructs them on how to maintain his shrine and effigy, and vanishes in a whirlwind of his own creation.

Nyikang, all Shilluk insist, did not and could never die. He has become the wind, manifest in animals who behave in strange and uncharacteristic ways, birds that settle among crowds of people; he periodically comes, invisible, to inhabit one or another of his many shrines (C. G. Seligman 1911: 220–26; 1934; Westermann 1912: xlii; Oyler 1918b; Hofmayr 1925: 307; P. P. Howell and Thomson 1946: 23–24). Above all, he remains immanent in his effigies, and in the sacred person of the king. Yet in the story, his transcendence of the bonds of mortal existence follows his rejection by the people. Neither is this mere mumbling and discontent: some versions make clear there was at least the threat of actual rebellion. In one (Crazzolara 1951: 126), Nyikang is speared in the chest by an angry follower, though he survives. He then assembles his people to announce his ascent. In every version, he is replaced by an effigy of *ambatch*, and remains as the vehicle of the prayers of his people,

---

31. Westermann (1912: 127–34) summarizes the origins of seventy-four different clans. If one discounts the three royal lineages included, and the six for whom no origin is given, we find that forty-nine were descended from "servants" of Nyikang, six from "servants" of Dak, six of Odak, one of Tokot, and, most surprisingly, three from servants of Queen Abudok, the last royal figure to play this role—another testimony to her one-time importance.

as their intercessor before God. It is through Nyikang, for example, that the king appeals to God for rain (Schnepel 1991: 58–59). Though even here the relationship of animosity does not disappear. Unlike more familiar gods, who, by definition, can do no wrong, the hero continues to be the object of periodic anger and recrimination:

> Their veneration of Nikawng does not blind their eyes to his faults. When a prayer has been offered to Nikawng, and the answer is not given, as had been hoped, the disappointed one curses Nikawng. That is true especially in the case of death. When death is approaching, they sacrifice to Nikawng and God, and pray that death may be averted. If the death occurs, the bereaved ones curse Nikawng, because he did not exert himself in their behalf. (Oyler 1918a: 285)

This passage gains all the more power when one remembers that illness itself was often assumed to be caused by the attacks of royal spirits—most often, Dak—and that mediums possessed by the spirit of Nyikang were the most common curers. Yet in the end we must die, as Nyikang did not; his transcendence of death resulted from, and perpetuates, a relation of permanent at least potential antagonism.

In fact, it was not just Nyikang. None of the first four kings of Shillukland died like normal human beings. Each vanished, their bodies never recovered; all but the last were then replaced by an effigy. Nyikang was replaced by his timid elder son Cal, who disappeared in circumstances unknown; then by the impetuous Dak, who vanished in yet another fit of frustration with popular grumbling over his endless wars of conquest; then, finally, by Dak's son Nyidoro.

Nyidoro, however, marks a point of transition. He vanished, but only *after* death. He was, in fact, murdered by his younger brother Odak, whereon his body magically disappeared. As a result, there was some debate over whether he merited a shrine and effigy at all, but in the end it was decided that he did.[32]

---

32. An alternative version from Howell's notes:

> In the past Shilluk kings never died but flew in the air. Now then Odak flew in the air trying to go away (die), then one man saw him flying. He shouted "there he goes!" Odak came down and said to the people, from this date no one of your kings will go away again. They have to be buried, and this is the last chance of your king. Odak is the person who started the burial of Shilluk king. (P. P. Howell n.d.: SAD 69/2/48–49)

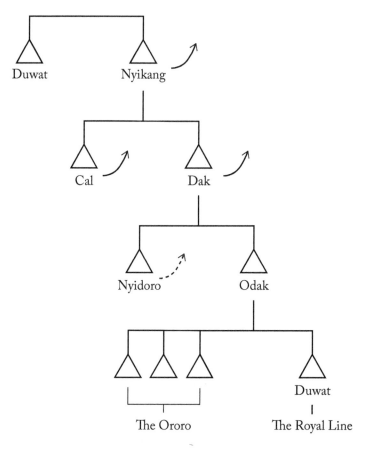

Figure 1. The mythic origins of the Ororo and the Royal line.
N.B.: solid arrows refer to rulers who, rather than dying, vanished and were replaced by effigies; the broken arrow refers to rulers who died but whose body vanished and was not replaced by an effigy.

If Nyidoro was the first king to die, his killer and successor, Odak, was the first to be ritually killed. This, however, was a consequence not of internal conflict (as in the case of his own usurpation), but of external warfare: Odak was defeated in a battle with the Dinka and the Fung. After witnessing the death of all of his sons except one, he threw Nyikang's sacred spears in the river in a gesture of despair, crying "Now all my sons are dead!" As one might imagine this greatly hurt the feelings of the one son who remained alive. This young man, named Duwat, had been often belittled by his father in the past, but this was the final straw. After promising his father he would degrade all those sons' children to commoners, Duwat snatched one of the spears from the river and single-handedly routed the enemy (Hofmayr 1925: 66–68, 260–62).

Apparently, Odak was discreetly finished off soon afterwards, and when Duwat became king, one of his first acts was to degrade the descendants of his brothers to a lower status than the royal clan. They became the Ororo, excluded from succession, but who nonetheless play a key role in royal ritual.

The story began with a Duwat, and with this second Duwat, one might say the first round of the mythic cycle comes to an end. It begins with stories modeled on birth and ends with stories of death: first, the nondeaths of Nyikang and Dak, rejected by their subjects; then, establishing the two typical modes of putting an end to a particular holder of the royal office, that is, either through internal revolt (challenge by an ambitious prince) or being ritually put to death.

The role of the Ororo is crucial. This is a class who represent a veritable institutionalization of this constitutive relation of hostility, and potential violence, on which the eternity of the kingdom is founded. Generally, the descendants of any prince who is not elected, should they grow numerous, become a named lineage within the royal clan, and the tomb of their princely ancestor becomes their lineage shrine. All members of such lineages are considered royals. In theory, the king can degrade any of these branches to Ororo status by attempting to sneak into their lineage shrine at night and performing certain secret rites, but the shrines are guarded, and if the king in question is caught, the attempt is considered to have failed. Some (e.g., Crazzolara 1951: 139) suggest that one reason a king might wish to demote a royal lineage in this fashion is that, since marriage is forbidden between royals, it is only by reducing a branch to Ororo status that a king can then take one of its daughters for his wife.[33] One *reth* (Fadiet) is remembered for having tried to reduce the descendants of Nyadwai—the famous bad king—to Ororo status in this way, but he got caught and the lineage remained royal; it's not clear if any king—that is, other than Duwat—has ever been successful (Hofmayr 1925: 66; Pumphrey 1941: 12–13; P. P. Howell 1953a: 202). Most sources suggest none have—another dramatic reflection on the limited power of Shilluk kings.

Moreover, it is precisely this degraded nobility whose role it is to preside over the death of kings. Male members of the caste who accompany the king during ceremonies are sometimes referred to as the "royal executioners," but here meaning not that they execute others on the king's orders, but rather that it is they who are in charge of presiding over the execution of the king. A *reth* would always have a certain number of Ororo wives; it is they who are

---

33. However, Charles and Brenda Seligman (1932: 48) say kings would only take Ororo wives if they were "unusually attractive," since no child of an Ororo could ever become king.

expected to announce when he is sick or failing in his sexual powers; as we've seen, according to some, it is they who actually suffocate the king after the announcement (C. G. Seligman 1911: 222). In other versions, it is the male Ororo bodyguards, who also preside over his burial.[34] All sources stress it is difficult to know anything for sure about such matters, about which discreet people knew better than to much inquire, and, doubtless, practices varied. The one thing all agreed, though, was it was critical that the king was constantly surrounded by those he had originally degraded, and who were eventually to kill him.

At this point we have reached historical times, which begin with the long and prosperous reign of King Bwoc, immediately followed by Tokot, Queen Abudok, and the historical creation of the sacred kingship at the end of the seventeenth century. Of this, we have already spoken.

* * *

Still, there is one last story worth telling before moving on. This is the story of the *mar*. The *mar* was some kind of talisman or element of royal regalia that had originally belonged to Nyikang. By the early twentieth century, no one quite remembered what it had been: a jewel of some kind, or perhaps a crystal, or a silver pot. According to some, it was a magical charm capable of assuring victory in war. According to others, it was a general token of prosperity and royal power (Hofmayr 1925: 72–75; Paul 1952).

According to Dietrich Westermann (1912: 143–44), the *mar* was a silver pot that, waved in front of one's enemies, caused them to flee the field of battle. Tokot employed it in many successful wars against the Shilluk's neighbors, many of whom he incorporated into Shillukland, but eventually—a familiar scenario now—his followers grew tired of fighting far from their wives and families, and began to protest and refuse his orders. In a fit of pique, Tokot threw the *mar* into the Nile. Here the story fast-forwards about a half-century to the reign of Atwot (c. 1825–35), who is elected as a warrior-king on the behest of a cluster of settlements plagued by Dinka raiders. Atwot attempts to drive off the invaders but is defeated. So, in a bold move, he decides to retrieve

---

34. In some versions, the Ororo men are responsible for killing the king "by surprise" if he is wounded in battle or grievously ill (Hofmayr 1925:178–80); the women kill him otherwise.

the talisman. The king consults with the descendants of Tokot's wives at his lineage shrine, and, defying widespread skepticism, rows out with his companions to the place where the *mar* was lost, sacrificing three cows along the way, and dives to the bottom of the river. He remains underwater so long his companions think he has surely drowned, but after many hours, he returns with the genuine article. Atwot proceeds to raise an army, repels and then conquers the Dinka, and is victorious against all who stand in his path. However, before long, the same thing begins to happen. He is carried from conquest to conquest, but his warriors begin protesting the incessant wars, and finally Atwot too throws the pot back in the river in frustration. There have been no subsequent attempts to retrieve the *mar*.[35]

The story seems to be about why the Shilluk kingdom never became an empire. It as if every time kings move beyond defending the home territory or conducting raids beyond its borders, every time they attempt to levy armies and begin outright schemes of conquest, they find themselves stymied by protests and passive resistance. To this the kings respond with passive aggression: vanishing in a huff, throwing precious heirlooms into the river. As we'll soon see, the scene of the king sacrificing cows and then diving down into the river to find a lost object appears to be a reference to a stage in the inauguration ceremonies in which the candidate must find a piece of wood that will be made into new body of Nyikang. Yet here, instead of an image of eternity, the river becomes an image of loss. According to one source (Paul 1952), the *mar* was "the luck of the Shilluk," now forever lost. It seems likely the debate over the nature of the *mar* reflected a more profound debate about whether military good fortune was always luck for the Shilluk as a whole—a question on which royal and popular perspectives are likely often to have differed sharply. And the fact that such arguments were said to be going on in the time of Tokot, in the generation immediately before the creation of the institutions of sacred kingship, once again underlines how much debate there was at that time about the very purposes of royal power.

---

35. This sort of behavior was occasionally noted even in colonial times. According to P. P. Howell and W. P. G. Thomson (1946: 76), there used to be ceremonial drums kept in Fashoda for royal funerals with special guardians, until *reth* Fafiti, annoyed that his predecessor had not used them to honor the previous *reth*, threw them in the Nile.

RETURN TO FASHODA

At this point we can return to those institutions themselves.

First of all, a word about the role of violence. Godfrey Lienhardt (1952) insists Nyikang (and, hence, the king) has to be seen only as a continuation of the Shilluk conception of God. God is ordinarily seen as neither good nor evil; anything extraordinary contains a spark of the divine; above all, God is the source of life, strength, and intelligence in the universe. Similarly, according to Lienhardt, Nyikang is the source of Shilluk custom, but not, necessarily, of a system of ethics; and kings—who are referred to as "children of God"—were admired above all for their cleverness, and for the ruthless ingenuity with which they played the game of power.[36] Royals regularly slaughtered their brothers and cousins in preemptive strikes; assassination and betrayal was normal and expected; successful conspirators were admired. Lienhardt concludes that intelligence and success (the latter typically reflected in prosperity) are the main social values: "Kings, and all others inspired by *juok* [divinity], are sacred because they manifest divine energy and knowledge, and they do so by being strong, cunning, and successful, as well as appearing to be in closer touch with the superhuman than ordinary men" (1952: 160; so too Schnepel 1988: 449).

All of these ideas are definitely there in the source material, but taken in isolation this is a bit deceptive. The situation appears to have been rather more complicated. God was also spoken of as the source of justice, the last resort of the poor and unfortunate. The king of course dispensed justice as well. The apparent paradox is, as I've emphasized, typical of divine kingship: the king, like God, stands outside any moral order in order to be able to bring one into being. Still, while a prince who successfully lured potential rivals to a feast and then massacred them all might be admired for his cunning, this was hardly the way ordinary people were expected to behave. Nothing in the literature suggests that if a commoner, or even a member of the royal clan who was not a prince, decided to act in a similar fashion to head off later quarrels over his father's cattle, this would be regarded as anything but reprehensible—by the king (if the matter was brought before him) or by anybody else. It was, rather, as if ruthlessness

---

36. Schnepel (1991) seems to agree with Lienhardt when he argues that the ingenious application of violence was valued in itself—or, at least, valued insofar as it was seen to contribute to the "vitality" of the Shilluk nation as a whole.

of this sort was to be limited to the royal sphere, and the royal sphere carefully contained and delimited from ordinary life—in part for that very reason.

Father Crazzolara, for instance, insists that this was precisely what the commoner chiefs (called *Jago*) who elected the king wanted: to ensure that everything surrounding kings and princes remained shrouded in mystery, so that it had no effect on ordinary life.

> Disputes and intrigues among members of the royal family were known to exist and were shared by the great *Jagos* and their councilors, but seldom affected the people at large. . . . Strifes and murders in the higher social ranks were settled among the great men, in great secrecy, and could never imperil the unity of the country. (Crazzolara 1951: 129)

Indeed, he observed, most ordinary Shilluk would never have dreamed of approaching the royal residence at Fashoda, and when the king did set out on a journey, "most people used to go into hiding or keep out of his path; girls especially do so" (ibid.: 139).

At the same time, the organization of the kingship those chiefs upheld, with no fixed rule of succession, but, rather, a year-long interregnum during which dozens of potential candidates were expected to jockey for position, plot and intrigue against each other, more or less guaranteed that only very clever, and very ruthless, men could have much chance of becoming *reth*. It also guaranteed that the violence on which the royal office was founded on always remained explicit, that *reths* were never too far removed from the simple bandit-kings from which they were presumably descended.

Everything is happening as if the *reth*'s subjects were resisting both the institutionalization of power, and the euphemization of power that seems to inevitably accompany it. Power remained predatory. Take, for example, the matter of tribute. The king's immediate power was based in the *Bang Reth*, his personal retainers, a collection of men cut off from their own communities: orphans, criminals, madmen, prisoners taken in war. He provided them with cattle from his herds, along with ornaments and other booty; they minded his cattle, accompanied royal children, acted as spies, and accompanied him on raids against Arab or Dinka neighbors. They did not, however, collect tribute. According to one colonial source, there was no regular system for exacting tribute at all. Instead, the king would intervene in feuds between communities that had resisted his attempts at mediation:

> The *Reths* . . . were extremely rich in cattle. They acquired these largely in the following way. Whenever one settlement waged unjustified war upon another or refused repeatedly to obey his order, the *Reth* would raise as a "royal levy" the adjacent settlements, who would go and drive off the malefactors' cattle and burn their villages. The strength of the levy would vary with the readily calculatable strength of the opposition but a good margin of safety would be allowed to ensure that the levy would win. It is said that such levies were in fact seldom resisted, the victim being glad to save their skins at the cost of most of their cattle. The participants in the levy got a percentage of the cattle taken but the majority went to the Reth. (Pumphrey 1941: 12; cf. Evans-Pritchard 1948: 15–16)

Significantly, it was precisely in the 1840s, when Shilluk kings, emboldened by an alliance with foreign merchants, began trying to move beyond raiding and create a systematic apparatus for the extraction of tribute, that many ordinary Shilluk began to cast doubt on the legitimacy of the institution of kingship entirely, and to throw in their lot with a different set of predatory freebooters (Mercer 1971: 423–24). As it turned out, the results were catastrophic. The Arab slave-traders with whom they aligned themselves turned out to be far more ruthless and destructive than anything they had previously encountered. But the pattern remains clear. As in the stories about the *mar*, popular resistance appeared at exactly the point where royal power tried to move beyond mere predatory raiding, and to formally institutionalize itself.

The kings' rather unsavory retainers lived at the margins of Fashoda. Its center was composed of his own compound, and the houses of his wives. All sorts of dark rumors surrounded the place. According to Seligman's account, quoted near-verbatim in *The golden bough:*

> During the day the king surrounded himself with his friends and bodyguards, and an aspirant to the throne could hardly hope to cut his way through them and strike home. It was otherwise at night. For then the guards were dismissed and the king was alone in his enclosure with his favourite wives, and there was no man near to defend him except a few herdsmen, whose huts stood a little way off. The hours of darkness were therefore the season of peril for the king. It is said that he used to pass them in constant watchfulness, prowling round his huts fully armed, peeping into the blackest shadows, or himself standing silent and alert, like a sentinel on duty, in some dark corner. When at last his rival appeared, the fight would take place in grim silence, broken only by the clash of spears and

shields, for it was a point of honour with the king not to call the herdsmen to his assistance. (Frazer 1911a: 22; Fraser 1990: 200–201)

This was to become one of Frazer's more famous romantic images, but in the original edition, it was immediately followed by a footnote explaining that Seligman also emphasized that "in the present day and perhaps for the whole of the historical period" succession by ritual combat "has been superseded by the ceremonial killing of the king" (Frazer 1911a: 22 n. 1). This would suggest we are not dealing with a Victorian fantasy here—or not only that—but with a Shilluk one, a legend about the ancient past.[37] Even here things are confusing: Seligman also contradicts himself by simultaneously insisting (i.e., 1911: 222; also Hofmayr 1925: 175) that even in his own day, *reths* did tend to sleep during the day and keep armed vigil at night, and that the drowsy behavior of the *reth*, the one time he did meet one, would appear to confirm this. In fact, such stories seem to be typical of the mysteries surrounding royalty. Very few people knew what really went on at Fashoda, and everything concerning kings was tinged with doubt and peril.[38]

All evidence suggests that, except perhaps during periods of civil unrest or when the *reth* had concrete evidence of some particular conspiracy, life in Fashoda was distinctly more relaxed. True, many observers do remark on the eerie quiet of the place, much in contrast with other Shilluk settlements. But this is for an entirely different reason: Fashoda was entirely lacking in children (e.g., Riad 1959: 197). As the reader will recall, not only was the settlement occupied almost entirely by women, the king's wives were sent back to their natal

---

37. Curiously, Evans-Pritchard (1948) ended up arguing exactly the opposite: that stories of ritual king-killing were the myth, and that in most cases one was really dealing with assassinations or rebellions. Mohammed Riad (1959: 171–77), however, went through all existing historical information and could only find two examples of important rebellions in all Shilluk history, only one of which was fully successful. Of twenty-six historical kings, he noted, fifteen "surely met their death in the ceremonial way" (ibid.: 176). Of the others, two were killed in war, three executed by the government in Khartoum, and six died of causes unknown. On the other hand, he includes the four known cases of murder by rival princes as ceremonial deaths, which does rather muddy the picture. At least it makes clear this did happen, but only rarely.

38. On both sides: Hofmayr writes "at night he [the *Reth*] is awake and walks heavily armed around the village. His hand is full of spears and rifles. Whoever comes close to him is doomed" (1925: 175, in Schnepel 1991: 50).

villages in order to give birth, and royal children were not raised in Fashoda. It was a place where there was sex, but no biological reproduction, no nursing, no child-rearing—but also, no old age, grave illness or natural death, since the king was not allowed to grow frail and pass away in the normal fashion, and his wives normally returned to their parents' settlements before they grew very old.

All of this very much recalls the villages described by Simonse further to the south, where birth and killing—or anything involving the spilling of blood—were considered "hot," violent, dangerous activities which should be kept entirely outside the confines of inhabited space. Even sacrificed animals had to be, like the Shilluk *reth*, smothered so that no blood was spilled. These restrictions were especially severe during the agricultural season, since they were the key to ensuring rain. Rain, in turn, was the temporary restoration of that happy conjunction of heaven and earth that was severed in the beginning of time. It seems hardly coincidental, then, that almost all of the *reth*'s ritual responsibilities involved either presiding over ceremonies appealing to Nyikang to send the rains, or conducting harvest rituals (Oyler 1918b: 285–86; C. G. Seligman and B. Z. Seligman 1932: 80–82)—or even, that it was considered a matter of principle that the king and his wives did work at least a few symbolic fields, and followed the same agricultural cycles as everybody else (Riad 1959: 196).[39]

These, at any rate, were the things that an ordinary Shilluk was likely to actually know about Fashoda. The overall picture seems clear. Fashoda was a little image of heaven. It was the closest one could come, in these latter days, to a restoration of the primal unity which preceded the separation of the earth and heaven. It was a place whose inhabitants experience neither birth nor death, although they do enjoy the pleasures of the flesh, ease and abundance (there was rumored to be a storehouse of plundered wealth and certain clans were charged with periodically bringing the *reth* tasty morsels), and also engaged in

---

39. I might add here that many of the more exotic-seeming practices of the capital seem to be adopted from ordinary Shilluk practice. All women, for example, were expected to leave their husbands and return to their natal villages in the sixth month of pregnancy (C. G. Seligman and B. Z. Seligman 1932: 69)—though in the case of nonroyals, they returned with their baby shortly after giving birth—and old people deemed to be suffering unduly from incurable conditions were often "helped to die" (Hofmayr 1925: 299). According to Howell, even the effigies had a kind of demotic precedent, since if someone dies far from home, her kin can hold a ceremony to pass her soul to a stick of *ambatch*, which is also the wood used to make effigies, so that it can be buried in her stead (P. P. Howell 1952a: 159; see also Oyler 1918b: 291).

agricultural production—if, like the original couple, Garang and Abuk, only just a little bit.

Fashoda is, then, an undoing of the dilemma of the human condition. Obviously, it could only be a partial, provisional one. The Shilluk *reth* was, as Burkhard Schnepel aptly put it (1995), "temporarily immortal." He was Nyikang, but he was also not Nyikang; Nyikang was God, but Nyikang was also not God. And even this limited degree of perfection could only be brought about by a complex play of balanced antagonism that would inevitably engulf him in the end.

THE INSTALLATION RITUAL: DESCRIPTION

All of this, I think, gives us the tools with which to interpret the famous Shilluk installation ceremonies.

One must bear in mind here that this ritual was one of the few occasions during which an ordinary Shilluk was likely to actually see a *reth* (the others were while he was administering justice, and, possibly, during raids or war). Almost every clan played some role in the proceedings, whether in the preparation of rebuilding of royal dwellings beforehand, by bringing sacrificial animals or regalia, or by presiding over certain stages of the rituals themselves. It was in this sense the only real "national" ritual. The sense of popular participation was made all the more lively since, the rituals being so endlessly complicated and there usually having been such a long a time since they had last been performed, each step would tend to be accompanied by animated debate by all concerned as to what the correct procedure was.

When a king dies, he is not said to have died but to have "vanished," or to have "gone across the river"—much as was said of Nyikang. Normally, Nyikang is immanent both in the person of the king and in an effigy kept in a temple in the settlement of Akurwa, north of Fashoda. This effigy too is destroyed after a king's death. The *reth*'s body is conveyed to a sealed hut and left there for about a year, or at least until it is certain that nothing remains but bones; at that point, the Ororo will convey the skeleton to its permanent tomb in the *reth*'s natal village, and conduct a public funeral dance. It is only afterwards that a new *reth* can be installed.

This interim period, while the king's body lies decomposing and Nyikang's effigy is gone, is considered a period of interregnum. It is always represented as a time of chaos and disorder, a "year of fear." According to P. P. Howell and

W. P. G. Thomson, who wrote the most detailed account of the rituals, messengers send out word that, "There is no land—the Shilluk country has ceased to be" (1946: 18). Others speak of the land as "spoiled" or "ruined," the same language used in Dinka and Nuer songs to describe the state of the world since the separation of heaven and earth (P. P. Howell 1952a: 159–60). At any rate, it is clear that with the rupture in the center, the image of perfection on earth and thus guarantor of the kingdom, everything is thrown into disarray. During this time, all important matters are put on hold, other than the frantic politicking surrounding the election of the new *reth*. There were usually at least a dozen potential candidates. Settlement chiefs lobbied for their favorites, princesses offered bribes, royals conspired and plotted, and there was a real fear that everything would descend into civil war. As the chief of Debalo explained in 1975:

> It is the period when we fear each other. I fear you and you fear me. If we meet away from the village, we can kill each other and no one will prevent us. So the meaning of *wang yomo* [year of fear] is that we are all afraid and keep to our own homes, because there is no king. (Singer in Schnepel 1988: 443)

This sounds very much like a Hobbesian war of all against all. Still, when the chief suggests that the chaos is the result of the mere absence of the king's power to impose justice, one must bear in mind that this is a local official who grew up in a time of strong state authority, during which the *reth* was subordinated to, but also supported by, Sudanese police. In earlier centuries, as we've seen, the *reth* did not play this role. Rather, it would seem that the interregnum was the time when royal politics—ordinarily kept at a safe distance from ordinary people's lives—really did spill over into society as a whole, and that, as a result, anyone became a potential enemy.

Traditionally, the interregnum lasted roughly a year, and ended during the "cool months" after the harvest in January and February, when the new election would be held so that the *reth* could be installed. It was considered important the installation be completed in time to allow the new *reth* to preside over rain-making ceremonies in April.

Neither was the election itself, conducted by twenty major chiefs or *Jagos*, presided over by the chief of Debalo, definitive. As Schnepel (1988: 444) notes, the college of electors did not so much select the king as identify the candidate the chiefs felt most likely to be able to successfully endure the series of tests and crises that make up the ritual. Every step was a kind of ordeal and, thus, another judgment. Candidates often feared assassination at critical points of the ceremony; it was said if they were so much as injured in the course of them, they would be declared unfit and disqualified. (For commoner participants, the rituals were also tinged with fear, but at the same time, enormously entertaining. The effigies of Nyikang and Dak, according to most sources, were seen as particularly amusing.)

Let me lay out the events, in abbreviated form, in roughly their order of occurrence.[40]

Once the electoral college, presided over by chiefs of the northern and southern halves of the country, had reached a decision, word was sent to the prince, who could be expected to be lingering nearby:

> The method of summoning the *reth* was interesting. . . . The chief of Gol Nyikang[41] sent his son by night to get him. Whether or not there was a mock fight between the selected candidate and the messengers I do not know, but the traditional form of the words announcing the choice was told to me. It is an interesting example of Shilluk "understatement" when talking of the *reth*—"You are our Dinka slave, we want to kill you" which means, "You are our chosen *reth*, we want to install you in Fashoda." (Thomson 1948: 154)

(Only at this point is it possible to finally proceed with the final burial of the old king and the initiation of his shrine—this, unlike the election, which is primarily an affair of commoners, is presided over strictly by royals.[42])

---

40. Schnepel (1988) provides the best published blow-by-blow summary. What follows is drawn from my own reading of the standard primary sources (Munro 1918; Oyler 1918b; Hofmayr 1925; P. P. Howell and Thomson 1946; Thomson 1948; P. P. Howell 1952a, 1952b, 1953a; Anon. 1956; but also Riad 1959, which adds some telling details). All these seem to be derived from three ceremonies: the installations of Fafiti (1917), Anei (1944), and Dak (1946).

41. The name given the northern half of the country during the ritual, the south being Ghol Dhiang. It is interesting of course that the northern half should be named after Nyikang, since this is the portion of the country Nyikang is said *not* to have conquered, but it is also where his effigy normally resides.

42. There is some confusion over when this ceremony takes place. Schnepel (1988) follows Howell and Thomson (1946) in placing it immediately after the election, but Riad (1959: 182) suggests the latter were describing an exceptional circumstance and that the funeral normally occurred well after the new *reth*'s installation.

The candidate-elect is now summoned, shaved and washed by Ororo women, and placed in seclusion. Immediately thereafter, select detachments of men from the northern and southern halves of the country set out on expeditions to acquire materials needed in the ritual, and, particularly, with which to remake the effigy of Nyikang.

This effigy is so important, and so famous, that it is fitting to offer a full description. Actually, Nyikang's effigy is one of three: in addition to his, there is also an effigy of his rambunctious son Dak, and, finally, one of his older, but timid, son Cal. The first two almost always appear together; the effigy of Cal is much less important, only appearing at the very last day of the ceremony. The body of Nyikang's effigy consists of a five-and-half-foot trunk of *ambatch* wood, adorned with cloth and bamboo, and topped with a crown of ostrich feathers. Dak is similar in composition but his body is much smaller; however, unlike Nyikang, his effigy is normally carried atop an eight-foot-tall bamboo pole. (The effigy of Cal consists primarily of rope.) Ordinarily, all three are kept in Nyikang's most famous shrine in the village of Akurwa—said to be the very place where Nyikang vanished into the whirlwind. Their traditional keepers are a clan called Kwa Nyikwom ("Children of the Stool"), inhabitants of the place:

> These effigies are not merely symbols. They may "become active" at any time, and
> when active they are Nyikang and Dak. The effigy of Nyikang is rarely taken on a
> journey in normal times, though it is often brought out to dance during religious
> festivals at Akurwa itself. The effigy of Dak makes periodical excursions through
> the country. Both effigies have an important part to play in the ceremonies of
> installation. The soul of Nyikang is manifest in the effigy for the occasion, and he
> must march from Akurwa to Fashoda to test the qualities of the new successor
> and to install him in the capital. (P. P. Howell and Thomson 1946: 40)

Before this can be done, however, the effigy of Nyikang—destroyed after the death of the former *reth*—has to be entirely recreated, and that of Dak, refurbished.

All the expeditions that set out of the country to gather materials are organized like war parties, and some of them—such as those sent into the "raiding country" to acquire ivory, silver, and cloth—originally were expected to acquire them by ambushing villages or caravans. In more recent times, those sent out have been obliged instead to buy them in markets to the north of Shillukland (P. P. Howell n.d.: SAD 69/2/1–13). However, whether they were sent outside the country to hunt ostriches or antelopes, or to gather rope or bamboo, all these parties are clearly seen as seizing goods by force, and little distinction is made between Shilluk and foreigners, since along the way "they are given, or take, what they want from Shilluk as they pass" (P. P. Howell and Thomson 1946: 38).[43]

All of these expeditions also seem to be under the broad aegis of Dak, whose effigy remains in the temple during the whole of the interregnum, except when leading occasional expeditions outside.[44] The "raiding country" to the north of Shillukland is seen as his particular domain.

The most important of these expeditions by far is the one dispatched to find the new body of Nyikang. It is led by the effigy of Dak, accompanied by his keepers from among the Children of the Stool, along with some men from the settlement of Mwuomo in the far north of the Shilluk country, who act as divers. After sacrificing a cow so that its blood runs into the river, they set out from Akurwa in canoes to an island in the midst of the "raiding country" called "the island of Nyikang." A drum is beaten; Dak scours the waters of the Nile; when a white bird appears to indicate the right spot, ornaments are cast into the water as an offering, along with a sacrificial ram, and a diver descends to search for an *ambatch* trunk of roughly the right size to make the new body of Nyikang (P. P. Howell 1953a: 194). If he finds one, the body is wrapped in a white cloth and carried back to Akurwa, where both Nyikang and Dak are outfitted with their newly acquired cloth, feathers, and bamboo. But luck was not guaranteed. Riad's informants emphasized that Nyikang himself has specifically instructed his descendants to observe this custom as an "ordeal," to test the *reth*-elect, since, although the latter does not participate in the ceremony, Nyikang will not appear if he disapproves of the electors' choice. In fact, they emphasized that if the trunk could not be found, the entire ceremony would have to be conducted again, starting from Akurwa, and that after ten failures, the *reth*-elect would be killed and another candidate chosen in his place (Riad 1959: 189–90)—though, as with most of the dire warnings of the ceremony's dangers, no one could remember a specific occasion when anything like this had actually occurred.

---

43. The Ororo who carry the king's skeleton to its final resting place have a similar right to "seize small gifts and ransom from those unfortunate enough to cross their path" (P. P. Howell 1952a: 160) and even those villages preparing gear for the ritual can do the same from anyone passing by at the time (Anon. 1956: 99). But, as we'll see, it is the effigies of Nyikang and Dak especially who are famous for this sort of thing.

44. For example, two months before the ceremonies begin, the effigy of Dak presides over an expedition to Fanyikang to obtain certain sacred ropes (P. P. Howell and Thomson 1946: 38).

Once Nyikang has been brought to life again in the form of an effigy, he and Dak march to the northern border of the country and begin to assemble an army, drawn from the men of the northern half. It is said that they retrace the steps of his original conquest of the country. The effigies are carried, and surrounded, by the Children of the Stool, many armed with whips to frighten away those who come too close, followed by a retinue carrying his drums, pots, shields, spears, and bed. No one is allowed to carry weapons in the effigies' presence, so when they stay overnight at village shrines, their hosts, who would ordinarily be carrying spears, carry millet stalks instead. During this time, Nyikang usually retires, and Dak comes out to dance with, and bless, the assembled crowds. Everyone comes out to see the show, and to ask for cattle, sheep, spears, and so on. But they also hide their chickens:

> It is usual for gifts of a sheep or a goat to be presented or exacted by Nyikang, and it was noticeable how all small stock or fowl were either shut up or driven away from the vicinity of Nyikang, for Nyikang has the right to anything he fancies. As Nyikang proceeds with Dak his son beside him, the escort chants the songs of Nyikang and Dak recounting their exploits of conquest. From time to time Nyikang turns round and dances back as if to threaten those following. When he does this, Dak rushes ahead, carried in a charging position, his body held horizontally pointed like a spear . . . . (P. P. Howell and Thomson 1946: 41–42)

Occasionally, though things could also get out of hand:

> It is accepted custom among the Shilluk that Nyikang and his followers may seize cattle, sheep or goats which cross their path (most Shilluk are wise enough to keep them out of the way) or to demand them as offerings together with other smaller gifts from the occupants of the villages through which they pass. This licensed plundering, which is often abused beyond the bounds of piety by Nyikang's retinue, is treated by the Shilluk with admirable tolerance . . . . At one point on the march at Moro, however, their demands were thought to be excessive and were resisted, a demonstration which nearly ended in armed conflict and which delayed the party for a while. (P. P. Howell 1953a: 195)

At the same time, the whole procedure is considered something of a farce. Howell remarks that "the effigies are treated by the Shilluk with a mixture of hilarity and dread: mixed emotions that are always apparent" (ibid.: 192).

It's clear enough what's happening. The effigies, assembled from pieces drawn from outside the country, descend on Shillukland like an alien, predatory force. On one level, what they are doing is all in good fun; on another, they represent forces that are quite real, and the consequences are potentially serious.

Nyikang and Dak proceed from settlement to settlement, gathering their forces, retracing, it is said, their original path of conquest. Often members of new communities will at first oppose them, then, energized, rally to their side. Finally, they approach Fashoda.

The king has all this time been in seclusion in the capital, but on hearing of Nyikang's passage through Golbainy, the capital of the northern half of the country, he flees at night to take refuge in Debalo, the capital of the southern half. During that night, all fires are put out in both villages. The chief of Debalo challenges the *reth*-elect, asking his business. He replies, "I am the man sent by God to rule the land of the Shilluk" (Hofmayr 1925: 145). Unimpressed, the chief has his men try to block his party from entering, leading to mock battles, where, after being repelled three times, the *reth*-elect finally enters. At this point the fires are relit, using fire-sticks. According to Riad, three are lit in front of the king's hut: one from the royal family, one from the Ororo, and one from the people. "These fires, one of the symbols of royalty, are never put out as long as the king lives, and are transported to Fashoda when the king moves to the capital" (Riad 1959: 190).[45]

Once in Debalo, the *reth*-elect gathers his own followers. At some times, he is surrounded by men seeking forgiveness for sexual misdemeanors: he grants this in exchange for gifts of sheep and goats. At others, he is himself treated "like a small boy," belittled and humiliated by the chief, made to sleep in a rude hut and to herd sheep or cattle. He is formally betrothed to an eight- to ten-year-old girl, called the *nyakwer* or "girl of the ceremonies," who will be his almost constant companion from them on. Gradually, the southern chiefs all arrive with their warriors, to match Nyikang's army of the north. Both sides

---

45. Actually, Riad claims these fires are traditionally lit at the same time as the water ordeal—but in order to make the claim, he has to also argue that in former times, the king used to move back and forth between Fashoda and Debalo during his seclusion. Whether or not this is the case, the parallel that he or more likely his informants are trying to draw here—between water in the north and fire in the south—is significant. Charles Seligman (1934: 9) adds that one of the three fires is transported to Fashoda as the "life token" of the king.

prepare for a ritual battle which is always fought along the banks of a river that represents the official border between the two divisions of the country.

The candidate marches up, surrounded by the Ororo, who are his body-guards but at the same time the symbols of his mortality. He proceeds north toward Fashoda sitting backward on an ox, which is led by its tail, and alongside a heifer, also walking backward. Nyikang dispatches messengers to mock him. Before crossing the river, he and the girl step over a sheep, then a black bull, before crossing the river, thus consecrating them for sacrifice. It is said in earlier days he used to step over an old man who was then trampled by the people after him, usually, to death. The two forces proceed to do battle, each side unleashing a volley of millet stalks in lieu of spears. Nyikang's followers, however, are also armed with whips, reputed to be so powerful that a direct blow could cause madness. As a result, the southern forces are put to rout, and at the height of the battle, the bearers of Nyikang and Dak sweep forward and surround the *reth*-elect, carrying him off as prisoner to Fashoda, together with the "girl of the ceremonies."

On their arrival, the heifer is ritually sacrificed.

Once in the capital, however, the two figures begin to fuse. Nyikang's sacred stool is taken from his shrine; a white canopy is arranged around it, and the effigies and their captives are brought inside. First, Nyikang is first placed on the throne, then removed and replaced with the *reth*-elect. He begins to tremble, and exhibit signs of possession—the soul of Nyikang, it is said, has left the effigy and entered the king. He's doused with cold water. At this point the effigies retreat to their shrine, and the *reth* is revealed to the assembled people, as his wives (newly transferred from the harem of the previous king) warm water for a ritual bath while he sits "like a graven image on the chair" (Munro 1918: 546), himself now an effigy, and later is led out before the assembled people. In one case, at least, observers remarked he seemed visibly in trance. After the sacrifice of an ox, he is led to a temporary "camp" just opposite the shrine, where he is bathed in great secrecy, with water alternately warm and cool, to express the desire that he "rule with an even temper" and avoid extremes (P. P. Howell and Thomson 1946: 64). This bath is part of a broader process of communion with the spirit of Nyikang, which was considered arcane knowledge about which outsiders should know little, but according to some, the *reth* spent many hours of contemplation as the soul passed fully into him.

The transfer of Nyikang's soul marks the new *reth*'s last public appearance for at least three days. Afterwards, the king remains in seclusion, guarded only by some Ororo and a few of his own retainers. Once again, he is treated like a boy, expected to tend a small herd of cattle, and accompanied only by his be-trothed child bride. At some point, though, adult sexuality intervenes. An Ororo woman (in some versions, there are three of them) lures the king away to the shrines on the mound of Aturwic in Fashoda and seduces him;[46] while he is thus distracted, Nyikang steals out from another of the shrines and kidnaps the "girl of the ceremonies." On the king's return, he discovers her gone and, pretending outrage, begins searching everywhere. On finally realizing what's happened, he confronts the chief of Kwa Nyikwom (who is acting as Nyikang's spokesman), explaining that the girl had been properly betrothed by a payment in cattle, and Nyikang had no right to her. The chief, however, insists that the herds used—which are, after all, the old *reth*'s herds—are really Nyikang's.

Finally it comes down to another contest of arms. Both sides marshal their forces in Fashoda. This time, Nyikang is accompanied not only by the ferocious Dak, but also by his hapless son Cal. A smaller mock battle ensues, but this time the northerners' whips prove ineffective. The *reth* sweeps in and recaptures the girl from Nyikang; finally, the effigies have to fight their way back into their own shrines, and negotiate their effective surrender. The girl remains with the king, who has, in his victory, demonstrated that he and not the effigy is the true embodiment of Nyikang. At this point the effigies disappear, and do not return for the remainder of the ceremonies.

At this point, too, the drama is also effectively over. The new *reth* spends the next day on his throne at Aturwic, holding court amidst an assembly of the nation's chiefs. Each places his spear head down in the ground and delivers a speech urging the new ruler to respect elders and tradition, protect the weak, preserve the nation, and similar sage advice. Drums salute their words; the king is invested in two silver bracelets that serve as marks of office; an ox is speared. Finally, the king is given a tour of the capital. Everything is back in place. The newly installed *reth* sends cattle for sacrifice to each of the shrines of Nyikang scattered throughout the country. Some weeks later he is ready to preside over his first major ritual, a series of sacrifices calling on Nyikang to call on God to send the rain. Once the first rains fall, the effigies leave Fashoda and return to their shrine in Akurwa, and do not return until the new king dies.

---

46. According to certain other versions, he now commits incest with a half-sister, a very outrageous act. This is incidentally the closest the *reth* comes to committing one of de Heusch's "exploits," and most sources do not even mention it.

Since the drama began with the people's representatives announcing, "euphemistically," that they wish to kill the candidate-elect, it might be best to end it by noting that even here, in the *reth*'s most benevolent function, there were similar, darker possibilities. While one would imagine a newly inaugurated *reth* would have nothing but enthusiasm for his role as rainmaker, this was not always assumed to be the case.

> The king is the only authorized person to refuse or permit sacrifices at the important ritual ceremonies. The act of sacrificing animals to appease Juok, the highest spirit, and Nyikang, the demi-god, cannot be correctly undertaken without the king's sanction. Without sacrifices the people's wishes cannot be granted. It follows that the king is the real power in religious matters, and sometimes he withholds his beneficial powers if he feels the disloyalty of his subjects or their hatred towards him. (Riad 1959: 205, citing Hofmayr 1925: 152 n. 1)

In other words, while the *reth* (unlike Simonse's rainmaking kings) was not personally responsible for bringing down rain through magical means, his role was, at least potentially, not so very different. A drought might well be blamed on royal spite—and, presumably, begin to spur a political crisis, even if it was unlikely to end with an actual lynch mob.

THE INSTALLATION RITUAL: ANALYSIS

To some degree, the symbolic structure of the ritual is quite transparent. There is a constant juxtaposition of north and south, the former the division of Nyikang, the latter, of the king. The north is identified with the eternal, universal "kingship"; the south, with the particular, mortal king. Hence as Evans-Pritchard put it, in the ritual, "the kingship captures the king" (1948: 27). Having been defeated as a human, the *reth*-elect becomes Nyikang, and is thus able to defeat the effigy and banish it back to its shrine.

Another explicit element is the opposition of fire and water. At the same time as the image of Nyikang emerges from the river far to the north, new fires are lit in Debalo, the capital of the south, that will burn for the rest of the king's reign and be put out when he dies. Water here is eternity. It doesn't even "represent" eternity, it *is* eternity; the Nile will always be there, and always the same. With the rains, it is the permanent source of fecundity and life. It is therefore utterly appropriate that Nyikang, whose mother was a crocodile and who is called "child of the river," should emerge from its waters.[47] Fire, on the other hand, is, like blood, the stuff of worldly transformation. In this case, the fires correspond to the mortal life of the individual king; they will exist exactly as long as he lives. It is thus equally appropriate that when the synthesis of Nyikang and *reth*, between the eternal principle and mortal office-holder, occurs, it should be accompanying by putting a fire to water. The "bath" during which the king becomes fully one with the demigod also unites the two elemental principles. Fire meets water as mortal man meets god.[48]

All these elements are, as I say, relatively straightforward. Other elements are less so. The most puzzling is the role of Nyikang's son Dak. Existing analyses—even those that have a great deal to say about the effigies (Evans-Pritchard 1946; Arens 1984; Schnepel 1988)—focus almost exclusively on Nyikang, who is always assumed to represent the timeless nature of the royal office. They rarely have anything to say about Dak. But in many ways Dak seems even more important than Nyikang: if nothing else, because (just as in the legends he is the first to transcend death through the means of an effigy) his is the only effigy that was genuinely eternal. When the king dies, Nyikang returns to his mother in the river. Dak remains. Dak's effigy then presides over the re-creation of Nyikang's. What is one to make of this?

It might help here to return to the overall cosmological framework. The reader will recall that the Shilluk Creator is rarely invoked directly, but largely approached through Nyikang.

> The all-powerful being who exists in the minds of the Shilluk as a remote and amoral deity is called Juok. Juok is the Shilluk conception of God and is present to a greater and lesser degree in all things. Juok is the explanation of the unknown, the reassuring justification of all the supernatural phenomena, good and bad, of which life is made up. The principal medium through whom Juok is approached is Nyikang. The distinction between them is not clear. Nyikang is Juok, but Juok is not Nyikang. . . . Further the soul of Nyikang is reincarnate in every Shilluk *reth*,

---

47. All this is actually quite explicit: "As soon as the king dies, the spirit of Nyikang goes to his mother Nyikaya in the river, and the people will have to go to the river and bring him, and they will have to beg him to accept" (Singer in Schnepel 1988: 449).

48. One might also point out that this appears to be the ritual inversion of Nyikang's mythic battle with the Sun, where the hero used water to "burn" him.

and thus exists both in the past and the present. Nyikang is the *reth*, but the *reth* is not Nyikang. The paradox of the unity yet separation is not easy to define. The Shilluk themselves would find it difficult to explain. Juok, Nyikang, and the *reth* represent the line through whom divinity runs . . . . The *reth* is clearly himself the medium through which both Nyikang and, more vaguely, Juok are approached, and is the human intercessor with God. (P. P. Howell and Thomson 1946: 8)

After many years of contemplation and debate, scholars of Nilotic religions have learned to read such paradoxical phrases (e.g., "God is the sky, but the sky is not God") as statements about refraction and encompassment: Nyikang is an aspect of God, but God is in no way limited to that aspect.[49] We are presented, as in a rainmaking ceremony, with a very straightforward model of a linear hierarchy:

God

Nyikang

the *reth*

the people

The *reth* intercedes for the people and asks Nyikang to intercede with God to bring the rains. If the rain comes, it temporarily joins everything together. However, as we've seen, at every point there is potential antagonism. The people may hate the *reth* or wish to kill him; they may curse Nyikang; the *reth* may withhold the rains out of resentment of the people; the king and Nyikang raise armies and do battle with each other. Only God seems to stand outside this, but only because God is so distant: in Nuer and Dinka cosmologies, where Divinity is a more immediate concern, we learn that the human condition was first created because of God's (apparently unjustified) anger against humans, and there are even stories of defiant humans trying to make war on God and on the rain

---

49. Though in this case made even more confusing by reversing the order in the second example. If this is not simply a mistake on the author's part, it could be taken as a telling sign of the reversibility of some of these hierarchies.

(Lienhardt 1961: 43–4). Antagonism here appears to be the very principle of separation. Insofar as the *reth* is not Nyikang, it is first of all because the two sometimes stand in a relation of mutual hostility.

This, too, is fairly straightforward. Certainly, there are ambiguities—for instance, about how and whether the people themselves could be said to partake of divinity, since divinity is, after all, said to be present in everything—but these are the ambiguities typical of any such hierarchical system of encompassment.

Things get a little more complicated when one examines prayers offered directly to God. Here is one in Westermann, pronounced during a sacrifice to cure someone who is sick:

> There is no one above thee, thou God. Though becamest the grandfather of Nyikango; it is thou (Nyikango) who walkest with God; thou becamest the grandfather (of man), and thy son Dak. If famine comes, is it not given by thee? So as this cow stands here, is it not thus: if she dies, does her blood not go to thee? Thou God, and thou who becamest Nyikango, and thy son Dak! But the soul (of man), is it not thine own? (1912: 171; also in Lienhardt 1952: 156)[50]

Here we have the same sort of hierarchical participation (God became Nyikang . . .) but the king is gone and Dak appears in his place:

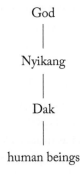

Dak's presence might not be entirely surprising here because it is most often his attacks that make people to sick to begin with. If so Dak, however much

50. Actually, Westermann claims this is the only prayer offered directly to God, but Hofmayr (1925: 197–201) and Oyler (1918b: 283) both produce other ones (namely, C. G. Seligman 1934: 5).

subordinated, also represents the active principle that sets everything off. This often seems to be his function.

Certainly, Dak is nothing if not active. This is especially obvious when he is paired with Nyikang, which he normally is. Nyikang's effigy is larger and heavier; it is clearly meant to embody the gravitas and dignity of authority. His image thus tends to stay near the center of things. In ordinary times, the effigy remains in the temple at Akurwa even when Dak's effigy leaves it to tour the country; when the two do travel together, it is always Dak who moves about, interacts, while Nyikang takes on a more "statesmanlike" reserve (Schnepel 1988: 437). True, one could argue this is simply a consequence of Dak's subordinate status: Nyikang is the authoritative center, Dak his worldly representative, his errand-boy. But even here there are ambiguities. Most strikingly, while Dak is smaller than Nyikang, he towers above him, always being carried atop an eight-foot pole. Nyikang, in contrast, stays close to the ground; in fact his effigy is often held parallel to the ground, while Dak's is ordinarily vertical. Similar ambiguities appear in stories about the two heroes' lives. Sometimes, especially in his youth, it is Dak who is always getting himself in trouble and Nyikang with his magical power who must step in to save him. But later, during the conquest of Shillukland, it is more likely to be the other way around: Nyikang is foiled by some problem, and Dak proves more ingenious, or more resourceful with a spear, and manages to solve it.

There is also the peculiar feature of Cal, Nyikang's feckless older son, who never accomplishes anything and whose image appears only when the effigies' forces lose. Dak and Cal seem to represent opposites: pure aggression versus absolute passivity, with Nyikang again defining the center. Yet in what way is Nyikang superior if he is more like the useless Cal?

What I would suggest is that this is not just a dilemma of interpretation for the outside analyst; it reflects a fundamental dilemma about the nature of political power that Shilluk tend to find as intractable as anyone else. Rituals can be interpreted as ways of puzzling out such problems, even as, simultaneously, they are ways of making concrete political change in the world.

Critical here is the role of the interregnum, the "year of fear." Wherever there are kings, interregna tend to be seen as periods of chaos and violence, times when the very cosmological order is thrown into disarray. But as Burkhard Schnepel (1988: 450) justly points out, this is the reason most monarchies try to keep them as brief as possible. There is no particular reason why those organizing the Shilluk installation ceremonies could not have declared, say, a three- to five-day period of chaos and terror—in fact, by the 1970s, that's exactly what they decided to do, abandoning the year-long interregnum entirely (ibid.: 443). If for centuries before they didn't, it indicates, if nothing else, that this year of fear was fundamentally important in some way.

Its importance, I think, is the key to understanding the importance of Dak as well. During the interregnum, royal politics, ordinarily bottled up in the figure of the *reth*, overflows into society at large. The result is constant peril. During this period, Nyikang is gone, and Dak alone remains. The return to normalcy begins with the stage of "preparations," conducted under Dak's general aegis, and often under his direct supervision. Expeditions set out to appropriate the materials with which to reconstruct the royal office, starting with the effigies. They uproot plants, they hunt and kill animals, they ambush and plunder camps and caravans. Nor do they limit their depredations to foreigners. They "take what they like" from Shilluk communities as well.

Dak's expeditions, then, represent indiscriminate predatory violence directed at every aspect of creation: vegetable, animal, every sort of human being. As I have pointed out, "indiscriminate" in this context also means "universal." Ordinarily, when one is in the presence of a power that can rain destruction equally on anyone and everyone, that is what Shilluk refer to as Juok, or God.[51] This is not to say that Dak is God (or, to be more precise, it is to say: God is Dak, but Dak is not God). Dak is the human capacity to act like God, to mimic his capricious, predatory destructiveness. In the stories, this is how he first appears: raining death and disaster arbitrarily. From his own perspective, "taking what he likes." From the perspective of his victims, playing God. During the interregnum, then, it is not just royal politics that spills over into society at large; it is divine power itself—the violent, arbitrary divine power that is,

---

51. God seems particularly immanent in violence or destruction. The above-cited prayer says "spear-thrusts are of Juok," and one of the few ways that God is regularly invoked in common speech is, as noted above, when people call out "Why, God?" when someone falls seriously ill. Among related Nilotic speakers in Uganda, "anything to do with killing must have *juok* in it" (Mogenson 2002: 424). On the other hand, in formal speech, God, so absent from the everyday life of ordinary Shilluk, pervades every aspect of royal existence. When speaking with members of the royal clan, one can never speak of their going someplace, or getting up, or staying someplace, or entering a house; instead they are "taken by God" to that place, "lifted by God," "nursed by God," "stuffed in the house by God," and so on (Pumphrey 1936).

as Shilluk institutions ensured no one could ever forget, the real essence and origin of royalty.

Of course, God (Juok) is not simply a force of destruction; he is also, originally, the creator of everything—and it is probably worth noting that this is also the only point in the ceremonies where anyone really makes or fashions anything. Still, this is not what's emphasized. What *is* emphasized is appropriation, which is perhaps the most distinctly human form of activity. Through a combination of appropriation and creation, Dak's people thus fashion Nyikang. Once they have done so, and Nyikang returns, he (unlike Dak) limits his depredations to his own Shilluk nation, retracing his original journey of conquest. But there seems to be a calculated ambiguity here. Do the Shilluk become Shilluk—Nyikang's subjects—because they collectively construct Nyikang (the classic fetish king, created by his people) or because he then goes on to conquer them (the classic divine king, raining disaster or the threat of disaster equally on all)?

The interregnum, then, is a time when divine power suffuses everything. This is what makes the creation of society possible. It's also what makes the creation of society necessary, since it results in an undifferentiated state of chaos and at least potential violence of all against all. Social order—like cosmic order—comes of separation, and the resultant creation of a relatively balanced, stable set of antagonisms. That one is, in fact, dealing with divine power here is confirmed by stories about the nature of the election itself. The electoral college is made up primarily of commoners, with a few royal representatives, but many insisted that "in former times" a delegation from the Nuba kingdom, the ancient allies of Nyikang, performed a ritual, a "fire ordeal," involving throwing either sticks or pebbles in a fire, that ensured that the new *reth* was chosen directly by God (Westermann 1912: 122; Hofmayr 1925: 451). Even in current times, the election is taken to represent God's choice: this is what allows the *reth* to tell the chief of Debalo that he is the man "sent by God to rule the land of the Shilluk" (Lienhardt 1952: 157).[52] The people and God are here interchangeable.

With Nyikang's return, God leaves the picture, and Dak is again reduced to his father's deputy. Divinity begins to be properly bottled up. Nyikang may

---

52. The presence of foreigners here—even if legendary—seems to be a reminder of the universality of the divine principle. Note, too, the opposition between this "fire ordeal," in which the candidate is chosen by God, and the "water ordeal," in which he is confirmed by Nyikang.

continue Dak's predatory ways, looting and pillaging as he reenacts his conquests, but it has all become something of a burlesque.

Over the course of the ceremonies, Nyikang's spirit, having been coaxed out of the river, is transferred first into the effigy, then, just as reluctantly, into the body of the *reth*-elect. In doing so, Nyikang is also moving forward in history: from his birth from the river in mythic times, to his heroic exploits in the beginning of Shilluk history, to his current incarnation in the body of a contemporary king. If one looks at what is happening in the south, surrounding the candidate, however, we see a very different kind of drama. I have already mentioned the contrast between the water symbolism surrounding Nyikang and the fire symbolism surrounding the king. This is also a juxtaposition between mortality and eternity. Nyikang might be constructed, but he is constructed of eternal materials. (There will always be a river, just as there will always be ostriches and bamboo.) He then moves from the generic—and thus timeless—to the increasingly particular, and hence historic. But he will never actually die, just disappear and begin the cycle all over again. The king, on the other hand, is from the start surrounded by reminders of his own mortality.

If the fires are the most obvious of these reminders, the most important are surely the Ororo. The Ororo preside over every aspect of the king's mortality. As degraded nobility, their very existence is a reminder that royal status is not eternal: that kings have children, that most of them will not be kings, that eventually, royal status itself can pass away. In royal ritual, Ororo have a jurisdiction over everything that pertains to sexuality and death. They are the men who carry out the sacrifices for the king by spearing and roasting animals, they are the women who wash, shave, and seduce the king; they will provide his highest-ranking wives; they protect but eventually kill him; they officiate over the decomposition and burial of his corpse. Throughout the ceremonies, the *reth*-elect is surrounded by Ororo. When he is defeated and seized by Nyikang, he is plucked from amidst his own mortality.

This is not to say that the *reth* is ever more than "temporarily" immortal. Even after his capture, the Ororo soon return.

This theme plays itself out throughout the ceremony. If the drama in the north is about the gradual containment of arbitrary, divine power, the drama in the south is about human vulnerability. The *reth*-to-be is mocked, treated as a child, forced to ride backward on an ox. His followers never wield arbitrary power over humans. Unlike Dak and Nyikang, they do not loot or plunder or hold passers-by for ransom. They do, however, constantly offer animals up for

sacrifice. Just about every significant action of the king is marked by his stepping over (thus, consecrating) some animal, which is later ritually killed.[53] In
one sense what the king does is the exact opposite of what Nyikang and Dak
are doing. Sacrificial meat is redistributed,[54] so instead of stealing live beasts, he
is distributing the flesh of dead ones. This is especially significant since, when
presiding over sacrifices meant to resolve feuds, Shilluk kings have been known
to state quite explicitly that the flesh and blood of the animal they sacrifice
should be considered as their own (Oyler 1920a: 298). Since in ordinary Shilluk
sacrifices the life and blood of the creature (unlike the flesh) are said to "go up
to God"—and to Nyikang—it would seem the king is here playing the part of
humanity as a whole, placing himself in a willfully subordinate position to the
cosmic powers that will ultimately take hold of him.

In a larger sense, sacrifice—in all Nilotic religions the paradigmatic ritual—is about the reestablishment of boundaries.[55] Divinity has entered into the
world, the ordinary divisions of the cosmos (e.g., between humans, animals,
and gods) have become confused; the result is illness or catastrophe. So while
sacrifice is, here as everywhere, a way of entering into communication with the
Divine, it is ultimately a way of putting Divinity back in its proper place. If the
interregnum, the reign of Dak, is a time of indiscriminate violence against every
aspect of creation, sacrifice is about restoring discriminations: respect (*thek*), to
use the Nuer/Dinka phrase;[56] separation, appropriate distance. In this sense, the
entire installation ceremony is a kind of sacrifice, or at least does the same thing
that a sacrifice is ordinarily meant to do. It restores a world of separations.

Of course, if the ritual is a kind of sacrifice, it is reasonable to ask: Who is
the victim? The *reth*-elect? A case could be made. The ceremony begins with the

---

53. It happens so often that most such examples I actually purged from my account,
    above, to avoid monotony.

54. This is not to say that Nyikang's passage does not include some acts of sacrifice, since
    otherwise there could be no feasts; only that this is not a particularly important
    aspect of what he does. With the king it is clearly otherwise.

55. In the absence of any detailed published material on Shilluk sacrifice, I am drawing
    here on Evans-Pritchard (1954, 1956) on the Nuer, but even more Lienhardt's
    work on the Dinka (1961) and Beidelman's (1966a, 1981) reinterpretations of this
    material.

56. On *thek*, see Beidelman (1981). The Shilluk cognate appears to be *pak*, usually
    translated "praise," which also refers to specialized formal language used within and
    between clans (see Crazzolara 1951: 140–42). As usual, though, there isn't enough
    material on Shilluk custom to make a sustained comparison.

people informing the candidate that they wish to kill him. During his time in Debalo, he is treated very much like an ox being prepared for sacrifice: sacrificial oxen, too, are secluded, manhandled, and mocked—even while those who mock them also confess their sins (Lienhardt 1961: 292–95).[57] Then in the end the ox's death becomes a token of a newly created community, its unity brought into concrete being in the sharing of the animal's flesh. Here one could almost see the humiliated princely candidate in a messianic role, giving of himself to man and god, sacrificing himself in the name of Shilluk unity. But if so, the obvious objection is that he doesn't seem to be sacrificing very much. To the contrary: the ceremonies end with the new king happily installed in Fashoda, accepting the allegiance of his subjects, inspecting the buildings, reassembling a harem; perhaps, if so inclined, plotting bloody revenge on anyone who has ever insulted him.

Still, all this is temporary. The king is, ultimately, destined to die a ritual death.

So, is the king to be considered a sacrificial victim on temporary reprieve? In a certain sense, I would say yes. Every act of sacrifice does, after all, contain its utopian moment. Here, it's as if the king is suspended inside that utopian moment indefinitely—or at least, so long as his strength holds out.

Let me explain what I mean by this. Normally, what I'm calling the utopian moment in sacrifice is experienced first and foremost in the feast, after the animal is dead, when the entire community is brought together for the collective enjoyment of its flesh. Often this is a community that has been created, patched together from previously unrelated or even hostile factions, by the ceremony itself. Even if that is not the case, they must put aside any prior differences. According to Lienhardt, for Dinka, such moments of communal harmony are the closest one can come to the direct experience of God—or, to be more exact, to Divinity in its aspect of benevolent universality:

> In Divinity the Dinka image their experience of the ways in which human beings everywhere resemble each other, and in a sense form a single community with one original ancestor created by one Creator. . . . When, therefore, a prophet like Arianhdit shows that he is able to make peace between normally exclusive

---

57. Admittedly, I am relying here on Lienhardt's detailed description and analysis of Dinka sacrifice, supplemented by Evans-Pritchard's Nuer ethnography, but this is, as I say, because no parallel Shilluk account exists. For what it's worth, Evans-Pritchard (1954: 28) felt it appropriate to use Shilluk statements to throw light on Nuer practices.

and hostile communities, to persuade them to observe between them the peaceful conventions which they had previously observed only internally, and to unite people of different origins in a single community, he proves that he is a "man of Divinity." . . . A man is recognized as a powerful "man of Divinity" because he creates for people the experience of peace between men and of the uniting of forces which are normally opposed to each other, of which Divinity is understood to be the grounds. (1961: 157)

It's in this sense that God "also represents truth, justice, honesty, uprightness," and so on (ibid.: 158). It is not because God, as a conscious entity, is just. In fact, like most Nilotic peoples, Dinka seem haunted by the strong suspicion that he isn't. It is because truth, justice, and so on, are the necessary grounds for "order and peace in human relations," and therefore, truth, justice, and so on, *are* God. The point of sacrificial ritual, then, is to move from one manifestation of the divine to the other: from God as confusion and disaster to God as unity and peace. Normally it is the feast which seems to act as the primary experience of God, but often the divine element takes even more concrete form in the undigested grass extracted from the cow's stomach. It seems significant that the one Shilluk sacrifice for which we have any sort of description—other than those meant to bring the rain—is aimed at creating peace between two parties to a feud (Oyler 1920a). The *reth* here plays the part of the Dinka prophet. After he emphasizes that the ox's flesh and blood are really his own, the animal is speared, and the chyme, the half-digested grass in question, is used to anoint the former feuding parties. "That was done to show their united condition" (ibid.: 299).[58] Nuer insist that chyme, like the blood and more generally the "life," is the part of the sacrificed animal that belongs to God (Evans-Pritchard 1956: 212; Evens 1989: 338). Generally speaking, in Nilotic ritual, chyme[59] is treated as the stuff of pure potential: it is grass in the process of becoming flesh; undifferentiated substance in the way of creative transformation. As such it is itself the pure embodiment of life.

It seems to me that this is the utopian moment in which the *reth* is suspended. Not only is he, as *reth*, the ground for "order and peace in human relations,"

---

58. "The thought was that the animal eats a bit here and there, but in the stomach it all becomes one mass. Even so the individuals of the two factions were to become one" (Oyler 1920a: 299).

59. And also chyle, which is the further digested grass in the animal's second stomach. This is the stuff even more closely identified with life, but I thought I would spare the reader all the niceties of bovine digestive anatomy.

of unity and hence of justice, he is the person actually responsible for mediating and resolving disputes. Peace and justice, then, is the social equivalent of rain, and chyme, like falling water, is the very physical substance of the divine in its most benevolent aspect. All this is stated almost explicitly in the peace sacrifice: the king is the ox, he is God, he is peace, he is the unity of all his subjects. This, too, is how the *reth* can be both sacrificial victim in suspense, and living in a kind of small version of paradise.

The installation ritual begins with a nightmare vision of a world infused with divine power, in which no separations exist, and all human relations are therefore tinged with potential violence. It is the worst kind of unity of God and world. It ends with the restoration of the best kind. In this sense, it is the transformation of divine king into sacred king. Dak, in his untrammeled form, embodies the former. The proceedings seem to be based on the assumption that the primordial truth of power—that it is arbitrary violence—has to be acknowledged so it can then be contained. One might argue the two main forms of sacred kingship identified by Luc de Heusch are the two principal strategies for doing this. Each plays itself out in a different division of the country. In the north, divine power is reduced to a fetish—literally, an effigy—which is constructed by, and hence to some degree therefore manageable by, ordinary humans. In the south, we see the making of a classic scapegoat king. Ultimately the two become one: the king not only becomes Nyikang, he also, at least momentarily, becomes an effigy. Ordered, hierarchical relations (God–Nyikang–king–people) are restored. The new king is (as Dak was originally) in a sense all of them at once, even as he is also the means to keep them apart, suspended in a kind of balanced antagonism. As such he is a victim himself suspended, temporarily, in a miniature version of the original unity of heaven and earth, in a strange village with sex but without childbirth, a place of ease and pleasure, devoid of hunger, sickness, and death.

The paradise, however, is temporary, and the solution always provisional, incomplete. Arbitrary violence can never be entirely eliminated. Heaven and earth cannot really be brought together, except during momentary thundershowers. And even the simulation of paradise is bought at a terrible price.

SOME WORDS IN WAY OF A CONCLUSION

I have framed my argument in cosmological terms because I believe one cannot understand political institutions without understanding the people who create them, what they believe the world to be like, how they imagine the human situation within it, and what they believe it is possible or legitimate to want from it. This is true everywhere, even though cosmological formulations themselves can vary enormously. Still, anyone coming at the Shilluk material from a background in Judaism, Christianity, or Islam is unlikely to feel on entirely here. There is a reason early anthropologists often saw Nilotic peoples as the closest living cousins of the biblical patriarchs: not only are Semitic and Nilotic languages distantly connected; in each case we are dealing with seminomadic pastoralists with a lineage-based form of organization, monotheists whose ritual life was dominated by sacrifice to a distant and arbitrary God. Actually, I suspect this affinity is true, in a more attenuated sense, for Africa more generally. It is easy to get the sense, reading African myths, that the basic dilemmas of human existence they explore—the reasons for suffering, the justice of God—are much the same as those grappled with in the Abrahamic tradition; if nothing else, certainly far more familiar to someone raised on the tradition of the Bible and Greek myths than equivalent stories from, say, Amazonia or Polynesia—or even ancient Ireland.

Though to some degree, too, they deal with issues that are universal.

It would have to be so, or it would not be possible to make cross-cultural generalizations about "divine kingship," "sacred kingship," or "scapegoats" to begin with. This essay is really founded on two such generalizations. The first is that it is one of the misfortunes of humanity that we share a tendency to see the successful prosecution of arbitrary violence as in some sense divine—or, anyway, to identify it with some kind of transcendental power. It is not entirely clear why this should be. Perhaps it has something to do with the utterly disproportionate quality of violence, the enormous gap between action and effect. It takes decades to bring forth and shape a human being; a few seconds to bring all that to nothing by driving a spear into his chest. It takes very little effort to drop a bomb; unimaginable effort to have to learn to get about without legs for the rest of one's life because they've been blown off by one. Even more, acts of arbitrary violence are acts which for the victims and their families must necessarily have enormous significance, but have no intrinsic meaning. Meaning, after all, implies intentionality. But the definition of "arbitrary" is that there is no particular reason why one person was shot or blown up and another wasn't; such acts are therefore by definition meaningless, in that they do not embody a conscious or even unconscious intention. This is just what allows arbitrary acts of weather to be referred to as "acts of God." Meaning abhors a vacuum. Particularly when we are dealing with actions or events of enormous significance, it is hard to resist the tendency to ascribe some kind of transcendental meaning, or at least to assume that one exists even though we can't know what it is. It is in this absolute absence of meaning that we encounter the Divine.

Of course, this is only a tendency. As I remarked earlier, it's not as if any bandit who finds himself in a position to wreak random violence with impunity is therefore going to be treated as a god (except perhaps in his immediate presence). But some are. It is also clear that the apparatus of sacred kingship is a very effective way of managing those who are treated in this way.

Here I introduce my second cross-cultural generalization. The sacred, everywhere, is seen as something that is or should be set apart. As much as an object becomes the embodiment of a transcendental principle or abstraction, so much is it to be kept apart from the muck and mire of ordinary human life, and surrounded, therefore, with restrictions. These are the kind of principles of separation that Nuer and Dinka, at least, refer to with the word *thek*, usually translated "respect." Violent men almost invariably insist on tokens of respect, but tokens of respect taken to the cosmological level—"not to touch the earth,", "not to see the sun"—tend to become severe limits on one's freedom to act violently. If nothing else, the violence can, as in the Shilluk case, be bottled up, limited to a specific royal sphere which is under ordinary circumstances scrupulously set apart from ordinary daily affairs.

We will never know the exact circumstances under which Shilluk royal institutions came into being, but the broad outlines can be reconstructed. The ancestors of the Shilluk were likely in most essentials barely distinguishable from their Nuer or Dinka neighbors—fiercely egalitarian pastoralists who settled along an unusually fertile stretch of the Nile. There they became more sedentary, more populous, but also began regularly raiding their neighbors for cattle, wealth, and food. To some degree this appears to have been born of necessity; to some degree, it no doubt became a matter of glory and adventure. An incipient class of war chieftains emerged who assembled wealth in the form of cattle, women, and retainers. These became the ancestors of Shilluk royalty. However, the royal clan itself only appears to have developed, at least in the form in which anthropologists came to know it, after a prolonged struggle over the nature of the emerging political order, the role of women, and the power and jurisdiction of commoner chiefs. A compromise eventually emerged, which has come to be known as "the divine kingship of the Shilluuk." This compromised formulation appears to have been brilliantly successful in creating and maintaining a sense of a unified nation, capable of defending itself and usually dominating the surrounding territories, without ever giving the royals with their fractious politics much chance to play havoc with local affairs. It was sustained by popular vigilance. Ordinary Shilluk appear to have resisted the emergence of anything resembling an administrative system. Communications between Fashoda and other settlements were maintained not by officials, but principally by relations with and between royal sisters, wives, and daughters. Any attempt at creating systematic tribute relations, at home or abroad, appears to have been met with such immediate and widespread protest that the very legitimacy of the kingship was soon called into question. As a result, the royal treasury, such as it was, consisted almost entirely of wealth that had been stolen—seized in raids either against foreigners, or against Shilluk communities that resisted attempts to mediate disputes. The playful raiding during installation rituals was simply a reminder of what everyone already knew: that predatory violence was and would always remain the essence of sovereignty. Above all, there seemed to be an at least implicit understanding that such matters ought not be in any way obfuscated—that the euphemization of power was essential to any project of its permanent institutionalization, and this was precisely what most people did not wish to see.

My use of the term "utopia" is somewhat unconventional in this context. I am defining "utopia," in the fairly colloquial sense, as any place that represents an unattainable ideal, particularly if that ideal involves an impossible resolution of what are otherwise taken to be the fundamental dilemmas of human existence—however those might be conceived. Utopia is the place where contradictions are resolved.[60] Part of my inspiration here is Pierre Clastres' argument (1962, 1977) that among the Amazonian societies he knew, states could never have developed out of existing political institutions. Those political institutions, he insisted, appeared to be designed to prevent arbitrary coercive authority from ever developing. If states ever could emerge in this environment (and it seems apparent now that, in certain periods of history, they did), it could only be through figures like the Tupí-Guraní prophets, who called on their followers to abandon their existing customs and communities to embark on a quest for a "land without evil," an imaginary utopia where all would become as gods free of birth and death, the earth would yield its bounty without labor, and all social

---

60. Or, better put, the place where existential dilemmas are reduced to mere contradictions, so that they can be resolved.

restrictions could therefore be set aside (H. Clastres 1995). The state can only arise from such absolutist claims, and, above all, from an explicit break with the world of kinship. Luc de Heusch's original insight on African kingship, which came out in the same year as Clastres' original essay (1962), makes a similar argument: kingship must always mark an explicit break with the domestic order. Perhaps this is not surprising as both emerge from the mutual confluence of revolutionary politics and structuralist theory.[61] Obviously, de Heusch was later to take it in what might seem a very different direction. But how different is it really?

Certainly, Shilluk kings do share certain qualities with Nuer and Dinka prophets, even if, unlike them, they don't predict the coming of a new world where all human dilemmas will be resolved.[62] Certainly, the organization of the royal capital did represent a kind of partial unraveling of the dilemmas of the human condition. But we can also consider de Heusch's idea of the "body-fetish." The reader will recall that the basic idea here is that rituals of installation turn the king's own physical person into the equivalent of a magical charm; he is the kingdom, its milk and its grain, and any danger to the king's bodily integrity is thus a threat to the safety and prosperity of the kingdom as a whole. If he grows old and sickly, defeats, crop failures, and natural disasters are likely to result. Hence the principle, so common in Africa, that kings ought not to die a natural death.

For this reason, the king "must keep himself in a state of ritual purity," as Evans-Pritchard stressed, and also "a state of physical perfection" (1948: 20). All sources agree on this latter point, and it is a common feature of sacred kingship. A legitimate candidate to the throne must not only be strong and healthy,

---

61. Before becoming an anthropologist and conducting fieldwork in the then-Belgian Congo, Luc de Heusch was known as a radical film-maker and part of the revolutionary art collective the CoBrA group, now remembered largely as the ancestor of the Situationist International. Clastres was famously an anarchist who became the main source for almost all of Deleuze and Guattari's anthropological interventions (the evolutionary stages in anti-Oedipus, the "war machine," etc). De Heusch's later work shows no obvious traces of revolutionary theory but this context must have influenced his initial framing of his problem.

62. Specifically, kings were like prophets seen as being possessed by divine spirits (Shilluk prophets, when they appeared, were often possessed by Nyikang), mediated disputes on a national level that local authorities could not deal with, and relied on a following of young men who were themselves cut off from the ordinary domestic order because, having no access to cattle, they could not ordinarily expect to marry.

he must have no scars, blemishes, missing teeth, asymmetrical features, unde-
scended testicles, deformities, and so forth. What's more, his bodily integrity
must be fastidiously maintained, particularly at ritual moments: we are told that
if during the installation ceremonies the *reth* is injured in any way, "even if the
king is only punched and blood appears" (Singer in Schnepel 1988: 444), he is
immediately disqualified for office. For this reason, some sources insist kings
could not even fight in war, but were rather borne along as a kind of standard
while others were fighting; historical narratives suggest this was not always the
case, but certainly, if the king were seriously injured, this could not be allowed
to stand, and he would be discreetly dispatched.

The very idea of physical perfection is strangely paradoxical if you really
think about it. What does it mean to say someone is physically perfect? Presumably that they correspond to some idealized model of what a human being is
supposed to be like. But how do we even know what humans are supposed to be
like? There is only one way: by observing actual human beings. But actual human beings are never physically perfect; in fact, when compared with the model
of a generic human we have in our heads, most seem at least slightly misshapen.
This is partly because, when moving from tokens to types, we wipe out change
and process: real humans grow, age, and so on; generic humans are, first of all,
caught forever at some idealized moment of their lives. But it's also an effect of
the process of generalization itself: in moving from tokens to types, we always
seem to generate something which we find more proper or appealing than the
tokens—or at least the overwhelming majority of them. In this sense, the king
is indeed an abstraction or transcendental principle: the ideal-typical human,
though here I am using the phrase not in Weber's sense, but rather from the
understanding that, like Leonardo da Vinci, when we try to imagine the typical, we usually end up generating the ideal.[63] Insofar as the *reth* is the embodiment of the nation, and of humanity as a whole before the divine powers, he
is a generic human; insofar as he is the generic human, he must be the perfect
human; insofar as he is an image of humanity removed from time and process,
he must be preserved from any harmful transformation until the point where,
when this becomes impossible, he must be simply destroyed and put away. In
the sense, the king's body is less a fetish than itself a kind of microutopia, an
impossible ideal.

---

63. This is, of course, what "ideal" actually means: it is the idea lying behind some
    category.

There is always, I think, a certain utopian element in the sacred. That which is sacred is not only set apart from the mundane world, it is set apart particularly from the world of time and process, of birth, growth, decay, and also simple bodily functions—ways in which the body is continuous with the world. I have explored this phenomenon in great detail elsewhere (Graeber 1997). What is most striking in the case of sacred kingship is that this is reflected above all in an urge to deny the king's mortality; and this denial is almost invariably effected by killing people.

Rulers of early states—Egyptian and Mesoamerican pyramid-builders being only the most famous examples—had a notorious tendency to develop obsessions with their own mortality. In a way, this is not hard to understand; like Gilgamesh, having conquered every other enemy they could imagine, they were left to confront the one that they could never ultimately defeat. Killing others, in turn, does seem one of the few ways to achieve some sort of immortality. That is to say, most kings are aware that there are rulers remembered for reigns of peace, justice, and prosperity, but they are rarely the ones remembered for all time. If history will accord them permanent significance, it will most likely be for either one or two things: vast building projects (which often themselves entail the death of thousands) or wars of conquest. There is an almost literal vampirism here: ten thousand young Assyrians or Frenchmen must be wiped from existence, their own future histories aborted, so the name of Assurbanipal or Napoleon can live on.

Shilluk refused to allow their *reths* to engage in this sort of behavior, but in the institutions of Frazerian sacred kingship we encounter the same relation in a far more subtle way. The connection is so subtle, in fact, that it has gone largely unnoticed. But it comes especially clearly into focus if one compares the Shilluk kingdom with its most notoriously brutal cousin: the kingdom of Buganda located on the shores of Lake Victoria a few hundred miles to the south. In many ways, the similarities between the two are quite remarkable. Ganda legends, too, trace the kingship back to a cosmic dilemma about the origins of death; here, too, the first king did not die but mysteriously vanished in the face of popular discontent; here, too, the next three kings vanished as well; here, too, there were elaborate installation rituals with mock battles, the lighting of ritual fires, and a chaotic year-long interregnum. Yet in other ways the Ganda kingship is an exact inversion.

Much of the difference turned on the status of women. In Buganda, women did almost all subsistence labor, while having no autonomous organizations of their own; men formed a largely parasitical stratum, the young ones organized into militarized bands, older ones into an endlessly elaborate administrative apparatus that seemed to function largely to keep the younger ones under control, or distracted in endless wars of conquest. The result was, by any definition, a bona fide state. It was also one of those rare cases when bureaucratization did not in any sense lead to any significant euphemization. While the king was not identified with any divine being, he remained very much a divine king in our sense of the term: a dispatcher of arbitrary violence, and higher justice, both at the same time. However, where the Shilluk king was surrounded by executioners whose role was eventually to kill him, the Ganda king was surrounded by executioners whose role was to kill everybody else. Thousands might be slaughtered during royal funerals, installations, or when the king periodically decided there were too many young men on the roads surrounding the capital, and it was time to round a few hundred up and hold a mass execution. Kings might be killed in rebellions, but none were ritually put to death. As Gillian Feeley-Harnik (1985: 277) aptly put it, regicide, here, seems to have been replaced by civicide.[64] When David Livingstone asked why the king killed so many people, he was told that if he didn't, everyone would assume that he was dead.

Benjamin Ray remarks that the capital was, as so often in such states, "a microcosm of the kingdom, laid out so that it reflected the administrative order of Buganda as a whole" (1991: 203); the king was the linchpin of the social cosmos, distributor of titles and spoils, and, hence, the ultimate arbiter of all forms of value. His was a secular court, with few of the formal trappings of sacral kingship. Even his close relatives insisted he just a man like any other. Still, the person of the king is always sacred, and the very fact that this was a regime based almost solely on force meant that the ritual surrounding the person of the king took on a unique ferocity. The *kabaka*, as he was called, did not leave the palace except when carried by bearers, and the punishment for gazing directly at him was death.

> The rules of courtly etiquette, such as the prohibition against sneezing or coughing in the king's presence . . . were considered as important as the laws of the state,

---

64. Probably literally: Christopher Wrigley, the grand old man of Ganda studies, makes a plausible case that what we are dealing with here is a very old and probably fairly typical institution of sacred kinship suddenly transformed, a few generations before, into a state (1996: 246). A bureaucracy was superimposed with disastrous results.

for behavior towards the king's person was regarded as an expression of one's allegiance to the throne he represented. Thus Mutesa sometimes condemned his wives to death because they coughed while he was eating. (Ray 1991: 172)

Foreign observers like Speke and Livingstone wrote in horror of even well-born princesses being dragged off to execution for the slightest physical infraction.[65] This might seem about as far as one can get from the Shilluk court, where women were sacrosanct and it was the king who was eventually executed. But in fact it is a precise inversion, a mirror image, and hence, on a deeper level, precisely the same thing. The constant element is the illusion of physical perfection at the center, which brings with it the need to suppress whatever are taken to be the most significant signs of bodily weakness, illness, or lack of physical control, and, above all, the fact that this illusion was ultimately enforced by threat of death. The difference is simply that the direction of the violence is reversed. It is, perhaps, a simple matter of balance of forces. In the war between sovereign and people, the *reth* was at a constant disadvantage. The *kabaka*, in contrast, held all the cards. One might even say that, for the moment at least, he had definitively won. His ability to rain arbitrary destruction was unlimited not just in principle, but largely in practice, and the bodies of royal women were simply the most dramatic means of its display.

Granted, the situation was not ultimately viable. Such victories can never be sustained. Even in the nineteenth century, it was assumed that every *kabaka*, driven mad by power, would eventually go too far, and be destroyed—if not by real flesh-and-blood rebels, then at least by the angry ghosts of his victims. By the end of the century, the entire system was overthrown and mass executions were abolished. What I really want to draw attention to here, though, is, first of all, the intimate connection between the otherworldly perfection of royal courts and their violence—to the fact that such utopias do, always, rest on what we euphemistically call "force." The second point is that the violence always cuts both ways. This is the truth that is being acknowledged in the Shilluk stories that show how Dak's effigy—which represents human capacities to become a god through violence—was created when the people as a whole set out to kill Dak, or how Nyikang vanished and became a god when everybody hated him.

---

65. No doubt some of this was simply to impress foreigners with the absoluteness of royal power; but such customs aren't improvised whole cloth.

What I would suggest is that this has remained the hidden logic of sovereignty. What we call "the social peace" is really just a truce in a constitutive war between sovereign power and "the people" or "nation"—both of whom come into existence, as political entities, in their struggle against each other. Furthermore, this elemental war is prior to wars *between* nations.

To call this a "war" is to fly in the face of almost all existing political theory, which—whether it be a matter of Carl Schmitt's argument that the first gesture of sovereignty is declaring the division of friend and enemy, or Max Weber's monopoly of legitimate use of force within a territory, or the assertion in *African political systems* (Fortes and Evans-Pritchard 1940) that states are entities that resolve conflict internally through law, and externally, through war—assumes there is a fundamental distinction between inside and outside, and particularly between violence inside and violence outside—that, in fact, this is constitutive of the very nature of politics. As a result, just about everyone (with the possible exception of anthropologists) who wishes to discuss the nature of "war" starts with examples of armed conflicts between two clearly defined political and territorial entities, usually assumed to be nation-states or something almost exactly like them, involving a clash of armies that ends either with conquest or some sort of negotiated peace.[66] In fact, even the most cursory glance at history shows that only a tiny percentage of armed conflicts have taken such a form. In reality, there is almost never a clear line between what we'd now call "war" and what we'd now call "banditry," "terrorism," "raids," "massacres," "duels," "insurrections," or "police actions." Yet somehow in order to be able to talk about war in the abstract we have to imagine an idealized situation that only rarely actually occurs. True, during the heyday of European colonialism, from roughly 1648 to 1950, European states did attempt to set up a clear system of rules to order wars between nation-states, and in this period one does find a fair number of wars that do fit this abstract model; but these rules applied only within Europe, a tiny corner of the globe. Outside it, the same European powers became notorious for disrespecting solemn agreements and their willingness to engage in every sort of indiscriminate violence. Since 1950, the rest of the globe has come to be included in the system of nation-states, but as a result, since that time, no wars have been formally declared, and despite hundreds of military conflicts,

---

66. Or sometimes they skip from description of monkeys, other sorts of animal behavior, or speculations about early hominids to wars between fully constituted nation-states. But generally there is nothing in between.

there have been only a handful that have involved the clash of armies between nation-states.

Obviously, the conceptual apparatus—the way we imagine war—is important. But it seems to me it is mainly important in occluding that more fundamental truth that the Nilotic material brings so clearly into focus. As those European travelers discovered, when asked by Nilotic kings to conduct raids or rain random gunfire on "enemy villages" that actually turned out to be inhabited by the king's own subjects, there is no fundamental difference in the relation between a sovereign and his people, and a sovereign and his enemies. Inside and outside are both constituted through at least the possibility of indiscriminate violence. What differentiates the two—at least, when the differences are clear enough to bear noticing—is that the insiders share a commitment to a certain common notion of utopia. Their war with the sovereign becomes the ground of their being, and thus, paradoxically, the ground of a certain notion of perfection—even peace.

Any more realistic exploration of the nature of sovereignty, I believe, should proceed from examination of the nature of this basic constitutive war. Unlike wars between states, the war between sovereign and people is a war that the sovereign can never, truly, win. Yet states seem to have an obsession with creating such permanent, unwinnable wars: as the United States has passed over the last half-century from the War on Poverty to the War on Crime to the War on Drugs (the first to be internationalized) and, now, to the War on Terror. The scale changes but the essential logic remains the same. This is the logic of the assertion of sovereignty. Of course, no war is (as Clausewitz falsely claimed) simply a contest of untrammeled force. Any sustained conflict, especially one between state and people, will have elaborately developed rules of engagement. Still, behind those rules of engagement always lies at least the threat—and usually, periodically, the practice—of random, arbitrary, indiscriminate destruction. It is only in this sense that the state is, as Thomas Hobbes so famously put it, a "mortall god."

I don't think there is anything inevitable about all this. The will to sovereignty is not, as reactionaries always want us to believe, something inherent in the nature of human desire—as if the desire for autonomy was always also necessarily the desire to dominate and destroy. Neither, however, does the historical emergence of forms of sovereignty mark some kind of remarkable intellectual or organizational breakthrough. Actually, taken simply as an idea, sovereignty, like monotheism, is an extraordinarily simple concept that almost anyone could have thought of. The problem is it's not simply an idea: it is better seen, I think, as proclivity, a tendency of interpretation immanent in certain sorts of social and material circumstances, but one which nonetheless can be, and often is, resisted. As Luc de Heusch makes clear, it is not even essential to the nature of government. Only by putting sovereignty in its place, it seems to me, can we can begin to look realistically at the full range of human possibilities.

CHAPTER 3

The atemporal dimensions of history
In the old Kongo kingdom, for example

Marshall Sahlins

INTRODUCTION: PARADIGMATIC HISTORIES

"There's something particular to Muslims. When I read I feel the behavior of people who lived a glorious past—in our consciousness, not in our experience—so we feel it keenly," he said. "And now in a quest to find that honor, there is a voraciousness to find it again and seize it once more."

Fathi Ben Haj Yahia, in *The New York Times* International: August 8, 2015

We are going to take the marvelous seriously: for we intend to reconstruct the mythological universe within which Bantu historical thought has developed.

Luc de Heusch, *The drunken king, or The origin of the state*

The ancient Greeks had good reason to deify Memory. Commenting on cosmogonic myths in Hesiod and Homer, Jean-Pierre Vernant noted that "the past thus revealed represents much more than the time prior to the present; it is its very source" (2006: 119). The observation has radical implications for historiography, insofar as it stipulates that historical causes in the mode of memory have no temporal or physical proximity to their effects; in that respect, they are not "historical realities" as commonly understood in normal historical science. They are inserted into the situation but they are not of it. On the other hand, anthropologists have come upon many institutional forms of a temporality that thus embeds the present in the terms of a remembered past, whether that past is "mythical" or more proximately ancestral or experiential. Such is the historicity of the omnipresent Dreamtime of the totemic ancestors organizing the world of Native Australians; of Maori chiefs who recount the deeds of their heroic ancestors in the first-person singular and consciously rehearse them in their own doings; of the installation rituals in which the king-elect of the Shilluk "becomes Nyikang," the immigrant founder of the dynasty (see chapter 2, this volume); of the positional succession and perpetual kinship relations among the chiefs of the Tongan Islands; or of Captain Cook, for example, greeted by Hawaiians at Kealakekua in 1779 as an avatar of Lono, the ancient god who returns annually at the New Year to fertilize the land. Here history is made analogically rather than sequentially—or what are traditions for?

A collective immortal in the form of tradition, Memory, mother of the Muses, indeed has the divine power of ordering human existence by revealing "what has been and what will be" (Vernant 2006: 120). Note that insofar as we are dealing with "myths" (so-called), as of the Dreamtime, the antecedents of events are rendered doubly disengaged from "historical realities": they are not even "true" by our ontological lights, let alone copresent with their effects. All the same, as Fred Myers reports in his excellent ethnography of Pintupi: "The Dreaming is experienced as the essential foundation to which human beings must conform" (1986: 245–46). Realized in the features of the landscape as well as current human action, "making first things continuous with last" (ibid.: 53), the Dreaming is a transhistorical condition of social action. Pintupi say, "from the Dreaming, it becomes real" (ibid.: 49). Myers explains: "The Pintupi see themselves as following the Dreaming. As the invisible framework of this world, the Dreaming is the cosmic prototype" (ibid.).

Myers, incidentally, is not the only one who, in writing of Pintupi "ontology," was far in advance of the *soi-disant* "ontological turn" in anthropology, as introduced with so much hoopla in the early twenty-first century. Irving Hallowell had already published a foundational article, "Ojibwa ontology, behavior, and world view," in 1960. The present essay could be viewed as an extended sequitur to Hallowell's essential point that "what we call myth" is not only for

the people concerned "a true account of events in the past," but a current account "of the manner in which their phenomenal field is culturally constituted
and cognitively apprehended" (ibid.: 27). Similar observations are features of
the ethnographic record the world around. As, for example, the New Guinea
Highlands: "For the Mbowamb myths are the truth, historical facts handed
down. The forces which they describe and represent are not of the type which
occur only once but are continuously effective, actually existing" (Vicedom and
Tischner 1943–48: 729).

Perhaps nothing better epitomizes the historiographic problem at issue as
that what we deem to be "myth," hence fictional, the peoples concerned hold
sacred and by that token unquestionably true, "what actually happened." Yet
as Maori say, "the problems of other lands are their own"; and for their part
they are proven masters in making current actualities out of collective memories
(Johansen 1954). Consider, for example, John White's (1874) reconstruction of
a scene from daily life of the Ngapuhi tribe of the North Island. The speaker,
Rou, a man of some prominence in the community, has lost a son in battle and
now protests the decision of the tribal chiefs that the enemies recently taken in
revenge be buried instead of eaten, as even the gods were wont to do. His disa-
greement with the chiefs thus begins at the origin of the world, with a reference
to the famous Maori cosmogonic narrative of the Sons of Rangi: a tradition
which among other precedents includes the origin of cannibalism on the part
of the god Tu, the ancestor and patron of man as warrior. Tu defeated and ate
his elder brothers, themselves ancestors of birds, trees, fish, cultivated and wild
foods, and thereby gained the ability to consume their offspring. "If the gods eat
each other," Rou says, "and they were brothers . . . why am I not allowed to eat
those who killed my child?" He concludes by citing another well-known tradition, this on the divine origin of witchcraft, which explains how evil came into
the hearts of men, including his own; and finally two proverbs which likewise
justify his personal project of cannibal revenge (ibid.: 185–93). Given this kind
of historicity, we can understand the perplexing problems of governmentality
confronting Sir George Grey as Governor of the New Zealand colony in the
mid-nineteenth century. Sir George soon discovered that he could not negotiate
critical issues of war and peace without a knowledge of Maori mythology and
poetry. "To my surprise," he wrote, "I found these chiefs in their speeches to me
or in their letters frequently quoted, in explanation of their views and intentions,
fragments of ancient poems and proverbs, or made allusions which rested on an
ancient system of mythology; and . . . it was clear that the most important parts

of their communications were embodied in these figurative forms (1956: n.p.).[1] "The Maori," as Prytz Johansen put it, "find themselves in history" (1954: 163; cf. Sahlins 1985: 54ff.).

As Valerio Valeri (2015) observed and demonstrated at length in the connection with the ascension of the great Kamehameha to royal power in Hawai'i, the past here functions paradigmatically as well as syntagmatically. And, one might add, consciously so—although it may otherwise transpire in the unremarked way traditions are realized in the normal course of cultural practice. The event at issue was a usurpation of the Hawai'i kingship by Kamehameha, who as a cadet brother of the royal heir had been entrusted with the war god as his legacy from the late king. Everything thus happened in the same way as the succession struggle of the great chief Umi-a-Liloa some generations previously, a well-known tradition that effectively served as the charter of the kingship. And it was again repeated in historic times, if with a different result, when Kamehameha's son and heir, King Liholiho, defeated the challenge of his younger brother, Kekuaokalani, who had inherited the war god and revolted against the ruler's turn to Christianity. The different outcome in this last iteration underscores Valeri's reminder that analogy is not identity, but always entails some difference: in particular, the contingent circumstances of the conjuncture, which are not foreseen in the paradigmatic precedent, but represent the syntagmatic dimension of what actually happened. Nor is the selection of historical antecedents in such cases given or predetermined, considering the complexities of tradition and the opportunities for the play of choice and interest. What remains, however, is that the course of events will unfold in cultural terms that are preposed to the current situation. Indeed, if anthropologists on the whole have been more sensitive than other human scientists to paradigmatic histories, it is because the appropriation of current events by already-existing traditions is, after all, what they have long known as the work of culture. Culture is what happens when something happened.

Another, similar instance of the deployment of dynastic traditions to current situations, this one close to the narrative of Kongo kingship which will be the focus of this essay, is provided by Victor Turner's (1957) comments on the Luba origins of the Lunda kingship among Central African Ndembu and other peoples. This classic stranger-king formation was the subject of a

---

1.   Sir George found that his translators rarely if ever could explain the historical allusions, probably because they were British, or if Maori, not of relevant tribes.

well-known structural analysis by Luc de Heusch (1982b). In the essential incidents, a Lunda king, Yala Mwaku, unseemly drunk, is insulted and badly beaten by two of his sons, and then nursed back to health by his daughter, Lweji Ankonde. In gratitude, he passes on to Lweji the palladium of the kingdom—the royal bracelet made of human genitalia that maintains the fertility of the realm—thus making her his successor and dispossessing his sons. Lweji later meets and marries a handsome young hunter, Chibinda, who turns out to be the youngest son of a great Luba chief; and when she gives him the bracelet because she must go into seclusion during menstruation, he becomes king of the Lunda. Chagrined, Lweti's brothers leave to found their own kingdoms, and their descendants spread Lunda rule far and wide among many other peoples, including the indigenous Ndembu population. But the events did not end there. Turner writes:

> Life, after all, is as much an imitation of art as the reverse. Those who, as children in Ndembu society, have listened to innumerable stories about Yala Mwaku and Lweji Ankonde know all about inaugural motifs. . . . When these same Ndembu, now full-grown, wish to provoke a breach or claim that some party has crucially disturbed the placid social order, they have a frame available to "inaugurate" a social drama. . . . The story itself still makes important points about family relationships, about the stresses between sex and age roles . . . so the story does feed back into the social process, providing it with a rhetoric, a mode of emplotment, and a meaning. Some genres, particularly the epic, serve as paradigms which inform the action of important political leaders . . . giving them style, direction, and sometimes compelling them subliminally to follow in major public crises a certain course of action, thus emplotting their lives. (1957: 153)

In the many instances of successive foreign dynasties in the same society, or serial stranger-kingship, where the advent of the later regime is clearly emplotted on a legendary original, the overall "course of action" takes the form of a historical metaphor of a mythical reality. For where the ancient regime is known by oral tradition and its recent successor is fully historical and archival, it would indeed appear that life imitates art. The West African realm of ancient memory established by the conquering hero Tsoede in the country of his Nupe maternal kin was essentially duplicated by the nineteenth-century Fulani conquest, as ruled by one Masaba—whose maternal kin, among whom he was raised, were likewise Nupe. The ethnographer S. F. Nadel explains:

In the tradition of Tsoede, that "mythical charter" of the Nupe kingdom, the essence of the Nupe state is already clearly expressed, structured, almost sanctified, by that paramount authority that attaches to prehistoric events: it outlines a system of political domination, growing by conquest and expansion, and governed by a group detached in origin and status from the rest of the population .... The twofold process of expansion over alien groups and cultures, combined with cultural assimilation and absorption, is reflected in both, in the ideological history of the Tsoede myth as well as the "real" history of the Fulani kingdom. In one there is Tsoede, who conquers Nupe with the help of alien magic, who brings into Nupe the insignia of alien rulership and culture, but who, himself half Nupe by [maternal] descent, creates a new, independent, and united Nupe. On the other, there is this remarkable piece of empire-policy when Masaba claims succession to the Nupe throne on the grounds of his being half-Nupe by birth and full Nupe by education. (1942: 87)

The Nupe, as Nadel says, are a historically minded people: "The highest, constantly invoked authority for things existing is, to the Nupe, the account of things past" (ibid.: 72). But then the common distinction Nadel draws between "ideology" and "real history" would have no value for Nupe, inasmuch as the "ideological"-cum-"mythical" status of the Tsoede tradition is, on exactly that basis, "real history"—proven source of what has been and what will be. Hence the credibility, too, of the observation commonly attributed to Mark Twain: "History doesn't repeat itself, but it does rhyme."

AFRICAN STRANGER-KINGDOMS

Stranger-kingdoms the likes of Lunda, Ndembu, and Nupe in Africa comprise the dominant form of premodern state the world around, on every continent.[2] They have developed in a great variety of environments and in combination with a considerable range of economic regimes: commercial, piratical, agricultural (both rainfall and hydraulic), slave-raiding, cattle-raising, and most commonly some form of mixed economy. These are distinctively dual societies: divided in privileges, powers, and functions between rulers who are foreign by origin and identity—perpetually so, as the condition of the possibility of their authority—

---

2.   See summary accounts in Sahlins (1981b, 2008, 2010, 2011a, 2014).

and the underlying indigenous people—who are characteristically the "owners" of the land and the ritual masters of its fertility. Not that the phenomenon is exclusively associated with kingship, let alone Africa, as it is also known among a number of tribal chiefdoms. "The chiefs come from overseas," a Fijian from the Lau Islands told A. M. Hocart (1929: 27), "it is so in all countries in Fiji." The same could be said for the Trobriand Islands and Tikopia, sites of classical ethnographic studies by Bronislaw Malinowski (1948) and Raymond Firth (1971), respectively. Stranger-kingship has also played significantly in famous colonial encounters: besides Captain Cook in Hawai'i and among others, there was James Brooke, "the White Rajah of Sarawak," whom local Iban considered the son or lover of their primordial goddess Keling; and Cortés, greeted by Moctezuma as Quetzalcoatl, the returning king and culture hero of the legendary Toltec city of Tollan. While the veracity and supposed historical effects of Moctezuma's purported identification of Cortés with Quetzalcoatl have been contested by a number of scholars, the Mexica king's own claim of descent from Quetzalcoatl and the Toltecs—by contrast to the common Mexica traditions of a "barbarian" Chichimec origin—does not come in for much notice (see chapter 4, this volume). Nor was Moctezuma unusual in this respect. Stranger-kings were the rule in Mesoamerican and Andean city-states and empires, including the classic and postclassic Maya, as well as the Inka and other South American states. Moreover, as is true of the phenomenon elsewhere, at least some of these kingdoms, the Mexica included, have constituted their historic order on the repetition of legendary events that never happened.

In several earlier publications, I have discussed stranger-kingdoms in their planetary extent and general characteristics; here the focus will be on the African forms, particularly the old Kongo kingdom of the sixteenth and seventeenth centuries, as these offer especially useful examples of histories that follow from (so-called) "mythical" precedents. Indeed, the apparent absence of verification in the archival sources has led some modern scholars to deconstruct the people's traditions of stranger-king origins on grounds they never really happened and thereby dissolve the basic structure of the society in an acid bath of Western positivism.

In an article on "The origin and early history of the kingdom of Kongo, c. 1350–1550," John Thornton (2001) makes the foreign status of the dynasty disappear for lack of confirmation in what he considers primary sources. Instead of this "myth," he prefers to invent his own origin story, according to which the Kongo kingdom was an internal political development among an

ethnically homogeneous population. It is difficult to say what kind of confirmation Thornton expected for the arrival of the stranger-prince Ntinu
Wene of Vungu, among a people without writing some six kings before the
Portuguese arrived. What is most relevant for the course of history and clearly
documented, however, is that the foundation of the kingdom from across the
Congo River by Ntinu Wene (aka Lukeni lua Nimi) was the official doctrine
of Kongo kings of the seventeenth century—and judging by certain chronicles,
the widely known charter tradition of their rule. The kingdom was established
by one "Motinu Wene," youngest son of the king of "Bungo," according to the
anonymous author of the *Historia do Reino Congo*, written in the first quarter
of the seventeenth century: "In Bungo, there are still kings that communicate
with the Kings of the Congo, sending gifts to each other. In that way, they recognize themselves as kinsmen, descended from one and the same family tree"
(in Sousa 1999: 509–11). Nevertheless, in writing of the origin of the kingdom,
Thornton does not recount the Ntinu Wene narrative, except for certain incidents that are written off as "mythical," "ideological," or "cosmological"—which
is to say, unbelievable. On the same grounds, the Australian Dreamtime, the
annual visit of the god Lono at the New Year in Hawai'i, the doings of the
gods and the ancestors by which Maori know themselves and emplot their
own deeds—in brief all such foundational traditions, which indeed would be
hard to prove actually happened, all these precedents of action and principles of
structure, could now be omitted from the histories of the peoples in question.
By conflating a paradigmatic history with a syntagmatic one, thus reducing the
template of historical action to the issue of whether it was "the literal truth"
(Thornton 2001: 108), the historian now bases his history of a nonliterate society on whether certain events referring to a remote past can be documented
from primary sources.

    For too many anthropologists and historians both, an axiomatic opposition
between "myth" and "historical reality," although quite the reverse of their essential identity in the societies concerned, has been an epistemological ground
of their study. Fictional by the Standard Average European understanding of
the term, "myth" becomes doubly implausible when it is functionally explained
away as a mystification of a stratified political order serving as its legitimation—
for then it could hardly reflect "historical reality," since it is meant to conceal
it. In their otherwise valuable survey of sub-Saharan African history, Robert O.
Collins and James M. Burns (2007: 117) warn that the oral traditions of royal
courts in Interlacustrine East Africa, insofar as they are often shrouded in myth,

given to hagiography, or enlisted in current political interests, would "obscure historical reality." From this it follows that we should discount the historical relevance of the ubiquitous stranger-king traditions of the region:

> Virtually all the oral traditions of the kingdoms of the Lake Plateau attribute their founding to the arrival of itinerant heroes from far away . . . . African dynasties throughout the continent have claimed external origins, justifiably or not, to legitimate their claims to authority. Scholars have been somewhat reluctant to accept the necessity to have the appearance of "the great warrior" or "hunter-stranger from afar" to explain state formation in Africa. Its very simplicity obscures what was probably a more complex process, and the story of warrior-pastoralists stimulating political centralization is reminiscent of the discredited Hamitic myth of John Hanning Speke . . . .
>
> Like Bunyoro and many other states of the Lake Plateau, the oral traditions emphasized the role of northern migrants in the founding of their kingdoms. Such traditions should be viewed skeptically, however, since they reflect the living memories of rulers, not subjects, and are devoted to insuring their legitimacy. (2007: 123)

That the foreign origin of the ruling dynasty would promote its legitimacy seems counterintuitive on the face of it, but it becomes all the more so in the case of Bunyoro, since the Nilotic founders of the historic dynasty were by their own traditions a rude and unsophisticated lot compared to the Bantu rulers of the fabled Kitara empire they replaced (Beattie 1971). The same would be true of the relatively crude or obscure foreign ancestors of the kings of Kongo, Mossi, certain Swahili cities, and a number of other such realms established by upstarts from the galactic peripheries. Whether the foreign origins of the kingship are lowly or godly, however, we shall see that there are profound structural reasons for their existence. In any case, the traditions of stranger-kingship—which are much more complex than this formulaic reduction to the advent of a great hunter or warrior would allow—are typically as well known to the subject peoples as they are to the rulers, if in certain contexts either may relate rather self-serving versions.[3] Yet most regrettably and ironically, the effect of all such reductions

---

3.   See above on the wide knowledge and relevance for social action of the Ndembu royal tradition among ordinary villagers. For an example of differing commoner and chiefly versions: the Shambala commoners emphasize their voluntary acceptance of

of stranger-kingship traditions to speculative political functions is precisely to ignore their historical reality, not only as presence but as cause—their own historicity. For inasmuch as these charter narratives lay down the fundamental relations between rulers and ruled, inasmuch as they are constantly rehearsed in rituals and continuously practiced economically as well as politically, to dismiss them as "mythical" or "ideological" is to efface their profound influence on the course of events. Inscribed in memories and practiced as *habitus*, the tradition lives on as a historical force—often for centuries.

Not to deny that "what actually happened" is important to know. In the many actual cases of a stranger-kingship structure without an event, that is, of native kings who become strangers rather than strangers who become native kings, this is important to know, since here history consists precisely in such inventions—however seemingly without material, formal, or efficient cause. In this connection, the claim of the rulers of the West African realms of Kanem-Bornu, the Hausa Emirates, the Yoruba states, and others that they descended from exalted personages of Mecca or Baghdad—or else, as in the instance of Borgu kings, that they come from one Kisra, the reputed enemy of Muhammad—reminds us of what is always implied in stranger-king formations: that the societies in question exist in larger, hierarchically ordered fields of intercultural relations. It follows that stranger-kingships are generated neither by internal conditions nor by external relations alone, but in a dialogue between them.

Africa probably deserves the title of the *locus classicus* of stranger-kingship. Of the many hundreds of African kingdoms large and small known to anthropology and history, it would be hard to find any that are not ruled by a dynasty of foreign derivation. Constituted in charter traditions, rehearsed in periodic rituals, and practiced in everyday social and economic relations, the dual division of society into indigenous subjects and rulers of external origins is here the normal if not the universal form of state. From traditions recorded in European travelers' accounts to the detailed reports of modern ethnographers—notably Aidan Southall on the Alur, Ian Cunnison on the Kazembe kingdom of the Luapulu, Michel Izard on the Yatenga Mossi, Jacques Lombard and Marjorie Stewart on Borgu kingdoms, among many others—sociopolitical formations of this description dominate the literature from every quarter of the continent. The

---

the chief, given his juridical functions and spiritual powers, while maintaining he holds power on their sufferance; while the chiefs emphasize or justify their coercive authority (Winans 1962: 77).

precolonial states ruled by stranger-kings noted in Lucy Mair's *African kingdoms* (1977; not a long book) include Oyo and other Yoruba kingdoms, Luba, Lunda, Kongo, Benin, Zande, Alur, Dahomey, Asante, Borgu, Malawi, Ngoni, Ndembu, Nyoro, Ganda, Rwanda, Nyakyusa, Sotho, and a good number more.

Whole regions of the continent—such as the Lake Plateau just mentioned—have been identified as realms of stranger-kingship (cf. Southall [1956] 2004: 229). Similarly, Kajsa Ekholm (1978: 121) observes of Central Africa: "In fact most of the ideology of Central African societies is marked by a dualism in which it is imagined that the population consists of two groups, the conquerors and the vanquished original inhabitants. The conquerors are 'men' and their subjects 'owners.'" What is mostly imagined is the "conquest," not the dualism of alien rulers and native subjects as such, which is not only ethnographically real but, according to Luc de Heusch, structurally intelligible. Referring broadly to West and Central Africa, de Heusch (1982b: 26–27) makes the critical observation that kingship does not develop organically and internally from lineage-ordered societies. In effect, he contradicts all those who since classical times have supposed the state evolves naturally from the extended family through the intermediate form of village or lineage systems. In a golden passage which is key to the understanding of stranger-kingship in general, de Heusch writes:

> Everything happens as if the very structure of a lineage-based society is not capable of engendering dialectical developments on the political plane without the intervention of a new symbolic structure. It is not by chance that so many mythical traditions in West Africa as in Central Africa present the founder of the kingship as a foreign hunter, the holder of a more efficacious magic. Whatever the historical origin of this politico-symbolic institution, mythical diachrony always involves an intervention of exterior events, whether or not the sound of arms accompanies them. Royalty thus appears as an ideological revolution, the instigator of which ancient history does not ignore . . . . The sovereignty, the magical source of power, always comes from elsewhere, from a claimed original place, exterior to society. (1982b: 26–27)

Speaking of Africa generally, Jan Vansina (1992: 61) observes that "elite migration" is a favored theme of traditions of state formation. Coming alone or with a few followers, the dynastic founder is a foreigner, often a hunter; and though the numbers of the newcomers are small, the sociopolitical consequences of their advent are "spectacular." In the same vein, while noting the analogous pattern of kingdom origins among the Mossi and related West African peoples, Dominique Zahan (1961: 6n) writes: "The traditions of African states on both sides of the equator practically without exception speak of the two social components: the aboriginal and the foreign or the invader. Nearly always they thus explain the origin of the state among these peoples."

In an extended essay on "The internal African frontier," Igor Kopytoff (1989: 60), recounting "the standard myth of the founding of most African polities," tells of the founders leaving their place of origin, entering a frontier, confronting the local population, "and instituting a new political order that was the origin of the society currently in being." In what is effectively a notice of the residual sovereignty marking the native people's status in these societies, Kopytoff observes that from their perspective, "the polity had issued out of the acceptance by the subjects of the ruler, and it continued to exist because of it. The rulers were intruders, outsiders, aliens, late comers" (ibid.). This also implies that stranger-king formations are basically contractual—for all the usual talk of conquest. A few pages on, Kopytoff observes that the alien rulers institute a new political era by taking on the local trappings and symbols of legitimacy. Hence "the crucial point in Africa" is that by way of the "compact" entailed in his ritual incorporation, the stranger-king is legitimated by the indigenous people. "In the constitutional perspective of the subjects," Kopytoff writes, "the people existed before the rulership existed since they were the grantors of authority; this was congruent with the subjects' paradigmatic myth of their precedence" (ibid.: 64–65). Consider, then, that the structure is inherently temporal as well as hierarchical, and that the encompassment of the native people in the rule of the stranger is effected through the encompassment of the stranger by the native people—all of which will be illustrated shortly. For now notice that in Kopytoff's own wording this history was made paradigmatically.

Recent research thus confirms what Lucy Mair (1977: 1) wrote on this account decades ago: "As the prehistory of Africa is reconstructed, it seems often possible to trace the imposition of chiefly authority by outsiders on 'tribes without rulers.'" Even tribes which are sometimes supposed to be without rulers, such as Tallensi—so classified and described by Meyer Fortes in the influential tome *African political systems* (1940)—turn out to in fact have them: in this case in the persons of immigrant Namoo chiefs from the Mamprusi kingdom peacefully settled upon the native Tale, who by ancestral right remain the "owners" of Taleland. As late as the mid-twentieth century, the Namoo chiefs were still appointed by a representative of the Mamprusi king. What Fortes had encountered was a marginal chiefdom in a regional galaxy of interdependent polities in northern Nigeria, including the substantial kingdoms of Dagomba and the Mossi, all of whom traced common descent to Mamprusi ancestors. Perhaps the peripheral position of the Tallensi accounts for their rather basic dual system in which the ethnically distinguished Namoo of aristocratic external origins—their main ancestor in most tellings was a disenfranchised and exiled son of a Mamprusi king—effectively divided power with important Tale lineage leaders presiding over the productivity of the land as Priests of the Earth. In Fortes' description, this "fundamental cleavage" in Tale society, headed respectively by the chiefs (*naam*) and the earth priests (*tenda'ana*), reads like an elementary form of African stranger-kingship:

> The complementary functions of chiefship and *tenda'ana*-ship are rooted directly in social structures but as also validated by myths of origin and backed by the most powerful religious sanctions of the ancestor cult and the cult of the Earth. The Namoos are believed to be descendants of immigrant Mamprusi who fled from [the capital] Mamprugu many generations ago. Hence, they claim remote kinship with the ruling aristocracy of Mampurugu. Their chiefship is derived from that of the Paramount Chief of the Mamprusi, and this is the ultimate sanction of its politico-religious status in Tale society. The Talis and other clans that have the *tenda'ana*-ship claim to be the aboriginal inhabitants of the country, and the ritual sanctions of their office are derived from the Earth cult. ([1949] 1969: 3–4).

> One is constantly reminded of the cleavage between Namoos and non-Namoos . . . for they are continually contrasting themselves. (1945: 25)

One might add that the Tale priests of the earth, like their counterparts throughout the continent, are known as the successors of the leaders of the aboriginal people, which helps explain their own sometimes-appearance as figures of chiefly authority. Indeed, the priests may represent the aristocracy of a former stranger-king regime, as in the cognate structures of Mossi states—whose priestly order notably interested Sir James Frazer (1918: 85–87). Citing an account of Louis Tauxier, Frazer observed that the Mossi rulers, as strangers in the land, were not entitled to minister to the local sprits, the divinities of the bearing earth:

It was only the vanquished, the ancient owners of the soil, with which they [the rulers] continued in good relations, who were qualified for that. Hence the political head of the aborigines was bound to become a religious chief under the rule of the Mossi. Thus . . . the king (Moro-Naba) never himself offers the sacrifices to Earth at Wagadugu, nor does he allow such sacrifices to be offered by his minister of religion, the Gande-Naba. He lays the duty on the king of Wagadugu (Wagadugu-Naba), the grandson of the aborigines, who as such is viewed favourably by the local divinities. (Tauxier in Frazer 1918: 86)

Note also Fortes' observation of the functional complementarity between the Namoo chiefs and the earth-priest leaders of the indigenous Talis, even as "one is constantly reminded of the cleavage" between the groups. Here as in many similar dual regimes, there is an oppositional tension in the relationship between the native people and their foreign-derived (and -identified) ruler: a tension that, among other expressions, is often a feature of royal installation rituals. But as will become apparent in the following discussion, the native and foreign components of the chiefdom or kingdom are each functionally incomplete without the other: whereas together they make a social, material, and cosmological totality. Hence their enduring coexistence—on the condition of their difference.

ON THE WAY TO THE KINGDOM

Charter narratives of the advent of the African stranger-hero consistently feature a number of themes that prefigure fundamental attributes of his future kingship. Three that are especially pertinent to the old Kongo regime are singled out here. First, to borrow from Aidan Southall ([1956] 2004) on the Alur, the *topos* of the "turbulent prince" or the "troublesome son": the hero is an ambitious offspring of the king in his own land, destined to rule by nature but condemned to exile for some fault or by losing out in a conflict royal with other pretenders to the kingship. Second, what Luc de Heusch (1958, 1962) called "the exploit": the hero commits a crime against kinship and common morality—incest, fratricide, parricide, murder of a close kinsman, adultery with a wife of his father, etc.—on the journey to his kingdom; perhaps it was the reason for his exile. Third, the theme Jane Guyer (1993: 257) refers to as "capture": the hero in the course of his migration demonstrates his prowess as a great hunter and/or a great warrior, thus proving his ability to control the vital and mortal powers of the wild—and thereby, provided such powers are properly domesticated, demonstrating his capacity to rule people.

The diaspora of turbulent princes is a main source of stranger-king formation. The succession struggles that give rise to it often go beyond fraternal rivalries, engaging a larger network of interested royal kin and loyal followers. For besides the force of ascribed rank or customary rules of succession which in principle disqualify princely candidates who nonetheless may have kingly ambitions, certain structural conditions function to expand and intensify these conflicts. In the common case of royal polygyny, many of the sons of the king who compete to succeed him are paternal half-brothers; and as each is backed by his own maternal kinsmen, their interpersonal contention becomes a multiparty conflict among collective factions. As, for example, in Ankole succession struggles, where, "even in a quite recent epoch, the primary heirs . . . each aided by their maternal kin, entered into a bloody conflict that lasted several months" (de Heusch 1966: 28). Or as Marjorie Stewart wrote of the Borgu kingdoms: "When the throne became vacant and competition for its possession became intense among the princes, matrilineal relatives of each prince played an important role" (1993: 92). Hence the well-known interregna of many African kingdoms, notable for their duration and carnage.

The princes not only menace one another, they may well be a threat to the general peace and even the life of the king. "For all those princes aspiring to the throne," writes Father Crazzolara of the Shilluk, "the main obstacle is the ruling *Yeth* [the king], Therefore they bide expectantly for his demise; and many a spear has been flung by royal hands in the past against the *Yeth*" (1951: 134). Azande, Shilluk, Ganda, Alur, and Borgu kings, among others, dispatched such unruly sons to peripheral provinces, often to the areas of their maternal kin, where they became semi-independent stranger-rulers themselves and potentially the founders of autonomous kingdoms. The effect is what Audrey Richards described for the Interlacustrine region as "multi-kingdom tribes": "Throughout the whole Interlacustrine area," she wrote, "the sons who became princes over subdistricts showed a tendency to assert their independence and even rebel against their fathers, forming separate states in what are called multi-kingdom tribes" (1960: 34).

A like effect may follow from the phenomenon that Hildred and Clifford Geertz (1975) identified as "sinking status" in Balinese royal lineages internally ranked by seniority of descent—often also found in African aristocracies.[4]

---

4.   See p. 431, where this diagram is reproduced and discussed by Graeber.

Owing to the growth of the senior line, the collateral kinsmen will be progressively distanced in status and disqualified for office over time—unless they
can muster the means to take by cunning or force what they can no longer
claim by right. Alternatively, they can move out as would-be kings in search
of a chosen people. It is relevant in this connection that many of the ruling
aristocracy of African states, inasmuch as they are possessed of marvelous powers by divine gift and entitled to rule by ancestry, have been known to exhibit a
certain *libido dominandi*. "The vocation of every Mossi," writes Michel Izard in
reference to the ruling group, "is to exercise power (*naam*) and thus to be a chief
(*naaba*), to command (*so*) and thus to have a command (*solem*)" (1985: 20). Of
the Shambala of Tanganyika, Edgar Winans (1962: 91) noted: "As all royal clan
members consider themselves rulers, an attitude which is reinforced by most or
all of their subjects, and as only a few hold regular and legitimate chiefship, then
tension in the system gives rise to the expansion of the state." According to the
robust Kongo tradition, Ntinu Wene's insatiable desires of rule were likewise
frustrated by his junior status among the sons of the king of Vungu—a modest
realm north of the Congo River—which was what moved him to cross the river
into the territory he would organize as the kingdom of Kongo, In general, the
centrifugal political impetus generated by the turbulent princes is probably the
most important source of stranger-king formation on the continent.

Having broken with their own kinsmen, stranger-heroes such as Ntinu
Wene then dialectically negate the kinship order they are on their way to
subdue by "exploits" that signify their power to do so. Here are the crimes of
fratricide, parricide, incest, and the like, which break through the limits that,
as Luc de Heusch observed, represent the inability of lineage systems to au-
tonomously transcend their own structure and give rise to a kingly state.[5] De
Heusch himself offered pertinent examples taken from the usual practice in
royal installation rituals of rehearsing the dominant tradition of the origin of
the kingship. Re-creating in this way the original stranger-hero, the Lunda
king (Mwata Kombana) of a number of Pende groups in Zaïre ritually unites
with his sister upon acceding to power; and several of his close kinsmen are also
secretly killed so that their ghosts may serve him (de Heusch 1982b: 19). In the
more complex case of the Luba king, he reproduces the "shameful legacy" of

---

5.   Credit to E. E. Evans-Pritchard too, who thus understood the imposition of the
     rule of the Sanusi brethren over the segmentary lineage order of the Bedouin of
     Cyrenaica (1949).

the founder of an earlier stranger-king regime—who was also the brother of his maternal ancestress—by uniting with his mothers and sisters at his investiture; and his own daughters and brothers' daughters become his wives. In this way, de Heusch observes, the king combines the incestuous qualities of the ancient regime with the superior culture of his own; and most importantly, "the Luba king finds himself projected into a zone of absolute solitude, beyond and above the profane cultural order" (1982a: 32). The founder-hero of the Nupe, Tsoede, effectively did the same when he introduced human sacrifice by making his mother's brother the first victim (Nadel 1942: 74). In still other traditions, the crime against kinship had occurred in the turbulent prince's own homeland and was the cause of his banishment. The ancestor of Shambala rulers, Mbegha, was deprived of the kingship in his natal country as a result of a demonstrable blemish of his person that mystically killed his relations: "because as an infant he had cut his upper teeth first, his presence was causing his kinsmen to die" (Feierman 1974: 43). The willingness of the youngest son of the Kerekere "conqueror" of the Zambezi Valley to commit "the forbidden act" of incest with his own sister when his older brothers refused is indeed what made him the heir to his father's rule (Lan 1985: 86). Sovereign exceptionalism: Schmitt *avant la lettre*.

Just so, when Ntinu Wene killed his pregnant "aunt" because she refused to pay the proper toll for crossing the Congo River, the crime not only initiated his departure from Vungu, but defined him as a "king" (*ntinu*) and prefigured his rule of Kongo. The report of this tradition from the Capuchin missionary Giovanni Antonio Cavazzi de Montecuccolo (in Kongo in 1664–65) relates that the woman was Ntinu Wene's father's sister—a paternal affine in the BaKongo matrilineal order—and that the deed infuriated his royal father, Nimi a Nzima, who wished to punish him (Sousa 1999). But this crime against kinship—and perhaps *lèse majesté* to boot—was the mark of Ntinu Wene's royal nature, for the exploit moved his henchmen to proclaim him "king" (*ntinu*). Indeed his following increased rapidly in the aftermath, upon which he led them across the Congo River, and embarked on a career of conquest and diplomacy that appended the state of Kongo to the kingly title he had already manifested. (Note that by tradition the conquest was not the origin of Wene's kingship but rather the other way around: his kingship was a precondition of his martial success.) Reflecting on this narrative, Georges Balandier underscored the same break with tribal society and the same manifestation of the power to create a new and greater order that Luc de Heusch had perceived:

> By killing his "kin," Ntinu Wene acquires the state of solitude necessary for the
> domination of men and the consecration of power . . . . The defiance of the
> fundamental principles of society is the mark of an exceptional being . . . . He
> has denied the ancient order; he has acquired an autonomy which can only be
> explained by the possession of extraordinary powers. . . . It is on the basis of these
> powers that he will construct *outside* the prevailing form a new society subject to
> his law only. (Balandier 1968: 37, emphasis in the original)

Instructive, you could say, is the contrast between the take of the anthropologists Balandier and de Heusch on such feats of royal exceptionalism and the interpretation of the Ntinu Wene episode by the historian John Thornton. Thornton finds the charter traditions of the Kongo kingship as a rule defective because of "the difficult problem of linking the secondary elements of tradition, like the narrative origin story, to documented reality" (2001: 96). This is like saying that for lack of any link to documented reality, we should have to eliminate the crucifixion of Jesus, let alone his resurrection, from an account of the nature and history of Christianity. Ironically, the particular fault Thornton finds with Kongo narratives, namely that they are only "interpretive histories" incorporating "secondary explanatory narrative," is a good description of how he provides alternative interpretations that purportedly reveal the historical realities by means of his own native commonsense explanations. The effect is rather to substitute ethnocentric banalities for ethnographic realities.

Although with regard to Ntinu Wene's murderous exploit, Cavazzi had commented that the BaKongo admired such bloodthirstiness, Thornton countered by a feckless analogy to the well-known story of the most Christian Kongo king Afonso (r. 1506–1543), who had his idolatrous mother buried alive "for the sake of the faith." Despite repeated remonstration by the king, she refused to part with a traditional amulet. In what amounts to a "secondary explanatory narrative" with the added defect of substituting his own commonsensical motive for a deed infused with Kongo meanings of kinship horror and royal violence, Thornton opines that both kingly exploits were legitimating signs of a "ruler who upholds the law"—which is rather the opposite of what they were doing. In any case, neither story could be true, he concludes, and the Ntinu Wene tradition in particular "is a tale we must not take too seriously, given its ideological significance" (ibid.: 109). Not take too seriously? Historiographic positivism would thus doubly distance itself from a historical anthropology: for in inviting us to commit the ethnological cardinal sin of not taking something too seriously because the people concerned do so take it, Thornton thereupon assigns what they take seriously to the louche status of "ideology." In the end, the truth value of the tradition for BaKongo having been ignored, so also is its effectiveness as a paradigmatic tradition thereafter neglected.

In any case, there is evidence early and late that exploits of kinship-killing are distinctive marks of Kongo kingship. Beside the stories of such deaths in royal installation rituals, Msgr. Cuvelier (1946: 288–89) tells of a certain clan device (other than the one vaunting King Afonso's pious murder) that claims: "Nlaza Ntotela [King Nlaza] killed his mother (*ngudi*) in the public square of Mbanza Kongo [the capital], without anyone questioning him for it." "This is a device," Cuvelier adds, "adopted by certain clans that reigned in Kongo." Nor were BaKongo kings the only rulers in the region who were renowned for so disposing of their mothers. Tired of his mother's foretelling that a rival would usurp his power, Nkongolo, first divine king of the Luba, "dug a ditch with his own hands and buried his mother alive in it" (de Heusch 1962: 17). Indeed, according to the master ethnographer Wyatt MacGaffey, the ability to kill a near kinsman still signified chiefliness for Congolese people in the twentieth century:

> Ideally the chief is a benevolent despot whose authentic relation to the ancestors is assured by some ordeal or test, such as a successful hunt for a particular kind of animal, or some other demonstration of the power to kill. Modern informants said, "If we choose someone to be chief, we would require him to kill one of his nephews. If he could not, we would have to find someone else to be chief." (1986: 176)

MacGaffey cites some legendary incidents in point, including one from the Yombe people in which the son who killed his brother at his father's command secured the latter's chiefly position and others of the family had to obey him. It is unlikely that these killings actually occurred; it is more likely they indicate that events which never happened can continue to have historic effects. Traditions need not have actually happened in order to then actually happen.

Resuming the journey of the stranger-prince: in the liminal period between leaving his own kingdom and establishing another, the hero proves his sacred violence is also a creative and beneficent power by controlling the ungoverned forces that everywhere pervade the African wild—and threaten to fatally penetrate the settled human communities. As Randall Packard reports for the Bashu of eastern Zaïre, their world is divided between the opposing spheres of the regulated human "homestead" and an untamed "bush" (*kisoki*) that surrounds and perpetually menaces it with "wild animals and plants, dangerous spirits, powerful medicines, and climatic elements" (1981: 26). Erratic and/or violent in their natural state, these presences are the usual sources of illness, death, and dearth in the homestead. So even as elements of the bush are essential for human existence—raw materials, foods (especially meat), sunshine and rain—people are in need of protection from many of them. Hence the distinctive figure of the hunter-king, who may also or alternatively be a warrior-king, and carry a reputation for capture or conquest even had his indigenous subjects voluntarily submitted to him (cf. Lombard 1965; Winans 1962). "Sacred violence" is the other side of a civilizing mission, as Balandier says of the advent of Ntinu Wene in Kongo.

If his own Vungu people knew Ntinu Wene was a king because he killed his aunt, upon which he forsook his homeland for a career of foreign conquests, the native Shambala people were moved to make the foreign hunter Mbegha their king because he had killed a lion—indeed because he *was* a lion. Mbegha was the disinherited son of the king of Kilinde in the Usambari mountains who became a great hunter when forced into the wild. One night he killed a lion that was menacing Shambala people—which motivated them to make him king the next morning. "The man has killed a lion," the people exclaimed, "The man is a lion" (Winans 1962: 80). Just so, on his way to the kingship, Mbegha lived the life of an animal, sheltering in rude camps and caves, and hunting wild pigs—a prized food that is also dangerous, whose capture would thus be a felicitous sign of kingly powers. Mbegha had occult knowledge of hunting and healing medicines; and after he fled his native land, he acquired a packet of magic that allowed him to control the clouds and the rain (thus agricultural fertility), and to foretell future events (ibid.). As Steven Feierman observed, however, the hero's life-giving powers were the obverse side of his destructive magic:

> The justification for the king's right to destroy is that of a rain magician: a magician of the fertility of the land must possess and dominate the entire land in order to be effective . . . . So if the king is a lion, if he eats the wealth of the whole countryside, then the land will be fertile. (1974: 59)

In everyday conversation in Shambaai one often hears that rain magic, the key to fertility, began with Mbegha. His magical powers, which were the powers to kill, and which derived from his wildness, were also the powers to bring fertility to Shambaai . . . . When all Shambaai became his possession, he was transformed from a killer to one whose power led to an increase of life. (1974: 62)

As such metahuman powers of life and death come from the outside, so do the human rulers who will instantiate them inside. (*Ergo*, Frazer *cogitates*.) And given such cosmic powers, one can see why a foreign identity is an enduring attribute of the ruling aristocracy: an ethnic distinction that may well survive their cultural assimilation by the aboriginal people—as the recurrent historic expression of a paradigmatic "myth." To follow the argument of Aidan Southall ([1956] 2004: 230), another such historical metaphor of a mythical reality was the early success of stranger-colonial rule in Africa, based likewise on the Europeans' apparent control of marvelous potencies: in this case as evidenced by their extraordinary wealth and terrifying firearms—that is to say, powers of life and death. "These things," writes Southall,

gave the quality of a unique marvel to their first appearance among any African people. To the latter, the newcomers appeared to have a complete mastery over the material world, and a degree of control over life and death through their medicines and their firearms which was generally terrifying. Even after the first shock wore off, the indelible expression of a mastery of fantastic forces of unknown extent remained. This induced many African peoples to submit to the establishment of European administration with little opposition . . . . ([1956] 2004: 232)

Only that, when the realities of European rule set in, frustration and resistance ensued in proportion to the extent that people's initial expectations had been deceived.

To return to the precolonial marvels, Mbegha was hardly the only African king identified with great beasts of the bush. The Dahomey ruling line famously descended from a leopard, as did the Igala kings by one well-known history— by other, subdominant versions, they were immigrant princes from Jukun or Yoruba royalty. All this helps explain why King Joao II of Kongo (r. 1688–post 1716) was pleased to style himself the one who "tramples the lion in the kingdom of his mother" (Thornton 2001: 98). Indeed, the phrase distills the whole process of stranger-king formation to its essence: the synthesis of an outsider endowed of transcendent powers with the indigenous masters of the bearing earth through his union with an esteemed daughter of the latter, thus giving rise to a dynasty that in its paternal and maternal ancestry combines the fundamental sources of life—and death.

ADVENT OF THE STRANGER-KING

Considering the process of kingdom formation as described in the historical traditions of rulers and ruled alike, conquest is too often invoked as the origin of sovereign power, the ferocious attributes of the stranger culture-hero notwithstanding. In this connection, with the Alur and other African peoples in mind, probably conquest has been overrated in Western scholarly traditions since Ludwig Gumplowicz (1899) mistakenly assumed that the ubiquity of an ethnic distinction between rulers and ruled in Africa and elsewhere was evidence that the state must have so originated. But Mbegha the hunter and lion-killer dominated the Shambala more by gifts of meat than by force; and in any case, the native people themselves claim to have initiated the process: "Whether or not it is true in an historical sense, nearly all commoners claimed that their ancestors voluntarily asked for chiefs, and, similarly, chiefs do not claim to rule by right of conquest" (Winans 1962: 76). Besides the gifts of meat, Mbegha's kingship owed more to making love than making war, for it was established when various villages, competing with each other by seeking a powerful ruler of their own, offered women to him and took the son born from the alliance for their chief. The elements of this process as narrated by Shambala are frequently repeated around the continent; the stranger-prince is peacefully accepted by the indigenous people, sometimes even solicited by them from some prestigious foreign king.

The kingship narrative of the Ekie of southern Zaïre is almost identical to the Shambala's: a great hunter of noble Luba origins kills a leopard menacing the main native village; he is invited to settle, given a wife, and their son becomes the first ruler of a united Ekie kingdom (Fairley 1987). Again, from West Africa, "Igala myths describing the origin of the kingship and the subsequent emergence of the state imply harmony and co-operation in the fusion of indigenous and immigrant elements; the transfer of sovereignty to the royal clan was made voluntarily and the indigenous clans were incorporated with their basic structure unchanged" (Boston 1968: 198). And East Africa:

> The oral traditions of the Fipa suggest that what happened was a peaceful takeover rather than a violent conquest. The newcomers did not dispel the chief of

Milansi, the ancient center of authority in Ufipa, but allowed him and his successors to remain in Milansi as chiefs of that village and the country for a few
miles about, and to be the senior pries of all Ufipa. (Willis in Roberts 1968: 85)

So were alien dynasties also peacefully founded in great kingdoms such as Benin
in West Africa or Bunyoro-Kitara in East Africa, among others, as well as in
lesser realms such as Acholi, Sogo, Bashu, Tallensi, or Alur, among numerous
others. In some instances, what passes for "conquest" is the usurpation of a previous regime, as Audrey Richards remarked for certain Interlacustrine societies.
It appears that more often than not, according to the broadly accepted traditions, the foreign rule was imposed without violence. There may be continuing
tensions between the native people and their foreign-derived rulers, but usually
sooner than later, the differences are synthesized in a unified kingdom of ritually
and otherwise complementary components. So the question becomes: What
makes the alien dominance legitimate?

In Aidan Southall's ethnographic experience, the Alur stranger-chief was
more revered for his ability to stop war than to raise war, and more to bring or
withhold rain than to muster punitive force. "Had his position depended on the
command of force or on personal prowess in war it appears that many units of
Alur domination of other peoples would never have come into existence, for no
irresistible force was brought to bear in their establishment" ([1956] 2004: 246).
Moreover, Southall was prepared to generalize the phenomenon: "The achievement of the Alur, in building up a new society out of diverse ethnic elements
submitting to Luo domination, seems to represent a type of largely peaceful
development which has been important elsewhere in the region, and which has
so far received little attention in African studies" (ibid.: 234). Or as he wrote in
another context:

It is very hard in this secular age, even in imagination, to conceive of one ethnic
group submitting and accepting subordination to another without some kind of
coercive force or solid material inducement, simply under the impact of belief
in more potent supernatural power. But such occurences evidently did occur in
many parts of the world, over and again, even if forceful conquest was more
common. (1988: 55)

There is no doubt that the currency of arguments in the human sciences pitting
"society against the state," with their emphasis on the "weapons of the weak"

wielded against draconian state power, has empirical as well as moral warrant, but it is not always or often pertinent to the kind of state formation at issue here. In regard to the too common scholarly claim that stranger-king narratives are fundamentally "ideological," having been perpetrated by the ruling class to legitimate their dominance, it should not be overlooked that agency in the matter also comes from the native subjects. In the same way as the Israelites petitioned Samuel for "a king like the other nations," the indigenous peoples may well have their own good reasons for acquiring a ruler. "It appears," writes Southall, "that many groups entered the Alur system to escape from factors operating within, not outside, their own societies" ([1956] 2004: 234). The spread of Alur lineages that occurred in almost every generation owing to the hiving off of the paramount's sons was not only attributable to their ambitions; it was also significantly abetted by "the fact that the chief's sons were a desirable element in any preexisting settlement" (ibid.: 54). Accordingly, Alur have traditions and rituals of chiefly installation which are rather the opposite of a foreign conquest: it is the native Lendu or Madi communities who sometimes literally and ofttimes ceremonially "kidnap" the son of an Alur ruler—to have a chief like other native groups (ibid.: 182ff.).

Yet if the agency in stranger-king formation may well come from inside the indigenous community, it necessarily involves an engagement in a larger political field composed of more and less powerful societies. The peoples concerned have been well aware of these gradients of power and sophistication—can we not say, these differences of "civilization"?—and they importantly influence movements of persons, groups, and cultural forms between the differences. Notions of cultural evolution were not the first invented by nineteenth-century anthropologists.

Virtually by definition, certainly as a rule, stranger-kingdoms were situated in regional, hierarchically ordered fields of interacting societies: core–periphery configurations such as Stanley Tambiah (1976, 1985, 1987) described for Southeast Asia as "galactic polities." Here is an almost ideal-typical description, very much like the regional Southeast Asian galactic orders, in this case regarding the Goba kingdoms of the Zambezi:

> Even petty Goba kings had appointees serving as palace guards, warriors, officials, and henchmen who bolstered their power at the center. They also had territorial subchiefs similar to those in East African Interlacustrine kingdoms. . . . These subchiefs exercised essentially the same kinds of power that the king formally

exercised over the entire territory, and each maintaned a more modest version of the king's staff. . . . The kingdom's sovereignty was relative, altenating [*sic*] through a series of zones of declining central power. There was so little control over the peripheries that some of them, in practice, joined other power chains that linked them one and sometimes several neighboring kingdoms. (Lancaster 1989: 108)

Just so, the galactic polity comprises a number of kingdoms and chiefdoms in varying degrees of subjugation to a dominant central state, the administrative, tributary, and cultural reach of which generally declines in proportion to distance from the capital. The peripheral realms often continue to function under their traditional rulers, provided they maintain their tributary obligations. Southall (1988) described the like as a "segmentary state," adding that the exalted magical status of the central ruler typically extends further than his actual authority. This is also to say that marginal societies, being thus dominated culturally before they are in fact, are in significant measure attracted to the center.

Reporting on the satellite Pabir sultanate of the Bornu "empire" (in present-day northeastern Nigeria), Ronald Cohen (1976, 1981) offers an exemplary description of the intercultural transactions in galactic polities, including the formation of stranger-kingships and chiefdoms in the outlying sectors. The central Bornu kingdom of Kanuri-speaking people was founded in the late fifteenth/early sixteenth century amidst great turmoil, forcing the local peoples to adapt to or otherwise flee from the developing predatory state. In the event, a ring of highly organized secondary kingdoms were formed along the southern edge of Bornu, including the Bura-speaking realm studied by Cohen. Here an immigrant ruling aristocracy from Bornu was established among the local Bura peasantry. As the tradition goes,

A small group of migrants under Yamta-ra-walla, the hero-founder of the royal clan who came from the Borno [Bornu] capital where he had failed in the succession to the throne [*sic*]. These adventurers subdued many of the locals, married Bura women, and settled down. They are said to have learned the local language and customs, but retained their own methods of warfare, the concept of political centrism, and a sense of superiority to the local population. These, then, according to legend were the original Pabir, and from them stems that peculiar variant [polity] that resembles the more complex cultures to the north. (Cohen 1976: 200)

From the sixteenth century, the Sultans of the Bura realm became subordinates of the Bornu rulers, tributary to them materially as well as culturally. Like the Bornu potentates, these Pabir were not only Muslim—by contrast to Bura peasants, who later were largely Christianized—but they also adopted Kanuri titles from Bornu, as well as dress styles, house styles, and Kanuri speech, among many other items. They even adopted Kanuri cross-cousin terms and marriage, in order to marry endogamously, unlike the exogamous Bura clans. The Bura, however, remained "owners" and priestly masters of the country, where their original ancestors had made covenants with the local spirits.[6]

In their actual-historical situation, galactic polities in various states of development or decline exhibit a variety of regional patterns: from centralized "empires" like the old Bunyoro-Kitara realm, or the Bornu and Lunda "empires," through multiple kingdom orders like Azande, to a series of greater and lesser domains acknowledging the spiritual authority of a quondam galactic center that has become politically decentralized like the Borgu kingdoms—and apparently Kongo before the Ntinu Wene regime (see below). Historians tell that at the beginning of the seventeenth century, Bunyoro, centered in a territory ranging south from Lake Albert, was ringed by a variety of smaller tributary kingdoms and chiefdoms, beyond which "other small stayed usually independent of Nyoro armies: Buganda on the east . . . and Rwanda on the south . . . are examples" (Alpers and Ehret 1975: 472). Moreover, Buganda, which was destined to largely displace Bunyoro as the core state of its own "empire," illustrates how great stranger-kingdoms may be developed from the galactic margins by smaller states—again, like the takeover of Kongo from Vungu across the Congo—as well as extended from the center by powerful armies or the migrations of turbulent princes.[7]

Another development on the northern borders of Bunyoro, leading to the creation of the Acholi chiefdoms under Luo domination, is an instructive example at once of stranger-king formation in the context of galactic-political

---

6.   See chapters 4 and 6 for a fuller discussion of galactic polities.

7.   The takeover of Bantu polities by marginal Luo immigrants, followed by the cultural assimilation of the latter by the former, was a common process in the Interlacustrine area. Alpers and Ehret (1975: 455) write: "over most of northern Busoga, the assimilation of Luo elements by the Bantu speakers preceded in accordance with the Interlacustrine pattern of immediately preceding centuries—immigrants acculturating to local language and customs but being able to move into positions of chiefly authority."

conditions and of the advantages accruing therefrom to the indigenous population—especially to its leaders (ibid.: 478; Atkinson 1989; Girling 1960). The
process began in the late seventeenth century and in the usual fashion when two
Paluo groups which had supported the losing side in a Nyoro succession struggle were forced to emigrate. Moving northward, they were able to set themselves up as rulers—complete with the paraphernalia and concepts of Nyoro
kingship—over several clans in what became the nucleus of Acholiland. Their
success stimulated other Luo parties to follow suit, until the former complex
of independent indigenous communities, usually composed of one clan, "had
become centrally-organized chiefdoms controlling an average of eight to ten
clans" (Alpers and Ehret 1975: 478). The centralization was often literal: the
village of the paramount, the *Rwot*, was encircled by a protective screen of subordinate native communities. In the usual dual pattern of stranger-kingship, the
Rwot had an indigenous counterpart in the figure of the "father of the soil," the
elder of the first lineage encountered by the Luo founding chief. F. K. Girling
notes that the "soil" (*won ngom*) in question referred to its aspect as the source
of food, for again the indigenous leader was ritually in charge of the productivity
of the land as well the fertility of the people: "The 'father of the soil' symbolized
in his person the mysterious forces of *jok* [spirits] which are responsible for the
fertility of the land and of human beings, and which also controlled hunting in
the area" (1960: 122). But if the indigenous authority instantiated the bearing
powers of the local earth and its inhabitants, the *Rwot* remained connected to
his foreign origins, and not only through the assumption of Nyoro trappings of
rule. "Frequently, disputes about the succession in Acholi domains were taken to
the kings of Bunyoro-Kitara for settlement" (ibid.: 8). Although they had long
since left Bunyoro, the Acholi paramounts still considered themselves under the
sway of Nyoro kings.

Meanwhile the native lineage heads of the Acholi chiefdoms were able enhance to their own powers and privileges under the sway of the Luo rulers.
Ronald Atkinson (1989: 24ff.) penned a detailed and persuasive argument to
the effect that the establishment of the Luo stranger-chiefdoms offered advantages to the local people not achievable under the previous lineage regime.
(One is reminded of Lucy Mair's observation of the African principle that it is
uncivilized to be without a king.) Socially and politically, the native headmen
not only continued to manage their own lineage affairs, "they also functioned
as the main advisors and councilors to the *Rwot* and as major spokesmen for
and representatives of their lineages within the polity as a whole." Economically,

they collected tributes for the *Rwot*, and perhaps retained a small portion. Religiously, they were "collectively the main ritual figures within the chiefdom" and, evidently referring to the father of the soil, "at least one lineage head—usually from the group acknowledged as the oldest in the area—became the primary ritual figure for the chiefdom as a whole." In the pages that follow it will be seen that these Acholi developments are hardly unique: at least some native authorities enhance their standing and powers under the aegis of stranger-kings. Given these benefits, it is not surprising that an important impetus for the formation of the stranger-kingdom may well come from the internal politics of the indigenous communities.

Engaged in their own rivalries, indigenous leaders and would-be leaders have been known to look upon the advent of a powerful stranger as a political resource, most useful for the prosecution of their own parochial ambitions. Competing for the leadership of the native community or region, one or another of the rivals will go outside the field and enlist a potent foreign ally—whatever the cost in submission and tribute his people would now pay to the latter. Or it may be the conflicts between local communities as such that lead one to enlist outside support—upon which the others will probably do the same. The competition in either case is of the form Gregory Bateson (1935, 1958) called "symmetrical schismogenesis," here involving the tactic of trumping the opposition by engaging an external political power beyond any that could be mustered within the arena of the contest.[8] Lloyd Fallers (1965: 145) recounts how the endemic struggles over succession in Soga states made them much more vulnerable to the penetration of powerful outsiders by invitation than by invasion: "Rulers and princes were constantly on the lookout for powerful allies, and both the Ganda and the Europeans were ready to supply such aid in exchange for overall control." In the same way the Soga had viewed the Buganda king, they saw the Europeans "as a powerful patron with whom they might ally themselves in the traditional manner." Similarly, among the Acholi in relation to outside Luo chiefs:

> Commoner households sought the protection of the *Rwot* for a variety of reasons and contracted affinal ties with him directly or with one of the branches of his agnatic lineage. Through the enjoyment of the ruler's favor, some of the

---

8.   Symmetrical and complementary schismogenesis, à la Gregory Bateson, are
     discussed in more detail in chapters 4 and 6.

household heads became the founders of separate commoner village lineages. (Girling 1960: 84)

Soga, Alur, and others also illustrate the cascading effect that the acquisition of an outside chief by one community can have on the aspirations of others. Speaking of Mbegha's accession to power among Shambala, Feierman (1974: 85) notes of the two densely populated regions of Vugha and Bumbuli: "Bumbuli could not accept the leadership of Vugha; Vugha would not be ruled by Bumbuli. But both made alliances with a powerful outsider." It is not only by the dispersion of turbulent princes or by conquest that galactic regimes are formed; they are also built up by certain impulses of "upward nobility" arising in the peripheries.

Indeed, beyond the native leaders, there may be substantial benefits of stranger-kingship for the underlying population in general. The advantages would include: greater political security; judicial means of resolving disputes and curbing feuds; a wider range of exchanges, notably by the establishment of markets where peace is enforced by regional authorities; a wider social range of intermarriage; and dividends from the ruler's distributions of wealth. Not to forget the latter's magical powers of prosperity: "To believe in the chief," writes Richards of Bemba (1961: 355), "is to cultivate in the hope and assurance that the land is sure to yield its utmost." The benefits of Alur chieftainship for the underlying population are summed up in his provision of "rain," the one blessing standing for "his general and ultimate responsibility in the minds of his subjects for both their material and moral well-being" (Southall [1956] 2004: 239). Indeed, like the Lovedu queen and the Shilluk king, the Alur paramount can be counted among African rulers who rain but do not govern. Just as the landed native people as wife-givers are to the immigrant stranger-princes as feminine is to masculine, so their capacity to make the earth bear fruit is protected and realized through the encompassing powers of the stranger-king over the natural conditions of human prosperity.

Providing prosperity is an aspect of the stranger-king's civilizing benefits, as usually acknowledged by all parties. His advent is frequently said to have raised the native people from a rudimentary state by bringing them cattle, crops, iron (tools and weapons)—even fire and cooking, hence a move from nature to culture. The Nyakyusa tell the story of the civilizing mission of the kingship—as well as the powers retained by the native villagers:

All are agreed that chiefs and commoners belong to different stocks; the commoners being descended from the original occupants of the country while the

chiefs trace their descent to a line of invaders from the Livingstone Mountains
eight generations ago . . . . Moreover, while the most sacred persons in the country were "divine kings," descendants of the original heroes, chosen each generation to become their living representatives, to take their name, and to sacrifice at
their graves, it was the commoners who chose them and . . . put them to death
when it was expedient for the good of the people . . . . The invaders were supposed to have brought into the country fire, cattle, crops, and iron; they were
creators, the guarantors and preservers of fertility; and it was to foster and increase fertility that men sacrificed and worshipped at the graves of the mythical
heroes. The aborigines, on the other hand, without fire, without iron, and feeding
on raw meat as the myth depicts them, possessed one weapon of terrible potency,
witchcraft, which no chief, not even a priest of the chief's lineage, could with-
stand or would dare to challenge. (M. Wilson 1959a: 1–3)

Once more: an enduring complementarity coupled to a residual hostility.

To return to the stranger-king effects of the competition between groups
in galactic fields, the same kind of schismogenesis when it involves competition between the most powerful states can generate a politics of the marvelous,
leading great kingdoms to conjure ancestors of universal renown from exalted
realms of ancient memory.[9] In the upshot, world-historical figures appear as the
founder of dynasties with whom they had no connection and progenitors of
rulers to whom they had no relation: Alexander the Great, for example, who in
his Islamic incarnation as Iskandar D'zul Karnain became the apical ancestor
of fifteenth-century sultans in Sumatra and the Malay Peninsula. The historic
dynasty of Benin was founded by the son of the Yoruba ruler of fabled Ile Ife,
Oduduwa, who had been solicited from his father by the representatives of the
autochthonous Edo people. The latter, the Uzama elders, were reportedly dissat-
isfied with the unkingly behavior of their existing ruler (Bradbury 1957, 1967,
1973). Following a pattern we have already noted more than once, the Yoruba
prince Oduduwa thereupon married a local woman, and their son, combining
the Edo and Yoruba identities and powers, became the first king of the new order. By a popular Yoruba narrative, however, the dynasty would have even more
fabulous antecedents: "The Yorubas are said to have sprung from Lamurudu,
one of the kings of Mecca whose offspring were: Oduduwa, the ancestor of the

---

9.   See the extended discussion of this phenomenon in chapter 6 and the related
      discussion of utopian politics in chapter 2.

Yorubas, and the founding kings of Gogohiri and the Kukuwa, two tribes in Hausa country" (Johnson [1921] 2006: 3). In the context of the dynamic West African Muslim states, a number of such dynasties competitively traced their origins to legendary Middle East ancestors: whether to purported enemies of the Prophet, such as the aforementioned Kisra of the Borgu kingdoms, or to prominent Muslims such as Bayajidda of Baghdad, whose sons by a local princess founded the Hausa sultanates. Thus, a real-politics of the marvelous.

As the tradition goes, the power of the historic Kongo dynasty was abetted by a similar conflict among the notables of the interior kingdom of Mbata, which issued in the inclusion of that rich realm and its satellites in Ntinu Wene's regime. Mbata appears in Duarte Lopes' late-sixteenth-century account as a great and powerful kingdom that submitted voluntarily and without battle to the oncoming Ntinu Wene owing to certain dissensions among its ruling chiefs (Pigafetta [1591] 1988: 61). In the outcome, the victor was one Nsaku Lau, the maternal uncle of the Kongo founding hero Ntinu Wene; he thus became the ruler of Mbata, the Mani Mbata, within Ntinu Wene's kingdom. Following the usual pattern of the union of the stranger-prince with a daughter or sister of the native leader, Ntinu Wene married a daughter of Nsaku Lau. Thenceforth it was enjoined on Ntinu Wene's royal successors to take a daughter of the Mbata rulers to wife, in principle as mother of the royal heir: her title *ne mbanda*, referring apparently to "authority" or "tributary rights," signified the conveyance of sovereignty entailed in the union. In the event, the Mani Mbata and his successors became the maternal "grandfather" of the kingship, a superior kinship status consistent with his bestowal of legitimacy on the alien rulers as well his continuing presence in the new order, including an important role as kingmaker. The old regime was folded into the new.

NATURALIZING THE STRANGER-KING

The marriage of the foreign prince with a daughter of the native leader is the final, contractual aspect of the critical process in which the stranger comes out of the wild to be domesticated by the native people, and thus become eligible to assume the rule of them. It is in this reining in of the king-to-be that oppositional tensions between native subjects and foreign rulers are particularly expressed. Ritual reenactments of the accession of the stranger-king have put social anthropologists in mind of "rituals of rebellion." But then, as Michel Izard observed for the realm of the Yatenga Mossi kings, the autochthonous "people of the earth," as the first to settle the region, were already practiced in transforming the wild into cultivated land, the dangerous into docile elements, the dead into benevolent ancestors (1985: 18).[10] Some or all of these transformations indeed have their counterparts in the installation rites of stranger-kings, which are always (as far as I can determine) under the control of leaders of the native people. But if indigenous leaders thereby confer legitimacy on their arriviste ruler, they may have to kill him first.

In discussing such an event among the Ndembu of Zambia, where the paramount chief of Lunda extraction, the Kanongesha, is installed under the aegis of the Kafwana, the senior headmen of the autochthonous Mbwela people, Victor Turner speaks of these protagonists as representing "a distinction between the politically or militarily strong [rulers] and the subdued autochthonous people, who are nevertheless ritually potent" ([1969] 2008: 99). What is then described is a rite in which an enduring precedence of the native Mbwela people is demonstrated by subduing the Lunda chief who would rule them. For in the critical period of the ritual drama, the chief-elect together with his senior wife or a slave representing the sacred regalia of Lunda rule, all clad only in ragged waist-cloths, are secluded on a hut named from the verb "to die" and decorated with symbols of death—"for it is here that the chief-elect dies" (ibid.: 100).[11] Here too the Kanongesha-to-be will be revived when washed with medicines mixed with water from the river crossed by the original Lunda conqueror when he entered Ndembu territory. Such waters are maternal-cum-autochthonous sources of life elsewhere in Africa, as we shall see shortly; but in any case it is clear that the death of the Kanongesha chief-elect as an outsider is followed by his rebirth as an insider through the offices of the Kafwana native headmen, one of whose titles is indeed "Mother of Kanongesha" (ibid.: 98). The headman then undertakes the new chief's maturation, as it were, by instructing him in the morality of the native society, while forcefully admonishing him to leave off the antisocial behavior of his previous existence—behavior characteristic of an unruly hunter living by and for himself in the wild:

---

10. "By the Mossi kingdoms is meant . . . composite socio-political formations resulting from conquest by warriors called Mossi of the Whie Volta Basin. However, the process of intermarriage and also infiltration by settlement carried out by Mossi peasants was certainly more decisive than military conquest" (Zahan 1967: 177).

11. Turner says he "dies from his commoner state," but as he is of Lunda origin, he would be no simple commoner, and it is rather from this external state that he dies and is transformed, naturalized (ibid.: 100).

You are a mean and selfish fool, one who is bad-tempered . . . . But today you are born as a new chief. . . . If you were mean, and used to eat your cassava mush alone, or your meat alone, today you are in the chieftainship. You must give up your selfish ways, you must welcome everyone, you are the chief! You must stop being adulterous and quarrelsome. ([1969] 2008: 101)

The foreign hunter-conqueror living outside the rules and relations of human society is domesticated by being put to death, reborn, and then socialized by the leader of the indigenous people. Not that his transcendent powers are eliminated, any more than his foreign identity is forgotten, but they are sublimated and put at the service of the society he will now dominate.

Hence if conquest there is, it is reciprocal. The Ndembu are hardly the only African people who integrate their foreign-derived ruler by a humiliating ritual death and rebirth in the seclusion of a specially constructed hut of sinister décor or location. The Acholi, Mamprusi, and Shilluk are among others who are reported to do the like—the Shilluk adding the repetition of a royal exploit when the king-elect also has incestuous relations there with a paternal half-sister. Some form of public humiliation of the royal heir followed by seclusion is even more frequently reported than what ensues in the clandestine rituals. However, what is often no secret in the periodic mock battles that ritually reenact the origins of the kingship is that the ruler and his party are defeated by priestly leaders and warriors of the indigenous stock— which defeat is what allows the king to then claim his realm. Rehearsing the kingship origins in the annual New Year ceremonies, the Yatenga Mossi king is bested in mock battle three times before he is allowed to enter his palace. In the Shilluk installation, the party of the king-elect is twice beaten by the host of the original king Nyikang in ritual battles whose prize was the "girl of the ceremonies": provided by a certain autochthonous clan—hence, again, at stake was the appropriation of the life of the land through a union with a marked daughter of the aboriginal population. Nyikang's victories were also initiated by crossing a certain stream outside the capital of Fashoda, and were followed by a reconciliation of this original king with his successor, in the course of which the latter gained the girl.[12]

---

12. The Shilluk installation involved a certain permutation of the confrontation of the foreign prince and the native authorities. Here the superseded kingly groups (the Ororo) led by Nyikang and his son Dak represented the ancient regime against an

The Mamprusi offer a clear example of subduing the stranger-king in the critical episode of the New Year ceremonies, where he was not only defeated by the priest-chiefs and elders of the previous regime, but also symbolically killed (Drucker-Brown 1975: 95–96). Marked by successive foreign-derived dynasties, the Mamprusi comprise a good example too of serial stranger-kingship wherein the priest-chiefs, the heirs of the former rulers, take the part of the kingdom's native element. In the rite in question, a group of drummers and dancers led by two of these great priests of the earth, war spears in hand, confronted a party of the king and his supporters in the enclosure in front of his house. At a certain moment, the dancers, also armed with spears, with the priest-chiefs apparently in their lead, moved toward the king with loud cries, "as if they were going to war." One prince, attempting to make light of the affair, told Susan Drucker-Brown, the ethnographer, that the menacing shouts of the priest chiefs were merely a "blood-dance." Nearing the king, the dancers raised their spears as if to hurl them at him, and then gently lowered them and stopped dancing. The king now wept "Just for the moment," explained a young royal, "tears come down from his eyes. That is the most essential part of the Damba [the New Year rites]." A commoner elder expressing the view of the subject people in general on their relationship to the king provided what Drucker-Brown deemed "perhaps the most accurate analysis of the ceremony: 'They (the priest chiefs) are saying "we own you" to the king. For that is how it is. We own the king and he owns us'" (ibid.: 96).

Just so, the stranger-kingdom is marked by the reciprocal encompassment of the indigenous subjects by the foreigner king and the king by his indigenous subjects. Even as the king instantiates the totality of the polity and the ruling aristocracy unifies the diverse native communities, the native leaders, by representation or in combination, naturalize and integrate their foreign royalty to the extent that in most African stranger-kingdoms, great "empires" partially excepted, the dominant identity, language, and customs of the society as a whole are those of the native "owners" rather than the immigrant rulers. The ethnic identities of both may have been developed in the course of the kingdom's formation, but that of the indigenous "owners" typically serves as the identity of the totality. Moreover, as perennial kingmakers, these native authorities not only legitimate

---

upstart king-elect who, coming from the south, would in effect reproduce Nyikang's original conquest—as indeed the new king famously became Nyikang in these rites. (See also chapter 2, this volume.)

the authority of the kings of foreign origin, they thereby demonstrate their own residual sovereignty—in many African kingdoms they are the designated regents during the extended interregnum that follows the death of the king. Nor do they ever surrender their "ownership" of the earth of the kingdom—with which they share an existential identity.

The kings of the old Kongo state were no exception to traditions and rituals of their sublimation and integration by an older aristocracy, especially those functioning as priest-chiefs (*kitomi*) of the kingdom and its several provinces. According to the dominant charter tradition, an important priest-chief (Nsaku ne Vunda) mediated the advent of Ntinu Wene, founder of the historic dynasty, as we shall see; and thereafter, no prince could be invested in the kingship without the endorsement of the titular successors of this priest. I am unaware of any detailed text on what happened in the eight-day seclusion of the king-elect during the Kongo installation rites, although a report from 1668 tells that the assembled people threw dust upon him as he was being escorted to the place of confinement (Dapper [1868] 1970). It is also reported that the installations of pre-Christian kings included draconian breaches of kinship on their part: they are said to have killed one or more junior kinsmen of their own clan and also had intercourse with a clanswoman. But we do have a revelatory notice of the installation rites of the "governor" or "duke" of the important Nsundi province in 1651 from the journal of the Capuchin father Giroloma da Montesarchio (Bouveignes and Cuvelier 1951: 97–101). Nsundi was the particular patrimony of Kongo kings, reputedly because it was the first realm subdued by the dynastic founder, Ntinu Wene, and the governorship was accordingly reserved for the designated heir to the kingship.

Before he could take office at the Nsundi capital, however, the prince, together with his wife and entourage, was obliged to travel to the village of the major priest-chief (*kitomi*) of the province, a personage "who was venerated as if he were the god of the country." Montesarchio continues:

> This Chitomi [Kitomi] was so esteemed that it was if it depended on him that one acquired the power and authority to rule the province. The Duke was convinced that if he did not go through the process at the Chitomi's, he would have no power over the people, who would accord him neither submission nor tribute, and indeed his life would be cut short. (Bouveignes and Cuvelier 1951: 98)

The encounter of the duke and the *kitomi* took place across a certain stream, apparently at the border of the village. On one side the duke, his wife, and party, arrayed as though for battle, faced the *kitomi*, his wife, and their people on the other. There followed a mock combat with bows and straw arrows, in which the stranger-prince was subdued: "The duke and duchess were obliged to acknowledge themselves defeated." But the defeat allowed them to cross the stream into the territory they would rule. For the *kitomi* then gave the duke a hand across, and his wife did the same for the duke's consort. Comments Montesarchio: "Without that ceremony, the duke would not be able to cross the stream" (ibid.).

The following day featured something of a reversal of the stranger-prince's defeat in what appears to have been the symbolic form of a sexual conquest: "The next morning, the duke and his wife lay down on the ground before the door of the Kitomi's house. The Kitomi and his wife came out of their house, took off their clothes so as to ostentatiously display their genitals, then dropped their clothes and trampled them underfoot." In the sequel, the priest-chief poured some water on the earth to make a muddy mixture with which, "as if it were blessed earth," he daubed the duke and his wife. The latter pair thereupon gave all their clothes to the priest-chief and his wife. The *kitomi* followed by entrusting the duke with several "objects of superstition" which had to be kept in the house of the duke's wife, "to be worshipped there as if they were sacred relics, if not more" (ibid.). He also gave him a certain firebrand from which "everyone" would light their fire; it had to be taken to the Nsundi capital, distant some six days' march. The firebrand also had to be kept in the house of the duke's wife. Thus ends the account of the ceremonies.

To comment only on the obvious: the stranger-prince is able to gain the rule solely on the condition of his own submission to the native priest-chief, god of the country, owner of the earth. There will be reason to suppose from comparable notices elsewhere that the remoteness of the *kitomi*'s village from Mbanza Nsundi, the capital, indicates that it is an old cultic center, the foyer of some of the earliest inhabitants of Nsundi. In any case, it is in this capacity that the *kitomi* and his spouse—the protagonists are conjugal pairs, as if to signify the reproductive aspects of the rites—offer themselves sexually as "wife" to the princely couple. Anointing the latter with earth mixed with water, the iconic patrimony of the autochthonous people, the *kitomi*, at once naturalizes the foreign royals, conveys the territory to them—and perhaps humiliates them. We are not told whether the clothes given by the princely pair to the *kitomi* and wife had special value. In any event, the firebrand the stranger king then receives from the *kitomi*, by which he will rekindle the hearths of the Nsundi people, implies he has become an inseminating source of their fertility of the land, analogously to his union with their priestly representative. Speaking of notices of such priest-chiefs in early missionary texts, Anne Hilton writes: "The *kitomi* also maintained one or two fires, which were closely associated with fertility, and sold firebrands to supplicants" (1985: 25).

Hilton also comments on this ritual by reference to another, more general-ized seventeenth-century account in which "the *kitomi* was said to tread the governor under his feet 'to demonstrate he must be subject' and the governor swore perpetual obedience" (ibid.: 47). In essence, the ritual consists of a transfer of sovereignty in the course of which the stranger-prince is appropriated by the native owners of the land, and vice versa. This recursive theme of royal ceremony and collective memory is not false historical consciousness, but rather, to bor-row a phrase from Clifford Geertz, it is "a model of and for" cultural order and historical action.

ON CROSSING THE RIVER AND MARRYING THE LAND

Not to forget a fundamental episode in the installation of the Duke of Nsundi in the role of stranger-prince: the crossing of the river. Crossing the river to take possession of the land is rather like marriage of the stranger-prince with a ranking woman of the native people that engenders the ruling chief. Symboli-cally, the crossing and the marriage are versions of one another. The similarities are cosmological at the same time they are political. For such very reasons, some Western scholars think they are not historical. They can't be real.

The genealogy of the founder of the Shilluk kingdom, Nyikang, leads back to the heavens and God (Juok) on the paternal side, and on the maternal, to earthly rivers. "His mother Nyikaya is associated with all riverine phenomena and beings, first and foremost with the crocodile, and she is associated with fertility and childbirth" (Schnepel 1988: 448). Nyikang is searched for in the White Nile at the beginning of the Shilluk installation rites, in the course of which he will be instantiated in the king. One of Nyikang's titles is in fact "Son of the River." Another is "The Crosser of the River," referring to Nyikang's initial traverse of the Bahr-el-Ghazal into the territory he then conquered and organized as the Shilluk (Col) kingdom. As we already know from several stranger-king narratives, including the Kongo in some detail, terrestrial waters as well as the bearing earth are the inalienable domain of the indigenous-cum-maternal component of the stranger-kingdom.[13]

These associations can be found even in nascent tribal forms of stranger-kingship. As reported by Godfrey Lienhardt (1961), for example, in Dinka charter traditions, cognate to the Shilluk's, Aiwel, first son of the God and ancestor of the priestly masters of the fishing spears, emerged at birth from a river. These masters of the fishing spears will marry off their sisters to the arriviste warrior chiefs, become the mothers' brothers of the latter, and thereby unite the dual ruling components of Dinka society. Lienhardt reports that rivers have influence on and are influenced by pregnant women: "The association to which we point . . . is between the river as a source of life for the Dinka, women as sources of life, and the prototype of sisters of masters of the fishing spear as dispensers of 'life'" (ibid.: 203).

As distant in space and language as the Bantu BaKongo are from the Nilotic Dinka, crossing the river has very similar implications for them. MacGaffey distills the sexual and reproductive symbolism from various legendary episodes:

> This concern with fertility is represented in the legends by the magical elements associated with the crossing of the river, in which sexual imagery is explicit: planting the staff that burgeoned . . .; the sister who insulted her brother by suggesting incest; the awl in the navel; hollowing a canoe; splitting a rock, where "the knife in the rock" is still a current sexual metaphor; or parting the water as did the chief Ma Kaba . . . by tying from shore to shore a woman's tumpline . . . a symbol of her reproductive capacity. (1986: 92)

The motif of crossing the river is a Rubicon moment in a goodly number of African dynastic traditions, the fateful move that will set an ambitious immigrant prince on a course to his kingship and introduce a new order among the native people of the land. "Indeed," writes Aidan Southall, "it was the crossing of the Nile and the process of incorporation of other groups that constituted the emergence of a new, composite society, called 'Alur'" (1989: 188). It is pertinent to add that the generic ethnonym, "Alur," referred originally to the indigenous Sudanic populations of the region: an identity that subsequently included their

---

13. For further details on the Shilluk installation, see David Graeber's account in chapter 2.

late-coming Nilotic chiefs, who for their part, however, preferred to vaunt their kinship with the Bito rulers of the once great Kitara-Nyoro kingdom. For more stranger-king ironies that have nothing to do with history except to create it, the Nilotic Bito, however, have long adopted the Bantu speech of their dynastic predecessors. Not coincidently, the Bito crossed the Nile on their way to the Kitara kingship. Again and generally: "the migration of the eponymous ancestor of the Bambara dynasties contains the theme of river crossing that is found in so many legends of origin in Africa" (Izard and Ki-zerbo 1992: 330).

Perhaps, then, we can up the symbolic ante on the meanings of narratives such as that of the installation of the Duke of Nsundi. In crossing the river and marrying the land, the stranger-hero effects a cultural synthesis of cosmic dimensions, as between the celestial and the terrestrial, masculine and feminine, the wild and the sown, foreign mobile riches and produce of the local earth, war and peace; in brief, the fundamental conditions of human order and welfare— the powers and sources of which are ultimately beyond society itself (cf. Sahlins 2014). Indeed, MacGaffey has emphasized that the motif of crossing the river takes its meaning from the Kongo conception of the universe as an upperworld of humanity separated by water from an underworld of the dead inhabited by the spiritual beings in control of the human fate. (Alternatively, the model is triadic, adding an upperworld of divine beings to the earthly plane and underworld of the dead.) Accordingly, in a text there will be occasion to revisit, MacGaffey says of the prescriptive crossing of the river in Kongo origin traditions, "the elsewhere from which the king comes is a land of spirits (Bupemba, Mpemba, Upemba), although it may be identified with a geographical location" (2003: 11).

The externality of the kingship is essential because power itself, the spiritual sources of human vitality, mortality, and prosperity, comes from beyond society:

> Bakongo see the ability to survive in the universe as a function of the play of power. The terms for "ordinary people" who lack *kindoki* or *kundu* (witchcraft power) are derogatory. People who have power obtain it directly or indirectly from the otherworld. They are relatively successful: they live longer and have more children and more wealth (both *mbongo*). Power obtained from the otherworld can be used for personal or for public benefit, with productive or destructive effect. (MacGaffey 1986: 190)

Considering the recent anthropological interest in cosmologies and ontologies as the relative cultural grounds of what there is and how such things came to be—not to mention the ethnographic evidence of the potency of alterity—it seems curious that the historian John Thornton should dismiss the longstanding Kongo traditions that the founder of the kingdom, Ntinu Wene, embarked on his kingly project by crossing the Congo River as merely a "cosmological necessity" surrounded by "ideological stories." In his important work on "The origin and early history of the kingdom of Kongo, c. 1350–1550," Thornton writes:

> The story of the first king crossing the Kongo from Vungu to conquer Mpemba Kasi, the first province of Kongo, may not have any basis, however; as Wyatt MacGaffey pointed out in his study of nineteenth-century tradition, the idea of a river crossing, surrounded by ideological stories, may be more of a cosmological necessity than a statement of literal truth. While there is little doubt that the seventeenth-century Kongo elite believed that their dynasty had originated in Vungu, or at least across the Congo River, this is not supported by earlier tradition. According to Lopes, Kongo began not across the Congo River, but in the province of Mpemba and annexed other provinces from that core. (2001: 108)

This search for "literal truth" becomes doubly curious by virtue of Thornton's methods for rewriting the documentary evidence in order to arrive at it. For one, there is his singular reliance on the 1591 text of the Italian humanist Fillipo Pigafetta—based on a manuscript penned by Duarte Lopes—for his own reconstruction of Kongo kingship origins, although this work says very little about it, and Thornton takes the liberty of boldly revising what it does say about it. A merchant who served as Kongo's ambassador to Rome, Lopes wrote "the first explicitly historical description of Kongo in 1588" (ibid.: 102). Thornton allows that, in fact, Lopes says little about the kingship origins, because "it was intended to convince Vatican authorities that Kongo was a Christian kingdom of good standing and thus worthy of having its own bishop, and did not deal very much with the pre-Christian period" (ibid.). (The pre-Christian period would be c. 1350–1500.) But at least equally important, apart from a few snippets of local traditions, Lopes does not even discuss the earlier kings because, for all he knew, the Congolese had no memory of them: "They preserve no history of the ancient kings, nor any memorial of past ages, not knowing how to write" (Pigafetta [1591] 1881: 111). Not a good start.[14]

---

14. Msgr. Cuvelier and Louis Jadin did not have good things to say about Duarte Lopes' reportage. Was it because he was a descendant of Jewish converts—which

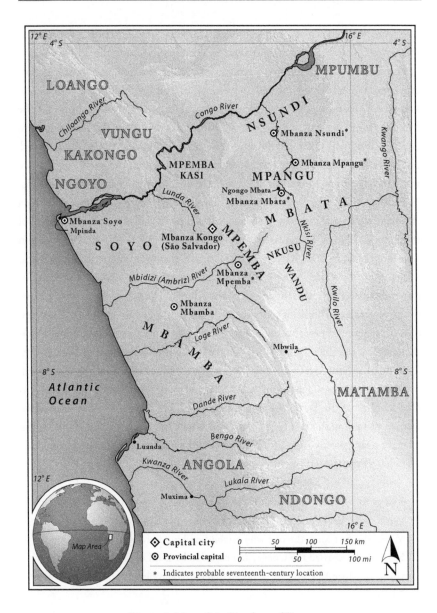

Figure 1. Map of the kingdom of Kongo.

they did not fail to mention? He was a trader, they said, neither explorer, voyager, nor historian. He seems not to have traveled beyond Loango and San Salvador. "His historical reports are without any exactitude. The errors and gaps in the *Relation* are numerous" (1954: 110).

Thornton will rely significantly on Montesarchio as well as Lopes for his historiographic project, which involves the deconstruction of the foreign origin
of the historic Kongo kingship in favor of a reconstructed truer history of its
endogenous beginnings immediately south of the Zaïre River in the region
known as Mpemba Kasi (aka Mpemba Nkazi, etc.) (fig. 1). Not only did the
dynasty really originate within Kongo, Thornton argues, but the founding hero
and first king was not really Ntinu Wene from Vungu, as commonly believed,
but his father, Nimi a Nzima of Mpemba Kasi. An important piece of evidence
was a passage from Montesarchio's journal describing his visit to Mpemba Kasi
in 1650 or 1651, which reads in part, "I went to Mpemba Casi, governed by a
chiefess having authority over several villages who held the title of Mother of
the King of Congo" (Bouveignes and Cuvelier 1951: 70)—to which Thornton
suggestively adds, "the KiKongo word '*ngudi*' means 'mother' but might also
mean 'origin' or 'source'" (2001: 108). So the text might also indicate she was, or
rather her ancestress was, the origin of the kingship. Possibly true, but to the opposite effect than Thornton supposes, as it rather implies an archetypal marriage
of the stranger-hero with a daughter of the autochthonous people, upon which
she will become the mother of the king and maternal ancestress of the dynasty.
(Like Joao II, who "tramples the lion in the kingdom of his mother.") Indeed,
the documentary evidence early and late makes it clear that the reference to
the "Mother of the King of Congo" recalled a hypergamous union of a native
woman of rank with a stranger-king from across the Congo River. So reads the
relevant passage of Montesarchio's journal, when taken in its entirety—including what Thornton left out:

> I went to Mpemba Casi, governed by a chiefess having authority over several
> villages who held the title of Mother of the King of Congo. Here is the reason:
> When the first king, the one who established his sovereignty over the Congo,
> left Coimba, crossed the Congo, and began to be Lord of Congo, it was at the
> village of Mpemba Casi that he began to reign. (Bouveignes and Cuvelier 1951:
> 70–71)[15]

Some centuries later, MacGaffey could provide a confirming report from his
own ethnographic study of the same area:

---

15. Thornton later quotes the second part of this text about crossing the river, but
separately and in a different context (2001: 107).

The likelihood is that Nkazi a Kongo has dominated Mbanza Nkazi [capital center of the region] continuously for five hundred years. The name is a title implying that the owners had the right to provide the king, Ne Kongo, with his official wife at the time of the coronation. This woman was probably his classificatory Father or Grandfather [by lineage . . .] and she would be known as Mpemba Nkazi, which is the first recorded name of the Manteke region. Probably this is what father Jerome de Montesarchio referred to when he gave the title of the chief he met in Mbanza Nkazi in 1650 as "Mother of the king of Kongo." (1970: 83)

A corollary problem with Thornton's thesis that Kongo began in Mpemba Kasi is that his primary documentary source, the Duarte Lopes text as transmitted by Pigafetta, distinctly says otherwise. It says that the cradle of the kingship was in the province of Mpemba, which is in the center of the Kongo kingdom—not to be confused with Mpemba Kasi in the north—where is located the capital Mbanza Kongo (later San Salvador). According to the Lopes' account as translated by Thornton, Mpemba was "the center of the state of Congo and the origin of the Ancient Kings and the land where they were born"—to which Thornton adds, "thus the original territory to which the other provinces were added" (2001: 104). The well-known tradition to which Thornton alludes, however, recounts how Ntinu Wene culminated his conquest of Kongo from Vungu north of the Congo by distributing the land to his followers from a mountain in Mpemba near the capital he would subsequently establish at Mbanza Kongo (Cuvelier 1946). Mbanza Kongo—another old name of which was Mbanza Wene—remained the royal seat of the Kongo state into the Christian era: which is not inconsistent with Lopes' statement that it was the center of the kingdom and the origin and birthplace of ancient kings—whose traditions were largely unknown to him. However, on the basis of his own choice of kingdom origins at Mpemba Kasi, Thornton simply asserts that Lopes (or Pigafetta) had gotten mixed up: that in describing Mpemba as the origin of the ancient kings, the author must have really meant Mpemba Kasi in the north. "What seems likely," to Thornton, "is that Lopes or Pigafetta conflated Mpemba, the large southern province, with Mpemba Kasi, the smaller northern province, thus putting both Lopes and the later Capuchins in agreement over the original core of Kongo" (2001: 108). How could this be? The Lopes text (Pigafetta [1591] 1881: 62–70) is perfectly clear about the location of—and unmistakably detailed in its description of—Mpemba province and its capital Mbanza Kongo. In this case,

Lopes must have known what he was talking about: he lived in Mbanza Kongo for some years, and he was the ambassador of Mbanza Kongo to the Vatican. As for the later Capuchins purportedly in agreement that Mpemba Kasi was "the original core of Kongo," besides Montesarchio, Thornton is invoking the 1687 text of Cavazzi—who was in the region in the mid-1660s—in which the founder of the kingdom came from across the Kwango River (rather than the Congo) and Mpemba Kasi was the first place in Kongo he had conquered (Cuvelier 1946; Sousa 1999).[16] In sum, Thornton's rewriting of the primary sources is perfectly arbitrary, except as it is motivated by his own empirically challenged, secondary interpretation purporting to be what actually happened.

In an earlier work (1983: 15ff.), Thornton had already sought to deconstruct the Kongo stranger-king tradition by asserting that "the supposed ethnic distinction" between the subject peoples generically known as Ambundu and the ruling elite, the Ashikongo (or Essikongo, etc.), was not really a difference between native inhabitants and immigrant rulers. The reputed ethnic distinction was merely an ideological supposition (on the part of the Congolese people), a mirage based on a more fundamental difference between the social systems of the countryside and the town as constituted in the seventeenth century. As we know, Thornton is not the only student of African societies who, by positing that stranger-king traditions are functional (cum-superstructural) reflexes of the real-political or real-economic structures at a given moment, consider that they have no real-historical value and can thenceforth be ignored. Since these traditions are time-bound, secondary rationalizations, and not "literally true" so far as the historian is concerned—it helps if they are called "myths"—they are supposed to have no real effect on the destiny of the people who continue to hold and practice them as timeless truths—transhistorical memories of what has been and will be.

In this matter of the confinement of the stranger-kingship of Kongo to the dustbin of real history, Thornton offers a quasi-Marxist explanation of the distinction between Ambundu subjects and Essikongo rulers as a "reflection" of differences in modes of production: the Ambundu social formation based on agriculture as organized by relations of kinship, and the Essikongo, based on tribute, slave labor, and foreign wealth obtained by levies on trade and war.

---

16. Not to mention the early documents, such as the 1620 H. R. C. and CIII of Paiva, which situated the founder of the kingdom respectively at Bungo and Bango (Vungu), north of the river (in Cuvelier 1946).

"More than just dialect or supposed ethnic origin," he writes, ". . . this distinc-tion was a social and economic one, a reflection of the way Kongo's production system and social relations were organized in the seventeenth century" (ibid.: 15–16).[17] But if stranger-kingship apparently mirrors the relations of produc-tion, is it not because the image has indeed been reversed: not that the distinc-tions of stranger-kingship reflect the relations of production, but that produc-tion is organized by the relations of stranger-kingship? The "ownership" and control of the means of production in the primary, agricultural sector by the underlying people is sequitur to the broad cultural distinctions of autochthony and alterity. It is the opposition between the descendants of first-settlers exis-tentially connected by ancestry to the spiritual sources of the earth's fertility, and the dominating late-comers of foreign derivation and violent disposition ruling by tributes and foreign wealth acquired by trade, warfare, and so on. Clearly, the relations of production are structured in the terms and forms of stranger-kingship as such, but the terms and forms of stranger-kingship are not those of production as such.

In any event, the distinction between the immigrant Essikongo nobility and the indigenous Ambundu peoples was structurally pertinent in the old Kongo kingdom, and it could not be so simply characterized as a difference between the denizens of the towns and countryside. In the beginning of his long reign (1506–43), King Afonso styled himself simply as "King of Kongo and Lord of the Ambundu," a title that was repeated by his successor King Diego in 1647 (Cuvelier 1946: 339). In later years, Afonso—as also Afonso II in a document of 1652—while naming all the principalities he claimed to rule (in European imperial style), added that he was "Sovereign Lord of all the Ambundu" (ibid.). Very likely the formation of the kingdom itself entailed the process of ethno-genesis by which these broad identities developed—each of them, and especially "Ambundu," including a considerable diversity of groups of different origins. The province of Nsundi alone "counted ten different tribes" (ibid.: 247).[18] The complementary formation of an Essikongo superstructure, moreover, involved the spread of the immigrant nobility into countryside settlements as ruling

---

17. As will be discussed presently, Wyatt MacGaffey takes a similar but more nuanced position on the determination of Kongo stranger-king traditions by the relations of production and social reproduction and their nonpertinence as history or for history.

18. Ravenstein (1901) writes—apparently from the dominant, Essikingo view—that "ambundu" meant "slaves," and "the conquered."

chiefs (cum-tribute collectors) in the provincial and district centers; even as the lower levels of this hierarchy were expanded by the bestowal of heritable titles—together with the distinctive bonnets signifying noble status—on local big-men and clan leaders who were prepared to pay the substantial qualifying fee. Probably, the question of the ethnicity of the town-dwelling rulers in the ancient Kongo was similar to what Nadel described for Fulani in Nupeland:

> The Fulani conquerors of Nupe, numerically an insignificant minority, were absorbed completely by the culture of the people whom they had subjugated . . . . Yet they remain a separate social group, conscious of its alien origin, and still distinguished by a special tribal name: they call themselves, and are called by their subjects, *goizi*, a name which distinguishes these settled, "town Fulanu" from the nomadic cattle people who are known as *bororozi*, never Nupe. They are a "representative" group in a different sense—the small elite of conquerors and rulers. The historical memory of their alien origin—for it is only this today—buttresses their detached social position. (1942: 71)

To take stock, then, in Thornton's notional reconstruction of "historical reality": Vungu was not the homeland of the kingship, notwithstanding that even seventeenth-century kings claimed that it was; Mpemba Kazi within Kongo was where the kingship originated, notwithstanding all tradition and documentation indicating it was the place the immigrant founder Ntinu Wene first conquered after crossing the Congo River; Ntinu Wene did not cross the Congo River, hence we can ignore the merely cosmological significance of that Rubicon moment and its presence in operative versions of the kingship traditions; anyhow, Ntinu Wene was not the founder of the Kongo kingdom, his father Nimi a Nzima was; and the dual society of indigenous Ambundu subjects ruled by a foreign-derived Ashikongo aristocracy was not really a distinction of historical origins and ethnic identities but an ideological reflex of the socioeconomic differences between rural peasants and the town elites. In sum, the Kongo state was not a stranger-kingdom.

But to return to the paradigmatic traditions of stranger-kingship that, "literally true" or not, are resources of real history: the ultimate integration of the foreign prince is his marriage to the daughter of the native ruler. This recurrent episode in narratives of the origins of stranger-kingship amounts to the contract of the new society, not only by allying its dual components but also by giving rise to a dynasty that encompasses the totality. The ubiquity of this foundational synthesis of foreign rulers and native owners is already evident in preceding paragraphs. Such unions or their symbolic equivalents are virtually universal conditions of stranger-kingship formations—around the world as well as in Africa. What Marjorie Stewart writes of the Borgu kingdoms in this regard could easily be duplicated from accounts of stranger-kingship origins anywhere: "It was common practice . . . when a powerful prince arrived in another chief's territory for the incumbent chief to offer his daughter in marriage to the new-comer to establish bonds of friendship and thereby acknowledge the latter's superior political power" (1993: 252).

More than "friendship," however, the two components of the kingdom are united by an ancestral and perpetual kinship. The chiefs of the old regime and their successors are related to the ruling kings as maternal "grandfathers" to their "grandsons" (Kongo) or "mothers' brothers" to their "sisters' sons" (Mossi); or else more generally, as in Borgu, "the [native] chief of the Earth becomes more intimately associated with political power and becomes for all the young princes the very incarnation of their maternal ancestor" (Lombard 1965: 186). Again, in another mode of generalizing the initial kinship connection, local indigenous headmen may be related to royals settled in their villages or districts as "wives" to their chiefly "husbands" (Luba, Tallensi, Nyakyusa). Note also that the status of the native chiefs as priests of the stranger-king realm is consistent with their maternal relation to the kingship insofar as it parallels Edmund Leach's classic formulation of the opposition between the "consubstantiality" of the own people (here, royals) and the "metaphysical influence" of the affines (here, natives). Affines of the kingship by origin, the indigenous priests are everywhere the sacrificers, the ritual intermediaries with divinity, even in some cases officiating at the sacrifices to the royal ancestors—though it be on behalf of the king as sacrifier.

On the other hand, by thus integrating the sacred powers of the autochthonous people with the violent potency of his own origins, the ruler himself becomes something of a divinity. Not only does he encompass the social totality in his own person, but he is endowed with the powers to create it. At least such are the attributes of the offspring of the original union. The immigrant prince himself may disappear, leaving behind a son by a native woman to become the first ruler and true founder of the kingdom—which he may then expand by conquest as well as enrich by civilizing gifts. This is the story in the kingships of Benin, Luba, Lunda, and, by implication, Kongo.

Not to forget that the native peoples have their own reasons for entering into an alliance with a powerful outsider, and accordingly they may have their own agency in the matter. Such was the experience more than once of the good Capuchin Montesarchio during his evangelizing travels around Kongo in the mid-seventeenth century. At one village in Mbata, he found the chief excessively attentive; for, "He wished at any cost to give me his own daughter for a wife" (Bouveignes and Cuvelier 1951: 151). A similar incident at the large principality of Congobella on the upper Congo River—apparently independent and rarely if ever visited by Europeans—gives some idea why the missionary was in such great demand: "They said I was a 'Banchita,' which is nearly saying that I was a man returned from the other world" (ibid.: 115). Here again, "The Congobella king wanted to give me one of his daughters in marriage, and many others wished to give a daughter or a sister to have descendants of a priest of the Pope" (ibid.: 116). Some people also expressed a desire to have his relics, never mind that he was still alive, and they offered him native cloth of the best quality for locks of his hair (ibid.: 117). A being returned from the otherworld to whom the native ruler proffers his daughter in marriage: Can one doubt the "historical reality" of stranger-kingship in the Kongo region, even the possibility of its peaceful establishment?

In the official tradition, the Kongo hero Ntinu Wene was himself the offspring of a union between the king, Nimi a Nzima, from Vungu across the Zaïre, and a sister of the Mbata ruler Nsaku Lau. It may be that Nimi had already threatened a decentralized galactic system from its margins and in the usual stranger-king pattern married an indigenous princess.[19] Hilton (1985) has argued this incursion actually happened; and as we know, Thornton (2001) takes the argument beyond its logical and empirical extreme to the conclusion that Nimi was of endogenous BaKongo stock and he rather than his son Ntinu Wene was the real founder and first king of Kongo. In this connection, both Hilton and Thornton stress the economic basis of Kongo kingship origins, especially its development at the intersection of long-distance trade routes, although neither (so far as I know) has addressed the dissenting scholarly opinions.

---

19. Alternatively, the Mbata ruler may have accorded the subordinate Vungu ruler a junior sister or daughter as a secondary wife of the latter. This would actually be consistent with the subdominant version of the tradition of Ntinu Wene's crossing of the Zaïre, wherein he takes on the ambition to become a conquering king when his mother, who had refused to pay the toll, was insultingly asked, "Who do you think you are, the mother of the king?" It would also be consistent with the recurrent motif to the effect that Ntinu Wene had no chance to succeed to the Vungu kingship.

Early on, David Birmingham (1975: 544–55) asserted there is no indication that Kongo before the Portuguese owed its wealth to monetary sources or any marketable product; it was essentially a prosperous farming regime, working through a tributary and redistributive political economy. Likewise, Luc de Heusch questions whether "the 'economist' hypothesis of Anne Hilton could not be reversed. Would it not be the very existence of the Kongo kingdom that structured the commercial development?" (2000: 69).

In any case, if Ntinu Wene's father was the original king of Kongo, one would have to draw a distinction between what actually happened and what became the historical reality. For inasmuch as the Congolese people have made their own history in tradition and in action, they have privileged the offspring of the foreign king and the native woman, Ntinu Wene, as the primary agent, founding hero, and original king of the historic dynasty. There is a difference between a happening and a historical event, rather on the order of the difference between fact and value, which is to say that nothing happens except as it is meaningfully appropriated and disseminated. Hence Wene, of mixed foreign and domestic descent, is the effective founder of the kingdom. As Balandier observes, by this synthesis of the foreign warrior with the sacred ancestral powers of the autochthonous people, the Kongo kingship derives "the means of converting into durable superiority what was merely vulnerable coercion, transforming into a permanent order what was merely a disorder favorable to innovation" (1968: 38).

THE DUAL SOCIETY

In a chapter on "Religion as a political system," Wyatt MacGaffey reviews an ethnographic report by Nestor van Everbroeck (1961) on the Bolia people living in the vicinity of LacMai Ndomba (former Lake Leopold II, Democratic Republic of the Congo), of whom MacGaffey says, "their ideology and social structure . . . are closely comparable to the BaKongo" (1986: 182). In MacGaffey's summary:

> The legendary first occupants of Bolia territory were the Nsese, forest dwellers and cannibals . . . . Every Bolia village has a political chief and an owner of the soil. These positions belong to clans described in the legends as invaders and autochthons respectively . . . . Traditions relating to occupation and ownership

of land resemble those of Kongo and are evidently political rather than historical material . . . . The political chief has the power of life and death and is responsible (with a committee of three assistants, as in the classical Kongo government) for justice, foreign relations, and war. The owner of the soil is responsible for the growth and well-being of the village. (1986: 182)

More than the resemblances to "classical Kongo government," however, the Bolia ethnography is classical stranger-kingship. Immigrant chiefs from the northeast, the Bolia took over the villages of the indigenous "owners of the soil," forming a series of chiefdoms in each of which the ruler was the collective "husband" of his native-subject "wives." For example: the charter tradition of the most important chiefdom in the area of the Sengele people, one of several indigenous groups, is quintessential stranger-king stuff (Van Everbroeck 1961: 31ff.). The advent of the arrogant Bolia hero Kengulu was initially conflictual but in the end peaceful. Kengulu appears as a hunter accompanied by his warriors who trail a wounded wild pig to its death in the forest near the Sengele village of Ngongo. Pleased by the location, Kengulu brings his people there to clear the forest for a settlement. As is often recounted in such charter narratives, the contact with the native population is made through a female relative of the native leader, in this case the wife of Yanganga, the "possessor of the land" of Ngongo and its environs. Hearing of the strangers through his wife, Yanganga confronts Kengulu with the demand of a thigh of the wild pig as his due as "possessor of the land." Kengulu refuses, and the native Yanganga not only backs down in light of the number of Kengulu's warriors, but returns the next day with a welcoming gift of a packet of vegetables, a chicken, and the shoulder of a wild pig (the chiefly portion?). Moreover, a few days later, having killed a leopard and desiring to remain on good terms, Yanganga sends a shoulder to Kengulu, who, standing on his chiefly dignity demands also the skin, teeth, claws, and thigh of the beast. Enraged, Yanganga, as the "legitimate owner of the soil," declares he would not submit to the domination of the strangers. Kengulu thereupon enters Ngongo with his warriors and demands damages. When the villagers advise appeasing the stranger-chief, Yangenga departs with his family, leaving only two sons at the village. In his absence, however, the victory of Kengulu soon turns to dust: the earth becomes sterile, and day after day fishing fails and the hunters return empty-handed. His advisors tell Kengulu he has acted badly toward Yanganga, and "for our life to return to normal, there is only one remedy: solicit the intervention of the owners of the soil." Upon the chief's request Yanganga's sons seek him out and ask him to return. Arriving at the village, Yanganga, first remonstrates with strangers for stealing his domain, and then agrees to restore its vitality—but only on three conditions: first, that Kengulu and his descendants shall give Yanganga and his descendants the thigh of every animal killed on his territory; second that each newly installed chief shall pay the owners a fee of four hundred pieces of the indigenous money; and finally that the strangers shall agree to give up their name and adopt the customs and identity of the native Sengele—particularly that they shall no longer mark their children with the Bolia tattoo, and they shall cease eating snakes and instead adopt the Sengele diet of frogs, cicadas, and winged ants. In the sequel, although life returned to normal when Kengulu agreed to these terms, some time later three of his sister's sons died shortly upon acceding to the paramount chieftainship. The fourth and youngest, suspecting Yanganga was the cause of his brothers' deaths and in order to avoid his own, demanded six wives from the native Sengele and had eleven children by them. One day, on assembling the notables of the Bolia and Sengele, he told them he could now die in peace, since Yanganga could no longer kill off his descendants: for his children, if Bolia by their father, were Sengele by their mother. He commanded the descendants of each of his six sons to take the chieftainship in turn. Such is the origin of the six clans that now succeed each other in power.

The story is ideal-typical down to the assimilation of the strangers by the native people, thus producing a cultural unity marked by the enduring tradition of an ethnic difference. But since such narratives among BaKongo as well as BaSengele "are evidently political not historical material," MacGaffey would dismiss the stranger-kingship thus described, not necessarily as untrue, but as historically irrelevant. The arguments differ from those of Thornton but they come to a similar banishment of stranger-kingship to a historical limbo of something like false consciousness; or more precisely their resolution to a redundant expression in discourse of other realities, even if disguised. For MacGaffey, what is substantially and logically at issue in the Bolia case is political: it is not historical content and should not be considered as such, but a useful or interested way that the people talk politics. Not that MacGaffey, as an exceptional ethnographer, is unaware of the enduring temporality, hence continuing historical effects, of charter traditions. He certainly recognizes this historicity, although he does not theorize it, and particularly in the matter of stranger-kingship, he effectively dismisses it. In the matter of the origin traditions of Kongo clans, however, MacGaffey writes:

> Because the narratives and related representations discussed so far refer to the
> "past" history of the clans, it may be thought that the way of thinking they em-
> body belongs to "the past" in the European sense, to tradition rather than to the
> present. Kongo conceptions of relations between European[s] and Africa show
> the same structure in contemporary thought and action, however, and discon-
> certingly incorporate elements of "the past," that is, of events that European
> thought considers over and done with. (1986: 61–62)

Add BaKongo to the peoples who find themselves in history. There will be occasion to again consider MacGaffey's position in these matters in the concluding
section of this essay. Suffice here to notice that since the foreign origin of the
Kongo dynasty has no existential standing of its own, the complex of relationships that are structurally entailed in stranger-kingship get lost to the cultural
order at the same time they are denied historical force. Although MacGaffey
(n.d.) freely allows that stranger-kingships could possibly have happened, he is
at some pains to doubt it. He cites the ubiquity of stranger-king origin legends
in Central Africa, and the fact that the Kongo version of the conflicts among
royals that lead to the founding of the dynasty are the matrilineal inverse of the
patrilineal Luba version, as if these were loose tales that easily diffused around.
Aside from the fact that being commonplace is not necessarily evidence of trivi-
ality, structural transformations of this kind among interacting societies—the
dialectic processes usually described as "symmetrical inversions" or "complementary schismogenesis"—are well-known modes of cultural production.[20]

In any event, what MacGaffey writes in another context about the resemblances of Kongo and Luba stranger-king traditions and rituals suggests
that considerably more is at stake than a complementary contrast in dynastic politics—although again, "these stories are not historical but sociological"
(2003: 11). This discussion is focused on the Rubicon moment, the crossing of
the river by the founding hero, initiating a new sociopolitical order. MacGaffey
is primarily comparing Kongo clan traditions of such crossings to Luba royal
traditions, thus little things to big things, but all the same the new order introduced in either case is culturally total and spiritually empowered:

> Stories on the grand scale describe transitions, often across a river, leading to
> the settlement of a new country. These stories are not historical but sociological,

---

20. See Bateson (1935, 1958) and Lévi-Strauss (1995).

sketching an ideally ordered society . . . . All this closely resembles, though not on an epic scale, the stories among Luba-related peoples in eastern Congo of heroes who come from across the river to introduce civilization as right marriage, right eating and right government [de Heusch 1982a]. In both east and west, the elsewhere from which the king comes is a land of spirits (Bupemba, Mpemba, Upemba), although it may be identified with a geographical location. It is a place visible to diviners in the reflecting surface of the water; in the form of a cemetery, a cave, a grove or a pool, it is a place of testing and investiture for chiefs and other persons whose special powers are signified by white kaolin clay, *mpemba*. The initiation rituals of chiefs retrace and recapitulate the migration stories of the myths. In much more detail than it is possible to recount here, Kongo [clan] chiefship rituals read like a reduced or provincial version of those found among Luba. (2003: 11)

Once across the river, the stranger-hero creates a dual cosmopolitical order of rulers and subjects whose respective identifications with outside transcendent powers and those of the local earth is existential, a difference of being. For Igala, J. S. Boston (1968: 15) speaks of a system of dual sovereignty:

In this political system rights of political sovereignty, in the widest geographical sense, are vested in large-scale clans of high rank, whilst rights of local sovereignty are vested in small-scale localized clans who are often regarded as being the "landowners" of the areas in which they are settled. The myth represents the basic division of functions and attributes in origin to the introduction of notions of aristocratic rank from other kingdoms with whom the Igala have been in historic contact.

Directly or indirectly, the indigenous people have an ancestral identification with the land: usually because their ancestors first occupied it and in death still do, being buried there; or else because their ancestors, having made a bond with the original spirits, continue to intercede with these ancient sources of fertility. As we have seen, whether the new order is established by conquest, peacefully, or by a combination of the two, the foreign rulers invariably forbear from appropriating the land as such, pretending neither to a proprietary claim to the soil nor to a spiritual relation to the ancestral sources of its fertility. Indeed it is reported of Mossi that their concept of elite power was foreign to that of work: "Their power is defined as the element of completion which achieves the construction of society after the world has been transformed by work" (Izard 1985: 14).

This cosmopolitical order is at the same time a dual system of political economy integrated by the dominant foreign aristocracy—whose constitution of the totality is founded on the occupation and work of their native predecessors. Even in the greater galactic polities such as the "empire" of the Luba, however, the foreign aristocracy's unification and dominance of the whole left considerable economic autonomy to the indigenous parts. "The political authority, as instituted by the leading family from the east, was a kind of superstructure, uniting and fusing the scattered groups living between the Lomani and Lualaba [Rivers]. The first occupants of the country remained the real owners of the soil" (Theuws 1983: 9). Accordingly, for all the tributary claims of Luba chiefs over the underlying population, they yielded precedence in the control of resources to the local earth priests:

> In this way they are acknowledging a fundamental problem: the Empire's political regime did not control village land. Only the village earth-priest could lay direct claim on the produce of village land, because he was the descendant of the village's founding ancestral spirit, who protected the land. (Reefe 1981: 46)

The dual economy was at the same time a division of spiritual labors. In an article entitled "The king comes from elsewhere," Luc de Heusch (1991:113), commenting on Alfred Adler's (1982) excellent ethnography of the Mundang of Chad, observes that the ruler alone can "assume command of the universe for the benefit of the group as a whole." A descendant of a royal immigrant from a former kingdom on the Benue, a great hunter who came in from the wild as a "sacred monster," the Mundang king "controls fecundity and fertility through the power he exercises over the sky" (ibid.: 114). Accordingly, the sovereign deploys his authority "in a space outside the jurisdiction of the [native] clans where, with the help of his men, he secures wealth by violence without interfering in the affairs of the clans" (ibid.). However, no one has such extensive powers over the earth, which belongs in severalty and on an equal basis to the autochthonous clans, each of whom has made a pact with the spirits of the area. Or as the Tale elder said to Rattray (1932, 2: 344), "We were once owners of the lands; since the scorpion Europeans came we have entered into holes. You have burned our bows and arrows; we once were keepers of the moons [i.e., custodians of the festival calendar for prospering the land]."

Linked to the ancestral sources of the earth's fertility, and often, by the same ancestral token, to human fertility, the autochthonous people's claims to the land had survived intact through the centuries of domination by rulers of foreign origin before European invaders changed the conditions of colonization. So do the typical narratives of kingship origins say—to which the normal relations of power, production, property, and piety correspond. In a well-known tradition of the Ouagadougou Mossi as recounted by Elliott Skinner (1964: 15), the conquest of the native Ninise villagers by a Mossi hero consisted of inducing or forcing them back to their villages from the forest into which they had fled, in order to resume the sacrifices to the local earth. As a corollary, many of the Mossi ruling lineages, the *nakombse*, are land-poor. Similarly, Jacques Lombard relates that the seminomadic Wasangari "conquerors" of the Bariba peoples of Borgu had little interest in land, as distinct from pillaging or otherwise exacting its fruits from the indigenous producers. What Lombard writes of the system of powers established in the formation of the Borgu states, the contrast he describes between the Wasangari control of the native people and the native people's control of the land, is typical of the political economics of stranger-kingship: "The conquest brought no impairment of the aboriginal rights over their land. The ruling aristocracy leaves the power of disposition to the Masters of the Soil, with all the prerogatives pertaining thereto . . . . The principle was that power should be exercised directly over men but not over land" (1965: 185). Lombard goes on to say, however, that considering the toll the Wasangari exacted on the people's output, they might as well have owned the land.

Maybe so, but that is not an intrinsic condition of stranger-king systems. Highly mobile ruling groups such as the Avongara of the Azande kingdoms exacted minimal tributes from the various peoples they subdued—one is reminded of Owen Lattimore's well-known observation that "the pure nomad is the poor nomad"—as is also true of small-scale stranger-kingships such as Alur (Evans-Pritchard 1971: 33; Southall [1956] 2004). What is invariant, rather, is the principle as succinctly enunciated by Nyoro people: "The Mukama [the King] rules the people, the clans rule the land" (Beattie 1971: 167). Referring to the Namoo chiefs of the Tallensi, R. S. Rattray writes: "'The people belong to me, the land belongs to the Tendaana [the Tale earth priest].' Is a statement I have repeatedly heard made" (1932, 1: xv). Likewise, it is said of Bemba chiefs that they count their wealth in people, not in land (Richards 1961: 245). In Loango, neighboring kingdom and quondam tributary of Kongo, the king does not possess the land and cannot dispossess anyone else. Divided into diverse territories, the land is the property of the spirits of nature. The king gets his authority from their representatives, dwarfs and albinos, and from the high priest of the realm (de Heusch 2000: 54). Michel Izard provides an exemplary summary of such dualism in relation to the Yatenga Mossi:

> The bipartition of the society of the kingdom . . . between "people of power" (the descendants of the Mossi conquerors) and "people of the land" (the autochthons) corresponds to two regimes of authority, the first which concerns men, the second which concerns land. One of the most fundamental functions of the king is to be the guarantor of the "alliance" between the power and the land. (1990: 71)

These economic distinctions are spiritual endowments, amounting to a complementary relation between the transcendent powers introduced by the stranger-king and the local powers of the earth inherited by the native people, as integrated by the former through his domestication by the latter. Where the native people mediate relations to the local earth through the ancestral sources of its productivity—or else to the earth spirits through their ancestors—the ruling aristocracy mediates the relations to the encompassing realm of natural and cultural resources, from which it derives material benefits by virtue of its own foreign identity and marvelous powers. Randall Packard provides a fine example in his ethnography of the East African Bashu:

> Of particular importance to the well-being of the land are the ancestors who first cleared the land of forest, for in so doing they established an important bond with the land. Their cooperation, obtained through the invocations of their descendants, is critical for the performance of any action involving land . . . . The Bantu view chieftainship, *bwami*, within the context of [a] wider view of man's relation to nature. The chief, *mwami w'ambita*, is the primary mediator between the world of the homestead and the world of the bush. Through the *mwami*, the mediating role of rainmakers, healers of the land, priests of earth spirits and ancestors are correlated and the forces of nature domesticated. The *mwami* is also ultimately responsible for separating the uncontrolled and dangerous forces of the bush from the world of the homestead. (1981: 29–30)

Motivated by their respective natures and powers, the native-descended subjects and their foreign-derived rulers are engaged in distinct and complementary economic spheres, coordinated largely through the distributive activities of the latter as funded largely by the productive activities of the former. Insofar as the ruling aristocracy "achieves the construction of society after the world has been transformed by work," the indigenous people are pretty much the working class in stranger-kingdoms, particularly in the primary sectors of agriculture, fishing, and hunting, as well as most craft production (the magical art of blacksmithing usually excepted). But then, "the clans rule the land": as the "owners" of the land by ancestral right, the subjugated working class of the stranger-kingdom have a monopoly control of the primary means of production. Moreover, as organized primarily through kin relationships, their production is oriented principally to their own domestic consumption. But where the indigenous people's relations to the land are proprietary and productive, those of the ruling aristocracy are tributary and extractive. The ruling class appear on the scene of production *post messem*, after the harvest, to levy a toll on its output, both in the products and in manpower they would put to their own uses. Their own uses have to do with the accumulation, strategic redistribution, and conspicuous consumption of circulating wealth with the aim of enhancing their power by the direct domination of people—rather than by control of people's means of existence. They are concerned with exchange and distribution more than production; with riches and sumptuary values rather than means of subsistence; with the returns of tribute and trade, and the booty of war rather than agriculture. The mobile wealth of this sphere—monies, luxury cloth, salt, metals, ivory, cattle, slaves, etc.—is generally of foreign or wild origins and ensouled with the vital potencies of these otherworlds, just as are the rulers who manifest such powers by acquiring and distributing them (Helms 1993; Sahlins 2014). As Beti-Fang people say: "We made war in order to have wealth, to have wives and slaves." Here "the very idea of power . . . involved the acquisition of the magical force of another person through warfare, that is, through capture" (Guyer 1993: 257). Considering that the native people *receive* their harvests by one or another form of spiritual bestowal, while the ruling elite *appropriate* their wealth by one or another form of predation, then our notion of "production" hardly applies at all to these societies (see chapter 1).

In any case, it need not be supposed that stranger-kingship as such represents a "determination by the economic basis." Not only because the subordinate class controls the primary means of production, but because, as Southall put it for Alur, the economic powers of ruling chiefs are insufficient to account for the concept of their authority. "Nothing more strikingly reveals the binding force of the concept of chiefship," he wrote ([1956] 2004: 190), "than the inability of the requisite material basis to confer its real essence." Besides Alur, there are stranger-chiefdoms and kingdoms large and not so large where the structural differentiation between the alien rulers and their autochthonous subjects is disproportionate to their minimal powers of economic domination and exploitation. Azande again, as well as Anuak, Lovedu, Shilluk, Tallensi, Nyakyusa, Moundang: all come to mind as instances of a radical differentiation of the superstructure unsupported by the inequalities of the infrastructure. Still, if Marx doesn't quite work here, Georg Simmel's classic essay on the "The stranger" is a fair description not only of the dualism of stranger-kingship, but also of the structural constraints that distinguish the localized native owners, connected in substance to soil, from the mobile stranger-traders and traffickers operating in an encompassing sphere:

> The stranger is by nature no "owner of the soil"—soil not only in the physical, but also in the figurative sense of a life-substance which is fixed, if not in a point of space, at least in an ideal point of the social environment. Although in more intimate relations [like marriage with the daughter of the natives], he may develop all kinds of charm and significance, he is not an "owner of the soil." Reduction to intermediate trade, and often (as though sublimated from it) to pure finance, gives him the specific character of *mobility*. If mobility takes place with a closed group, it embodies that synthesis of nearness and distance which constitutes the formal position of the stranger. For the fundamentally mobile person comes in contact, at one time or another, with every individual, but is not organically connected, through established ties of kinship, loyalty and occupation, with any single one [—he is encompassing and transcendent]. (Wolff 1950: 403–4, original emphasis)

SERIAL STRANGER-KINGSHIP

> I uncovered an increasing number of first occupants and former chiefs, to the point that it began to appear that there were as many first occupants among the Bashu as there were New Englanders who claim came over on the Mayflower, and as many chiefs as subjects.
>   Randall M. Packard, *Chiefship and cosmology*

Probably the majority of precolonial African states, including Kongo, have known serial-kingship histories, sometimes involving several successive foreign dynasties. For the most part they were nevertheless organized in the classic binary terms of "native" and "stranger": that is, by recursively categorizing all earlier regimes, their rulers and subjects alike, as native "owners" relative to the latest foreign dynasts. The historical complexities were systematically recuperated by the master dualism of native owners and foreign rulers—if not without some residues of contradiction. For insofar as the latest dualism did not cancel the earlier ones, the effect was a polity structured as a series of encompassing iterations of the same structural duality.

To this effect, Michel Izard writes of the Yatenga Mossi: "The duality Mossi/People of the Earth can be interpreted as the last of a series of homologous distinctions of the type conquerors/autochthons" (1985: 18). The Mossi conquerors had deposed of the Fulse rulers of the earlier stranger-kingdom centered in Lurum, from which the realm took its name; whereupon the Fulse became "People of the Earth" or "Sons of the Soil" in the kingdom of their successors. Moreover, the Fulse leaders took on the functions of "Priests of the Earth" or "Masters of the Earth" throughout the Mossi realm, those of highest rank becoming the head priests of the Mossi state—a recurrent pattern in stranger-kingships, as will be seen. The Fulse rulers of the ancient regime are said to have imposed themselves on a still earlier population of Dogon, who, as original inhabitants, were "Masters of the Earth" relative to their Fulse overlords. This original duality was for the most part unrecognized by the Mossi, who would reduce both the old Fulse rulers and their Dogon subjects to the generic identity of native "Fulse" or "Ninise." Yet the Dogon did not entirely lose their identity or prestige as indigenous earth priests in the new Mossi order. In the areas they shared with Fulse, they still functioned in that capacity relative to the old Fulse nobility, and as the original occupants of the land, they maintained a reputation for great spiritual powers throughout the Mossi kingdom.

In his rich works on the Kazembe kingdom in the Luapulu Valley, Ian Cunnison (1951, 1957, 1959) describes a somewhat more complex history of successive dynasties similarly folded into the binary opposition of native subjects and foreign rulers. When the latest "conquerors" led by the Lunda hero Kazembe took over the country, the erstwhile Shilla rulers of Bemba derivation together with their own original subjects, the Bwilile people of Luba derivation, collectively became the indigenous "owners" of the land, at least from the kingdom-wide perspective of Lunda. The Bwilile had displaced the original pygmy population in the hunting and fishing heartland of Kilwe Island, and they became "owners" when the Bemba under their chief Nkuba took over the country.

Indeed, in a process of ethnogenesis typical of stranger-king formations, they became "Bwilie" under the Bemba occupation, even as the Bemba were now known as "Shilla." When the Lunda arrived, the Bemba/Shilla leader, titled Nkuba by positional succession, was made the "chief wife" of the conqueror, Kazembe, as well as the paramount "owner" of the kingdom land. However, this did not erase the earlier historical distinction between Shilla rulers and native Bwilile owners, which continued to function within the areas occupied by these peoples. So while Shilla together with Bwilile were owners relative to the Lunda chiefs, Shilla were chiefs relative to Bwilile owners. The master dualism thus accommodated a triad of ethnic groups, which, moreover, were broadly distinguished in function: the Lunda as rulers, the Shilla as fishers, and the Bwilile as ritual experts. "The first of the annual ceremonies to 'unlock the fish' in many of the lagoons shows that there are Bwilile about" (Cunnison 1959: 202). But then the Bwilie's ritual knowledge had come from their autochthonous pygmy predecessors. The overall effect is a complex polity constituted by the interplay of complementary and opposed relations of precedence: complementary in regard to the control of land and people, but opposed in regard to the virtues of autochthony and alterity. In the event, the rule over society as a whole in serial stranger-kingdoms passes to the later and greater of the several peoples, while the ritual authority over the land devolves upon the earlier and lesser of these peoples. Paradigmatic history.

Also relevant to Kongo, when one important stranger-kingdom replaces another of similar magnitude, the earlier realm leaves certain residual marks on the organization of its successor. For insofar as the quondam rulers are now the dominant owners and priest-chiefs of the new order—the way the Shilla under Nkuba became the primary owners under the Lunda kingship of Kazembe while remaining secondary rulers, as it were, of the enduring older regime —the subject population is more broadly and centrally organized than the congeries of small-scale, autonomous communities that make up the indigenous stratum of an elementary stranger-kingdom. Serial stranger-kingship structures do vary, depending on more or less contingent conditions: whether the immigrant rulers come with their own native subjects, like the Ambonu complement of the Avongara rulers of Azande kingdoms or the Bakabilo priests of the Bemba, for example; or whether the latest dynasty is centered in the same capital as the ancient one, as in the successive dynastic occupations of Mbanza Kongo or the West African kingdom of Bussa in Borgu (Nigeria). For that matter, Borgu itself, as a multikingdom region of six major principalities, rather resembles the regional configuration of polities referenced in the narratives of Ntinu Wene's advent (Lombard 1965; Stewart 1993). A brief aperçu of the Bussa kingdom offers further clues to the Kongo.

The Borgu peoples are collectively known as "Bariba," itself apparently a generic term for the various Voltaic speakers who comprised the principal native chiefs of the earth in the latest precolonial regimes. Together with Yoruba, Mandingo, and other custodians of the earth, the Bariba are said to have arrived in Borgu as hunters and to have once ruled in various areas. The historic kings who displaced them were descendants of the legendary Kisra, the enemy of the prophet in Arabia, who himself (or else his son) led the mounted warrior aristocracy known as Wasangari (or Wangara) westward into Borgu from Bornu. The Wasangari kings first settled at Bussa, whence certain of their descendants dispersed to found their own domains—among which Bussa remains superior for its antiquity, although surpassed in size and power by others, particularly Nikki. The complex hierarchy at Bussa of priestly owners-cum-former rulers is indicative of the process by which the recursive deployment of these identities in serial stranger-kingdoms generates native officials of wide authority in the state, the latest owners especially exercising temporal functions as well as acting as major priests of the realm. As Marjorie Stewart explained:

> Even in an earlier era the same processes had been unfolding. Before the arrival of the Kisra rulers, the priests of the earth or owners of the land, when they belonged to a group coming from elsewhere, also acquired a greater degree of political power and control over a larger territory than had previously been the case of earlier priests. (1993: 127)

> The most important officials at Bussa were the kingmakers, who, apart from the addition of the Imam in recent years, consisted of the custodians of the land and priests of the earth, whose ancestors ruled over the area in pre-Kisra times. (1993: 176)

Since these prominent priest-chiefs ministered to the divine dead rulers effectively in the same way they ministered to the sacred living king, there is in fact little point in differentiating their temporal from their spiritual functions. The four greatest priests and owners of the earth at Bussa had various duties and privileges in relation to the kingship: they acted as counselors to the ruler; electors and installers of his heir; stewards of the king's household; keepers of the

royal regalia; officiants at royal sacrifices; and, not least, they were in charge of
what may be called the "second installation," the royal funerary rites, whereupon
they repeated their earthly role as priests in relation to the entombed kings.
Of these native custodians, "the principal chief of the earth at Bussa" was the
Bakarabunde—whose title appropriately translates as "The Old Man Who Was
There"—with powers such as to evoke notices of him as the "prime minister"
of the kingdom. Mandingo by origin, his ancestors were the previous rulers of
Bussa, the ones who gave Kisra permission to settle and thereupon assumed
the status of native owners. The priest-chiefs subordinate to the Bakarabunde
evidently represent several successive ethnic regimes, and whereas they appear
to be ranked according to how recently they arrived, they are notably associated with the cults of the earliest gods, particularly the pre-Kisra great god
Lashi. Thus. second to the Bakaraburde was the head priest of the earth, the
Badaburde, who, besides being in charge of the burial of the king, offered the
sacrifices in times of general crises to Lashi. Likewise, for the third of these
priest-chiefs, the Beresoni: described as the priest to the owners of the land, in
a sense priest to the priests, he officiates at an ancient shrine of Lashi and other
pre-Kisra spirits at Dogon Gari. The god Lashi and this shrine in particular—to
which the Bussa king also sends an annual sacrifice—are linked to certain of the
oldest ethnic groups of the kingdom, notably the Kamberi people, who speak
a Yoruba dialect, and also certain Dogon clans. As this is a shrine of the native
owners dedicated to the ancient god, what is characteristically at stake in the
annual sacrifice is the fecundity of the earth; for until the Bussa king's sacrificial
ram is offered, the chief of Dogon Gari did not send the season's yam crop.
Stewart (ibid.: 75) observes: "Many of the ancient shrines and spiritual places
in Borgu are associated with the Kamberi and it is believed as other groups settled in the area, the last to arrive submitted to the sacred rituals of the earliest
inhabitants." This helps account for the report (ibid.: 194) that the pre-Kisra regime was actually dominated by two "families": not only the Bakarabundi at old
Bussa, but in the outlying village of Monai, the group headed by one Bamoide,
who, though of Kamberi origin, was known as the "brother" of the Bakarbundi
(of Mandingo origin). Accordingly, the prominence of the Kamberi and Lashi,
representing the autochthonous people and their own earthly powers, is another
form of the tendency to reduce the complexities of serial kingship orders to the
master dichotomy of foreign rulers and native owners—which is also to say, to
the structural chiasmus formed by the interaction of the complementary and
opposed values of autochthony and alterity.

ORIGINS OF THE KONGO KINGDOM

The structures and traditions of serial stranger-kingship in the Kongo region were much like those of Borgu, although, so far as I am aware, they have largely gone unremarked as such by the early chroniclers and the later scholars alike. The issue of the integration of successive foreign dynasties has been foreclosed notably as it is presented as a discrepancy between competing versions of Kongo history, rather than a temporal sequence synthesized as a structural palimpsest. The reports of an original BaKongo migration from the interior, beyond the Kwango River, are generally taken as disposable exceptions to the dominant tradition of Ntinu Wene's coming from beyond the Congo. Or else the serial kingship is recognized but not conceptualized, as though it were of no particular significance that Ntinu Wene incorporated several older kingdoms in the course of the epic journey to his own. In the climactic episode of this charter tradition, also often widely noted and little theorized, Ntinu Wene submits to and is installed by a Chief-Priest of the Earth, Nsaku ne Vunda, in the ancient capital of Mbanza Kongo—the characteristic function of the native owner whose own ancestors were once the rulers. For the most part, however, everything happens in the Europeans' accounts as if they were content to follow the authoritative discourse of the latest Kongo powers-that-be in reducing the perduring structures of successive stranger-kingdoms to the master dichotomy of immigrant rulers and autochthonous subjects by conflating all previous regimes in the latter category. As, for example, the early eighteenth-century account by Bernardo de Gallo:

> It is necessary to know that there are two peoples in this kingdom. One arriving as immigrants and the other truly of the land, the latter composed of those who submitted or subjugated and the other the dominant ones. The dominant ones came with king Lukeni [aka Ntinu Wene] and they were called Essikongo or Congolese nobles, inhabitants of the royal city. The others, the subjects, are those who are found in the lands and provinces of the kingdom, and those called Akkata, Alumba or peasants and rustics. (Cited in Randles 1968: 57)

Some years earlier, the Capuchin missionary Cavazzi noted a similar distinction, also observing that the BaKongo did no productive work, leaving that to slaves; although rather than completing society, they passed their days smoking (ibid.: 57, 59). In any event, the countryside at that time also had some aristocratic inhabitants, including those from previous regimes as well as Essikongo bearing the graded titles of European nobility in charge of various districts. Taken together with the ethnic diversity of the underlying population, the collapse of this complexity into the binary opposition of immigrant rulers and native subjects is the structural condensation I am talking about. Among the anthropologists, Balandier (1968) alone takes note of two distinct incursions of immigrant rulers and suggests they refer to different historical periods, but otherwise the general scholarly opinion follows the dualist model—which is no doubt the ethnographic reality. "The conqueror [Ntinu Wene] created a new system when he founded the kingdom of Kongo," writes Kajsa Ekholm, "but he remained a foreigner. The land did not belong to his forefathers and for that reason he was dependent on the first occupants and primarily on their representative, Nsaku ne Vunda" (1972: 155; cf. Vansina 1992; de Heusch 2000).

By contrast, a number of chroniclers of Kongo charter traditions since the seventeenth century have been reporting one or another of two fundamentally different versions of the kingdom origins, with different casts of characters migrating from different homelands across different rivers. Indeed there are many modern groups who claim to have founded the old capital of Mbanza Kongo, let alone those who claim to have originated there, but the widespread traditions of an origin from the east across the Kwango River and from the north across the Congo (Zaïre) have the warrant of early as well as recent documentation. As can happen in serial stranger-kingships, the dynastic stories may get conflated such that elements of one appear, more or less incongruously, in traditions of the other. Based on information collected in 1665, the account of Ntinu Wene's advent by Cavazzi is one of the most informative narratives on the origins of the reigning dynasty, except that instead of Vungu it situates the hero's point of departure as "Coimba in the region of Kwango": that is, east of the Kongo kingdom. The Jesuit Mateus Cardoso, writing in 1622, got Ntinu Wene's homeland as Vungu ("Bungu") alright, but he also recorded the names of six earlier rulers not found on any other extant king list. What these anomalies evidently represent is the subjacent tradition of a prior kingship that had indeed come across the Kwango. Consider, for example, a text of 1680 by the soldier-historian Antonio de Oliveiro de Cadornega:

> Concerning the origin of this kingdom of the Congo, the old conquerors of Angola testified that the *mexicongo* nation was always reputed to be foreign . . . that they had come from the interior to dominate the kingdom, just as we say of the Romans . . . . In that way this *mexicongo* people came from the interior

and expanded. They came from the lordly lands of *Congo de amulaca*, [and] took possession of the powerful kingdom of the Congo, the natives of that kingdom being the *Ambundos*, of another stock. (Cited in Paiva Manso 1877: 266)

As Amulaka extended considerably beyond the Kwango, this is something completely different.

Yet it is not completely different from certain legends recorded in the late nineteenth and early twentieth centuries. Not to forget that Ntinu Wene's own story involves contacts with previous regimes, including the one at the capital of Mbanza Kongo, which he is otherwise supposed to have founded. The Protestant missionary Karl Laman, writing of Nsundi province, says the eponymous Sundi people "had immigrated and established a great kingdom before the foundation of the Congo" (1953–68, 1: 1). In one version of the kingdom origins, the story he reported is much the same as Vungu tradition, with Ntinu Wene (aka Lukeni) as the main protagonist, except that the river he crosses is the Kwango and the relations he kills for not paying the toll are his brother-in-law and the latter's wife (1957: 137).[21] Laman was convinced in general that the people came from across the Kwango, as indeed the tradition current among them was "our ancestors came from the East" (1953,1: 10). In this regard, the traditions of an original Bantu kingdom in the Congo established by migrants from the right bank of the Kwango River collected by the Jesuit missionary J. Van Wing (1959) are particularly suggestive for their resonance with local references to ancient kings reported in the sixteenth and seventeenth centuries. From the Bankanu people, for example, who inhabit the region watered by several tributaries of the Kwango on the Congo side: "Their principal town was Mbansa Kongo, situated at the angle formed by the Kwilu and its tributary the Tawa. They say that their Kongo was founded by a great chief, Na Kongo, when he crossed the Kwango" (ibid.: 38). Or again, from the Inkisi region:

The Bakongo of the Inkisi region still know that their ancestors came from the Kwango, and it is from the Kwango that they left to found Kongo di Ntotila, or

---

21. Killing his brother-in-law is not radically different from Ntinu Wene's killing his father's pregnant sister. In all probability the victim was not his sister's husband as the wife in question would then be his sister; given the BaKongo preference for father's sister's daughter marriage, the brother-in-law was more likely his father's sister's son. Hence as in the Ntinu Wene exploit as reported by Cavazzi, the principal victim was the hero's paternal affine.

San Salvador [that is, the "Kongo of the King," San Salvador being the renamed capital, Mbanza Kongo]. Most traditions and legends known to the masses do not go back beyond San Salvador to the origin-place of the population. But several chiefs distinctly affirmed to me that the first chiefs of the tribe came from the Kwango. (1959: 38)

Then there are the complementary accounts from clans in Mpangu province that trace their genesis to a dispersal from Mbanza Kongo ordered by this Na Kongo, the king of Kwango origins. From these several sources, Van Wing (ibid.: 40) constructs an alternate history to the Vungu tradition, a narrative of migration and kingdom formation under the aegis of Na Kongo, "the principal chief of the Bakongo clans," and his successors of the same title and distinction.

Beginning with the crossing of the Kwango and the initial residence on the Kwilu in the northeast, the story takes Na Kongo and his people through the Congo heartland to the ancient capital of Mbaza Kongo in Mpemba province, leaving people along the way to form dependent chiefdoms (see fig. 1). That is how the important Mbata province was generated, including certain Kwilu and Inkisi settlements under a ruler who acknowledged the suzereignty of Na Kongo. By the tradition, Mpangu province was constituted in response to the growth of population in Mbanza Kongo, which prompted the king, Na Kongo, to dispatch a levy of people from each resident clan to other areas on a mission of conquest. This dispersal of ruling groups from Mbanza Kongo is repeated in the traditions of Ntinu Wene and the Vungu dynasty; but what is also paradigmatically relevant in the early historical chronicles is that a set of interdependent kingdoms and chiefdoms centered in Mbanza Kongo preexisted the installation of the Vungu kings in the same sacred center. Moreover, in their notices of local traditions, these sixteenth- and seventeenth-century records correspond closely to significant elements of the Na Kongo traditions that Van Wing collected much later from much the same places.

With regard to Na Kongo's initial residence in the Kwilu Valley, there is the 1664 text of Cavazzi relating that "in Esquila [Nsi a Kwilu in the Kwilu River Valley . . .] they revere a site hidden deep in the forest, which by ancient tradition was the residence of the first kings." Cavazzi was told that anyone who looked upon the site would die (in Thornton 2001: 109–10).[22] The Kwilu

---

22. A descendant of the Kwilu rulers came to the Kongo throne in 1568 as Alvaro I. It may be this was a reprisal of the ancient Kwango kingship. The argument the other

sites noted by Van Wing were in the domain of the ruler of Mbata (the Mani Mbata), whose incumbent figured prominently in the Ntinu Wene tradition as the latter's maternal uncle. In the Lopes/Pigafetta work of 1591, the Mbata ruler is described as a stranger-king in his own right—as might be expected from the narrative of the Na Kongo incursion: "The Prince of Batta has many Lords under him, and the natives are called Monsobos, their language being understood in Congo. They are a much ruder tribe than the Mocicongo [the Bakongo rulers], and slaves coming from them prove extremely obstinate" ([1591] 1881: 62). Regarding the information gathered by Van Wing of the colonization of the Mpangu area by Na Kongo's people, a passage in Pigafetta indicates that the Mpangu ruler of the sixteenth century indeed belonged to the "oldest nobility" of the kingdom: "The present governor is called Don Francisco Manipango, and belongs to the oldest nobility of the chiefs of Congo. In councils of state he is always present, being already an old man and of great prudence, and for fifty years he has governed this province without any outbreaks" (ibid.: 60). The Mpangu notable's political functions in the historic Kongo regime are consistent with the typical role of former rulers in serial stranger-kingships.

Finally and more recently comes strong linguistic evidence of a pre-Ntinu Wene dynasty from across the Kwango in an article, "On the origin of the royal Kongo title ngangula," by Koen Bostoen, Odjas Ndonda Tshiyavi, and Gilles-Maurice de Schryver.[23] Of this "traditional king's title," the authors write:

> Thanks to a distinctive diachronic sound change, it is even possible to locate quite precisely the term's origin within the KiKongo dialect continuum. Its provenance gives new credibility to an earlier but dis carded hypothesis situating the origins of the Kongo kingdom in the eastern part of the lower Congo, somewhere in-between the Inkisi and Kwango rivers. (2013: 54)

In contrast to the dominant Ntinu Wene narrative, the authors would accordingly revive the "older and alternative scenario [in which] the Kongo kingdom was founded by conquerors who subjugated an autochthonous population

---

way around, that Alvaro's reign motivated the Kwango tradition, would not seem persuasive, as the Kwango, at that time the territory of the kingdom's Yaka enemies, would not be logically pertinent or politically desirable as a newly invented source of the kingship.

23. Many thanks to Cécile Fromont for bringing this work to my attention.

commonly recognized as Ambundu and came from region known as *Kongo dia Nlaza* between the Inkisi and Kwango Rivers" (ibid.: 72). In this connection they cite a "highly relevant" notice from Montesarchio's account of his travels in 1650 though the eastern part of the Kongo kingdom and beyond. Here the ruler of a place called Elema styled himself "Grandfather of the King of Kongo": a title analogous to that of the Mbata ruler in the Ntinu Wene regime, a, the linguists correctly observe (ibid.: 73)—and which, as mother's father to the king, also signifies the founding marriage of the stranger-prince with the daughter of the native ruler. One need only add the linguists' reiterated assurance that the royal *ngangula* title "could only have originated in one specific region of the Kongo, i.e., east of the Inkisi River" (ibid.: 73).

Following Thornton's (2001: 104) translation of Pigafetta, Mbanza Kongo in Mpemba "was the center of the state of Congo and the origin of the Ancient Kings of the land where they were born." A priori, then, it would be highly unlikely that "the origin of the Ancient Kings" referred to Ntinu Wene, inasmuch as the Vungu tradition says Mbanza Kongo was already inhabited by the priest-chief of an older regime when Ntinu Wene arrived. By all evidence, the political configuration of the Kongo region when Ntinu Wene arrived was like Borgu in more ways than one. A galactic polity in a phase of decentralization, Borgu consisted of several independent kingdoms and chiefdoms acknowledging the nominal superiority of the original state of Bussa, founded by the famous Kisra, from whom the rulers of the others had derived. Recall also the Bakarakundi, "The Old Man Who Was There" in Bussa: the descendant of former rulers, who gave the immigrant warrior Kisra permission to settle, installed him in the kingship, and became "the principal chief of the earth" in the kingdom at large. Just so, in the Vungu tradition, Ntinu Wene came upon a congeries of autonomous principalities south of the Zaïre centered on Mbanza Kongo of sacred memory, where one Nsaku ne Vunda was established as "lord of the earth." Also known in the chronicles as Mani Vunda and Mani Cabunga, Nsaku ne Vunda was the descendant of former rulers, with kinship ties to the first inhabitants. There was a local political chief of Mbanza Kongo, but his title of Mani Pangalla evidently could not match the scale, prestige, or authority attending the Nsaku ne Vunda's hegemony over the earth—which would have reflected the past glory of Mbanza Kongo as the dominant center of the region as well as "the origin of the ancient kings." That Ntinu Wene came from a peripheral chiefdom to take over a declining galactic center is a process common enough in regional polities of this kind (Ekholm 1980, 1985b; J. Friedman 1992; chapter 6 in this volume). That Vungu had already accumulated considerable power under the reign of Ntinu Wene's father, Nimi a Nzima, as Thornton and Hilton have argued, seems likely in that the important Mbata king had accorded the Nimi a sister to wife. As previously noted, then, Ntinu Wene, who thereby combined the native and foreign kingly virtues, was destined to be immortalized as the conquering hero, even as the tradition of his fateful interaction with the indigenous priest-chief Nsaku ne Vunda would become the paradigmatic charter of the Kongo kingship.

Residing in Mbanza Kongo, the Nsaku ne Vunda was effectively the epitome of the quondam ruler become the priest-chief of the indigenous owners of the country. Under the cognate name of "Mani Cabunga," he is described in the anonymous, seventeenth-century *History of the Kongo kingdom* as "the Supreme Pontiff (speaking in our way)" among the Congo nobility. In Cuvelier's references to his powers, he was the intermediary between the living and the ancestors—who were "the real owners of the fields, the forests, the rivers, and the streams" (1946: 80). The Nsaku ne Vunda was the person to whom one appealed for help in all circumstances, on whose authority one planted and harvested, who had the magical powers of the hunt and the remedies for madness and convulsions; and although he himself did not reign in the country, neither could anyone who had not been recognized by him (ibid.: 15). We have encountered this kind of Kongo figure before: the *kitomi* who as priest-chief of the province installs the foreign governor from across the river—although not before humbling him into acknowledging the *kitomi*'s own precedence in the land (see above). "Considered by many as a god on earth, according to Cavazzi, the *kitomi* was the plenipotentiary of the heavens, and was offered the first fruits of every harvest" (Randles 1968: 39). In Hilton's generalized depiction: "The *kitomi* were described as the owners, masters, lords, or chiefs of the land and gods of the earth, seed, or region, and it was believed that . . . they could grant or withhold the rain, thereby making the world fecund or barren" (1985: 25).

By all evidence, then, Nsaku ne Vunda was the *kitomi* of Mbanza Kongo, and insofar as the earth priests of a region were hierarchically ordered (MacGaffey 1986: 195–97), he would be endowed with such powers on a scale commensurate with the ancient preeminence of Mbanza Kongo.[24] Hence his traditional

---

24. It is consistent that certain Nsaku people (*kanda*) claim pygmy ancestry, thus an association with the original inhabitants—in the maternal or paternal line? (Cuvelier 1946: 252).

and historical role as kingmaker: "It is certain, according to the documents as well as tradition, that Nsaku ne Vunda had the privilege of being the principal elector of the kings, of installing them, and of receiving the portion of the tribute rendered when they acceded" (Cuvelier 1946: 252). Nsaku ne Vunda shared the kingmaking privilege with others whose chiefly ancestors had also submitted to Ntinu Wene, notably the Mani Mbata or Nsaku Lau, and they continued in this office well into the Christian era. What had distinguished Nsaku ne Vunda as so-called "principal elector" is that he alone could proclaim the king-elect to the assembled Kongo nobility, hence his assent to the decision was deemed essential. And the reason for this distinction was that in so recognizing the king, the Nsaku ne Vunda reprised in historical practice the paradigmatic tradition of the inauguration of the Kongo dynasty at Mbanza Kongo, where his ancestor transferred the sovereignty to Ntinu Wene—although not before suitably humbling him. Like stranger-heroes elsewhere, Ntinu Wene was legitimated at the price of his domestication as a conqueror from the dangerous outside.

Ntinu Wene had defeated the overlord of Mbanza Kongo, the Mani Pangala, and was installed on a mountain some four leagues distant, where he divided his conquests among his followers. (I am following Cuvelier's [1946: 11ff.] recounting of the tradition, based largely on Cavazzi and the anonymous *History of the kingdom of the Congo*.) But because Ntinu Wene had failed to secure recognition of his authority from Nsaku ne Vunda, he now fell ill with convulsions. His people thereupon went to Mbanza Kongo and, bowing before Nsaku ne Vunda, pleaded with him for a cure: "Lord, we know that you are the elder, the one who first occupied this region, or in the expression of the country, the one who was first in the nostrils of the universe. Ntinu Wene has fallen into convulsions, make him calm." At first incensed, Nsaku ne Vunda protested against what he deemed an invasion, but he relented and agreed to accompany them to Ntinu Wene. Here the latter addressed him, saying: "You are the eldest among us. Strike me with the buffalo tail, that my convulsions may cease." Cuvelier explains the symbolism: the cure was the making of Ntinu Wene as king; striking with the tail of the buffalo stands for the sprinkling of the king-elect with lustral water in the royal installation ceremonies. Hence by this request, writes Cuvelier, Ntinu Wene recognized the authority of Nsaku ne Vunda, and implicitly confessed that the illness he suffered was due to his negligence of the indispensable formality of acquiring the consent of "the religious chief." Nsaku ne Vunda responded to the plea and sprinkled the Ntinu Wene with the water. "That is how we know, Congo people still say now, that in order for every king to rule, Nsaku ne Vundu must be present and strike with the tail of the buffalo or sprinkle the water. If Nsaku is not there, his [the would-be-king's] authority will not be recognized."

The reconciliation of the king and Nsaku ne Vunda was sealed by the usual contract of stranger-kingship: the marriage of the foreign hero with a daughter of the native authority, here Ntinu Wene with a daughter of Nsaku ne Vunda. According to a 1665 text, Ntinu Wene also ordered his followers to marry daughters of the native people, "nobles with nobles and commoners with commoners"—which again implies the presence of a distinctive, preexisting ruling group. His installation by the native chief of the earth accomplished, Ntinu Wene then left his mountain redoubt and settled in Mbanza Kongo. "He took the title of mani Kongo or ne Kongo, Lord of Kongo, from the name of the locality founded by the Nsaku clan." Reading from Cuvelier, this union between Ntinu Wene and Nsaku ne Vunda was instrumental in bringing about the voluntary incorporation of Mbata province in the Kongo kingdom. If so, the submission of Mbata would be further testimony of an ancient regime centered at Mbanza Kongo. In any event, as we know, the Mani Mbata (Nsaku Lau) now became the primary wife-giver to the king, providing a daughter to the inheritor of the crown, a practice still faithfully observed through the early seventeenth century. Also still observed were the powers of the Nsaku ne Vunda and the Mani Mbata in kingmaking and other respects. Both were "grandfathers" of the king in that their daughters' sons inherited the rule—Nsaku ne Vunda's grandchild originally and Mani Mbata's regularly; and the Mani Mbata was also the king's maternal uncle, as originally the brother of Ntinu Wene's mother. After the king, these two were the most important personages in the realm, although over time Christianity and the Mani Mbata's political support of the crown apparently made him the more prominent, albeit the Nsaku ne Vunda remained no less indispensable. For that matter, neither was the political chief of Mbanza Kongo, the Mani Pangala, forgotten: every year the title-holder mounted a ritual protest of Ntinu Wene's usurpation. Details are unknown to me; it would be interesting if the rituals again involved the submission of the foreign king to the native ruler as a condition of the submission of the native ruler to the foreign king.

In the matter of serial stranger-kingship, everything happens in the traditions and the historical texts as if the Nsaku ne Vunda and Nsaku Lau represented dispersed branches of the royal clan which previously ruled the central and eastern portions of the Ntinu Wene kingdom. As in the ideal-typical stranger-kingship pattern, these Nsaku notables of the ancient regime became the electors, councilors, and wife-givers of the historic Kongo dynasty. Cuvelier writes of the Nsaku under the new dispensation: "At Mbanza Kongo, the Nsakus (Nsaku ne Vunda and Nsaku Lau) occupied the highest rank. Among the Congolese the Nsaku clan is considered the oldest of the clans. Nsaku Lau, whose family governs Mbaka, is of royal blood. One can presume that the Nsakus were the principal councilors of the king" (1946: 305).[25] Not only are the royal Nsaku the oldest clan (relative to Essikongo latecomers), but according to Van Wing, the Nsaku Lau clan "is very widely spread through the Bakongo country" (1959: 32). That the Nsaku Lau in Mbata ruled a rustic people called "Monsobos" indicates they were stranger-kings in their own right. In sum, the Nsaku people, extending over the country they once ruled, exercised a certain residual sovereignty as a condition of the legitimacy they conveyed to their alien successors. Serial stranger-kingship.

HISTORIOGRAPHY (THE END)

Something must be said, then, for the distinctive ways that different peoples are the authors of their own histories. Particularly at issue are the people's ongoing re-creations of how their society came to be, in practice as well as discourse, thus endowing their charter traditions with a certain historicity. In this connection, it deserves reiteration that stranger-king structures are distinctively and inherently temporal. The entire cultural order, from its dual modes of production through its social and political and religious cults, is predicated on a diachronic narrative. Accordingly, like Maori, people in these societies find themselves in history. So it should not surprise that Ndembu accounts of their kingdom's origins are not one-off stories. And inasmuch as they are rehearsed in connection with the activities and relationships they underwrite, tradition and structure reciprocally affirm the truth of the other—or indeed, by way of awakened memories, they reproduce each other. Ian Cunnison observes of another kingdom of Lunda origin, the Kazembe realm of the Luapulu Valley: "The whole justification of the existence of the kingship and its customs is referred back to its origins in the state of [the Lunda ruler] Mwata Yamvo" (1959: 149). Similarly for Tallensi:

---

25. The councilor role would belong specifically to Nsaku Lau, supposing the report that after the installation of the king the Nsaku ne Vunda could not come into contact with the king was accurate and referred to the pre-Portuguese period.

> All that matters of the past which lies beyond the span of man's recollection lives on in the social structure, the ideology, the morality, and the institutions of today. These are palpable proofs of things that happened . . . "in the days of our forefathers and ancestors." (Fortes 1945: 24)

Nor was Kongo an exception. Speaking of Kongo matters such as war, the death of the king, and the royal installation, Balandier recounts: "At each decisive moment in the life of the kingdom, reinforcement was sought in a symbolic return to the origins, in a sort of communion in which the notables and the people were associated" (1968: 201). Although the deceived wisdom may have it that because so-called "mythical" charters are merely narrative justifications of the sociocultural order, they cannot be historically true, in practice it follows rather that because people put these foundational traditions into their ongoing relationships, they must be historically true. It's true because they do it, and they do it because it's true: society endures on such tautologies.

The big issue here is the status of "myth," its historiographic value, arising from the fact that in the received language of Western scholarship it denotes something fictional, whereas for the African peoples whose story it is, it is certainly true and frequently sacred. The effect can be a fateful disconnect: the people's sacred truth is the historian's axiomatic falsehood. Together with some historically minded anthropologists, historians seem especially prone to thus oppose "myth" to "historical reality." As, for example, Collins and Burns when writing of the rulers of certain Swahili city-states who trace their origins to Shiraz in Persia: "These assertions are more myth than historical reality" (2007: 103). For these Swahili, however, this *is* the historical reality upon which they are organized and in terms of which they act; and as it is truly their historical consciousness, it cannot simply be ignored as false consciousness.

Of course, not all historians are disposed to thus write off the distinctive ways that other peoples may know and make their history in favor of an archival determination of what actually happened—or, more often, what probably happened. As for anthropologists, the classic statement of the fallacy of myth was penned by their armchair ancestor, Sir James Frazer:

> By myths I understand mistaken explanations of phenomena, whether of human life or of external nature. Such explanations originate in that instinctive curiosity concerning the causes of things which at a more advanced stage of knowledge seeks satisfaction in philosophy and science, but being founded on ignorance and

misapprehension they are always false, for were they true they would cease to be myths. ([1921] 1976: xxvii)

Likewise well known, however, was the critique of Frazer and his like by the Africanist anthropologist William Bascom (1965). In the course of rescuing myths from Frazer's calumnies, Bascom offered a useful typology of three kinds of prose narrative: myth, legend, and folktale—and one mixed category, notably common in African societies, of "myth-legends." Concerned with superhuman persons and the origins of the world, mankind, death, and other such cosmic themes, myths, wrote Bascom, "are prose narratives which, in the society in which they are told, are considered to be truthful accounts of what happened in the remote past . . . . Myths are the embodiment of dogma; they are usually sacred, and they are often associated with theology and ritual" (ibid.: 4), whereas legends "are prose narratives which, like myths, are regarded as true by the narrator and his audience, but they are set in a period less remote, when the world was much like it is today" (ibid.). Concerned with such things as wars, chiefs and kings, heroic deeds, and dynastic successions, legends are like our "history" in their content, if not in their science. The third category, folktales, consists of entertaining stories not told as truths, nor in the social or ritual contexts that suppose they are. The African "myth-legends" are the product of a simpler dichotomy of true and fictional narratives: cosmic and historical traditions are thus grouped together and distinguished as "historically true," as distinguished from folktales—by Yoruba, for example:

> The Yoruba recognize two classes of tales: folktales (*alo*) and myth-legends (*itan*). Myth-legends are spoken of as "histories" and are regarded as historically true; they are quoted by the elders in serious discussions of ritual or political matters, whenever they can assist in settling a point of disagreement. (1965: 11)

Note the implication: these "historically true" narratives function as paradigmatic precedents.

Two different issues of historicity are entailed in these myths and legends: whether they make history—that is, as paradigmatic precedents—or they are history—that is, as reports of what actually took place. Too often, however, in opting for one alternative, Western scholars are apt to ignore or discard the other. Considering that the myths and legends are a priori true for the people concerned, hence that they function continuously as precepts of order and action, for some analysts (mainly but not exclusively anthropologists), whether the events reported in the narrative truly happened is irrelevant. Alternatively, in concluding that that these traditions are a priori untrue and could never have happened, either because of their fabulous character or because they are merely functional reflexes of existing institutions, other scholars (mainly but not exclusively historians) eliminate them from historical consideration altogether, either as being history or as making history. For reasons to be explained, I will here argue against both these extremes. But for the same reasons I would also reject the common average scholarly refuge in "the answer lies somewhere in-between": that these traditions may well harbor some historical realities, which we can determine by subtracting their obviously fantastic and irrational elements.

This common, average historical wisdom about myths might be labeled the "kernel of truth" thesis. The supposition is that the traditions are more-or-less valuable means of discovering real-historical events provided their fantastic aspects are debunked and discarded. The object is to find the "kernel of truth" in an otherwise unbelievable story, upon which the rest of it is best ignored. Or else, as in the case of certain traditions of stranger-king origins, the rest is written off as a counterfeit claim of legitimacy. Among scholars of African history, Jan Vansina (1985) has been the great master of this kind of historicist exegesis. In an interesting way, it involves an inversion of the relation between "myth" and "fact" that has been argued above concerning the analytic value of a demonstrable discrepancy between traditions of origin and what actually transpired. In the typical kernel-of-truth practice, one subtracts the "fanciful" from the "mythical" in order to arrive at the "truly historical." But if the so-called "myth" is known to be the historical reality by the people concerned, what actually happened becomes the means of historical wisdom rather than the end: for the comparison with the tradition shows how these happenings have been appropriated within a given sociocultural scheme. The relationship between what happened and how it was construed, which is also to say what historical effects it may have, is the work of culture—or, more precisely, of people making what happened intelligible by means of cultural standards of what there is. Too often, scholars have worked from the tradition to the event by a process of rational abstraction, supposing historical truth is factual; whereas a comparative anthropology would work from the event to the tradition by a process of exegetical elaboration, supposing the cultural truth is historical.

A parenthesis here, lest I be charged with the crude notion of relativism to the effect of "any morality is as good as any other" by which critics too often

slander an anthropological sensitivity to the ways other cultural orders, and correlatively other histories, differ from our own (cf. MacGaffey 1976: 116f.). My
understanding of cultural relativism has always been the following:

> Cultural relativism is first and last an interpretive anthropological—that is to
> say, methodological—procedure. It is not the moral argument that any culture or
> custom is as good as any other, if not better. Relativism is the simple prescription
> that, in order to be intelligible, other people's practices and ideals must be placed
> in their own historical context, understood as positional values in the field of
> their own cultural relationships rather than appreciated by categorical and moral
> judgments of our making. Relativity is the provisional suspension of one's own
> judgments in order to situate the practices at issue in the historical and cultural
> order that made them possible. It is in no other way a matter of advocacy. (Sahl-
> ins 2012b: 46)

Cultural relativism is an anthropological way of discovering cultural differences, rather than a charitable way of granting them moral absolution. End of
parenthesis.

By contrast to "the answer lies somewhere in-between," some scholars would
endorse the radical argument that since myths are sacred truths, all that matters
is that they function as historical paradigms, regardless of their factual status.
For Edmund Leach, what is structurally and historically effective about myth is
that the people believe it is true; that it may or may not have "really happened"
is "irrelevant." In the Frazer lecture of 1988, he offered a most un-Frazer-like
take on the historical value of "myth":

> In the language of contemporary anthropology, the assertion that a particular
> story (either oral or literary) is a myth need not imply that it is untrue. Stories are
> myths if they are used as . . . justifications or precedents for social action, whether
> secular or religious. Whether the precedent story in question was or was not true
> as factual history is entirely irrelevant . . . . Myth is believed to be true by those
> who use it. In this sense, all the Christian gospel stories are myth for Christians.
> Although practicing Christians are deeply committed to a belief that the key
> events recorded in the gospels "really happened," the fact is that the historicity
> of the stories (if any) is irrelevant for the religious implication of what the texts
> contain. (2011: 283–84)

In his excellent treatments of history in the Kazembe kingdom of the Luapula Valley, Cunnison comes to a similar conclusion, but with an important caveat about the nature of the truth-values at issue:

> What actually happened matters little unless the people concerned have means of knowing that what they say happened, did happen, or did not. The important thing is this: what the Luapula people say now about the past is what they *know* actually happened in the past. Simply to say they believed it happened in the past is too weak, for they do not doubt it. (1959: 33)

> It thus seems sociologically irrelevant whether the history is in quality possible, improbable, or downright mythical . . . . What is important to Africans about their histories is not their probability or reliability, which are unquestioned and outside discussion, but it is the implication present in the form which the history finally takes; and nowadays this conception has found currency among some of the people by the use of the English word "meaning." And in the mythical histories of clans and subclans and tribes the meaning is the *raison d'être* for the group's coming there in the first place, of their position in regard to the occupation of land, and their relation to other neighboring groups, or groups with whom they live together. (1951: 22)

Clearly Cunnison's stronger contention that traditions of the past involve indubitably known, objective judgments—this happened—is preferable to the dubitable subjective propositions entailed in belief—I hold that this is what happened. Moreover, given that this history organizes the relations between groups, it also has to do with what *will* happen. Considering the sense of fiction that ever attends the word, then, why continue to call these unquestionable narratives "myth"? Even Malinowski's "charter myth" is an ethnological oxymoron, inasmuch as a tradition that establishes the constitution of the society could not be fictional in the society in which it so functions. On the other hand, if "belief" and "myth" are too weak for a proper anthropological understanding of these origin stories, to say that their relation to what really happened is irrelevant goes too far in just that anthropological respect. Especially if by archival or archaeological means one could determine a discrepancy between *wie es eigentlich gewesen* and the tradition thereof, it would be an intellectual bonanza. To repeat: it would expose the cultural work in the organization of a historical praxis, how

what happened has been effectively recuperated in the terms of a particular
sociocultural order. What the discrepancy between "fact" and tradition would
reveal is the way—which is never the only possible way—the events have been
culturally construed by some social process of valuation. For historians and anthropologists both, the fundamental question is not what actually happened, but
what it is that happened.

But that cannot be a question addressed through the Kongo indigenous
traditions of the past according to Wyatt MacGaffey. MacGaffey could agree
with Leach and Cunnison that whether or not such narratives are factual is
irrelevant; for in his own view, they are not really about the past. Whatever
their relation to the actual past, they have no place in a historical account, since
historical is not what they are. Merely epiphenomenal is what they are: discursive expressions of social institutions whose logic, purpose, and content they
embody, syntagmatically or metaphorically, explicitly or in disguise. For Mac-
Gaffey, to give charter traditions any historical credence is to make the major
methodological error of suborning the analytical position of the anthropologist
by an indigenous point of view beholden to its own structures and functions.
Speaking of conventional attempts to separate historical fact from the magical
aspects of traditions, he writes:

> The conventional ethnographic view regards such magical details as accretions
> upon an historical core. Tradition, that is to say, is implicitly sorted into a class of
> events that seem likely to the European mind, and thus as possibly or probably
> historical and a class of unlikely events that are discarded the procedure is arbi-
> trary and unjustified . . . . Real history cannot be inferred from tradition in any
> simple way. To accept as historical even such portions as look real to the foreign
> eye is to submit unawares to the authority of indigenous cosmology as much as
> though one had also accepted the magical portions as historically real. In fact,
> there is no boundary between the two: the myth is all one piece and all of its
> parts make sense from the same point of view. (1974: 420–21)

And since the traditions of stranger-kingship too are functionally dissolved in
and as religion or some other social institution, since they cannot be "real history," everything is then written as if they had no temporality or historical significance of their own.

The point of view from which BaKongo construct these traditions and
which thus comprises their native logic and substance is variously determined

by MacGaffey as ritual, political, sociological, religious, or cosmological. And while any and all such kinds of narrative or practice cannot then be "historical material," in a recurrent deference to Marxist anthropologies they are deemed to have ultimate sources in the relations of production and social reproduction. In one of MacGaffey's latest statements of this position, the dual system of stranger-kingship featuring the complementary relations between immigrant chiefs and autochthonous priests, as summarized for Kongo by Luc de Heusch (2000), is referred to the even more abstract basis of Space and Time:

> De Heusch dwells quite rightly on what he calls "dual systems," but evidently the pairing of earth-related and dynastic rituals is independent of the narratives that purport to account for them . . . . The pairing can be understood sociologically, in that every community exists both in space and time, which are the necessary dimensions of production and social reproduction and will be ritualized to some extent in every agricultural society. Space is the earth itself and the forces of nature on which all depend in common. Time, on the other hand, is the source of authority and the measure of social differentiation; reference to the past purports to distinguish older from younger, first-comer from late-comer, aristocrat from commoner. These two dimensions are what Victor Turner called *communitas* and *societas*, although he thought of *communitas* as occurring only in marginal situations outside the reach of *societas*. As Michael Jackson put it, "The complementary principles of social organization which are variously called lineage/locality, kinship/residence, ancestors/earth, descent/territoriality, can be abstractly and heuristically polarized as a distinction between temporal and spatial modes of structuring." Not the origin of this polarity but how it works out in practice is a contingent, historical question. (MacGaffey 2005: 195)[26]

We are not specifically informed either by Thornton or by MacGaffey how one accounts for the particular attributes of stranger-kingship by the mode of

---

26. Speaking of Lele religious symbolism involving animals, Mary Douglas observed that it is not relevant to ask how accurate the observation of the creature's behavior need be.

> A symbol based on mistaken information can be fully effective as a symbol, so long as the fable in question is well known. The dove, it would seem, can be one of the most relentlessly savage of birds. The pelican does not nourish its young from its own living flesh. Yet the one bird has provided a symbol of peace, and the other of maternal devotion, for centuries. (1959: 56)

production. A Marxist "determination by the economic basis" involves the forces and relations of production, but in this MacGaffey text all the explanation
we get by "production and social reproduction" is a generic reference to "agricultural society." As a technical means, agriculture does not entail any particular
structure of society. Certainly it does not specify that the working class of native
subjects monopolize the ownership and control of this primary means of production by virtue of their forebears' original settlement of the earth in life and
continued occupancy in death, such that the descendants of these first-comers
are uniquely able to ritually nurture the growth of crops which are in effect the
transubstantiation of their ancestors. Rather than explicating stranger-kingship
and its rituals by determinate properties of production, then, MacGaffey's treatment becomes more and more abstract. Now we are told that the dualism at issue is an opposition between Time as the source of authority and of the measure
of differentiation and Space as the nature upon which we depend in common:
Time is to Space as *societas* is to *communitas*. But perhaps nowhere is space so
radically differentiated as in the pervasive African distinction between the human community of the settled and the wild populated by powerful evil and beneficial forces—through the associations with which the stranger-king derives
the measure of his authority. Finally, we learn that not only are the dualisms of
stranger-kingship forms of Time and Space, but likewise the complementary
principles of lineage and locality, kinship and residence, ancestors and earth,
"can be abstractly and heuristically polarized as a distinction between temporal
and spatial modes of structuring." We are thus encouraged to explain differences
by a constant and particulars by universals—to which MacGaffey, by invoking
history to bridge the epistemological abyss, thereupon adds an explanation of
the recurrent by the contingent.

Although MacGaffey and Thornton have their more principled reasons
for dismissing the historical value of Kongo origin traditions, whether of the
kingship or the clans, they also on occasion pooh-pooh them for the trivial or
unlikely causes these stories may assign for large events. So Thornton (2001:
109) follows MacGaffey in writing off the so-called "Cabbage Patch Wars," a
recurrent motif in clan traditions which alleges that an original ancestral group
was definitively divided as a result of a quarrel between women over the ownership of a cabbage patch. (I have seen the like in traditions of Fijian clans and
the origin of the Hawaiian ruling chiefs, not to forget the Luo kingships that
were sequitur to a brother's child swallowing a certain bead.) Without claiming
to assess the possible symbolic weight of the incident, one could easily suggest

from our own Judeo-Christian traditions that though such episodes may seem unlikely, they can serve as the reasons for major real-historical consequences. Or is it not partly because they have accumulated such effects over time that to the rational-positivist eye, they seem disproportionately trivial? In any case, for two thousand years Christians have known that they are inherently marked by sin and condemned to labor, suffer, and die, all because Adam ate an apple. There is, however, no historical record of the event. Or of Adam, for that matter. Perhaps Augustine's influential notions of the inheritance of acquired characteristics in regard to original sin were instrumentally designed to combat the alternative interpretations of the rival doctrines abroad in North Africa, even as they would be of functional value to the exercise of Roman imperial power (Pagels 1988). Still, the stigma of the original sin together with its many doctrinal complements has survived all manner of regimes, including the medieval, feudal, and the modern democratic, notwithstanding the mythical and irrational—not to say ridiculous—tradition of its origin. It also has been successfully perpetrated on colonized peoples who needed to be persuaded they were inherently evil. All that grand history has been sequitur to a trivial event that never happened.

Yet because MacGaffey and Thornton are convinced that events described in the Kongo traditions of stranger-kingship never happened, or in any case that they are of no historical moment, they dismiss these traditions as precedents and thereby ignore their specific structural entailments—as in the relations of agricultural production—as well as their historical reiterations—as in the political functions of the Nasku ne Vunda (Mani Vunda) in the Christian kingdom. Otherwise said, they confound a syntagmatic history with a paradigmatic one, and having denied the facticity of the former, that also precludes the possibility of the latter. This is not to say that for MacGaffey this is standard ethnographic or historiographic procedure. In regard to other aspects of Kongo history, he is prepared to recognize the historicity of Kongo traditions that, like stranger-kingship, suppose that power comes from a spiritually charged other world:

> The conversion of the king and the leading nobles to Christianity in the fifteenth century meant from their point of view, as Randles effectively indicates, their initiation into a new and more powerful cult which, like all the other cults known to them, offered privileged access to the powers of the other world through contacts with the dead. The subsequent religious history of the BaKongo down to the present day is the history of this misunderstanding. The misunderstanding is as fundamental as the definition of death (lufua) which to BaKongo is a condition

of life in another place, or as the definition of race, which to BaKongo is a matter of changing one's skin. Any foreigner attempting to understand must be prepared to recognize a logic totally unlike his own. (1974: 426)

The numerous working misunderstandings that have attended Western colonial enterprises afford perhaps the best demonstration of the historical significance of the difference between "what actually happened" and "what it is that happened." The Whitemen thought they were buying Maori land; by the same transaction, the Maori understood they were acquiring Whitemen. One can understand why Luapulu people translate their traditions as "meaning": the same happening can have different meanings, hence different historical effects, for peoples of different cultural heritage. In 1779, Hawaiian women of ordinary rank ate with their sailor paramours aboard Captain Cook's ship during his fateful sojourn at Kealakekua Bay (Sahlins 1981a). That is what actually happened; but what it is that happened, among other meaningful things, is that the women broke the Hawaiian taboos on codining with men and eating sacrificial foods, pork and bananas, strictly forbidden them. For the sailors what happened was something like a date for lunch, an expression of intimacy. For the Hawaiians, it was a significant historic event, which—along with other exchanges of mundane significance to Europeans that amounted to violations of the human and divine order for Hawaiians—contributed to the climactic abolition of the indigenous religion in 1819. At that time, in a symmetrical and inverse act of codining, King Liholiho launched a cultural revolution by eating in public with women of the highest nobility. Consider, then, that the syntagmatic event is as much dependent on cultural conditions that are not coterminous with it as are events that are paradigmatically inspired by ancient memories. One might say that the happening becomes an event insofar as it is recuperated by values originating outside of it, that is, by the meaningful or symbolic values of a particular cultural scheme. Indeed, the event as such is doubly beholden to phenomena external to it: both to cultural values preposed to it and to subsequent events that retrospectively make it more-or-less consequential. Not that these values determine what actually happens, as this also depends on contingent circumstances not specifiable as such in the relevant cultural scheme. The British explorer Captain Cook was not foreseen in the Hawaiian order of things, however much the annual visitation of the god Lono, with whom Cook was identified, became the cultural template of his fatal end.

However circumstantial, history is necessarily atemporal and cultural through and through. Whether the pertinent causation is sequential or analogical, syntagmatic or paradigmatic, the transhistorical cultural context is the condition of its possibility—of what it actually is that happens. Otherwise, without the culture concerned, what actually happens would be as significant as a tree falling in an uninhabited African forest.

CHAPTER 4

The stranger-kingship of the Mexica

Marshall Sahlins

According to Cortés, upon first meeting Moctezuma, the Mexica ruler famously told him:

> It is now a long time since, by means of written records, we learned from our ancestors that neither myself nor any of those who inhabit this region were descended from its original inhabitants, but from strangers who immigrated hither from a very distant land; and we have also learned that a prince, whose vassals they all were, conducted our people into these parts, and then returned to his native land. He afterwards came again to this country . . . and found that his people had intermarried with the native inhabitants, by whom they had many children and had built towns . . . . And when he desired them to return with him, they were unwilling to go, nor were they disposed to acknowledge him as their sovereign; so he departed from this country, and we have always heard that his descendants would come to conquer this land and return us to subjection. (1843: 87–88)

For all the scholarly controversy that has ensued about the veracity of Cortés' account, when one considers the worldwide distribution of stranger-king dynasties with quite similar structural features and historical traditions as are entailed in Moctezuma's discourse, what he is reported to have said is quite unremarkable. Stranger-kingdoms of this description constitute the dominant form of premodern state (Sahlins 2010, 2014). The rulers of a remarkable number of societies the world around have been foreign by origin to the peoples they rule. As rehearsed in ongoing traditions and enacted in royal rituals—notably the rituals of their installation and of the New Year—the kings come from elsewhere. Moreover, as their cosmic-cum-celestial powers derive from their external origins, the foreign identity of the kingship is perpetual, a condition of their sovereignty, in contrast to the earthly powers and identity of their indigenous subjects. A common counterpart of the fabled origins of the stranger-kings is their cultural superiority: just as in the Moctezuma text, they are (literally) the civilizers—they built cities. Yet most indicative of stranger-kingship is the marriage of these powerful foreigners with native women—in the paradigmatic case, the union of the original stranger-king with the daughter or daughters of the autochthonous ruler—an alliance that is in effect the fundamental contract of the new society. Sovereignty here is embodied in and transmitted by women of rank. In the sequel, the union of the native woman with an immigrant prince engenders a succession of kings who combine in their own persons the essential components of the new regime: foreign and indigenous, celestial and terrestrial, masculine and feminine—each component incomplete in itself, but taken together they make a reproductive totality. Have you ever wondered why vassal lords address Moctezuma as "my child"? I have heard the like in the Fiji Islands, where the indigenous chieftains similarly assume the status of the paramount's elders, for he is the offspring of their clan, their ancestress. First in the land, giving birth to the king, the subject people are senior kinsmen of their ruler.

The return of the original king, ruler of the native people—the Quetzalcoatl figure in the Moctezuma text—is another common narrative of strangerkingdoms, as well as an annual ritual drama. The king of ancient memory and godly status comes back to reclaim his sovereignty, only to be deposed again by the usurper now in power, although usually not before he renews the fertility of the land during his temporary ascendency. Also not uncommon is the tragic irony involved in the identification of the colonizing European with the returning popular god-king: the way Captain Cook was considered an avatar of Lono in Hawai'i, or Sir James Brooke, the "White Raja of Sarawak," was taken by some Iban people as the son of their primordial progenitors, Keling and Kumang—then again, in another version, Sir James was Kumang's lover, thus replicating the contractual union of the stranger prince with the ranking woman of the native people (cf. Sahlins 2010: 113). Similar marvelous tales of Whitemen are told in Amazonia and Melanesia. For the Micronesians of Ponape and Truk, things that drift ashore, including the founders of chiefly lineages, have come from the spirit world; which is why, as Ward Goodenough explained, Europeans, on their first arrival, were greeted as denizens of that divine realm (1986: 559). The parallels with Moctezuma's alleged greeting of Cortés would not be worth further discussion were it not for the disputable speculation of some scholars that the identification of Cortés with the lost god-king of Tollan greatly facilitated the Spanish Conquest. That this does not necessarily follow is demonstrated in the case of Captain Cook, whose identification with the ancient deity Lono merely got him killed. What will happen in the showdown between the returning god and the king whose ancestors came to power by usurping him depends on contingent circumstances of the historical conjuncture. Moctezuma hardly had to give in as a result of the tradition; he could have as well concluded from it that Cortés was a threat and got rid of him. What is structural is that either outcome, the death of the god or the king, is a logical but not inevitable sequitur to opposition between them in the indigenous cultural order: one might say it is structurally sufficient but not historically necessary. That is one possible conclusion from Mexica history on the relation between structure and event.

Another is the remarkable similarity between the Mexica history and that of the Bunyoro kingdom of the East African Rift Valley—itself a lacustrine basin geographically similar to the Valley of Mexico. The resemblances include the Banyoro people's notions of early European visitors, who were sometimes identified with the Bachwezi rulers of the fabled Kitara "empire" that once dominated the Valley and peoples beyond. "Europeans," reports the ethnographer John Beattie (1971: 50), "were sometimes taken for Bachwezi returning to their old kingdom, and . . . were said to have possessed marvelous skills and marvelous powers"—should we not say, like the Toltecs? Indeed the Banyoro relate that they inherited the great realm and high culture of the Bachwezi in much the same way as the Mexica became the successors of the glorious Toltecs, including the parallel saga of their origin as uncultured barbarians who migrated from the northern peripheries of the empire to its interlacustrine heartland. So the resemblances continue: the Bachwezi of ancient Kitara are analogously described as "a mysterious race of semi-divine rulers," of whose extraordinary wisdom and achievements stories are still told, including their takeover of the country from "an even more shadowy dynasty" (ibid.: 25, 45). (Hint: Teotihuacan.) And the Bachwezi kings, too, were high priests of their Kitara realm, as wealthy as they were wise, reigning over many lesser kingdoms of the Rift Valley and beyond.

Just as the Bachwezi resemble the Toltecs, so the Banyoro who replaced them were like the Mexica in their original Chichimec state. Their own traditions stress the Banyoro's "ignorance and uncouthness when they first arrived from their uncivilized homeland" (ibid.: 59). Like the common depictions of the Chichimecs, the Banyoro are described as rough hunters, naked and savage, without knowledge of riches, courtly manners, or diplomacy—as it were, "*sans roi, sans loi, sans foi.*" Speakers of the uncivilized Nilotic Luo tongue, this, too, the Banyoro would give up when they adopted the customs and language of the Bantu Bachwezi. It is remarkable, comments the historian Roland Oliver (1955: 115), that the successor kingdoms of the Bachwezi in the Rift Valley— Buganda, Toro, Nkole, Sogo, and Bunyoro, among others—attribute most of the social and cultural practices that mark them off from surrounding regions to their glorious Kitara predecessors. Many "are at pains to describe how they learnt and copied the kingship customs" of these ancient rulers, from whom indeed their own kings claim to be descended—like Moctezuma, who similarly transcended Chichamec origins by virtue of an ancestral connection to the fabled Toltecs (see below).

In juxtaposing the Mexica and the Banyoro, I join a small cottage industry in Mesoamerican studies that has turned out a number of such cross-cultural comparisons: likening not only the Mexica's polity to various African states, but also their hegemony to the Roman empire and their kings to sovereigns of Polynesian islands. In the latter connection, Susan Gillespie's (1989) adaptation of the Polynesian stranger-king model to Mexica history, including her appropriate emphasis on the passage of sovereignty through high-ranking women, is most pertinent to the present discussion. So is David Carrasco's (2000) analysis of core–periphery relations in the Valley of Mexico on the model of the "galactic polities" of Southeast Asia, as described in influential works by Stanley Tambiah (1976, 1985, 1987). Still, these excellent studies are also relevant to Mexica history and culture in a way that is not usually envisioned, for, like the Banyoro, we are here considering a stranger-kingdom established by a peripheral, relatively undeveloped society over the legendary "high culture" core of a galactic polity. Although such takeovers of dominant centers by hinterland peoples are not all that unusual, everything thus happens in reverse of the ideal-typical case where foreign kings from legendary homelands subjugate uncultured aboriginals. The structural permutations and contradictions that ensue from this reversal—Mexica who proudly know themselves at once as Toltecs and Chichimecs, for example—make up the main subject matter of this essay.

STRANGER-KINGS, GALACTIC POLITIES

To make these points, I will need some further preliminary discussion of stranger-king formations and a summary of the dynamics of galactic polities.

In the prototypical stranger-king traditions, the heroic founder of the dynasty comes from some fabled homeland, terrestrial or celestial, actual or legendary. Commonly, he is the son of a powerful king in a realm of great repute who failed to succeed his father, perhaps because he was bested by a fraternal rival, perhaps for some fault that led to his banishment. Or in a higher register, the dynastic founder is the offspring of the gods, perhaps expelled from their presence by some similar conflict or offence, who descends upon an autochthonous people from the heavens—always a good address for persons with royal ambitions. In a common *topos*, the hero undertakes an arduous journey to his future kingdom, mastering both natural and human forces along the way, thus demonstrating his transcendent powers and prefiguring the royal gifts of fertility and victory he will bring to his native subjects. As has been said of certain African kings, their powers of destruction were powers of creation. The hero is often known as well for more sinister exploits such as fratricide, parricide, incest, or other crimes against common morality, which likewise puts him above and beyond ordinary society and proves he is stronger than it. Both Quetzalcoatl and Huitzilopochtli were notorious for betraying or slaying close kinsmen--sisters, paternal uncles, brothers, and sisters' sons among them—on the way to their respective kingdoms. They were something else, not like the kinship-ordered peoples they were destined to rule.

Endowed with cosmic potency and stronger than society, the stranger-king is in a position to reorganize it. The advent of the foreign hero is a civilizing mission, bringing the aboriginal people out of their original state of naked savagery. Such was the condition of the primordial Chichimecs: a people without idols or storehouses, living in straw huts, subsisting on game that was not always cooked, as well as wild roots, fruits, and herbs—"in short, they lived like brute animals" (Motolinia 1951: 27). In the paradigmatic Mesoamerican tradition, the Chichimecs were delivered from this primitive condition by "advanced" peoples

such as the Toltecs, and in particular by Quetzalcoatl (or Kukulkan), who introduced marvelous crafts, precious goods of various kinds, houses and temples of
stone, clothing of cotton, and a lot more. But not necessarily by conquest.

Stranger-kingdoms may be established by conquest, and the kings are typically ferocious by nature, but notwithstanding certain popular nineteenth-century theories of state formation to that effect, conquest is often overrated as the
source of foreign dynasties. Noticing the prevalence of an ethnic distinction
between rulers and ruled in premodern states, Ludwig Gumplowicz (1899) famously concluded that might must have made right in all such cases. While
this ethnic divide does indeed suggest the ubiquity of stranger-kingdoms, in the
traditions at issue the dominance of the foreign ruler is not necessarily generated by forcefully overcoming the autochthonous people, since his superiority is
an original condition. Arriving from an exalted realm, his power derived from
gods of universal scope; the stranger-king is a ruler a priori, whereas the native
people, insofar as they approximated an Aristotelian definition of barbarism,
would be subjects if not slaves by nature. In the charter traditions at issue, the
rule of the foreign hero is often peacefully accepted for a variety of divine or political benefits, ranging from bringing rain to suppressing feuds and protecting
the native communities against even worse regimes in the neighborhood. Frequently enough, for some such reason, an indigenous group will actively solicit
a ruler of their own from a more powerful king: just as the Mexica elders did
from the king of Culhuacan, himself of Toltec heritage. There will be more to
say of this in the context of Mesoamerican galactic polities, but for the present
note that the Mexica had good precedent in certain traditions of Quetzalcoatl
that tell of how the Toltecs brought him from Cuextlan to install as their king
in Tollan. According to *The annals of Cuauhtitlan*. 5 House (AD 873) was the year
"the Toltecs went to get Quetzalcoatl to make him their ruler in Tollan, and in
addition he was their priest" (Bierhorst 1992: 29).

As Rousseau famously argued in *The social contract*, force alone is not enough
to make a society. The strongest, he said, will never be strong enough to rule unless he turns might into right and obedience into duty; for "to yield to force is an
act of necessity, not of will—at the most, an act of prudence. In what sense can
it be a duty?" (1997: I.3, 44). Just so, conquest or not, the kingdom is established
by contract: the aforementioned union of the immigrant prince with a high-
ranking woman of the land. So far as I can make out, marriage of this kind is a
condition of the formation of stranger-kingdoms everywhere, notably including
the Indo-European ancients, as in the origin traditions of Greek city-states,

whose ruling lines were established by unions of the daughters of autochthonous kings with strangers fathered by Zeus (on human women, another union
of the same kind). The eponymous Pelops (namesake of the Peloponnesus), also
of Zeussian descent, became ruler of Pisa when he conspired with the king's
daughter, Hippodamia, to win her hand in a chariot race with her royal father.
Marseille (Masila) was founded when the local Celtic princess chose to give
the drink of sovereignty to a handsome Greek immigrant youth from Phocaea.
Again, sovereignty is embodied and transmitted in the women—whose marital
congress with the stranger is a replication in miniature of the celestial royal's
appropriation of the bearing earth. Marriage makes a structurally analogous
pair with the kingship by virtue of the common feature of an outsider (as by
the incest taboo) who fertilizes the land. Speaking of a number of such Indo-
European kingdom origins, J. G. Preaux (1962: 112) writes:

> Every foundation of a city, every conquest of royal power becomes effective the
> moment the stranger, charged with sacredness of the gods or the fates, endowed
> moreover with the force of the warrior, symbolically gains possession of a new
> land either by receiving peacefully, or by conquering valorously or by ruse, the
> daughter of the king of the land.[1]

Yet everything in the Valley of Mexico is by all appearances the inverse of classical stranger-kingdoms, since here the foreign rulers are the barbarians. They
are Chichimecs by origin, and although they indeed founded their dynasties
through marriages with the daughters of autochthonous leaders, the latter were
Culhhuacan kings of sacred Toltec descent.[2] In the event, it was the primitive
foreigners who were civilized by the highly cultured aborigines. And this would
not only be true of the Mexica, but also of the Acolhua, the Tepaneca, and
others of Chichimec or Otomi origins whose rulers ennobled themselves with
Toltec affiliations. In some respects, the prototypical sequence is reinstated by a
compensatory story alleging that the Chichimec invaders were the autochthons
of the Valley who had early on left it and latterly returned. But more particularly,
it is the stranger-king system of society that is turned around and restored by

1. For these Indo-European and other such stranger-king formations, see Sahlins
   (1981b, 2010, 2011a, 2011b, 2014).
2. This was also true at the divine level: the Mexica tutelary deity Huitzilopochtli
   married the goddess of the Culhuacan, the earth goddess Tuci (Gillespie 1989: 55).

these hypogamous marriages of Toltec royal women with Chichimec leaders. For insofar as the Chichimec rulers have been differentiated and elevated by their Toltec affiliations, the polity assumes the classic form of a late-coming civilized aristocracy of glorious ancestry imposed upon a stratum of primitive first settlers. The effect is a recuperation of the paradigmatic structure of stranger-kingship that leaves a permanent residue of ambiguity: a Chichimeca-Tolteca aristocracy (cf. Clendinnen 1991; Nicholson 2001).

But then, the paradigmatic structure of stranger-kingship is everywhere inherently ambiguous by virtue of the residual authority retained by the underlying native people as the original settlers and owners of the country. It is a general rule of stranger-king formations that even as the foreign rulers impose their authority on a subjugated native people, they are in turn domesticated in the process. In critical respects, the stranger-kingdom is a system of dual sovereignties in which the immigrant rulers and their indigenous subjects reciprocally encompass one another. Having transformed the country into habitable and productive space in the first place, the native people are already practiced in taming the wild. They do something similar in taking charge of the installation rites of their rulers of foreign derivation—who come out of an uncontrolled outside world with antisocial dispositions as well as beneficial powers. The successors of the indigenous chieftains—or of the previous dynasty, in the case of successive stranger-king formations—are the constituted kingmakers, who in legitimating the royal heir demonstrate their own residual sovereignty. It is not unusual in the royal installation rites for the king-elect to suffer a symbolic death as an outsider at the hands of the native authorities, who then preside over his rebirth and maturation as their own sacred child.[3]

Something quite similar occurs in the installation of the Mexica king when he is seized by the kingmaker-priests, evidently the successors of the *teomama*, the four native bearers of the tutelary god Huitzilopochtli who led the migration to Tenochtitlan (Sahagún 1953–82, 8:18; Townsend 1987). Brought before the assembled leading lords and warriors by these priests, the heir to the kingship is stripped naked, hence deprived of all signs of rank, status, and property and placed in a state of weakness. Thereupon, the upper part of his body is stained black by the chief priest, and he is dressed in a black cape decorated with skull and crossbones. "The attire symbolized death," Richard Townsend observes (ibid.: 392), as would the subsequent self-sacrificial bloodlettings of the king before Huitzilopochtli.

---

3. For much more on the nature and implications of the juvenile status of the king, see David Graeber's discussion in chapter 5.

Probably, then, the ensuing four-day seclusion of the king-elect with his entourage involved a ritual rebirth and maturation; as indeed the god being supplicated here was Tezcatlipoca, who, beside being regarded of Toltec origin, "was identified with the life force that animates all beings and things" (ibid.: 393). Subsequently, the new king moved to the palace for the spectacular sacrifices and brilliant rites of his investiture. Everything thus happens as if the heir to the kingship goes through a symbolic death, rebirth, and growth to maturity—which is also a domestication of the foreign prince by the indigenous authorities.

Nor do the powers and privileges of the native notables end in stranger-kingdoms when the foreign regime begins. Speaking again in ideal-typical terms, the native chieftains, beside maintaining control of their own communities, are often titled councilors of an outsider king who has reason to fear the ambitions of his own kinsmen. Noteworthy in this connection are the diarchies of various forms involving queen mothers who represent the indigenous powers or second kings whose affiliation with the indigenous population gives them the active leadership in temporal affairs. Most significantly, as just said of the Mexica, the leaders of the ancient regime become the principal priests of a country whose enshrined ancestors and gods are their own rightful heritage—which makes the health of the bearing earth their responsibility. Even the king's own cosmic powers of prospering and protecting the people, as by the rain he brings to fertilize their earth, may only become effective when mediated by the sacrificial offices of the indigenous priesthood.

As mentioned earlier, because the external sources of the stranger-king's power, including his privileged relations to his own ancestral gods, are significant means and necessary conditions of his authority, the kingship is perpetually foreign to its own realm. Even where the immigrant aristocracy is acculturated by the native population, which is usually the case, "the king comes from elsewhere" (de Heusch 1991).[4] By contrast, in many parts of Africa, Oceania, and Southeast Asia, the autochthons are explicitly known as "the owners" of the land."[5] We shall see similar notices of the Mexica. Likewise certain passages of

---

4. "The king comes from elsewhere" is the title of an illuminating article by Luc de Heusch (1991), commenting on a study of the Mundang kingship of Chad, studied by Alfred Adler (1982). See the discussion in chapter 6.

5. The autochthonous clans in Fijian chiefdoms are designated by a term (*i taukei*) that at once means "owners" and "first settlers." They are likewise the "land people" (*kai vanua*) or "the land" (*na vanua*). Similarly the Nyakyusa common people are "the earth."

the *Codex Chimalpopoca*, for example, identify the "landowners or founders" with the Chichimeca (Bierhorst 1992: 46; cf. ibid.: 117). Accordingly, the people of the Valley of Mexico as a whole are in certain contexts "Chichimeca": the totality is known by its underlying native inhabitants. What the Banyoro say in such regards holds for many a stranger-kingdom: "the Mukama [the King] rules the people, the clans rule the land" (Beattie 1971: 169). Or again, as it is said of the Kongo king of old: in relation to "those who are there," who hold the land, "he remains a stranger" (Balandier 1968b: 38). Historical materialism notwithstanding, in the premodern states of this description, the subordinate class controls the means of production in the primary sector of subsistence.[6]

By contrast, "the king rules the people": the economic powers of the ruling class are a function of their politico-religious domination of the producing people; hence they mainly take the form of taxation or pillage as opposed to the control of capital and the productive process as such. The economy has something of the same dual structure as the polity, divided between a native sphere primarily concerned with subsistence production and an aristocratic sphere critically concerned with the acquisition of wealth from abroad. The native economy is based in real property, organized largely by kinship, and oriented to domestic consumption. The relation of the ruling class to the native sphere—apart from their ritual access to the divine sources of prosperity—is for the most part extractive rather than productive: they appear on the scene *post messem*, after the harvest, to take a toll on people's products and manpower. But as Mary Helms has shown in a series of remarkable works (1988, 1993, 1998), the aristocratic economy, likewise by means of its powers over people, is primarily oriented to the acquisition of moveable valuables from abroad by raid, trade, and/or tribute: the accumulation of riches whose value objectifies the life-and-death potencies of the realms from which they come, as well as exotica that represent the submission of distant peoples. Strategically redistributed, conspicuously consumed, or offered to the gods, the valuables of the aristocratic economy sustain the greater order of the kingdom—not least by sustaining its ruling powers-that-be.[7]

---

6. Likewise. the merchants usually owned their stocks-in-trade and craftsmen owned their tools, workshops, and raw materials (Calnek 1974: 194).

7. "Those who create and/or acquire goods and benefits from some dimension of the cosmological outside are not only providing goods and benefits per se but also are presenting tangible evidence that they themselves possess or command the unique qualities and ideals generally expected in persons who have ties with distant places

I have indulged on this account of stranger-kingship particularly because, as will be described presently, the Mexica of the fourteenth and fifteenth centuries underwent a revolution from above that produced a classic version of it. The summary of the galactic polity which follows will also be useful in this regard, since its structures and dynamics were clearly in play in this creation of a Toltec aristocracy ruling over a Chichimec peasantry.

Stanley Tambiah introduced the galactic polity as a worldly realization of the cosmological mandala form well known in South and Southeast Asia.[8] Here was a scheme of creation spreading "from a refined center outwards and a refined summit downwards, each outer reality or circle being a progressively weaker representation of the preceding . . . grosser in constitution and more imprisoned on sensory pursuits and desires" (1985: 322). By further reference to famous Buddhist and Hindu texts on universal Cakkavatti and Devaraja kings of kings, Tambiah transposed the cosmic dynamics to a political register:

> We are told that the wheel-rolling emperor solemnly invokes the wheel to roll outward; the wheel rolls successively to the East, the South, the North, and the West. As the mighty monarch with his fourfold army appeared in each quarter following the wheel, the rival kings prostrated themselves in submission. The *cakkavatti* allowed them to retain their possessions on the condition of observance of the five moral principles binding on Buddhist layman. (1976: 45–46)

When Tambiah still further objectifies the model in terms of actual galactic polities, more needs to be said: for instance, some further notice of the progressive reduction in the imperial center's hegemonic power as it moves to peripheral sectors of the galaxy, where tributary dues may have to be exacted by force. In this respect, the reach of the center is typically beyond its political grasp: not only in that the galactic potentate usually claims a greater domain than he rules; but also in that his grandeur and divine potency are known to the peoples

---

of supernatural origins and, therefore, are themselves 'second creators.' Evidence of inalienable connections with places of cosmological origins thus conveys a certain sacrality which readily translates into political-ideological legitimacy and facilitates successful exercise of power" (Helms 1993: 49–50).

8. The galactic polity as Tambiah described it is essentially the same as the core–periphery "world systems" of premodern civilizations analyzed by Ekholm, Friedman, and colleagues, and the "segmentary state" concept developed by Aidan Southall, among other, similar regional hierarchies otherwise identified (see chapter 6).

beyond, in distant and uncontrolled hinterlands. This imagined imperium of the galactic outer reaches is an important factor in the attraction and movement of peripheral peoples toward the "high cultures" of core regions—like the movement of the Chichimecs into the Valley of Mexico, apparently taking advantage of a weakening Tollan.

Among Tambiah's historical examples of galactic polities is the fourteenth-century realm of Sukhothai (Sukhodaya), a kingdom in the Upper Chao Phraya Valley of Siam that flourished under immigrant Tai rulers who had replaced an earlier Mon dynasty (Tambiah 1976). Incidentally and coincidently, a number of Tai peoples had poured into and taken over Southeast Asian valleys from their original homeland redoubt in the southern borderlands of China, rather in the same way (and the same direction) the Chichimec groups established themselves in the Valley. In certain respects, Sukhothai's own success was also like the Mexica's god-driven ascent to power, including a history of competitive relations with other kingdoms within its own galactic system and beyond. Aided by the importation of Sinhalese Buddhist concepts of universal kingship and a famous image of the Buddha that became the palladium of their rule, the Tai sovereigns of Sukhothai transformed their realm from a tertiary outpost of the Khmer kingdom of Angkor Wat in Cambodia to the independent ruler of a number of other principalities in the region, even as they developed pretensions of empire in regions beyond.

The Sukhothai capital was a mandala in itself: centered in the royal palace and principal temples, quartered by roads laid out in the cardinal directions, and encircled by three concentric ramparts. This was the area of direct administrative control by the Sukhothai king. Beyond were further concentric zones marked by diminishing powers of the center and weakening versions of its royal forms and practices. The sphere immediately outside the capital zone consisted of four major provinces (*muang*), governed by sons of the king from secondary centers situated in the cardinal directions. Beyond lay an outer ring of more or less independent kingdoms controlled by their own traditional rulers—whose allegiance to the Sukhothai ruler was often problematic. For all that the layout of the Sukhothai realm in the cardinal directions signified a universal extension of the ruler's authority, the monarch's hegemonic ambitions exceeded his real-political powers. For that matter, like all the Southeast Asian potentates claiming to be the king of kings, the Sukhothai monarch periodically sent tributes to the Chinese emperor for the purpose of legitimating his authority relative to rival princes and vassal kings within his own domains as well as the rulers of rival galactic regimes—who likewise affected cosmocratic titles: for example, the erstwhile tributary kingdom of Ayutthaya—reputedly founded by a Chinese merchant prince—which defeated and absorbed Sukhothai in the early fifteenth century. The Ayutthaya rulers created a Siamese imperium of their own, achieved recognition from the Chinese emperor, and claimed authority over such distant realms they could not rule as the important sultanate of Melaka in the Malay Peninsula. A great commercial empire in its own right, Melaka was ruled by descendants of Alexander the Great in his Koranic persona of Iskandar D'zul Karnain (C. C. E. Brown 1952). That is another story, illustrative of many aspects of stranger-kingship, including the practice known in Mesoamerica where, rather than strangers becoming native kings, native kings sometimes become strangers: that is, they take on the identities of legendary world-historical rulers.

If you will forgive the English pun, galactic systems are marked by a politics of "upward nobility," whereby the chiefs of satellite areas assume the political statuses, courtly styles, titles, and even genealogies of their superiors in the regional hierarchy—who for their part imitate the galactic hegemon, while the latter, in invidious contrast to ambitious vassals and rival emperors, claims to rule the world. In the event, the structural effect is a certain "galactic mimesis," insofar as peripheral groups assume the polities and cosmologies of their regional superiors. Recall Edmund Leach's descriptions in *The political systems of Highland Burma* (1954) of hinterland Kachin chiefs who "become Shan," acquiring the cultural trappings and political backing of Shan princes—even as the Shan princes retire to their Burmese or Chinese palaces and the lifestyles of their own imperial paragons. For all the apparent delusions of grandeur, these pretensions could be calculated political moves, as when a highland Kachin chief marries a daughter of a lowland Shan prince, perhaps acquiring a Shan title as well as making himself a client of his princely father-in-law. As Leach tells, this did not make him any less a Kachin chief, but potentially too much of one in the view of his countrymen—who would then be inclined to rebel and return to an egalitarian state.

These upward moves in the galactic hierarchy are typically motivated by competition with immediate rivals in a given political field, who are thus trumped by the chief who goes beyond the shared structures of authority by adopting a politics of higher order. Gregory Bateson (1935, 1958) called this "symmetrical schismogenesis," a type of conflict that works on the principle that "anything you can do I can do better." Competition of this kind occurs within and between groups at all levels of the galactic system, including the attempts of subordinate groups to displace their superiors. As we shall see momentarily, it marks the ascent of the Mexica of Tenochtitlan from their contest for superiority with the fraternal town of Tlatelolco to the overthrow of their Tepanec imperial predecessors, the Mexica rulers taking progressively greater titles at critical junctures along the way. Such practices of galactic mimesis suggest that the upward and inward movement of groups such as the Mexica or Banyoro from the barbarian periphery to the imperial core may well be anticipated in structural form before it is achieved in historical practice. Indeed, the Mexica of the long march from Aztlan were an agricultural people, not simply Chichimec hunters, and they had paramount leaders before the institution of a Toltec kingship. Taken together with the imposition of kingly forms and practices from the center in the course of extending its rule, the dynamics of galactic polities are at once centrifugal and centripetal, involving displacements of power and culture in both directions.

In the event, the galactic polity becomes a main forcing ground of stranger-king formations, both as emanating from the politics of the center and as emulating the center from the peripheries. Regarding the former, the fallout from fratricidal battles royal among princes contending for the rule of the center is a major source of the spread of stranger-kingdoms to outlying sectors of galactic regimes—and beyond that, into the barbarian fringe. At least some of the princes who fail to win the crown, including some for whom discretion was always the better part of valor, are then likely to move to peripheral regions where they can establish kingdoms of their own, whether as dependencies of their homeland or as autonomous realms. Hence the constitution of society as previously implied, consisting of a single royal kindred or lineage spread over a set of diverse native communities. A similar effect is achieved where the galactic hegemon establishes his sons as rulers of dependent provinces. This practice is usually confined to areas in and near the capital, however; in the outer regions, particularly among peoples of other cultural and ethnic identities, the local kings are normally left in charge of their traditional domains. (The long-reigning ruler of the Tepanec empire, Tezozomoc, seems to have been an exception, installing many of his sons as kings of subordinate cities such as Tlatelolco, where they gave rise to new dynasties.) Here it is worth remarking that the greater galactic systems often called "empires" in the historical literature were primarily regional systems of tribute collection rather than unified, bureaucratically ruled regimes. Apart from the supervision of tributary dues, they were not directly administered by officials from the capital; even in the aftermath of a conquest, it was often more politic to leave the kings and chiefs of the outlying sectors in place.[9] The only problems came when these chiefs did not know their place and defiantly took on great ambitions and exalted titles of their own.

Another mode of stranger-king formation from below is what Fijians call "to beg a chief" (*kere turaga*), that is, to solicit a ruling chief of their own from a higher and greater power, most commonly a son of a renowned ruler of the region. Perhaps the best-known African example concerns the ruling dynasty of Benin, founded by a Yoruba prince who had been granted by the ruler of fabled Ile Ife on the request of the Benin elders (Bradbury 1967). Then there were the elders of Israel, who, when besieged by dissension within and enemies without, petitioned Samuel to have a king, "that we may be like all other nations; and that our king may judge us, and go out before us, and fight our battles" (Samuel I 8:20). Put out because he was not deemed sufficient to rule his own chosen people, God instructed Samuel to tell the Israelites if they got a king they'd be truly sorry; and although Samuel laid it on about the evils of kingly power, the Israelites insisted, and the omnipotent God had to give in. You will recognize the origins of the Mixteca stranger-king in the person of Acamapichtli, solicited by the elders from the ruler of Culhuacan in (suspiciously) similar terms: "We are all alone and forsaken by all nations. We are guided only by our god. . . . We must have a ruler to guide us, to direct us, to show us how we are to live, who will free us, who will defend us and protect us from our enemies" (Duran 1994: 49). Alternatively, a native chief may simply claim membership in a dominant or legendary foreign dynasty: the way that certain "barbarian" rulers on the Chinese borderlands took on prestigious Han ancestry (Backus 1981); or certain Gaulish leaders claimed descent in the Julian or Augustan line of Roman emperors (Drinkwater 1978). Nor were the Mexica kings the only rulers of Chichimec origins to appropriate a Toltec identity, but as that ambitious move was most fateful for the history of Mexico, I conclude by considering it in a bit more detail.[10]

---

9.   This was certainly the case of the Mexica "empire" (cf. Calnek 1982).

10. Cf. Ixtlilxóchitl (1840); Tezozomoc (1853); Sahagún (1953–82, 8 and 10); Soustelle (1964); Davies (1974, 1977, 1980); Bray (1978); Clendinnen (1991); Nicholson (2001); E. de J. Douglas (2010).

CHICHIMECA AND TOLTECA

The stranger-kingship developed by the Mexica in the fourteenth century was not only typical in form; it was motivated, at least in part, by a classic dynamic of galactic systems: a schismatic rivalry among compatriot adversaries, leading one faction to put down the other by appropriating a higher political form drawn from the larger region. I mean Tenochtitlan's conflict with the fellow Mexica community of Tlatelolco. That Tlateloco originated by splitting off from Tenochtitlan indicates their relationship had been antagonistic from the beginning (Duran 1994: 47). As recounted in the *Codex Ramirez*, when the elders of Tenochtitlan decided they needed a king of their own, and such as they had never had, it was because of "the seditious activities of their co-citizens at Tlatelolco" (Ranirez 1903: 37). According to Frey Duran, the Tenochca feared that Tlatelolco was out to dominate them, and by obtaining a king they proposed rather to turn the tables and rule their Mexica fellows. Although that didn't happened for some time—the Tlatelolco people refused to acknowledge Tenochtitlan's rule, and soon enough they solicited their own stranger-king in the person of a son of the Tepaneca ruler Tezozomoc—by a characteristic process of symmetrical schismogenesis, the Tenochca did get a king like the other nations. And apart from the quarrel with Tlatelolco, this king could stand the Tenochca in good stead in relation to the Tepanec rulers of Azcapotzalco on whose land they were squatting.

The problematic relation of the Mexica to their Tepaneca overlords in Azcapotzalco was the other part of the motivation of the Mexica elders in begging a ruler from Culhacan. At least the Tepaneca must have thought so, for they promptly doubled the Tenochtitlan's tributary obligations, including imposing some peculiarly difficult forms of payment. Still, the Tenochca elders would trump the Tepaneca as well as Tlatelolco by acquiring a ruler of supreme status in Mesoamerica, a ruler of Toltec descent through the Culhuacan monarch of that lineage, which thus connected the Mexica with the great Tollan of ancient memory and its own original king Quetzalcoatl. The Mexica elders, playing the paradigmatic native part of kingmakers, created a polity of imported Toltec rulers of indigenous Chichimec subjects, thus reproducing a recurrent Mesoamerican tradition of kingship—one might even say, the normative form of Mesoamerican kingship.[11]

---

11. The Mexica assumption of Toltec kingship, by contrast to the Tepanec "lord of the Chichimecs," also involved an element of a second form of schismogenesis: a competition by invidious differentiation of the kind that Bateson called

All the same, the historiography of the Mexica kingship has been vexed by the multiple versions of the lineage of the dynasty's ancestor, Acamapichtli. While some of the alternatives are clearly outliers inspired by the chroniclers' own civic loyalties, the more credible texts offer two contradictory versions which, by the prevailing norms of patrilineal descent and succession, would make Acamapichtli either the Toltec king of the Mexica or the Mexica king of complementary Toltec filiation. As related notably by Motolinia (1951: 77–78), the strong Toltec version includes another classic feature of stranger-king traditions: the founder of the dynasty is a prince of a great land who fails to succeed his father and instead migrates to a country where his royal virtues are recognized by the native people, who thereupon install him as their ruler. In this text, Acamapichtli's father, the thirteenth in the main line of the Toltec kings of Culhuacan, was assassinated by a rebel who then usurped his throne, forcing the young prince to flee the city and take refuge in Tenochtitlan. In the contrasting version, however, Acamapichtli's father was a true Mexica notable who had remained in Culhuacan from the time his people sojourned there in the course of their migrations; and there he married a daughter of the Culhua king, the mother of Acamapichtli. Although this version may be the less plausible—as by its implication of the existence of a high Mexica nobility before the letter—it has to be considered historically relevant, not least because it is the more popular of the two. Indeed there is good reason to suppose both were current at the time of the Conquest, since they have valid if different political values and would be functionally appropriate in different contexts. Each has its place.[12]

Basically, the Toltec identity of Mexica kings looks outward, making a claim of higher pedigree against rival potentates; this is kingship in its foreign-encompassing aspect. Whereas a dominantly Mexica identity looks inward, at the

"complementary schismogenesis"—of which another, striking example will be discussed below in connection with Texcoco.

12. I say the paternal Culhuacan ancestry of Acamapichtli is the "strong Toltec version," not only because nobility among the Mexica would have to be patrilineally determined—given the maternal descent of Acamapictli's children rather from *calpulli* elders—but for incidents such as are described in Duran (1994: 68), where Tezozomoc fails to prevent certain Tepanec nobles from seeking the death of his daughter's son, the Mexica ruler Chimalpopoca, they arguing "that even though Chimalpopoca came from the lineage of the Tepaneca, this relationship was through a woman, that because on his father's side he was the son of an Aztec, he would always be inclined towards his father's people and not his mother's." In Sahagún's discussion of kinship relations, "one's father" is described as "the source of lineage, the beginning of lineage" (1953–82, 10.1); but there is no such valorization of maternity.

preeminence they achieved by the aid of their particular tutelary god, Huitzilo-pochtli; this is kingship in its indigenous-exclusive aspect. Giving the Mexica rulers a purely Toltec genealogy clearly makes them different from and superior to their "Chichimec" subjects, not only in Tenochtitlan but in the whole region of Mesoamerica inhabited by peoples of that description. It gives the greatest legitimacy to the Mexica's representations of themselves and their empire as "Culhua," and to the title of their king as "Lord of Culhua"—notably by op-position to the Tepanec ruler, who styled himself "Lord of the Chichimecs." On the other hand, the Mexica paternity of the kingship remained relevant, insofar as it directly connected the rulers to the divine source of their sovereign power, their patron god Huitzilopochtli. The distinctive guardian of their fortunes from the time of their Chichimec origins in the barren north, Huitzilopochtli was also identified with the sun. In the latter capacity he was a central figure in the human sacrificial rites that at once sustained that celestial body and testified to the sovereign's earthly domination. In short, the Mexica paternity of King Acamapichtli, thus linking him to Huitzilopochtli, was as critical for legitimacy of his royal descendants as his Toltec paternity. Indeed, as the source of Mexica rulers' power, the affiliation with Huitzlopochtli was the condition of the pos-sibility of their Toltec hegemony. It follows that both genealogies remained his-torically relevant so long as the Mexica remained politically dominant—much to the consternation of the later professional scholars who need to know which one is "true." If in fact one were true and the other not, it would only confirm Nigel Davies' astute observation (1977: 71) that Mexica history can consist in the reenactment of legendary events that never took place—as in the return of Quetzalcoatl or Lono (Captain Cook), for example.

Indeed, to believe the *Codex Chimalpahin* (Chimalpahin 1997: 69–71), the dual genealogy of Acamapichtli reenacts the ambiguous origins of earlier rulers, sometimes described as "captains-general," who presided over the last stages of the migration of the Mexica from the Chichimec homeland. Here again were stranger-kings who may also have claimed affiliation with the Toltecs: for as the first of them, Huehue Huitzilihuitl descended from the ruler of Xaltocan; and Xaltocan by some accounts was founded by migrants from Tollan following the fall of that city (Bierhorst 1992: 41; Davies 1980: 91).[13] Deemed "the very first

---

13. However, Xaltocan is most commonly identified as an Otomi city (Davies 1980; E. de J. Douglas 2010); albeit there are suggestions its rulers had more exalted genealogical connections, including Culhaucan (Davies 1980: 91, *et passim*).

ruler of the Mexica" in the Chimalpahin text, Huehue Huitzilipochtli was by one version the son of a Xaltocan prince and a daughter accorded him as wife by the Mexica, among whom he had lived.[14] By the symmetrical and inverse version, Huehue Hutzilihuitl was the offspring of a daughter of the Xaltocan ruler and a Mexica man, hence Toltec in the maternal rather than the paternal line. Still, as the *Codex* indicates, one way or another "the very first ruler of the Mexica" was a grandson of a foreign king, and thereby set over the native priests and elders who were erstwhile leaders of the migration from Aztlan. Serial stranger-kingship.

Returning to the kingship of Acamapichtli, this Toltec-minted ruler inaugurated a new order of society, dominated by a newly formed aristocracy. As in stranger-kingdoms in general, the contractual foundation was again the union of the foreign prince with daughters of the native leaders. The "elders" of Tenochtitlan, as many as twenty *calpulli* heads (according to the version), voluntarily provided wives for Acamapichtli: out of sympathy, it is commonly said, for his principal wife, a Culhuacan princess, was barren. The effect would be a kingship that integrated in the royal persons the two fundamental components of the society, native and foreign, Chichimec and Toltec. Descended from a common ancestor, the offspring of these alliances of Acamapichtli with Mexica women would form a kinship-integrated, Toltec-affiliated nobility (*pipiltin*)—one might even speak of a royal lineage—spread over a set of discrete groups of Chichimec origins, each such group being the maternal kin of some subset of the nobility. (There are dozens of African stranger-kingdoms of the same description.) If in the early period of Tenochtitlan these nobles, without lands of their own, went to live with their native maternal kin, this may account for the presence of persons of high rank in the several *calpulli* of the kingdom.

But then, some of the native leaders who were involved in the establishment of Acamapichtli's kingship themselves became "lords" under the new regime. As we have seen, this, too, is a normal feature of stranger-king formations: the bestowal of offices of state on indigenous leaders, notably as the councilors of kings and major priests of the realm. Just so, the *Codex Ramirez* (Ramirez 1903: 38)

---

14. Huehue Huitzilihuitl was killed at Chapultepec by the Culhuaque in1299, to be succeeded by Tenoch, who led the Mexica to Tenochtitlan. Tenoch was the predecessor of Acamapichtli, first of the new *tlatoani* regime. (Huehue Huitzilihuitl [I] is not to be confused with Acamapichtli's son and successor as *tlatoani*, likewise Huitzilihuitl [II].) Davies (1980: 202) considers that a Mexica nobility had surely existed for long before the dynasty inaugurated by Acamapichtli.

relates that at the time of Acamapichtli's kingship there were "still some of the old men who had made the pilgrimage from the distant country to Mexico, old men who became the elders, the lords, charged with grand offices and the conduct of the nation" (ibid.: 36). At least through the succession of Acamapichtli's son Huitzilopochtli, the native notables continued to act as kingmakers, operating as an "electoral college of priests, elders and calpulli officials" (Davies 1977: 198). And they continued to be a major force in the government until the victory over the Tepanecs in 1427 ushered in the imperial era, at once enriching the nobility by the distribution of booty and patrimonial estates, and empowering them by military and political office. "Although Acamapichtli's sons and grandsons appear to have collaborated closely with traditional leaders until 1426," writes Edward Calnek, "they were evidently not permitted to make or execute important decisions until first obtaining consent of a strong popular assembly in which traditional leaders retained a dominant voice" (1982: 53). Following the defeat of the Tepaneca at Azcapotzalco, the *tlatoani* Itzcoatl bestowed titles on the nobility—and also burned the books so the common people would not need to know what did not concern them. Even so, "Until the end of Ahuitzotl's reign (1502), commoners continued to hold powerful positions within the imperial court, and in some instances must have outranked hereditary noblemen by virtue of their offices" (Calnek 1974: 203; cf. P. Carrasco 1971). Moctezuma II abolished all that in a famous reform that restricted official service in the palace, the city, and the provinces to noblemen of unimpeachable pedigree, excluding persons born of "a lowly woman"; for "he considered that anyone born of a lowly woman or a slave might take after his mother and be, therefore, ineligible for his service" (Duran 1994: 395). What is here repudiated is the original formation of polity through the marriage of the stranger-king with the daughters of the native leaders, thereby constituting a nobility of indigenous maternity. Still, the fundamental duality of the stranger-kingdom, consisting of foreign newcomers and indigenous owners of complementary natures and functions, remains evident in many aspects of the culture—as witness the enduring notion of a world basically composed of Chichimecs and Toltecs.[15]

More generally than the native leaders' political powers, the chronicles speak of their presence in many parts of Mexico in terms that indicate their antiquity, their priestly functions, their kinship seniority, and especially their privileged

---

15. "There are two types of people in this land, that still exist today, according to various histories, Chichimec is the first, and Toltec the second . . ." (Davies 1980: 79).

relations to the land. Having given rise to the chiefly children through their daughters, they may be described as "grandfathers" of the rulers and the realm, the "elders" or "fathers" relative to the parvenu aristocracy, or the "original leaders" or "founder chiefs." All these are again common attributes of the underlying autochthonous peoples in stranger-kingdoms, but most significant in this regard is the association of the native people with the land, by contrast to the foreign-cum-celestial aristocracy. I alluded earlier to the entry in the *Codex Chimalpopoca* referring to certain Chichimecs as the "landowners" as well as the "founders" of the country. Another entry rehearses the opposition between foreign rulers and indigenous landholders in a Chalco town:

> This was the year [7 Rabbit, 1486] a dynasty began in Chalco Tlacochcalco, starting with Itzcahuatzin, who was made lord [apparently by the Mexica] at this time. Those who tolerated him there, since they had no ambitions of being princes themselves, were the landholding Tlatecacayohuaque Chalca. (Bierhorst 1992: 117)

Analogously in practice if not also in name, the native *calpulli* of Tenochtitlan were the main landowners. Apparently the nobility were not a landed class until they acquired estates as spoils of Mexica conquests (e.g., Tezozomoc 1853, 1: 40–41). The distribution of conquered lands by Itzcoatl to the noble captains of the early wars of Mexica expansion is described by Tezozomoc (ibid., 1: 40–41, 69–70) as an act of charity, given the impoverished conditions of these prominent men and the necessity to provide for their families and descendants. As opposed to the estates—together with their inhabitants—awarded to the king and the warrior nobility, the booty of the Mexica commoners consisted only of common lands for the upkeep of the *calpulli* temples (Duran 1994: 81–82).[16]

Moreover, the opposition between an indigenous population associated with the land and a conquering aristocracy of foreign derivation was replicated by the two main gods, Tlaloc and Huitzilopochtli, and their respective priests, in the principal temple of Tenochtitlan. In contrast to the solar deity of the upstart

---

16. In Ixtlilxóchitl's (1840, 1: 242–43) discussion of tenure referring to the same period, the *calpulli* lands constituted the greater part of the territory of the city or village, and while held by ordinary people and inherited by their children or relatives, the same were also described as lands of the king and nobility—meaning governed by them? Ixtlilxóchitl also refers to a category of land held by the "old nobility" or "former nobility," a symptom of stranger-kingship.

Mixteca, Huitzilopochtli, Tlaloc was the chief among the old gods of the land, and indeed associated with earthly, agricultural fertility. "Their double presence at the head of the religious world," comments Jacques Soustelle (1964: 58), "consecrated the union of the two basic ideologies of Mexica, which the Mexica had brought together when they became the ruling nation." And more particularly, as Edward de J. Douglas observed:

> Tlaloc's half of the temple, like Huitzilopochtli's, represented a mountain, Tonacatepetl, "Mountain of our Sustenance," the counterpart to Coatepetl, ["Serpent Mountain," Huitzilopochtli's birthplace and site of his initial conquest—of his sister and brothers]. A diphrastic metaphor, the building's complementary opposites—Coatepetl and Tonacatepetl, south and north, sky and earth, sun and rain, fire and water, young and old, foreign and native, Mexica/Chichimec and pan Mesoamerican/Toltec—evoke the fundamental quality of being and, more specifically . . . war, the creative force of existence. (2010: 100)

Most striking is the way the basic dualism of the stranger-kingship polity is recreated at the kingdom level in late pre-Conquest times in the relations between the Texcoco "Chichimecs" and the Mexica "Toltecs" (Ixtlilxóchitl 1840; Townsend 1987; Douglas 2010; Duran 1994). The Triple Alliance was rather more of a diarchy in which the Texcoco ruler–particularly the famous King Nezhualcoyotl–bearing the inherited title of "Lord of the Chichimecs," appears as second in authority to the Mexica "Lord of Culhua." The Texcoco kings adopted the Mexica tutelary god, Huitzilopochtli, and enshrined him alongside Tlaloc in the central temple of their own city. Moreover, at least from the time of the Moctezuma I, inaugurated in 1440, the Texcoco rulers were the kingmakers in Tenochtitlan. The Chichimec kings of Texcoco legitimated the Toltec kings of the Mexica: Nezhualcoyotl and his successor Nezhualpilli were the principal electors of the Mexica *tlatoani*, and the ones who actually crowned the latter in the investiture ceremonies.

The Texcoco rulers' claim as Lord of the Chichimecs represented their descent from the legendary Chichimec conqueror Xotlotl, said to have created a great "Empire" in the Valley of Mexico.[17] True to classical stranger-king traditions, the Texcoco people's own story is that the "primitive" Chichimecs

---

17. The other title of the Texcoco king, "Lord of Alcohua," as the heritage of the "empire" of Xolotl, bore the same Chichimec connotation as "lord of the Chichimecs."

led by Xolotl predated the "civilized" Toltecs in the occupation of the Valley. In Eduardo de J. Douglas' reading of the old Texcoco documents such as the *Tlohtzin Map*, the Chichimec ancestors are depicted as "self-generating and autochthonous, like the Mixtec ancestors"; while in the *Codex Xolotl* and the *Quinitzin Map*, "the Toltecs are the migrants, and the Chichimecs, the native inhabitants . . ." (2010: 55, 58; cf. Bierhorst 1992: 5 for an analogous tradition). In thus depicting their ancestors as the autochthons, the Texcoco traditions differ from the common narratives of Chichimec migrations into the Valley following the collapse of Tollan of the Toltecs. But that is not the only anomaly of Texcoco's Chichimec identity.

The more interesting anomaly is that the Texcoco rulers, for all their Chichimec identity, were affiliated genealogically and assimilated culturally to the Toltecs in the same fundamental ways as the Mexica kings who claimed to be the Lords of Culhua. Beginning with Xolotl's immediate descendants, Nopaltzin and Tlohtzin, the founders of Texcoco dynasty repeatedly married and fathered their successors by Toltec women: brides and mothers who, as Douglas notes, "transmit civilization, and the Toltec legacy, to their daughters and eventually their male descendants" (Douglas 2010: 105). But only eventually to their male descendants, who rather follow their fathers as Chichimecs for some generations. Xolotl's grandson Tholtzin was a Chichimec, although his mother, Nopaltzin's wife Azcaxochiti, was a Toltec, a daughter of the royal house of Culhacan—the same kind of alliance that produced Acamapichtli and launched the Toltec heritage of Mexica kings. In another example, two members of Xolotl's court move away and marry the daughters of the ruler of a Toltec city; each couple has a daughter and a son, and the daughters are born Toltecs and the sons Chichimecs (ibid.: 223 n. 46). The implication of ethnic affiliation descending in separate male and female lines, the former Chichimec and the latter Toltec, is what actually is pictured diagrammatically in Texcoco documents. Whether this was an expedient the illustrator devised for representing double descent—patrilineal and matrilineal—is hard to say.[18] But safe to say, the self-representation of the Texcoco aristocracy as "Chichimec" is arbitrary: as arbitrary as it is politic.

---

18. In this connection, an emphasis on matrifiliation in an otherwise patrilineal order is not necessarily an indication of a cognatic or a double-descent system (cf. Calnek 1974; Kellogg 1986), inasmuch as a kinship order of preferred patrilineal succession and group affiliation commonly involves vital complementary relations to affinal/maternal kin (Leach 1961; Sahlins 2013).

"Do not forget that you are Chichimec," the dying Texcoco king Ixlilxochiti told his son Nezhualcoyotl (Ixtlilxóchitl 1840: 127).

It follows that the Toltec identity of Mexica kings is equally arbitrary, since their maternal descent from Culhuacan kings does not differentiate them from Chichimec rulers who could claim as much. Rather than some sort of pre-scriptive identity, the process in play is a high-stakes mode of complementary schismogenesis in which major kingdoms selectively position themselves vis-à-vis each other by adopting contrasting values from a common stock of cultural traditions. Texcoco was already involved with the Tepanecs of Azcapotzalco in a conflict of the symmetrical schismogenesis variety before the rise of the Mexica and the formation of the Triple Alliance. Not long after the Tepanec ruler Tezo-zomoc proclaimed himself "Lord of the Chichimecs," which was something of a usurpation in the Alcohua view, the Texcoco king Ixlilxochiti went him one or two better by having himself installed as "Universal Monarch" and "Lord of All the Earth" (Davies 1980: 56). When the Mexica came along as Toltecs, their ruler assuming the title of "Lord of Culhua," it was not so much a play of a symmetrical kind as what Bateson called "complementary schismogenesis," which works rather on claiming a status "different to and better than" the other party.[19] By virtue of such oppositions, a complex set of values may come into operation: the way the Chichimecs are mere "barbarians" from the perspective of the civilized Toltecs, but in their own view "hardy and great warriors" of the hinterlands as opposed to the city-dwelling Toltec artists and craftsmen. On the other hand, as Bateson (1935, 1958) pointed out, insofar as such contrasting values are complementary and interdependent, the conflict between them may reach a point of equilibrium and reciprocal exchange.[20] It seems fair to say that this is what happened in the case of the Texcoco "Chichimecs" and the Mexica "Toltecs," no doubt motivated by a political situation in which alliance was the better part of valor.

I close, then, with one of the many anthropological lessons that could be drawn from such histories of interacting and interdependent societies. Clearly, these societies are formed in relation to one another: perhaps to the extent that

---

19. In other registers, the Mexica double claim of being Chichimecs and Toltecs—or alternatively worshipers of Huitzilopochtli and Tlaloc—thus as Lords of Heaven and Earth—would indeed symmetrically top even the Lord of All the Earth.

20. For an excellent example, see Lévi-Strauss' (1971) study of the differentiation and reconciliation of the Native American Mandan and Hidatsa peoples.

the legitimacy of their own rulers depends on their foreign origins—stranger-kingship—or that these rulers take on borrowed notions of authority that are beyond their own political means—galactic mimesis. The lesson is that anthropology has long been implicated in a major theoretical scandal, insofar as it has been futilely engaged in various ways of explaining cultures from within, as if they were self-fashioning, although even their differences are formed in relationships to others—schismogenesis. "Human societies are never alone," as Lévi-Strauss (1952: 9) said, although he might have added that anthropologists—as others in the human sciences—have generally acted as though they were. I won't go into the reasons, which range from the prevalence of nationalist concepts to the limitations of ethnographic practice, hence the habitual epistemological inclination to know cultures as isolated monads. Suffice it to note that, with some important exceptions such as globalization and world-systems studies, virtually all our received paradigms of cultural order and development—functionalism, structural-functionalism, cultural materialism, evolutionism, Marxism of base and superstructure, the new ontology and the old ecology, patterns of culture, even postmodern discourses, epistemes, and subjectivities—all these paradigms suppose that the forms, relations, or configurations at issue are situated within a more or less coherent cultural scheme, and that the articulations and dynamics of that scheme are the theoretical matters at issue. French structuralism has had an interesting history in this respect, likewise inner-directed so long it was based on Saussurean notions of a systematic semiotic field in which "*tout se tient*," but from which it broke out in Lévi-Strauss' intercultural permutations of mythical structures. By and large, however, as Fredrik Barth succinctly put it decades ago, "Practically all anthropological reasoning rests on the premise that cultural variation is discontinuous: that there are aggregates of people who essentially share a common culture, and the interconnected differences that distinguish such culture from others" (1969: 9).

The scandal is that this is empirically not so and evidently never has been so. The great majority of societies known to ethnography and archaeology, as remote in space and far back in time as we can get, are formed by their situation within fields of cultural others. Even as Immanuel Wallerstein (1976) was developing the notion of a capitalist world-system, Stanley Tambiah had worked out the galactic polity, and Kajsa Ekholm (1980) and Jonathan Friedman (1992) had discovered the five-thousand-year-old history of regional core–periphery configurations focused on dominant civilizations (cf. Ekholm and Friedman 1979). Not to forget Alfred Kroeber's (1945) similar discussion of the Eurasian ecumene and its underdeveloped margins, Morton Fried's (1975) arguments about the relations between pristine states, secondary states, and dependent "tribes," and Aidan Southall's (1988) depiction of "segmentary states." Early on, Kroeber (1947) and Clark Wissler (1938) were mapping Native American "culture areas" that were likewise centered on certain "dominant cultures" or marked by "cultural climaxes." More recently, Deborah Gewertz (1983), Anthony Forge (1990), and Simon Harrison (1990), reporting on the peoples of the Middle Sepik, New Guinea, and Dan Jorgensen (1990c, 1996), on the Sepik Headwaters, have ethnographically recorded just such regional systems, focused on the Iatmul and Telefol peoples, respectively. These studies show that by means of the demonstration-effects of punctuated warfare and the demonstrated efficacy of the spirits and rituals of the leading peoples, regional patterns of core–periphery relations analogous to the galactic polities of "high cultures" exist as well in the tribal zone. They may even involve a degree of economic domination, insofar as the agricultural prosperity of the peripheral peoples depends on rituals controlled by the central groups. In sum, this hierarchical system of "interculturality," as it may be called, is the normal state of cultural affairs in many places. Perhaps everywhere. Certainly from my own limited knowledge of the primary texts on Native Mesoamerica and the brilliant scholarly analyses made of them, I suspect that such interculturality is equally a feature of Mexica history. It seems appropriate, then, to leave the last word to the greatest student of intercultural relations among Native American peoples, Lévi-Strauss:

> It is high time that anthropology freed itself from the illusion gratuitously invented by the functionalists, who mistake the practical limitations imposed on them by the kind of studies they advocate for the absolute properties of the objects with which they are dealing. An anthropologist may confine himself for one or more years within a small social unit, group or village, and endeavor to grasp it as a totality, but this is no reason for imagining that the unit, at levels other than the one at which convenience or necessity has placed him, does not merge in varying degrees with larger entities, the existence of which remains, more often than not, unsuspected. (1990: 609)

CHAPTER 5

The people as nursemaids of the king

Notes on monarchs as children, women's uprisings, and the return of the ancestral dead in central Madagascar

David Graeber

The institution of kingship embodies a kind of paradox. Kings are both omnipotent and helpless. On the one hand, the essence of sovereignty is the sovereign's power to do as he likes with his subjects and their possessions, and the more absolute the monarchy, the more absolute, arbitrary, and unaccountable this power tends to be. On the other hand, kings are, in part for this very reason, dependent on their subjects. They are fed, clothed, housed, and have their basic physical needs attended to by those ostensibly under their power. And the more absolute their power, the greater that dependency will also tend to be.

For those educated in European philosophy, this observation will immediately call to mind Georg Wilhelm Friedrich Hegel's master–slave dialectic, where the conqueror, in reducing his rival to servitude, becomes dependent on him for his means of livelihood, while the conquered at least achieves a kind of paradoxical autonomy, and mastery, in work. But Hegel was by no means the first to have noticed this dynamic. There have been times and places, far from

Ranavalo Manjaka, reine de Madagascar, et ses héritiers présomptifs. (Page 186.)

Hegel's Germany, where the paradox is seen as lying at the very center of the idea of kingship; not just in the reflections of philosophers but in the ritual life surrounding kings themselves.

In this essay I'd like to explore one of them. In the Merina kingdom of the north central plateau of Madagascar, kings were quite often represented as infants, toddlers, or petulant adolescents. They were assumed to be both willful, difficult, and utterly dependent on their subjects. Framing institutions of government in this fashion created a peculiar moral alchemy whereby selfishness, imperiousness, even occasional outbursts of vindictive violence, could actually be seen as endearing, or, at the very least, as reinforcing the feeling that it was the duty of commoners to attend to royal needs. Yet this way of imagining royal power clearly cut two ways. For one thing, it was accompanied by a sense that, while the living ruler could be seen as a kind of perpetual minor, it was dead kings—the royal ancestors—who really represented mature authority. For another, it gave subjects a language with which to chasten and admonish rulers, whether in their own names or the names of those ancestors, whenever they were seen to have gone too far.

This aspect of Merina kingship has largely been ignored in the existing scholarly literature. But as soon as you start looking for it in the primary sources, it's everywhere.

It is one of the unique pleasures of studying the Merina kingdom that these sources are so rich. After King Radama I invited foreign missionaries into his kingdom to set up a system of primary education in 1820, literacy became widespread, and the result was an unprecedented outpouring of texts, official and unofficial—ranging from histories, compendia of customs, poetry, oratory and folklore, including a 1,243-page collection called the *Tantara ny andriana eto Madagascar* ("History of the kings of Madagascar") which consists of a detailed history and ethnography of nineteenth-century Merina[1] society in pretty much all of its aspects, drawn from a wide variety of authors. Infuriatingly, since most of this material only reaches us through missionary sources, almost none of the authors' names have been preserved. (The *Tantara*, for instance, is remembered as the work of one Père Callet, a Jesuit priest who assembled and edited the manuscripts.) Still, combined with the detailed correspondence, legal records, and official registers preserved in the National Archives, they provide an almost unparalleled window on nineteenth-century Merina society.

What I'm going to do in the following pages, then, is to examine how the theme of king as child works itself out in this literature. I'll start with a story that I heard while I was carrying out my own fieldwork in 1990 and 1991, about an arrogant prince who literally fell from power. Stories like his, it seems to me, raise obvious questions about the nature of authority in the highlands: first and foremost why, if kings really did receive the unquestioning devotion of their subjects, as all foreign observers insisted they did, are they now remembered largely as bullies and tyrants? To understand that, in turn, will require an examination of the overall organization of the kingdom itself, conceived as a vast structure of ritual labor; then, reexamining moments in the past when royal authority was challenged through that lens. Finally, I will ask whether the apparently exotic formulations of Merina kingship, in which the people regularly represented themselves as "nursemaids" of the king, might not also provide insights into more general questions about the nature of social authority.

---

1.   The name "Merina" is rarely used nowadays, and even in the nineteenth century was one term among many (Larson 1996). Generally speaking, I avoid the term when speaking of the contemporary descendants of those known in the literature as "Merina," but it seems appropriate in this historical context.

INTRODUCTION: LEILOZA AND THE PROPHET OF VALALAFOTSY

Leiloza, the last prince of Imamo

I carried out my doctoral research in the northern hinterlands of the town of Arivonimamo, in Western Imerina. This is rolling country, dotted by small granite mountains, valleys full of tiny streams and terraced rice fields, broken by expanses of tapia forest—tapia being a tree that looks a little like a dwarf oak, and sports silkworms from whose webs a native cloth is manufactured. This is what the area has long been famous for. Until the very end of the eighteenth century, too, this territory, along with all the lands west of the Ombifotsy River, were part of an independent kingdom called Imamo, distinct from Imerina to the east. Or, to be more specific, they were considered to have once, long before, been unified under a great wise king named Andriambahoaka, just as in the same time Imerina was considered to have been created by a great wise king named Andriamasinavalona. Such great wise kings always seem to have existed a few generations in the past, just beyond living memory. In the case of Imerina and Imamo, the same story was told: the great wise king, unwisely, split his territory between four sons, resulting in endless civil wars.

In the case of Imamo, however, these rival princes did all share a single tomb. In the nineteenth century, this tomb was known as Fondanitra ("in the heart of the sky"), a huge stone structure which sat atop the sugar-loaf mountain of Ambohitrambo—a mountain that dominates the landscape of the region, visible for miles around.

The mountain, and the tomb, is still there; and it's still a place of pilgrimage. But now the tomb is remembered not as the burial place of the collectivity of Imamo's kings—just about all of these have been forgotten—but as the tomb of a boy named Lailoza, or Leiloza, remembered as a childish, tyrannical young prince who, it is said, never actually came to the throne of Imamo.[2] Still, everyone knows his story. According to the legend, Leiloza was so literally high and mighty that he refused to walk along the hillside paths like ordinary humans, but instead employed the women of the kingdom constantly weaving silk, which he had turned into giant cable bridges between Ambohitrambo and other nearby mountains; bridges reserved for his personal use. This caused such

---

2. The name means "the great disaster," though used of a person *loza* can also mean "fierce" or "angry."

suffering that one day, his father could no longer stand it, and cut the cable while his son was on the bridge, sending his only child plummeting to his death.

The place where he is said to have fallen is a village now known as Manjakazaza, which literally means "a child rules." "Because he was just a child," people told me, "but he bossed everyone around." (*zaza fotsiny fa nanjakajaka*; cf. Graeber 2007a: 90).

These elements of the story appeared in every version I heard, or am aware of. Some added further embellishments: random executions, whimsical orders—in one version, the prince is even said to have forced all the women in the kingdom to cut off their hair to provide materials for his bridge. By at least the 1960s, such actions had become proverbial. One French ethnographer who worked in the region cites an informant as follows:

> This Leiloza loved to make the population suffer for his own pleasure; now, he had a herd of cattle; sometimes, he would give the order to take the entire herd up some hill for no reason, and then bring them down again; hence the saying *"Akaro toy ny andry ombin'i Leiloza."* [Go up the hill like those minding Leiloza's cattle.] (Augustins 1971: 553)[3]

When asked why Leiloza acted the way he did, people would usually just say that he was *maditra*—a word that can probably be best translated as "naughty," since it's mainly used for children who misbehave. In dictionaries it's sometimes translated "stubborn," in the sense of actively resisting parental authority, rather in the way English-speaking parents will say a child "won't listen" when they mean "won't do as he's told."[4] It's unusual to spend any length of time with a Malagasy woman taking care of, say, a toddler without hearing the word evoked at least once or twice, often called out in a chiding tone that seems

---

3.   Augustin's informant continues: "Or again, when, at Antongona, a village twenty-five kilometers away from Ambohitrambo, something was burning. Leiloza would say 'put out that fire at Antongona, the smoke from it might choke me.' And from that comes the saying *'Efa ho lava ny afon'Antongona,'* 'interminable like the fire of Antongona'" (ibid.). This story I never heard myself, but it seems to distantly evoke myths where upstart heroes challenge the divine powers by setting fires to send smoke to heaven to choke the children of God.

4.   Hence Richardson defines *maditra* as "obstinate, stubborn, pertinacious" (1885: 123). This makes sense because the root, *ditra*, also refers to things that are hard and resistant, such as a knotty piece of wood that cannot easily take a nail.

simultaneously indignant and at least a little bit bemused. Yet the same word, *maditra*, was also employed to refer to princes, kings, or other figures of high authority when they behaved unjustly and arbitrarily. In one early source, the bad prince of Ambohitrambo is actually referred to not as Leiloza, but simply as Rakotomaditra, or "Naughty Young Man" (Callet 1908: 573 n. 1).

Leiloza, then, is the very embodiment of selfish, childish, royal behavior.

The curious thing is that this term, *maditra*, is not really a generic word for irresponsible or headstrong behavior. It's used when referring to children or figures of authority—especially royalty—but only rarely anybody else. When I was still doing my fieldwork, I often wondered why this should be. What was it about powerful people, and recalcitrant children, that people found analogous?

It also always struck me as curious that while one might think the real hero of the story was Leiloza's father—he, after all, was the one who was ultimately willing to sacrifice his own posterity for the sake of his subjects—*his* name was never mentioned. I often asked; but few were even willing to speculate as to what it might have been.[5] Leiloza's fame, in contrast, has only increased since his death. This is in part because his death redeemed him. He has become a royal ancestor, one of a pantheon of spirits called on to possesses mediumistic curers, and help them to cure the sick, answer vows, and battle the designs of witches. His tomb has become a *doany*, a portal and a place a pilgrimage—perhaps not nearly so important a one as Andriantsihanika, the most famous royal tomb in Imamo, located further to the west, but this is largely because Ambohitrambo is far from any paved road, and Andriantsihanika is very close to the highway.

Most large mountains are said to be marked by royal tombs of one sort or another, and many of these have become *doany*, a word which literally means "customs office," opening on a kind of spectral universe inhabited by heroic figures from "Malagasy times." They are referred to collectively as "kings" (*andriana*). But the stories associated with them tend to be, like Leiloza's, markedly antimonarchical in tone. Andriantsihanika, for example, is remembered now as a descendant of a king who voluntarily abandoned his *andriana* status and became a commoner because he "didn't want to have slaves" (Peetz 1951a). Others were magicians who defied unjust royal power, women betrayed by royal friends or lovers, or simply notable historical figures—diviners, water-nymphs—with

---

5.   One informant suggested "Ratrimo," but there's no other record of such a figure. Augustin (1971: 553) suggests Andriantokanandy, but this seems to be taken somewhat arbitrarily from a different royal genealogy.

no particular relation to royalty at all. Some bear the names of documented historical rulers, but rarely, if ever, even in those cases did I hear anyone who frequented, made vows and offerings at, such rulers' *doany* have anything good to say about their behavior when they were still alive. Perhaps few went so far as Ratsizafy, the old and venerable astrologer in the community where I did my own fieldwork, who insisted that all the famous kings of Madagascar were actually witches, who only since their death had returned to cure the diseases they once had caused (Graeber 2007a: 302). But everyone seemed to feel that dead kings were very much preferable to live ones.

Still, there was a universal acknowledgment that, however cruel and disastrous monarchs might have been in life, as soon as they were placed inside the stone chambers of the tomb, everything changed, and monarchs were immediately transformed into "holy spirits" (*fanahy masina*) capable of protecting the living from the very disasters they used to inflict on them in life.

The uniformity of this attitude surprised me. Almost no one had anything good to say about past monarchs—this despite the fact that almost everyone had learned at least a little Malagasy history in primary school, where historical monarchs were presented in a far more favorable light. In fact, the only real exceptions I encountered were a handful of educated history buffs who had memorized the names and dates of ancient rulers from textbooks. They, at least, would often take the view common amongst the intelligentsia and see at least some of the past rulers as nationalist heroes of one sort or another. But I never heard such sentiments from anybody else. Ask an ordinary farmer, trader, or laborer, one would invariably hear some variation of the same story: the *andriana* of "Malagasy times" (*tany gasy*) had abused their authority, they had kept slaves, or treated their subjects like slaves, or both; and for this they had been punished, like Leiloza's father, by the loss of their posterity. Even after they were deposed, many insisted, they often proved infertile, or their children came to bad ends, their numbers dwindled, the few left falling into madness or poverty. This was God's judgment, said those who considered themselves pious Christians. The less pious cited the famous Malagasy proverb, "divine retribution may not exist, but what you do comes back" (*ny tody tsy misy fa ny atao no miverina*).

Such statements were all the more striking because in the nineteenth century there is simply no sign of such sentiments at all. They are nowhere to be found in the voluminous Malagasy literature of the time, which tended to represent ancient kings as wise and benevolent founders of contemporary institutions. Neither can one see anything like it in the observations of foreign visitors, who would uniformly remark on the absolute, unquestioning devotion of the Merina population to their queen. Yet as soon as the colonial period (1895–1950) begins, such stories seem to pop up out of nowhere. So how did popular views of royalty change so rapidly?

My first attempt at an answer to this question—the one I develop in my book *Lost people* (Graeber 2007a)—was that the change of attitudes had something to do with the shock of colonization. Practically the first thing the French colonial regime did after conquering Madagascar in 1895 was to dissolve the monarchy—but they also abolished slavery at the same time. The fact that under the police state regime that followed, Christianity became about the only institutional form in which it was possible to express nationalist sentiments, combined with the continued presence of a population of ex-slaves living in uncomfortable proximity to their former masters, created an environment where slavery became a continual source of guilt and embarrassment. It became the kind of issue that everyone didn't want to talk about, but almost invariably ended up talking about anyway: a reality that had to be so constantly hidden it ended up seeming the hidden reality behind everything. When I asked rural people about precolonial history, almost no matter what I asked about, my interlocutors would half the time assume I was *really* asking about slavery.

All powers of command—whether royal or colonial power—seemed to fuse together in people's minds as so many extensions of the principle of slavery, of making one person an extension of another's will.[6] As a result, even wage labor was frowned upon, at least among adults. Curiously, this moral condemnation of relations of command was particularly marked among the descendants of the free population, the descendants of *hova* ("commoners"), or *andriana*. The actual descendants of slaves, who constituted roughly a third of the population, do not feel they are in a position to be nearly so punctilious about such matters: in fact, they were not only more likely to become Zanadrano, that is, mediumistic curers who still tended the tombs of royal ancestors, they were also the most willing to join the actual military, work for wages, or otherwise subordinate themselves to others in ways that would ultimately extricate themselves from poverty.

---

6.   Hence, people would often refer to both kings and the French as having treated their ancestors as slaves, slaves were often described as "soldiers," and fundamental institutions of the royal period, such as *fanompoana*, or royal "service," which was once what distinguished free subjects from slaves, were now seen as simple euphemisms for "slavery."

In fact, the cult of the Zanadrano, which has also existed at least since the colonial period (cf. Peetz 1951a, 1951b; Bernard-Thierry 1960; Cabanes 1972), has been dominated, from the beginning, by descendants of slaves. Royal tombs, for example, the kind that become places of cult, are almost invariably accompanied by small outlying tombs of figures who are usually referred to as the king's "soldiers," who still serve their old masters, and whose spirits do the hard work of actually fighting the witches and retrieving the evil charms they have planted in patients' houses, fields, wells, and gardens. It would often be explained to me that the word "soldier" here was really just a polite way of saying "slave." It was the presence of such slave-tombs that marked the royal tomb as royal. But at the same time, the mediums, too, would refer to themselves as the "soldiers" of the divine spirits who—wicked in life, benevolent in death—possessed them and rendered them extensions of their will.

Such was my reading at the time. I still stand by it. It's clear that the shock of colonization, and the end of slavery in particular, did play havoc with existing conceptions of authority. And there is certainly no precedent for any of this in the cult of the "twelve sacred mountains," each with its purely benevolent royal ancestor, that existed under the monarchy. Still, political ideas don't come out of nowhere. It's all a matter of where you look. And if one turns back to the nineteenth-century literature and looks in the right places, one can, I think, already find strong evidence that the nature and legitimacy of the power of kings was, indeed, being contested, and often quite openly. The most compelling evidence is the fact that almost all the foreign observations about subjects' unquestioning obedience to the sovereign referred not to kings, but to queens. In fact, during the seventy-eight years where foreign observers were present, from roughly 1816 to 1895, only two men (Radama I and Radama II) sat on the throne, for a total of fourteen years between them, and both faced significant popular opposition. All other heads of state were women.

Here is the canonical list of Merina monarchs, to give a sense:

- King Andriamasinavalona (c. 1675–1710)
- [period of civil wars, c. 1710–87, all contesting parties male]
- King Andrianampoinimerina (1787–1810)
- King Radama I (1810–28)
- Queen Ranavalona I (1828–61)
- King Radama II (1861–63)
- Queen Rasoherina (1863–68)

- Queen Ranavalona II (1868–83)
- Queen Ranavalona III (1883–95)

Now, the standard narrative of the Merina kingdom runs like this: once upon a time, there was a wise old king named Andriamasinavalona, who managed to unify the numerous tiny kingdoms of the northern highlands into what was later to become the Merina state. After his death, the kingdom descended into civil wars, with his various male descendants vying for power. Up to this time, in fact, there is no record of female monarchs of any sort, other than legends about the very distant, misty past. Eventually, the ruler of one of these principalities managed to conquer the rest, took on the name Andrianampoinimerina ("the desire of Imerina"), and laid the foundations of the Merina state—insisting his ultimate goal was to bring the entire island of Madagascar under his suzerainty. His son, Radama, managed to accomplish his father's vision by entering into an alliance with British agents from Mauritius, who sent military aid and advisors to help him create a standing army, and invited foreign missionaries to enter his kingdom on condition they establish a school system on which he could train civil service. But Radama's early death threw the kingdom into crisis. Commoner generals seized power, and placed his widow, Ranavalona, on the throne.

Ranavalona reigned for the next thirty-three years, and is remembered both as a terrifying tyrant who fostered endless wars against coastal "rebels," and a protonationalist who restored the ancient rituals, expelled missionaries and other foreign agents, and demanded world powers recognize Madagascar as a fully independent modern state. Her death provoked another crisis, and after a brief attempt by her son Radama II to open Madagascar to foreign powers once again, another military coup in 1863 led to a compromise where from then on, only women would actually sit on the Merina throne. The last three queens were all selected by, and secretly married to, the commoner prime minister, Rainilaiarivony, the general who actually held ultimate political authority.

Such is the canonical version. The story is true as far as it goes. But one must ask: If what we are dealing with is essentially a ploy, a series of queens put up as figureheads by what was really a commoner military junta, what was it that made the generals think such a ploy would be effective? As I've noted, there was little precedent for women rulers in Merina history.[7] Even

---

7.   According to legend, in very early times there were two female monarchs named Rafohy and Rangita, but these were "Vazimba" monarchs, Vazimba often being

in world-comparative terms, what they came up with was an extraordinarily unusual arrangement. In fact it may well be unique. I am not aware of any other kingdom on record, anywhere in the world, where a clique of commoners seized power and legitimated their rule by placing a series of exclusively female monarchs on the throne.[8]

Even more, one has to ask why the ploy actually *was* effective. Because while both Radamas faced strong popular resistance, by all accounts, the queens—however oppressive the military cliques that actually ran their governments (and they were often very oppressive indeed)—did not. Even the terrifying Ranavalona I seems to have inspired genuine devotion.

* * *

So far the story of Leiloza, which purports to explain the end of the monarchy in Imamo, has led us to a series of historical puzzles. Let me arrange them in reverse order:

1. Why is it that in the nineteenth century, the legitimacy of male kings fell into question, but the legitimacy of female ones did not?
2. Why is it that after the French conquest, popular history was quickly rewritten so that all ancient monarchs were represented as being oppressive or even outright evil during their lifetimes, but benevolent and protective after their deaths?[9]
3. Why is it that when describing their unjust and oppressive behavior, kings are so often represented in their lifetimes as petulant, egotistical, "naughty" children?

---

represented as an early, aboriginal people expelled by the current inhabitants of the country.

8.   There are a few cases where the paramount political position is always expected to be held by a woman: the Lovedu "rain queen" (Krige and Krige 1943) being perhaps the most famous. But it is surprisingly rare.

9.   It's worth pointing out here that almost all documented eighteenth- and nineteenth-century rulers, including the queens, were quickly forgotten in the colonial period. The founder of the Merina state, Andrianampoinimerina, is still an important curing spirit, and there are still shrines to a few earlier kings, but the latter are of virtually no ritual importance. The "kings" remembered now are a peculiar hodgepodge of ancient figures almost none of whom were actually rulers, let alone important rulers, during their lifetimes.

The best way to start to think about answers to these questions, it seems to me, would be to reexamine the history of Leiloza himself. Because there was a historically documented prince of Imamo named Leiloza, who did in fact fall from power, and it happened just around the time that the fabled Leiloza of Ambohitrambo is supposed to have tumbled from his bridge. It's actually rather remarkable we know the story, because most stories from Imamo have been irrevocably lost. By a peculiar historical accident, history has been preserved, in the unpublished journals of one James Hastie, a British infantry sergeant dispatched to the court of king Radama by the governor of Mauritius in 1817, and who was at the time acting as the king's chief military advisor. In this very early account, many of the key elements that were later to come together in Merina attitudes toward their rulers—from mediumship to female rule—are already very much present, and might be said provide a kind of structural foretaste of what was to come.

Let me begin, then, with Hastie's account.

The real Leiloza and the bandit queen

The Leiloza in Hastie's account was not from Ambohitrambo but from a small kingdom called Valalafotsy, also part of the region of Imamo, but on the very western fringes of the highlands, where it drifts into uninhabited no-man's land. His story appears in account of the death of Leiloza's son, Rabevola, at the hands of the Merina king, Radama I.

In October 1824, Radama's new British-trained army, fresh from its conquest of the Sakalava kingdom of Boina, was marching south through a territory called Mivamahamay. It was largely open country, dotted with occasional forests, renowned for its dense herds of feral cattle, which the soldiers stopped to hunt. The only inhabitants of this desolate land were a band of several thousand runaways from the highlands, most of them Manendy—members of a famous warrior caste who had once served Radama's father (Domenichini and Domenichini-Ramiaramanana 1980; Rakotomanolo 1981). They had presented themselves at the court of the king of Boina, who granted them leave to establish themselves in this no-man's land. There they formed what Hastie referred to as a "Manendy Republic," welcoming a variety of other refugees from the highlands, who ranged from escaped slaves to various unseated princes and their retainers. This motley crew soon became notorious for launching marauding raids on Radama's subjects in the highlands, and in the process, accumulating a great deal of moveable wealth.

In fact, the "Manendy Republic" was only a republic in a certain very broad sense of the term. It had a supreme leader: a "prophetess," as Hastie describes her, widely feared across the region. This woman went by the unwieldy name of Triemanosinamamy.[10]

This is where the story becomes relevant to us, because in describing the origins of this prophetess, Hastie begins telling stories, obviously culled from her followers, about events in the highlands several generations before. As it turns out, Sergeant Hastie explains, Triemanosinamamy was not originally the name of the prophetess, but the name of an earlier ruler of Valalafotsy, a kingdom on the very western marches of Imamo. What's more, the prophetess was the successor to the recently deceased former chieftain of the Manendy Republic, who was, precisely, Leiloza. Leiloza had himself originally been king of Valalafotsy:[11]

It is said that four generations back, a Chieftain named Triemanosinamamy governed the district Valalafotsy in so equitable and successful a manner as to render himself highly respected and even revered by all his subjects. His good actions had such an effect that they transferred his influence and popularity to his descendants and particularly to the Chieftain from whom the late Leiloza was descended. During the reign of Leiloza, a slave boy that was sent for firewood returned with a dry faggot and placed it under the cave, outside his master's house, where it was soon discovered to grow luxuriantly, and the boy ran into a little building or cemetery which was erected over the remains of Triemanosinamamy; a place considered so sacred by the natives that they suppose any person not of noble blood would die immediately on entering it. The boy, however,

---

10. Since the text was written just before Malagasy spelling was standardized in its current form, I follow the version adopted by the English missionary William Ellis, who summarizes Hastie's account in his *History of Madagascar* (1838, II: 345–48). Ellis' version abbreviates the narrative, leaves out several elements such as the magical charms and prophetess' harem, but otherwise remains fairly faithful to the original. The most peculiar omission is the name Leiloza, whose name is written Lahilooza in Hastie's text—Ellis for some reason renders this Sahiloza and incorrectly ascribes the name to the first "prophet" in the story, rather than to the king. There's also the question of the old king's name, which takes an unusual form. Trie- is a rare prefix, and *manosimamy* would literally mean "to confiscate that which is sweet," which doesn't seem to make a lot of sense. I follow Ellis but suspect the real name was different. Hastie's first mention of the name is *Tsiemamoshima maam*, which seems better rendered Tsiemamotsiramamy, which would make slightly better sense.

11. I have kept the original, but changed the spelling of the Malagasy names to standard form.

soon began to sing, and roar loudly; and after singing, and roaring alternately for some time, he declared himself to be filled with spirit, and ultimately to be the absolute person of the long-deceased Chief Triemanosinamamy, whose voice it was imagined by those on the outside he had assumed. Under this assumed title he issued from the tomb and was received by many as a true prophet; the miracle of the dry faggot growing being considered an incontrovertible proof, that he was not an imposter, and it so occurred that he gained confidence with the people by happening to foretell, with exactness in several instances, their success or defeat in marauding expeditions.

Leiloza finding his own power declining, and that of the prophet fast increasing, charged him with being an imposter and urged that his dark colour and particularly his curly head proved that he could not be the personage that he represented himself to be. And Leiloza caused him to be put to death.

At that period commenced the victorious career of Radama's father Andrianampoinimerina, who, aiming at conquest, attacked the district of Valalafotsy, and met little opposition from Leiloza, who was deserted by the greater part of his subjects; it being their belief that in the prophet they had lost the only means by which the invaders could be restrained. And Leiloza, with a few followers, sought safety in the Boina district, where they were joined by the Manendy and other immigrants or runaways from Imerina. They all settled at Mivamahamay, where Leiloza died, leaving the settlement without a leader of distinction.

Much confusion succeeded until a female of more than ordinary talent raised herself to notice among them, and in confidence told Rabevola (the son of Leiloza) that she was the identical person that his father had caused to be put to death; in testimony of which she showed the wounds inflicted on her former person, when in the character of a man, and this she asserted to be the cause of her now assuming the character of a female.

Rabevola gave full credit to her story, and several of the persons who had witnessed the execution of the slave boy prophet testified that the report she made of the wounds was correct. She had no difficulty consequently in getting herself installed as the leader of the people. However she always permitted Rabevola and Tsiafondrazana [her second husband, the Manendy leader] to appear to share the power of Government with her; and the several petty Chieftains that have since joined the population under her sway have been allowed to form their parties, and enjoy all the privileges of royalty, within their respective divisions; so that she has thus kept in favor with all. And though she had only two reputed husbands, she exercised her extensive prerogative in that respect as a true-born Princess of the country is entitled to do. (Hastie n.d.: 402–6)[12]

After having defeated the main force of Manendy a few days previous, Radama's soldiers had captured the prophetess and her chief followers red-handed, trying to make off with some royal cattle. Curious to meet so extraordinary a figure, Hastie accompanied two officers who had been sent to interrogate the captives. Her people, probably numbering not more than a few hundred, had, it would seem, established a certain reputation for themselves, not so much for military might, as for knowledge of dangerous medicines. Their forest camp, serving as temporary capital, was guarded only by *ody*: "pieces of sticks, and roots in various forms, and rubbed with oils, were suspended on the trees around them" (ibid.: 402) without, to Hastie's surprise, any more conventional fortification. At the center of the camp, they encountered the prophetess herself. Hastie found her decidedly unimposing in appearance: about twenty-five-years of age, short and fat, dark of complexion, with frizzy hair but excellent teeth, she appeared flanked by her two "copper-colored" husbands. Backed up by Leiloza's son Rabevola, "she launched into vigorous protestations of innocence, swearing endless fidelity to the Merina king" (ibid.). Rabevola added that any accusations of their being in possession of *ody mahery*, or evil medicine, were entirely unfounded: they had

---

12. Some liberties have been taken with punctuation. That Leiloza was indeed a historical ruler of Valalafotsy is confirmed in the *Tantara ny andriana* (Callet 1908: 567), a series of manuscripts assembled sometime in the late nineteenth century, where the king reigning in Valalafotsy at the time of Andrianampoinimerina's conquests is called alternately Andriandeiloza or Andriandailoza—the prefix here just meaning "lord" or "king." Otherwise the name is the same. No indication is given of his ancestry, but he is said to have made common cause with the last high king of Imamo, Andrianampoetsakarivo, who led the western resistance against the Merina king, but then is said finally, on realizing his kingdom would inevitably fall, to have buried his wealth somewhere in his ancestral lands and "fled to Sakalava." The story now attributed to Leiloza, about Mount Ambohitrambo and its bridges of silk, does appear in the *Tantara* (ibid.: 573 n. 1), but the imperious prince is referred to instead as Andriankotomaditra ("lord naughty young man"), though the author adds, "who some call Andriandahiloza." (To make matters even more confusing, Rakotomaditra is nowadays remembered instead as the name of a faithful slave of Andriantsihanika, the king who gave up his throne, who is buried next to his tomb and still assists him in doing battle with witches.) So two generations later, the legend of Leiloza's bad behavior and consequent fall was already beginning to take on its current form—but it had not completely done so.

only such as were required to protect them from the envy of their enemies, but even those they would gladly abandon should it please the king.

Radama assured Hastie he had abundant proof that they were lying in all these matters, and were guilty of numerous crimes. He ordered their immediate execution.

> When Radama's commands were communicated to the heroine, she stood up, and taking her spear and shield, both of which she handled with skill, she attempted to harangue her followers. She used much gesticulation and said that those who believed her to be the spirit of Triemanosinamamy were right, and tho' her person might now again suffer, she would still be victorious and she roared out "never despair never despair."
>
> When the infatuated woman was conveyed to the place in which she was to suffer, she requested that she might be dispatched with a spear, as she had a great antipathy to being shot. Her wish was complied with, and Rabevola suffered at the same time. (Hastie n.d.: 402)

Such, then, was the real ignominious end of the line of Leiloza. Radama ordered the entire settlement razed, and the bulk of its population returned to Valalafotsy.[13]

Hastie's text is particularly intriguing because it appears to represent the very earliest reference we have to spirit mediumship in the Malagasy highlands. Written in 1824, it refers mainly to events that must have taken place in the 1760s, 1770s, and 1780s. Hastie lacks the language to describe it—hence his talk of "prophets" and "reincarnations"—but, clearly, this is what he was talking about. The slave boy in the story was possessed by, and spoke with the voice of, the ancient king. When acting as his medium, he would have possessed all the authority the king would have had in life. (Hastie implies it was a permanent state, but this is very unlikely to have been the case.)

What's especially interesting for present purposes is the fact that mediumship is clearly operating here as a form of political contestation: the people rally to the boy who speaks with the voice of their ancient king, though the boy

---

13. Cf. Edland (2006: 103–4) for a brief summary of the campaign and its significance, which, however, relies only on European sources. Some Manendy remain there to this day (cf. Raison 1984, I: 267; Raison, incidentally, claims the Manendy, too, were originally from Valalafotsy, but this seems a misreading of the evidence).

himself is of the lowest possible social status;[14] the current king eventually reacts with simple violence, but thus delegitimizes his rule. After his fall, yet another "prophet" appears—this time, not just a former slave but also a woman—who quickly becomes effective leader of the rambunctious "republic" of Valalafotsy's refugees.

EMBLEMATIC LABOR AND THE KING AS CHILD

The historic Leiloza was a tyrant so jealous of the child possessed by the benevolent spirit of his grandfather that in the end he killed him. Thus did he lose the loyalty of his subjects and precipitate his fall from power. The legendary Leiloza of today is a tyrannical child who, after his fall, himself became a benevolent spirit that possesses mediums. Between the two stories, it seems to me, you have all the themes and elements required to start writing a proper history of Merina attitudes toward their rulers—that is, if one wishes to understand the crisis of authority that engulfed Merina kings from at least the beginning of the nineteenth century, these stories tell you precisely where to look.

Let me give an example. One of the striking elements of the Leiloza story as it's told around Mount Ambohitrambo today is that it talks about forced labor. Under the Merina kingdom, *fanompoana*, or royal service, was the overarching principle of governance. Every subject was expected to perform some form of labor for the sovereign. And indeed the story echoes much of what ordinary subjects seemed to have considered most obnoxious about *fanompoana* at that time: the tending of vast herds of royal cattle; industrial projects; transporting lords too high-and-mighty to walk on the ground (real Merina royalty didn't employ silk bridges, but they were regularly carried about in palanquins). All this is extremely unusual. While stories about kings told nowadays regularly

---

14. That is, a slave. Hastie emphasizes the African appearance of both "prophets," but in fact he seems to be projecting a Euro-American racial bias onto the Malagasy. At that time, African descent would not in itself have been taken as a sign of servile status; in fact, while northern highlanders were, then as now, more phenotypically Asian than coastal populations, they were then more likely to be enslaved by coastal populations than the other way around. However, it is possible that spirit mediumship itself reached the highlands from Africa via Malagasy populations on the coast.

emphasize their injustice and cruelty, those stories almost never have anything to say about *fanompoana*.[15]

Nineteenth-century sources, on the other hand, often seem to talk of nothing else. Foreign observers would regularly remark that the bulk of an adult Merina subject's waking hours was spent either performing *fanompoana* for the queen or avoiding doing so, and everything from school attendance to military service was considered a form of royal service. Not only was *fanompoana* the central principle of governance, it was key to the status system and the animating principle of royal ritual as well—if, indeed, royal work and royal ritual can even be entirely distinguished.

What I'm going to do in this next section, then, is explore the internal logic of that system of ritual labor that characterized the old Merina kingdom, since I think it's the key to understanding Merina kingship itself.

* * *

Malagasy ritual provides an unusual challenge to the interpreter because ritual gestures often seem to be saying two quite contradictory things at exactly the same time. Malagasy rhetoric (or *kabary*) is quite similar; it often seems that everything is double-edged, in the sense that it can be read in at least two different ways, sometimes even three. Blessings can be curses in disguise, and curses, blessings; statements of submission are often covert challenges; assertions of power often take the form of mock self-effacement. Anyone who has spent much time in a Malagasy community knows this is one of the things audiences find most enjoyable about good *kabary*: observing the agility with which skillful rhetoricians use professions of support or agreement to subtly slice each other apart. Yet when analysts turn to ritual, they tend to assume, instead, that ritual statements must all be taken at literal face value.

Merina royal ritual is a perfect case in point, since it's often subject to this kind of heavy-handed reading. Most existing literature on the subject (e.g., Lejamble 1972; Delivré 1974; Bloch 1977, 1982, 1986, 1989; Berg 1979, 1988, 1995, 1996, 1998; Raison-Jourde 1983b; S. Ellis 1985, 2002) emphasizes that the legitimacy of kings was bound up with a concept referred to as *hasina*. Here's a fairly typical example:

---

15. This is largely because *fanompoana* has now become a euphemism for "slavery" (Graeber 1996, 2007a: 43).

Common to those kingdoms in old Madagascar which succeeded one another, rising and declining in the extent of their influence, was the notion of hasina. This designates the invisible essence of power and fertility that can be channeled to human beings, particularly through ancestors. Maintaining this life-force demands respect for ritual obligations and taboos that in effect bind members of a family or a community to each other, to nature, and to the land. The foremost principle of political authorities throughout the island was that they should embody hasina and bestow it on their subjects. (S. Ellis 2002: 103; cf. Randrianja and Ellis 2009: 109)

Statements like this are not so much incorrect as extraordinarily crude. They annihilate all the subtlety and ambiguity that, in Malagasy eyes, give concepts like *hasina* their conceptual power. The passage above would be a little like announcing that the English political system is organized around a notion of "force" or "power," then explaining that English people assume force and power to be basic constituents of the natural universe, and finally concluding that English political and bureaucratic institutions exist primarily to channel force and power in benevolent directions. None of these statements are exactly false. But as with *hasina*, this, first, suggests a very naïve understanding of what are in fact quite sophisticated concepts, and, second, assumes everything fits together in a far neater fashion than it actually does. In fact, if one examines how the term *hasina* is used in ritual contexts today, it is clear that it is in no sense some kind of liquid fertility or power that flows one way or another, let alone something that powerful figures "bestow" on anybody else. *Hasina* is first and foremost a way of talking about powers that no one fully understands. Royal rituals always play on this: subjects are constantly "giving *hasina*" to the king, in the form of unbroken silver dollars,[16] which express their desire to create a unified kingdom; but it is utterly unclear, and indeed people seem to have been of very much two minds, as to whether those desires created the kingdom, or whether it was the mysterious allure of royal power that created the desire. Royal ritual often seems to be declaring that the people recognize the power of the king, and that the people create the power of the king, at exactly the same time. But this was simply typical of those domains that we would label "magic" or "politics"—they

---

16. Most cash transactions in highland markets made use of imported silver coins cut up and weighed: whole coins were unusual, and in this context were said to represent the unity of the kingdom such acts of allegiance were meant to create.

were precisely those domains where no one could ever completely understand what was going on.

On ritual labor

How, then, might we attempt a less heavy-handed approach to Malagasy royal ritual?

Until now, the most creative and insightful work on Merina royal ritual has surely been that of Maurice Bloch (1977, 1982, 1986, 1999). I suspect his work stands out not just because of the quality of the theoretical insight, but also because Bloch is virtually the only writer on the subject who has comes at it armed with detailed first-hand knowledge of ritual life in the northern high-lands today.[17] Bloch is most famous for his analysis of the Merina circumcision ritual (1986)—a ceremony that is typically performed on quite small children: boys are usually circumcised between the ages of two and four. His analysis of *fahasoavina*, or circumcision rituals, is his starting point for analyzing the whole ritual system, royal ritual included. My own ethnographic work has focused more on mortuary ritual (*famadihana*: Graeber 1995) and curing rituals car-ried out by spirit mediums (*fanasinana*: Graeber 2007a, 2007c). But I think it's significant that even though these rituals aren't typically held for children, meta-phors about children, and the raising of children, do also appear prominently in both of them as well.

What I'm going to do in this next section, then, is to read eighteenth- and nineteenth-century royal ritual, as it were, backward—through the kind of ritu-als I myself witnessed in the Merina countryside.

First, mediums. Mediums, and curers in general, are often referred to as *mpitaiza olona*, the nursemaids, nurturers, or carers for others. The verb *mitaiza*

---

17. About the only other body of work that sets out from contemporary ethnographic observation and moves from there to Merina royal ritual is that by archaeologists Susan Kus and Victor Raharijaona (e.g., 2000, 2001, 2008). Francophone literature on the subject is largely by historians, and mostly unabashedly diffusionist, more interested in representing the kingdom as an unstable amalgam of elements of Austronesian, East African, Arab, or even South Asian origin than as an emergent totality in itself. (This is most dramatically true of the work of Paul Ottino: e.g. 1983, 1986, which, while often intriguing in its own right, is of quite limited help in solving the kind of questions being asked here.) This is not to say there have not been ethnographically based studies of other Malagasy systems of royal ritual, in French and in English—I am speaking strictly of the northern highlands here.

is ordinarily used for either breastfeeding an infant, or, by extension, taking care of a small, dependent child.[18] It can also be used for caring for the sick, as here, but in this context the implication is somewhat broader than simply "taking care of":[19] rather, as in the case of a child, it implies the benevolent, nurturant authority of someone more able and knowledgeable. In the case of mediumistic curing, of course, there are in effect two levels of such benevolent authority: the mediums, and the royal spirits that possess them. Ordinarily, mediums are simply "pressed down" (*tsindriana*) by these spirits, which means that while in trance they remain at least partly conscious, yet hear disembodied voices, or even see visions, directing them. But if they fall deeper into trance, the metaphor reverses: they are no longer "pressed down by something" (*tsindrin-javatra*) but "carried by something" (*entin-javatra*), and they become the spirit, their ordinary personality entirely effaced.

A similar reversal lies at the center of the *famadihana* ritual, where the bodies of ancestors are temporarily removed from tombs and rewrapped in native silk shrouds. (The word *famadihana* literally means "reversal.") When people talk casually about their communities, they often make it sound as if ancestors are the only real adults—living people are often referred to as *ankizy*, "children," in comparison. (If you ask who are the local elders, you will almost invariably be told that the real elders are all dead: "Only we children remain.") Yet during *famadihana*, ancestors themselves are turned into children; they are first placed across women's laps—the word used for this is *miampofo*, "to nurse a child carried on one's lap"—given candies and honey and small change (though also rum), coddled as one would a child. Only then, once the ancestral relation has been thus reversed, can the bodies be taken up by everyone, danced with, rewrapped, and in the process, largely pulverized before being locked back in the ancestral tomb, where they can no longer trouble the living (Graeber 1995). A

---

18. So one current dictionary defines the word "to breast-feed, to take care of a child not yet capable of taking care of its own needs" (Rajemisa-Raolison 1985: 909), with nurture, attend to, etc., as secondary derivative meanings. Richardson suggests "to nurse, to take care of" (1885: 662); Abinal and Malzac suggest "allaitar, nourrir, élever un nourisson; prendre soin de quelq'un, comme une mère s'occupe de ses enfants" (1899: 624).

19. That would be *mikarakara* or *mitandrina*, or, if the meaning was just curing, *mitsabo*. It's important to emphasize in what follows that *mitaiza* has never been used as a general term for any relation of caretaking, but only those of a particularly intimate or, alternately, ritually significant kind.

celebration of the ancestral dead thus ultimately turns into a war against death itself, and just as an unlocked or unattended tomb can lead to ghosts escaping to steal one's babies, the most appropriate response to locking one, I was often told, was to immediately go home and have sex, preferably with one's wife or husband, if not with anyone who's willing and available, since doing so at that moment was most likely to bring new babies into the world.

These are obviously extremely abbreviated descriptions, but they serve to bring home two points I believe to be critical. The first is that the theme of nurture, and, especially, women's labor in the rearing of children, is a key way of imaging the creative power of ritual; the second, that such relations tend to become the locus of reversals of authority structures, where ancestors turn into children, or slaves turn into vehicles for kings. These reversals don't necessarily overthrow or challenge relations of authority (though they can), but they definitely become a way of negotiating such relations. All this is important when one turns back to royal ritual, because the moment one begins to look, one starts seeing all sorts of obvious parallels—even though these are precisely the elements that might otherwise be most likely to be overlooked if one did not have this larger ritual context in mind.

Understanding the ritual logic is all the more crucial because highland kingdoms—whether the various warring principalities of the eighteenth century or the great imperial state of the nineteenth—were essentially organized on ritual terms. This is not to deny that they were not also vast forms of labor extraction; rather, it is to suggest that within them no clear distinction between what we would call "work" and what we would call "ritual" could be made (cf. Sahlins 1985: 113). Both were seen as necessary, and overlapping, aspects in the constant human efforts required to create and maintain the material and social universe.[20]

We might state the matter this way: What we call "societies" are always vast coordinated systems of ritualized labor. Always, too, the elementary unit of any such system is some kind of household; however it might be configured (and as anthropologists know, there are an enormous number of possibilities in this

---

20. It is worth noting that while there is a Malagasy word for "work" (*asa*), there is no generic word for what we'd call "ritual"—the closest is, perhaps, *fanasinana*, which is the term for the actions of making things *masina*, powerful or sacred. But not all forms of ritual were considered *fanasinana*—mortuary ritual, for instance, was not. What's more, many types of ritual—notably, mediumistic curing—could often themselves be referred to as "*asa*" or work.

regard), this household is the elementary unit of work, solidarity, domination, and the creation and fashioning of human beings. In this sense women's labor, which tends to predominate within households, is also the most fundamental form of work itself. These statements, I think, can be made of any known human society. Obviously, this is never all. Anything we feel merits the name of a "society" will also have more encompassing structures through which all this is coordinated: clans, temple complexes, joint-stock corporations, and so forth. Usually, these look quite different from households. What makes monarchies unique is that, much though there might be all sorts of things going on in the middle of the hierarchy, the very top almost exactly resembles the very bottom. Kingdoms not only begin with households, they also end with one. This apical household is, of course, the royal household.

Now, certainly, royal households are almost invariably far more elaborate than any ordinary households (which do not, for instance, ordinarily involve harems attended by eunuch slaves, dancing dwarfs, and so forth), and often they are organized in ways that can only be described as intentionally perverse, in the sense of violating the basic moral principles that govern ordinary households (led by men who murder their fathers, marry their sisters, and so forth), but they are considered households nonetheless; in the final analysis, they are the same sort of unit, a domestic unit creating, nurturing, and educating children—that is, producing people—as the household units at the very base.

The difference, of course, is that the royal household, in the vast majority of cases anyway, was *only* about the creation of people, and did not involve all those other forms of production—of food, clothing, ironware, basketry, and so on—that in ordinary households served as essential material elements for that process of tending, growing, and nurturing human beings. In fact, the tendency in those ordinary households is for what we would label "work," "play," "ritual," and "education" to be, not indistinguishable perhaps, or not usually, but in every way entangled, overlapping, and mutually entailed. In contrast, royal households could be seen as the first prefiguration of the modern consumer household, which at least ideally is set in a sphere entirely opposed to the "production" of material goods, which is just about the creating and shaping and maintaining of people. Royal households largely divorce the making, shaping, and maintaining of people from the making, shaping, and maintaining of things. They also separate work, ritual, and play—at least, when royal figures do plow fields or lay the foundations of buildings, it's almost invariably as a form of ritual play; it's not considered actual labor. Royal households will tend to be full of servants and retainers, some of whose work is to continually teach members of the royal family how to behave like proper royalty, just as, say, presidents and prime ministers nowadays tend to be surrounded by hosts of aides and advisors whose function is to teach and remind them how to be proper heads of state. But rarely do they do a lot of what we'd consider productive work. What we'd call "material production" tends to be outsourced onto other households.

This might seem an odd way to frame things. Surely, kingdoms are not run by a royal household. They're run by an individual called "the king." Which is, of course, true: no kingdom has ever been ruled by a household collectively (at least, not officially), and in principle, the entire purpose of the royal household is to produce that one single individual—the monarch—who is, properly speaking, the entire focus of all ritual labor. But the apparatus for the creation of such individuals is nonetheless crucial, since such individuals, for all their occasional insistence to the contrary, are mortal, and can be replaced at any time.

I'm emphasizing all of this—at least some of which might seem self-evident—because I think it's important to problematize received categories in order to understand what's really going on in monarchies, which are, after all, an extremely common form of government historically, even if they seem strange and exotic to most people today. The terms of political economy, invented in the North Atlantic world around the same time that modern republican forms of government were being instituted in the late eighteenth century, really don't seem adequate to describe them. These terms propose a very simple schematic version of what an "economy" is, one that has become so much a matter of common sense that we have to remind ourselves that for most people, the very idea of a division between spheres of "production" (in workplaces) and "consumption" (at home) would simply make no sense. Some of the attendant political economy categories have been thoroughly critiqued by anthropologists. Others have not.

Take, for instance, the commonplace notion that labor is basically about "production": that it's typically directed at making things, transforming the world by combining raw materials into finished products. This is simply assumed in most theoretical literature. But it's a very odd assumption. Even a moment's reflection should make clear that nowhere in the world is most activity we would ordinarily refer to as "work"[21] directed at making anything. This is

---

21. Let us define "work" here as repetitive or formalized activity not performed for its own sake, but primarily to change the state of something else.

true even if we restrict ourselves to work directed at material objects. Most such labor isn't aimed at producing things, but at cleaning or maintaining them or moving them around. A ceramic coffee cup is "produced" just once; it's washed and stacked a thousand times. Even if it's a disposable paper or styrofoam coffee cup, far more time and energy is spent transporting, storing, and disposing of it than in the relatively brief moment of its actual fabrication.[22]

This blindness has any number of pernicious effects, but for present purposes I am just invoking it to make three points which I think are crucial to understand the organization of labor in Merina kingdoms. The first is the obvious anthropological one: that we cannot presume Malagasy assumptions about what work is and what is important about it necessarily mirror our own. And they are indeed quite different. The second is that, as I've argued elsewhere (Graeber 2007c), assumptions about the nature of work tend to be organized around certain forms of what I will call "paradigmatic labor"—that is, certain varieties of work effectively stand in, in the popular imagination, for a whole class of other ones. In contemporary social science, and, to a large extent, popular discourse as well, the two most important of these are factory work and childcare. The first has become the paradigm for all paid work, the second, for unremunerated, domestic labor. This is the imagery lurking in the background, for instance, when Marxists speak of "productive" versus "reproductive" labor; this is what can allow popular commentators to blithely declare that the decline in the number of factories in Britain or America means there is no more working class in such countries, even though there's probably never been a single place in the history of the world where the majority of working-class people were employed in factories.

The third point is that in monarchies like the Merina kingdom, the easiest way to understand how work was imagined is by examining the forms of ritualized labor surrounding kings.

Let me introduce another distinction here, and cite a term I introduced in an earlier work (Graeber 2007c): "emblematic labor." If paradigmatic labor is what you imagine to be the model for work in general, or a whole broad category of work, emblematic labor is work seen as typical of a certain group of people, a kind of work that defines what sort of people they are seen ultimately to be. A "fisherman" might spend only a relatively small proportion of his time actually fishing, he might even get a larger proportion of his income from something

---

22. In this sense, even my previous comments about households and production aren't precisely right.

else, but a "fisherman" is nonetheless what he is basically seen to be. In many societies, this emblematic labor is the kind of work that sort of person does in ceremonial contexts. Caste systems are an obvious case in point: drummers or washermen or barbers in an Indian village do not spend most of their working days making music, washing, or cutting hair. Yet those activities define their role in the larger society, largely by determining what role they play in important cosmological rituals.

A. M. Hocart (1950) in fact insisted that caste systems of this sort originate specifically in royal rituals, where, as in Fiji, different groups in a kingdom were defined by the kind of labor they performed specifically for the king. Thus in Fijian kingdoms, there were certain groups identified as fishermen—not because they spent most of their time fishing, or even because they spent more of their time fishing than anyone else (everybody fished), but because it was their responsibility to provide fish to the court or royal rituals. Each Fijian clan was characterized by its own form of emblematic labor, and this was seen as establishing what kind of people they really were. Eighteenth- and nineteenth-century Merina arrangements have been referred to as "caste-like" for similar reasons (e.g., Bloch 1977): different ancestries, and different orders of nobility, were defined by the work they performed for the royal household (particularly, the products they brought as first-fruits or *santatra*), and the role they played in building royal houses and royal tombs.

I think examining emblematic labor in the Merina kingdom in this fashion is the best way to understand the structure of the kingdom, and the role of the royal household. But in order to do so we first must say something about paradigmatic labor. In highland Madagascar, the paradigm for work in general is not production or even, precisely, childcare. When people think of "work," they think first and foremost of the bearing of burdens: moving, dragging, and, especially, carrying things, which includes everything from carrying babies to dragging trunks of wood to moving earth with shovels. The semantic range and web of associations is quite different than we are used to. But once we understand this, a lot of other things begin to make much better sense.

Speaking, carrying, and making

The essentials of the matter do not seem to have changed much since the nineteenth century. Then as now, work was seen as centered on the household, and was primarily the business of women. This is not to say men did not work at all—often they worked very hard—but women spent more of their time in activities viewed as working (*asa*), and women's general dispositions were seen as pragmatic, industrious, and generally work-oriented in a way that men's simply were not.[23] If I were to guess what kind of paradigmatic image was called to mind by the idea of work—parallel to the clock-punching industrial worker of our own imagination—it would most likely be a young woman, infant slung over her back, laboring in a rice field, or carrying water or produce on her head. Domestic labor here represents the perfect fusion of child-rearing and physical work because women tend to attend to children and carry out other duties simultaneously.

The paradigmatic form of work, then, was—and is—not seen as a making or building anything, or even maintaining anything, but, rather, lifting things up and moving them around. The importance of such matters can be seen in that fact that, traditionally, who carries what for whom in what circumstances is carefully regulated, at least in formal or ritual moments—indeed, formal or ritual moments are above all those in which the niceties of etiquette in such matters are strictly enforced.[24] Who carries what for whom is probably the most important way of indicating rank. Even well-educated, not particularly traditional women, I found, would on trips occasionally make (half-hearted) offers to carry my backpack, noting that, properly, if a man and woman are of roughly the same age, the man shouldn't be the one shouldering the burden. But mainly these rules applied to seniority. As elsewhere in Madagascar, the ranking of children by age is especially important. Indeed, insofar as one can speak of an "atom of hierarchy'" in highland society, it is embodied in the principle—repeated in proverbs—that elder brothers or sisters should speak for their juniors, and juniors, carry burdens for their seniors.[25] Often this is treated as a reciprocal

---

23. Women in general endlessly denounced males as lazy (*kamo lahy*), either individually or as a category. The reverse was never heard. I once asked a woman if the phrase "lazy woman" even existed, and she seemed rather taken aback. "That," she said, "would be outrageous. It's not even all that insulting to call a man lazy because all men are lazy really; in the case of a woman it would be a genuine insult."

24. Traditionally, modes of carrying are also strongly gendered: it's often noted that women carry objects on the head or hips; men on the back or shoulders.

25. Hence the well-known proverb, *Manan-jandry, dia afak'olan'entina; manan-joky, dia afak'olan-teny*: "if you have a younger sibling, then you'll have no problems with carrying, if you have an older one, then you'll have no problems with speech" (Cousins [1876] 1963: 37; Camboué 1909: 385; Houlder [1915] 1960: #1901).

obligation: a younger sibling (*zandry*) has the right to demand an elder (*zoky*) speak for them in court, or in a communal assembly, an elder sibling has the right to demand the younger one carry their bags. But it is also considered scandalous for a *zandry* to speak for *zoky*, a *zoky* to carry a *zandry*'s things—at least, if the *zandry* is old enough to carry anything.

In fact one could define the first stages of a child's life through the gradual application of this principle. I observed this even in contemporary households. Infants were themselves carried by their mothers or older sisters, toddlers were often sent off on play-tasks of fetching and carrying things, greeted as heroes if they succeeded, or with indulgent laugher if they refused or wandered off; then, gradually, play-tasks turned into real ones, and as soon as a child is physically capable, she finds herself thrust into situations where the youngest sibling is, paradoxically, expected to carry the heaviest burdens. This happens earliest, again, for girls, and it's not uncommon to see girls even of eight or nine toting baskets on their heads or infants on their backs. But the same thing eventually happens to boys. "By the age of about ten, children begin to help in the gardens and rice-fields by carrying burdens and packages. What is remarkable about the practice is that: it is to the youngest that the heaviest parts usually fall" (Camboué 1909: 385).

The Malagasy word for "oppression" is, precisely, *tsindriana*, to be pressed down. And it makes a great deal of intuitive sense that it should, since one can only imagine the first deep feeling of injustice a child will have is at precisely this moment when being a child suddenly pivots from having no responsibilities, to having the most onerous responsibilities of all (Graeber 2007a).

This opposition between speech and carrying is crucial. It runs through all political affairs. Speech, particularly formal speech, is seen as essentially constituting political society. Public assemblies are called "*kabary*," which is also the word for formal rhetoric. On the level of the kingdom, the opposition between speaking and carrying was even further elaborated because speaking was paired with making, what we'd call "production," and the carrying of burdens became instead the general figure for any sort of labor that, rather than being creative, was about nurturing, sustaining, and maintaining things.[26]

---

26. Many of the paragraphs that follow in this section are adapted from an essay called "Oppression" (Graeber 2007c). Normally I don't like to reproduce whole paragraphs of my own work, but in this case it seems justified since as far as I can make out the article has never been cited by anyone, and I have no reason to believe that even many scholars of Madagascar have ever read it.

* * *

Highland kingdoms were organized around a figure called the *Andriana*. The word, as I've mentioned, literally means sovereign, or king. But as much as a quarter or third of the free population in the heartland of the kingdom were also called *andriana*, either because they could claim descent from the royal line, or because their ancestors had been ennobled because of some outstanding service to royalty. By the end of the eighteenth century, these *andriana* were divided into seven ranked orders. Other free subjects were referred to as *hova*, or "commoners." Like the lesser *andriana*, *hova* were divided into ancestries (called *foko*, or *firenena*), each with their own ancestral lands. While all but the very most exalted *andriana* were expected to do some form of royal service, or *fanompoana*, *hova* were defined first and foremost as those who performed work in the service of the king.[27] Slaves were those who did *not* do so. Slaves served their masters. In fact, royal service was considered the primary mark of free status within the kingdom: legally, if a slave could demonstrate that he or she had been part of a royal work crew, especially if it was engaged in something intimate like clearing ground for a royal palace, then that was considered grounds for manumission in itself.

Almost everyone who writes about the Merina kingdom emphasizes the importance of *fanompoana*, since it really was the central organizing principle of just about everything: the political system, the economic system, the status system as well. The rank and character of any given ancestry was determined by the kind of service it traditionally performed for the royal family. These traditional tasks were especially important because, while in theory a local king could demand most anything from his subjects, evidence suggests that—at least before the nineteenth century—a ruler's ability to extract goods and services from anyone who did not happen to live in the immediate vicinity of a royal residence was actually quite limited. Therefore, those services they did receive revolved largely around these traditional emblematic tasks, especially those involved in building and rebuilding royal houses and royal tombs, or participating in great public ceremonies like the circumcision of royal children or the annual

---

27. There were other groups, such as the Mainty Enin-Dreny, who are often referred to in European sources as "royal slaves," but are actually specialized groups of warriors or retainers with a direct relationship to royalty. The Manendy, whom we have already encountered, and Manisotra, whom we shall meet in the next section, were among their numbers.

New Year's festival. It's important to bear in mind that in terms of how they earned their livelihoods (again except for those who belonged to the very highest *andriana* orders), nearly all of these groups were almost exactly the same. All devoted most of their energies to growing rice in the summer, and to handicrafts or petty trading in the agricultural off-season. It was largely during these rituals that each was assigned some specific task or set of tasks as emblematic labor, which was seen as defining their place in the kingdom, and, hence, what kind of people they ultimately were.[28] As a result, even though subjects might flee or mutiny if rounded up for certain tasks, like clearing out drainage ditches, the same subjects might come to physical blows over the privilege of carrying out other ones—say, being allowed to raise the central pillar in a royal house (Kus and Raharijaona 2000; cf. Clark 1896.)

So the next question is: *How* did emblematic labor define the nature of groups, and what did this say about the structure of the whole? Our material is uneven, but there's enough of it to see that the speaking/carrying division is indeed reproduced on the level of the kingdom. *Andriana* were seen as monopolizing powers of creativity. *Andriana* spoke first at council and were seen as being the masters of oratory and poetic speech (Callet 1908: 288; Rasamimanana and Razafindrazaka 1909; Andriamanantsiety 1975; Domenichini-Ramiaramanana 1982). At the same time, *andriana* also fashioned beautiful objects. *Hova* conveyed things from place to place.

What this meant in practice is that while carrying out work for the king, tasks involving what we would consider "productive" labor, the actual making, shaping, or fashioning of material objects, were almost invariably assigned to those at the very top of the social hierarchy. The building and repair of royal tombs might serve as an example—just because we happen to have a fairly good breakdown of how those tasks were divided up. Malagasy accounts written in the 1860s divide the necessary work into two broad categories. The first involved the actual building of the tomb and manufacture of the objects that would be placed inside. These tasks were monopolized by *andriana*. The noble orders of the Andriamasinavalona and Andriantompokoindrindra, for example, provided the stonemasons and carpenters who made the tomb itself; the Andrianandranado provided the smiths who produced the huge silver coffin in which

---

28. The notion of "emblematic labor" might be compared to Barth's idea of ethnic "diacritics" (1969), where one or two apparently minor features can become the reference to distinguish otherwise overlapping or similar social groups.

kings were buried, and, later, who made the tomb's tin roof; women of the An-driamasinavalona and Zazamarolahy orders wove the mats that would be hung on the walls inside. Three others were expected to provide the silk shrouds used for wrapping the dead (Callet 1908: 260–62, 267, 1213–14). The second set of tasks were phrased as matters of "carrying": especially, carrying off the tattered mats and other rubbish from inside a tomb when it was opened or repaired, and gathering and conveying baskets full of the red clay that was used to seal it af-terward (ibid.: 164, 307, 490, 534–53, 812–31). These tasks were never assigned to *andriana* but always to *hova*, though, since having the right to do any sort of labor on royal tombs was considered an extraordinary privilege, generally only *hova* ancestries who had rendered some extraordinary favor to royalty.[29]

In such ritual moments, *andriana* were indeed defined as the kind of people who make things; commoners, as those who fetch and carry them. These em-blematic tasks could influence what people were considered apt to do outside of royal ritual as well. The Andrianandranado, for instance, the order of *andriana* who provided the smiths for royal rituals, also produced all the gold and silver objects used at court; as a result, they eventually managed to win a formal mo-nopoly on gold- and silverworking within the kingdom. During the nineteenth century, other branches of this same order provided almost all the tinsmiths and a large number of the skilled ironworkers in the capital. Similarly, the Andri-anamboninolona, the *andriana* group with whom I did my own fieldwork, were famous as smiths, and ironwork was considered not just an art but something of a privilege; while there was no formal monopoly and little way to enforce one, if anyone not of *andriana* descent were to have taken it up, it would have been considered quite presumptuous (Graeber 2007a: 99–100, 338). Similarly, Andrianamboninolona women were seen as having a de facto monopoly of the weaving of native silk. But in other places such a monopoly did not exist.

As a rule, *andriana* were seen as producers, makers; it was their basic identity in the structure of the kingdom. This fact was perhaps most clearly revealed when, in 1817, British envoys asked King Radama I to chose a handful of boys from his kingdom to study artisanal trades in England. Every young man the king chose was *andriana*.

---

29. I note that one group of former *andriana*, of somewhat ambiguous status, did have the special privilege of providing one silk shroud on such occasions. Another group of similar ambiguous status receiving the privilege of actually "carrying" the royal body to be placed in the tomb—the most exalted form of carrying, but still one not relegated to a group considered royal kin.

Royal service as principle of government

When we turn to actual governance, however, things get a bit more complicated. Like so many key Malagasy concepts, the notion of *fanompoana* was double-edged. On the one hand, it refers to a meticulously graded system of ritual labor. On the other, it was the power of the sovereign to make anyone do anything at all.

It's not hard to imagine how this situation might have come about. As I mentioned, for much of highland history, rulers' powers of compulsion were fairly limited. Archaeologists confirm that from the sixteenth century, most lived on hilltop or mountaintop fortresses—the higher the better, since in principle a king's domains corresponded to everything he could see from the summit—and Maurice Bloch is probably right in adding that most were little more than successful brigands, which, as we've seen, is exactly the situation to which unsuccessful monarchs like Leiloza would be likely to revert (Bloch 1977; Dewar and Wright 1993: 448; D. Rasamuel 2007: 171–75). When a heavily armed band appears in a defenseless village its leader can, of course, make anyone do pretty much anything he orders them to do. What he can make them do when he is not actually physically present is quite another matter. The apparent contradiction at the heart of *fanompoana* no doubt originates in this very practical circumstance. But that hardly explains why this pragmatic circumstance (being able to order anyone to do anything) should be preserved as a ritual principle—indeed, as the definition of sovereignty itself.

It's also not hard to see how, if a ruler insists on building his house on the top of a mountain, the real challenge entailed in constructing and maintaining that house will not be finding skilled craftsmen to do the metalwork or carpentry, but rounding up people to do the really onerous work of dragging the building material, and, later, daily supplies of food, fuel, and water, up the slopes. This is what stories like that of Leiloza are clearly playing on. Given the cultural context in which all this took place—all those distinctions between speaking, making, carrying, which were already so important in the internal organization of families and households—it was hardly surprising that as a result, the production of material objects, and particularly magnificent objects, should have ended up becoming a special privilege to be allotted to kin and loyal followers, while bearing burdens should be seen as both the essence of real work and, in a broader sense, the key to the creation and maintenance of actual human beings.

The fact that the arbitrary will of the sovereign remained the core of *fanompoana* allowed the principle to regularly be put to new purposes, whenever sovereigns were, in fact, in a position to impose their will in any sort of systematic way. In the late eighteenth century, King Andrianampoinimerina used the principle of *fonompoana* to marshal the manpower to reclaim thousands of hectares of arable land from swamps; in the nineteenth, his son Radama, to compel children to attend mission schools and teenagers to serve in a newly created standing army. At the same time, wars of expansion brought thousands of slaves into the country. All of this meant that in practice, actual labor arrangements transformed quickly and dramatically. Still, in principle, *fanompoana* remained the basis of the monarchy.

As I remarked, pretty much all observers made a point of emphasizing this. Here's a typical comment from a late nineteenth-century missionary named Houlder. He begins by noting actual power was held by a commoner prime minister named Rainialarivony, who was secretly (not that secretly, since everybody knew it) the consort of the queen:

> Under the rule of this strong personality, as under that of his predecessors, no direct taxes, or next to none, were levied. In lieu thereof came fànompòana, or compulsory unrequited service, such as a slave renders to his master, a very onerous duty and a very questionable exchange.
>
> Fànompòana is the genius of the native government, and seemed to be its principal end. The rulers were most concerned, not with the promotion of the prosperity and happiness of the people, but with the proper carrying out of service to the Queen. The whole of a native's life is taken up with doing fànompòana of one sort or another. . . . Anything in the nature of service was fànompòana, from the superintendence of all the arrangements of Her Majesty's household down to the cleaning of her royal shoes; from presiding over the council of Government, or the running of a province, to the shouldering of a musket in war, and the carrying of a stone or lump of earth in peace. Any and every labor could be exacted at any and every time at her sovereign will and pleasure.
>
> Fànompòana for the government, whether civil or military, was bad enough; but it was made a hundred times worse by the fact that the system involved, not only a multitude of petty oppressions and exactions by the persons duly appointed to carry it out, but also the fànompòaning of one another. The theory was that the unrequited service was rendered to the Queen, but unfortunately it did not end with service to royalty. The organization requisite for getting work done for Her Majesty was a system of subordination, by means of which any person who had authority over another could make that person work for his own benefit, and the inevitable result was that there was infinitely more

fànompòana done for private individuals than there was for the Government.
The peoples' lives were often made a perfect misery to them. (Houlder 1912:
37–38)

Most accounts by foreign observers from the period contain similar observations
about the simultaneous legitimacy, universality, and abusiveness of *fanompoana*.

The principle that royal service was by its nature the unlimited personal
power of the sovereign helps explain one of the more peculiar features of the
archival record: the fact that, much though everyone who observed the functioning of the kingdom talks incessantly about it, there is almost nothing about
forced labor in the government's administrative documents themselves. This
never ceased to puzzle me while I was doing my own archival researches. Especially after the 1860s, almost everything has been preserved: the National
Archives contains thousands and thousands of school and military registers,
property censuses, court transcripts, grievances, audits, and administrative correspondence of every sort. By compiling everything I could find concerning the
area immediately surrounding Leiloza's tomb in Ambohitrambo,[30] I was able to
reconstruct a quite detailed sense of how the government worked and what the
day-to-day experience of governance was like. I was even able to reconstruct the
organization of work brigades for *fanompoana*, since "100s" and "1000s", that is,
districts responsible for providing teams of either a hundred or a thousand male
or female workers for royal labor projects, were the basic administrative units.
The one thing on which I could get virtually no information was what those
teams were actually made to do. It was all the more surprising since, for all the
fact that, say, taxes were, as Houlder remarked, very light and largely symbolic,
tax assessments and receipts were meticulously registered, down to the penny.
But on labor duties there was virtually nothing written down at all.[31]

---

30. The region selected was, to be more precise, what was often referred to as "Eastern
    Imamo." It included everything between the Ombifotsy and Onilahy Rivers, from
    Ambohibeloma in the north to Arivonimamo in the south. Ambohitrambo is its
    center.

31. The only exceptions I could find in the region in question was one document
    concerning ironworking in a town called Vatolevy, and a couple of very late registers
    of people summoned for gold prospecting in the desperate days before the French
    invasion. The LL series in the royal archives does contain a few more detailed
    documents from other parts of the kingdom, but, again, there are far, far fewer of
    these than almost anything else.

Apparently, then, the personalized, arbitrary nature of *fanompoana* was seen as so essential to its nature that to subsume it within the bureaucratic apparatus would have been seen as a violation of principle—so much so that even registering who was sent on what task might be considered to compromise the absolute power of the queen.

So, what did people actually do in service of the queen at the height of the nineteenth-century kingdom, and how did they conceive it? The question is important because, as foreign observers uniformly insisted, the sense of absolute legitimacy of *fanompoana* as personal service to the queen was really what held an otherwise corrupt and often brutal government together. Here, we have to turn, I think, from lists of what people had to do—which mostly don't exist—to lists of what they *didn't* have to do: that is, lists of tasks from which especially privileged groups were considered to be exempt. These do exist, and they give us a sense of what generic *fanompoana* was thought to consist of. The lists of exemptions, in fact, are strikingly uniform. They almost always include four primary sorts of work which always occur in the following order:

1. *Manao Hazolava*, or "dragging trees." Since Imerina proper was largely devoid of timber, it was necessary to form crews of workmen to drag the vast trunks needed for royal houses and palisades from the edge of eastern forests up to the center of the country.
2. *Mihady Tany*, or "digging earth." This mainly refers to leveling and the making of embankments for royal building projects.
3. *Manao Ari-Mainty*, or "making charcoal." In practice this mainly involved transporting baskets of charcoal produced in the eastern forests to the royal court in the capital, Antananarivo.
4. *Mitondra Entan'Andriana*, or "carrying royal baggage." Most often this involved transporting imports bound for the court from the port of Tamatave to the capital, but it could include any number of other transport duties, including literally carrying the palace baggage when the monarch was traveling.[32]

---

32. This follows the same order as the list given by Standing (1887b: 358), though I left out Standing's fifth category (building and maintaining roads and bridges) since it does not appear in any Malagasy-language account. For evocations of the standard list in nineteenth-century legal cases, see National Archives IIICC 365 f1:43–48 (Tsimadilo, 1872), IIICC37 f2 (Ambohitrimanjaka, 1893); for standard lists of exemptions in the *Tantara ny andriana*, see Callet (1908: 411 [Andriamamilaza]

Once again, in every case, we have tasks which centered on dragging or carrying heavy objects—usually, in baskets on one's back or on one's head. ("Digging earth" might seem a partial exception, but in fact anyone who has ever taken part in a large-scale digging project knows the lion's share of the labor does in fact consist of hoisting and carrying away containers of displaced earth.)

Now, obviously, to some degree the list is just reflective of material realities: nineteenth-century Imerina lacked beasts of burden or wheeled vehicles; even the now-ubiquitous ox-carts had not yet come into general use; it was also notoriously lacking in decent roads. As a result, just about everything had to be moved by human beings, and often with great difficulty. But there's clearly more to it. Many of the more onerous tasks reported by foreign sources (tending royal cattle, repairing streets and bridges) are conspicuously absent from the list. Choosing these tasks as paradigms of *fanompoana* clearly drew on a sense that, in the kingdom as in the household, carrying things for someone else was emblematic of subordination. Indeed, in the case of royalty the principle was taken even further, because, as noted above, royals and officers of state did not walk on the ground for long distances; like foreign visitors, they were carried everywhere on palanquins borne on the shoulders of trained bearers. Royal bearers were themselves a class of relatively esteemed specialists, of a status similar to royal warriors (in the documents they are referred to as *alinjinera*, or "engineers.") Important court figures, or local grandees, tended to keep specially trained bearers of their own, who usually formed an elite corps amongst their slaves.

Still, bearing the palanquin remains one of the most potent symbols of oppression (*tsindriana* again) throughout Madagascar: as on the East Coast, where memories of colonialism always seem to focus on the way local people were arbitrarily summoned to carry officials and missionaries and planters about.[33]

---

and 545 [Antehiroka]); see also entries in the *Firaketana* (an early-twentieth-century Malagasy encyclopedia) for Ambohibato, Ambohimalaza, Ambohimirimo, Andriana, and Antsahadinta, all of which provide variations on basically the same list.

33. A later ethnographer working on the East Coast reports:

Countless people—both those who had lived through colonial times and those who were born well after it was over—told me about the palanquin. They never failed to mention the fact that people riding in them urinated and defecated on those below. Josef once commented, with his usual gentle, rueful smile, "They must have deemed us Betsimisaraka less than human to act that way." Surely there is no more appropriate symbol of one people's exploitation by another than the image of the colonial official carried on the very backs of

Thus the lists of exemptions will, when they come to the fourth, occasionally write, instead of "not to carry the royal baggage," *tsy milanja andriana*: "not to have to carry the king" (e.g., Domenichini 1982: 15)—or, even more colorfully, *tsy mibaby andriana,* "not to have to carry the king 'like an infant on one's back'" (Callet 1908: 545).[34] And in nineteenth-century Imerina, at least, one of the most dramatic images of royal power—and one which, as we'll see, made a profound impact on the popular imagination—was the rounding up of people to carry royal baggage when the monarch set out on a trip. This practice became particularly destructive during the reign of Queen Ranavalona I (1828–61); whenever the queen traveled abroad, she brought her entire court and enormous quantities of furniture and provisions with her, so much so that she was obliged to send ahead agents at each town along the way calling up almost the entire able-bodied population as porters. This was a very ambivalent demand, since carrying royal baggage was indeed personal service to the crown and hence seen as inherently legitimate; but the results were usually frequently lethal. Since those recruited were not fed, and the queen's party tended to absorb all available provisions in the regions through which it passed, hundreds if not thousands would perish of a combination of exhaustion, hunger, and disease. "Never," wrote the queen's secretary Raombana, after one particularly disastrous trip to Manerinera, "was an excursion of pleasure more productive of famine and death" (n.d.: 488).

Reversals: The king as child

If there is an "atom of hierarchy" in highland culture, I have suggested, it is the dichotomy between the elder child, who speaks, and the younger one, who carries. Children in fact learn about the nature of social rank largely through the experience of carrying burdens—of being literally "oppressed," pressed down by the weight of objects balanced on their heads, or backs, or shoulders—objects which, significantly, belong to someone else (or, in the case of babies, since small

---

the Betsimisaraka? Few indeed were the older men who had not suffered the indignity. (Cole 2001: 165)

34. Perhaps unsurprisingly since carrying the queen's packages was considered, in a sense, almost the same as carrying the queen herself. William Ellis (1867: 256) notes that inhabitants of the capital were expected to doff their hats and bow down as anything belonging to the queen passed them on the street, much as they would if the queen's own person were to pass.

children are sometimes obliged to carry even smaller ones, actually *are* someone else). Carrying is thus both the paradigmatic form of work and emblematic of subordination; production, creation, is, in contrast, seen as much more similar to speaking, which can create social realities, *ex nihilio*. One might say, in phenomenological terms, that the experience of physical compression implied by being "pressed down" by something contrasts here with the ability to expand, or extend oneself into the world.

The contrast can be observed in the most important forms of work within the household itself—when a man is working a forge or a woman weaving, it is generally the most senior person who actually fashions the object, while younger ones scurry back and forth carrying supplies—and in formal settings (feasts, funerals, etc.) it is meticulously applied, as elders speak first, and it is often considered strictly taboo for them to so much as pass a plate to their juniors. It recurs on the level of the kingdom: when the ruler assembled his people to pass down rulings or ask their permission to begin some project (say, dragging trees to make a new palace), it was the representatives of *andriana* orders who had the privilege of speaking first (Rasamimanana and Razafindrazaka 1909: 31).[35]

So far, these arrangements seem simple enough. But we've already seen hints—in the image of the mother carrying her baby, in the peculiar concept of the people carrying the sovereign, like a baby—that there might be something more subtle going on. That as with the spirit mediums, at a certain point, subordination itself was seen as "turning" into a kind of covert power. And indeed, just as in the *famadihana* and possession rituals mentioned earlier, the royal rituals also contained at least a potential element of reversal. The ritual emphasis on the people's support for the king shaded into the notion that the king was himself a dependent child cared for by the people. Much like a toddler, kings were assumed to be egocentric, irresponsible, petulant, given to destructive tantrums, certainly not entirely in control of themselves; and thus it was sometimes the responsibility of their subjects to chasten or admonish them. Some nineteenth-century texts state the matter outright. Here is a quote from the *Tantara ny andriana* about the immediate family of the king:

---

35. In doing so, they represented the kingdom, in the same way an elder does his junior (Callet 1908: 288). Cousins (1873, [1876] 1963) provides samples of the sort of *kabary* made on such occasions.

The Royal Family are like infants nurtured by their parents. And it's just like taking care of children; this is why they're referred to as "Children and Descendants." And it's the people who nurse, nourish, and support—and by doing so, honor —the Royal Family. (Callet 1908: 364)[36]

The verb here translated "nurture" is again *mitaiza*, which literally means "to nurse."

Let me take this step by step.

Even in ordinary usage, "carrying" has a double meaning. The verb *mitondra* means not only "to bring" or "to carry," but also "to lead." Hence one can say a person arrived "carrying a shovel" or "leading a detachment of a hundred soldiers": it's exactly the same word. Authority itself can be spoken of as a burden, so that one "carries" a certain responsibility or public office; active governance is a matter of "carrying the people" (*mitondra vahoaka*), and the most common word for governance is in fact an abstract noun, *fitondrana*, which might here best be translated as "the manner of carrying." This is also the word being used in the quote above for "taking care of" children—*fitondrana*, literally how one carries them around.

These idioms, too, go back to relations of seniority in the family. In the household, the duties one owes to one's elders are often framed in terms of a kind of reciprocity. Let's return here to the woman with the baby on her back, which I've suggested is the primordial figure for labor. In speaking of child-rearing, carrying children was often invoked as a paradigmatic image that summed up all the work of caring for, feeding, clothing, cleaning, teaching, and attending to a child's needs which parents—and of course particularly mothers—were acknowledged to provide. Obligations of support which adult children later owe to their parents and ancestors, in turn, could be collectively referred to as *valim-babena*: "the answer for having been carried on the back."

---

36. Original Malagasy: "*ny Havanandriana no toy ny zaza taizainy ny raiamandreny, dia tahaky ny fitondrana ny zana'ny hiany, dia atao ny hoe Zanak'amam-para; ary koa ny ambaniandro no mitaiza sy mamelona sy manampy ka manome voninahitra ny Havanandriana.*" Note here the term for "nurture" is literally "nurse," but the word for "taking care of" is literally "carrying." Compare the same collection, "*Fa ny vahoaka no mitaiza ny andriana, ary ny andriana koa sady mitondra no mandidy ny vahoaka rehetra*" ["for it's the people who nurture the king, and the king, too, both carries and commands the whole people"] (Callet 1908: 366). As in all subsequent cited Malagasy text, the translation into English is my own.

Alternately, they can be called *loloha* or *lolohavina*, "things carried on one's head" (and it's important to remember here that carrying on the head was considered paradigmatic of *women's* work in particular; men carried packages and similar burdens instead on their backs and shoulders). The term *lolohavina* was used as way of referring to any responsibility to support others, but particularly the obligation to maintain ancestral tombs, and provide the ancestors within with cloth and other gifts at *famadihana* (during which they were, as noted, symbolically rendered children once again).[37]

Perhaps unsurprisingly, some nineteenth-century documents use the term *filolohavina*, "things carried on the head," to refer both to one's responsibilities to one's ancestors, and to one's responsibilities to provide taxes and labor to the state.

There's kind of a continuum here from carrying as pure subordination, to carrying as nurture, to carrying as outright authority. It's the second term, the woman with the baby on her back, that marks the point of transition between the other two. She is precisely the pivot around which one flips over, and turns into its opposite.

I would argue that the exact same thing happens in royal ritual. If one returns to the most prestigious ceremonial moments of *fanompoana*, where labor becomes most emblematic, and different ancestries defined their place in the kingdom as a whole, one finds these are also the moments where the idiom of nursing or nurturing (*taiza*) is most likely to be evoked. This is true above all in first-fruits ceremonies (*santatra*), where various representatives of the kingdom's many ancestries "carried" not just the first of the rice crop:

> Once the first rice harvest is brought in, then the people present the first-fruits
> to the Andriana, each variety of rice crop, and it's only once they have done so
> that the people can eat of it. . . . This was the custom from olden times: to honor
> him, as he is the child nursed by the people, as he is the master (*tompo*) of the
> land and the kingdom.[38]

---

37. Compare Cole (2001:214-15) and Lambek (2002) for parallels among the Betsimisaraka and Sakalava, respectively.

38. *"Dia manome santa-bary ny andriana ny vahoaka, isan-karazana ny mamboly vari-aloha, vao izay no maka ho hanina. Raha tsy ny andriana no manantatra, dia tsy mahazo homana ny vahoaka . . . .. izany no fomba fanao hatr' izay hatr' izay: fanajana azy fa izy no zanaka taizany ny ambanilanitra, fa izy no Tompo ny tany sy ny fanjakana"* (Callet 1908: 61–62).

As in most Austronesian societies, sacrificial ritual is a way of invoking the gods' power only to banish it again; most often, in order to lift some taboo those gods might otherwise impose. First-fruits are a variation: in principle, the entire crop could be said to belong to the gods (because the gods caused it to grow) or the king (because he owns everything). By accepting a small symbolic sample, the true owner (*tompo*) releases his claim over the rest.

This ritual, too, is modeled on household practice, where the eldest member of the family receives the same *santa-bary* from the family's lands after the harvest, and must taste it before anyone else is allowed to eat. Now, the process of the "ripening" and harvest of the rice crop is spoken of in much the same terms as the gestation and birth of infants, and the ceremony of first-fruits, as several of my own informants emphasized, is identical in form to an infant's first haircut, conducted when he or she is three to six months old (Graeber 2007a: 284–85; cf. Standing 1887a: 35–37; Camboué 1907: 988; Molet 1976: 37–39). This is the ceremony that marks the child's debut as an autonomous social being (it's sometimes the occasion for giving a child a name). Like the rice, the clipped hair is cooked with milk and honey, though while the rice is first eaten by the head of the household, who then releases the remainder of the harvest to everyone else, the hair is placed in a banana-leaf spoon and sampled by everyone, particularly young women, since it is said to convey fertility. In the case of the rice, then, a release of ancestral authority; in the case of the haircut, a general distribution of human vitality.[39] Yet each implies the other, and in the case of the royal *santatra*, the two are, at least rhetorically, combined. Much as in the *famadihana*, where ancestors were turned into infants so as to free the living from their (often petulant, arbitrary) demands, here the monarch, "owner" of the land and the kingdom, is presented with the product of those lands in a way that

---

39. There are other parallels. The bearers of first-fruits, for instance, had to be *velond-rai-aman-dreny*, that is, men and women both of whose parents were still alive. This is true also of those who conduct the haircut ritual (*fanala volon-jaza*). The ceremony is also a sort of foreshadowing of the circumcision ritual to be conducted perhaps two or three years later, when another part of the child is removed, though in this case, the precipice should be swallowed instead by the child's mother's' brother. Finally, it is probably relevant that this is a presentation of *vary aloha*, that is, of a double-cropping system said to have been developed by rulers who used *fanompoana* to drain the swamps surrounding the capital, and thus from fields the monarch would have laid particular claim to. In this context, Andrianampoinimerina was said to have declared, "me and the rice are the same" (*izaho sy ny vary dia mitovy*, Callet 1908: 746).

transforms him into a dependent child, helpless but for the nurturant support of the kingdom's inhabitants.

Reflections on the king as toddler

How, then, do we think about this notion of the king as child nurtured by the people?

In much of Madagascar, kings typically represent themselves as foreigners: they trace their genealogies to far-away kingdoms, exotic half-forgotten lands like Mangalore or Mecca. As Marshall Sahlins (1981b, 2008) has demonstrated, this circumstance is not at all unusual. Most kings insist they come from someplace other than the lands they rule. In myth, and also ritual, the stranger-king scenario, as Sahlins describes it, follows a fairly predictable narrative sequence: the king first arrives from far away as a kind of holy terror, an alien, outrageous power, whose absolute vitality is signified by a tendency to engage in arbitrary acts of violence. But in conquering his people, he is also, subtly, conquered by them; often this culminates in his marriage to a daughter of the people of the land, who thus become the closest thing he has to parents; in the process, he is surrounded, incorporated, domesticated, even symbolically killed and reborn as a child of his people.[40]

Might something like this be happening here? It's tempting to make the connection. But there's a problem: Merina sovereigns didn't really represent themselves that way. In other parts of Madagascar, royal lineages certainly did. They tended to see themselves as conquering outsiders, imposing their dominion on an autochthonous population who were seen as the true "owners of the land" (*tompon'tany*)—and who therefore, nonetheless, maintained certain crucial ritual privileges, such as the right to nominate or install the king. While there are traces of such arrangements early in Merina history, by the late eighteenth century, at least, traces were all that remained. Official histories instead represented the entire Merina population, *andriana* and *hova* alike, as foreign invaders, and the country's true aboriginal inhabitants, the Vazimba, as elf-like

---

40. Hence in the original essay, about Fiji, Sahlins notes "the usage that long puzzled Hocart, that the Fijian nobility are styled 'child chiefs' (*gone turaga*), while the native owners of the land are the "elders' (*qase*). The relation is one of offspring to ancestor, as established by the gift of the woman" (1981b: 119). Kings in Benin were also addressed as "child" (Bradbury 1973: 75). No doubt other examples could be compiled.

primitives who had been defeated and driven from the country. Merina kings claimed absolute command of everything, including all land and labor, within their kingdoms (Fugelstad 1982).

Still, one could say that the image of the king as child—and particularly the king as naughty child, like Leiloza—takes the two moments of the stranger-king story—the king-as-extramoral-outsider and king-as-tamed-by-the-people—and effectively fuses them together.

In my essay on the divine kingship of the Shilluk (chapter 2, this volume), I suggested a slightly different way these same pieces often come together. One can also pluck two more general principles out of this scenario that are always simultaneously present, and in constant mutual tension. I referred to these as divine and sacred kingship. The first applies not so much when kings are taken to be gods (this happens surprisingly rarely), but rather when they *act* like gods—that is, with arbitrary impunity. Divine kingship corresponds to sovereignty in Carl Schmitt's sense in *Political theology* ([1922] 2005); it is something that stands entirely outside the legal order, and can therefore, constitute it. Sacred kingship is very different. To be "sacred" is, as Durkheim long ago recognized, drawing on the logic of Polynesian taboo, to be "set apart," and what setting the king apart as a sacred being always means in practice is surrounding him with such an elaborate system of restrictions, protocols, and taboos ("not to touch the earth, not to see the sun") that it becomes extremely difficult for a sovereign to exercise that arbitrary divine power except in very carefully circumscribed ways. In fact—and this is true particularly in nonbureaucratized kingdoms—the more elaborate the court ceremonial, the less effective personal power the monarch was likely to wield.

What I am suggesting here is that the pomp and protocol that surround powerful figures are rarely, if ever, the creations of those powerful figures themselves—any more than King Tugo, sometimes credited with having "invented" the Shilluk sacred kingship, is himself likely to have simply decided one day that it would be a neat idea to create a body of armed executioners with the power to kill him whenever his senior wives decided he was no longer capable of adequate sexual performance. Deference is always double-edged. On the one hand, violent men invariably demand "respect," a certain kind of ritual deference; on the other, the more extreme forms of such respect can easily become ways of isolating and controlling such violent men. This continues to be true even if a monarch remains in other respects a despot, capable of ordering executions and similar acts of spectacular cruelty or destructiveness at whim: first of all, because all kings worthy of the name are to a certain degree despotic, "sovereignty" and "despotism" being at root the same thing; and, secondly, because the tension between the divine and sacred aspects of kingship is always to some degree constitutive of kingship itself. True, it is possible for ritualization to overwhelm and entirely hollow out the crown, leaving it a purely ceremonial or constitutional monarchy. But the opposite cannot really happen. Even in the case of Leiloza, who descended from monarch to something very like a simple bandit, his son's need to establish himself as something more than just the son of a bandit compelled him to quickly pass most of his power to someone else.

One might well argue that both the classic stranger-king narrative and the baby-king image are two different ways of elucidating this fundamental tension.

Within the Merina kingdom, that tension was above all summed up in the phrase *mpitaiza andriana*, literally, the "nursemaids of the king." All major royal aides and advisors—that is, those who created and maintained that court ceremonial—were called this. The term was applied to the *tandapa*, or palace attendants (Cousins [1876] 1963: 50; André 1899: 55–56 n. 1; Callet 1908: 324, 361, 500, 634, 832, 895, 904, 1053, 1063, 1084, 1187, 1100; Soury-Lavergne and de la Devéze 1913: 312), to royal councilors (Callet 1908: 425, 691, 832, 943, 962, 1028–29, 1006, 1146), and to the diviners and keepers of the charms that protected the kingdom (Jully 1899a: 325; Callet 1908: 19, 165, 440; Domenichini 1977),[41] as well as to the retainers assigned to support various lesser lords assigned to *menakely*, or local estates (Callet 1908: 148, 439, 492, 1043)—these latter were said to "nurse" or "nurture" these children of the royal line in the same way as the people did the king himself.[42] The term could thus be applied either to those who fed, cared for, and physically sustained the king, or to those

---

41. This one is a little more complicated, as the *mpitahiry sampy*, or keepers of such guardian "palladia" (Berg 1979), were the *mpitaiza* not only of the king but also of the sampy themselves (Callet 1908: 188, 194–97, 203, 213, 222, 227). (Sampy was the name given to the major political charms that protected larger groups, up to and including the kingdom.) Finally, insofar as the charms were also used to heal, one could also speak of the charm as "nurturing" its patients, much as one would now (ibid.: 231).

42. So, for instance, the very first *andriana* to receive a *menakely* were the Andriantompokoindrindra, and they were assigned a lineage of attendants, the Zafitsimaito, who are alternately described as their *mpitaiza* (ibid.: 149) or "those who carry their bags" (ibid.: 1211). The subjects of those minor lords could also be said to *mitaiza* them, in much the same way as the subjects of a king. I could find only one reference, though, to slaves who *mitaiza* their adult owners (ibid.: 189).

who might be said to provide for the king's ongoing education: reminding him of his duties and responsibilities, guiding him toward appropriate conduct.[43] Neither were these simply metaphors. In the histories, *mpitaiza* regularly speak to kings using terms of address—notably the informal second person, *ialahy* or *leiretsy*—which would be utterly scandalous if directed at anyone of higher status in any other context (there is no precise English equivalent, but it would be roughly analogous to addressing the king as "boy"[44])—and kings respond with the terms of address a child would use for a father, guardian, or elder: *ikiaky* or *idada*.

These same *mpitaiza andriana*, of course, were those responsible for the actual creation of royal ritual as well.

* * *

Earlier, I observed that royal households always stand at the pinnacle of an elaborate system of ritual labor. They also tend to be somewhat different from the households that make up the base of the kingdom, because while in ordinary households, the creation and sustenance of people was inextricably bound up in the creation and maintenance of things, royal households, for the most part, produced *only* people. To this we can add: but they did not produce those people

43. About the only scholarly source that discusses the use of the term is a footnote in Bakoly Domenichini-Ramiaramanana's book on Merina court poetry (1982:406 n. 148), which is worth quoting in full. "The term '*mpitaiza*' which is commonly translated 'intimate councilor' when it appears in the phrase '*mpitaiza andriana*' (*mpitaiza* of a prince), currently designates a nurse-maid, governess (male or female), curer (male or female), priest or priestess who assures moral guidance, and seems to indicate that the king was in some sense an eternal minor simply insofar as he was *andriana*" (my translation from the French). This seems exactly right. Yet this profound insight into the nature of Merina kingship was not further pursued, as far as I'm aware, either by the author or by anyone else. Standard histories of the kingdom continue to follow Édouard Ralaimihoatra (1969: 164–65), who claims that the title of *mpitaiza andriana* was invented in the 1830s to deal with the unprecedented situation of having a woman on the throne. Hence the entire phenomenon has somehow been excluded from discussions of Malagasy kingship: for example, of the seventeen essays brought together in the volume *Les souverains de Madagascar* (Raison-Jourde 1983c), not one makes any mention of *mpitaiza andriana* at all.

44. To get a sense of how shocking this would ordinarily be, in my experience, men never used terms like that even to men of equal age or status unless they were drunk and trying to start a fight.

all by themselves. In a larger sense—and this is clearly the case here—the organization of kingdom-wide ritual labor was itself directed not just toward the material provisioning of royal households, but also toward the active shaping of those offspring royal families produced. Everyone, in their own way, contributed to the raising of royal children, not just in terms of feeding and clothing them, but even in the broader sense of bringing them to full maturity: certain groups carried out the circumcision rituals for princes, others were assigned to play with princesses, and so on. Yet as a paradoxical result of the enormous focus on the task of raising royal children, that task would always remain incomplete. Kings and queens never quite grew up and never quite became autonomous. They were, in a sense, permanent toddlers. This was both the key to their legitimacy—they were cherished, their health and well-being were the common project of the Ambaniandro, the common people or "under the day"—but also an obvious limit to the exercise of power, since while childish displays of petulance were only to be expected, as we shall see, the framing of the king as child allowed everyone, in principle, to step in and impose gentle but firm maternal discipline when the monarch was seen to have overstepped his bounds.[45]

What I am suggesting is that this is precisely the idiom through which the relation between divine and sacred kingship here plays itself out. The idiom of the king as dependent child provides a framework through which the arbitrariness of power, even the arbitrary violence of individual kings—and there was quite a bit of that in Merina history—not only makes sense, but can itself become a token of legitimacy, if one that can also be easily contested.

The ritual system seen from the perspective of the child-king

So, why were Merina kings represented as children?

One obvious reason was that, for all they might be occasionally be hailed as "fathers of the kingdom," they ruled *because* they were children of someone else. A king is a king because his ancestors were kings. Hence the constant invocation, at every ritual event, of the names of the royal ancestors. In the case of commoners, this situation was reversed: their importance for the kingdom was

---

45. Similarly, there is a proverb everyone knows, *ny marary no andriana*, "sick people are kings," which suggests the same logic: sick people are the objects of constant nurturant attention, must be indulged, but are at the same time helplessly dependent on their carers. It's no coincidence that curers can, in certain contexts, also be known as *mpitaiza*.

the fact that they produced and fostered children themselves. This was brought home most clearly in naming practices. Queen Ranavalona I, during her reign, was known as Rabodon'Andrianampoinimerina—literally, "King Andrianampoinimerina's little girl." Her son, who became Radama II, is always referred to in official texts as RakotondRadama, which in turn means "Radama I's little boy." These names continued in use even after the rulers themselves became quite advanced in years. Queen Ravanavalona was still being called "the little girl" when she was eighty. Commoners, in contrast, tended as soon as they had offspring to name themselves after their children, adopting teknonyms such as "Rainikoto" (father of Koto) or Renibe (mother of Be).[46]

Similar naming practices have been documented elsewhere in the Austronesian world (e.g., Geertz and Geertz 1964; Brewer 1981; Schrauwers 2004). It seems a common side-effect of the tendency of aristocratic lines to monopolize genealogies: once the royal line becomes the core organizing principle of the kingdom, and local ancestors become unimportant, then only nobles are, properly speaking, descendants. Certainly this came to be the case in Imerina, where the ritual advisors of King Andrianampoinimerina, who reunified the kingdom after its period of civil wars and is generally regarded as the founder of the Merina state, first laid out the kingdom-wide arrangement of "twelve sacred mountains," each with its royal ancestral tomb of one of the "twelve who reigned"—the great royal ancestors—which meant the memory of any local royal ancestor who was not integrated into the new system became simply irrelevant, for ritual purposes. (This is, for instance, why no one remembers the kings of Imamo buried in Fondanitra today. They didn't make it into the new system, so no one had any reason to remember them.)

The keepers of these royal tombs were, paradoxically, a group of men called the *velond-rai-aman-dreny*, "Those Whose Mothers and Fathers Are Still Living," whose task it was to present various kinds of *santatra*, or "first-fruits," at royal ceremonies. From the late eighteenth century, they were drawn from eight key ancestries, and these were considered to have the very highest and most exalted position in the great system of royal service that anyone could possibly

---

46. In the nineteenth century, virtually every *hova* official who served in the government bore such a teknonym. Since it seems unlikely that each one had children, one has to assume that some had adopted or fostered children just to be able to do so. Monarchs, on the other hand, only became defined as parents on their deaths: Ranavalona I, known in her lifetime as "King Andrianampoinimerina's little girl," became Ranavalonareniny, "Ranavalona the Mother," afterwards.

have. These *santatra* were not limited to rice. Almost any object dedicated during a ritual was considered *santatra*. *Santatra* of one sort or another had to be brought for every major action or project the monarch undertook, from the building of a new cattle pen to a military expedition, every time the monarch appeared in public, and, crucially, at every major ritual marking the life-course of royal offspring: birth, first haircut, circumcision, marriage, and so on. Hence Those Whose Mothers and Fathers Are Still Living were sometimes said to "care for (*mitaiza*) the king when living, and bury him when dead" (Callet 1908: 260, 1185).

Whereas the cult of ancestors focused on the great kings of the past, first-fruits were all about creating something new. Technically, all this followed from the logic of Malagasy astrology.[47] As our sources emphasize, all these rituals were created by court astrologers and followed the basic astrological principle that, just as the fate of a child is determined by the hour of its birth, so is the success or failure of any undertaking determined by the moment of its beginning. Still, destinies are never inexorable. Hence, much of the Malagasy astrologer's art, then as now, consisted of "adjusting" or "repairing" destinies (*manamboatra vintana*), through the assembling, manipulation, preservation, or disposal of various symbolically potent objects: in this case, animals for sacrifice (not just oxen but eels, or forest animals like hedgehogs), rare woods and plants, incense, honey from a living hive, baskets, stones, and even the unbroken coins presented to the sovereign. These are the objects brought (literally "carried") by Those Whose Fathers and Mothers Are Still Living, and the *Tantara* provides us with elaborate lists of them. So, despite the fact that these are the same men and women who take care of the royal tombs, their principal work is not commemorating the past, but preparing the way for the future. Insofar as royal ancestors are relevant to these rituals, they, too, rather than the ancestors in *famadihana* nowadays (who are locked back in the tomb after the ritual), are something to be propitiated and then shunted off to someplace safe where they cannot interfere with everyday human affairs. As the French colonial ethnographer Charles Renel (1920: 157–58) observed when speaking of *santatra*: the ancestral order being seen as fixed, the creation of anything new was always a

---

47. There is a traditional system of astrological calculation common to the island, which is based on the Arabic lunar calendar; at one time, knowledge of it was a monopoly of certain in-marrying groups of Muslim immigrants and the Merina court employed some of these, but by this time it had also been more widely popularized.

certain sense an act of defiance, and, therefore, seen as requiring an act of propitiation directed at the ancestors themselves. This is presumably why calling such actions "first-fruits" made sense to begin with: in each case, there is a similar logic of appealing to authorities (whether king or ancestors) to lift some taboo or restriction they could otherwise impose, and in doing so, subtly, banishing them, at least temporarily.

* * *

All this matters because presentation of *santatra* was the apogee of the system of ritual labor as a whole. First-fruits were presented either at moments when subjects performed some great project for the king, or when royal children were being shaped into proper adults. The obvious implication is that these two moments were in some a sense equivalent—that royal service, even if it involves dragging trunks or making charcoal, extends the principle of caring labor for the royal household to the population at large, infantilizing the king at precisely the point where the royal will was, by definition, absolutely sovereign and unconditional.

It might be helpful to turn again here to the above-quoted passage about the presentation of first-fruits of the rice harvest to the sovereign. In fact it occurs at the very end of the exposition on *santatra* in general in the *Tantara* (Callet 1908: 48–61), as if this is what everything is leading up to. Recall the language: "This was the custom from olden times: to honor him, as he is the child nurtured by the people, as he is the master (*tompo*) of the land and the kingdom." *Tompo* means both "owner" and "master." It refers not only to command of land or other resources, but also to command over others' labor. It's also the root of *fanompoana*, which literally means "the action of making someone else an owner or a master." So even the king's mastery of his people, or ownership of the land, is not an intrinsic quality. The people make him the master and owner by doing whatever he says.[48] What's more, that willfulness, the tendency of the master to give orders, the pure arbitrariness of sovereign power, is also what reduces the sovereign to a permanent minor, and hence a cherished object of devotion.

---

48. In a similar way, the misconception that *hasina* "flows" can largely be traced back to the existence of the abstract noun *fanasinana*, from the verb *manasina*, an identical construction which means to "the action of causing someone or something to have *hasina*"—for instance, by making offerings or observing taboos (cf. Graeber 2007a: 37–38).

As representatives of Queen Ranavalona I's subjects announced to her in one famous speech, spoken on the occasion of her assembling her people for *fanompoana*, royal service was a matter of performing "whatever your heart desires, whatever sweetens your belly, whatever you wish to do with us, your playthings" (Cousins 1873: 42).[49] She was the sovereign with the power to do with her subjects what she would. But by that same token she was ultimately a beloved, but helpless, dependent child—and thus not fully responsible for her actions, because in a certain sense, like any child, she stood outside the adult moral order. If a toddler breaks the teapot, you might get angry, but you can't really say it was "wrong" of her to do so. Similarly, since it was the sovereign's right to do anything she liked, she could be "naughty," but she couldn't actually be wrong.

POPULAR CONTESTATION, WOMEN'S REBELLIONS, AND THE RETURN OF THE ANCESTRAL DEAD

At this point, I think, it is possible to pull the threads of this essay together. The reader will recall that I began by describing how, after the abolition of the monarchy in 1895, almost all past kings were immediately recast in the popular imagination as oppressive and unjust, even as spoiled children, and suggesting that this apparent overnight transformation couldn't really have come out of nowhere. At this point, we can certainly understand where the notion of the king as child was coming from. It's the linchpin of the system of ritual labor on which the kingdom was founded. The question, instead, is how is it that royal immaturity came to be considered objectionable, and not endearing.

The other question is why the uneasiness with royal power first manifested itself in a broad rejection of male kings in favor of female ones. Why did kings come to be viewed like the contemporary image of Leiloza, as self-indulgent child-princes endlessly making up oppressive new tasks for their subjects, while even notoriously violent and tyrannical female sovereigns like Ranavalona continued to inspire the devotion of their subjects?

It might not be possible to answer this last question definitively, but if we reread Merina history through the terms that have been laid out so far in this essay, it becomes a lot easier to understand. If nothing else, the story begins to

---

49. "*Fa izay sitraky ny fonao sy mamin' ny kibonao sy tianao hatao aminay amin' ny filalaovana.*"

look very different to the received official history. Because, in fact, at just about every point in that history where one finds an acute crisis of royal authority, one also finds these same themes cropping up: the childishness of displays of arbitrary royal power; the people as nursemaids, or as embodiments or avatars or royal ancestors, or both.

* * *

Now, it's easy enough to see how the notion of the people as nursemaids could become a language of political protest. And indeed it regularly did. Here's a speech reported to have been made by representatives of the town of Alasora, appealing to King Andrianampoinimerina to remove the local lords (*tompomenakely*) who had been appointed to rule over them:

> Children are sweet, but when they bite the breast, they must be pushed away. . . . Don't give us any more children to take care of, but if you please, let this become land directly under your own control. Alasora is a place of abundance, but those who've wound up here in the past have revealed the evil of their ways; let us no longer take care of them, because you have naughty children, and we the people have been fooled. (Callet 1908: 1043)[50]

Oral traditions suggest that in the seventeenth and eighteenth centuries, the nature and extent of royal power were under constant negotiation. While in principle, there were no limits at all on what a king might do, and kings did, often, act quite arbitrarily, the *mpitaiza andriana* had the power to admonish, chasten, or even mobilize the people to remove them. This was particularly true of royal councilors, who at the time acted as the principal representatives of the commoner population (Rafamantanantsoa-Zafimahery 1966). The first record we have of a ruler actually being deposed was that of a monarch named

---

50. *"Mamy ny zanaka: raha manaikitra ny nono, tsy maintsy akifika. . . . Aza omen-jaza hotaizanay; aoka ho menabe io raha tianao; fa tany manana zina Alasora, ka izay mivilivily eo miseho ny ratsy atao; ary aoka izahay mba tsy hitaiza intsony, fa maditra anaka hianao, koa izahay vahoaka no voafitaka."* The distinction here is between *menakely* (land granted by the king for the support of some lesser *andriana*) and *menabe* (land that provided all its taxes and services directly to the king.) It was commonplace to refer to these lesser lords both as "children" of the king, and as "children nursed by" the population of their *menakely*.

Rajakatsitakatrandriana (c. 1670–75), long remembered as the quintessence of selfish, tyrannical irresponsibility. After five years in power, he was unseated at the instigation of his father's aged former chief councilor and astrologer, Andriamampandry.[51] There are several contradictory accounts of how the old man managed to effect this. All agree that it began with his summoning a great *kabary*, or assembly, to win popular consensus that the king must be removed, where it was agreed that his younger brother be placed on the throne in his stead. According to some accounts, Rajakatsitakatrandriana then simply collapsed before the power of the elders' imprecations; in others, he was tricked out of the palace by divination (only to later make a failed attempt to find foreign allies to recapture it); yet others imply an actual uprising, since Andriamampandry is said to have set fire to the village of Andohalo just outside the royal precinct in order to drive away the king's most faithful followers (Callet 1908: 284–88; Julien 1909, I: 126–27; D. Rasamuel 2007: 218).

Andohalo was never rebuilt. Instead, the open space where the village once stood became the site of the great *kabary* held between kings and people from that point on. Later visitors describe it as "natural amphitheatre, in which some eighty to one hundred thousand persons may conveniently assemble" (W. Ellis 1838, I: 103), and in the nineteenth century, it was the scene of gaudy royal ritual and proclamations.

The *Tantara* claims it was King Andriamasinavalona (c. 1675–1710), the ruler Andriamampandry placed on the throne after the rebellion, who first made a systematic practice of consulting with the people before making important decisions (Callet 1908: 386). Often these consultations seem to have been mere formalities. At other times they involved serious negotiations between well-balanced powers. It was at these *kabary*, as well, where *hasina* was presented, oaths and vows of loyalty were pronounced, and the kingdom as a whole effectively created and re-created the kingdom, and thereby the king. Yet such actions could only have meaning if all were also aware that the people could, in the last instance, act otherwise. It was possible to withdraw one's oaths. And surely, the fact that all these oaths and consultations took place on the very site

---

51. As astrologer: Callet (1908: 31). Raombana (1980: 44–45) has him use divination as
      a pretext for removing the king from the palace. Some contemporary scholars make
      out Andriamampandry to be of noble descent, presumably because of his name, but
      both the *Tantara* (Callet 1908: 284) and Raombana (1980: 41) clearly identify him
      as *hova*.

of an earlier popular insurrection could only have constantly underlined the possibility that such things could, in the last instance, happen again.

* * *

According to the tradition, Andriamasinavalona lived long and wisely, but in his dotage made the unfortunate decision to divide his kingdom between his four favorite sons. (Andriamampandry strove mightily but failed to dissuade him.) The result was a chaotic descent into civil disorder. The histories refer to this as the period of civil wars. They ended only after a prince of Ambohimanga—the one who was eventually to call himself Andrianampoinimerina, roughly "the desire of Imerina"—managed, through a skillful combination of brutal force and delicate diplomacy, to patch together the various warring kingdoms into a single, unified, state.

It is especially difficult to assess Andrianampoinimerina in retrospect, since by the 1860s, when the histories were put down in writing, he had already become something of a folk-hero, the paragon of the old wise king against whom contemporary monarchs and their councilors could be judged. Earlier sources present a much more ambivalent picture: of an enterprising monarch sincerely dedicated to the prosperity of his subjects, but who was also responsible for the deaths of thousands, both in calculated massacres, and in the constant submission of the populations of whole towns and villages to the poison ordeal, or *tangena* (e.g., S. Ellis 2002). Even in the idealized accounts preserved by Callet, he is constantly threatening to kill law-breakers and dissenters. And some later sources preserve popular memories of the king that must have circulated among his enemies of the time, as a brutal usurper, ally of foreign slave traders, and murderer of innocents—memories still vividly alive—especially in *andriana* circles—long after his death.

Case 1: Andrianamboatsimarofy, an unstable king

In the stories collected in the mid-nineteenth century, Andrianampoinimerina is always represented as the stern but principled monarch, the one true adult on the throne. Since he is universally recognized as laying the foundations of the later Merina state, historians usually focus on him as the paradigm for kingship; but in fact, he seems to have tried to completely reinvent the institution. To get a sense of what early monarchs were like, it seems to me, it would be better to focus on his chief rival, King Andrianamboatsimarofy, king of Antananarivo.

Tsimarofy, as he is sometimes called, is regularly contrasted to Andrianampoinimerina as an almost comical figure, an impulsive blowhard given to every sort of indulgence and vice. In the *Tantara*, his court is represented as a kind of madhouse, its denizens constantly wasted on rum, cannabis, and opium. One typical passage: "There was one palace attendant who was smoking marijuana, and when high on marijuana chased a dog and fell into ditch, and for a while they didn't know if he would survive; but the king was not alarmed, neither did Tsimarofy forbid it but just let him carry on preparing the stuff anyway" (Callet 1908: 761).[52]

Typically, such passages are followed by declarations by Andrianampoinimerina that he would order the execution of anyone who indulged in such dangerous pastimes.

For over a decade, Andrianampoinimerina and Tsimarofy fought a see-sawing war over the control of the great city of Antananarivo, in which the capital repeatedly fell to the usurper's armies, only to be snatched back again by the Manisotra—Tsimarofy's most devoted troops. The Manisotra were (like the Manendy, whom we've met already) a kind of military order or specialized warrior caste. The sources often refer to both as "royal slaves." In reality, they were also a powerful descent group with their own ancestral towns and villages, and a peculiar relation of privileged familiarity with the royal household. Not only did the Manisotra lead and form the elite core of the king's armies; they alone were allowed to play with royal children.[53] There are long passages in the *Tantara*, many clearly meant for comic effect, purporting to record Tsimarofy's interactions with his protectors (ibid.: 964–69).

The first time the Manisotra drove Andrianampoinimerina out of the city and recovered the capital, they brought their king to show him,

> And the Manisotra took Tsimarofy to Antananarivo, and they said, "Did we lie to you, Tsimarofy? Here is your land and your government; if you don't care for it, then give it to someone else."

---

52. "*Nisy tandapa nifoka rongony, ary dia mamo rongony ka manenjika alika, na hady aza dia ianjera'ny, ka tsy mahalala ny ho faty, dia tsy matahotra andriana, ila hananika ny rova; koa tsy no raran' Andrianamboatsimarofy avela ny hiany hanao.*"

53. Domenichini and Domenichini-Ramiaramanana (1980) make a strong case that the Manisotra, like the Manendy, traditionally have a *ziva*, or joking relation, with the king (cf. Hébert 1958).

And Tsimarofy said: "I am happy, daddy Manisotra, I put my faith in you. Yes! You truly did not deceive me, so I thank you for that. Because here is my son Maromanompo, who dwells together with you and lives in the same house as you. So I have absolute confidence in you that you should live with him." (1908: 965)[54]

The Manisotra then inform him that they are returning to their own ancestral lands of Ambohijoky, where they will be available in case the king should be so careless as to lose his capital again. They also propose he send his (roughly eight-year-old) son Maromanompo with them, "as he isn't settled happily here, he'll enjoy Ambohijoky, and [your daughter] Ravao too wants to play with the girls at Ambohijoky." It's not clear whether the king assents, but he does order a great celebration, presumably replete with rum and other intoxicants, and tells the Manisotra to bring their wives and children. The Manisotra women dance and rejoice, but while they do so, they gently chide the king, urging him not to fall asleep or become distracted once again.

After a few years, Andrianampoinimerina again seizes the capital, and Tsimarofy is once more forced to appeal to his servants: "Come again, daddy Manisotra, because Antananarivo is lost once more, and once more I don't know what to do."[55] The Manisotra representatives immediately ask him: Did not our women tell him not to fall asleep on the job? A proper king doesn't play games but thinks about the government. Andrianampoinimerina only thinks about the government. If you prefer to play games, perhaps we should turn the government over to him and leave you to your games in peace.

Tsimarofy was roused up by this, and took up his shield and spear, fired off a shot of his musket, and declared: "If you still love me, then I myself shall fight at the head of my army. I will fight in the manner of the Sakalava, where the king himself leads the army, because the people may be powerful, but if the king is defeated then the people are defeated too."

---

54. *"Ary dia nentiny Manisotra Andrianamboatsimarofy nankany ao Antananarivo, ka hoy Manisotra: 'Mandaingia va izahay, Andrianamboatsimarofy? Indro ny tany nao sy ny fanjaka' nao, fa raha tsy tia· nao omeo ny olona.' - Ary hoy Andrianamboatsimarofy: ' Faly aho, ray Manisotra, matoky aho. Hay·! Tsy mamitaka ahy tokoa hianareo, ka misaotra anareo aho. Fa indro lahy Ramaromanompo, f'iny miara-monina ami' nareo ary miara-mitoetra ami' nareo."*

55. *"Alao indray i kiaky Manositra, fa lasa indray Antananarivo, koa tsy hitako indray izay hatao ko."*

"God forbid," said the Manisotra, "And where exactly did you come up with this 'Sakalava manner of fighting,' you with your bright ideas? You'll just hand the kingdom over to Andrianampoinimerina! Because that's all you'll accomplish with this 'let's do the Sakalava manner of fighting' nonsense. It's not the ancestral way; the king is to be guarded. You think you're going to lead the army, boy? All you're going to do is get yourself killed."[56]

The Manisotra leaders noted that great though their love was for the king, they were equally loyal to his ancestor, King Andriamasinavalona, who first granted them their lands in Ambohijoky, to which they were now inclined to return. When Tsimarofy persisted in his plan to personally lead his army into combat, they finally turned to their sometime playmate, the little princess Ravao: "Goodbye Ravao. Your father has abandoned you. Your daddy doesn't want to be king any more, ... so we must go home. Farewell!"

At this point Tsimarofy conceded: "I'm sorry, fathers, I will not continue in my foolishness. I put my faith in you. Do what you must to recover Antananarivo."[57]

* * *

Since all these stories are so clearly arranged to contrast the stern but efficient king of the north with the silly, feckless, self-indulgent king of the south, one might wonder how much of this is simply literary embellishment. But as a matter of fact there is good reason to believe the accounts are substantially correct. As it happens, a French slave-trader named Nicholas Mayeur personally visited Tsimarofy's court on at least two occasions, and has left us two different

---

56. "*Taitra indray Andrianamboatsimarofy ka nandray ny ampinga sy ny lefona, dia nipoa-basy tokana nanao hoe: 'Raha mbola tia'nareo hiany aho, dia izaho no voalohan' ady hitari-dalana, hanao adi-ntSakalava ka ny andriana mpitari-dalana, dia mahery ny vahoaka, ary raha resy ny andriana dia resy ny vahoaka.' 'Sanatria,' hoy Manisotra, 'Iza no mahalala izay adi-ntSakalava ny ialahy, ialahy hanao hevitra: fanjakana atolotr' ialahy an' Andrianampoinimerina! k' izany no anaovan' ialahy hoe "aoka hanao adi-ntSakalava." Fa tsy fanao ndrazana izany, fa ny andriana no ambenana; ary ialahy kosa no hitari- dalana? Ka hamono tena ialahy.'*"

57. The Manisotra's farewell: "*Veloma ry Vao, fa lasa ray nao. Ray nao tsy tia fanjakana . . . fa hody izahay ka dia hanao veloma.*" .. And the king's reply: "*Hivalo aho, ry kiaky, fa tsy hanindroa intsony ny fahadalana, fa hanome toky anareo aho, hatao lahy izay hahafaka an' Antananarivo.*"

descriptions of it, written eight years apart (Mayeur [1777] 1913, [1793] 1913). These accounts provide striking confirmation of some of the details of the account in the *Tantara*, while at the same time showing that Tsimarofy's misconduct at one point became so outrageous it inspired an outright revolt.

Mayeur is, in fact, the first foreign observer to have left us any sort of detailed eyewitness account of the Merina kingdom, which he called "the Kingdom of Ancove."

While visiting the small highland kingdom of Ankay in the spring of 1777, Mayeur was, by his own account, approached by a small delegation who explained to him that they were agents of Tsimarofy, and that the king would be very interested in establishing direct commercial relations with French traders operating on the coast. Mayeur was, at first, hesitant. The king of Ankay was clearly very hostile to the project, and Mayeur himself had not heard good things about Ancove. When the head of the delegation asked why he came to Ankay, rather than the much larger kingdom to the north:

> I responded that this preference was only natural; that several times, caravans of people from the coast had been pillaged by the subjects of his master; and this was reason enough to strictly avoid his province.
>
> "It is true," he replied, "that in the past the Manisotra have committed some excesses; because this class of men, who are slaves of the king, enjoy an unlimited liberty during such time as the king is not of age to govern. But he has now established order throughout his realm; I can assure you that foreigners will now enjoy the same security among us as they would enjoy in their own homes." (Mayeur [1777] 1913: 155)[58]

The next morning one of Mayeur's bearers took him aside and explained to him in confidence that he recognized the man claiming to be Tsimarofy's chief envoy —he was not an envoy at all; he actually *was* Tsimarofy, who had traveled incognito into his enemy's kingdom, at great personal risk, in order to effect the alliance. If nothing else, this impressed Mayeur of the man's seriousness. When the king admitted it was true, Mayeur agreed to set out together with him to Ancove.

---

58. My translation from the French. Translations from either Malagasy or French are mine unless otherwise indicated.

Along the way, the two men struck up a friendship. Mayeur ended up leaving an enthusiastic account of his capital, Antananarivo, a city that rose like a startling acropolis from the middle of a vast plain of terraced rice fields crowded with villages whose industrious inhabitants appeared, despite their complete lack of contact with foreigners, to have mastered the agricultural, industrial, and even administrative arts with far greater sophistication than any other inhabitants of Madagascar. (Mayeur was particularly impressed that Ancove's silversmiths could perfectly counterfeit European currency and that its blacksmiths were able to manufacture functional replacement parts for European guns.) The king took a great interest in promoting and regulating circulating weekly markets. The inhabitants of Ancove, Mayeur observed, seemed a fundamentally peaceful people, more interested in commerce than in war; though he must also have noted with some professional interest that the division of the country into numerous warring principalities, and resultant instability, ensured it was in a position to supply unusually large numbers of slaves.

When Mayeur returned eight years later, in late August 1785, matters were not going nearly so well for his old friend. The king was perpetually drunk, and had become addicted to opium purveyed by Arab merchants. Tsimarofy seemed at constant war with all his neighbors, especially Andrianampoinimerina, who seemed, Mayeur estimated, at this point to be gaining the definite upper hand. Finally, Tsimarofy's own people had indicated there was a very definite limit to their patience with his behavior.

Three years before, Mayeur reported, Tsimarofy had killed his chief wife in a drunken rage. His people, outraged, convoked a general assembly in order to decide whether to remove him from office and pass his formal title on to their preadolescent son. In the end, the answer was affirmative. Mayeur summarizes the message presented to the king in the *kabary*—it was presumably held at Andohalo—in his characteristic, slightly stuffy, style:

> Prince, here is your legitimate successor. He is now under our watchful care; we wish to teach him how to govern us, because it is true that currently, if he remains with you, he will only witness bad examples. We wish for tranquility, far from the vexations which your continual inebriation has imposed on us. The innocence of your son, and the respect that the *hova* have for their sovereign, mitigate against the vow we have already taken to change our ruler. Yet the crime you have committed against your wife, your own first cousin, which marks the very culmination of our indignation, cannot remain unavenged, so we have assembled

to deliberate on the matter. It has been decided that you will no longer receive either our allegiance or our tribute; that we will regard all those among us as remain attached to you as enemies of the Hova people, up to such time as you solemnly declare that you have completely renounced the use of strong liquor. We have also taken a vow to allow you a fixed term to reflect on this matter. Until that term is expired, all authority you have over us shall be suspended. Our allegiance will be directed to your son. (Mayeur [1793] 1913: 39)

The declaration was followed by the firing of muskets, and the conferring of Maromanompo to the protection of the Manisotra. After the appointed term was over, a second *kabary* was held, and the king determined to have remained sober in the interim. His people therefore renewed their vows of fealty again.

Still, according to Mayeur, this newfound sobriety was short-lived. Before long the king had lapsed, Andrianampoinimerina returned, and the resulting popular disillusionment played no small role in his ultimate military defeat.

* * *

The role of the Manisotra and Manendy, collectively known as the Mainty Enin-Dreny, the warrior orders of ancient Imerina, has always been something of puzzle for historians. While referred to as "royal slaves," they have many of the same privileges as *andriana*; they seem to rank in certain ways above, in other ways below, the bulk of the population. The understanding of the ritual structure of the Merina kingdom developed in the course of this essay suggests one way to understand this apparent paradox. Such warriors were (like the Tsiarondahy, the palace attendants with whom they were often grouped), a particularly intimate kind of *mpitaiza andriana*, not just because they protected the king in battle, but because even in ordinary times, the king's own children were relegated to their care. Here their playful intimacy with little princesses like Ravao. As a result, if the monarch was not yet of an age to rule, or else if he was simply not acting as if he were, his sovereign power—that is, his right to engage in arbitrary, essentially lawless violence—devolved onto them.[59] This is

---

59. The impunity of the Manisotra probably refers to a status known as *tsy maty manoto*, a privilege granted in recognition of extraordinary favors to royalty (as in the story of Trimofoloalina: Kingdon 1889; Callet 1908: 316–21). The Manendy, the other major warrior caste, were said to be *tsy maty manoto* as well (Rakotomanolo 1981: 7). Those who held it could not be held accountable for certain crimes, notably, theft.

why during Tsimarofy's minority, the Manisotra could revert to simple banditry, preying on foreign caravans at whim. But even when, as an adult, he attempted to take full command of his armies, they treated him as a child again, and put him firmly back in his place, in such a way as to ensure he was aware their loyalty was as much to his family (whether his ancestor Andriamasinavalona, or his six-year-old daughter Ravao) as it was to him. He was neither the eldest nor the youngest of his lineage.

And in the end, what was true of the Manisotra was, in an attenuated sense, true for all of his subjects as well, since, in the event of the king's proving himself utterly unfit to preside over the royal family (by killing his wife), they were willing to temporarily convey power to a minor (his son, Maromanompo, restored to the supervision of the Manisotra) until he could prove himself capable of ruling even within those parameters to which he was allowed.

If so, it makes it easier to understand the fate of the historical Leiloza, and his son Rabevola, as well. Having been expelled from his kingdom in Valalafotsy, Leiloza fell in with a faction of Manendy, who took on exactly the same role: they offered him their nurturant protection, but at the same time used that relationship as the moral basis for effectively turning bandit and launching raids against all around.

Case 2: Radama I and the first women's uprising

Andrianampoinimerina was ultimately victorious, and in his new united Merina kingdom, he marginalized both Manisotra and Manendy, relying instead for military support on two large *hova* ancestries from his native Ambohimanga, the Tsimahafotsy and Tsimiamboholahy. These were to provide his royal councilors, who were his own principal *mpitaiza andriana*, and the military commanders who were to effectively run the kingdom from then on. Yet, like his son Radama, who took power at the tender age of seventeen, Andrianampoinimerina allowed the *mpitaiza* only a modest role in government. Other than the councilors, his chief *mpitaiza* were the guardians of the royal sampy (i.e., the keepers of the "political" charms that protected the kingdom): it was Andrianampoinimerina who seems to have systematized the elaborate ritual system outlined in the *Tantara*, with its pantheon of twelve royal ancestors, twelve sacred mountains, and twelve national charms. Radama, once he had entered into alliance with the British governor of Mauritius, who recognized him as "king of Madagascar," threw everything into the creation of his new red-coated army, drilled and provisioned by British advisors, and no longer seemed to have found much use for *mpitaiza* of any kind.

Radama also largely abandoned his father's habit of calling grand assemblies to consult with his subjects about policy issues; increasingly, the great *kabary* at Andohalo became places to make proclamations and convey royal orders, or to make a display of military formations, but very little else.

Radama was the ultimate adolescent king, and it's not hard to see him as a distant inspiration for the myth of Leiloza.[60] He fancied himself a new Napoleon, whose portrait he in fact kept in his private chambers:[61] an enlightened despot determined to employ his unlimited powers to reshape society in modern, progressive terms. He established a school system and a civil service. He sponsored industrial projects, and campaigns to modernize building techniques, clothing styles, and standards of public hygiene. He divided the entire male population of Imerina into two broad categories, military (*miaramila*) and civil (*borizano*), and invoked the principle of *fanompoana* to call the first up to service in the army, the second, to labor teams assigned to increasingly onerous royal corvée. At the same time, Radama played the enlightened skeptic in relation to the mumbo-jumbo of his father's ritual system: he was especially famous for entertaining himself by posing impossible tests for astrologers and magicians and trying to expose the various tricks and stage illusions employed by mediums.

One of the king's most notorious comments was rendered to a French artist hired to paint his portrait, one André Copalle, himself apparently an Enlightenment skeptic of sorts. Copalle wrote the followed account of a conversation he had with the king, after the latter's return from a journey to the shrines of the royal ancestors, to petition them for rain:

---

60. Back in the 1960s, Radama was still an important healing spirit, at least in the region immediately surrounding Antananarivo, and he was sometimes also known as Rakotomaditra ("Naughty Boy"), which was the original name given to the spirit whose *doany* is of Ambohitrambo later to be known as Leiloza (Cabanes 1972: 52-3). See above, footnote 12.

61. Many sources speak of Radama as modeling himself on Napoleon. After the breakdown of his alliance with the governor of Mauritius, Radama replaced Hastie with a French-Jamaican sergeant named Robin, who had deserted Napoleon's army and eventually fled to Tamatave. When the King first met him, he asked if he'd really served under Napoleon's orders, and on hearing that he had, "he then showed him a portrait of the Emperor, saying, 'behold my model! Behold the example that I wish to follow!'" (Ackerman 1833: 49). Radama eventually named Robin his supreme military commander.

> The prince was long returned from his pilgrimage, from which he had obtained all the success he had wished for. Radama, moreover, did not believe in these spells and devotions, and even less in the divine power which superstition attributed to them. He sometimes laughed at it, and told me, between us, that it was all just a matter of politics. He questioned me one day on my religious opinions, and, I having in my turn addressed several questions on the subject, replied to me among other things that religions were nothing but political institutions, fit to lead children of all ages. (Copalle [1826] 1970: 37)

The latter remark takes on renewed significance coming from the mouth of a thirty-year-old monarch (in other words, himself little more than a child by Malagasy standards) in a political system where kings were regularly themselves treated as de facto minors. It sounds very much as if Radama was using his privileged relation with foreigners to reverse all this, to cast himself as a kind of stranger-king in the making, and, by that very token, render those who might otherwise have been considered his *mpitaiza* (astrologers, sampy guardians, the people as a whole) as so many benighted children in their turn.[62]

This attempted realignment did not go unchallenged. Matters came to a head, in fact, over precisely the sort of personal household issues—the care and nurturing of the king, and royal family more generally—that were the traditional focus of the system of ritual labor. It will be recalled that the act of bringing first-fruits was also modeled on the ritual of a child's first haircut, the point where a child effectively begins to become a social being, capable of forming relations with others. In commoner households, this was a ceremony presided over primarily by women; and women continued to play a critical role in the care and maintenance of hair—their children's hair, their menfolk's, and each other's—throughout their adult lives. This is more important than it may seem because traditional highland hairstyles were quite elaborate and required a significant investment of care and labor to maintain:

---

62. My interpretation here in part contrasts with Gerald Berg's (1998) reading of the same statement. Berg argues that rather than being cynical, Radama was simply restating an ideology which made no distinction between what Copalle would consider politics and ritual—in this I certainly agree—but goes on to argue that this ideology was based on a notion of "the flow of *hasina*" from king to subjects whereby "Merina rulers had always been considered as 'fathers' of their subjects" (ibid.: 70). In fact, as we've seen, despite some lip service to this idea, matters were ordinarily quite the reverse.

> From all accounts the various styles of plaiting the hair were innumerable. Men
> seem to have fully appreciated this mode of ornament as well as the women, so
> much so that King Andrianampoinimerina is said to have had a special style for
> himself, which was called *Ny bóko antámpona*, i.e. "The knob on the top of the
> head," as all of his hair was gathered together into one big plait at the crown of
> the head. Another famous mode, called *sàlo-bìta*, consisted of plaiting the hair
> into an equal number of very fine plaits, which hung down in an even row. . . .
> The special feature of this plait consisted in the addition of a row of coral beads,
> sewn along each of the exterior angles, if the person was of the andriana, or
> noble class; whereas among the Hova, or commoners, it was the custom to sew
> on small silver chains or coins. The time spent in plaiting must have been very
> considerable. (Edmonds 1895: 471–72)

The careful maintenance of elaborate hairdos was, it seems, seen as one of the
main preoccupations of women and itself became a kind of paradigmatic labor:
a synecdoche, one might say, for the broader process of shaping human beings.
If responsibilities to one's parents and ancestors could be referred to as *valim-
babena*, "the answer having been carried on the back," the two main marriage
payments to a bride's family were (and still are) called the *akana kitay* ("fetching
firewood") and the *alana volo fotsy* ("plucking out white hairs"), in both cases a
recognition of the loss of the services the daughter might otherwise have provided to her family, in the first carrying things again, in the second, carefully attending to the tresses of her aging parents. Second to bearing burdens (firewood,
babies, etc.), hairdressing seems to have been a paradigmatic form of female
labor, just as female domestic labor was the paradigmatic form of labor itself.

As on the domestic level, so on that of the kingdom as a whole. Andrianampoinimerina not only had a unique hairstyle, his hair had to be elaborately renewed before every major royal ritual. For instance, an early-twentieth-century
Jesuit source recalls this of the royal circumcision ritual, which was the occasion
of one of the great national festivals:

> Under Andrianampoinimerina, when everyone wore their hair long, the first of
> the holy days was consecrated to the needs of coiffure. The sovereign's hair, along
> with that of the fathers and mothers having some infant to be circumcised, had
> to be plaited according to a particular rite, in the middle of the public plaza of
> the capital. This initial ceremony began with the sacrifice of a white-spotted ox,
> it ended with the firing of canons. (Camboué 1909: 376)

The dressing of the king's hair was itself a form of *santatra*, performed at Andoha-lo by the most senior among Those Whose Mothers and Fathers Are Still Living (Callet 1908: 30, 73–74; Soury-Lavergne and de la Devèze 1912: 342–43; Molet 1976: 41; Bloch 1986: 122–27, 135). Similarly, in the early part of Radama's reign, the king wore his hair long, in a style so full of plaits and curls it was said to take up to three days to properly dress it (W. Ellis 1838, I: 287). In the spring of 1822, however, Radama made a momentous decision: to sheer off his locks, and adopt a military-style crewcut in the European fashion. What's more, orders soon went out that all subjects of *miaramila* status were to cut their hair in the same way.

This order was the culmination of a series of reforms that had the cumulative effect of transforming *fanompoana* from a system of ritual labor, focused on the royal household, to the organizing principle of a modern state. The unlimited power of the sovereign to call his subjects up for labor was being used to justify everything from the responsibility of children to attend mission schools, to the calling up of recruits to be sent to war, or simply to be stationed for indefinite terms in coastal fortresses—the latter leading to serious rates of mortality from malaria and other diseases.

> Against the above innovations, a spirit of daring resistance was evinced by a number of females in a neighboring district [Avaradrano], and a large meeting was held, to which the discontented repaired. Information of these proceedings soon reached the capital. About two thousand soldiers were immediately summoned; they renewed their oaths of allegiance, promising that whoever should be found guilty of creating a disturbance, even if their own parents should be implicated, they required but the king's order or permission to put them to death: after these assurances of fidelity, the soldiers were ordered to guard the capital. On the following day, four or five thousand females assembled at Ambatoraka, a village to the east of Tananarivo, and sent a kabary, or message, to the king complaining of his having adopted foreign customs, and having allowed his people to be taught by Europeans. In reply, Radama sent to ask them what were their grievances; if they were too heavily taxed, or if they were displeased at having their sons employed in the army; whether he were their king or not, and whether they had chosen some other king in his stead? They replied to these questions in the negative; *but said, they were the nurses of the king*,[63] and complained because he

---

63. Larson, who reproduces this passage, oddly renders the word incorrectly as "caretakers," but correctly notes the Malagasy word was "probably *mpitaiza*, a word suggesting the relationship between nurse and child" (2000: 249).

had adopted the customs of the foreigners; had allowed them to teach him and his people; had changed the customs of the ancestors; and finally, he had cut off his hair, and drank spirituous liquors. Radama sent back a message to ask if, being king, he had not a right to do as he pleased with his hair without consulting women; reminding them, it was the inalienable right of the twelve monarchs to do as they pleased, and added, that he would presently give them a proof of this, by taking care that their hair should never grow again. (W. Ellis 1838, I: 288, emphasis mine)

According to Ellis, five ringleaders were identified and summarily executed with bayonets. Others were flogged to within an inch of their lives. The rest of the "rebellious females" were surrounded by troops, held for three days without food or water, and forced to watch the bodies of their companions be "devoured by dogs and birds." Finally, the king proclaimed the survivors would be allowed to return to their homes "to attend to their domestic duties, but must leave the business of government to himself" (ibid.: 289; for a detailed analysis of the events, see Larson 2000: 240–53).

This was the most overt popular challenge to royal policy during Radama's reign and it was quite in keeping with traditional forms. The protestors represented themselves as *mpitaiza andriana* ("nurses of the king"). The fact that this was an all-women's assembly appears new—at least we have no record of earlier all-women's assemblies in the highlands—but this might just be due to the bias of our sources, which overwhelmingly represent the perspectives of men.[64] At any rate, it's easy to see how, if the plaiting of hair was a major part of women's daily occupations, and was an intrinsic part of the gradual process of rendering and maintaining their children as fully human, then abruptly removing this responsibility by forcibly shearing their children's heads might seem the most vivid, and obviously outrageous, aspect of a series of royal edicts designed to remove them from domestic control and turn responsibility for their growth and

---

64. In other parts of Madagascar, women's *kabary* have been documented, but not in Imerina itself. The *Tantara*'s account of these same events, recorded almost a half century later (Callet 1908: 1078–80), is already beginning to downplay the women's role (claiming it was men put the women up to it), which suggests that if there had been women's revolts in earlier times, we wouldn't necessarily have any record of them. Neither do we have any way of knowing if women were prominently involved in Andriamampandry's revolt, or the *kabary* held to temporarily remove Tsimarofy, though women were presumably present in some capacity as they generally do participate in highland *kabary*.

development over to foreign-trained schoolteachers and drill sergeants working directly for the state. From their perspective, there simply was no meaningful distinction between "domestic duties" and "the business of government"; and reminding Radama of the people's role as *mpitaiza andriana*, and admonishing him over his own domestic misbehavior—drunkenness, consorting with foreigners, neglect of customary usages, making major changes in how his very physical person was to be maintained without prior consultation with those charged with maintaining it—was the obvious way to make this point.

In doing so, they also not only cast the king in the role of nursling, but also identified themselves, at least tacitly, with his own royal ancestors. In the *Tantara*, the delegates are instructed to appeal to the "twelve kings," none of whom ever shaved their heads.

> We have come to admonish you, Sir, do not cut your hair because this is not a custom observed by kings. . . . King Andriantsimitoviaminandriana did not cut his hair. Andriambelomasina ruled and never cut his hair. Andrianampoinimerina, too, ruled and never cut his hair. And now we have you, Radama, and you make soldiers, and you shear off all your hair. (Callet 1908: 1079)[65]

Radama's personal reaction, as remembered inside the palace, is recorded by later court historian Raombana:

> With the greatest brutality (for he was rather drunk or completely drunk, I do not know which), he exclaimed that these abominable women want to stir a rebellion to upset him from his kingdom, but that he will disappoint them, *for that he is not a child*, and that he will be beforehand with them and cut short the rebellion which they meditate against him. (Raombana 1994: 79.803–4, emphasis mine)

Any act of mass political contestation—and this is true above all of nonviolent ones—is an act of political theater in which the audience is not just the

---

65. "*Mananatra anao izahay, Tompokolahy, fa aza boriana ny volonao fa tsy fomba fanaon'ny Andriana nanjaka izao mibory volo izao. . . . Nanjaka Andriantsimitoviamanandriana, tsy notapahina ny volony; nanjaka Andriambelomasina, tsy notapahina koa ny volony; nanjaka koa Andrianampoinimerina, tsy notapahina koa ny volony. Ity mby aminao Radama, ka manao miaramila hianao, ka hianao no manao sanga ka borianao ny volonao.*"..

government, but if anything, even more, those charged to carry out the government's orders. Successful rebels tend to be keenly aware of this. You win if you can either create a situation where those sent to shoot you refuse to do so, or else convince the government that those they would otherwise be inclined to send to shoot you cannot be relied on, and therefore that compromise is the only course. In Madagascar itself, movements of nonviolent resistance against standing governments, starting with the Forces Vives in 1990, have tended to prepare the ground beforehand by using family connections, or often church ties, to reach out to the commanders of the security forces to ensure their neutrality before street actions began. Clearly, the rebels of 1822 were employing a similar strategy. According to the *Tantara*, the great assembly that made the decision to hold a women's march on the capital also decided to send women primarily from the province of Avaradrano: this was, significantly, the home province of the bulk of Radama's officer corps and most loyal troops as well. This no doubt explains the king's initial panic: calling in thousands of troops and asking them to swear to follow his orders to execute dissidents "even if their own parents should be implicated"—since there was a very real prospect that that this exact circumstance might arise. Once he did secure that loyalty, the game was effectively over.

Or at least it was for the moment. In the longer term, it's not nearly so clear who really won.

Case 3: Ranavalona I, the toddler queen and the return of the dead

On the surface, Radama's victory in April 1822 would appear to be absolute. The survivors were terrorized into silence; no further movements of public opposition occurred. In retrospect, some of the demands of the women's assembly—for instance, that all foreigners be immediately delivered over to them—seem so presumptuous that one wonders how those who made them could have imagined things might turn out any other way. But a mere twelve years later, their core program had been largely realized. A woman sat on Radama's throne, and she did indeed call in these same foreigners for ultimate expulsion; ancestral customs put into abeyance by Radama were, indeed, restored. What's more, all of this was carried out under the aegis of the very officer corps to whom the women of Avaradrano had so—apparently—unsuccessfully appealed.

What happened?

According to the standard history, after Radama drank himself to death at the age of thirty-six in 1828, several high officials, led by a general named

Andriamihaja and an old judge named Andriamamba, effected a kind of coup. Pretending the king had named his long-neglected senior wife as successor, they quickly moved to assassinate all rival claimants. The new queen, Ranavalona, already fifty-one at the time of her coronation, went on to reign for thirty-three years, the longest of any historical Merina monarch,[66] and while she maintained Radama's standing army and school system, she eventually effected a radical break with most of her ex-husband's other policies. Above all, she abandoned his attempt to open Madagascar to the larger world economy, adopting instead a policy of self-sufficiency which ultimately led to almost all foreign-born residents of the island being expelled. The only ones allowed to remain were a tiny handful of favored advisors, such as Jean Laborde, a wanted criminal from France who was therefore assumed to owe no loyalties to his homeland, and who, being in possession of a set of technical encyclopedias, was put in charge of the government's industrialization campaign.

The expulsions, the prescription of Christianity, and subsequent execution of a number of Christian converts ensured that Ranavalona soon became the object of intensely hostile propaganda from abroad. Foreign histories came to depict her as a monster, a "mad queen," even a "female Caligula," whose endless wars and purges of suspected witches devastated the country—according to some of the more surrealistic claims, killing off between a third and two-thirds of the entire Malagasy population. Such numbers are obviously absurd, and might be forgivable, perhaps, coming from the pens of angry exiles at the time, with access only to sensationalistic horror stories; the peculiar thing is that it's still possible to find them reproduced in the works of influential historians like Gwyn Campbell, who, completely ignoring the voluminous demographic material in the royal archives, treat the most extravagant claims of foreign observers as literal historical fact.[67]

---

66. Andriamasinavalona is also said in most accounts to have reigned thirty-five years, but the dates are an approximation.

67. Campbell's works cite only European sources, almost entirely uncritically, while systematically ignoring almost all sources written in the Malagasy language— whether because Campbell disdains such sources, or simply cannot read Malagasy, I cannot know. For instance, in his *An economic history of imperial Madagascar, 1750–1895* (2005), he provides a chapter with what he claims is a comprehensive list of sources on nineteenth-century Merina demography containing no Malagasy sources that have not been translated, and shows no awareness of the fact that Ranavalona's government actually carried out a census in the 1840s, and that the census documents still exist, easy accessible, within the Malagasy National Archives.

* * *

A real social and economic history of Ranavalona's reign thus remains to be written. What evidence we do have from sources inside the country (and there's actually considerably more of it than historians like Campbell let on) suggests largely continuity with what was already happening under Radama. Young people continued to be drafted into the army and sent off on military campaigns against "rebels" in the provinces; these continued to lead to massacres and a constant flow of coastal women and children into highland slave markets; all much as before. Inside Imerina, the main change was a withdrawal of state authority. While the government kept a firm hand on the capital and major ports, it seems to have left small towns and rural communities in the highlands largely to themselves: the administrative apparatus set up under Andrianampoinimerina, and vastly increased under Radama, fell into abeyance.[68] True, when government intervention did occur, it was often spectacularly destructive. Much as under Andrianampoinimerina, whole communities were sometimes put to the poison ordeal (*tangena*) on suspicion of being in possession of subversive magic.[69] And the queen's notorious pleasure excursions—these were the ones which led to the rounding up of thousands of subjects as porters— did wreak havoc on the communities through which they passed through. But state intervention of this sort was sporadic at best; there is no evidence that such depredations, when they did occur, were significantly worse than they had been under Andrianampoinimerina or Radama; the difference was that otherwise, for the most part, rural communities were largely left alone.

Meanwhile, in the capital, the royal household became the focus of endlessly baroque and spectacular forms of public ritual.

As Pier Larson (2006) has pointed out, Campbell's numbers are often bizarre: he once estimates the population of all of Imerina at 25,000, and, at the same time, the population of its capital at 800,000. Yet for some reason his argument that Ranavalona's regime committed autogenocide on a scale two or three times worse than Pol Pot is taken at face value by numerous historians.

68. During Ranavalona's reign, internal administrative documents in the National Archives largely disappear, aside from census documents and some judicial registers. Military and diplomatic correspondence, however, continues unabated.

69. Those who underwent the *tangena* were forced to imbibe water infused with scrapings of a poisonous nut, and three pieces of chicken skin. If they vomited up the chicken skin, they would be considered innocent; if they did not, they would be pounded to death with pole-like pestles used to pound rice.

Since the unification of the island, Madagascar has witnessed a continual
ebb and flow of state power in the countryside. In many ways, the regime of Ranavalona I seems to most resemble that of President Didier Ratsiraka between
1975 and 1993: he, too, cut off most external trade and expelled foreign-botn
residents, while simultaneously withdrawing state authority (up to and including police) from most of the countryside. What's important in Ranavalona's case,
however, is the ideological formula through which such arrangements came to
be justified. Because, say what you will about the queen herself, the formula
clearly worked. Her government was stable, successful, and long-lasting, and, in
marked contrast to earlier reigns, it saw very little in the way of popular unrest.

Now, certainly there have been other times and places where rule by arbitrary, spectacular, but occasional violence is considered preferable to more apparently gentle, systematic, but intrusive, forms of governance. My essay about
the Shilluk (chapter 2 in this volume) addresses precisely this kind of situation.
So Ranavalona's case is hardly unique. In kingdoms that take this path, royal
power is often seen as analogous to powers of nature; the sovereign becomes a
kind of divine force standing outside the moral order. There is some evidence
something like that was happening here, too. Ranavalona, like other Merina
kings, was often greeted on her public appearances by songs comparing her
to God, or to the sun. Still, there is no reason to assume such effusions had
much more significance than they might have in, say, the court of Louis XIV.
No one appears to have evoked them when speaking of the queen's actual conduct.[70] The arbitrary willfulness of the sovereign was instead directly identified with her childishness. As observed above, she was regularly referred to as
Rabodon'Andrianampoinimerina, "King Andrianampoinimerina's little girl," or
just Rabodo, "the little girl"; her advisors were her "nursemaids," the people her
"playthings" to do with as she pleased. Unlike the solar metaphors, these weren't
mere rhetorical effusions. These terms cropped up regularly when people discussed the regular conduct of political affairs.

---

70. The one song referring to Ranavalona as "God seen by the eye" and comparing her
    to the sun is, however, widely cited in foreign sources at the time (e.g., Sibree 1889:
    176; 1896: 214; Renel 1920: 71–72), presumably since it conforms so well with the
    current stereotype of Oriental despotism. As a result of this and one or two other
    references (most in folklore), the idea that Merina sovereigns were "visible gods" has
    been take up almost universally in contemporary scholarship (probably via Raison-
    Jourde 1991: 78, though strongly echoed in Ottino 1986, 1993). But the sentiment
    is almost entirely absent from nineteenth-century Malagasy-language sources.

* * *

We are fortunate enough to have a long and very detailed history of the reign of Ranavalona I, written by her personal secretary, Raombana, in English so that no one else at court could read it. Raombana, who had studied in London, considered the queen's regime to be an utter catastrophe. His narrative reads like something halfway between Tacitus' *Annals* (with its prolonged accounts of prominent aristocrats being unjustly put to death) and Procopius' *Secret history* (with its shocking revelations of madness and debauchery at court). But it also makes clear that, despite many historians' claims to the contrary, Ranavalona was in no sense a mere figurehead. If anyone was in a position to know who was actually in charge at court, surely it was Raombana; and in his version of events, Ranavalona makes all important decisions, from the general direction of policy (should Radama's imperial ventures be maintained?) to the exact wording of diplomatic correspondence or military communiqués. Yet for all this, she's constantly treated like a self-indulgent child by everyone around her.

Raombana himself attributes much of the organization of Ranavalona's court to her previous sexual frustration. The queen had been named Radama's senior wife largely because Andrianampoinimerina had wanted to pay off a political debt to her father; being ten years older than her husband and "not at all pretty," Raombana explains, she was almost completely neglected by the prince; though at the same time, she was avoided by other men who feared the king's wrath should they take up with her themselves. As a result, when she came to power, her first priority was to acquire a coterie of lovers:

> Such being the propensity of the Queen, and not having for years been embraced by a man, no sooner therefore was she seated on his throne and before Radama was even buried when she formed the project of getting several paramours.
>
> Before Radama was consigned to his grave, she took to her bed Andriamihaja, Rainiharo, Rainimaharo, Rainijohary; and subsequently Rainiseheno etc. etc., and by these paramours she got to be with child about five months after the death of the King, a thing which neither she nor anybody else in Madagascar ever expected for she as I have already stated was about fifty-five [sic][71] years of age . . . .
>
> During the first months of her pregnancy she was very ill and often had falling fits, and it was thought that she would not survive long. Whenever she

---

71. In fact she was fifty-one.

recovered from these fits, she drank enormous quantities of rum and arrack; and
lay with her paramours even in the day times and thus satisfied her lusts in an
extraordinary manner. (Raombana n.d.: 76.1308–10)

Obviously, Raombana is taking a somewhat jaundiced view of things. For
Malagasy royal women, establishing one's sexual freedom was clearly a key part
of the establishment of one's political autonomy. We have seen the same thing
in the case of Hastie's "prophetess": formally married to powerful political figures, but reserving the right to choose other lovers freely among their subjects
too.[72] Ranavalona's situation was actually slightly different from theirs since her
"paramours" were all, in fact, generals and men of state: Andriamihaja commanded the army; Rainiharo was prime minister; Rainijohary, as guardian of
the sampy Kelimalaza, effectively became the kingdom's high priest. Raombana
observes that these men very quickly combined to convince the queen that expanding her circle of lovers beyond palace officials would open her up to mortal
dangers of witchcraft; they took particular care to keep her away from any men
who were not, like them, of commoner descent.

So Ranavalona's taking on multiple lovers was in no way scandalous in itself;
this was exactly how a woman in her circumstances was expected to behave.
To convey a sense of scandal, then, Raombana has to emphasize the extreme
nature of the queen's behavior, and the degree to which it interfered with affairs
of government—not to mention, endangered her own health and safety, which
was the ostensible raison d'être for the entire apparatus of state. Ranavalona, by
his account, would veer from indulgence to illness, needing to be literally nursed
back to health; terrified of witchcraft, she continually forced those surrounding
her to undergo the *tangena* ordeal, falling into panic and depression when she
feared her lovers might perish as a result, often rising from her sickbed to dance
with joy on learning they'd survived. The queen is represented in his account as
imperious, gullible, vindictive, quick to shame but equally quick to anger—that
is, as very much the spoiled child.

---

72. The same applies to Matavy, the famous wife of the founder of the Betsimisaraka
    confederation, Ratsimilaho. She was daughter of a Sakalava king to whom
    Ratsimilaho wished to ally, but, apparently, on realizing his whole kingdom was
    something of a fraud cooked up in alliance with European pirates, she immediately
    began to flagrantly take multiple lovers from among his subjects. He seems to have
    felt incapable of raising any objections to her behavior and was forced to raise what
    everyone assumed to be another man's child as his son and heir..

Raombana, of course, is giving the view from inside the palace; he was also writing in English, presumably, for an imagined future audience abroad. The *Tantara* allows us to have some sense of how such matters were represented outside the walls of the *rova*, or royal enclosure. The chapter on Ranavalona's government is entitled "*Lehilahy mpitaiza ny andriana,*" or, "Men who were nursemaids of the queen" (Callet 1908: 1146), and in the official historical record, all the queen's lovers are officially referred to as her "nursemaids," or men "taken by the queen to nurture her" (*nalain'ny andriana hitaiza azy*).

Here's, for instance, how Raombana begins his account of the downfall of Andriamihaja, the general who was primarily responsible for placing Ranavalona on the throne, and who was widely assumed to be the real father of her infant son. According to European sources, the general represented a progressive faction, friendly to Christians, keen on pursuing Radama's modernizing project, and opposed to Rainiharo and Rainimaharo's traditionalists. Raombana first notes his role in bring the queen to power:

> She was therefore fond of him, and trusted to him almost the whole management of the state affairs, so that in fact, he acted as the first judge or minister, as chief secretary of Her Majesty, and as commander-in-chief of the army, which business he managed in the most admirable manner. As a paramour however, Her Majesty loved Rainiharo and his brother Rainimaharo more than him, especially Rainiharo who was the best looking man in Madagascar, and of the finest shape . . . .
>
> Andriamihaja was not a very good looking man, but he had more talent than his opponent, so that literally speaking Rainiharo ruled the will of the Queen while in bed with her; and Andriamihaja, while he was out of bed and ruled almost as a sovereign when out of the palace: for he had the sole management of the different affairs of the kingdom, the continual sickness of Her Majesty, and she being continually in bed with her paramours both night and day, made her trust to Andriamihaja the affairs of her kingdom as already stated. So that a few months before his death, he was very seldom admitted into the palace on account of his business, besides so enamored was Her Majesty with Rainiharo and her other paramours that she did not much want his presence in the palace, as his presence there awes them, and keeps them from mirth, and while he is admitted into the palace, he always lays at night with Her Majesty for she was also afraid of him and dare not lay with the other paramours while he is in the palace. Therefore in order that she may be more in the company of Rainiharo,

etc., she said to Andriamihaja that the sikidy or divination does not allow him to remain in the palace for some time; and that he is to remain outside of the palace and manage all the business there. (Raombana n.d.: 12.448–53)

Andriamihaja, he goes on to explain, was an intimidating presence who had the presumption of occasionally rebuking the queen for dallying with other men. He felt he should really be her only lover. Early in Ranavalona's reign, the queen's solution had been to send him off on frequent military expeditions. (In fact Raombana implies that many of the wars that plagued Madagascar in those years were occasioned primarily by her desire to get him out of town.) But finally, her lovers made common cause to remove him. They charged him with possession of *ody mahery*, evil charms, claiming these were the real cause of the queen's frequent illnesses, and, furthermore, that he had contrived to falsify the results of the poison ordeal. In addition, several testified that the general had come to refer to himself, among his friends, as "Bonaparte"—a very disturbing choice of nickname, they emphasized, considering that Napoleon Bonaparte was a commoner who had placed himself on the French throne after an uprising that led to the previous monarch's public execution. The queen was still hesitant, so in the end, Raombana says, her lovers were obliged to send an assassin to Andriamihaja's home to murder him with a butcher's knife, and then retroactively claim he had failed the *tangena* ordeal.

Such, anyway, was Raombana's palace-gossip version. The version preserved in the *Tantara* (Callet 1908: 1147–50) is entirely different. The author begins by observing that "under Rabodo, the chief men were her nursemaids, and Andriamihaja, from Namehana, was chief among them."[73] Knowing he had the absolute support of the queen, the author says, caused the general to engage in much high-handed behavior, and matters eventually came to a head when he decided to round up a number of slaves belonging to free subjects and put them to work manufacturing shoes and cartridge boxes for the army. This was considered a violation of the principle that only free subjects perform *fanompoana* for the queen, and therefore an outrageous precedent that threatened the very foundations of the social order. Important court figures, including Ranavalona's other *mpitaiza* and the twelve chief royal women, who were the still-surviving widows of Andrianampoinimerina, began to meet in secret to decide how to

---

73. "*Ary taminy Rabodo ny lehibe nitaiza azy tao, Andriamihaja, avy amy ny Namehana, izy no lehibe.*"

respond. Local leaders were consulted. Finally, a decision was made to send a delegation to the queen.

Yet when this delegation approached Ranavalona, they chose not to frame the issue in terms of the employment of personal slaves for state purposes; rather, they insisted, the general was violating the principle of *fanompoana* by his demand for exclusive sexual access to the queen:

> We don't know what Andriamihaja is thinking, but no one has ever treated a monarch in the way he's treated you. No matter whom the queen may love, there's never been anything like this. Look! What he's done to you is not like service (*fanompoana*), living with you and nurturing you (*itaizany anao*); he is treating you like he would a wife in his own home, like a person of the same status. So we can't accept that, even if that is what you want. There's no lack of people for you to love in this land, for you are a queen for whom nothing is forbidden. Whoever you desire, take him! So here are our thoughts, your fathers and your mothers: pretend to be sick, and we will request the poison ordeal. (Callet 1908: 1148)[74]

Presumably this was so as to arrange matters in such a way that Andriamihaja should be determined to be responsible.

The author goes on to explain that the queen first balked at the prospect of exposing her immediate circle to the *tangena*, but finally the intervention of some of the old surviving wives of King Andrianampoinimerina was decisive, and she agreed. In other words, in this version, the entire story about the queen's illness was actually a ruse, and what Raombana represents as a purely bedroom affair was the result of extensive political consultation and debate among different powerful interests in the kingdom, with royal women playing the ultimately decisive role.

The above passage is revealing, however, because it lays bare the ideological foundations of Ranavalona's reign. The entire apparatus of government—up to

---

74. "*Tsy fantatray ny hevitr' Andriamihaja, fa tsy mbola nisy nanao ny manjaka toy izao nataony aminao izao; na iza tian' andriana na iza tian' andriana, tsy mbola nisy toy izao. Ka he! ity ataony anao tsy ohatry ny fanompoana ny itoerany sy ny itaizany anao atoana, ataony anao ohatry ny fitondrany vady ao an·trano, ohatry ny olona mitovy hiany. Ka tsy mety izahay, na dia tianao aza izy. Fa tsy lany olona hotiana amin' ity tany ity hianao, ka mpanjaka tsy manam-pady hianao amin' ity tany ity hianao; izay tianao alaina, alao. Ary dia izao no hevitray ray aman-dreninao . . . modia marary hianao, izahay hangataka finomana.*"

and including the military—was indeed seen as ultimately just a means of providing for the queen's personal needs, whims, and indulgences. It was still all a vast system of nurturance. Yet as such it is necessarily a collective affair, involving every subject in the kingdom; the only thing the queen could *not* do, then, was to violate the latter principle, by allowing any one of her *mpitaiza* to stake an exclusive claim.

* * *

It is telling, then, the closest there was to an overt popular challenge to Ranavalona during her thirty-three years in power played on that very image of the queen as the old king's "little girl." This was the event that, according to Raombana, caused Ranavalona to make her final break with Christianity, and, ultimately, to ban "the praying," as it was called, entirely.

One of the effects of early Christian evangelizing was, in Madagascar as in so many other places, the appearance of millenarian movements prophesying the imminent end of the world. In 1834, a certain Rainitsiandavana, a minor sampy guardian from Mandiavato to the north of Antananarivo, unlettered and with, our sources assure us, only indirect knowledge of Christian doctrine, began to claim to have learned in visions that the end times were near, and the dead would soon return to life. When that day came, he announced to his followers, Ranavalona would reign as queen of the entire world, the time of wars and recruitment drives and poison ordeals would be over, crops would grow of their own accord, and men and women would live in universal peace, harmony, and equality (Freeman and Johns 1840: 91–97; Rabary 1910: 54–55; Raison-Jourde 1991: 131–38). Several hundred devotees marched with him to the capital, carrying the sampy, to inform the queen of the good news. According to the version of events that soon became canonical in the Christian literature, Ranavalona sent envoys to interrogate the prophet, until, finally, he was asked whether the story of Adam and Eve implied that the queen was of the same descent as Mozambican slaves—and was outraged when Rainitsiandavana affirmed that it did. Raombana, as usual, gives us a rather different view. The way the story was remembered inside the palace was that what really terrified the queen were the political implications of the return of the dead:

> Before they could arrive in town, news was immediately spread in it, that Rainit-siandavana has received power from God to raise the dead up to life again; and

that his object in coming to town is to raise them up; and that he will first raise up Radama, and the sovereigns who are interred in the palace; after which he will go about all Imerina and raise up all the dead . . . .

These reports were received with avidity and joy by the superstitious populace of Antananarivo who fully expected that they will soon see and embrace all their dead relations again.

They whispered and asked one another who will reign when all the dead sovereigns are raised up; whether it will be Her Majesty, or Radama, or Andrianampoinimerina or Andriamasinavalona, or who. Some said that Her Majesty would not deliver the kingdom to any of them but will retain it, as she has felt and enjoyed the sweetness of reigning. Others said that she will be obliged to resign the throne to one of the old sovereigns who has reigned better than her. And others in the gravest manner said that they fear there will be civil wars in Imerina again between these sovereigns, for that each will have their partisans. (Raombana n.d.: 41.161–65)

The queen ordered Rainitsiandavana and his main confederates be placed head down in a ditch and drowned in boiling water; others were made to undergo the *tangena* ordeal; many died; the survivors were sold into slavery.

It would appear that one critical weakness of any monarchy where the ruler is conceived as a child whose legitimacy derives from royal ancestors is what might happen if those ancestors actually reappear. It's not a danger that most kings have to worry much about. But in the northern highlands of Madagascar from at least the time of Leiloza onward, dead monarchs were to begin appearing among the living with increasing frequency.

Case 4: Radama II and the second women's rebellion

About a year into her reign, Ranavalona gave birth to a son who, despite the circumstances of his birth, was declared to be Radama's offspring by some form of mysterious spiritual conception. He was given the name Ikotoseheno, though in official documents he is universally referred to as RakotondRadama, or "King Radama's little boy." From his teenage years onward, the prince began to take more and more after Andriamihaja, who was widely rumored to be his actual father: aligning himself with the progressive faction at court, and becoming the devoted companion of the few foreigners allowed to remain in the city, and protector of the kingdom's Christians. (The prince, however, considered himself a Deist.) The queen had by this point swung decisively into the camp of traditionalists; but in her eyes, the prince could do no wrong. By the 1850s, they were operating openly at cross-purposes. RakotondRadama began cultivating a circle of liberally minded young companions, known as the Menamaso, or "red-eyes," purportedly because of their fondness for wild late-night parties. As the queen relied more and more on the pantheon of royal sampy, her son began openly ridiculing the cult, once even setting fire to the shrine of Kelimalaza. As the queen, increasingly ill-tempered and arbitrary, began flying into rages at the slightest provocation and sentencing dozens at a time to death, her son adopted the habit of simply walking into prisons holding those he considered unjustly accused, releasing their fetters, and providing them money for a safe trip home. Some claimed he'd released literally thousands in this way (Régnon 1863: 57–64; Anon. 1900: 486). It's not clear whether his mother simply wrote it all off as youthful hijinks, or whether her advisors were afraid to tell her this was even happening.

In 1855, six years before his mother's death, RakotondRadama had already signed a secret entente with French representatives promising to open the country to foreign investment once he came to power. He also began putting his Menamaso companions into positions of authority, particularly in the judiciary, as counterweights to the traditionalist military elite who controlled public affairs. And when he did finally come to power, in 1861, at the age of thirty-one, he moved swiftly to reverse almost all of his mother's policies. Indeed, if Queen Ranavalona might be said, on taking power, to have attempted to put into effect the demands of the women's uprising of 1822, the new King Radama II might well be said to have tried to institute a kind of liberal, this-worldly version of Rainitsiandavana's millenarian vision of 1834—the one his mother so brutally suppressed. Radama called an end to military recruitment; he sharply reduced the employment of forced labor, abolishing capital punishment and the poison ordeal; he declared freedom of religion, abandoned most spectacular public ritual, eliminated customs tariffs, and opened the country to foreign trade. He also made clear his ultimate aim was to abolish slavery, and to dissolve the kingdom's standing army entirely.

Within a very short period of time, this did indeed lead to something very like an apocalyptic scenario.

The problem with Radama's project was that while his mother's isolationist strategy might have seemed cruel and barbaric, given Madagascar's larger geopolitical situation, it actually made a lot of sense. The moment the country was opened, and particularly the moment it was made legal for foreigners to buy land, Antananarivo was instantly invaded by a small army of corporate agents, diplomats, speculators, purveyors of get-rich-quick schemes, and flimflam artists pretending to be any of the above. The kingdom's infrastructural development, even its mint, was turned over to one giant French conglomerate that under Napoleon III's encouragement proposed to give itself the historically unpromising name of the French East India Company; foreigners began buying up slaves and establishing sugar plantations in the plains surrounding the capital; and word began to spread that foreign interests were preparing to acquire large chunks of the island wholesale.

Before long the capital was subsumed by a sense of social breakdown and rampant criminality. None of this was helped by the fact that, under the influence of the Menamaso and some French advisors, the young king's own court began to very much resemble that of Tsimarofy: marijuana, hashish, and opium, now being produced in quantity alongside the rum being distilled at the new sugar plantations, were openly consumed in nightly champagne orgies at the palace. Again, sexual indulgence of this sort, for all it disconcerted the missionaries,[75] was not in itself considered particularly scandalous—this was more or less the way a young prince was expected to behave—but in the context of the times, the combination of intoxication, foreign influence, erratic policy decisions, and immature self-indulgence clearly must have been seen as a repetition of just the sort of behavior that sparked rebellions against male monarchs in the past—only now, writ exceptionally large.

In the late winter of 1863, rumors began to reach the capital of an epidemic of spirit possession, a "dancing mania" as the missionaries came to call it. Those affected first felt stiffness and fever, and reported feeling as if they were struggling under a heavy weight; gradually, they fell into a trance-like state, marked by the constant need to dance. Here is how its beginnings were described by

---

75. A typical comment:

> The ruin of poor Radama was accelerated, and his untimely end very much hastened by the conduct of some French officers and others who got to the capital, and who aided and encouraged him in his sins, and in those orgies that were practiced in his palace. They probably taught him many sins he had never dreamt of before. They had champagne suppers night after night, for weeks and months, followed by scenes that dare not be described, and for many months the poor King could seldom be said to be in his senses. (Matthews 1881: 20)

Radama's court physician, one Dr. Davidson, assigned at the time to diagnose the phenomenon, in an article he was later to publish in the *Edinburgh Medical Journal*:

> In the month of February 1863, the Europeans resident at Antananarivo, the capital, began to hear rumors of a new disease, which was said to have appeared in the west or southwest. The name given to it by the natives was *Imanènjana*, and the dancers were called *Ramanènjana*, a word which probably comes from a root signifying to make tense. . . .
>
> After a time, however, it reached the Capital, and in the month of March began to be common. At first, parties of twos or threes were to be seen, accompanied by musicians and other attendants, dancing in the public places; and in a few weeks these had increased to hundreds, so that one could not go out of doors without meeting bands of these dancers. It spread rapidly, as by a sort of infection, even to the most remote villages in the central province of Imerina, so that having occasion to visit a distant part of the country, we found that even in remote hamlets, and more wonderful still, near solitary cottages, the sound of music, indicating the mania had spread even there. . . .
>
> Those affected belonged chiefly, but by no means exclusively, to the lower classes. The great majority were young women between fourteen and twenty-five years of age; there were however a considerable number of men to be seen among the dancers; but they certainly did not exceed one fourth of the entire number, and these also belonged mostly to the lower orders of society. (Davidson 1867: 131; 1889: 21–22)

The sudden appearance of musicians everywhere might seem puzzling, but there is a longstanding tradition, throughout Madagascar, of musical diagnosis and cure. If there's any reason to believe an illness might be caused by some invisible being wishing to make itself known—and there are many such: Bilo, Tromba, Salamanga, etc.— it is necessary first of all to determine what sort of spirit it is by the sort of music it responds to; then, if possible, to allow the intruder to dance itself out, and in the process, to express any message it might be intending to convey. The latter is important. A frustrated spirit might well prove fatal to its host.

The Imanenjana soon took on a character halfway between an epidemic and a popular uprising. One French historian (Raison-Jourde 1976; 1991: 269–84) has even labeled what happened a kind of revolution through spectral theater—which seems about right: I would only add, one that soon came to combine the most salient themes of 1822 and 1834. Certainly, women, slaves, and enslaved women in particular had the most to lose if Madagascar really did become a plantation economy under the aegis of foreign corporations and investors.[76] Yet anyone contemplating open defiance of the government would surely also be aware of the fate of the women who marched on Antananarivo under the last Radama—or, for that matter, of what had happened to Rainitsiandavana himself. Somehow, in the visions and trances of the dancers, in the stories reconstructed by those who tried to cure them, in subterranean political alliances that thus began to be made, a form of rebellion began to take shape that proved utterly impossible for the government to suppress. We do not know precisely how the pieces came together, but we know what happened when they did.

At first, the kingdom filled with rumors. Neither Western medicine nor Christian exorcism seemed to have any effect on those afflicted. Royal ancestors, it was said, were returning in some form, but there was not yet a consistent narrative as to why and which. William Ellis, envoy of the London Missionary Society, caught the king at a point, quite early on, when rumors were just beginning to reach the palace:

> When I went to the king I found him greatly excited by some reports of a new kind of sickness which had made its appearance in some of the villages at a distance from the capital. These reports had been coming in from different parts for two or three days past. The people, he said, had seen strange sights in the air, and heard unearthly sounds. The spirits of his ancestors had been seen in the heavens, and were coming to Antananarivo, and some great events were about to occur, but what, he did not know. He did not believe, he said, in ghosts, but since the reports came from such a number of people—nearly forty—and continued for three days, he did not know what to think of it. "Was it a sign," he asked, "of the end of the world?" (W. Ellis 1867: 253)

Ellis assured him it was not, since that would only come after all nations were converted to Christianity.

---

76. This is not really the place to enter into the matter, but the 1860s began to see a broad change in the conditions of slavery in Imerina, whereby many slaves began winning increasing de facto, if not de jure, autonomy. While Radama II aimed to abolish slavery entirely, whether or not he had done so, establishing a plantation economy would certainly have reversed these trends decisively.

Gradually, the stories did begin to coalesce. Women were being possessed by the spirits of royal baggage carriers. It will be recalled that one of the most dramatic forms of oppression under the old regime had been the queen's periodic pleasure excursions, for which all the finery of court had to be transported, and thousands of villagers swept up to be employed as porters, given no food or provisions, until many collapsed and died. Now the spirits of these unfortunate victims were descending from Ambondrombe, the mountain of the dead, because Ranavalona I was determined to come and admonish her son for having allowed the Christians to return to the capital (he had even visited their chapels and accompanied them in their prayers!). The *Tantara* gives us a sampling of the kind of stories that began to circulate—some that spoke of just the kind of civil war between former monarchs some had feared in the days of Rainitsiandavana. The following account, for instance, appears to have been partly occasioned by the sighting of distant forest fires along the slopes of Ambondrombe:

> When Mother Ranavalona died and came to Ambondrombe, the *andriana* and commoners on Ambondrombe were happy and rejoiced, and the people cried out for joy, and soldiers stood in formation, and music played, and cannons fired all around. The celebrations lasted over half a month. Many oxen were presented to Mother Ranavalona, and many cannon, so even on Ambondrombe the whole town was agog at the grandeur of the queen's ascent. After a while some palace attendants from Antananarivo came to Ambondrombe [presumably because they had died], and told Mother Ranavalona, "Radama II and the people are praying."
>
> And Mother Ranavalona was furious and spoke with Radama, saying, "They say that Ikotoseheno and my subjects in Antananarivo are praying."
>
> And, purportedly, Father Radama told her, "He belongs to both of us. Let him do what he likes, because he's our only child."
>
> When Mother Ranavalona heard what Radama said she cried out in a rage, "So what mortal person is it who's caused Ikotoseheno to start praying?"—calling here to the people of Antananarivo.
>
> Furious, she set out for the capital. Radama tried to stop her, but she wouldn't let him; Radama tried to block off the road, but he wasn't able to block it; Radama ordered the forest around the highway set on fire, but even then he couldn't stop her; she was determined to seize her son anyway, because there was absolutely nothing she hated so much as praying.
>
> And when she'd gone, Radama was frustrated, because he hadn't been given many soldiers, there were a mere handful consigned to follow him when

he set out for Antananarivo. So Mother Ranavalona in her anger said, "I put my faith in you, you Army that follow me, and you others who refuse to abandon your Mistress (referring to the small numbers of soldiers and civilians with her). We must set out this very night!" (Callet 1908: 640)[77]

Neither monarch had, apparently, managed to scrounge up sufficient forces in the land of the dead to support a march on the capital. The queen, however, knew how to gather reinforcements; and so, the account goes on to say, when the next day her followers began to flag under the weight of her baggage, she ordered them to seize anyone they passed on the road as porters—apparently, since Radama I plays no further part in the story, leaving her late husband languishing helplessly behind.

Before long, possessed women and their escorts were occupying the sites of tombs and tops of sacred mountains, where they danced with bottles of water on their heads, or flung themselves from heights, to return unscathed; others were donning their finest apparel and marching in processions toward the capital, snatching the hats of all men they passed, claiming they had to be removed out of respect for the passing queen. Often they'd eat nothing for days on end, yet still showed themselves capable of impossible feats of strength. Slaves joined the

---

77. "*Raha tonga tao Ambondrombe Ranavalonareniny efa niamboho, dia faly sy ravo ny andriana sy ny ambaniandro tao Ambondrombe; ary nihoby ny vahoaka, sy nilahatra ny miaramila, sy velona ny mozika, ary nipoaka ny tafondro manodidina, ary izany fifaliana izany naharitra tapabolana mahery. Ny omby betsaka no nentin- dRanavalonareniny, ny tafondro betsaka, ka mahagaga tokoa tany an-tanana n' Ambondrombe tamy ny izany fiakarany ny andriana izany. Ka nony efa tonga elaela Ranavalonareniny, dia misy olona tandapa taty Antananarivo tonga tany Ambondrombe, ka nilaza tamy ny Ranavalonareniny:'fa mivavaka Radama II sy ny vahoaka.' Dia tezitra Ranavalona, ka niteny tamindRadamarainy hoe:'Mivavaka, hony, Kiotoseheno sy ny vahoaka ko any Antananarivo.' Dia niteny, hony, Radamarainy nanao hoe: 'Iny no antsika, ka avelao izy hanao izay tia' ny, fa zaza tokana amy ntsika.'—Raha nandre ny fitenindRadama Ranavalonareniny, dia tezitra ka nanao hoe 'Olombelona iza moa no hampivavaka any Kiotoseheno!' miantso ny olona aty Antananarivo. Dia tezitra izy, ka niezaka hankaty Antananarivo; ka no sakanan–Radama, ka tsy azo no sakanana; ka nambenan-dRadama ny lalana, ka tsy azo nambenana izy; nasain-dRadama no dorana ny ala lalambe, ka tsy azo izy, fa miezaka haka ny zana' ny hiany: fa tsy tia ny dia tsy tia' ny indrindra ny mivavaka. Ary nony efa nandeha izy, dia tezitra Radama, ka tsy nomena miaramila betsaka, fa vitsy foana no nome'ny hanaraka azy hankaty Antananarivo. Ka tezitra Ranavalonareniny ka nanao hoe: 'Toky no ome' ko anareo ry foloalindahy izay manaraka ahy, sy hianareo tsy mahafoy Tompo, (miantso ny tsimandoa sy ny borizano vitsivitsy), dia tsy maintsy handeha isika anio alina.*"

caravans, some shackled in invisible chains; others would suddenly fall writhing as they were lashed by unseen overseers, stripes from spectral whips appearing mysteriously on their flesh. Numerous raids were carried out on the new plantations around the capital, cash crops were seized and deposited on tombs, and dancers descended on the city from all directions carrying stalks of sugarcane.

Many converged on the plain of Mahamasina, a wide-open space at the foot of the hill of Antananarivo, containing the sacred stone on which Merina kings are traditionally invested in office. "This stone," Davidson noted, "was a favorite rendezvous for them. They danced here for hours on end, and concluded by placing the sugarcane, as a sort of offering, upon the stone" (1867: 133).

The king, increasingly drug-addled and confused, wavered between paternalistic indulgence and occasional ineffective attempts at police repression:

> [The Ramanenjana] conveyed the fruits of the land, they seized whatever they liked, whether oranges, or sugarcane, or bananas. And they didn't have the slightest fear of the thorns, as often owners would surround such fields with thorny hedges, but they just walked across the thorns, and no part of their bodies were injured in the process; they did whatever was required to seize the fruit of the land to carry to the king. Even if it was land guarded by its owner, they just took it, and their kin would pay money later; because Radama II put out an edict: "Whoever stands in the way of those who are sick, I declare guilty, do not stand in their way, let them take what they want to take, for they are ill." And there at the sacred stone at Mahamasina they took the things they'd appropriated; they didn't eat it, not at all, they placed it atop the sacred stone, or on top of mountains, or at the head of tombs; and every now and then, one would carry it home to place in the Corner of the Ancestors. And when they presented the sugarcane and other fruits of the land, sometimes, their fevers would abate.[78]

---

78. "*Dia manatitra ny vokatry ny tany, ka maka voankazo na fary na akondro . . . . dia tsy matahotra ny tsilo akory izy ireny; fa matetika mifefy ny saha n'olona ka be tsilo manodidina, ka manitsaka ny tsilo be iny izy, ka tsy maratra ny tena ny rehetra amy ny izany, fa atao ny izay ahazoa' ny ny vokatra ny tany ho entina amy ny andriana; fa raha tany miaro ny tomponjavatra, dia alain' ny hiany, fa ny havana no mandoa vola; fa tamy ny Radama II namoaka didy izy nanao hoe, 'raha misakana ny marary dia atao ko meloka, fa tsy sakanana izy, fa avela haka izay tia'ny halaina ireo, fa olona marary,' dia eny amy ny vato masina eny Mahamasina, no mametraka ny zavatra alaina, fa tsy dia hani'ny tsy akory, fa atao ny eny ambony ny vatomasina, eny antendrombohitra, eny andoha fasana; indraindray enti'ny mody ka apetra'ny eo an-jorofirarazana; ary rahefa manatitra ny fary na zavatra hafa vokatry ny tany, dia miafa ny sasany.*"

And they say there were some, ill with the Ramanenjana, who entered the *rova* [the royal compound] saying "Where is Radama II?"

And the guards said, "He's here inside the *rova*."

And the sick women spoke again, "Let us enter, as his mother has sent us here to see him."

The guards relayed those words to Radama, and he allowed the sick women to enter, and once before him the sick women said, "Be well, my Lord! Live long, my Lord! May you grow old beside your mother!"

And Radama was taken aback by the words, "may you grow old beside your mother." But, he asked himself, isn't my mother dead?

Then the sick woman spoke, and said, "My Lord! Your mother is waiting for you over in Mahamasina."

Radama II was shocked again to hear that, but then he ordered the woman arrested, because there wasn't anything at all at Mahamasina, aside from innumerable sick people around the sacred stone, and those singing for them. And when Radama saw the sick woman, having been tied up, was on the point of dying, her ordered her released . . . . (Callet 1908: 641)[79]

The "fruit of the land" referred to here were treated exactly as *santatra*, which were conveyed to the king as a gesture of homage which also recognized him as a child, nurtured by the people. In fact, every aspect of the proceedings—conducted almost exclusively by the laboring classes—might have been designed to reinforce the message that human labor is properly directed to that larger ritual system which nourishes the sovereign (and not, presumably, toward internationally oriented commercial enterprise). The carrying of sugarcane, for instance, recalls processions carried out during circumcision rituals—the prince's

---

79. "*Ary misy koa, bony, ny marary Ramanenjana niditra tany anaty rova nanao hoe: 'Aiza Radama II?'—Dia niteny ny mpiambina nanao hoe: 'Ato anaty rova.'—Dia niteny indray ny marary: 'Avelao aho hiditra, fa asain-dreny ny mankaty amy ny.'—Dia lazainy ny mpiambina amindRadama izany teny izany; dia navela ny hiditra ny marary; dia niteny ny marary eo anatrehan dRadama II nanao hoe: 'Sarasara Tompo ko e! trarantitra Tompo ko e! mifanantera amy ny reny nao.'—Dia taitra Radama amy ny teny hoe mifanantera aminy reny nao.—'Moa, hoy Radama anakampo ny, tsy maty ny reny ko!'—Dia niteny ny marary nanao hoe: 'Tompokolahy o!: reny nao etsy Mahamasina miandry anao.' Taitra indray Radama II nandre izany, ka nasai'ny ho samborina ny marary, fa teo Mahamasina tsy nisy na inona na inona akory, afatsy ny marary be dia be manodidina ny vato masina, sy ny mpihira ny marary. Ary rahefa voa fatotra ny marary, dia saikia maty, dia nasain-dRadama nalefa . . .*"

own circumcision, many years before, had been a nationwide festival of unparalleled magnificence—but these were precisely the kinds of great public ceremonial he was currently abandoning. The fact that the women who now filled the streets of the city, surrounding the palace, claimed to have been sent there by the king's own mother to admonish him only made the message unusually transparent.

Even when the king tried to propitiate the Ramanenjana, his gestures tended to backfire. According to one foreign observer, after the "crazy dancers" had descended on the palace, Radama even issued an edict that all who passed them on the road should, indeed, doff their hats as to his mother—an order which then caused no slight indignation on the part of members of the elite now obliged to render respect to what many considered mere mobs of rebellious female slaves (S. P. Oliver 1866: 94–95).

Before long, the sampy guardians, stalwarts of the anti-Christian faction, began to come out into the streets in support of the dancers. The Christians tried to mobilize their own marches against them. The city began to experience something like a general insurrection. Whole regiments of soldiers seized by the "disease" marched on the city, bringing their guns and even toting pieces of artillery; companies of workers summoned for *fanompoana* abandoned their assignments and converged on Mahamasina. The military high command—who were mostly from the traditionalist faction—became increasingly restless as the king's behavior seemed to grow ever more unhinged and bizarre. Finally, in mid-May 1863, they found a pretext in a royal order legalizing dueling: considering the state of the capital, this must have seemed like a veritable invitation to civil war. The commander in chief, the later Prime Minister Rainilaiarivony, ordered two thousand troops into the city to besiege the *rova* and slaughter the Menamaso. A few days later, the king himself was strangled with a red silk cord, and the kingship allowed to pass to his wife—but only on condition she agree to reverse her late husband's decision to allow foreigners to buy land in the country. (Christians, however, were still allowed full freedom to pray and to proselytize.) That August, the new queen Rasoherina duly appeared on the stone of Mahamasina to accept the people's vows.

So ended the brief reign of the last of Madagascar's would-be Napoleonic reformers. In a *kabary* held on April 24 of the next year, her new prime minister introduced Rasoherina to the Ambanilanitra—the "below the sky," or people of the country—in the following fashion:

And as for the common people, whether white or black, may you live! But also, do not be the nurses of many; because it is Queen Rasoherina who is the nursling of the people. (Cousins 1873: 49)[80]

CONCLUSIONS

If half of wisdom is knowing how to ask the right questions, then we are, perhaps, roughly halfway there.

It would seem that something about the integration of the Merina kingdom into the larger world economy triggered a crisis in its very conception of sovereignty. Traditionally, monarchs were seen as very much like children: willful, egocentric, yet totally dependent on the people whose willingness to tend to their needs made their lives possible, and whose willingness to obey even their most arbitrary orders made them sovereigns. Infantilizing rulers in this way had a double effect: on the one hand, it made it possible for their subjects to forgive even the most occasionally brutal behavior; on the other, it provided a language through which those subjects, as the king's nursemaids, could intervene when a consensus arose among them that things had gone too far.

One might argue that it was really King Andrianampoinimerina who first marked a break with this tradition. But matters seem to have really come to a head in 1816, shortly after his death, once European missionaries and advisors appeared on the scene. From that moment on, an unmistakable pattern appears. All male sovereigns—including near- or apparent would-be ones like Andriamihaja—see themselves as Napoleonic reformers,[81] and each is directly challenged by women: Radama I by the women's assembly of 1822; Andriamihaja by the former wives of Andrianampoinimerina who convinced Ranavalona to destroy her ambitious lover; Radama II by the trance dancers of 1863. Radama I seems to have been most effective in fending such challenges off, but in fact it wasn't long before he fell into the drunken malaise that destroyed him—one

---

80. *"Ny ambani-lanitra, na ny fotsy, na ny mainty, veloma, koa aza maro fitaiza; fa Rasoheri-manjaka no taizany ny ambani-lanitra."*

81. Radama II never self-consciously identified himself with Napoleon as far as we know, but he actually entered into an alliance with one, Napoleon III, and clearly saw himself as an Enlightenment reformer on the same model.

could argue, as a direct result of the dismantling of the ritual system which was, ultimately, designed to nurture and sustain the king.

Why did this happen?

In the existing literature, such overly ambitious kings tend to be identified with a mythic figure, derived from highland folktales, of the Andriambahoaka or "universal sovereigns" from the center of the four quarters of the cosmos,[82] and hence a revival of heroic figures of the past—even, kings who took seriously the notion that they were "Gods seen by the eye." They represent a kind of bursting into the present of mythological times. Worldwide, this is not at all an uncommon conception, but in this context it seems particularly inappropriate. What's unusual about the vision of history that emerges from the *Tantara* and other nineteenth-century texts is that it does not follow the common pattern where time is, as it were, layered; accounts do not begin with some great cosmological epic full of gods and primordial beings, where fundamental institutions such as cooking or marriage or death came into existence, move on to a heroic world where cities and nations are founded, and only then, finally, to the more modest imitations of such primordial gestures by the lesser beings of today. Quite the contrary. The earliest beings, in such stories, were disorganized primitives known as Vazimba, and the conquering invaders who displaced them, ancestors of the *hova* and *andriana*, were led by rulers who were said to have gradually created the basic institutions of society—everything from ironworking to circumcision rituals to the protocols of deliberative assemblies—all by themselves (Delivré 1974: 185–99).

Kings were thus expected to be innovators and inventors.

All this is familiar enough to scholars of Malagasy, but it seems to me few are willing to consider the full implications. If it is possible for kings to be innovators and inventors on this scale, it is because the powers of creativity that in so many traditions exist only in a distant *illo tempore* (as Mircea Eliade famously named it), that is, in mythological times, are distributed evenly across history. But if this is true that means that for all intents and purposes, Malagasy people were *still* living in mythological times. I think the same is true today. It took me

---

82. Andriambahoaka actually just means "Lord [of] the People," but in some of the myths recorded in the nineteenth century this name is given not just to a legendary king of Imamo, but to a kind of generic all-powerful king of the center, matched by princes of the north, east, west, and south (Dahle and Sims [1877] 1986). The argument is that this is an essentially Javanese conception of sovereignty. It's never been clear to me what the Andriambahoaka concept is actually supposed to tell us that we don't already know.

a while to come to grips with the situation when I was conducting my own research in Betafo. I had been taught to look for cosmological myths, and then try
to understand ritual as small-scale, latter-day imitations of the great primordial
gestures they encode. I found it quite impossible to apply this sort of cosmological analysis. Almost no one knew anything that might be described as a cosmological myth, and if they did, they did not take them in any way seriously. It was
only gradually I came to realize that any wondrous powers—to cast lightning,
become invisible, transform landscapes, speak with animals, turn bullets into
water, etc.—that might have featured in such stories, and that still featured in
historical stories about "Malagasy times," were still believed to exist today. Now
as then, they were simply a matter of knowing how to manipulate medicine
(*fanafody*).[83] And such knowledge could be acquired, if one knew where to look,
had a knack or natural facility, or were just willing to pay a great deal of money.
There was no fundamental difference between the present and the mythic past.

In such a world, the role of ancestors is necessarily ambivalent. On the one
hand, who one is in the world depends largely on the status and location of one's
ancestors. On the other hand, to achieve anything significant in life, one must
break away from one's ancestors' shadow at least to some degree. This is all the
more the case for royalty. In fact, most of the *mpitaiza andriana* who created
royal ritual—the astrologers, diviners, keepers of charms—were technicians of
the future, not guardians of the past. And as Charles Renel (1920: 157–58) as-
tutely pointed out, the secret of the *santatra* borne by the guardians of the royal
tombs was the desire to propitiate the royal ancestors, to effectively get them out
of the way, so that one could create something radically new.

But since one is living in mythological times, one also must accept the possibility that the ancestors might not accept this, even that the dead might personally intervene to bring matters back under their control.

This is the final implication of the king as child: sheer potentiality. One does
not really know yet what a child might become. Royal children were expected to
do something new and surprising. Thus perhaps it only stands to reason that once
the Merina court was in direct contact with Europeans offering new and powerful social and mechanical technologies, young princes would tend to eagerly
embrace them, identify with them, fancy themselves enlightened despots, toss
aside old technologies for new. Neither is it particularly surprising that women

---

83. So characters in legends with wondrous powers are often specifically said to have
    acquired them through *ody*, or charms, and even when not stated, it could be said to
    be implied.

regularly appeared to remind them that these old technologies they were toss-
ing away were an intrinsic element of a vast system of caring labor that began
with commoner households, but culminated in their own. What is surprising,
perhaps, is that so many of the men in power were forced to acknowledge this.

Placing queens on the throne, then, was above all a way of acknowledging
this. Even the traditionalists who supported Ranavalona I were not conserva-
tives in the strict sense of the term—the queen didn't abandon the tradition of
royalty as a source of innovation; she even sponsored her own crash industrialization program—but they ensured that no one in the kingdom could forget
what the kingdom ultimately was: an intricate system of ritualized caring labor.
That we may still live in mythic times, but, as women know and men tend to
forget, myth is founded on work.

In part, this was effected by a startling reversal. The royal household at the
very pinnacle of the kingdom became an exact inversion of the households on
the bottom, being composed of a child-queen served and supported by her male
"nursemaids." That arrangement itself operated as a kind of magical charm that
transformed even the most onerous unpaid male work assignments—dragging
trees, toting fuel, digging ditches, carrying baggage, military service in distant
garrisons—into caring labor, analogous to their own mothers' or *mpitaiza*'s
when they had been infants carried on a woman's back.

In the end, this was not successful as a geopolitical formula to fend off
European aggression; but it's not clear that any other approach would have
worked particularly better. The resulting system was certainly oppressive. But
if nothing else, reformulating all free labor as care and nurture to the queen,
that is, establishing principles that were exactly the opposite of those of European political economy, also made it absolutely impossible for such commercial,
agricultural, or industrial relations to make any significant headway while the
island did remain independent. Even after Queen Ranavalona II's conversion to
Protestantism in 1869, which led to Christianity effectively becoming the state
religion, British missionaries tried in vain to explain concepts such as capital
and wage labor to their parishioners, and complained endlessly of the impos-
sibility of convincing the queen's freeborn subjects that working for wages was
fit for anyone but slaves.[84] Even after sixty-five years of French colonial rule, and
over a half-century of independence, many are still convinced this is the case.

---

84. For instance, the very first issue of the Malagasy-language mission journal *Ny
    Mpanolo Tsaina* ("The Advisor") began with a piece explaining the concept of

* * *

It would be interesting to consider the case of the Merina kingdom in relation to contemporary theories of caring labor. Feminist theories of caring labor, from Nancy Folbre (1995) to Silvia Federici (2012) to Evelyn Glenn Nakano (2012), have tended, for obvious reasons, to examine how these matters are framed in the terms of political economy, since this is the logic behind the institutions that affect the vast majority of women today. In the world as imagined by political economy, (tacitly male) "productive" labor is always assumed to be the primary form, and (tacitly female) "caring" or "reproductive" labor becomes its usually unacknowledged mirror image. Still, even if one does acknowledge both sides of the equation, that primary division remains. This is by no means the only way to divide things up. In the highlands of Madagascar, everything was different. Labor was assumed to be first and foremost women's business; the paradigm for work was bearing burdens; but bearing burdens was seen as combining a range of activities that we would classify into such different domains as transport, building, digging, and nurturance. Moreover, labor was also seen as continuous with ritual, the ritual element was seen as making it truly creative, and the ritualization of labor—and the most ritualized forms of labor as well—was preponderantly the domain of men.

Even under the queens, powerful men were obviously the primary beneficiaries of the system. One would not wish to idealize it. But it was only because it was based on fundamentally different assumptions about what labor, and what we call an "economy," is basically about that it both allowed women such powerful ways to influence politics, and managed to resist the incursions of those who would have reduced Madagascar to a plantation economy so effectively for so long.

* * *

Once the queens were no more, the entire ritual apparatus simply disintegrated, and the concept of *fanompoana* as caring labor appears to have been forgotten

capital, followed in the next issue by a piece on the nature of wage labor (Anon. 1879a, 1879b). Missionary accounts are full of complaints about how difficult it is to convince government officials to contemplate eliminating forced labor and substituting a regime in which the government taxes and then hires its subjects.

almost instantly.[85] Memories of the old kingdom quickly came to center on male figures like Leiloza, unjust oppressors who, insofar as they were seen as children, were anything but lovable.

I've been emphasizing relations with the outside world as crucial in setting off the crisis in Merina kingship. But one could make the argument it all really began with Andrianampoinimerina, who knit the various principalities into something that is universally acknowledged to qualify as a state. Maurice Bloch (2006) has made a case that, historically, something about the creation of states in particular had the effect of disorganizing domestic ritual, causing it to become partial and incomplete, and that, at least in the case of powerful and successful states, matters simply could not be put back again the way they had been—and that this remained the case if those states themselves collapsed or otherwise passed from history. (He argues that religion, as an autonomous institution, first emerged to fill the resultant gap.) The Merina kingdom is one of his prime examples. The more elaborate and beautiful its royal palaces became, Bloch argues, the less care and ritual attention subjects tended to invest in their own houses, until, finally, when the kingdom collapsed, houses never recovered their former ritual importance, but instead, the ritual focus shifted to ancestral tombs (Bloch 1995).

It's a compelling argument. In fact, one could argue that the two great contemporary ritual complexes around which I first framed my analysis of royal ritual—*famadihana*, and the network of *doany* with their mediumistic curers—are both transformations and reappropriations of royal ritual itself. Already in the waning days of the kingdom, commoners had begun shifting their focus from royal ancestors to their own: the habit of periodically opening tombs to rewrap the dead (Haile 1891; Larson 2001) and defining themselves as descendants

---

85. As part of my research for this essay, I consulted a number of Malagasy-language histories of Merina ancestries, compiled over the course of the twentieth century (Zanak'Andriantompokoindrindra: Rasamimanana and Razafindrazaka 1909; Zanak'Andrianetivola: Ratsimba 1939; Tsimiamboholahy: Rabeson 1948; Zanak'Antitra: M. Rasamuel 1948; Terak'Andriamanarefo: Andriamifidy 1950; Zanak'Andriamamilaza: Ramilison 1952; Antemoro-Anakara: Kasanga 1956; Ambohitrimanjaka: Randriamarosata 1959; Zanak'Andrianamboninolona: Andriamanantsiety 1975; Manendy: Rakotomanolo 1981), examining the language used to describe relations to royalty. Remarkably, even in the earliest, no trace of the language of *taiza*, ubiquitous in the *Tantara* and other nineteenth-century texts, could be found.

rather than ancestors.[86] But the deep, hidden logic of royal ancestral ritual was preserved. Just as those bearing *santatra* effected a double reversal, first neutralizing the ancestors so that the living king could create or do something new, then infantilizing and thereby neutralizing the king himself so that living commoners could enjoy the fruits of their labor, so too did *famadihana* rituals honor the dead so as to ultimately lock them away and prevent their interfering with the living. At the same time, the spectral theater created by the Ramanenjana has now become permanent. The old cult of the "twelve sacred mountains" has been definitively appropriated by the descendants of commoners and slaves, who have turned its cast of characters, once celebrated in the *Tantara ny andriana*, into a kind of prolonged meditation on the moral perils of arbitrary, coercive power.

* * *

Outside of Madagascar, the notion that kings are a little bit like children is unusual (notable exceptions being Schwartz 1989, 1990; Springborg 1990), but the notion that children, especially infants and toddlers, are a little bit like kings is commonplace. In China they speak of "little emperors." Freud referred to "his majesty the baby."

It's not hard to see why: it's for all the reasons outlined in this essay. Monarchs are regularly expected to behave in ways that, were any of their ordinary adult subjects to imitate them, would be likely to be taken as profoundly immature. And all of us—women especially, of course, but everyone to some extent—are also used to reacting with love and affection to egocentric tantrums or even outright cruelty on the part of actual children; this is true whether our culture teaches us that the proper way to respond is with nurturant indulgence or by stern rebuke. There's no need to appeal to evolutionary arguments here; it's necessary to do this, on a fairly regular basis, in order to bring children to maturity at all. And endlessly repeated, it can only become something of a habit.

I have suggested, in this essay, that herein lies the secret of the ideological power of monarchy. Because it cannot be denied that monarchy is, in

---

86. The most telling sign here was the change in naming practices: teknonymy was almost entirely abandoned, and especially in the early years of colonial rule, more and more names took the form instead of, for example, Razanadrakoto or Razafindrabe, that is, "Child of Rakoto" or "Grandchild of Rabe."

world-historical terms, a very common form of government, and often a stubbornly effective one; apparently, there is *something* about taking one single household, with all its inevitable household dramas, and placing it at the pinnacle of a political system that manages to grab hold of the imagination and affections of subject populations in a way that few others manage to do. Part of the reason is, of course, that monarchs actually produce babies; in almost any other form of government, children and babies are definitively off-stage. It's not far from here to suggest that monarchs in many ways *are* babies. Childishness—childish snits, childish indulgence, childish self-aggrandizement—is what court life is largely about.

In the first chapter of this volume, Marshall Sahlins makes the argument that insofar as there is a primordial political state, it is authoritarianism. Most hunter-gatherers actually do see themselves as living under a state-like regime, even under terrifying despots; it's just that since we see their rulers as imaginary creatures, as gods and spirits and not actual flesh-and-blood rulers, we do not recognize them as "real." But they're real enough for those who live under them. We need to look for the origins of liberty, then, in a primal revolt against such authorities. I do not mean to argue that ontogeny exactly reproduces phylogeny in this case; but it's easy to see how the argument being developed here might be seen as complementary in a sense. Every human being has a primordial experience of autocracy, far earlier than any experience of equal relations could possibly be—and here I refer not, as usually supposed, to the apparent absolute power of mothers or other adults (since, at first, infants cannot even recognize others as autonomous beings with power or intentions), but in their own behavior. Children are would-be autocrats. They are at first incapable of anything else, since they lack the capacity to even comprehend another's point of view.

Perhaps these truths are unusually apparent in a place like Madagascar with an explicit ethos of consensus-based communal decision making. In local assemblies, *fokon'olona*—really this word just refers to any meeting that brings together everyone affected by some common problem—the only criterion for participation is if one is mature enough to formulate a reasonable argument. But they also explicitly reject any principle of representation or leadership. Children, and kings, are thus the only people who are in a sense incapable of the mutual understanding and compromise that defines mature deliberation.

It's helpful to bear this in mind when we think about what raising children actually consists of. The text in the *Tantara* says that taking care of the royal family is "just like taking care of children," but really it isn't, since the point of raising children is that they eventually grow up. The people's nurture, in contrast, traps rulers in permanent immaturity. Time after time, in my own circles, I've heard parents with antiauthoritarian politics agonize over to what degree it is appropriate to discipline children, or even, sometimes, to control or guide their behavior in any way. It obviously can't be avoided to some degree. Does that mean that on a certain level authoritarian behavior is not just legitimate but inevitable? I myself puzzled over the problem for many years until one day it occurred to me: Is it necessarily "authoritarian" to intervene to stop a child from behaving in an egocentric and harmful fashion? Surely it all depends on how you do it. There's nothing intrinsically authoritarian about doing so because it's normally only really required when children themselves behave like would-be autocrats. If it is done in such a way as to gently guide a child toward the eventual capacity to engage in mutually considerate, mature, egalitarian behavior, it's not authoritarian at all: it's actually antiauthoritarian. This would suggest that not only do we all share a primordial experience of (our own) autocracy, but we've all experienced a form of love designed to allow us to transcend it, and move us on to at least the capacity for something else.

CHAPTER 6

The cultural politics of core–periphery relations

Marshall Sahlins

My intent is to put the issue of "soft power" in a world-historical frame. I speak here of the anthropological experience of core–periphery systems, which are much more extensive, ethnographically and historically, than the modern "world-system" of capitalism described by Wallerstein and colleagues. Similar configurations of domination are in fact planetary in scope—they are common even in tribal zones—and are doubtless even older than the history that began at Sumer. The effect is a multicultural order of intercultural relations in which no participating society is sui generis. So, for example, the relations between valley civilizations and the upland "tribals" of Southeast Asia—a major focus of this essay—as described by James C. Scott:

> Both hill and valley peoples were planets in a larger galactic system (Indic or Sinic) of mutual influence. Hill peoples may not have been subjects of valley states, but they were active participants in the economic system of exchange and in the even wider cosmopolitan circulation of ideas, symbols, cosmology, titles, political formulas, medical recipes, and legends. (2009: 305–6)

And conversely:

> Histories of the classical lowland court-states, taken in isolation, risk being unin-
> telligible or vastly misleading. Lowland states (mandala or modern) have always
> existed in symbiosis with hill society. (2009: 26)

I hasten to add that although they are often recognized, these multicultural
orders are rarely theorized. They are largely ignored by a normal anthropological science of autonomous and self-fashioning cultures, each a world unto itself.
There is a radical disjunction between functionalist, structuralist, evolutionist,
and other such paradigms of cultural self-determination, and the often observed
fact that the cultural differences which distinguish interacting peoples—not to
mention the similarities that unite them—are largely dependent on the relations between them. Consider this notice of Randall Collins (1992: 373), from
the introduction to an article on "The geopolitical and economic world-systems
of kinship-based and agrarian-coercive societies":

> I want to suggest that there is no type of society in any period of human exist-
> ence in which world-system relationships do not affect its structure and dynam-
> ics. That is to say, economic and political/military connections among organized
> social units affect these units as an overall pattern; all societies are in important
> respects structure from the outside in.

Not to mention "spiritual" connections. Human societies the world over are not
only interdependent with societies of other kinds, they are also dependent for
their own existence on relations with humans of other kinds. I mean the gods,
ancestors, ghosts, demons, species-masters, and other such metapersons, including those inhabiting plants, animals, and natural features: in sum, the host of
"spirits"—wrongly so-called; they are this-worldly and indeed have the attributes of persons—the host of whom are endowed with life-and-death powers
over the human population. "Each society," writes Georges Balandier, "links its
own order to an order beyond itself, and, in the case of traditional societies, to
the cosmos" (1972: 101). Lest you think I am going astray, everything I now
say on this score is in support of the observation that the cultural-cum-political
authority of dominant societies in many traditional core–periphery formations,
notably as this authority extends as "soft power" into regions beyond the coercive reach of the center, is based rather on an indigenous anthropology of the

metahuman sources of human welfare. No battle is won, no child is born, no gardens flourish or pots come whole from the kiln without the intervention of the metapersonal powers-that-be—to whom the human powers-that-be have privileged relations. The kingly gifts of fertility and victory, wealth and health, beauty and monumentality manifested in the center resound in the peripheries as so many demonstration-effects of divine life-giving powers. Unlike their material manifestations, such powers are discursively communicable, socially transmissible, and ritually accessible. In the event, hinterland peoples may be attracted and subordinated to the center culturally while they are still independent politically.[1]

As noted previously (chapters 3 and 4), this soft power of acculturation appears by definition in Aidan Southall's discussion of the "segmentary state," a multicultural order of the core–periphery kind found in many parts of Africa—in which, however, "the spheres of ritual suzerainty and political sovereignty do not coincide. The former [the ritual authority] extends widely towards a flexible, changing periphery. The latter [political authority] is confined to a central core domain" (1988: 53). Described in fine detail by Southall, the Alur chiefdoms in Uganda west of the Nile, where immigrant rulers of Nilotic Luo origin dominate a variety of Sudanic, Bantu, and Nilotic communities, are classic examples of the segmentary state. Southall's succinct characterization of the spatial structure of Alur rule could indeed serve as a model of core–periphery systems in general—even the imperial systems of cosmocratic ambitions, including the East Asian "world-systems" that will occupy much of this essay:

> In Alurland, the greater chiefs are focal points of rudimentary political specialization, from which an almost spatial zoning of authority spheres radiates, from that of chiefship in the center, through that of chieflets with non-Alur subjects, to that of peripheral non-Alur groups vaguely recognizing some aspects of the charisma of [Alur] chiefship but continuing with their own autonomous kinship authorities. ([1956] 2004: 124)

Also exemplary, and more pertinent for the moment, are the spiritual sources of the Alur chiefs' domination of peripheral groups. Alur rule was not established by conquest or sustained by force. "Had his [the chief's] position depended on the command of force or on personal prowess in war it appears that many units

---

1. The cosmic polity of metaperson powers encompassing human societies is discussed at length in chapter 1.

of Alur domination of other peoples would never have come into existence, for no irresistible force was brought to bear in their establishment" (ibid.: 246). Rather the reverse: it is the Alur chief who is effectively conquered by the subordinate people, as happens often enough in practice and prescriptively in ritual, when chiefly Alur men are "kidnapped" and carried off by other ethnic communities—who have their own reasons for wanting a chief to rule them. Prominent among these reasons is "rain":

> Rain (*koth*) stood for material well-being in general, and a chief's ability to demonstrate his control over it was a crucial test of his efficacy. The chief's control of rain and weather, together with his conduct of sacrifice and worship, stood for his general and ultimate responsibility in the minds of his subjects for both their material and moral well-being. (Southall [1956] 2004: 239)

As Frazer, Hocart, and numerous ethnographers have taught: the world around, the king is the condition of the possibility of the people's welfare by virtue of his privileged access to the divine sources of prosperity and life itself. Note, in particular, Southall's observation that the Alur chief gains authority over "the *minds* of his subjects"—not their bodies. This is a political economy of social subjugation rather than material coercion. Here, as in many such chiefdoms and kingdoms (see chapters 3 and 4, the means of production in the primary, subsistence sectors are "owned" by the underlying producing population, and more particularly by the ancestors or local spirits indwelling in their lands. Accordingly, kingly power does not work on a proprietary control of the people's means of existence so much as on direct command of the people themselves—and thereby on some portion of their product in goods and manpower. The powers-that-be have an extractive rather than a productive relation to the economic process. By contrast to capitalist enterprise, which aims at the increase in productive wealth as such, the objective of the palace economy is to increase the number and loyalty of subjects, as by beneficial or awe-inspiring effects of royal largess, display, and consumption. Wealth here is a strategic means of power, although not the only means, and not the ultimate end. And beyond any material advantage to the people-at-large, what the king's disposition of riches demonstrates is his access to its divine origins—from which follow the benefits he promises to others.[2]

---

2.   This politics of manpower rather than capital power as such is discussed in some detail in chapters 3 and 4.

"Soft power" may thus become real-political power even in tribal zones As Mary Helms observes: for all that the best examples of superordinate centers are known from "centralized societies," similar formations are commonly found in so-called "non-centralized societies." Indeed, they are present "at least to some degree in any setting in which a polity extends its skillfully crafted symbols and encapsulations ('regalia') of political-ideological identity to at least select outside groups and/or acquires resources from some portion of the geographical outside realm." (1993: 157).

Just so, the dominance respectively achieved by the Iatmul and Abelam peoples over other groups in the Middle Sepik region of New Guinea peoples was essentially similar to the reign-cum-rain of the great Alur chief over Bantu and Sudanic villagers, or for that matter the superiority of the Celestial Emperor over the "raw" barbarians of the Chinese borderlands. Indeed, speaking of the Sepik "regional systems," Deborah Gewertz (1991: 236) specifically likened them to "a world system . . . predicated on power asymmetries." But, of course, the asymmetries of power did not entail the Iatmul's governance of the peoples who respected it and desired to share its benefits. Working from secondary centers subordinate to Iatmul, Gewertz from among the nearby Chambri and Simon Harrison from the Manambu people, the ethnographers describe a regional system quite like Southall recorded for the Alur: a series of concentric zones of decreasing cultural influence emanating from the dominant Iatmul core, as conveyed by intermediate groups to the less powerful hinterlands.

> The Manambu . . . seem to have imported throughout their history very many elements of Iatmul culture, particularly ritual, magic, totemism, and myth. To the Manambu, the cultural forms of the Iatmul are surrounded by an aura of especially dangerous power, and are therefore valuable to acquire. The Iatmul seem to have a similar domineering influence on all the groups they traded with. They exported many elements of their culture to the Sawos and Chambri, for instance, as well as to the Manambu, while the Chambri and the Manambu were in turn exporters of their culture to their respective sago-suppliers to the south. (Harrison 1990: 20)

The intermediately situated peoples, notably the Chambri, also appropriated powers and even ancestors from the marginal "bush" groups; but throughout the region it was particularly Iatmul metapersonal potency that was highly coveted. In many ways, Harrison (ibid.: 78–79) explains, the Iatmul were deemed by Manambu to be associated with "the 'invisible' world of spirits." Such spirits spoke through their Manambu shaman mediums in a language laced with extraordinary Iatmul features: a language that conveyed the beings and forces of a widespread totemic cosmology. More than any other of their neighbors, Harrison says, the Iatmul "embody" this hidden realm "which is the perceived source of all power." It perhaps goes without saying that the power thus imported, as it gave access to the life-giving totemic ancestors, included the indispensable means of human fertility and material livelihood.

So run the reports of the Abelam hegemony as well. The extraordinary cultural achievements of the Abelam represented "spiritual" powers that were themselves dangerous, attractive, and useful to others. These were all-purpose achievements, not just material or military but also aesthetic and demographic distinctions that by invidious contrasts to surrounding societies could engender an indigenous anthropology of cultural evolution. In Anthony Forge's summary:

> Effectiveness in warfare and skill in growing yams, particularly the phallic long yams, were in local terms merely the material manifestations of a more fundamental Abelam domination, that of power conceived fundamentally in magical and ritual terms. The Abelam were admired and feared for what was believed to be superior access to supernatural power in all forms and the concrete expression of this command in rituals, buildings, and an immense array of objects, decorations, and styles loosely classifiable as "art." In Sepik terms, it was the Abelam's superior access to supernatural power that made their long yams larger, their gardens more productive, and their occupation of land previously the undoubted property of others so conclusive. (1990: 162–63)

This emphasis on the "superior access to supernatural power," which underwrites also the dominant status of major Alur chiefs among peripheral groups of various ethnicities, will be a recurrent theme in the pages that follow in regard to the similar reach of even major kingdoms into hinterland realms that they have neither conquered nor directly rule.

THE ANTHROPOLOGY OF CORE–PERIPHERY RELATIONS

For all their ethnographic and theoretical obsession with self-determining sociocultural monads, anthropologists have long recognized that societies were never alone and were always interdependent. Long before world-systems theory made core–periphery relations a critical issue in the human sciences, it was a common anthropological observation—if not common cultural theory—that societies were set in regional systems of dominant centers and dependent hinterlands, hence adapted to one another in structural form and cultural content. (I am reminded of something I learned from Althusser: just to recognize a phenomenon is not the same thing as knowing its right theoretical place.) By all evidence, cultural order has always been regional; or at least since the Neolithic, it has been marked everywhere by gradients of political-cum-cultural authority focused on apical centers thereof.

As in the Native Americas, North and South, tribal to imperial, where "one could not go far in the study of an area," as Clark Wissler wrote, "before recognizing that one or more tribes dominate" (1938: 261). Along with Alfred Kroeber, Wissler was a key figure in the development of the largely forgotten and little-lamented culture area studies of the early twentieth century. Although their primary interest was in the reconstruction of history from the distribution of "culture traits," both Wissler and Kroeber were thereby led to recognize the core–periphery relations in play among the societies of a given region. Conscious of their power, the dominant tribes of the area, Wissler wrote, were "centers of influence" (ibid.). For his part, Kroeber, in the *Cultural and natural areas of Native North America* (1947: 5), endorsed Wissler's contention that the dominant center was "the integral thing about the area." The center was a "cultural climax," whence radiated the forms and practices that united and distinguished the societies of the region. Both Kroeber and Wissler also recognized certain dynamic features that only many decades later were comprehended as recurrent and systemic properties of these multicultural configurations: that the centers rise and fall, competitively expanding and contracting, to the extent that erstwhile peripheral societies often become focal, even as the thresholds of the culture area prove unstable—which is also to say that important political forces are in play at the peripheries as well as the core of the system (cf. Helms 1993: 187f.). Wissler made the point particularly in discussing the rise of the Teton Dakota and Cheyenne from marginal positions to dominance in the Great Plains during the nineteenth century. "They formed a focus for a central cluster of tribes whose influence is seen throughout the area and its corresponding regional development" (1938: 261). Nor, then, was such domination characteristic only of the greater American civilizations such as the Inka, Maya, or Mexica: "We have found the higher centers of culture in Mexico and Peru to be not really unique growths but to possess many of the fundamental traits common to the wilder folks in the marginal areas of both continents" (ibid.: 383).

The decades following World War II saw several increasingly sophisticated—though apparently unrelated—anthropologies of cultural order radiating outward from dominant centers on a regional or world scale, the latest of these in dialogue with modern globalization paradigms. Beside Southall on segmentary states, there was Kroeber (1945) on the Old World *oikoumene* of interconnected "high civilizations" developing from around 1000 BC from the Straits of Gibraltar to Java, each with their culturally dependent hinterlands. In a related discussion in his encyclopedic textbook *Anthropology* (1948), Kroeber noted the "reduction" of culture as it spread from the more developed regions: "the basic idea" being that "culture gradually radiates from creative focal centers to backward marginal areas, without the original dependence of the peripheries precluding their subsequent independent development." And in the latter connection, he drew attention again to the instability of these regional hierarchies, noting that the high centers may shift as new ones emerge, even at the edges, "until what was peripheral has become focal" (ibid.: 701–2).

Then there was Morton Fried's (1967, 1975) critique of anthropological notions of the "tribe" as a self-determined indigenous form, contending rather that all tribes ancient and recent were created by colonial impulses of already-existing states (in contemporary terms, a "state-effect"); even as most states were likewise secondary formations, constituted directly or indirectly by influences emanating from the pristine few that had evolved independently. Supposing this derivation of secondary states from the original ones, together with the derivation of tribes from existing states, the world according to Fried would again consist of multicultural constellations of core–periphery form.

Speaking of intercultural relations, in the middle Sepik region of New Guinea, Deborah Gewertz was hardly the only anthropologist to find a "world-system" among "tribal" societies in the wake of Immanuel Wallerstein's celebrated analysis of the modern capitalist world-system in the 1970s. Some were put in mind of the earlier culture area discussions (e.g., Kowalewski 1996), yet even those who rejected the comparison described regional configurations of "stateless" societies in much the same terms. Barry Craig and George E. B. Morren, Jr. preferred to speak of "culture spheres" in their survey of the several regional systems of Lowland and Highland New Guinea, but in a way quite reminiscent of Wisslerian culture areas: "A sphere is a politically expansive, segmentary, reticulated mosaic of local groups that, notwithstanding observable ethnolinguistic diversity, share a common tradition and are strongly influenced by one or more core populations at the historic-geographic center(s) of their region" (1990: 10). In such terms, the authors describe the Mountain Ok sphere, whose ritually sustained core–periphery relations were a subject of interest in chapter 1 above. In an extensive study of relations between the Wintu and neighboring peoples of the aboriginal California region, Christopher Chase-Dunn and Kelly M. Mann (1998) also reject the analogy to classic culture areas, although taken in larger compass what they describe is an even greater multicultural order centered in the Pomo and Patwin peoples. Nor would it be altogether an oxymoron to speak of such regional hierarchies as "world-systems," inasmuch as for the peoples concerned they are the human world. The centers from which cultural influences spread were typically superior to the outlying societies in wealth, population, ritual powers, ceremonial pageantry, artistic and architectural achievements, and military prowess—and would be so acknowledged by the hinterland peoples. But when it comes to the economic exploitation of the peripheral societies by dominant ones, or the material dependency of the former on the latter in the manner of a global industrial order, here the resemblances end. Introducing a collection of papers on world-systems theory and archaeology, Peter Peregrine (1996: 3–4) writes:

> What all these redefinitions of core/periphery relations seem to have in common is the notion that world systems did exist in prehistoric, pre-capitalist situations, but that Wallerstein's definitions of core/periphery relations are too strict to be directly applied to them. . . . Most of the scholars have argued in one way or another that dependency or exploitation is a basic characteristic of the capitalist world system but may not have been for pre-capitalist world systems. Models of core/periphery relations in the absence of this dependency open the world system perspective to a variety of pre-capitalist and non-capitalist situations . . . .

The ethnographic argument—as in the Sepik and Mountain Ok regions—would be that the cultural attainments of the dominant peoples function as demonstration-effects of their superior relations to the metaperson powers of human welfare. Hence the movement of rituals and other cultural forms of cosmological import from the center to outlying peoples, including even gods, ancestors, clans, and totems.

In another critical reflex of world-systems theory, Kajsa Ekholm, Jonathan Friedman, and colleagues have argued in a series of ambitious works that a political economy of planetary—or at least hemispheric—dimensions has been in existence since its origins in the Mesopotamian civilizations of five thousand years ago (J. Friedman and Rowlands 1978; Ekholm and Friedman 1979; Ekholm 1980; J. Friedman 1992; K. E. Friedman and J. Friedman 2008). There may have been some other original civilizations, as in China, but they were integrated into a single historically connected global network of regional polities—the modern European-based world-system included, having been a late relay from the Middle East. Although Friedman has explicitly argued against the explanation of particular cultural formations as such by their mode of production, his analysis of core–periphery relations reproduces classical utilitarian arguments—in fact, the lineaments of the modern world-system of industrial capital—at this intercultural level. The dominant regional centers are manufacturing hubs exploiting peripheral societies organized as specialized suppliers of raw materials: until a surfeit of capital wealth at the center causes a production crisis, a rise in the price of raw materials, the flight of capital to outside societies, followed by the collapse of the core and its replacement often by one or another external group. Without subscribing to Friedman's economics of core–periphery relations, we should retain the observation of their unstable, competitive character, especially the challenges to the center from the margins—a process typically preceded and made possible by a soft-power assimilation of the margins to the center.

Of the several extant anthropologies of core–periphery relations, the one I believe best serves as a general model is the "galactic polity" as formulated by Stanley Tambiah in the late1970s and early 1980s—and complemented by Mary Helms' discussions of the like (Tambiah 1976, 1985, 1987; Helms 1988, 1993).[3] Tambiah coined the term in reference to premodern Southeast Asian civilizations such as Sukhotai, Ayutthaya, Angkor Wat, Pagan, Srivijaya, and Madjapahit; but as we already know, similar constellations of apical centers reproducing themselves in diminishing versions as they spread into underdeveloped hinterlands have been ubiquitous modes of intercultural order from the beginnings of recorded history and anthropology. Unlike the Ekholm–Friedman economic model, however, the galactic polity was for Tambiah a cosmopolitical order: cosmology and polity being two modalities of the same fundamental structure (see chapters 3 and 4). Just as in the classic mandala system of the universe, the states ruled by Buddhist (*chakkavatin*) and Hindu (*devaraja*) kings of kings

---

3.   The following paragraphs reprise the discussion of galactic polities elsewhere in this volume, sometimes in the same terms. Aside from the fact that the chapters at issue were written on different occasions, I can offer little excuse for the repetition except that it is indispensable for what follows here.

realized in another register the creative force and moral virtue radiating with progressively declining effect from an original, refined center to the gross beings of the world's outer reaches:

> We are told that the wheel-rolling emperor solemnly invokes the wheel to roll outward; the wheel roles successively toward the East, the South, the North, and the West. As the mighty monarch with his fourfold army appeared in each quarter following the wheel, the rival kings prostrated themselves in submission. The *cakkavati* allowed them to retain their possessions on condition of their obedience of the five moral principles binding on Buddhist laymen. (Tambiah 1976: 45–46)

Tambiah makes the important observation that the galactic polity was "centered" rather than "centralized," inasmuch as the authority of the sovereign, although in principle extending indefinitely through the world in all directions, in practice was limited to the governance of the capital and surrounding provinces, beyond which were self-governing, tributary-paying principalities; and beyond these, an untamed zone at best linked to the core by raid and trade. While it is often noticed that the cosmocratic reach of galactic kings exceeds their administrative grasp, we should not forget that the repute of their divinely endowed potency does indeed extend beyond their ability to enforce it—thereby creating a far-reaching cultural subordination among hinterland peoples without the benefit of real-political coercion.

Soft power thus begins at the cosmic center, which in these Southeast Asian kingdoms was the center of the world, an *axis mundi* running through the royal palace and the nearby temples of the dominant kingdom cults. In many of the major realms, this central establishment was identified with the famous cosmic mountain of the Indian tradition, Mt. Meru, through which were transmitted the divine powers that enabled the sacred ruler to "conquer" in all directions. Here also were housed the regalia and palladia of rule: statues of the Buddha, *linga* of Shiva, famous *krises*, sacred jewels, and other royal heirlooms whose subjective powers of sovereignty were as much objectified in the kingship as the kingship was objectified in them—the *moi subtil* of the king, as some ancient texts have it (Coedès 1968: 101).[4] Or else, as in the case of the Emerald

---

4. The founder of the Angkor empire, Jayavarman II, is said to have doubled down by installing a *linga* originally obtained from Shiva in a sanctuary atop a natural or artificial mountain at the center of the royal city.

This map was originally created for Sheldon Pollock's *The Language of the Gods in the World of Men* (2009) and is reproduced here with some modification with permission.

Buddha, the Sinhala Buddha, and other historic palladia of Thai kingship, the statue was "animated" by the "presence" of the Buddha himself, whence radiated a "fiery energy" that blessed and fecundated the world (Tambiah 1984: 204ff.). Tambiah meticulously documents the process by which the images are linked by a series of "reincarnations" to the Buddha himself, then consecrated in rituals that render him immanent in the statue, as by recitations that inject his biography into it, culminating in ceremonies for opening the statue's eyes. Prominent among the other fructifying effects that could now be spread abroad by the Buddha's fiery energy was rain. The pervasive animism of the outlying hill tribes of Southeast Asia thus had its counterpart in what might be called the "political animism" of the civilized centers (cf. Århem and Sprenger 2016). Apart from the dynastic heroes, Indic gods, or the Buddha who might be enshrined in such sovereign objects, giving them agentive powers of prosperity and protective force, some might have come from the hinterlands—like the amulets of Thai forest monks, which, as Tambiah also documented, conveyed potencies of the wild to the kingdom's civilized centers.[5]

The capital of the exemplary fourteenth-century kingdom of Sukhotai was something of a mandala in itself: the royal palace and principal wat at the center, set within three concentric ramparts with gates situated at the cardinal directions (Kasetsiri 1976; Tambiah 1976). Surrounding the capital, which was under the king's direct control, was a zone of four major provinces (*muang*) ruled by sons of the galactic sovereign from secondary centers aligned with the capital by their location in the cardinal directions. In structure and courtly practice, these semiautonomous princely establishments replicated the galactic center in reduced form. Beyond lay an outer ring of more or less independent principalities, populated by diverse ethnic groups, and governed by their own traditional rulers. Some of these rulers acknowledged the overlordship of the Sukhotal king and rendered him tribute; whereas the inclusion of others ranging as far off as the Malay Peninsula in the Sukhotai domain was evidently more nominal than political. The successor Siamese kingdom of Ayutthaya had essentially the same structure during its early history, with sons of the rulers in charge in the four

---

5. Indeed, the sacred palladia of the Bugis and Makassar kingdoms of Sulawesi were nourished and maintained by their own rice fields, forests, fish ponds, and slaves (Andaya 2006). And as will be seen presently, these were not the only animistic powers available to galactic potentates, who characteristically knew how to appropriate the potent subjective forces embodied in nature—in the wild peripheries of their realms—as well as in culture.

major domains east, west, north, and south of the capital, and an outer zone of sovereignty extending eventually into cosmocratic ideology—but also effectively encompassing Sukhotai among the tributary "vassal states" in 1385, and its satellites in 1438. Not incidentally, this galactic pattern of three circles and four directions is a common one—and not only in Southeast Asia (cf. Lincoln 2007).[6]

CULTURAL DYNAMICS OF GALACTIC POLITIES

Galactic polities are never alone. Constitutionally inspired by hegemonic pretensions of indefinite extent, each is engaged in a wider competitive field of galactic and would-be galactic powers whose rulers were ever prepared to defend their own claims of world superiority. "Whoever he may be, he shall be my enemy in the world if he is an equal on earth," is a statement attributed to Hayam Wuruk, ruler of the Javanese empire of Madjapahit at the acme of its power in the fourteenth century (Wolters 1986: 37n). At about the same time, Sukhotai on the mainland was surrounded by just such "world conquerors" contending with each other for the lesser kingdoms and principalities between them. Besides Ayutthaya to the south, there was the other Thai realm of Lan Na (Chiangmai) to the north, the Burmese power of Pagan to the southwest, and the famous Khmer empire of Angkor to the southeast—from which Sukhotai had won its independence in the late thirteenth century and which Ayutthaya would invade and defeat in 1431–32. This competition engaged a characteristic dialectics of theocratic regimes, in the course of which Sukhotai made a state cult of Theravada Buddhism (derived largely from Sri Lanka), thereby opposing its singularly empowered *chakkavatin* kings to the primarily Brahmanic rulers of first its Angkor overlords, and then its Ayutthayan successors. Not only

---

6. In a comprehensive work on mainland Southeast Asian history from the ninth to the nineteenth centuries, Victor Lieberman (2003: 33) prefers the term "solar polity" to Tambiah's "galactic polity," while describing the system in the same general terms—if according to a more sustained celestial metaphor. He also provides many excellent summaries of historic galactic systems: including those of Pagan, Ava, and Pegu in Burma; Funan and Angkor Wat in Cambodia; and Ayutthaya (Ayudhya) in Thailand. Lieberman is careful to note variations between those more ("Pattern A") or less ("Pattern B") effectively ruled from the center, He is also notably attentive to the structural and conjunctural sources of instability in these kingdoms.

is there god in these details but a general politics of cultural order, endemic in core–periphery systems, with the effect of bringing a transcendent series of encompassing cosmopolitical authorities into the regional conflicts between galactic sovereigns. Reading from this same Southeast Asian context, James C. Scott took some note also of the wider distribution of the phenomenon: "Much as the Romans used Greek, the early French court used Latin, and the Vietnamese court used Chinese script and Confucianism, so the rise of Sanskritic forms staked a claim to participation in a trans-ethnic, trans-regional, trans-historical civilization" (2009: 112).

O. W. Wolters (1999: 110) talks of a process of "self-Hinduization," by which the early Khmer courts of Cambodia, the Malay kingdoms known as Srivijaya, and the Javanese powers of Kendari and Madjapahit, among others, took on the gods, cosmology, protocol, ritual, art, architecture, and Sanskrit vocabulary of southern Indian states of grand repute. In his magisterial work on the Sanskrit cosmopolis, Sheldon Pollock (2009) emphasizes the historic singularity of this process by which, beginning in central India early in the first millennium AD, such regimes spread in a few centuries through Southeast Asia as far as Java—without the benefit of outside political impositions of any kind. There is no evidence of the colonization of Southeast Asian regions from India, Pollock observes; nor of ties of political subservience to the South Asian subcontinent; nor of forms of material exploitation or dependency relations; nor of large-scale settlement by Indian peoples, or anything resembling military conquest and occupation (ibid.: 123). And yet,

> All across mainland and maritime Southeast Asia, people who spoke radically different languages, such as Mon-Khmer and Malayo-Polynesian, and lived in vastly different cultural worlds, adopted suddenly, widely, and long-lastingly a new language—along with the new political vision and literary aesthetic that were inseparable from it and unthinkable without it—for the production of what were often defining forms of political culture. In itself this was a remarkable development, but given the manner in which it occurred—without the enforcement of military power, the pressure of an imperial administrative or legal apparatus, or the promptings of religious evangelism—it is one without obvious parallel in history, except indeed for South Asia itself. (2009: 124–25)

Subsumed thus in realms of universal power, the Southeast galactic regimes would assert their superiority to any and all worldly rivals. Moreover, this is only one of many examples in these pages of why the famous "determination by the economic basis"—or for that matter any such internal functional dynamic—is an inadequate explanation of the cultural order, inasmuch as the cosmopolitical "superstructure" is of historically distinct and structurally surpassing attributes relative to the "infrastructure." We see the like at every level of core–periphery systems.

When the Biak Islanders of Western New Guinea returned from their long voyages carrying tribute to the sultan of Tidore (in the Malukus), they passed the *barak*—the life-giving potency they had absorbed from the sultan's presence—to their relatives by shaking their hands, upon which the latter promptly rubbed their faces with it. As Danilyn Rutherford has documented in rich ethnographic works on Biak, these same powers, indwelling in the titles, silver jewels, fine cloth, and other wealth bestowed by the sultan, amounted in Biak to a "currency of value, in both its functions: in the form of objects that reflected a person's past achievements, and in the form of an invisible substance that conveyed the capacity to act" (2003: 16). Passed on locally—notably in affinal exchanges in which human reproduction appeared as the sequitur to foreign wealth—these things from a great and distant realm bestowed the honorable status of "foreigner" on the donors as well as productive and reproductive talents on the recipients—the children so empowered becoming ardent lovers as well as exceptional fishers, hunters, smiths, or singers.

There is a considerable history to this traffic in Malukan goods, titles, and power along the western New Guinea coasts: a network of exchange relations also involving islands in-between, altogether comprising a provincial galactic polity of its own (Elmberg 1968; Ellen 1986).[7] It has been speculated that the tributes to sultans were set up in the wake of an Islamic holy war in which the local peoples purchased exemption from the depredations of the Maluku fleets at the price of an annual tribute in Papuan goods. Biak apparently was involved in some such arrangement by the end of the fifteenth century, receiving among the other returns for its tributes certain Tidore titles that suggested actual administrative authority: the Malay *radja* for the head of an independent domain, and others for district chief and village chief. Alternatively, and more likely,

---

7.   It appears that Chinese goods had already reached Western New Guinea in Han times. When Chinese traders themselves appeared is uncertain, but some coming out of Manila were active in the area during the seventeenth century. As early as 1616, the Dutch found Chinese porcelain and Indian coral beads in Biak Island. In the eighteenth century, Chinese traders were still active on the shores of Geelvink Bay.

the titles referred particularly to tribute-collecting functions in these places. In time the titles became "incorporeal property which, like the various forms of esoteric knowledge and personal names constituted part of the status of the individual and his descendants" (Ellen 1986: 59). But in still another use, Biak Islanders themselves bestowed these Malukan titles on trading partners on the New Guinea coast in return for exotic goods obtained by the latter from interior peoples—goods that could then be conveyed to Tidore on Biak canoes. A similar tributary and status system reached the western New Guinea shores from Tidore via the intermediate Radja Anpat Islands and eastern Ceram. At least some Ceramese people settled as rulers (*radja*) of local Papuan groups; and it was reported as late as 1902 that some still spoke their ancestral Ceram language. In a classic competitive move, however, one of their stranger-chiefs reckoned his lineage from a Javanese ship's captain who had married a local woman (Elmberg 1968: 129).

Meanwhile back in the Malukus, the sultans of the clove islands of Tidore and Ternate had been taking on the trappings of the renowned rulers of distant realms whose presence in the form of impressive commercial and naval vessels had long reached their shores. European realms were not excluded: toward the end of the sixteenth century, "Sultan Hairun of Ternate dressed like a Portuguese, spoke their language fluently, and governed his kingdom with the assurance of long familiarity and friendship with Portuguese officials" (Andaya 1993: 58). Whereas in the seventeenth century, a Ternate sultan who owed his power rather to Dutch support named two of his sons "Amsterdam" and "Rotterdam" (ibid.: 177; cf. ibid.: 208). But as is obvious from the title of "sultan," this was not the first time the Malukan rulers had assumed foreign identities. Indeed, their European imports adorned an Islamized royalty that for its part had long been fitted out with Chinese attributes.

Call it "the real-politics of the marvelous." Not only because, in line with our own sense of the political, it is motivated by competitive ambitions of domination, but because in the local anthropologies these exotic forms of power are effective means thereof: transcendent sources of human prosperity and victory, whose human agents are thus worthy of the deference of others. When the sultans of the flourishing fifteenth-century commercial empire of Melaka in the Malay Peninsula claimed descent from Alexander the Great—that is, in his Koranic manifestation as Iskandar D'zul Karnain—it made an invidious contrast to the important rival state of Melayu-Jambi in Sumatra (C. C. E. Brown 1952). For Melaka thereby laid claim to the legacy of the fabled ancient kingdom of Srivijaya, where the prince, Sri Tri Buana, who was the sultan's Alexandrian ancestor, first appeared, and along with two of his brothers turned the rice fields into silver and gold. A few generations later, Sri Tri Buana's descendants converted to Islam and metaphorically repeated the miracle by the commercial enrichment of Melaka. Malayu Jambi, however, may have gained the last word, according to an edict issued in the eighteenth century by the sultan of its successor state of Minangkabau. On it were three seals representing three descendants of Alexander: the sultan of Rum (Constantinople); the sultan of China; and, himself, the sultan of Minangkabau. As the youngest, the Minangkabau ruler was the privileged successor, fulsomely described in the edict as "king of kings . . . lord of the air and clouds . . . possessor of the crown of heaven brought by the prophet Adam" (Marsden 1811: 339). In the same connection it is notable that during the T'ang dynasty Srivijaya sent multiple missions to the Chinese emperor, which apparently were intended to legitimate that realm's successful subordination of Melayu (Wolters 1986: 38).

Likewise in the Sung dynasty, the Srivijaya dispatched several missions to China, which, according to Wolters,

> were certainly occasions when the rulers could trade with China, but I believe the rulers had another and more important intention . . . . Foreign rulers in Sung times were anxious for imperial favors which signified their superiority vis-à-vis other Chinese vassals and especially those that were their neighbors and political rivals. Distinctions of rank were part of the political culture of Southeast Asia, and, when granted by the [Chinese] emperors, helped to establish status among Southeast Asian rulers whose spheres of influence overlapped. (1986: 37)

"Status," yes, but should we not add that the indwelling aura of the Celestial Emperor transmitted in these "imperial favors" not only differentiates the recipient from his rivals but also commands the loyalty of his followers?

Clearly we have to do with a longstanding Greater East Asian Galactic Polity centered in the Middle Kingdom. China was similarly the high-stakes, soft-power arbiter of political legitimacy in Ayutthaya and other distant kingdoms which it neither reached nor feared militarily. Still, China was present commercially and politically: by the common tradition, Ayutthaya was founded by a local Chinese merchant prince who strategically married the royal daughters of two important kingdom centers in the region. His descendants by these women would then compete bitterly for the encompassing kingship of Ayutthaya for decades—as by means of tributary submissions to the Chinese court. Between 1369 and 1433, Ayutthaya royals sent fifty-eight such embassies to the emperor or members of his family, mainly in the interest of promoting their chances of succession in Ayutthaya. In the period 1370–1482, the Chinese court dispatched eunuch officials on seventeen celestial embassies to Ayutthaya, not all of them friendly. Among their functions: conveying condolence on the death of the Ayutthaya king; investing the new king; presenting royal gifts; and declaring imperial edicts, including instructions on conduct toward other states (Kasetsiri 1976). This kind of diplomacy was not that unusual, considering that the strategic demand for soft power in high places is common in galactic settings.

Marked by the civilizing mission of the Celestial Emperor and manifest in the petitions and tributes of distant peoples, a huge East Asian force field of Chinese influence was created, extending even to the island kingdoms and principalities of Java, Borneo, and beyond, where "Sina" was a political identity to conjure with. Chinese commerce has been long and widely spread beyond the borders of the Middle Kingdom. Chinese monks and other religious figures also traveled early and far. Chinese military might has been demonstrated periodically on the northern frontiers; and regarding the southern borderlands of particular interest here, the Mongol invasion and famous voyages of the Ming admiral Cheng Ho penetrated deep into Indonesia. Yet the Greater East Asian Galactic Polity centered in the imperial capital has endured longer in time and space than the presence of any Chinese coercive force.

In AD 484, a petition reached the Southern Qi imperial court from the ruler of the original Khmer kingdom in the lower Mekong Delta, a distant Cambodian place that had never known the presence of the Chinese arms it now solicited (Pelliot 1903). True, northern Vietnam had been successfully invaded by Chinese forces in Han times, but in Cambodia, as Keith Taylor comments,

> there was no experience with the soldiers and officials of a neighboring empire, nor the awareness of boundaries, in terrain and culture, that such an experience produced among the Viets and Chams. Information about the outside world arrive to Khmer leaders as news about Hindu gods and forms of Buddhist and Hindu devotion as well as cosmological notions of political space that were expounded in the Sanskrit language. (1993: 157)

Still, King Kaundinya Jayavarman of the Khmer realm the Chinese knew as "Funan" must have been aware of the Son of Heaven's might when he complained to him about a certain "slave" who had rebelled against his own authority and enlisted support from a neighboring kingdom ("Lin-yi," evidently the predecessor regime of Champa in southern Vietnam). The Chinese ruler in question was probably the Emperor Wu of the short-lived Southern Qi dynasty. The mission is recorded at the beginning of the sixth century in *The history of the Southern Qi dynasty*, and accordingly presents a Chinese—indeed Confucian—perspective on what transpired. Jayavarman did not lead the embassy in person, although some Funan kings did so act; he sent a Hindu bonze as his representative. His petition begins properly with a profession of submission to the sage and saintly Celestial Emperor. "Your subject, Jayavarman," it reads, "bows his forehead to the earth and fulsomely praises the divine civilizing virtue" of the "saintly master," wishing him all kinds of happiness, including that "the concubines of the six palaces be perfectly beautiful"; and voicing confidence that earth will know peace, harmony, and prosperity "because of the brilliant civilizing influence of your majesty." Such is the preamble to King Jayavarman's complaint about his "slave" rival, followed by the offering of "meager presents" in tribute to the "saintly and virtuous" majesty, including a golden image of the king of dragons. Jayavarman asks the emperor for troops to put down the rebel, promising in return to aid the imperial throne in "repressing the realms that border the sea." Or if not an army, would the Divine Majesty issue a special edict authorizing a small number of Chinese troops to join his own forces in order to "exterminate this nefarious lowly one"? The emperor's response is equivocal. Taking note of his benevolence, his reform of Buddhism, and his own resemblance to Indra, king of the gods, the emperor declares that: "For me, it is only by culture and virtue that I attract the distant peoples; I do not wish to have recourse to arms." However, considering that King Jayavarman "comes from afar and with a loyal heart to ask for the aid of the imperial forces," the emperor will refer the matter to his tribunal—where, as far as I can determine, the request for military aid died. Apparently it was soft power from beginning to end.

In AD 252, the Chinese military did intervene in Yunnan: an event that was inscribed in ritual memories and tribal polities for many centuries beyond, even as its political impulses also rippled further than the actual extent of the invasion. The famous Shu Han minister and strategist Zhuge Liang led the campaign in the aim of restoring the imperial authority that had lapsed with the decline of the Han dynasty. Sensing he could not rule what he had conquered, Zhuge withdrew, leaving the area in charge of the leaders of indigenous ethnic groups on whom he had bestowed Chinese offices and surnames—a practice of letting "barbarians rule barbarians" apparently in effect since Western Zhou times, later commonly known as the "bridle and halter" policy, and, since Yuan, as the *tusi* system. For centuries after Zhuge's withdrawal, he was numbered among local deities in temples built in his honor. As late as the twentieth century, Bai peasants, reputed to be the aborigines of Yunnan, were using a carrying yoke whose design was attributed to Zhuge, claiming their ancestors had learned the style when serving in his armies. Other longstanding traditions of local non-Han peoples related that their chieftains' bronze drums—not merely a "symbol" of their authority, as often reported, but an active-animistic agent thereof—had been given their predecessors by Zhuge. Richard van Glahn tells that when a drum of this kind was forcibly surrendered to an invading Ming army in 1573, the chief lamented, "with two or three of such drums, one could proclaim himself king. Striking the drum at the summit of a hill will cause all the tribes to assemble. But now, all is lost" (1987: 15). Various signs and traditions of Zhuge's conquests were long preserved in central Yunnan, some into modern times, although his forces had never reached that far. And in a phenomenon of the kind frequently recorded in the Sino-Southeast Asian borderlands, important chiefs of non-Han peoples in the areas he did pacify were known to convert their Chinese surnames into claims of Han ancestry (cf. Backus 1981; Giersch 2006; Took 2005). Stranger-kingship: the cultural politics of core–periphery relations have real-political effects.

GALACTIC MIMESIS: UNEVEN DEVELOPMENT IN CORE–PERIPHERY SYSTEMS

"Barbarian" chiefs of Chinese ancestry; New Guinea villagers who adopt clans, totems, ancestors, and rituals of their dominant neighboring peoples; Cambodian or Javanese kingdoms ruled in Sanskrit terms by Hinduized kings; Indonesian rulers become Islamic sultans who assume a Portuguese lifestyle: in sum, a recurrent impulse of upward mobility—more exactly upward *nobility*—runs through these galactic systems, no less at the peripheries than at the center, as well as among the several secondary and tertiary societies in-between. Even the kingdoms at the apex of the regional hierarchy aspire to a hegemony of yet higher order—a project that also engages them with exotic hinterland groups, thereby opening prospects of grandeur at the underdeveloped galactic margins.

The world over, would-be kings of kings would institute something approaching a cosmocratic regime by laying claim to ancient or current predecessors of widespread and exalted renown: whether by descent, incarnation, or other privileged association; and whether these paragons be great gods such as Shiva, world-historical heroes such as Alexander, fabled cities such as Rome, or mighty empires such as the Chinese. Buddhist rulers in Southeast Asia invoke Ashoka. West African Islamic rulers and their nearby pagan counterparts trace their dynasties to Mecca: the former often to descendants of the Prophet, the latter to his reputed enemies. The Gauls and Spartan kings come from Herakles, although after the Roman conquests some Gaulish chiefs had Julian or Augustan ancestors. The kings of the Banyoro, Baganda, and several other East African realms claim to be heirs of the Bachwezi rulers of the fabled Kitara empire. Later Mexica emperors overlaid their barbaric Chichimec origins with an exalted Toltec identity by importing a ruler of known descent from that legendary civilization and its renowned god-king Quetzalcoatl. Aeneas of Troy, stranger-king of the Latins, became the ancestor of Roman emperors through Romulus, and thereby of the Holy Roman emperors and the Habsburgs, among others; whereas the Greek heroes who returned from the Trojan War, the Nostoi, particularly Odysseus, gave rise to the ruling aristocracy in city-states of northern Greece, Italy, and Sicily. Enough said, except that the ambitions of galactic sovereigns which thus impel an upward cosmic reach are complemented by a policy of outward expansion through war, trade, and diplomacy, going even beyond the strategic material returns with the aim of encompassing the potent animistic powers of the barbaric wild.[8]

These upward and outward ambitions were interrelated: everything happens as if the appropriation of the diverse earthly powers of the galactic hinterlands would thus validate the claims of universal hegemony entailed in the ruler's privileged relations to transcendent cosmic authorities. Consider, for example, Lorraine Gesick's description of Southeast Asian galactic orders:

> Linked with the conviction that living things were ordered along a continuum from the bestial to the sacred, we found a circular conception of space in which politically charged centers were thought to radiate power outward and downward

---

8. To document some of the most marvelous claims, see C. C. E. Brown (1952) on Alexander the Great, Malkin (1998) on the Nostoi, Tanner (1993) on Aeneus, and Drinkwater (1978) on Romanized Gauls.

toward the less charged peripheries . . . . In the landscape, palaces, temples, sacred mountains, and capital cities were similarly surrounded by secondary and tertiary centers and villages, all of which participated in and reflected, in varying degrees, the power of the center. Finally, at the extreme periphery, civilized, cultivated lands and villages gave way to jungles and mountain ranges—"wild" territory beyond the reach of the center's power. These territories were by no means impotent; on the contrary, they were filled with power; but it was anarchic, chaotic, primeval. Only a person who was extremely "civilized" in himself could, by meditation and self-discipline, subdue these forces. (1983: 2)

Underlying it all, the reach for both celestial and terrestrial powers beyond the cosmocrater's own, is the alterity of the sources of human life and death, and thereby of the welfare of the social totality. Speaking of "traditional societies" in general, Mary Helms refers to a "cosmologically-charged outside" from which are drawn materials, intangible energies, and original knowledge and culture "that allow the production of human life and social being" (1993: 7). And among a series of astute observations on the dynamics of core–periphery systems in general, Helms notes that in taming the wild hinterlands with their cultivated exports, the civilizing mission of dominant centers has a counterpart in the centers' acquisition of "naturally endowed" imports that increase their "ideological and political potency by virtue of the autochthonous forces believed to be inherent in that which is exotic, curious, or different" (ibid.: 180). Here again is a real-politics of the marvelous, in the course of which the untamed forces of the periphery are transformed into the potency and prosperity of the center. As Helms describes, by trade and tribute from the hinterlands come rare animals, strange foreigners, precious stones and minerals, rare woods, spices, and drugs, and the horns, tails, furs, and feathers of exotic beasts and birds. One is of course reminded of the Celestial Emperor's mission of bringing order to All Under Heaven, and particularly of the demonstration of his virtue (*te*) by incorporating the tributary wonders and monsters brought from afar by the barbarian inhabitants of fabulous countries. So likewise would the tribute-bearing peoples be culturally transformed, domesticated, and civilized by coming into the imperial presence and thereby under its power as manifested and transmitted by his person: that is, bodily as well as ritually, architecturally, and in the banquets, gifts, and honors the outlanders receive and consume. The overall effect is a two-way traffic in animistic potencies, political and wild, in which the subjective forces of things endow vitality on both the central and outlying societies—and notably elevate and empower their leaders.

The center "desires the resources, the potency and the potentiality, the 'alien powers' of the periphery, the wild, the forest. Both center and periphery seek to restore 'vitality' in the exchange of powers" (Turton 2000: 25–26). So Andrew Turton describes the exchanges between lowland Shan states and the hill peoples they call *kha*, "serfs" (or "slaves")—although typically the hill peoples are the residual autochthonous "owners" of the fertile lowlands. For their part, the Shan states, historically tributary to Burmese or Chinese potentates, were included in the Greater East Asian Galactic system that stretched southward from the Middle Kingdom into Malaya, Sumatra, Java, and beyond.

Edward Schafer tells that the aromatics and other exotica from Southeast Asia that reached China "partook of the godly and the beneficial, and at the same time the deadly and the devilish" (1967: 193). The animistic force was not merely a Chinese sense of the exotic; it was quite familiar to the tribal people who collected these potent things. Something like the divine and the deadly were already ensouled in the camphor crystals and other aromatics sought out by the indigenous peoples of the Indonesian forests. In his useful compendium of *Malay magic*, Walter William Skeat (1900: 212ff.) relates that camphor was controlled by indwelling spirits who had to be propitiated so that it could be discovered and harvested. Communication with these metapersons, moreover, required a special language, ordinary Malay being taboo. Transmitted thence to the Chinese court, the ensouled forces of the Malay wild redoubled the political animism of the emperor. As Schafer observed, incense from Southeast Asian aromatics "marked the presence of the royal afflatus, breathing supernatural wisdom through the worlds of nature and human affairs" (1963: 156). In imperial levees of the T'ang ministers, a table of these aromatics was placed before the Son of Heaven. Inhaled then by the court officials, the scent of camphor from Malaya or sandalwood from Borneo insinuated the emperor's virtue into the persons of his officials, whereupon it could be realized in statecraft and disseminated through the world—to ultimately subdue and civilize the barbarians who had originally appropriated these powers. (That was long before Marx talked of the surplus value that returned in fetishized form to rule its producers.)[9]

---

9. I have discussed this use of Southeast Asian aromatics by T'ang emperors in much the same terms elsewhere (Sahlins 2010).

On being informed that the Chinese protector-general had been chased from Vietnam by a rebellion, an imperial court official and poet wrote:

Remember when the North was on good terms with the Yueh [the Viets]. For a long time both were nourished by the southern fragrance.

All the same, the ensuing Ly dynasty (1009–1225), having established an independent Dai Viet state, proceeded to organize the kingdom on basic principles of the Chinese imperium: a "Vietnamized version of Chinese political theory," as Keith Taylor characterized it, with a "southern emperor" counterposed to the Chinese "northern emperor," ruling his "southern kingdom" by the grace of his own "mandate of heaven" (1999: 147). Chinese sources identify the third Ly ruler, Ly Nhat Ton (r. 1054–72), as the first Viet king who had the presumption to claim imperial status; Vietnamese sources corroborate that he "adopted many of the formalities of China's imperial court, from the official name of the realm, to the attire of his officials, to the ranks and titles conferred upon officials, upon members of the royal family, and upon the royal ancestors" (ibid.: 144). For all that the Dai Viet opposed imperial China, they did so by replicating it—just as certain Maluku rulers took on Chinese, Portuguese, or Dutch attributes; the Prussian court imitated the French; the Nilotic rulers of Nyoro assimilated to their Bantu predecessors of fabled Kitara; many a Khmer, Siamese, or Malay ruler became an Indic king, and some of the latter became Islamic sultans; and so on.

As already noted, the phenomenon is endemic in core–periphery relations. A certain impetus of "galactic mimesis" runs through the regional system, whereby outlying rulers assume the political culture of the higher powers with which they are engaged. Virtually a law of political science, this dynamic is in play at every level of the intersocietal hierarchy: down to the pretensions of peripheral tribal headmen like the Kachin chiefs who famously "become Shan [princes]"; whereas, for their part, the Shan princes rule in the style of Burmese or Chinese kings—which perhaps accounts for the rudimentary forms of the imperial Chinese temples of Heaven and Earth in certain villages of Kachin hill people (Leach 1954; cf. Scott 2009). The same acculturation from below is current even in purely tribal zones, absent a dominant civilization, as in the avidity of various Sepik peoples for the cultural powers of the Abelam or the Iatmul. In any case and every place, however, the spread of the cultural forms of dominant societies is not all of their own doing. Something has to be said for this demand of higher culture from below.

This mimetic process is notably in evidence in the Greater East Asian Galactic Polity. James C. Scott documents many particular instances in his treatise on relations between the greater states of the region and upland tribal peoples. More generally he writes:

> We have often noted what might be called the great chain of mimicry that extends from Angkor and Pagan through pettier and pettier states right down to hamlets with the slightest pretensions among, say, the Lahu or Kachin. The classical states similarly modeled themselves after the states in South Asia. (2009: 306; see also above)[10]

The cultural exchanges in core–periphery systems do not emanate from the higher centers alone. Motivated especially by local political conflicts, there is agency at every level of the galactic hierarchy in the course of which politico-religious forms of ruling societies are appropriated by subordinate ones, thus migrating downward through the system without the benefit of compelling initiatives from above. The soft power of dominant societies may thus be potentiated by the people subject to it—inasmuch as it also empowers them. This galactic mimesis develops either as a mode or resistance to the encroachment of a higher power, a dynamic George Devereaux and Edwin Loeb (1943) called "antagonistic acculturation," or by something like the "symmetrical schismogenesis" of Gregory Bateson's devising (1935, 1958), wherein local rivals try to outdo each other by scaling up the competition to another level. We have already seen instances of both—some of which suggest both were in play at once.

Antagonistic acculturation: by matching point for point a Southern Empire against the Chinese Northern Empire, Vietnamese rulers of the eleventh century took the contrarian process to a remarkable structural extent. Making their own polity the same as and yet different from the ostensibly superior Chinese realm, the Ly dynasty kings thus undertook to separate from the latter and ward off its colonizing ambitions. Subsequent Vietnamese dynasties continued

---

10. Curiously, neither here nor elsewhere in his major work (2009) on relations between upland and lowland peoples in Southeast Asia, and despite his occasional use of the term, does Scott refer to Tambiah's work on "galactic polities."

to differentiate their realm from the Chinese by the fact that they had their own Chinese imperium—as in this 1428 proclamation by a Le dynasty official, upon the eviction of a Ming administration of two decades standing:

> *Now our Great Viet is truly a cultured country;*
> *The features of our mountains and our rivers are different,*
> *Just as the customs of the North [China] and South [Vietnam] are also different.*
> *From the time of the Viet, Trieu, Dinh, Ly, and Tran dynasties' establishment of our*
> *state,*
> *And from the time of the Han, Tang, Song, and Yuan dynasties of the North,*
> *Each emperor has ruled over his own quarter.*
>
> (Dutton, Werner, and Whitmore 2012: 91)

Not that antagonistic acculturation is imperial politics only, for it is also encountered in the outlying tribal societies—which in the Southeast Asian uplands may resist lowland states with their own kingdoms, whether legendary ones of the past, messianic ones of the future, or current imitations of the greater regional powers. Like the Karen of Burma, whose history, writes James C. Scott, "seems to illuminate the preservation of a culture liberation and dignity fashioned, for the most part, from the cosmology of lowland [Shan and Burmese] states" (2009: 285). He cites verse from a prophetic tradition:

> *That a Karen King would yet appear*
> *The Tabin [Mon] Kings have had their season*
> *The Burmese Kings have had their season*
> *And the foreign Kings will have their season*
> *But the Karen King will yet appear*
> *When the Karen King arrives*
> *There will only be one monarch . . .*
> (2009: 287)

Just so, F. K. Lehman describes the characteristic polity of the Kayah, a Karen people of eastern Burma, as "a quasi-state level political system developed among an essentially tribal people as an adaptation to the Shan-Burmese environment" (1967: 15). By common local traditions, these states were formed when a Kayah chief was victorious in a skirmish with a Burmese force; whereupon an honorable peace was negotiated, recognizing the boundaries of the Kayah domain and of its ruler under the title of a Shan prince (Sawbwa) or lord (Myasa). Over time the differences and similarities increased together: the Kayah founder's victory over the Burmese was celebrated as a miraculous feat, even as this charter narrative was coupled to a Kayah regime with a Burmese cast—including courts that interfered in otherwise independent affairs of the villages. As Lehman observed, "This was essentially an exercise in foreign power within or attached to Kayah society" (ibid.: 26) It was an imitation of Shan princely practice, including the organization of the Kayah chief's house in the ritual form of a Sabwah's palace, with the aim of contracting marriages between Kayah and Shan ruling families.

Seeking alliances with lowland Shan nobility, however, suggests something other than resistance is in play. Consider the common report that the pretensions of Kayah chiefs to Shan princely status are a matter of competition within their own communities, "something the leaders and would-be leaders were constantly contending for" (ibid.: 30). The suggestion is that beside the opposition to foreign superior others that drives imitation of them—by way of antagonistic acculturation—competition with similars likewise drives identification with foreign superior others—by way of symmetrical schismogenesis:

> The acquaintance with foreign social and economic techniques of organization gave the Kayah leaders several sorts of advantage at home. In the first place, it gave them charismatic authority among their Kayah followers. That is, insofar as they remained successful in dealing with the Shan and Burmans with some measure of economic advantage to their Kayah "subjects," they came to be thought of as *phre phraw*. This expression means wonder-worker, miraculous person, seer, prophet, supernaturally endowed, and of miraculous birth . . . . As a result, those villages and persons who acknowledge a particular Sawbwa often had a considerable attachment to him, and in principle to his line. (Lehman 1967: 26)

Miraculous person, wonder-worker: notice that this is still a real-politics of the marvelous, in which the dividend of successful upward nobility is the assimilation of the metahuman powers of the "cosmological outside"–giving a hold, then, on the people inside.

Where antagonistic acculturation involved conflictual relations between lower and higher or outer and inner peoples, symmetrical schismogenesis is typical of the competition between more or less equivalent parties at a given level of the regional hierarchy. The adversaries may be individuals or factions within the same group with the leadership thereof at stake; or they may be groups of the same order in the galactic hierarchy contending for a superior position therein. The way Bateson described it, symmetrical schismogenesis works on the principle of "anything you can do, I can do better," as in an arms race where each side strives to accumulate more destructive power than the other. Rather than "the same as and different from," the favored competitive move here is "equal to and better than." Indeed, the best move is to "go outside the box," to introduce an unprecedented lethal weapon into the conflict, thereby trumping any and all adversaries competing by only conventional means. Or as Clifford Sather (1996: 92) reported of Iban of Kalimantan, competition among members of the community is essentially waged outside of it: "It is largely through deeds performed beyond the boundaries of the long house that unequal status within it was, and continues to be, measured." In the context of galactic systems, the privileged tactic is to go above and beyond one's own group to acquire the cosmopolitical powers of proximate superiors—whether by identification, alliance, predation, or some such mode of cultural assimilation.

Motivated thus by internal competition, these aspirations for the marvelous powers of galactic superiors have been effective means of cultural mimesis in core–periphery relations. As has been noted elsewhere (Sahlins 2010), they are a recurrent mode of stranger-king formation worldwide: native rulers who become foreigners rather than foreigners who become native rulers. The self-Hinduization of Southeast Asian kings is a case in point. Another is the Malay sultans contending for local supremacy by adopting Alexandrian bona fides. An example so good I have already used it more than once concerns Hawai'i, where, within a decade of Cook's death in 1779, three of the island paramounts had named their sons and heirs "King George"; and even before the great conqueror Kamehameha ceded the archipelago to his "brother" King George in 1793, he was flying the Union Jack from his house and canoe. Early in the nineteenth century, the prime minister of the Sandwich Island kingdom was Billy Pitt Kalaimoku, the governor of Maui was Cox Keeaumoku, and John Adams Kuakini ruled Hawai'i Island (Sahlins 1981a, 1992). Instances could easily be multiplied, but for convenience I cite one of James C. Scott's general notices of the phenomenon in Southeast Asia—with the added indication of the major powers' own interest in the politicization of the uplands:

> The State's desire for chiefs and the ambitions of upland local strongmen co-incided often enough to create imitative state-making in the hills, though such

achievements were seldom durable. Local chiefs had ample reasons to seek the seals, regalia, and letters conferred by a more powerful ruler; they might overcome rivals, and confer lucrative trade and tribute monopolies. Recognition of a lowland ruler's implied charisma was, at the same time, entirely compatible with remaining entirely outside its administrative reach. (2009: 114)

Like Scott, virtually all the scholarly chroniclers of the region have stressed the endemic instabilities of core–periphery relations: egalitarian (*gumsa*) revolts against the pretensions and exactions of (*gumlao*) local chiefs who assume the style of superior foreign rulers; underlying villages or principalities that switch allegiance from declining to rising outside powers; the overthrow of local rulers affiliated with an external power by a rival party affiliated with a different realm; high-level competition resulting in the defeat and displacement of one apical state by another. As many of these shifts suggest, an intrinsic evolutionary impulse is generated throughout the system by the cultural politics of galactic mimesis. Indeed there is always the potential that marginal societies, by virtue of some strategic advantage—military, commercial, or other—will fully realize in practice the greater foreign regime they had previously identified with by now overcoming and succeeding it. It may be that as a general rule, all great civilizations were peripheral once, outliers of galactic polities: like the Mongols and the Manchus were to China; or the Siamese kingdoms were to Khmer predecessors, who were themselves marginal to South Asian realms. For that matter, the Greeks were marginal relative to the Persians; the Romans to the Greeks; and the Gauls, Franks, and Britons to the Romans; and so on. Virtually all of this begins in soft-power politics, moreover, set up by the demonstrable cosmic potency of dominant centers, to which peripheral societies are oriented and subordinated culturally while they are still independent politically.

Recall, moreover, that there is a reciprocal search for vital power, from above as well as from below: a centrifugal expansion from the center outward toward the peripheries, as well as a centripetal movement from the peripheries toward the center. As Tambiah observed, while the central kingdom moves outward to incorporate the lower-standing territories of the "wild" hinterlands, "in the opposite direction, the lower attempts to raise itself by emulation of, and contact with, the immediately superior" (1985: 322). Except that typically there is no political "incorporation" of the hinterlands by the central kingdom, although, as a consequence of diffusion of its "high culture," there is an interesting disconformity between the cosmopolitical superstuctures and the material infrastructures of societies throughout the field of core–periphery relations. Given the pervasive operation of galactic mimesis, the political and cosmological order of the greater states is more or less replicated beyond their borders through a wider domain of effective influence than their practical means of domination could reach; whereas, by the same mimetic token, the lesser societies know more developed institutions of governance than their own "economic basis" could generate. "One major characteristic of any of the hill societies of Southeast Asia that live in symbiosis with civilizations," as F. K. Lehman observed, " is the marked disparity between what their supravillage political system attempts to be, on the models provided it by its civilized neighbors, and what its resources and organizational capacity readily permit it to achieve" (1967: 34). All this is to say that the conventional notions of the systematic coherence of the sociocultural totality, these paradigms of "anthropology-cultures" or "national-cultures," whether Marxist, Durkheimian, structural-functional, cultural-materialist, or whatever, supposing as they do in one way or another that the political and spiritual forms of any given society are reflexes of more fundamental social or material realities, are inappropriate to the uneven development of structural registers in societies situated in galactic polities.

We are back to the beginning of this essay and a repeated theme of this book: the specious assumption that societies are all alone and self-generating; and, accordingly, left thus to their own devices, they develop functionally consistent cultural wholes. But the diverse societies set in hierarchical core–periphery systems are nether isolated nor sui generis. They are interdependent structurally to the extent that their cosmological and political forms are in significant respects not of their own making, and accordingly without basis in the coexisting infrastructures. Uneven development is the structural norm in galactic polities. And since, as far as we know, human societies virtually everywhere and everywhen have been situated in such fields of core–periphery interactions, our main theories of cultural order are, to put it benignly, in need of revision.

Also worthy of reconsideration are the premodern "empires" so-called, which, the world around, are not extraterritorial governments of colonized societies so much as predatory overlordships, ruled typically by hubristic kings of divine potency exacting tributes from subordinated proxy regimes—in other words, galactic polities as described here for Southeast Asian civilizations. The lineaments of the same also appear in earlier pages on Africa and Middle America. And the argument can be extended to famous empires of Mediterranean and Western Asian antiquity: Median, Achaemenid, Seleucid, Sasanian,

Parthian, Egyptian, Akkadian, Aassyrian, and their like—even the Roman, particularly during the republic. Of course they vary considerably in structure, but all take the form of a core region under the direct administration of the dominant ethnic group, whose powers and cultural influences diminish in proportion to distance from the center and inversely to the self-determination of the outlying peoples. As has been noted of the Roman imperium—and is true of these galactic orders more generally—the relations of the center to subordinate peoples are effected in severalty, as so many bilateral arrangements; hence, unlike the uniform government of national states, these empires are characterized by heterogeneous forms of submission of peripheral collectivities to the galactic core (Ando 2015: 13). Generally, however, the effect is a system of three concentric zones, the circle beyond the ruling core consisting of vassal polities obedient to it, and a further region where submission to the center is nominal and tributary obligations are minimal. All the same, the pretensions of the galactic rulers are typically world encompassing, figured as extending indefinitely along the cardinal directions, the whole taking the form of three circles and four quarters. Characteristically also, the cultural achievements and cosmic powers of the dominant people and their famous kings are respected beyond any actual political presence or authority, thus generating an orientation of marginal peoples toward the center that may presage their ultimate usurpation of their erstwhile superiors. Indeed, the dynamic phenomena of upward nobility and galactic mimesis, involving progression culturally and politically from below, as motivated by competition within subordinate groups or resistance to dominant groups, are likewise endemic in imperial regimes. The outward reach of the dominant center is thus complemented by a centripetal impulse of peripheral peoples, producing chronic instabilities in a system that is otherwise envisioned, insofar as it is impelled by the search for the security of divine, life-giving benefits—elsewhere.

CHAPTER 7

Notes on the politics of divine kingship
Or, elements for an archaeology of sovereignty

DAVID GRAEBER

This essay is meant to draw some threads together from the other pieces assembled in this collection; but also to propose some new ideas and possible directions for research. It's an essay about the politics of divine kingship—as well as about the origins of the principle of sovereignty, since one of the main arguments is that the two are intimately linked.

"Sovereignty" is a complicated word and nowadays it is often used to simply mean "national autonomy," but as the etymology suggests, it originally referred to the power of kings. Sovereignty in the sense of royal power has always been fraught with paradoxes. One the one hand, it is in principle absolute. Kings will, if they have any possibility of doing so, insist that they stand outside the legal or moral order and that no rules apply to them. Sovereign power is the power to refuse all limits and do whatever one likes. On the other, they often tend to lead lives so circumscribed, so ringed about by custom and ceremony, that they can barely do anything at all. What's more, this paradox has never gone away. It still lingers in the peculiar way we imagine the modern nation-state, where sovereignty has in principle passed from the king to an entity we refer to as "the people," who are simultaneously viewed (in their capacity as "the people") as the source of all legitimacy, as capable of rising up in revolution and creating an entirely new constitutional and legal order, and also (in their capacity as just "people") as those bound and constrained by those very laws.

What I want to do in this essay is to try to trace this paradox back to its origins. If we define sovereignty in its broadest sense as the ability to "lay down the law," either literally or figuratively—that is, to both break all accepted rules of law, morality, or propriety at will, and to thus step outside the social order and impose new rules, or simply give arbitrary orders backed up with threat of punishment—then its historical origins are long since lost. They must surely to go back long beyond the advent of written records. But it's possible, I think, to turn to the ethnographic record to create a conceptual model of the logical possibilities, as they have worked themselves out in cases that we actually know.

The essays collected in this volume all share at least three common premises. The first is that A. M. Hocart was largely correct in arguing that what we have come to call "government" originally derives from ritual. The second is that recognition of this fact forces us to radically reconsider what we mean by both. And the third is that what Marshall Sahlins has termed "stranger-kingship" provides an ideal point of entry from which to do so. For the moment, let me focus on the second point. Despite occasional protests to the contrary, anthropologists still largely accept the premise that there is some kind of inevitable division between the cynical world of *Realpolitik* and the airy domains of ritual, which—even if they take the form of rituals of state—are assumed to consist of statements about the ultimate meaning of human life. Or perhaps the ultimate forms of authority. Or visions of an ideal social order. Or some kind of alternative, "as-if" reality. But anyway, always at a fundamental remove from the pragmatics of political action. This division between ritual and politics is maintained whether one insists that royal ritual exists largely for the sake of reinforcing pragmatic authority (e.g., Bloch 1989), or whether one instead insists that pragmatic authority exists largely for the sake of enabling those in charge to perform rituals (e.g., Geertz 1980). To some degree, this division is just an effect of the dogged persistence, in both the British and American traditions, of the theoretical assumption that society and culture, action and expression, must be treated as different levels of human reality, and one must therefore develop different sorts of theoretical tools to understand each. But to be fair, it's not just that. Often those who organize and carry out rituals will themselves insist on a similar division. This may be because they see ritual as providing access to another dimension of reality, as famously with the Australian Dreamtime, or it may be because intellectuals in charge of conducting such rituals—Confucian, Brahmanical, or Rabbinical—have developed their own theory of ritual as representing a kind of ideal, as-if, "subjunctive" universe standing apart from a chaotic and tawdry everyday existence (A. Seligman et al. 2008); but whatever the theory, rituals are always to some degree set apart, framed as different from mundane life, and in pragmatic terms, it is the creation and maintenance of those frames that is key to rituals' power.

In this, at least, the Durkheimians were not entirely wrong.

Nonetheless, it is precisely in royal ritual and the politics surrounding it that such frames seem most in danger of collapse, where sometimes they do indeed collapse—where it is possible, even, to say that ritual really is politics by other means, but only to the measure that it is also possible to say that politics becomes ritual by other means. I think this is why Sir James Frazer's stories about the killing of the divine kings continue to resonate among poets, mystics, and Hollywood script-writers down to the present day. Killing is one symbolic act of which it is simply impossible to write off as "just" symbolic—because, whatever you may or may not be communicating through the ritual, when the rite of sacrifice is over, the victim continues to stay dead.

This is why anthropologists found ritual regicide so compelling back in the days when it was common to imagine people in earlier stages of history as themselves still living in a kind of poetic Dreamtime, and also why those most insistent on maintaining the division between symbolic expression and political reality were so assiduous about insisting that such things never really happened, that kings were never really killed (e.g., Evans-Pritchard 1948, 1951). Or alternately, that if they were, such acts were really political acts dressed up as ritual, rather than moments when the frames collapse and it's simply no longer possible to say there is a difference between the two. But in fact, as practitioners of cold-blooded *Realpolitik* from Pizarro to the Bolsheviks discovered to their irritation, king-killing is always, necessarily, a mythic and ritual act, whether or not those who perform the act feel it ought to be.

At the same time, no one can possibly claim it's not political.

This essay, then, is not just an exploration of the politics of kingship, or even sovereignty; it's also an exploration of what happens when such frames implode. One might even say that's what sovereignty itself is: the ability to toss frames about. In the first part of the essay, therefore, I want to offer some suggestions about how sovereignty might first have burst out of the ritual frames in which it was originally encompassed, thus allowing divine kings to come into the world in the first place. In the second two, I will again take up a notion I first proposed in my essay on the Shilluk (chapter 2 above): to consider what happens when kings either definitively win, or definitively lose, that war.

SOVEREIGNTY CONTAINED IN TIME AND SPACE

> *Claire*: How do you know you're God?
> *The Earl*: Simple. When I pray to Him, I find I'm talking to myself.
> Peter Barnes, *The ruling class*

It's a premise of this volume, as I've noted, that A. M. Hocart was correct to argue that forms of governance first appeared in the ritual sphere, as a part of a larger politics of the creation, channeling, and maintenance of life, and only later came to be applied to what we consider the political domain. As Marshall Sahlins has pointed out earlier in this volume, forager societies do have kings, even if they are not mortal ones. Mortal kings were modeled on gods and not the other way around. But the fact that this is true in the broadest historical sense does not mean that, for instance, Frazer was also correct in assuming that human government itself begins in divine kingship: the absolute rule of humans taken to be gods.

It might seem like a logical step, but the archaeological and historical evidence in no way supports it. What we know—and our knowledge is decidedly uneven—suggests a longer and more twisted path. The first bits of evidence we do have for marked social inequality appear surprisingly early, in the Pleistocene, where, despite the fact most people do not seem to have been buried at all, a few clearly extraordinary individuals were not only placed in tomb-like graves but their bodies were festooned with enormous quantities of bead-work and other precious materials. Yet these "princely" burials (as archaeologists sometimes call them) appear in isolation, often thousands of years apart, and, despite the enormous amounts of human labor that must have been mobilized to create their costumes, never seem to lead to anything that otherwise resembles a kingdom or a state. What's more, the majority of these bodies appear to have been physically anomalous in some way: some were extremely tall, others were marked by dwarfism, yet others had markedly deformed skeletons (Formicola 2007), and there is reason to suspect the burials might have been as much about containing and neutralizing their power as in honoring them (many, for instance, are topped by very heavy slabs of stone). Norse myth notwithstanding, it seems unlikely the Paleolithic had really produced a hereditary aristocracy that largely consisted of giants, dwarfs, and hunchbacks. We can only guess, but the appearance of such striking characters in sumptuous and elaborately fashioned costumes, some thirty thousand years ago, in such magnificent isolation, does rather suggest that insofar as we are speaking of Ice Age "princes"—as some of these individuals have been called—any powers they may have held was strictly limited in time and space: perhaps even to very specific ritual contexts (Wengrow and Graeber 2015: 604–5).

All this does not necessarily mean that the first princely figures in human history were, as a Hocartian reading would suggest, impersonators of divinities in dramatic rituals whose authority began to extend further during the ritual season. Other interpretations are possible. But that one would certainly fit the evidence, which, it must be admitted, most contemporary interpretations, caught up as they are in evolutionist categories, really don't. What's more, there *are* precedents for societies in which powers we normally associate with government—and particularly sovereignty, even only in the minimal sense of the power to issue commands and back them up with the threat of punishment—exist only in ritual contexts, even, specifically, when participants are impersonating metahuman beings. It's just that neither they, nor the gods they impersonate, are ever anything remotely like Zeus, Jehovah, Vishnu, or other familiar "King of the Gods"-type figures.

* * *

What I am suggesting is that, while the emergence of sovereign powers most likely did follow a path from kingly divinities to divine kings, this path is in no way straightforward. It passed through a veritable circus-world of oddities. The region from the western littoral of North America to the Great Plains provides, I think, the closest we can get to a glimpse of what must have happened. Here one can see a clear progression from societies (central California, Northwest Coast, etc.) where direct orders between adults (or, in the latter case, free adults) are given only during ritual dramas in which mortals impersonate gods, even to the point where certain characters in those dramas are regularly referred to as "police" who enforce the rules of the ceremony; to those in which, as Robert Lowie was first to point out (1948b; cf. Wengrow and Graeber 2015),[1] specific

---

1.   Kroeber (1922: 307–8) note that Californian cult associations never took on the broader police functions they did elsewhere in North America.

police powers are assigned (usually on a rotating basis) to clans or warrior societies during the three-month hunt and ritual season as a whole, even if, during the rest of the year, society reverts to its usual egalitarian decentralized political state, chiefs have to rely on powers of persuasion, not compulsion, and the former police have no more say in public affairs than anybody else.

The really striking thing about the powers of command that could be exercised only during rituals, though, is that, most often, they were exercised by clowns.

Some examples from north central California might prove illustrative. In indigenous Californian societies, with very few exceptions, chiefs and other explicitly political authorities—where they existed—held no powers of command or punishment; neither were explicit orders given or taken by adults in the domestic sphere. Even children were no longer punished after a fairly young age. The great exception was during the great Kuksu, or God-Impersonating rituals (Barrett 1919; Kroeber 1922: 307; 1925: 364–90; Gifford 1927; Loeb 1932, 1933; Halpern 1988), held in the winter months. During the Kuksu ceremonies, cosmic powers became manifest to mortal humans in the form of costumed dancers, who trained young boys in arcane ritual and older boys and girls in curing, or participated in the renewal of the universe.

On one level, these were fairly unremarkable examples of a broad type of spirit-impersonation ritual widely practiced in Australia, Melanesia, and parts of South America as well: involving elaborate disguises, the use of bull-roarers to create terrifying unearthly noises, and the pretense that those excluded (young boys and many women) actually believe they are witnessing spirits. But in these dramas, the spirits almost never give orders. Mainly they just terrify people (or else people pretend to be terrified; it's never entirely clear who's really fooling whom), and then reveal to a certain elect the ritual knowledge that lets initiates themselves play spirits in their turn. The elders who impersonate the spirits in some contexts might, in others, beat and admonish the initiates, and order them around; but these initiates are children and the elders' behavior is just a harsher or more exaggerated version of how parents normally treat small children. What we see in central California is in certain ways quite different.

The most important spirit was known as Kuksu, or "Big Head," the god who had revealed all the arts and sciences to humans long ago. Yet at least equal in importance were the clowns. Clowns were a fixture of many Californian rituals. They behaved like gluttons, lechers, and buffoons; they accompanied almost all rituals, no matter how solemn or important, with burlesque mimicry and slapstick routines, making fun of the officiants, musicians, and even gods. All this is much

discussed in the literature. But if one picks carefully through accounts of the actual ceremonies, one surprising feature emerges that has largely escaped previous
comment. Clowns were also the only figures in those rituals, or, for that matter,
in Californian life more generally, who had the power to issue direct orders to
anyone else. Or at least, they were the only ones who could issue orders directly
backed up by threat of punishment—since clowns also had the power to levy fines
or other penalties for misbehavior. This might mean enforcing the various rules
and regulations of the ceremony, though it might also mean whimsically making
them up, and sometimes "misbehavior" might mean just laughing at their jokes,
since unlike in ordinary life, during rituals, laughing at a clown's jokes was strictly
forbidden. During Pomo Kuksu rituals, if anyone cracked up at the clown's antics,
the clown—who we are told also acted as "sergeant at arms" for the ritual—was allowed to (playfully) attack the culprit and then levy a fine (Barrett 1917: 417, 422;
cf. 1919: 457 n. 24).[2] Of the Wappo coyote dance, another Kuksu ritual, we read:

> While the dance was open to women, it was only the men who made up as
> clowns. The latter danced naked, with stripes on their bodies, and colored clay
> on their faces. They made funny faces. . . . If a man (or woman) laughed, he was
> thrown up in the air. Then he had to pay a fine, give a feast, or do anything which
> the clowns demanded. (Loeb 1932: 111)

In other words, clown orders could be completely arbitrary and, in principle, at
least unlimited. Among the Wintun *hesi* ritual, S. A. Barrett observed that *moki*
clowns, described elsewhere (Loeb 1933: 171) as "policemen" of the ceremony,

> are privileged to levy a fine on one who does anything contrary to custom, and
> especially upon those who show displeasure at their ridicule or refuse to do their
> bidding. When, therefore, they ask someone to sing, he must accede or pay a fine.
> It is said that nearly all individual singing is due to the commands of the clowns.
> (Barrett 1919: 458)[3]

---

2. So among the Northern Maidu the director of ceremonies issues "commands"
    (Dixon 1905: 253); in Loeb's description of the Pomo ritual, the clown or ghost-
    clown has the role of fining dancers who make mistakes (1932: 50) or who laugh at
    their jokes (ibid., 5, 27, 110–12); on fines for laughing, see also Kroeber (1925: 264,
    450); Loeb (1933: 224); and Steward (1931: 199–200).

3. Here the clown's behavior seems to echo the behavior of shamanic spirits, who, at
    least among the Shasta, will demand the shaman sing and threaten punishment if

Clowns were the only performers who could break all the rules. Often they carried out tasks literally backward, or upside down. But they also made up rules, and enforced existing ones. Sometimes clowns did both at the same time, like the Yuki clowns, who would tell initiates to do the exact opposite of what they were supposed to, then impose fines on anyone foolish enough to take them at their word (Kroeber 1925: 187).[4] It was as if the clowns were the personal embodiment of the principle that only those not bound by rules can create rules. Clown commands were supposed to be whimsical—hence, arbitrary—but clown commands were the only genuine commands anyone gave or received in most Californian societies, since only they were enforced by the threat of sanction. What's more, while clowns were not, like the costumed masqueraders, identified with specific gods, they appear to have represented the divine principle in general. Rather than humans impersonating gods, they were gods impersonating humans, the absurdity of their behavior a way of conveying to us how ridiculous we appear in divine eyes (Park 1990: 270; cf. Makarius 1970; Hieb 1972; Handelman 1981).[5]

For present purposes, though, what's important is that the divine and arbitrary power clowns wield is strictly confined to rituals. Some Californian communities did have their own village clowns; but those clowns had no right to give orders under regular circumstances. In fact, neither did anyone else: the main authorities among the Pomo, Wintun, Maidu, and their neighbors, whether chiefs, shamans, or heads of initiation societies, did not have the power to command others. What's more, the clowns were most often drawn from a class of hobos and beggars, who were the last people who could be seen as holding authority of any kind, coercive or otherwise (Brightman 1999).

Pueblo clowns similarly embodied gods, acted as "police" during rituals, and had the power to whip and punish children. Clowns become more of an autonomous force here, as there are warrior societies that combine police

---

they don't (Dixon 1907: 473–76). The name Moki is used both for the master of ceremonies and for the clowns. In other instances the roles are combined.

4. "They direct each other to step in the wrong place, which is their way of indicating where they are to stand. Should one really go where he is told, he has to pay" (ibid.).

5. "The key to understanding these ludic displays—their obscenity, their disrespect for property, and their seemingly irrational disregard for self—is a simple one: we are meant to view them not as perverse humans but as gods impersonating humans, showing us what clods we are in the gods' eyes" (Park 1990: 270).

functions and clowning.[6] But perhaps the most impressive expression of police powers in the hands of buffoons is to be found among the Kwakiutl, during the Midwinter Ceremonials. During this ritual season, the normal social structure was suspended, people even took on different names, and society came to be organized around rights to dance certain roles in the great ritual dramas: Cannibal dancers, Thunderbirds, Grizzly Bears, Killer Whales, Seals, Ghosts, and, critically, Fools (Boas 1897: 498–99; Curtis 1915: 156–58). The system seems in many ways a transformation of a graded set of initiation societies, with additional military functions added on: many of the dancers are specifically said to be warriors, and this alternative social structure also pops into action, replacing the normal one, whenever society goes to war (Boas 1899: 101–2; cf. Codere 1950: 119).[7]

The highest order during the ritual season is represented by the Hamatsa or Man-Eater, a human seized by a terrible cannibalistic spirit who must gradually be cured over the course of the ceremonies. But it's the clowns—the Fool Dancers or *nutlmatl*, often aided and accompanied by the Grizzly Bears, armed with great bear claws—who functioned as "the tribal police during the winter period of aggregation and ceremonial" (MacLeod 1933: 339). According to Boas,

> [The] "fool dancers" are also messengers and helpers of the Hamatsa who help to enforce the laws referring to the ceremonial. Their method of attack is by throwing stones at people, hitting them with sticks, or in serious cases stabbing and killing them with lances and war axes. (1897: 468)

---

6. "Pueblo clowns served as police during ceremonies to ensure that people attend performances and that they obeyed the taboos during ritual periods. Clowns might be given considerable power over others at these times. . . . Among the Pueblo Indians clowns are also disciplinarians for children, and are used as bogeymen. Wearing masks and impersonating supernatural beings, they threatened to whip children and frighten them in other ways" (Norbeck 1961: 209, cited in Crumrine 1969: 15, who provides a similar analysis of Mayo clowns). Similarly, Else Clews Parsons writes "the clowning society is dangerous and fear-inspiring. The clowns are licensed to do as they choose; they are punitive and have express police or warrior functions" (1939: 131). On police functions of Southwestern clowns in general, cf. Parsons and Biels (1939: 499, 504); Whitman (1947: 15).

7. It is probably significant that in the Southern Kwakiutl winter dancing societies documented by Drucker (1940), Fool Dancers were largely absent, though "warrior" dancers appear to have taken their place.

The Fools are said to menace or attack anyone who stumbled while dancing (Morland-Simpson 1888: 82; Boas 1890: 67), laughed, or coughed during a performance (Boas 1897: 506),[8] mistakenly called someone by his or her summer name (ibid.: 517), or even took too long eating (ibid.: 551). Even if Boas' informants were obviously sometimes exaggerating for theatrical effect ("if anyone makes a mistake in dancing he is killed by the *Nutlmatl*" [ibid.]), Kwakiutl clowns were clearly far more dangerous characters than their Californian cousins. Most in Boas' time were experienced warriors. They are also even more grotesque. Fool Dancers wore tattered clothing, blackened their faces, or donned masks with exceedingly long noses. Their noses were always running and they became excited if anyone touched or even mentioned them. They flung mucus at one another. They carried out tasks backward and became furious if anyone tried to correct them. They were constantly pretending to throw rocks at crowds. Some would feign stabbing themselves, using bladders of fake blood to feign injury. But some of their destructiveness was not simulated. "They are armed with clubs and stones, which they use on anything that arouses their repugnance for beauty and order," wrote Edward Curtis (1915: 216); "they dislike to see clean and beautiful clothing," one of Boas' informants added. "They tear and soil it. They break canoes, houses, kettles, and boxes; in short, act the mad man in every conceivable way" (Boas 1897: 469). Sometimes a crew of Fools in a berserker rage would soil everything in sight, filling houses with filth and ordure, even pulling houses apart[9] (Boas 1890: 66–8; 1897: 468–73, 506, 516, 564, 566–69; 1921: 1160; 1930: 146–50; Curtis 1915: 215–16, 231–32).

So once again those who are not bound by any sort of order—indeed, who express revulsion toward the very idea of order—are also those in charge of enforcing it.

Northwest Coast society was in no sense egalitarian. Perhaps a third of the population held aristocratic titles, and in pre-Conquest times roughly a fifth were slaves (Donald 1997).[10] Still, there was nothing like a state, no apparatus of rule. Free adults did not issue commands to one another, let alone commands

---

8.   For other examples of punishment for laughing: Boas (1897: 525–26, 642).

9.   Since they were obliged to compensate the owners later for any property damage, the office was actually rather expensive. For Goldman, the Fool Dancers are "lesser forms of war dancers. The *nutlmatl* represent the madness, the wildness, and the obscene side of war and destruction" (1975: 118–19).

10. One role of the Fools prior to conquest had been to sacrifice and carve up a slave for the Man-Eater (Boas 1897: 339).

backed up by threats of force.[11] Ordinarily there was nothing like a "tribal police." Yet between November and February, when a whole series of "secret society" initiations spilled over into a "Winter Ceremonial" season of dances and potlatches, the authority of the Fools seems to have spilled over as well.

Unlike the Californian clowns, they could not give arbitrary orders in their own right; they were strictly deputies of the Man-Eater, who alone could issue commands.[12] We are already beginning to see a process of division of sovereignty. The right of command in the Northwest Coast belonged properly to "supernatural power" (divinity in the undifferentiated sense);[13] when that divinity manifested itself in human form, it was as the crazed Hamatsa, lusting for human flesh. But the Hamatsa mainly just made inarticulate noises; it was incapable of ordering anyone to do anything other than fetching food. The Man-Eater in this context is almost like a stranger-king *manqué*, a pure force of vital energy bursting into the world of the living, needing to be tamed; with the exception that, once domesticated, his sovereignty is destroyed and he is rendered once again an ordinary mortal. The Fools, in turn, seem to be stripped of any autonomous power of command, and so simply act as enforcers.

The Kwakiutl (like the Pueblo) are also already halfway to the situation described by Lowie for so many Plains societies, where throughout the summer months—a time when otherwise scattered bands gathered together first for the great bison hunts, then for the Sun Dance rituals—certain clans or warrior societies would be assigned temporary police powers, allowing them to keep discipline in the hunt, impose arbitrary resolutions to disputes, and enforce their judgments by the destruction of property, beatings, and even in extreme

---

11. In fact, they did not even really have chiefs.

     Although titleholders are usually referred to as "chiefs" these men and women were not political office-holders as such. Indeed, we might say that political office-holding as we understand it did not exist on the Northwest Coast. Titleholders led or were important in their kinship or residential group. In many winter villages, the heads of the component villages were ranked, but though this gave the "village chief" considerable prestige and some ritual authority, it bestowed little or no power or authority to command in what is usually thought of as the political arena. (Donald 1997: 26)

12. "When a Hamatsa wishes to obtain food he may send anyone hunting or fishing, and his orders must be obeyed" (Boas 1890: 64).

13. So in Boas' later account, speeches at the Winter Ceremonial make frequent invocations of following "orders given by the supernatural power" (1930: 97, 124, 126–27, 166, 172), the latter apparently referring to the divine generically.

cases killing of recalcitrants, even though, during the rest of the year, disputes were resolved through mediation and the last summer's police no longer had any more power than anybody else (Lowie 1927: 103–04; 1948b: 18–19; cf. 1909: 79, 82, 89, 96–98; 1948a: 40, 162, 325–26, 350; MacLeod 1937; Provinse 1937: 344–53; Llewellyn, Hoebel, and Adamson 1941). At all times, ultimate authority in such societies still rested with councils of elders. But in the ritual season, "police" or "soldiers" could act with a fair degree of discretion and impunity—even though there was always a system of rotation to ensure no individual or group held such powers two years running. There were some traces here of the association of police power with clowns and contraries—in writing of his own original fieldwork on the Assiniboine, for instance, Lowie observed that some insisted their own Fool Society used to hold police powers in the summer months (1909: 72)—but ended up concluding that despite frequent convergences between "clowning" and "police functions" across the Plains, there was no systematic relationship between the two.[14] In fact, warrior societies, ritual fools or contraries, and temporary police associations seem to have largely split apart, and there no longer seems to have been any sense in which those assigned police powers embodied deities of any sort.[15]

We can observe, then, three stages of a logical progression:

1. (California) clowns as embodiments of divine power, with a moral logic external and contrary to society, wielding arbitrary powers of command and punishment, but only during the course of rituals.
2. (Northwest Coast) Fools as delegates of divine power, with a moral logic external and contrary to society, wielding arbitrary police powers during ceremonies that extended across the ritual season.
3. (Plains) temporary police societies, no longer divine or external, but wielding arbitrary powers of enforcement delegated to them over the course of the ritual season, but not limited to the rituals themselves.

---

14. "Clownish behavior and police functions likewise occur in varying combinations and cannot be taken to define any one type of organization of the Plains Indians" (Lowie 1909: 98).

15. "During the Sun Dance police were selected for the preservation of order by the Dakota, Crow, Assiniboine, Blackfoot, Sansi, Iowa, Plains-Cree, and the Kansa; among some of the groups these police also supervised the conduct of the dance ritual" (Provinse 1937: 348). Often in that specific context their power was delegated by the officiating priest or master of ceremonies, but they do not seem to have been themselves in any sense an extension of metahuman beings.

I should emphasize that this is a logical progression, and in no sense an attempt at historical reconstruction. The actual course of events, in any given instance, was likely far more complicated.[16] Still, it represents one way that sovereign power could, as it were, burst through the its frame, even while still being carefully contained within the ritual season in such a way that it could not, as in the modern state, suffuse and inform the entirety of everyday existence.

In fact, why it did not was precisely Lowie's problem. Lowie's 1948 Huxley Lecture, "Some aspects of political organization among the American Aborigines" (1948b), was specifically concerned with why states had largely failed to develop in the Americas, and concludes that indigenous Americans had created institutional arrangements to ensure that they did not. If this sounds similar to Pierre Clastres' argument in *Society against the state* (1977), that chiefship among most North and South American societies was constructed in such a way that arbitrary, sovereign power—authority that could not be questioned since it was ultimately backed up by force—could not possibly develop out of it, there is a reason. Clastres' argument was directly taken from Lowie.[17] Clastres even ended his own essay in the same way as Lowie's Huxley Lecture: by concluding that since secular chiefship was designed to prevent the emergence of powers of command, the latter could only have emerged from the religious sphere, from prophecy, or some similar appeal to exterior cosmic authority (Lowie 1948b: 21–2; P. Clastres 1977: 183–86).

As far as I know, no one has really developed a theory of the prophetic origin of the state. Presumably this is because there's so little evidence to support it. One of the few to have taken the argument seriously, Fernando Santos-Granero (1993), makes the obvious point that this kind of charismatic authority is notoriously unstable, and that even in those places where it does seem to have become institutionalized, such as among the Amuesha of the Peruvian Amazon,

---

16. Morphologically, the Plains societies, with their extreme seasonal variation and annual concentration for hunting of megafauna, probably are (despite their limited reliance on agriculture) if anything more analogous for Paleolithic societies across much of Eurasia, while the Californians and Northwest Coast societies would, at least in comparison, be more Mesolithic. But such analogies are always extremely inexact.

17. In his first exposition of the idea in *L'Homme*, Clastres does acknowledge the debt, noting for instance that his list of chiefly functions is taken directly from Lowie's 1948 essay (Clastres 1962: 53, 55, 58), but the relationship has been ignored by Clastres' later avatars (with a few exceptions: e.g., Santos-Granero 1993; Wengrow and Graeber 2015). What Lowie called "libertarianism," Clastres referred to as "anarchism," but in the context of their times, the two words meant pretty much the same thing.

it leads to a kind of constant *gumsa/gumlao*-like rise and collapse of priestly do-mains.[18] While there are examples of prophets founding states (Muhammad is an obvious example), such events are surprisingly rare in human history.

Still, the insight does ring true in a certain very broad sense. The principal example Clastres himself invoked were the Tupí-Guaraní prophets who up-rooted whole communities to go off in search of a "land without evil," in which the basic dilemmas of death and reproduction would be finally resolved and the sundering of the worlds of gods and men undone (see also H. Clastres 1995). This kind of utopian vision does, indeed, seem to lie behind the very project of creating kingdoms and, later, states. I have myself noted the analogy of the role of Nuer prophets, and the Shilluk *reth*: one might say that where prophets fore-tell a total resolution of the great dilemmas of human existence in the future, divine kings embody a partial resolution of those same dilemmas in the present, their courts constituting a kind of paradise.

Does this mean that divine kingship represents the final explosion of the divine into the human domain, a kind of final shattering of its ritual, or seasonal, containment? I think this is true only to a very limited degree. Ordinarily, we are speaking only of a frail and diminutive sort of paradise.

To illustrate, let me turn to one final North American example, the Natchez kingdom of what's now southern Louisiana. It is considered the only genuinely unambiguous example of divine kingship north of the Rio Grande.

The divine kingship of the Natchez

In 1739, the Jesuit missionary Father Maturin Le Petit put forth the argu-ment that the Natchez, who called themselves Théoloël or "People of the Sun," were the only American people to have a system of beliefs worthy of the name "religion."[19] Natchez religion, he observed, centered on two enormous earthen platforms that dominated their Great Village; on top of one of them was a Tem-ple, atop the other, the house of their ruler, known as the Great Sun, capable of holding perhaps four thousand people—that is, the entire Natchez population at the time. A spacious plaza lay between. The Temple contained carved images

---

18. Santos-Granero suggests one might see the emergence of states when the prophets ally with autonomous warrior bands, and become self-reproducing lineages. But again, this is basically speculation.

19. It would appear that "Natchez" was really just the name of what the French called the "*grand village*" in which the Sun resided.

and an eternal flame, as well as baskets holding the charred remains of the former rulers and their servants; common people brought offerings to ancestors buried within, but aside from four temple guardians, only members of the royal family were allowed to enter:

> The Chief of this Nation, who knows nothing on earth more dignified than himself, takes the title of brother of the Sun. To enable them better to converse together, they raise a mound of artificial soil, on which they build his cabin, which is of the same construction as the Temple. The door fronts the East, and every morning the great Chief honors by his presence the rising of his elder brother, and salutes him with many howlings as soon as he appears above the horizon. Then he gives orders that they shall light his calumet; he makes him an offering of the first three puffs which he draws; afterwards raising his hand above his head, and turning from the East to the West, he shows him the direction which he must take in his course . . . . (Le Petit 1848: 269–70)

Le Petit's description is matched by many others. We have multiple accounts of the protocol surrounding the Great Sun, as he was ordinarily called, and his close relatives, also called Suns. "Their subjects, and even the chiefs of the villages, never approach them but they salute them three times, setting up a cry, which is a kind of howling"—that is, hailing the Great Sun exactly as he himself greets the Sun each morning. "They do the same when they retire, and they retire walking backwards" (Charlevoix 1763: 315). None might eat with the Sun, nor touch any plate or vessel he had touched; his meals were meticulously choreographed; when he left his house, carried on his warriors' shoulders on a litter, his subjects had to prostrate themselves and call out when he passed.

Similar but less stringent etiquette surrounded the Tattooed Serpent, the Great Sun's brother and military commander, and the White Woman, his eldest sister, whose child (the Natchez being matrilineal) was to be the next Great Sun. All three, they emphasized, had the power of life and death over their subjects. "As soon as anyone has had the misfortune to displease any of them, they order their guards, whom they call *allouez*, to kill him. 'Go and rid me of that dog,' say they, and they are immediately obeyed" (ibid.). The Suns could also help themselves to their subjects' possessions.

> The submissiveness of the savages to their chief, who commands them with the most despotic power, is extreme. They obey him in everything he may command

them. When he speaks they howl nine times by way of applause and to show
him their satisfaction, and if he demands the life of any one of them, he comes
himself to present his head. (Dumont in Swanton 1911: 104)

Similarly, Le Petit:

The people blindly obey the least wish of their great chief. They look upon him
as absolute master not only of their property but also of their lives, and not one
of them would dare refuse him his head. (1848: 271)

The Suns were divine in every sense of the term. They were literally gods—descendants of two children of the Sun, a radiant brother and sister, who had come
to earth to establish peace by creating the institutions of government—and they
were also divine in the broader sense that they could act with absolute arbitrariness and impunity. The only limit, in fact, on the actions of Suns is that they appear to have been forbidden to do violence toward other Suns: members of the
royal family, who numbered perhaps twenty, could not be harmed under any circumstances. One unusual result was that royals, and apparently some of the lower
grades of nobility as well, could only marry commoners—since a Sun's wives
or husbands, along with their servants and retainers, all had to be put to death
as part of the obloquies at their funeral, and this would be impossible if they
had themselves been of equal rank. The result was a complex system of sinking
status: while the children of female Suns remained Suns, children of male Suns
descended one rank down each generation (to "Noble," then "Honored" status)
until their great-grandchildren became commoners again. The actual dynamics
of this system (it was complicated by the fact it was also possible to move up
ranks by accomplishment in war) have kept anthropologists busy for generations
trying to figure out exactly how it could work in practice, without the top three
classes eventually running out of commoners to marry (on the "Natchez paradox," see MacLeod 1924; Josselin de Jong 1928; Haas 1939; Davis 1941; Hart
1943; Quimby 1946; Tooker 1963; J. L. Fisher 1964; Mason 1964; Brain 1971;
D. R. White, Murdock, and Scaglion 1971; Knight 1990; Lorenz 2000: 153–57).

The technicalities need not concern us.[20] Suffice it to say the divine quality of even male Suns was passed on, but only to a certain attenuated degree.

---

20. In fact there's no particular reason to assume Noble and Honored classes could
    only marry commoners in the first place (MacLeod 1924; Tooker 1953; Mason

Scandalized French observers noted how women of the ruling matrilineage could take lovers as they pleased, but order their commoner husbands' heads be clapped against blocks of wood if they so much as suspected them of infidelity; such husbands, one observed, took on the air of masters among the numerous household servants but stooped like slaves in the presence of their wives, on whose death they would, like the rest of the household, be strangled. All members of the royal family were assigned servants at birth, many culled from infants born on the same day, who were expected to form part of their household in life, and accompany their master or mistress in death, along with any "voluntary slaves" (Swanton 1911: 100; Milne 2015: 38) who joined the household afterward.

This seems as close to absolute sovereignty as one might imagine. There seems no check at all on royal power. But if one reads the original sources carefully, cracks in this façade begin to show. Take the word "Stinkard." In the anthropological literature, the commoner class is regularly referred to as "the Stinkards," since the French sources regularly use the term, but it turns out this word was just one of many ways the nobles expressed contempt for ordinary people when speaking with each other. It was never used before the commoners themselves:

> The Natchez Nation is composed of nobility and people. The people are called in their language Michi-Michi-Quipy, which signifies Puant ("Stinkard"), a name, however, which offends them, and which no one dares to pronounce before them, for it would put them in a very bad humor. The Stinkards have a language entirely different from the Nobility,[21] to whom they are submissive in the last degree. (Du Pratz 1774: 328, translation after Swanton 1911: 108)

"Submissive in the last degree," that is, unless one used a word they didn't like.

Such apparently contradictory statements are commonplace in early European accounts of distant kingdoms. One encounters them in descriptions

---

1964), or that "Honored" were a class at all, for that matter. For what it's worth, I find Knight's (1990) argument that the Natchez system is a transformation of a ranked exogamous clan system of a sort that had likely been common within the Mississippian civilization, and Lorenz's reconstruction (2010: 153–57) of how the system might have worked, largely convincing. The phenomenon of sinking status will be discussed in greater detail in the final part of this essay.

21. This does not appear to have been true, though there were certain differences in vocabulary.

of courts in Asia, Africa, and the Americas alike. In much the same way that European observers would often assert that a given people "go naked"—and then go on to describe their clothes—they would often first insist on the unlimited, "despotic" power of their king—and then go on to elaborate its (often very considerable) limits. In the case of the Thécloëls, the confusion has caused most recent authorities (e.g., Hudson 1978: 210; Lorenz 2000: 158–59; Balvay 2008; Milne 2015: 33–38) to conclude that French observers—who were, after all, loyal subjects of their own Sun King, Louis XIV—were simply confused by unfamiliar forms of deference, and that their assertions of the Great Sun's absolute power had almost nothing to do with the Natchez at all, but were mere projections of their own absolutist monarchy.

This is not entirely untrue. Certainly, in purely political terms, the Great Sun's power *was* sharply limited.[22] War councils would often ignore his advice; most of the six subordinate districts—even the three that had members of the royal family imposed as governors—pursued independent trade and foreign policies that often completely contradicted the king's; a royal order to turn over rebels might simply be refused (Lorenz 1997). On the other hand, accounts of arbitrary executions at whim within the king's "Great Village," or of retainers willingly offering themselves up for sacrifice at the death of a member of the royal family, do not appear to be fabricated. George Milne is probably right to speak of the French being overawed by the spectacle of an elaborate Mississippian "monarchical theatre" (2015: 37); much of what happened in the Great Village did have a theatrical quality—except, of course, it was the kind of theatre where, if a character died, they actually did die.

As a result, the royal village grew smaller and smaller:

> The great Village of the Natchez is at present reduced to a very few Cabins. The Reason which I heard for this is that the Savages, from whom the Great Chief has the Right to take all they have, get as far away from him as they can; and therefore, many Villages of this Nation have been formed at some Distance from this. (Charlevoix 1763: 312)

This might help explain the contradiction between reports of extreme obeisance, and the royals' reluctance to use the term "Stinkard" in commoners' presence. Foreign observers almost never got outside the Great Village, a place largely

---

22. But, of course, so was that of Louis XIV.

reduced to Suns, Nobles, and their servants. The only commoners they were likely to encounter were the royals' own wives and husbands, or the visiting delegations that would periodically appear to offer contributions of choice meats and delicacies—neither of whom it would have been wise for the Suns to gratuitously humiliate.

Archaeology confirms that not only were the other settlements larger than the "Grand Village," they were actually wealthier (Lorenz 1997: 106–8; 2000: 168–72). What's more, relations between center and periphery often seem to have taken the form of ritualized hostility. On the one hand, we are told that "relatives of the Sun regard the other savages as dirt" (Swanton 1911: 100); on the other, we find descriptions of how the common people, in their role of warriors, would every year pretend to ambush, capture, and prepare to kill the king, until a second mock war party intervened to rescue him (Du Pratz 1774: 319–20). Afterward, those same warriors would combine to cultivate a special field of maize whose harvest the female Suns would subsequently mimic stealing.[23]

What sort of power, then, *did* the Great Sun have? And how do we characterize such a polity? Most contemporary literature is of little help here. Even those who see the French accounts as largely a projection of their own absolutism are content, insofar as they take on the question at all, to fall back on the evolutionist language favored by most contemporary archaeologists and describe it as a "complex chiefdom" (Lorenz 1997; Milne 2015: 6, 10)—which doesn't really tell you much other than that they think the Natchez should be considered one notch lower than a state. Not only is this unedifying, it tends to obscure the key feature of arrangements like the Shilluk, or Natchez, or even for most of its history the Merina kingdom: that the question of the king's sovereign power (i.e., his absolute ability to impose his will in any way he wished to

---

23. The mock battle was ostensibly a reenactment of a historical event when the Great Sun actually was nearly captured by an enemy war party, but it's hard to read it as anything but a reminder of how much his life is ultimately in his warriors' hands. Du Pratz provides a description of two feasts; this one, and a harvest festival, of which we have several other accounts as well (compiled in Swanton 1911: 113–23). The first feast, in March, corresponded to the equinox, and maize planting, and the ultimate victory of the white-plumed warriors of the Great Sun over the red-plumed "enemy" warriors led by the war leader, the Tattooed Serpent, no doubt also implied a transition to the half of the year marked by agricultural activity. Warriors then go on to plant and tend the special field for the king, which is harvested in July, and female Suns pretend to run away with the crop. For present purposes, though, I only wish to stress the element of ritualized hostility.

when he was physically present) and the question of his political power (i.e., his ability to influence events when he was not physically present) are completely separate. The first, kings' ability to place themselves beyond and outside the laws which they uphold, was always absolute in principle (however much it might not be in practice).[24] If a king cannot, at least in theory, kill his subjects without reason, he can hardly be said to be a king at all. But it is notoriously difficult for monarchs to wield such power in situations where they are not physically there.[25] The Great Sun, then, seems to have been in a situation quite similar to the Shilluk *reth*: largely confined to a peculiarly constituted village largely consisting of his wives and attendants (and in his case, his brother and sisters and their spouses and attendants), presumably along with the motley assortment of criminals, orphans, and runaways who ordinarily collect around such courts, inside which his whim was law, outside which his ability to control the course of events was almost entirely dependent on his guile and political savvy.

The Great Sun's capacity to bring health, prosperity, and fertility to his people, on the other hand, was entirely independent of that political influence. In fact, there is even some reason to believe it might have been seen as dependent on its containment. According to one account, the secret holy of holies within the Great Temple was not the eternal fire, but a stone image which was considered to be the petrified body of the original lawgiver. Apparently that original Sun who had "formerly been sent to this place to be the master of the earth, had become so terrible that he made men die merely by his look; [so] in order to prevent it he had a cabin made for himself into which he entered and had himself made into a stone statue" (St. Cosme, in Swanton 1911: 172; 1946: 779), a secret which was known only to the Suns and their closest confidants. In

---

24. It is surely significant, for example, that the laws Du Pratz was told were conveyed by the founder of the kingdom—"we must never kill anyone but in defense of our own lives; we must never know any other woman besides our own; we must never take anything that belongs to another" (1774: 314)—seem precisely those most likely to be ignored by the Great Sun and his close relatives. I should emphasize that in reality, no one ever really has absolute power in this sense: there are always lines one cannot cross, at least without eventually being destroyed for it. But kings quite regularly insist that they do, in principle, have this power anyway.

25. Even Tudor kings had trouble with this: their power was so caught up with their physical being that in order to get subjects to accept delegated authority they often had to rely on members of court who were known to be in the most intimate possible physical contact, such as the famous Groom of the Stool of Henry VIII (Starkey 1977).

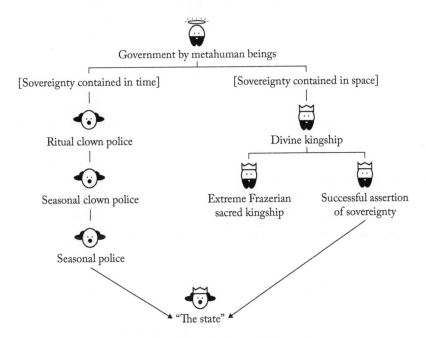

Figure 1. The "declownification" of sovereignty.

other words, the Great Sun, who regularly interceded with his ancestors in the Temple to bring the powers of life to his people, also kept the potential deadly powers of those ancestors contained in precisely the way that his people sought to contain his own deadly powers. Again, much as among Shilluk, the divisions between heaven and earth were maintained, however tenuously, by the maintenance on every level of at least potential hostility.

* * *

While the Natchez situation might at first seem a far cry from the kind of careful circumscription of police powers we saw in California, the Northwest Coast, and societies of the Plains, on another level, all of these can be seen as structural variations on a single principle. In every case, sovereign power—the power to violate the terms of the ordinary moral order, to create rules, give unquestionable, unaccountable orders backed up by threat of punishment—is held by humans only insofar as it is an embodiment, extension, refraction, or delegate of metahuman beings. In each case, too, the contexts in which such power can be exercised are carefully defined, and—since marking something off as sacred is always a way of creating, preserving, or maintaining its power—this circumscription itself plays a role in generating the power of which sovereignty is a practical expression.

Seen this way, the difference between the Kwakiutl and the Théoloël is perfectly straightforward. The Kwakiutl contain divine sovereignty in time, giving the Fools police powers during the ritual season, but not otherwise. The Théoloël, in contrast, contain divine sovereignty in space, limiting it to the theatrical arena of the Great Village and the area immediately surrounding the physical body of the king. If the Plains societies' seasonal police represent a partial secularization of the first, then more familiar forms of kingship might equally be said to be a partial secularization of the second. Yet this secularization is always partial. Kings are always sacred, even when they are not in any sense divine.

ON THE CONSTITUTIVE WAR BETWEEN KING AND PEOPLE

> The sovereign is not bound by the laws.
>
> Ulpian

> Government is civil war.
>
> Anselme Bellegarrigue

In "The divine kingship of the Shilluk" (chapter 2 in this volume), I suggested that monarchies—and, by extension, modern states—are marked by a kind of primordial, constitutive war between king and people, one that is prior, even, to Carl Schmitt's purportedly foundational distinction between friend and enemy. It is constitutive in the sense that it is through this (antagonistic) relation that both king and people can be said to come into being to begin with. This is why even when a kingdom is founded on purely voluntary arrangements (as many do appear to be), it is nonetheless framed as conquest, or even, as Marshall Sahlins observes (chapter 3), the mutual conquest ("encompassment') of king and people.[26]

In stranger-kingship, one might say that the "social peace," the truce in that war that makes stable kingdoms possible, takes the form of those diarchical

---

26. It is worth recalling that immediately after the passage when the Israelites tell Samuel they wish to have a king "like other people," the prophet warns them, prophetically, that they'll soon come to see their relation as adversarial (Samuel 8: 11–19).

arrangements so beautifully described in Sahlins' essays on the BaKongo and Mexica in this volume (chapters 3 and 4, respectively). In these, royal control over the lives of subjects is typically matched by popular control over the land and its products, with the indigenous people represented by earth priests or other autochthonous authorities with ritual power over the soil. Still, I think the idiom of war between king and people draws on and is expressive of an even deeper structural reality—the ability to step outside the moral order so as to partake of the kind of power capable of creating such an order is always by definition an act of violence, and can only be maintained as such. Transgression is not in itself necessarily a violent act. The kind of transgression that becomes the basis for a power of command over others necessarily must be. It is a form of compulsion that lies behind any possible accountability. This is also the deep truth about the modern state whose disturbing implications Schmitt ([1922] 2005)—the German jurist credited with creating the legal basis for the Nazi concentration camps—was perhaps the first to work out in a systematic fashion. To say a state is "sovereign" is ultimately to define its highest authorities as beyond moral accountability. This not just war; it is total war. Insofar as the sovereign intends to apply such compulsion to an entire population within a given territory, it ultimately must always be. (The only limitation on such total war is that the sovereign cannot wipe out the entire population, or his sovereignty would itself cease to exist.) Hence, as I remarked at the end of the Shilluk essay, the tendency for modern states to frame their greatest projects in terms of some sort of unwinnable war: the war on poverty, crime, drugs, terror, and so forth.

Sometimes, this structural conflict can become explicit: Simon Simonse's (1992: 204; 2005: 84) memorable image of the rainmaker king, armed with a rifle, single-handedly defending himself against his outraged subjects being only one dramatic case in point. History is full of occasions when things actually did come down to weapons: massacres, insurrections, mutinies, and reigns of terror. There is always a continuum, too, between rites of rebellion, actual rebellions, and outright revolutions; as we have come to learn (e.g., Berce 1976), almost any of these things can unexpectedly flip into any of the others. I'm hardly saying anything new here. All this has been endlessly debated and discussed by historians for many years; but once again, the perspectives and materials assembled in this volume suggest that war is by no means the only way that the structural conflict can work itself out. And even when it does, armed conflict, even between nations, always involves rules, and one might say (as I have argued for unarmed street actions: Graeber 2007c, 2009) that in any war, there are always two levels of conflict: within the frame (in which each party tries to win), and about the frame (in which they argue about the rules of engagement; ultimately, about what winning even means). Here, sovereignty is, again, one of those points where such frames implode; where the two levels collapse into one another. When a divine king breaks the rules of conventional morality, marries his sister or massacres his brothers, this is never just a political move (though it might also be a savvy political move), it is always simultaneously a metapolitical move, a way of shifting the frame of reference upward to a level where it is possible to rule over—and hence fight over—the nature of the rules themselves.

I understand this might seem confusing. My distinction between divine and sacred kingship is actually meant to provide a way to navigate this often vexed territory. So clarification might be helpful. In proposing that we apply the term "divine kings" to monarchs who act like gods—that is, with arbitrariness and impunity—rather than those who are actually considered to "be" gods, I am in no way suggesting that kings are never considered to be gods (as we'll see, some certainly are), or even that, historically, the attribution of divine status, when it does occur, must be considered some sort of secondary elaboration on certain forms of practice. I do think Hocart was basically right to say royal powers were ultimately modeled on and seen to be derived from those of gods; even if I think the devolution was likely to have proceeded in a far more circuitous fashion than he would likely have imagined.

So that's what I'm not saying. What I *am* saying is this: if you look at the literature on divine kingship as we know it from the anthropological record— that is, for roughly the last five hundred years—what is really striking is the degree to which there is no systematic relation between the *theology* of kingship—that is, the degree to which a monarch is or is not considered to be a god (or the avatar or incarnation of a god, or priest, prophet, or earthly representative of a god, etc.)—and the degree to which they *behave* like one. Let us compare the Shilluk *reth* and Ganda *kabaka in* this context. The *reth* is explicitly considered to be the embodiment of a divine being: Nyikang. But while he is able to wield arbitrary and questioned power in principle, his subjects are careful to ensure he has virtually no opportunity to do so in practice. In Buganda, in contrast, even members of the *kabaka*'s family insist he's in no sense a deity and just a human being. Yet he still commits outrageous "exploits" that place him beyond mor(t) al society, still is able to issue commands and order executions with arbitrariness and impunity, even, like some Jovian thunder god casting lightning, to stand at the door of his palace with a rifle and pick off random subjects on the street.[27]

The two examples, by the way, weren't chosen entirely at random. The contrast between the Shilluk and Ganda kingships has long puzzled outside observers. Sir James Frazer himself was befuddled by it. His discovery of the Shilluk in the 1910s led him to believe most of his boldest hypotheses about the divine nature of kingship had been spectacularly confirmed; excited, he sent one of his few students, a certain Reverend Roscoe, to investigate the Ganda— then quite famous in England owing to testimonies of Speke and Burton—as a second likely case. The results were endlessly frustrating. True, Roscoe found, the *kabaka* was occasionally referred to as a *lubaale* or "god," but typically when he was doing something outrageous that only gods could otherwise get away with, or directly challenging the gods by raiding their temples and "plundering their women, cattle, and goats" (Roscoe and Kaggwa in Ray 1991: 49). But the *kabaka* was rendered no cult, and even the periodic ritual massacres over which he presided were never framed in sacrificial terms. What's more, royal histories affirmed that those kings who became too audacious in defying the gods were invariably destroyed (Kenny 1988: 611). Despite heroic efforts to shoehorn the results into his theoretical model, Frazer found it simply wouldn't fit. He ended up so frustrated he briefly came near to abandoning the idea of divine kingship entirely (Ray 1991: 51–52).

In purely sociological terms, the difference between the two kingdoms is obvious. The *kabaka* might have been far more powerful than the Shilluk *reth*, but unlike the latter, he also had to contend with an entrenched and jealous priestly class who had no intention of allowing him into their pantheon. As a result, he was a divine king in every sense except that of being formally recognized as such. But cases like these only serve to underline the point that, when it comes to divine kingship, questions of explicit (as opposed to tacit) theology are at best secondary—and, anyway, are likely to be matters of debate rather than consensus, even in kingdoms which remain entirely outside the influence of Islam, Christianity, Buddhism, or, for that matter, secular republicanism or Marxism-Leninism.

---

27. On the debate on the *kabaka*'s divinity, see Roscoe (1911); Irstam (1944); Gale (1956); Ingham (1958: 17); Richards (1964); Southwold (1967); Kenny (1988); Ray (1991: 39–50); Wrigley (1996: 17, 126–28); Claessen (2015: 11).

* * *

Insofar as sovereignty is precisely where the frames ordinarily separating ritual and politics, human and metahuman, immanent and transcendent, tend to collapse, this is much as one should expect. It is one of the misfortunes of humanity, I have suggested, that even the most awful crimes—mass murder foremost among them—will tend to take on at least a potentially numinous quality, and can, under the right circumstances at least, be made to seem divine. But just as most profane acts can be turned to cosmological purposes, so can the elaboration of ritual itself become a political weapon.

Hence my distinction between divine and sacred kingship. Each, one might say, crosses the same line in an opposite direction.[28] Kings will try to turn acts of arbitrary violence into tokens of divinity; those who wish to control them will try to impose ever-more elaborate ritual restrictions that recognize them as sacred beings, but, at the same time, make it increasingly difficult for them to impose their will in arbitrary ways. If one conceives the long war between king and people instead as a strategic game (I know I am multiplying metaphors here, but I can only beg the reader's indulgence), we can say that kings will, generally speaking, attempt to increase their divinity, and the people, to render them more sacred. From this perspective, many of the classic institutions of divine kingship, including most of those made famous by Frazer, could be seen as moves, gambits on a conceptual chessboard, with the sovereign attempting to maneuver his way out of the various forces marshaled to contain him. Even the emergence of what we call "the state" might be seen as just one possible outcome of this game.

Normally, the sides are not entirely mismatched. But the lopsided cases are perhaps the most revealing, because they give a sense of what's ultimately at stake. Let me divide the remainder of this essay, then, into two sections, one which describes what things look like when a monarch is definitively checkmated, the other, the new sorts of problems that arise when a monarch definitively wins.

---

28. Just to be absolutely clear, let me provide an example of what I'm speaking of in each case. An example of profane acts turned to cosmological purposes might be a situation where a ruler kills his brothers and marries his sister as an act of simple political expedience, but where it nonetheless contributes to the sense that a king is a metahuman being. Or where a coup d'état becomes a ritual sacrifice. An example of ritual becoming a political weapon might be one where a principle that the king's blood must never be spilled might not prevent assassination (he can always be strangled), but has significant effects on his ability to lead his troops in war.

When kings lose: The tyranny of abstraction

> All these antique fancies clustered, all these cobwebs of the brain were spun about the path of the old king, the human god, who enmeshed in them like a fly in the toils of a spider, could hardly stir a limb for the threads of custom.
>
> Sir James Frazer, *The golden bough*

> Thus also the taboo ceremonial of kings is nominally an expression of the highest veneration and a means of guarding them; actually it is the punishment for their elevation, the revenge which their subjects take upon them.
>
> Sigmund Freud, *Totem and taboo*

> Often enough it is difficult to draw the line between political and sacral king-murders.
>
> Sture Lagencrantz, *The sacred king in Africa*

We have already seen one vivid example of hobbled kings in the Shilluk *reths*, who, foiled in their periodic efforts to create an administrative apparatus, ended up largely at the mercy of their wives and local village chiefs, surrounded by "royal executioners" whose ultimate task was to kill them. Since the Shilluk represent the closest approximation yet documented for what might be termed Frazerian sacred kingship, it suggests the latter might itself be the form (or at least one form) checkmate might take.

I will refer to this as "adverse sacralization"—the imposition of ritual restrictions on a ruler as a way to control, contain, or reduce his political power.

It might be useful to examine the defining features of African sacred kingship (Irstam 1944; Lagercrantz 1944, 1950; de Heusch 1981, 1982a, 1997), to see how many fit this model. It began with Sture Lagercrantz outlining a fairly simple list of common features—taboos on mobility, regicide, and incest—but has since been expanded to something that might be summarized as follows:

1. *The king is a sacred monster*, exterior to society, often seen as a powerful witch or sorcerer, a wielder of terrible transgressive power. This power expresses itself through a fundamental break with kinship morality, either
   a. some form of *incest* (typically brother–sister marriage, real or symbolic), or
   b. some act of *cannibalism* (real or symbolic).

2. *The king's health and vitality is bound up with the health, prosperity, and fertility of the kingdom* (droughts and natural disasters being considered signs of the king's sin or infirmity); this leads to:

3. *The king is bound by multiple taboos*: for example, he is forbidden to cross water, see large bodies of water, or even in a few cases touch water; these restrictions always include severe limits on mobility that culminate in complete seclusion.

4. *The king cannot die a natural death*: some kings are sacrificed after fixed terms of four or seven years; even if they are not, if injured, in failing health or strength, or in a state of ritual impurity, or if some disaster (failure in war, plagues, etc.) demonstrates fading powers that endanger the kingdom, the king may be required to commit suicide or, more often, be secretly put to death.

Most of these seem to be just local versions of more general principles of kingship already discussed. The first is the particular form which the principle of sovereignty, or divine kingship, takes in this particular tradition. The second, the idea that sovereign power is directly linked with the health, fertility, and prosperity of the population, exists almost everywhere where there is a king or king-like figure; Frazer compiled endless examples, and the connection can be observed from China to the court of Charlemagne (Oakley 2006: 93). Even in the United States, one of the best indexes of whether a sitting president will be reelected is the number and intensity of tornados during his term of office (Healy, Malhotra, and Mo 2010; Healy and Malhotra 2013). The third is sacred kingship itself. By which logic, the fourth, the actual killing of the king, is, as Frazer also hinted, simply the culmination of his adverse sacralization.

The latter would be consonant with the Shilluk material as well, where kings become transcendent at the moment when popular hatred becomes the most intense.

René Girard, of course, provides a psychoanalytic analysis of why rancor and sacralization coincide: the community projects its internal hatreds onto a single figure who is first reviled and destroyed, then, in an abrupt reversal, comes to be an object of adoration in implicit recognition of his or her role, as scapegoat, in creating social unity. (Christ is his primary example.) Much of the recent debate on king-killing has indeed turned on the scapegoat principle: to what extent is the king seen as taking on the sins and transgressions of his people, and somehow disposing of them, either through purification rituals, or through his own seclusion or death (Simonse 1992, 2005; de Heusch 1997, 2005b; Quigley 2000; Scubla 2002, 2003, 2005). The critical question has become: Could it be said that the "exploits" or transgressions that establish the king as beyond morality also make him a potential scapegoat in waiting, so that, when things go well, he can be as a transcendent being, but when they do not, he becomes once again a simple criminal, and the legitimate object of rebellion, challenge, or sacrifice? Some such dynamic does often appear to be at play. But again, it's just as possible to see scapegoating simply as an inevitable consequence of the fact that kings are always both sacred figures embodying their people's unity, and politicians. One can just as easily say, "this is just how hardball politics will necessarily work itself out under a regime of divine kingship," than to see in it any dark hidden secret of the human soul.

One thing seems clear: there is simply no systematic relation between sovereignty, scapegoating, regicide, and ascriptions of divinity. In the Equatorian societies described by Simonse (2005), rainmakers were often killed during droughts by outraged mobs, after a long game of bluff and maneuver. They were clearly scapegoated, but they were in no sense gods. Many weren't even kings. At the other extreme, in South Africa, the Luvale "rain-queen" was very much considered a divine being in human form. She had to be physically perfect, and she was considered impervious to human woes and ailments; she never became ill and could not die of natural causes; she was therefore expected to, and apparently did, discreetly end her own life by taking poison after roughly sixty years on the throne (Krige and Krige 1943: 165–67).[29] Still,

> ritual suicide is not conceived to have any relation to the welfare of the country. People do not say the country will suffer if the physical powers of the queen fail. But ritual suicide does elevate the queen to a divinity; only by her act, not because of susceptibility to the weaknesses of man, can she die. (Krige and Krige 1943: 167)

---

29. "Among the Lovedu, tradition decrees that the queen shall have no physical defect and must poison herself, not when she is old, but at the end of the fourth initiation (*vudiga*) of her reign" (ibid.: 166), but in fact this was when she was old, since *vudiga* were "held by the whole tribe every twelve to fifteen years," though "an interval of twenty years is not considered extraordinary" (ibid.: 114)—so a period of four *vudiga* was minimally forty-eight years and maximally eighty. In fact, at the time the Kriges were writing, there had only been three queens in the last hundred and forty years (ibid.: 165).

The Luvale rain-queen, then, was in no sense a scapegoat. Neither, however, did she wield anything in the way of sovereign power. Among the Rukuba of Nigeria, the king's sanctity is preserved when, every fourteen years, any impurity affecting him is passed on to an old man who is expelled from the community and lives as a beggar for seven years, then dies (Muller 1980; 1990: 59). That king actually governs. Among the Ewe of Togo, the "king" does not govern at all, but is himself reduced to a scapegoat; banished to a forest on accession, there he must remain, celibate, performing rainmaking rituals, until after seven years he is put to death—or earlier, in the event of bad harvests. He is only referred to as a god (if a bad god) after his death (de Surgey 1990). Similar cases can be endlessly elaborated.

If the relation between these elements is indeed contingent, the particular configuration they take in any given case can only have been the outcome of the particular play of historical forces. That is, it is an effect of the politics that lie behind it. This is what I mean by the politics of kingship. The Rukuba king has maneuvered himself himself into a fairly strong position; the Ewe king, if one can even call him that, has fallen victim to almost complete adverse sacralization. Let us turn, then, to one of the most famous examples of African divine kingship, that of the Jukun of Nigeria, to get a sense of how this might come about.

* * *

According to the standard history, the Jukun as a people are said to have reached the Benue River valley around AD 950, and their ruling lineage still claim to be migrants from Egypt or Mecca (Meek 1931: 22; Stevens 1975: 186). What's sometimes referred to as the "Jukun Empire," based in the city of Kwararafa, peaked in the seventeenth century, after which its military expansion was checked by the stubborn resistance, among others, of the egalitarian Tiv to the south. By the nineteenth century, the kingdom also came under intense pressure from attacks by jihadis from the north, who sacked their capital and forced them to relocate (Abraham 1933: 10; Apata 1998: 79–81).

Their transformation, during this period, was so profound that many have begun to question whether the Jukun were ever a military empire at all (Afigo 2005: 70–73), but the likeliest interpretation of the evidence is that the Jukun were at first the center of a classic galactic polity, but one whose rulers, once their military ambitions were foiled, gradually came to redefine themselves less as alien warriors and more as the ritual leaders of a people who claimed autochthonous status as the original owners of the land (Isichei 1997: 235; Afigo 2005: 72).[30] In the process, the king's role was likewise transformed: he was largely confined to his palace, his person identified with the crops and agricultural fertility, every aspect of his life regulated by elaborate taboos (Meek 1931: 126–33, 153–63). It seems Jukun kings were always in principle scheduled to die at the end of a seven-year term, but in early times, unless they failed as warriors, this fate was always postponed, and any disabling impurities they may have taken on were transferred to a scapegoat slave killed in their stead (ibid.: 139–44; Muller 1990: 58–59). By the time our evidence kicks in, in the 1930s, this scapegoat ritual had long since fallen into abeyance. Instead it was the king himself who had become a potential scapegoat; he could be executed for any number of reasons, whether for crop failure or violation of taboos (see also Abraham 1933: 20; Lagercrantz 1950: 348).

Though the Jukun king was never referred to as a god but merely as a "son of a god" (it is never said precisely which), and though all things surrounding the divinity of the king are, as often, left vague, or kept secret, some notion of godlike status seems consonant with the general tenor of the taboos that surrounded him. These kept him from any regular contact with his people. The king rarely left his compound, and then under carefully choreographed situations: none might gaze at him directly, or touch anything he'd touched; most subjects could never come into his presence at all, but only hope to communicate with him through layers of officials. Not only contact between king and people, but intimate contact between the king and surrounding world of any kind had to be negated, hidden, or denied:

> Jukun chiefs and kings . . . are not supposed to suffer from the limitations of ordinary human beings. They do not "eat," they do not "sleep," and they never "die." It is not merely bad manners, but actual sacrilege to use such expressions when speaking of a king. When the king eats he does so in private, the food being proffered to him with the same ritual as is used by priests in offering sacrifice to the gods. . . .

---

30. I should emphasize this is my own reconstruction; earlier colonial historians saw the Jukun as a fallen empire, and most contemporary Nigerian historians believe that they were always more of a spiritual federation—as Afigo (2005) adds, with a core group claiming autochthonous status as earliest settlers of the land. Isichei (1997; see also Afolayan 2005: 144) suggested a gradual transformation from a warlike power to a ritual one, on the model of Benin, which, she notes, took a similar course. I have simply synthesized these views.

> The Jukun king must not put his foot on the ground or sit on the ground
> without a mat, possibly because he is a god of the Upper Air or because his dy-
> namism might escape into the ground and blast the crops . . . .[31] It is taboo for
> the king to pick up anything from the ground. If a Jukun king were to fall off his
> horse, he would, in former times, have been promptly put to death. Being a god
> it may never be said of him that he is ill, and if serious illness overtook him he is
> quietly strangled. (Meek 1931: 126–27)

Any way that the royal body was continuous with or in contact with the physical world—eating, excretion, sex—was not only performed in secret, but had to
be treated as if it did not occur at all (excrement, hair or nail clippings, spittle,
even sandal-prints, had to be hidden away). The king could not directly touch
the earth, and was often referred to as an airy spirit: when he slept or died, he
was said to "return to the skies."

While there was the usual ideology of the king's absolute power,[32] there's
little indication of arbitrary executions or other high-handed behavior. Instead,
royal anger was seen as dangerous in itself:

> It is a disastrous thing, also, for the Jukun king to fly into a rage, point his finger
> at a man or strike the ground in wrath, for by doing so, he would let loose on the
> community the anger of the gods immanent in his person, and the whole land
> would be infected by blight. If the king were so far to forget himself the offenders
> would immediately render their apologies and take steps to induce him to recall
> or cancel his hasty word or act. They would request one of his sisters' sons, the
> king's acolyte, to approach him and calm him, and persuade him to dip his fin-
> gers in water in order to purge or rather quench the "fire of his hand," and when
> this rite had been performed the acolyte would withdraw backwards, sweeping
> the ground in front of the king, in the same way as a priest withdraws when he
> has offered sacrifice to the offended gods. (Meek 1931: 128)

---

31. It is often difficult in Meek's text to know what is report and what is speculation,
but this does seem rooted in Jukun ideas, as we'll see.

32. Meek notes that "the Jukun system of government is, in theory at least, of a highly
despotic nature" (ibid.: 332), but emphasizes this was in no sense true in practice. "If
the harvests were good people were prepared to put up with a moderate amount of
tyranny. But excessive tyranny would lead to a demand for his death even if harvests
were good" (ibid.).

This passage gives a particularly vivid glimpse of the intimate, indeed, mutually constitutive, relation between violence and sacralization. Jukun kings may not be gods. but they bear within them a divine element, identical with their power of command, or sovereignty, and which resides in the heart and right arm (Young 1966: 147–49). Each new king acquires this power by consuming the powdered heart of his predecessor, mixed in beer, during his coronation; the old king's right hand is also preserved as an amulet (Meek 1931: 168; Muller 1981: 241). This is presumably why pointing is considered so particularly dangerous. It blights the crops. But in a broader sense the king—at least, his human, non-divine element—*is* the crops: at public appearances he is regularly hailed as "Our Corn, Our Beans, Our Groundnuts" (Meek 1931: 129, 172; Young 1966: 149–50). And if the crops fail for too long, rather than being mollified and propitiated, the king himself can be killed; whereon it is said—as it is always said when any monarch dies—that he ascended to heaven and became a god owing to the malice of his people (Meek 1931: 131; Young 1966: 148).[33]

All this clearly recalls the curious dialectic of hostility and sacralization we've already seen in the myths and rituals surrounding the Shilluk *reth*. Nyikang and his immediate successors, we are told, did not die; they ascended into the heavens and became disembodied gods in the face of the rancor of their people. Among the Jukun, *all* monarchs do this.

However, the ceremonial surrounding the king also suggests that such cosmological statements are themselves expressions of a deeper truth, inscribed in the very nature of formal etiquette, hierarchical deference, and gestures of respect. Recall that the formalities surrounding the Jukun king are simply more elaborate versions of those surrounding chiefs and elders, on the one hand, or of gods, on the other. In fact, in their most basic elements, such formalities can be said to have certain common structural features that can be observed in forms of formal deference anywhere— indeed, the very nature of what we call "formality." I've offered an analysis of these structural features in an earlier work (Graeber 1997); here I can only offer the barest summary.

---

33. "When the king became sick, or infirm, or broke any of the royal taboos, or proved himself unfortunate, he was secretly put to death. Whether any king was, in the olden days, permitted to die a natural death cannot be known" (Meek 1931: 165), but "when a Jukun king dies (even if he has been secretly murdered as a result of a famine) it is commonly said he has forsaken the world and gone back to the heavens in consequence of the wickedness of men" (ibid.: 131).

Essentially, the argument is that what anthropologists have traditionally called "joking relations" and "relations of avoidance" are simply exaggerated forms of a kind of playful familiarity, and formal respect, that might be considered among the universal building-blocks of human sociality. Deference tends to expressed not only by the inferior party averting eyes, or otherwise avoiding contact with the superior (gestures generally accompanied by feelings of shame), or by the fact the superior party remains relatively free to engage in or initiate such contact if desired, but also by a suppression of any acknowledgment of ways that bodies, and particularly the superior's body, are continuous with the world around them, where, as Bakhtin (1984; cf. Stallybrass and White 1986; Mbembe 1992) so aptly put it, the borders between bodies in the world become permeable or are cast into doubt entirely. These usually include eating and drinking to a degree, but almost always they include sexual intercourse, pregnancy and labor, excretion, mucus, mutilation, menstruation, death and decomposition, flatulence, suppurating wounds, and so on. There is an enormous degree of cultural variation in which of these are considered most shocking in polite company, which relatively trivial; and, as Norbert Elias ([1939] 1978) so carefully demonstrated, the borders of shame and embarrassment can advance and retreat over time. Still everywhere, the basic list remains the same. And topics considered shameful and suppressed in one context are exactly those to which people will also appeal when making rude jokes, and celebrated in "joking relations,"[34] which are less humorous than enactments of playful egalitarian competition, insult, or hostility, in a kind of systematic inversion of the principles of avoidance. In such relations, that hierarchical superiority instead turns into a constant game of back-and-forth—a sometimes literal wrestling in the mud—where the very materiality of the interaction, the lack of clear borders between bodies, also emphasizes the temporary, even momentary, nature of any victory.[35]

To be sacred, as Émile Durkheim reminds us, means "to be set apart," which is also the literal meaning of the Tongan word "*tabu*." "Not to be touched." By constituting the object of hierarchical deference as a thing apart, and therefore

---

34. I should emphasize that "joking relations" of the classic anthropological variety are often not all that funny; they tend to involve play fighting or simple insults ("my, you're ugly") more than witty banter, though one could argue that witty banter is the same thing in an attenuated form.

35. I should also hasten to add that I am not suggesting that all human behavior can be placed on a continuum between joking and avoidance; it's one axis among many.

at least tacitly as a perfectly self-contained and disembodied entity, floating above the muck and mire of the world, such taboos effectively render that object an abstraction. Hence it makes sense that kings, and gods, are so often rendered homage in similar ways. But the logic of deference also helps explain an apparent paradox: that the more exalted, hence more set apart, a superior is from his surroundings, including his inferiors, the more he is also seen as hierarchically encompassing those very same inferiors. Because "abstraction" in such situations always has a dual meaning. It does not just refer to disembodiment; it also means being, as it were, moved upward on the taxonomic ladder.

Lévi-Strauss referred to this as "universalization" versus "particularization" (1966: 161). An easy example will suffice: consider the difference in our own society between the use of first and last names. A first name (Barack) is yours alone, and is hence used to express familiarity; a family name encompasses a plethora of first names, and is hence more generic, hence more formal and deferential (Mr. Obama)—and of course a title (Mr. President, et al.) is even higher up the taxonomic ladder, hence more deferential yet.[36] In this sense, Marshall Sahlins' language of "metabeings" is decidedly apt. Gods are often seen as almost literally Platonic Forms: the Master of the Seals is also the generic form of all seals, which are but tokens of their type. The same tacit logic is at play here as well. Consider the common insistence that a sacred king be "without blemish" or "physically perfect." As noted in chapter 2, the very idea of physical perfection is itself a kind of paradox: Can one so perfectly embody the generic human form that one is set apart from other humans as unique?

How does all this relate to sovereignty?

Well, if nothing else, I think it now makes the opposition between clowns and kings worked out in the last section begins to make a great deal more sense. In my original essay (Graeber 1997), I emphasized how the great "reformation of manners" in early modern Europe might best be considered a generalization of avoidance relations, attendant on the rise of possessive individualism, which posited everyone as self-contained within the circle and compass of his or her property: hence, everyone was now to address everyone else as inferiors had once addressed feudal lords. This was the exact opposite of the festive generalization

---

36. This is *not* to say that we are always talking about the relation of (profane) individual and (sacred) office in the ritual surrounding sacred kings, as structural-functionalist anthropology tended to assume, but rather that that relation is one specific form this more general relation of particularization and universalization might take.

of joking relations that Bakhtin referred to as "the carnivalesque." (Obviously, this equalization is never perfect. There is always a residual—women, the poor, some racialized underclass—which the possessive individual also avoids talking about in formal situations, in the same way as one pretends not to notice when one's superior blows his nose or farts.) But the opposition between clowns and kings is different. Normally, joking and avoidance relations are between individuals, or sometimes between groups. One might say the sovereign clown is an individual with a joking relation with absolutely everyone; the sacred king, in an analogous way, is in a relation of avoidance with everybody else. Hence in the first case, the violence essential to the nature of sovereignty is wildly exaggerated, in a kind of mock chaos that actually disguises a maintenance of a certain form of order (the clowns double as police); in the second, it is largely euphemized, along with all the bodily functions that clowns are so notoriously fond of celebrating—though, in fact, the form of the euphemization can itself become an insidious form of violence: since the only way to render a human being a complete abstraction, a self-enclosing Idea divorced from material entanglements, is to destroy their body entirely (adverse sacralization taken to its last degree).

* * *

A case could be made that all etiquette has an element of potential violence in it. When the rich and powerful feel utterly humiliated (it does sometimes happen), it usually has to do with being discovered in some scandalous breach of protocol or decorum. But clearly, not all sacralization is adverse. Systems of deference overall tend to operate very much to the benefit of those who are deferred to. To turn such a system so against itself is unusual. It almost only happens to monarchs of one sort or another, or others at the very apex of some sort of hierarchy. Why, then, does it happen to them?

In the Jukun case, the king seems to have been demoted from war leader to a kind of fetish object, whose secular powers, while they did exist, appear to have been entirely outbalanced by those of various palace women (particularly the king's mother and sister, who had their own court and observed similar taboos but were never killed), a governing council, and a whole panoply of priests and officials (Meek 1931: 333–45; Tamuno 1965: 203; Abubakar 1986). Any attempt by the king to exercise his "absolute" power too aggressively would, Meek noted, lead to those surrounding him claiming he had violated some taboo and ordering him to be strangled in his sleep (ibid.: 333).

In this case, Frazerian sacred kingship was a consequence of political decline. Might this be a more general tendency? It's very hard to judge, because there have been so few attempts to look at the phenomenon in any sort of broader historical perspective. What evidence there is is certainly suggestive. Kajsa Ekholm (1985a; also 1991: 167–78), for instance, made a detailed examination of the BaKongo evidence—one of the few cases where we have good historical evidence going back more than five centuries—and concluded that Frazer had got things precisely backward. The more extreme forms of royal ritual, she argued—especially the killing, scapegoating, and imprisonment of monarchs—was in no sense primordial. As Phyllis Martin (1972: 19–24, 160–64) had documented for the Loango kingdom, early rulers (called "Maloango") might have been seen as "quasi-divine" beings (their meals, for instance, were conducted in secret), but it didn't stop them from taking an active role in every aspect of political life. It was only after the kingdom had largely collapsed under the pressures of the slave trade that a rising merchant class turned the Maloango into a sacred being effectively confined to his palace, forbidden to cross water, or touch foreign-made goods.

Even more extreme customs emerged around the dozens of tiny potentates who emerged from the collapse of the BaKongo kingdom. The old Kongo king was, as we've seen (chapter 3), a divine king of the classic stranger-king type, if not an especially sacred one. But the kingdom collapsed into civil war, and before long, the great capital city of San Salvador lay sacked and abandoned, replaced by thousands of tiny villages; the slave trade and subsequent machinations of foreign traders then brought the equivalent of criminal gangs to power in many parts of the country. In the process, Ekholm (1985a) writes, divine kingship underwent a process of "involution." Nineteenth-century sources unveil a veritable Victorian wonder-cabinet of strange and exotic political forms: kings executed on the first day in office who then reigned as ghosts; kings exiled to forests like the Priest of Nemi; kings regularly beaten and mutilated by their guards and companions; kings who actually *were* regularly put to death at the end of their four- or seven-year terms.

BaKongo kings had always been elected from among a host of candidates, through the offices of the earth-priests who represented the indigenous "owners of the land," and, by extension, the whole people. But now those indigenous authorities effectively seized, and decentralized, power (Ekholm 1991: 171–72). "The people" had won the war, and the king was transformed into a kind of Clastrean "anti-chief, divested of all real power and immobilized by a plethora of taboos" (Ekholm 1985a: 249). The most extreme form of such adverse sa-cralization is documented from Nsundi. According to the account of one later BaKongo catechist (Laman 1953–68, 2: 140–42; Janzen 1982: 65; MacGaffey 2000: 148–49), around 1790, the first Nsundi king of Kibunzi, whose title was Namenta,[37] was a boy kidnapped by his lineage's wife-givers (i.e., lineage of the indigenous priests themselves), and put through a kind of savage parody of a typical Central African puberty ritual. Secluded in the forest by his future of-ficials, he was whipped, starved, and generally mistreated until he came of age. "When he was a grown man, he was castrated by the use of a feather of a fishing eagle. Then they left him alone, but he was not yet Chief, because he was still a prisoner" (MacGaffey 2000: 148). Finally, when it came time for him to take office, he was, like kings of old, expected to conquer the capital (defended by these same wife-givers) in a ritual battle—except, in this case, it was not a mock battle but an actual battle, and if the candidate was killed in combat, the office would lie empty until another candidate could be raised again. Offices often lay empty for very long periods. But even if Namenta passed the ordeal, and was duly invested in the royal leopard-skin regalia, he was treated essentially as a magical charm, created by his people, and his main responsibility was in main-taining various onerous taboos. (He was also ritually married to a woman of the wife-giving clan whom his brother was expected to impregnate.)

This represents perhaps the lowest a monarch can fall. Small wonder then that some wealthy BaKongo chiefs around this time never went outside without weapons, for fear they might be kidnapped and forced to become king (Bastian in Ekholm 1991: 168).

Ekholm's conclusion is that Frazerian kingship is effectively a side-effect of European imperialism. As the BaKongo descended from a mighty empire to the impoverished prey of predatory merchants, gangsters, and colonialists, cosmology itself transformed: the powers of nature were redefined as dangerous and evil, and stranger-kings, embodying powers of the wild, became forces to be quelled and controlled. Even the ritual scapegoating of kings, Ekholm suggests, is a result of this dilemma. This is heady stuff. But she also appears to suggest this is a more general pattern, and here we are on much shakier ground. Even the

---

37. Laman (1953: 68, 2) says he was the last of his dynasty, and Ekholm (1991: 168) echoes this, but as MacGaffey observes, the text actually describes him as the first of the dynasty, and names various successors (2000: 150). He concludes there likely was no real person named Namenta; he was just the titular founder and a kind of template for the investiture of later kings.

unfortunate Namenta's successors eventually managed to reassert themselves, breaking out of ritual isolation to become judges, merchants, and conquerors, and eventually suppressing the unpleasant investiture ritual (MacGaffey 2000: 150). It's very hard to see a single direction of development.

The only other comparative historical analysis I am aware of, by the Russian anthropologists Dmitri Bondarenko and Andrey Korotayev (2003), points in precisely the opposite direction. They suggest that, with certain significant exceptions, kings become more sacred as their governments become stronger.

Some background would be useful. Bondarenko's research has focused on the West African kingdom of Benin, a classic stranger-kingship ruled by a monarch of Yoruba descent. The king, called the Oba, was a god who never died, who often acted in defiance even of other gods. (The royal symbol, the "bird of disaster," commemorated an early warrior-king who, warned that a bird spotted on the way to battle was sent by a god to warn of impending defeat, shot and ate the bird but nonetheless marched to victory: Okpewho 1998: 71.) At the same time, the Oba's day-to-day power was balanced against that of the town chiefs who represented the indigenous population (Ryder 1969; Bradbury 1967, 1973; Rowlands 1993; Okpewho 1998). After an age of expansion in the fifteenth and sixteenth centuries, there followed a long period of civil wars, culminating in a popular rebellion in 1699 which led to the destruction of the capital, and forced the king to reach an accommodation with the town chiefs:

> The struggle between the *Oba* and the chiefs took the form of constant and gradually successful attempts of the latter to limit the sovereign's profane power by means of inflicting new binding taboos on him, and hence *volens nolens* increasing his sacrality inversely proportional for "lists" of royal taboos . . . . The final act ran high in the early seventeenth century when the chiefs succeeded in depriving the *Oba* of the right to command the army in person. Relations of the Europeans who visited the Benin court in the late sixteenth–nineteenth centuries are full of vivid stories and surprised or contemptuous remarks testifying to the "king's" complete impotence at the face of his "noblemen." (Bondarenko 2005: 32)

While every newborn child in the kingdom was duly brought before the Oba, visitors were only allowed to see his foot (the rest was hidden behind a curtain), and the king himself could only leave the palace twice a year. It was the queen mother, instead, who was delegated the task of judging important trials and mediating disputes (Kaplan 1997).

The result in many ways resembles the situation Ekholm describes for the BaKongo, from the dominance of merchants, the sequestering of the king from any contact with foreigners, even the visions of a terrifying and hostile natural universe (Rowlands 1993: 298). But the hidden king gradually took advantage of his new position to develop ever-more elaborate ritual powers. Again the situation can be likened to a chess game, each move followed by a countermove. The king's sequestration was ostensibly due to his terrifying, witch-like powers, which might otherwise devastate the land. The king responded by importing a new god from the Yoruba town of Ife—the royal ancestor, Oduduwa, father of the original stranger-king—accompanied by ferocious cannibal stranger-priests (ibid.). The new priesthood instituted human sacrifices to the royal ancestors to protect the kingdom, and these did indeed devastate the land, increasing in scale and terror until, by the end of the nineteenth century, hundreds of subjects might be rounded up and crucified or beheaded during important rituals or national crises. (Members of the indigenous chiefs' clans, however, were immune.) These spectacular displays, which so horrified foreign visitors, were in part simply demonstrations of sovereignty: though the Oba no longer had direct contact with his people, he alone could take life (Bradbury 1967: 3). This in turn led to further taboos.

Intrigued by such dynamics, Bondarenko and Korotayev (2003) created a "Ruler Sacralization Index." Basing themselves on Henri Claessen and Peter Skalník's database of twenty kingdoms in their book *The early state* (1978; cf. Claessen 1984, 1986), they ran a statistical analysis and discovered that, overall, the more powerful the state apparatus—they defined this in terms of the presence or absence of impersonal laws and administration—the more sacred the ruler becomes. The great exceptions, they note, are Axial Age civilizations, or what they call the "Axial Historical Network" (Bondarenko and Korotayev 2003: 119), from Europe to China, which take off in the opposite direction—presumably, they say, because of the importance there of priests of the great universalistic religions, Christianity, Buddhism, Hinduism, and Islam. Otherwise, whether among the Mexica, Yoruba, or in Japan, strong, autonomous bureaucratic systems will regularly declare the monarch a quasi-divine being and lock him in his palace.

All this is intriguing, but the sample is skewed in so many ways it's a little difficult to know what to make of it. First of all, the list is of "early states," so kingdoms that can in no sense be considered states since they have no significant administration—like the Shilluk, or the Natchez—simply aren't included.

But of course these include many of the prototypical examples of "divine kingship." So: Does sacred kingship tend to decline when kingdoms first turn into states (presumably under the aegis of ambitious warrior-kings), only to return once they have developed an autonomous administration?

The Axial Age argument seems biased by the relatively small sample as well. The authors argue that the creation of a priestly class in the "Axial Historical Network" traces back to Indo-European age-sets, where they see elders as transforming into priests (ibid.: 121–23), and suggest something similar might have happened in very early times in the Middle East. But this still doesn't explain why China became an Axial Age civilization, and rejected divinization of the emperor, but Japan developed in precisely the opposite direction; or why Hindu kingdoms, which have the strongest priestly castes of all, are also most likely to have sacred and divinized kings.

I have myself (Graeber 2011a: 223–50) proposed a rather different argument: that Axial Age civilizations found their origin in the emergence of new social and military technologies (especially, professional armies paid in coined money), and followed a remarkably similar pattern, whether in China, India, or the Mediterranean. The rise of standing armies and eventually slave-based empires led first to a highly materialistic phase, where rulers began to treat wealth and military power as an end in itself divorced from any larger cosmological framework; then, to popular movements of contestation which included what were to be remembered as the great religious and philosophical traditions; then, finally, to a phase when, as the empires reached their limits, their rulers embraced one or another of the religious movements in a last-ditch attempt to preserve their rule. This historical process led to kingdoms where the constituent war between king and people was partly displaced onto a war between kings and priests, or, anyway, between secular and religious authorities. Or better, perhaps, it became a kind of three-way contest. God, King, and People all existed in dynamic tension with one another.

Nonetheless, adverse sacralization of the monarch was a trick that could still be played, and indeed often was. The institution of the harem plays a key role. It's interesting to note that while in most of the kingdoms discussed so far, kings had multiple wives, the women were in no way sequestered. Often, in fact, it was the king who was confined to the palace, and women who moved back and forth, communicating freely with the outside world. Historically, the practice of confining palace women can only be traced back to the Sumerian Third Dynasty of Ur (2112–2004 BC), though over time the practice seems to have become commonplace across much of Eurasia, with the exception of the Christian West.[38] There is no reason to believe Mesopotamian kings, whether Sumerian, Babylonian, or Assyrian, were in any sense confined to the palace, but their wives and concubines increasingly were; by Assyrian times, one already reads of harsh punishments for anyone who so much as chatted with or gazed on one unveiled (Barjamovic 2011: 52).

The problem, of course, is that if one designs a trap, one can oneself fall into it. Eurasian history is full of examples of royal figures who ended up sequestered in much the same way as their womenfolk. Probably the most famous example are the Ottoman sultans of the late sixteenth to eighteenth centuries, notorious in Orientalist fantasy for being, as historian Peter Baer once put it, "hidden in the palace like a pearl in an oyster, aloof, secluded, and sublime, hermetically sealed from the world, confined and condemned to a wilted life in the harem" (2008: 20). As it turns out, the stereotype in this case was not too far off the mark. During this period, sultans—not unlike the Byzantine monarchs who had come before them—were surrounded by such rigid protocol that ordinary subjects were not even allowed to converse with them:

> [They] withdrew from subjects and servants and from public view. Because or-
> dinary speech was considered undignified for sultans to use, they communicated
> by sign language. Unable even to speak, the sultan became out of touch, and was
> visible only on rare, carefully staged processions through the capital. The sultan
> had become a showpiece and sat silently on his throne in a three-foot turban, like
> an icon, immobile. (Baer 2008: 141; see also Necipoğlu 1991: 102–6)

Once again, too, the effective confinement of the ruler occurred at a time of widespread popular unrest: by the mid-sixteenth century, sultans were deprived of most of their military functions, there followed a series of Janissary uprisings in the capital, then rural upheavals which left large stretches of countryside in the empire's heartlands lost to Celâli rebels (Neumann 2006: 46–47).

Leslie Peirce (1993) has described the period from 1566 to 1656, from the point of view of ruling circles, as "The Age of the Queen Mother." Prominent court women were often in de facto power. The key turning point was Mehmed

---

38. This was partly owing to royal monogamy, a custom which goes back at least to Rome. Of course, for much of Christian history, many women were cloistered for religious purposes, but they were expected to remain celibate.

IV's transformation of the system of succession. Earlier, the children of a reigning sultan had been sent off to cut their political teeth as rural governors; then, on the sultan's death, they were expected vie for the throne (often through outright warfare), a drama which would end with the winner killing off his remaining brothers. Under the new dispensation, the brothers remained alive, but confined to a section of the Topkapi Palace in an extension of the harem called the *kafes* ("cages"), in near-complete isolation (Necipoğlu 1991: 175, 178; Peirce 1993: 99–103;).[39] Each would take the throne in turn until none were left and then power would revert to the son of the first. This ensured that by the time most did come to power, they were not only quite old, but also lacked any experience of the world, and often were struggling with severe mental health issues caused by decades of solitary confinement. Most reigns in this period were therefore short. The most notorious, perhaps, of the period's rulers, Ibrahim I ("the mad," r. 1640–48), exercised absolute and arbitrary power inside the palace, at one point ordering his entire harem be tied into weighted sacks and drowned; at the same time, he knew almost nothing of life outside, and his interventions in public life were largely whimsical. (At one point he is said to have ordered his officials to locate the fattest woman in the empire, whom he ultimately made governor of Aleppo.) Eventually he was deposed and a child was made sultan in his place.

During this period, day-to-day power in the palace was wielded above all by royal women, the chief consort and queen mother, who were technically slaves. Outside it was increasingly in the hands of an emerging bureaucracy. Occasionally a relatively energetic sultan would "escape from the palace" to organize a military campaigns or some other royal project. But this was considered a notable achievement in itself.

I could go on from here to describe the self-enclosing paradises created by such walled-up kings, whether in Persia or in China, or the dynamics whereby warrior elites would relegate existing kings to boxed-in ceremonial status (as the Seljuks did to the later caliphs, or shoguns to the emperor of Japan). But space does not permit. Suffice it to say the dialectic of divine and sacred never entirely goes away. Even since the rise of republican forms of government in the late eighteenth century, and displacement of sovereignty itself—that is, divinity—entirely from living monarchs onto an even greater abstraction called "the people, in practical terms, their defeat has always taken the same form.

---

39. The confined princes were above all forbidden to procreate, so once a set of brothers were all dead, office passed to the eldest child of the first of them.

When kings win: The war against the dead

Alexander, who was invincible on the battlefield, was completely helpless in his personal relationships. For he was ensnared by praise; and when he was called Zeus, he did not think he was being mocked, but honored in his passion for the impossible and his forgetfulness of nature.

Agatharchides of Cnidus

Let Alexander be a god if that's what's so important to him.

Damis the Spartan

Let him be the son of both Zeus and Poseidon at the same time if he wants for all I care.

Demosthenes of Athens

What happens, then, when kings definitively win? When sovereign power is not bottled up in a palace or other bounded utopia, but can operate relatively untrammeled across a king's dominions? It seems to me this introduces an entirely new set of dilemmas, and that these dilemmas also take a fairly predictable form.

It is one thing to take a palace garden, or even a palace, and turn it into a tiny model of perfection, a paradise outside of time, process, and decay where the fundamental dilemmas of the human condition are—at least momentarily—resolved. It's quite another to do this to a city or a kingdom. Few even try. What's more, a king's power breaks out of such a diminutive paradise: that is, the less the king's power is contained in space, the more self-conscious he becomes about the fact that power is nonetheless contained in time, and, thus, the more he confronts the contradictions of his own mortality.

In a medieval Hebrew version of the Romance of Alexander the Great, the great conqueror faces this dilemma directly. Having subjugated the kingdoms of the world, he proceeds to scour the earth in search of immortality. Finally, winning his way into the Garden of Eden, he locates and is about to take a drink from the Waters of (eternal) Life when he hears an unearthly voice:

"Wait! Before you drink of those waters, do you not want to know the consequences?" Then Alexander looked up and saw a radiant being standing before him, like the one at the gate of the Garden, and he knew it must be an angel. . . . Alexander said simply, "Yes, please tell me." Then the angel Raziel—for that was who it was—said to Alexander: "Know, then, that whoever drinks these waters will know eternal life, but he will never be able to leave this garden." These words greatly startled Alexander, for had the angel not stopped him he would already have tasted of those waters and become a prisoner in paradise. (Cited in Anderson 2012: 97)

At this, Alexander realized that, given the choice, he preferred to be contained in time than in space after all, and abandoned Eden forever.

Every tradition calibrates the basic quandaries of human existence slightly differently: the relative importance and particular significance of dilemmas surrounding work, sex, suffering, reproduction, or death. Still, there is none in which human life is not seen to involve impossible dilemmas, and none in which the reality of death is not at least prominent among them. It is a tragedy of human existence that we conceive the world in timeless categories, but we are not ourselves timeless. Kings tend to become a focus of such problems because they are simultaneously a kind of Everyman, an exemplar of the human condition, but at the same time, beings which have at least the potential to transcend that condition. As we've seen, even when kings lose, the most effective way of controlling them is to force them to pretend that they are bodiless immortals. One need only consult ancient fantasies about all-conquering heroes like Alexander to see how much the dilemma continues to haunt them when they win. The Epic of Gilgamesh is only the earliest and most famous: Gilgamesh, notoriously, having conquered everything he considered worth conquering, became depressed contemplating the inevitability of death, and set off on a quest to secure the herb of immortality in a far-off Land of Darkness. As most readers five thousand years later will still know, he succeeded, only to carelessly lose it, and immortality, to a serpent. At the end of the story, Gilgamesh consoles himself by gazing at the walls of Uruk, which he had built, and which will remain his enduring testimony.

Variations of this story appear again and again. Wonder-tales accumulated around great works of architecture, typically centering on monarchs who in one way or another tried to cheat death.

Some of these monarchs were, obviously, more successful than others. Among the most successful, in legend at least, was the Assyrian queen Semiramis, whom Diodorus Siculus called the "most renowned woman of whom we have any record" (2.3.4) and who, by Alexander's time, was said to have conquered nearly the entire known world (Herodotus 1.155, 1.184; Diodorus

Siculus 2.3–20; Voltaire 1748; Gilmore 1887; W. R. Smith 1887; Sayce 1888; Frazer 1911c: 349–52, 366–68; D. Levi 1944; Eilers 1971; Roux 2001; Dalley 1996, 2005; Kuhrt 2013). It's worth dwelling on her story for a moment because in the ancient world, for a time, she seems to have become a paradigm for the greatest possible realization of human ambitions.

Scholars still argue about what historical figure, if any, the legendary Semiramis was based on. She appears to have originally been an amalgam of a number of Mesopotamian queens, most prominent among them Sammuramat, wife of the Assyrian King Shamshi-Adad V (823–811 BC), possibly Armenian in origin, who might have ruled as regent during her son's minority.[40] Scholars, needless to say, contest pretty much every detail, but it would seem Sammuramat became the Mesopotamian prototype for any autonomous female ruler who led military campaigns, patronized sages, and sponsored great works of architecture and engineering (Dalley 1996: 531; 2005: 18–19; 2013b: 123–24). Her story only seems to have really taken off under the Persian empire (Eilers 1971; Roux 1992), such that by the time Herodotus visited Babylon three centuries later, Semiramis was remembered as the creator of its earthworks and other marvels. Herodotus hints at, but does not spell out, more scandalous legends (W. R. Smith 1887: 304). Two generations later, Ctesias, a Greek doctor living in the Persian court, provides us with the details (Nichols 2008).

By the time of Ctesias' account, the queen has become of semidivine origins, her mother cursed to turn into a fish, herself raised by doves. Above all, though, her story seems to have become a patriarchal fantasy about the terrible—if titillating—things that men in that epoch suspected women would get up to if allowed to compete with them on equal footing (cf. Slater 1968; Asher-Greve 2006).[41] In many versions, Semiramis' rise to power is literally a ritual of inversion run amok. She is a beautiful courtesan, or maybe servant girl, who tricks King Ninus into allowing her to be queen-for-a-day during a festival; then quickly sounds out his disaffected generals and orders him locked up. In

---

40. Many even cite specific dates for her reign, 810–806 BC (e.g., D. Levi 1944: 423; Eilers 1971: 33–38), but Kuhrt (2013) insists all this is presupposition based on her later fame, since there is no direct evidence she was ever regent.

41. We only know Ctesias' account from Diodorus and a few other later sources, but the latter author seems to have cleaned out many of the more romantic, magical, or scandalous elements. All these were later developed in the Greek "Romance of Ninus and Semiramis" (D. Levi 1944; Dalley 2013a), which was very popular in the Hellenistic and Roman periods.

others, she merely marries the infatuated king, impresses him with her military acumen, and takes power when he dies,[42] but either way, Semiramis sets out to outdo her former husband's achievements—no mean feat, as in the stories he's the original founder of the Assyrian empire. She sets off on a series of conquests that carry her from Ethiopia to the gates of India, founding the cities of Babylon (she builds its hanging gardens) and Ecbatana in the process, and becomes responsible for virtually every impressive monument in western Asia whose author was otherwise unknown. Semiramis was also said to have shunned remarriage, preferring to take lovers from among the most handsome of her soldiers, whom she would order killed when she grew bored of them; hence, by the time Alexander's armies were passing through Asia, any mysterious artificial hill was referred to as a "mound of Semiramis" and assumed to contain the body of one of her paramours. Smith (1887: 306–7) and Frazer (1911c: 372), for this reason, felt Semiramis was in part just a secularization of the Mesopotamian goddess of war and fertility Inanna/Ishtar/Astarte, whose annual lovers met a similarly unhappy fate.[43]

Most spectacularly: Semiramis never died. Forewarned by the oracle of Ammon in Libya that someone close to her would betray her, but not to resist, when she learned her son Ninyas was conspiring with court eunuchs to overthrow her, she called him in, announced she was turning over the kingdom to him, and simply vanished and became a god. ("Some, making a myth of it," adds Diodorus [2.19.20], "say that she turned into a dove.") This is particularly important for this study because Semiramis appears to be the first monarch we know of (the first I know of certainly) who was said not to have died but to have disappeared this way—the paradigm for Nyikang, and dozens of other African

---

42. Diodorus' version, in which she married a general and then eventually the king, whom she impressed by her ingenious stratagems that allowed him to capture the city of Bactra, seems to be an attempt to deromanticize the story. Berosus' lost history of Babylon (fr. 5–6) calls Semiramis daughter of a prostitute, or perhaps of a holy recluse; Plutarch (*Moralia*, 243c, 753e) and Pliny (*Natural History* 6.35) both make her a slave-girl in Ninus' royal household; an otherwise unknown Athenaeus whom Diodorus cites as the alternative version, like Aelian (*Varia Historia* 7.1), makes her a courtesan or prostitute herself. Wilder versions of her sexual exploits seem to have been circulating as well: Pliny, for instance, has her, like the later legend about Catherine the Great, arranging to have sex with a horse (8.15).

43. Gilgamesh himself, Frazer remarks, refused Inanna's bed for just this reason (1911c: 317). On the other hand, insofar as he was divinized, he ended up a god of the dead, which presumably would have been his fate as Tammuz-figure as well.

founders of dynasties, for instance, who likewise vanish and become gods in the face of hostility of kin or people.[44]

Alexander was quite self-conscious in seeing himself as trying to emulate, and if possible outdo, the achievements of Cyrus, the founder of the Achaemenid empire, but even more he saw Semiramis as his rival. His disastrous march across the Gedrosian desert to India was meant to match one of her exploits, and even at the end of his life, he is reported to have expressed frustration that, unlike her, he had never conquered Ethiopia (Arrian 6.24.3, 7.15.4; Stoneman 2008: 68, 129, 140–43). Like Semiramis, Alexander made himself a god on the basis of a visit to the oracle of Ammon in Libya, to the bemused shrugs of statesmen back in Greece; he also founded cities, raised monuments, and did all the things a great conqueror was supposed to do. But he only truly defeated his rival after death, when the *Alexander Romance*, a marvelous version of his life story, was translated into dozens of languages and became perhaps the single most popular nonreligious book of the next millennium, easily eclipsing the fame of the competing *Romance of Ninus and Semiramis*. Almost instantly, Alexander himself became the measure of the ultimate possibilities of human ambition, and his stories go even further than that of Semiramis, not only granting him Ethiopia and India, but having him pursue mastery all human knowledge and wisdom as well, attempting to attain heaven in a flying machine powered by griffons, explore the bottom of the sea in a diving bell, even, by the Middle Ages, finding his way to the Garden of Eden. At the same time, he outdid all predecessors in fame not by what he achieved, but by what he didn't: in the Romance, his conquests become simply so many attempts to overcome mortality; he is constantly trying to achieve eternal life or at least learn the hour of his death, and in this he fails. Like Gilgamesh, he embarks on an impossible quest through

---

44. The obvious common feature is that having disappeared, none of these monarchs have burial places. Semiramis is said to have built a famous monumental tomb for her husband Ninus, but despite leaving tombs of her lovers across western Asia, and endless cities, bridges, canals, towers, tunnels, and so forth, there is no evidence in any of the sources of her having a tomb—except in one case, as a kind of joke:

    Semiramis caused a great tomb to be prepared for herself, and on it this inscription: "Whatsoever king finds himself in need of money may break into this monument and take as much as he wishes." Darius accordingly broke into it, but found no money; he did, however, come upon another inscription reading as follows: "If you were not a wicked man with an insatiate greed for money, you would not be disturbing the places where the dead are laid." (Plutarch *Moralia* 173b).

a Land of Darkness to obtain the Waters of Life, but in the end, he loses it to someone else—not a snake, this time, but his own cook and daughter, whom he then punishes by casting them out to live forever with nothing further to show for themselves (Dawkins 1937; Stoneman 1995: 98–99; Szalc 2012).[45]

One can actually see this as a little structural inversion: Semiramis was a queen betrayed by her son, responded with uncharacteristic grace, and thus achieved immortality; Alexander was a king betrayed by his daughter, responded with uncharacteristic fury, and thus did not. In any case, in every version of the Romance, his quest to become a god proves unsuccessful.[46] As an Axial Age hero, the best he can do is finally listen to the various sages, angels, yogis, and philosophers he encounters in his journeys and learn to understand and accept his mortal limitations.

* * *

Alexander, then, did attain immortality but only by becoming a kind of Everyman foolishly pursuing immortality.

The advantage of these stories, however fantastic, is that they bring home what was felt to be at stake in absolute sovereignty. It's important to be explicit about my use of terms here. Sovereignty, in the sense we've been using it here, was something of a latecomer in Bronze Age Western Asia, whose political landscape had long been a checkerboard of temples, palaces, clans, tribes, autonomous cities, and urban neighborhoods. Not only were most "empires" really galactic polities of one sort or another, rulers rarely had sovereign (i.e., arbitrary) power outside their own palaces, and those who insisted on creating something

---

45. In the original Romance, the cook, Andreas, discovers the Waters of Life when, ordered to boil a fish for dinner in the Land of Darkness, he takes some water from a fountain, and observes the fish come back to life. He drinks some, and preserves some in a bottle, which he offers to the king's daughter Kale in exchange for sexual favors. Alexander has him tossed into the ocean with weights tied to him and he becomes a sea god, Kale is merely exiled. In later versions, she becomes the sea goddess Nereis. In the Islamic tradition, however, Andreas the cook becomes al-Khidr, the "Green Man," who, though he does make his home in the sea, is also a sage and mystic who wanders the earth eternally, helping strangers or guiding them to enlightenment.

46. In fact, he fails to attain immortality in both the divine, and genealogical sense: in the story his daughter becomes an exile; his son, in fact, was killed in a palace coup not long after his death.

like an empire of conquest and either declaring themselves world-rulers (e.g., Sargon, c. 2340–2284 BC; Frankfort 1948: 228; Liverani 1993) or claiming divine status (Naram-Sin, c. 2254–2218 BC; the kings of the Third Dynasty of Ur, c. 2112–2004 BC) achieved immortality only in the sense of being remembered for centuries thereafter as models of wickedness (Cooper 1983, 2012). Rulers of the Akkadian, Assyrian, Median, and Achaemenid empires aspired to universal sovereignty in principle. But it's largely in the wildly exaggerated stories that accumulated around figures like Semiramis and Alexander —who not only rule the world, but seem to encounter no significant popular resistance—that we have a clear sense of what was ultimately at stake even in success. Each of these rulers became obsessed with outdoing earlier ones. Each sought immortality by (1) transforming the landscape by works of monumental architecture or engineering, (2) having their exploits and achievements preserved in legend and romance, and (3) attempting to found an enduring and flourishing dynasty (here again Semiramis did better than Alexander: her son Ninyas was said to have been succeeded by a long line of descendants).[47]

The problem is that the first two often appear to be in direct contradiction to the third—so much so that one might be justified in saying we are in the presence of a structural contradiction. The more one succeeds in transcending the frames of mortal existence, the more one's latter-day epigones are placed in a position of structural rivalry to one's memory. Here we might consider the case of Egypt, where, quite unusually in the Bronze Age world, kings did indeed attain the status of gods with absolute sovereign power over their dominions. Pharaohs were incarnate divinities, manifestations of Horus; they did not die, and many of their tombs were so enormous that (as we are periodically reminded on TV) they can still be seen from outer space. Yet for this very reason the greatness of any one pharaoh must have been an enormous burden on his children, who literally existed in the shadow of the dead. By the time we reach the reign of the last pharaoh of the fifth dynasty, Unas (c. 2352–2322 BC), that is, the end of the pyramid age, we also find a king who had to contend with the existence of nineteen different monumental pharaonic tombs, each of a known predecessor, who was also a deity, lingering immortally inside it.

---

47. This is not an exhaustive list of ways that successful rulers might seek immortality. At the very least one could add: (4) the creation of laws or institutions that endure long after one's death; (5) the collection of famous heirlooms and exotic/distant treasures (Helms 1993); and (6) the accumulation of knowledge and wisdom, such as Alexander did in founding the Alexandrian Library. But these are less immediately relevant to the argument at hand.

Back in the 1960s, Lewis Mumford (1967: 168–87, 206–23; cf. Fromm 1973) made the argument that the divine kingships of the Bronze Age were in part the result of the emergence of new social technologies. While Egyptian mechanical technology was extremely limited—they had little more than pulleys and inclined planes—they had already developed production-line techniques of breaking up complex tasks into a series of very simple machine-like actions and then distributing them across a vast army of people. The first complex machines were thus made of human beings. These human machines, in turn, were brought under the control of sovereign power through hierarchical chains of command that, Mumford suggests, probably first emerged in military contexts. The result was unprecedented. It gave ancient rulers power on a scale no human being had ever previously experienced, and that very much went to their heads. One reads of rulers ordering conquered cities torn down one day and rebuilt the next; boasting of bizarre acts of mass sadism such as ordering the murder or mutilation of tens of thousands in a day (whether these claims were actually true or not is in a way of secondary importance). As an illustration of the emotional tone of the violent megalomania that he saw as arising alongside this new mechanical order, Mumford (ibid.: 184) refers us to Unas' tomb inscriptions, which have come to be referred to by Egyptologists as "The Cannibal Hymn":

> The sky darkens; the stars go out; heaven's vaults tremble; the bones of the earth shake; the decans are stilled against them. They have seen Unas rising up in power, as a god living on his fathers, feeding on his mothers . . . Unas it is who devours people, and who lives upon gods . . . .
>
> It is Shezemu [god of judgment] who butchers them for Unas, cooking what's inside them on his evening hearth stones. It is Unas who eats their magical powers, who swallows their souls. The great ones serve for his morning meal, the middle-sized ones for his evening meal; the little ones for his meal at night. Of the old gods and goddesses he makes his cooking hearth . . . .
>
> Unas is the God; older than the eldest. Thousands go round for him; hundreds offer to him. . . . Unas has risen again in the sky; he is crowned as Lord of the Horizon. He has broken the joints of their vertebrae; he has taken the hearts of the gods . . . . (After Eyre 2002: 7–10; cf. Piankoff 1968)

Mumford did have a point. It's hard to imagine anything more megalomaniacal than a man who claims to literally eat gods for breakfast. At the same time, it's hard to discount the fact that Unas' pyramid was also one of the smallest of the Old Kingdom, perhaps half the size of most of those around it in the Saqqara tomb complex (Bárta 2005), which were themselves a fraction of the size of those at Giza. We seem to be witnessing an epic instance of overcompensation. One is tempted to speak of pyramid envy.

Still I would argue that there is a deeper, and more fundamental problem behind such grandiloquent posturing: How does one reconcile claims to absolute and universal sovereignty with the lingering existence of previous monarchs who continue to claim exactly the same thing? It's difficult enough when one is still a live king. The problem is only compounded when one is just another dead one. This dilemma took a particularly acute form in Egypt, where the dead were almost constantly present in one form or another: not only were their tombs visible from the capital, each with attendant staffs of soul priests and funerary estates, but, as David Wengrow (2006: 142–46, 220-31, 266) has shown, bureaucratic structures of production in Egypt had originally emerged largely through the need to manage their domains, and Old Kingdom records suggest they continued to make up a very large part of Egypt's economy (Muhs 2016: 42–45, 106, 125–26.) Another large chunk of the kingdom's revenue was paid directly to gods via various temples. Nineteen pyramids then meant nineteen dead pharaohs, each with his own lands and administrative organization, competing not only for ritual attention, but also for their share in the total surplus production—that is, the grain, meat, and vegetables being extracted from the peasants who inhabited rural estates. Unas' claims to devour the gods (including his own ancestors) might be seen as a defiant assertion of ultimate sovereignty from one god surrounded by a host of equally hungry rivals.

* * *

Curiously, Egyptian monarchs were not the only ones to face this dilemma. The situation for Inka emperors was if anything even more extreme.

The Inka succession system (Cobo [1653] 1979: 111, 248; Conrad 1981; Zuidema 1990; Gose 1996a, 1996b; Jenkins 2001; Moore 2004; Yaya 2015) is rarely discussed outside of the work of specialists, which is odd because it's clearly the key to understanding the rapid expansion of the Inka empire. The latter is one of the few political entities that existed in the American hemisphere before Columbus that is universally recognized to be a state, and it was quite a formidable one, extending a uniform system of administration over a territory that at its peak spanned some two thousand miles, from Ecuador to Chile. The basis of the almost frenetic pace of its expansion (its rulers conquered a territory that stretched two thousand miles in little more than a century) lay in a system which ensured that dead rulers continued to hold almost all the powers and privileges they had in life.

Inheritance was patrilineal, and sovereign power passed from a dead Inka to his eldest, or most capable, son. Sovereign power, however, was almost the only thing the new Inka inherited. Old kings were mummified, and the mummies had to be treated in much the same way as a living person.

> Upon the death of an Inca ruler the rights to govern, to wage war, and to impose taxes on the empire passed directly to his principal heir, who became the next head of state. However, the deceased emperor's buildings, servants, chattel, and other possessions continued to be treated as his property and were entrusted to a corporate social group (*panaqa* or royal *ayllu*) containing his other descendants. These secondary heirs did not actually receive ownership of the items named above; they derived their support from the *panaqa*'s own holdings. Instead, they managed their ancestor's property for him, using it to care for his mummy and maintain his cult. In effect, a deceased emperor's *panaqa* treated him as if he were still alive. (Conrad 1981: 9)

Each new ruler, or *Sapa Inka* ("Unique Inka," his singularity consisting in the fact that he was still alive), was therefore expected to gather together a company of warriors and conquer new territories with which to support his own court, wives, and retainers. In the meantime, his father's mummy carried on much as before, attending rituals, managing his property, holding regular court at his urban palace or country estates, and throwing feasts for visiting notables, at which his will would be conveyed by mediums (Gose 1996a: 19–20).

Not all rulers would become estate-owning mummies: some died "bad deaths" and their bodies were destroyed or not recovered; others died before they had managed to conquer any territories of their own to begin with (Yaya 2015: 651). Still, the accumulation of palaces made Cuzco, the Inka capital, into a very unusual sort of city, with an ever-increasing number of fully staffed royal palaces (Rowe 1967: 60–61), each the ritual focus on an ever-burgeoning *panaqa* made up of all descendants of the (non-succeeding) children of the former king.

One reason such an arrangement is so unusual is that it brings out a fundamental contradiction in the logic of dynastic rule—one which most systems attempt to finesse in one way or another, but which is impossible to ignore in situations when old kings are still physically present in such dramatic ways. The contradiction is that while older monarchs will always tend to outrank younger ones (partly simply by the principle of seniority, partly in most cases too because they are closer to the charisma of the original stranger-king founder of the dynasty), their descendants will tend to be ranked the other way around: those particularly identified with the earlier rulers will tend to rank lower than those identified with more recent ones, and their position in the total genealogical order will continue to decline steadily as time goes on.

This sounds counterintuitive at first, but it makes perfect sense if you consider how such ranked lineage systems work. If you imagine a genealogy starting with King A, and proceeding through A's eldest son, King B, then B's eldest son, King C, and so on, then the descendants of the younger (noninheriting) sons of King A have only declining status to look forward over time. After all, the younger sons of King B are still descended from King A (King B's father), the younger sons of King C still descended from A and B as well, and so forth, down to the children of the present king today, who are of course princes, and of the highest rank of all. Nonetheless, a lineage founded by the younger children of King A, the founder of the dynasty, and only descended from King A and not any of the others, will tend to be identified with King A, typically be charged with taking care of his tomb or shrines or relics, or otherwise maintain a special ritual status based on their identification with the founder of the dynasty and greatest of all kings. And the descendants of King B will likely enjoy a slightly lower ritual status, of C lower than that, and so on.

Thus, the lowest-ranking royal lineage will be the guardian of the memory of the highest-ranking royal ancestor.

Lineages where everyone is ranked in order of birth are referred to in the anthropological literature as "conical clans" or "ramages," and their implications have been worked out in detail (Kirchhoff 1949, 1955; Sahlins 1958; for application to the Inka case, Jenkins 2001). If the founder of a lineage has three children—let's assume for simplicity's sake that whether they are sons or daughters doesn't matter, which is in fact often the case—then they are ranked numbers 1, 2, and 3, but if each of those has three children, the children of the second are no longer number 2, but numbers 4, 5, and 6, in the next generation, numbers 10–19, and so on. The technical term for this is "sinking status" (H. Geertz and C. Geertz 1975: 124–31; C. Geertz 1980: 26–32). If one does not become king, one's descendants have no place to go but down, and one can expect one's line to become lower and lower in rank as time goes on. It's commonplace in such a system to have a cut-off point: thus, among both the Natchez and Merina, it was said that after seven generations royal descendants lose any noble privileges and become commoners again.

In reality, of course, things are never this simple, since human beings normally have two parents, not one, and marriage allows one to avoid the inevitability of decline—either by marrying back up, or by marrying outside the system entirely (the stranger-king principle again). But the more a unilinear genealogy, matrilineal or patrilineal or cognatic, is determinant of status, the more will the principle of sinking status, inevitably, apply.

In the Inka case, for instance, in 1532, the Valley of Cuzco surrounding the capital came to be entirely occupied by members of the ten *panaqa* descended from former kings, and these were indeed ranked by genealogical distance from the core lines (Zuidema 1964, 1989; Gose 1996b: 405; Jenkins 2011: 179–81). All claimed descent from Manco Capac, founder of the empire, but the *panaqa* specifically identified with Manco Capac, Chima Panaqa, and which kept the founder's image and conducted rituals on his behalf, in fact ranked lowest (Bauer 1998: 125–26).

What I am proposing here is that, in the case of royal genealogies at least (and these are, by definition, ranked), there are in fact two different kinds of sinking status at play, and that they work at cross-purposes. On the one hand, collateral branches will inevitably spin off the royal line, just like the *panaqa*, and each new one that spins off pushes all the older ones even further downward in rank. We can refer to this "collateral" or "horizontal" descending status: the further a lineage gets from the center, the less exalted it becomes. On the other hand, we can also distinguish a principle of vertical descending status, that applies within the core dynastic line itself.[48] All things being equal, the founder of a dynasty will necessarily rank higher than his descendants, for the same reason that fathers outrank sons, and because the longer a dynasty endures, the more distant the current ruler will be seen to fall from the original (often alien) sources of his or her power.

I think this is a structural feature, or, at the very least, a constant tendency within any dynastic system; but the problem becomes all the more acute in traditional societies where history itself is seen as a process of rupture or decline from mythic or heroic times. Michael Puett has argued that in Bronze Age China, during the Shang (c .1600–1046 BC) and Zhou (1046–256 BC) dynasties, this problem became systemic. Each ruler's ritual role was to sacrifice to his father, who would then intervene with his own father, and so on, up the chain to

---

48. The terminology was first suggested to me by Marshall Sahlins; it somewhat echoes Clifford Geertz, who speaks of genealogical status "dimming" both vertically and horizontally in Bali (1980: 16), but the usage is not identical.

the original founder of the dynasty, who would intervene with God (or heaven) for the well-being of his people:

> In such a sacrificial system, however, there was a built-in inevitability of decline. . . . Since it was defined genealogically each subsequent generation would grow ever more distant from the ancestors serving Heaven. . . . As reigning kings grew ritually weaker, rival claimants from powerful lineages inevitably began seeking allegiances that would allow them to overthrow the king and begin a new dynasty. (Puett 2012: 214)

Puett makes the intriguing argument that the First Emperor (259–210 BC) attempted to break the cycle by declaring himself a god, who could therefore remain available for direct contact for his descendants, no matter what the genealogical distance; but the project failed, leading, ultimately, to the distinctly human Chinese conception of kingship we find in the Han and thereafter (ibid.: 216–18; cf. 2002: 237–45). Still, Chinese sages simply found other reasons to insist that dynasties tended toward inevitable decline.

The term "sinking status" was originally coined by the Geertzes (1975) to describe the ranked lineage system of Bali, where lineages that spin off core descent lines are always in danger of losing status over time, but here too one can speak of both vertical and horizontal sinking status. All Balinese kings claim descent from the princes who fled from the downfall of the Javanese kingdom of Majapahit, but the Babad Dalem chronicle recounts how even the highest-ranking branch of the royal line, the kings of Gelgel and Klungkung, steadily decline from their divine origins when one misstep or another leads to a fall from grace: hence even the rank of kings, as indicated by their titles, descends from godlike Mpu, to priestly Sri, to the relatively modest warrior titles Dalem and Dewa (see C. Geertz 1980: 15–18; Weiner 1995: 105–35; Acciaioli 2009: 62–65). Here, the contradiction between vertical and horizontal principles plays itself out explicitly, since each lineage that splits off from the royal line should rank properly higher than those who split earlier, but, in fact, the effect is countered by the fact that the ruling line itself was losing rank—no doubt creating all sorts of opportunities for neighbors to develop deeply felt disagreements about who is ultimately superior to who (see fig. 2).[49]

---

49. For some reason, all the spin-off lines in figure 2 are represented as descended from Satria lineages that are formally of the same rank, but there were *dadia* or lineages descended from later monarchs as well.

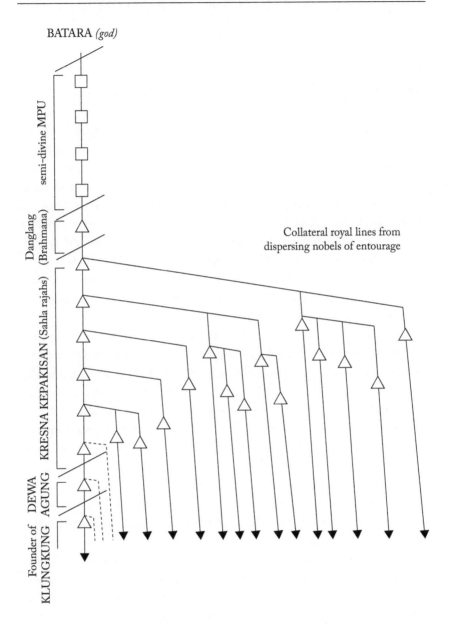

Figure 2. Sinking status (Acciaioli 2009: 63).

* * *

Rather than multiply examples (the idea that royal dynasties are often seen as prone to decadence is hardly controversial), let me sum up the argument so far.

I have proposed that when kings definitively win what I've called the constitutive war between sovereign and people, succeeding in extending sovereign power to their kingdom as a whole, they will tend to take the assumption of their godlike status (the very weapon used against them when popular forces win) as inspiration to actually try to transcend mortality. They will make themselves legends, transform the landscape, create dynasties. However, insofar as they succeed, this will always create problems for their successors, especially if those successors wish to do the same. Generations fall in rivalry with one another. Living kings find themselves choked and surrounded by the dead.

Now, I do not think this problem is peculiar to royal dynasties. Actually, something like this is likely to happen wherever the status of the living is dependent on ancestors who are similar to themselves.

I first came to this conclusion when thinking about mortuary ritual in highland Madagascar (Graeber 1995), where *famadihana* ceremonies, which people of all social backgrounds now perform, have a peculiar double-edged quality. Such rituals simultaneously celebrate the memories of the dead, and allow descendants to efface those memories by literally pulverizing the ancestors' bodies. This ambivalence can be observed wherever ancestors take human form. On the one hand, if one has no ancestors at all, one is not really a social person (in Madagascar one becomes a "lost person," which is a polite way of saying "slave"); on the other, if an ancestor is simply someone who succeeded in keeping his children around him and being remembered as the founder or great ancestor of a village or clan or tomb, then that ancestor will inevitably be in a position of rivalry in relation to any descendant whose ultimate ambition is to do the same.

I suspect we are in the presence of a general sociological principle here. When ancestors are seen as being fundamentally different from their descendants, or as existing in a fundamentally different *kind* of time (the Australian Dreamtime, for example), they tend to be seen as sources of power for their present-day descendants; when they are fundamentally similar and living in the same sort of time, like Malagasy ancestors, they tend to be seen as rivals and sources of constraint. The former is particularly true of those societies of Australia and North and South America that are marked by totemism, where ancestral figures are not even human, or exist in a kind of mythological time where present-day differences between gods, humans, and animals did not yet exist; the latter tends to be the case in societies in Africa, East Asia, and the Austronesian world, where one instead finds widespread worship or propitiation of named human ancestors.

Highland Malagasy mortuary ritual, I also suggested, is to a certain degree a popularization of royal ritual. This raises the intriguing question of how often and to what extent ancestor cults on the popular level are always appropriations of, or at least influenced by, royal or aristocratic practice. The matter can only be resolved through further research, and no doubt the relation is one of mutual appropriation; but for present purposes, I will merely point out that it is in precisely in those parts of the world marked by ancestor worship where one also encounters kingdoms, whereas in the totemic zone, monarchy effectively does not exist.[50] There are, as in all things, a few exceptions (largely in East Africa, including curiously both Ganda and Shilluk), but the Americas would seem to provide strong confirmation, since it is precisely in those places where we do find kingdoms—in the Andes, and among Maya and Zapotec—where totemism is weak or nonexistent, and one finds ancestor cults instead.[51]

Be this as it may, throughout the totemic zone, ancestors, while often seen as dangerous, give various forms of power to their descendants; throughout the zone

---

50. Obviously it is hardly the case that all societies that practice ancestor worship are kingdoms; I am merely pointing out that in those parts of the world where ancestors are propitiated, monarchy is a common form of government, whereas in those parts of the world marked by totemic clan systems, it is not. The argument is much more complicated than I can develop here. On the one hand, as I noted in the case of the Merina monarchy in chapter 5, monarchic and aristocratic systems tend to deny commoners genealogies, which helps explain why it is often in the more egalitarian polities around kingdoms (Nuer, Tiv, Tallensi, et al.) that one finds the most generalized systems of ancestor worship; on the other hand, in appropriating royal practices, commoners also end up with the same problems in that the ancestors tend to be demanding, vindictive, and so on.

51. This seems to hold true even in North America—the Natchez had totemic clans by 1900, but the consensus seems to be they borrowed them from neighbors after the kingdom was destroyed (Swanton 1905: 667; Knight 1990: 14). The fact that cults of aristocratic ancestors appear to have flourished under the Mississippian kingdoms, and largely vanished with the monarchy itself (Knight 1986: 683-84; Ethridge 2010: 224) suggests that at least in the Americas, it is not so much that societies with ancestor worship are more likely to develop kingdoms, but that the presence of kingdoms are likely to lead, eventually at least, to the dissemination of ancestor cults. The one possible exception is among the Mexica, where neither ancestor worship nor totemism is present.

marked by propitiation of named human ancestors, royal, aristocratic, or otherwise, ancestral spirits tend to impose themselves in unwanted ways: at best, they
need to be constantly propitiated, at worst, they make themselves known through
the vindictive or arbitrary (i.e., sovereign) infliction of disaster and death.[52]

Kings invariably have ancestors of the human type, and those ancestors regularly tend to become a problem. Typically, the original stranger-king founder
of a dynasty is seen as a source of legitimacy and power rather than a constraint
(unless, that is, the current monarch is particularly ambitious), but the closer
one comes to the present, the more of a burden ancestral memories tend to
become. The Egyptian and Peruvian mummies are just extreme examples of a
more general tendency. Just as much of the panoply of Frazerian sacred kingship
can be seen as a series of techniques for reining in and controlling monarchs, so
too can many of the ritual institutions one sees in kingdoms where sovereignty
has, indeed, broken out of its initial frame, where kings have won, as I've put it,
be seen as consisting of so many strategies for coping with this problem—itself
mere one manifestation of the more general problem of vertical sinking status.

Space does not permit a detailed exposition, but a rough list of such strategies would at the very least include:

1. killing or exiling the dead, in the sense of erasing or marginalizing their
   memories;
2. becoming the dead, in the sense of creating a positional succession system;
3. outdoing one's ancestors in some dramatic way, the most historically important of which appear to have been:
   a. the creation of monuments;
   b. the conquest of new territories;
   c. mass human sacrifice; and
4. turning history on its head and inventing a myth of progress.

---

52. This is clearly true in most African and Austronesian cases; Japan, China, and
    other East Asian societies might seem exceptions, since ancestors there are
    always represented at least superficially in a benevolent light. But in fact ancestors
    everywhere are represented in a superficially benevolent light; the veneer just seems
    much thicker in these cases, largely I suspect owing to the existence of intellectual
    traditions such as Confucianism that have turned the idealization into a moral
    exercise. In neither the elite nor popular tradition, though, do ancestors benefit
    their descendants, and on the popular level, if unpropitiated, they are apt to turn
    into dangerous ghosts (Kwon 2008: 20–25; Puett 2013).

Let me end by considering these briefly, one at a time:

1. Killing or exiling the dead

"Genealogical amnesia" (or "structural amnesia") is an inevitable feature of any system of descent. Not all dead can be remembered. Clans, for instance, are descent groups that claim descent from a single ancestor but cannot trace the intermediary links to their own grandparents (or however far back they remember), everyone in between is simply forgotten. But even in a segmentary lineage system like the Nuer, where ostensibly everyone can trace back to the founders of their descent groups through an unbroken chain of ancestors, there is an "amnesiac space" (M. Douglas 1980: 84) five generations back, a memory hole into which ancestors must disappear to ensure that there are always only ten to twelve generations between the founding ancestors, who always remain the same, and the present.

When the bodies of ancestors are physically there (as in highland Malagasy tombs, or Inka mummies), or ancestors otherwise memorialized in physical shrines, relics, or other material tokens, this obviously becomes much harder to do. The objects themselves must be dealt with in some way. The same is true when genealogies are preserved in writing, as with Chinese ancestral tablets, or when there are institutional structures (such as the Egyptian funerary priests, or Shilluk royal lineages) whose existence is based on keeping those memories alive. In the case of royal ancestors, any or all these things are likely to be the case. There is always a social and material apparatus of memory. For this reason, kings often find it very difficult to efface the memories of particular royal ancestors even if they wish to. I've already mentioned the story of the Shilluk king who tried, and failed, to sneak into the shrine of a royal ancestor in order to demote his descendants (see chapter 2). Even the much more powerful Ganda kings were sometimes foiled in similar attempts. When one particularly high-handed *kabaka* ordered the shrine of a divinized ancestor be burned to the ground, "a spark from the burning shrine flew up and burned the Queen Mother's breast," leaving a wound that continued to pain her until the king finally relented and ordered the shrine be restored to its former state (Kagwa 1971: 74; Wrigley 1996: 211).[53]

---

53. Generally speaking, it would seem that royal ancestors were seen as not particularly remarkable ancestral spirits by royals, and as gods by everyone else (Ray 1991: 150–53).

For kings to erase ancestral memories, then, requires extreme measures, and those measures may backfire. Attempts to wipe ancestors out of history, as, for instance, the New Kingdom pharaoh Thutmoses III famously tried to wipe out his mother Hatshepsut and her steward Senenmut, rarely succeed (though admittedly if such a project did succeed completely, we would not know about it).[54]

Still, even when ancestors cannot be destroyed, they can be marginalized or made irrelevant. Stranger-kingship itself might be seen in some cases as a way of wiping the slate clean by starting over somewhere else. Another approach is to mark some sort of fundamental break or rupture so as to announce a new dynasty. Obviously, this is more likely to be an expedient used by popular forces or court officials *against* sitting kings, but there are also cases where the dynastic break appears to be internal. The case of Unas is again instructive. He is considered the last ruler of the Fifth Dynasty, but in fact there is no evidence his successor, Teti, was an outsider in any particular sense (W. S. Smith 1971: 189–91; Rice 2003: 210; Grimal 1988: 79–81)—most of Unas' court officials remained in place, and the new pharaoh, presumably from at least a collateral branch of the ruling line, appears to have married one of the old pharaoh's daughters to preserve continuity. He also founded a new capital further from the old burial grounds and built two pyramids, in addition to his own, for his primary wives, all of which suggests an effort to restart the historical memory—and, presumably, limit the postmortem ambitions of the overweening Unas. In the latter endeavor he had only very limited success, since Unas was later revived as a local deity, and was still receiving popular cult around Saqqara many centuries later during the Middle and New Kingdoms, by which time Teti would appear to have been largely forgotten (Malek 2000: 250–56).

This leads to the final peril of attempts to marginalize earlier rulers, ancestors or otherwise: that even if the social apparatus by which their memories are maintained is thoroughly uprooted, they may become popular heroes, taken up as a weapon on the other side of the constitutive war between king and people. This often happens at the end of dynasties. The first recorded case we have is, surprisingly, the Emperor Nero, the last of the Julio-Claudians. Nero is now

---

54. I should emphasize that I am speaking here of the difficulty of destroying the memories of a king's *own* ancestors. The systematic destruction and/or desecration of the apparatus of memory for conquered rulers is a regular practice; our first historical record of such practices coming from the Assyrian empire, which would regularly attempt to uproot and destroy the memory of conquered dynasties (Suriano 2010: 65–67), but the practice is commonplace.

remembered through the eyes of his enemies as a monster, a bloodthirsty psychopath who, ridiculously, fancied himself a great poet, actor, and musician. But even in the official accounts there are strong indications that his eccentricities actually cut quite the other way: during his early reign he systematically refused to sign death warrants, and even ordered that gladiators no longer fight to the death at games he sponsored. (He did, however, on one occasion order that senators themselves take part in the now bloodless fencing contests, which might begin to explain some of the vitriol.) He also attempted to negotiate a permanent peace with Rome's main imperial rival Parthia.[55] Odd though it may seem, Nero was about as close to a pacifist as Rome produced. He might have gone a bit further than some in trying to glorify his name and preserve his memory ("he took the former appellations from many things and numerous places and gave them new ones from his own name. He also called the month of April Neroneus and was minded to name Rome Neropolis" [Suetonius, *Nero* 55]). After Nero was overthrown in a military coup in AD 68, all of this apparatus of memory was immediately dismantled, he became one of the few Julio-Claudians never to be deified,[56] and attempts were made to paint him as a tyrant so awful that the subsequent imposition of military rule was entirely justified (Henderson 1905; Griffin 1984; Champlin 2003).

Most of Nero's former subjects, apparently, disagreed. Already in AD 96, we read that "even now, everybody wishes Nero were still alive; and the great majority believe that he is" (Dio Chrysostom 21.10). Three different pretenders

---

55. Nero's misfortune was that while he was anything but brutal by Roman standards, those relative few on whom he did vent his wrath—Christians, who were widely held to have been responsible for the fire that devastated Rome in AD 64, and the senatorial class, after many, including his former mentor Seneca, were implicated in an assassination plot in AD 65—were precisely those who wrote later histories. For what it's worth, I have always personally suspected that Christians (perhaps the Peter faction) actually were at least partly responsible for the great fire—some certainly can be seen to be gloating about it in Revelations 18.8-20—and that Nero might not have actually died in AD 68 at all, since the account of his suddenly abandoning a plan to flee to the east for no particular reason and instead killing himself (Suetonius *Nero* 48–49) seems novelistic and implausible. For all we know, the "imposter" who ended up in Persia was really him.

56. Normal practice was to deify emperors only after their deaths so the reigning *princeps* could be referred to as "son of a god" (*divi filius*). Nero thus duly deified his adopted father Claudius, and later added his wife Poppaea and daughter Claudia, but for obvious reasons he did not receive the same honors after his own death (Woolf 2002: 250).

claiming to be Nero appeared in the eastern provinces, at least one sparking a widespread revolt; the Parthians kept another as a bargaining chip; and as late as AD 410, St. Augustine of Hippo wrote that pagans still insisted Nero was sleeping somewhere, waiting "until the time is right" to reclaim his throne, just as Christians feared that, though dead, he would rise from the grave as Antichrist (*Civ. Dei* 20.19.3). As one biographer writes:

> The persistent expectation that Nero would return from hiding (or from the dead, in the negative formulation of the Antichrist) puts him into the select company of historical figures whom people wanted to return, figures like King Arthur, Charlemagne, Saint Olaf, Frederick Barbarossa, Frederick II, Constantine XI, Tsar Alexander I, and Elvis Presley. (Champlin 2003: 21)

The latter, significantly, referred to as "the King."[57] To which list one might add Cuatemoc in Mexico and Tupac Amaru in Peru. Almost every one of these was a figure whose memory his successors had attempted, vainly, to suppress.

2. Becoming the dead

Another way to solve the problem is by declaring oneself the same person as a previous, more famous ruler, or, even more, through a system of positional succession, saying that all kings are effectively the same person. Think of this perhaps as the ultimate extension of Marshall Sahlins' "kinship" or "heroic I," whereby a Maori chief can tell an enemy, "I killed your grandfather," referring to an event that happened many centuries before (Prytz-Johansen 1954: 29–31; Sahlins 1983a: 522–23; 2013: 36–37).

Stephanie Dalley (2005: 20) has argued that the former approach was quite common in the ancient Middle East, where living monarchs could assimilate themselves to more famous antecedents, "prototypes" of great rulers—as, say, Sargon I of Assyria (722–705 BC) simply took on the name and persona of Sargon of Akkad (c. 2340–2284 BC), or various independently minded queens in the same part of the world all became "Semiramis."[58] One might say there is

---

57. For an excellent Durkheimian analysis of Elvis as messiah figure in the American religion of consumerism, see Stromberg (1990).

58. "A striking feature of ancient Mesopotamian history is the naming of a new king after a much earlier king of a different dynasty to whom he was unrelated. Sargon, Naram-Sin, and Nebuchadnezzar are three obvious examples" (Dalley 2005: 20).

a strong form and a weak form of such identification. Almost all kings will play this game in the weak sense: either by identifying with past heroes (as Edward IV, to take a fairly random example, presented himself as a reincarnation of King Arthur [Hughes 2002]), or just by all taking the same name: this is why in the High Middle Ages almost all English monarchs were named either Henry or Edward, and France had sixteen different kings named Louis. Attempting this strategy in the strong sense of claiming to actually *be* Sargon, or Arthur, or the last Louis, is relatively rare. All Shilluk *reths* are embodiments of the founder, "Nyikang," but one reason the Shilluk kingship is considered so interesting and exotic is because they are one of the few to take this principle to its logical conclusion, and even among the Shilluk, it's not as if the historical personalities of individual sovereigns are actually wiped out.

In fact, positional succession systems, whereby whoever takes a given office is assimilated to some historical prototype, are much more typical of relatively egalitarian political orders like the seventeenth-/eighteenth-century Haudenosaunee ("League of the Iroquois"), where the characters said to have been involved in the creation of the League centuries before were still very much alive: the fire-keeper of the central Onondaga lodge was always Thadodaho; the Roll Call of the Founders recorded the names of fifty original chiefs who were still present at every League council (Morgan 1851: 64–65; Graeber 2001: 121–29; Abler 2004). But these were societies where there was no real difference between names and titles, since each clan had a fixed stock of names, which could only be portioned out by clan matrons one at a time, and the entire effect seems to be to minimize the scope for personal self-aggrandizement.[59] Kings tend to avoid positional succession for exactly this reason. It might allow them to destroy their ancestors' ability to make a unique name for themselves, but only by the sacrifice of their own.

There are few exceptions. Perhaps the most famous is the Luapulu kingdom of Central Africa, whose ruler is always Kazembe (Cunnison 1956, 1957, 1959)—but only because the Luapulu dynasty appears to have conquered a group of people who, very unusually for Africa, practice positional succession in their lineages. (When a man or woman dies, for instance, another is given their name, and accedes to their possessions and even family, though they are

---

59. For this reason, the two most famous figures in the epic, considered the founders of the League—Deganawideh and Hiawatha—still exist as titles, but their positions are never filled.

allowed after a brief decent interval to divorce an unwanted spouse acquired in this way.) By far the more common pattern is the weak version exemplified by the medieval notion of the "King's Two Bodies" (Kantorowicz 1957), where the king is a flesh-and-blood individual, capable of receiving personal allegiance, and an immortal concept at the same time.

3. Outdoing the dead

This one is fairly self-explanatory; we've already seen how even kings who accomplish feats so extraordinary their own ancestors vanish (does anyone know or care who Alexander's grandparents were?) will make up some imaginary rival like Semiramis to compete with. We've also seen how monarchs dealt with the continued presence of mummified ancestors in political life in two very different circumstances: in Peru, where each new Inka had to conquer a new territory to feed their dependents; and in Egypt, where, the Nile Valley being circumscribed and further opportunities for conquest rarely available, the result was an efflorescence of monumental architecture unparalleled before or since.

Building monuments, of course, is effective only if one manages to attach one's name to that monument over the long term. It can be difficult to make names stick. As we've seen in the case of Semiramis, if you establish enduring fame—however you manage to attain it—you will also tend to get credit for all sorts of monuments you did not build and probably never even touched or saw, in much the way that all witty things said in late-nineteenth-century America now tend to be attributed to Mark Twain, or in England, to either George Bernard Shaw or Oscar Wilde, leaving those who actually did say the witty things or build the various earthworks, walls, towers, and cities ascribed to the queen to languish in obscurity.

There is another option I haven't really discussed, however, and that's a hypertrophy of sovereignty itself, in the specific sense of arbitrary destructive power. It is hard to find any other explanation for why, when kings do manage to accumulate enough power that their kingdoms can be called "states"—basically that tipping-point at which kings can be definitively said to win—one of the first things they do is embark on some kind of campaign of ritualized murder. Such massacres include the acts of mass sadism that, as Lewis Mumford used to point out (1967: 183–85), we so often squeamishly write out of history—the massacres, torture, mutilation—but typically, in this initial phase at least, they can justifiably be labeled human sacrifice.

For archaeologists, for instance, it is notorious that the mass slaughter of retainers at the burial of rulers tends to mark the very first stages of the emergence of states.[60] It can sometimes escalate to the massacre of entire courts. The phenomenon has been thoroughly documented among other places for early Egypt, Ur, Nubia, Cahokia, China, Korea, Tibet, and Japan; as well as the Moche in Peru, Scythians, and Huns (Childe 1945; Davies 1984; Parker Pearson 1999; van Dijk 2007; Morris 2007, 2014). It has also been documented ethnographically in West Africa, India, and among the Natchez. As the final example makes clear, when one is dealing with kings whose absolute and arbitrary power was largely confined to the circle of their own court, such mass killings might best viewed as a kind of final supernova of sovereignty—but a sovereignty still incapable, for all its blazing out in glory, of bursting through its frames. It's also important to remember these sacrifices were organized not by the former king (who was after all dead) but by his successor. In this light it's telling that at least two of the more dramatic cases of retainer sacrifice (Peru, early Egypt) are in precisely places where later we find dead kings maintaining their own courts and retinues, and competing with the living for a share of the surplus—suggesting one motive might simply be to ensure this did not occur. Instead, in a curious twist, a final display of divine power that ostensibly catapults the ruler into godhood also serves to wipe out the entire human apparatus that had served to, in Audrey Richards' (1964) felicitous phrase, "keep the king divine."

Why, then, does it stop? Ellen Morris (2014: 86–87) suggests that, historically, retainer sacrifice tends to lead to a dangerous game of one-upmanship. Other royal households, or just wealthy and powerful ones, will adopt the practice; kings will then feel they have to kill even more retainers to assert their exceptional nature. They will also, inevitably, come to measure themselves against former kings. We have some good descriptions of what the process might look like at its peak from the West African kingdoms of Asante, Benin, and Dahomey (Law 1985; Rowlands 1993; Terray 1994), as well as Buganda (Ray 1991), which seem to roughly approximate, in scale and general tenor, what has been documented archaeologically from Bronze Age China (R. Campbell 2014). As the circle of those slated for death expands from intimates, who one can at least imagine gave up their lives voluntarily, to entire courts, to massacres

---

60. "Large-scale retainer sacrifices are typically witnessed when a state suddenly and dramatically expands in geographic domain and coercive power. At such times the conception of the ruler is ripe for reformulation" (E. F. Morris 2007: 17 n. 3).

of hundreds or even thousands of prisoners or war, criminals, or simply random subjects swept up on the roads, in displays of sheer arbitrary power.

> The royal funerary process ended with an orgy of killing, called *kiwendo*, or "mass execution," which inaugurated the shrine of the deceased king. Such killings occurred whenever a royal shrine was rebuilt or on the rare occasions when the king visited such a shrine in person. In 1880, Mutesa reportedly had two thousand people killed at [his father] Ssunna's shrine after it was rebuilt. The victims, who were peasants traveling to the capital and transporting goods in the service of their chiefs, were captured by the royal police as they approached the narrow bridges leading to the capital . . . . (Ray 1991: 169)

Here, sovereignty does break through its containing frames—as part of a curious double game whereby living kings, in an ostensible bid to honor their ancestors, actually vied to outdo them. But the fact of sovereignty exploding its limits and challenging the dead in this way also tended to render it untenable. In many African cases, we find kings remarking on the burden of constantly having to display their vitality through the deaths of others.[61] Mutesa, as it happened, had no such compunctions, but as a result his memory became infamous and after his reign the executions largely ceased.

This is what usually happens. In all the cases we know best, at least, once matters reach such a pass, some kind of moral backlash eventually begins to set in. Or popular unrest. Or both. This may lead to abandoning the custom entirely, usually when converting to a world religion (e.g., Buddhism in Korea: Conte and Kim 2016; Christianity in Buganda and Benin); it might lead to gradual adoption of symbolic substitutes, such as the armies of terracotta soldiers in Anyang (R. Campbell 2014); it might even lead to a kind of attenuated popularization, where broad sections of the elite adopt the practice but only in carefully limited form. The latter appears to be the case with *sáti* in certain parts of India, where the widows of high-caste men were expected to commit suicide at their husbands' funeral (E. J. Thompson 1928; Morris 2014: 84),[62] but the fact that

---

61. So, for example, David Livingstone was told if the *kabaka* didn't kill people, people would think he was dead (Ray 1991: 179), and Benin's *oba* told one foreign visitor he was "sick of it all," but felt he had no choice (Roth 1903: 66).

62. This statement is somewhat contentious. Retainer sacrifice used to be referred to in the archaeological literature as "*sáti*-burials" until Trigger (1969: 257) pointed out there was no evidence for retainer sacrifice in India. Still, the fact that the practice

the practice spread from rulers' households via warrior castes is certainly sugges-tive. It also brings home the deep logic of such sacrificial projects: to telegraph, as clearly as possible, that certain lives have value only for the sake of others. Foreign observers often expressed shock at the willingness of many wives, serv-ants, and other intimates of dead kings and grandees to voluntarily follow them to the grave (though, invariably, some were more enthusiastic than others). The high-caste Hindu household where the wife is taught to address and treat her husband like a god, and to throw herself on his pyre, is just a more explicit form of the same logic of self-sacrifice that expects widows in Mediterranean coun-tries to spend the rest of their days wearing black in mourning (or, in parts of India where *sáti* is not practiced, white in mourning); but at the same it is also a microcosmic version of the patrimonial kingdom, which, as described by Hocart (1950), is itself seen as a giant household where each social group ultimate ex-ists primarily for its allotted role in feeding, maintaining, and deifying the king.

One might go further. Are not these mass ritual killings—especially those that ensue when the violence explodes the framework of the royal household and does become veritable civicide (Feeley-Harnik 1985: 277)—moments when the contradiction between two notions of the relations of king and peo-ple, one, the notion of kingdom as household, the other, of the constitutive war, is actually exposed? As always, the sheer arbitrariness, the lack of meaning[63] in the selection of victims—who are often swept up entirely at random—is itself a way of conveying the absolute nature of royal power. If one cannot kill everyone, the closest one can come is to demonstrate one might kill *any*one. This remains true when the massacres are specifically intended to appease royal ancestors (as in Benin), when they are sacrifices to gods, but not to ancestors (as among the Mexica), when they are directed against witches (as in Madagascar: S. Ellis 2002), or, finally, when they serve no purpose other than to demonstrate the king's absolute "power of life and death over his subjects" (as in Ganda coronation rituals: Mair 1934: 179). Whatever the excuse, the same logic of es-calation seemed to apply—likely leading to the eventual abandonment of mass

---

began with rulers and then spread via the warrior castes, and foreign accounts of hundreds of women sacrificing themselves at royal funerals (e.g., Barbosa [1518] 1918: 213–14), suggest something on the scale of the most dramatic examples of retainer sacrifice elsewhere.

63. I am using "meaning" in the hermeneutic sense of intentionality behind a statement or an act.

killing for fear that the contradictions of sovereignty might eventually destroy the kingdom itself.[64]

4. Reversing the direction of history

Just about all of these expedients, then, are fraught with difficulties, or likely to self-destruct. There is one final approach. One can challenge the logic of sinking status directly, by reframing history not as a story of inevitable decline, but as one of incremental progress.

We are used to assuming that the idea of progress is a recent innovation, and that all "traditional" societies (i.e., all societies up until, say, Renaissance or even perhaps Enlightenment Europe) assumed, instead, that they descended from gods rather than having evolved from savages. In fact, a significant number of human societies seemed to have held both positions at the same time. As Arthur Lovejoy exhaustively documented for Greco-Roman antiquity, it was nearly universally assumed, by most ancient authors, that humans once lived in caves and subsisted on nuts and berries, before the discovery of the arts and sciences brought about urban civilization (Lovejoy and Boas 1935; cf. Adelstein 1967; Nisbet 1980). What they differed on—and here they often differed quite sharply—was not the reality of progress, but its moral significance: whether the earliest days of humanity should be considered a Golden Age, or a time of benighted savagery. Advocates of "Primitivist" and "Anti-Primitivist" positions continued to debate the question until Christianity succeeded in temporarily settling matters in favor of Eden for roughly a millennium. (Then, of course, it started up again much as before.)

These debates are relevant because very often the inventions or discoveries that made civilized life possible were ascribed to kings. Or gods; but for this very reason, the two categories, kings and gods, often came to overlap. Hecataeus represented the Egyptian gods as great inventors, made kings for their creations: of writing (Thoth), agriculture (Isis), viniculture (Osiris), and so on (Diodorus Siculus 1.13.3, 1.14–16; 1.43. 6). Later Euhemerus was to turn his account into a general theory, arguing that all stories about gods were really memories of kings, queens, and other remarkable mortals, and it became regular

---

64. One might speculate that the common folktale motifs of wicked kings cursed with insatiable demands for human flesh or blood, of whom the prototype perhaps is the Persian Zahhak, might reflect to some degree on this structural condition.

practice, even among those who were not outright Euhemerists, to ascribe discoveries to rulers who had gone on to become deities: Semiramis, for instance, was credited by Pliny with the invention of both weaving (ibid.: 7.417) and certain types of long-hulled ships (ibid.: 7.57).

China around the same time witnessed similar debates. There, too, was the assumption of a gradual invention of arts and techniques, and the "sages" who made these inventions and discoveries were frequently represented as monarchs. (The Yellow Emperor, for example, was held to be have been personally responsible for the invention of house-building and weaving, and his wife invented silk.) There, too, a lively controversy about the moral status of technological progress ensued, with Mohists seeing technological and social invention as a rise from savagery, Taoists as a fall from a Golden Age, and Confucians taking a variety of nuanced positions in between (Needham 1954: 51–54; J. Levi 1977; Puett 2002).

If all one is doing here is taking stories of the creation of cultural institutions by primordial gods, and transposing them to stories of their creation by primordial kings, the ramifications might not be particularly profound. It still leaves kings of the present day very much in the shadow of their ancestors. In fact, if one represents the founder of one's kingdom also as the inventor of farming, or metallurgy, or music, competition would seem absolutely hopeless. Still, if one sees history, instead, as a gradual and ongoing series of discoveries and inventions—as some Hellenistic Greek and later Chinese writers did do—then this at least allows for the possibility of competition, even the possibility of introducing revolutionary innovations in the present day. Perhaps the best way to see it is this: a monarch who considers himself one of a long line of inventors can treat the principle of sovereignty, which allows him to step outside traditional structures and institutions, in the same way as that by which he can step outside law and morality, to make himself a kind of internal stranger-king, capable of injecting new infusions of creative power to disrupt existing traditions from within. As a result—and this is what is crucial in this context—it allows a king to both identify himself with an ancient tradition (of kings as innovators) and at the same time to assert his ultimate superiority to them, by laying claim to the cumulative legacy of all their innovations, and his own besides.

I've already noted, in chapter 5, that the history of the Merina kingdom was conceived along such lines. The *Tantara ny andriana*, a twelve-hundred-page history and ethnography of Imerina written in the 1860s or 1870s by Merina authors and assembled by a Jesuit missionary named Callet (1908), represents the history of the kingdom as the progressive invention, discovery, or appearance of key institutions by successive Merina kings (the terminology used seems to be intentionally vague as to which):

- *Andriamoramorana*—division of game, basic principles of hierarchy.
- *Andriandranolava*—political oratory.
- *Rafohy, Rangita*—astrology, first-fruits (*santatra*) rituals.
- *Andriamanelo*—iron weapons, metallurgy, pottery, canoes, circumcision rituals, money and commerce.
- *Ralambo*—domestication of cattle, sheep, divination, medicine, protective talismans (*sampy*), marriage customs, New Year's festival.
- *Andrianjaka*—customs of burial and mourning, royal ancestor cult.
- (*Andriantompokoindrindra*—ancestor of noble order, did not reign: writing.)
- (*Andriandranando*—ancestor of noble order, did not reign: muskets.)
- *Andriantsitakatrandriana*—riziculture, irrigation, court etiquette.
- *Andriamasinavalona*—legal principles, poison oracle, slavery, additional marriage customs (divorce, polygyny).

What's crucial for our purposes is that where in most cases of inventor kings (such as the Chinese, Vietnamese, Javanese, Persian, Inka, or Mexica traditions), it's the earliest kings who discover the most important principles and institutions, here it's the three kings in the middle, Andriamanelo, Ralambo, and Andrianjaka, who are the most creative. These three are in fact represented as marking a dramatic break with those who came before, who are generically referred to as "Vazimba," fundamentally uncivilized beings familiar with magic and certain elementary social forms, but innocent of metallurgy and agriculture.

There has been a great deal of debate about the exact meaning of this word "Vazimba," which nowadays can be used to refer either to an ancestor whose body was never properly buried or whose descendants have forgotten them, and whose spirit thus lurks in wild and watery places, or, in many oral histories, to an aboriginal population driven out by the country's current inhabitants. When early missionaries heard stories about Vazimba, they inevitable assumed they represented some kind of primitive "race," possibly pygmies, who had been driven out by the country's current "*hova*" inhabitants, who they assumed to be a wave of later immigrants from Malaysia. ("*Hova*" in fact just means "commoner.")

This was clearly not the case, and as a result, many contemporary historians (e.g., Berg 1977, 1980; cf. Dez 1971a; Domenichini 2007) have come to discount the stories entirely, suggesting, for instance, that when oral histories speak of earlier rulers as "Vazimba," they merely mean that they were buried in lakes or their bodies were otherwise lost. But the matter is slightly more complicated. On the one hand, numerous stories, often from quite early on, actually do speak of wars between *hova* and Vazimba, with the former, led by King Andriamanelo, taking advantage of their newly invented iron-tipped spears to put the latter to rout and drive them fleeing to the west (W. Ellis 1838, II: Callet 1908; Savaron 1928, 1931; G. Ralaimihoatra 1973; Raombana 1980). On the other hand, they also insist that Andriamanelo was himself the son one of the last two Vazimba Queens—sources differ as to which—who bear the intentionally unappealing names of Rafohy and Rangita ("Short" and "Frizzy").[65]

There is no space here to go into the details—people have spent lifetimes trying to figure these stories out, there are endless traditions with endless subtleties of interpretation—but one thing seems abundantly clear: we are dealing here with a classic stranger-king narrative that's been rewritten. For instance, the father of Andriamanelo the great inventor is either not mentioned at all, or treated as completely insignificant.[66] He is spoken of as if the only thing important about him is that he was the child of Rafohy or Rangita (the sources differ as to which). If we consult figure 3, however, it becomes clear what's really happening.[67]

---

65. In fact, our earliest printed source, William Ellis (1838, II: 117) even says Andriamanelo himself was a Vazimba, presumably because his mother was. If nothing else, this shows how fluid the categories were.

66. It is given either as the otherwise unknown Ramanahimanjaka (Callet 1908: 9) or equally unknown Manelobe (Jully 1898), but the overwhelming majority of sources are content simply not to bring up the question of the king's father at all. Jully attempted to link "Manelobe," which seems a made-up name, to the Zafindraminia, but these do not seem to be based on anything in the Malagasy accounts, just what colonial writers assumed ought to be the case.

67. The diagram is my own schematized synthesis; needless to say almost every detail is contested by someone or other. Delivré (1974: 77–99) provides the most comprehensive review of sources for royal genealogies, starting with the Rabetrano manuscript of 1842; Berg (1977) and David Rasamuel (2007: 205–19) offer important critical reviews; I have made extensive use of Gilbert Ralaimihoatra (1974) here as well, which uses an alternate tradition based on manuscripts also said to go back to the 1840s, as well as Savaron (1928, 1931).

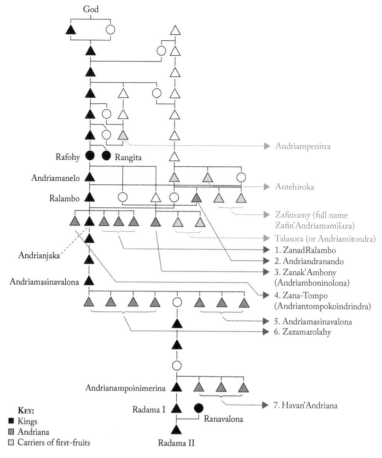

Figure 3.

There are, in fact, two royal genealogies.[68] The first, the one on the left, stretches back through an unbroken line of fathers and sons to the very earliest days of humanity. Once upon a time, the story goes, one of God's children descended to the earth to play with the Vazimba in the great eastern forests, but was trapped there after being tricked into inadvertently eating some mutton (Callet 1908:

---

68. Actually considerably more than two—for instance, the Zanak'Andriamamilaza, though represented here, have their own genealogy, which claims to stretch back to a stranger-king founder Andriantomara, purportedly from Indonesia in the thirteenth century AD (Ramilison 1952; Rakotomalala 2011). Any number of others had to be integrated, or effaced, in order to patch together the existing one.

11 n. 1). God punished the Vazimba—who are represented as being primitives, innocent of agriculture or herding—by leaving his son to rule them, and also provided a daughter for him to marry. The fruit of that incestuous union became the royal line. Their tombs (still remembered in the early nineteenth century when all this was first written down) trace a steady movement westward from the edge of the forests to the center of the Great Plateau, which was eventually to become the heartland of the Merina kingdom.

The royal line on the right occupied that future heartland all along. So one would imagine that they would normally be the "Vazimba" line. And indeed some of their descendants (the Antehiroka and Talasora in particular) are still referred to as "Vazimba" and occasionally as "owners of the land" (Fugelstad 1982; Domenichini 1982, 2004).

There are also hints this opposition, between forest and interior, must have once been central to royal ritual. As explained in chapter 5, in this volume, at least since the reign of Andrianampoinimerina (1787–1810), there was an elite group with the somewhat daunting title of *velond-rai-aman-dreny* ("Those Whose Mothers and Fathers Are Still Living") drawn from certain privileged ancestries,[69] who were charged with maintaining royal tombs, conveying first-fruits, and presiding over key events in the life of the royal household. While some of these were ancestries rewarded for having performed some special service for the monarchy, any team of *Velondraiamandreny* had to include at least one group that lived on the edge of the Great Forest, and one Vazimba group from the central highlands. In the diagram above, the Andriampenitra and Zafimamy represent the foresters, and the above-mentioned Antehiroka and Talasora are the indigenous "owners of the land."[70]

---

69. Most highland descent groups are localized, and in principle endogamous; they focus on *tanin-drazana* (ancestral lands) containing their founder's tomb. Maurice Bloch (1971) proposed to call these "demes," but the term has not been largely taken up; in the nineteenth century they are referred to as *firenena* (literally, "motherhoods," though they are cognatic with a patrilineal bias), or *foko* (just "group"). Nowadays, there does not seem to be a regular term for them at all. I'm here adopting "ancestry" as a generic usage from Feeley-Harnik (1991).

70. These were the only four for whom clear genealogical information was available. Sometimes it's ambiguous: for instance, the Tahiamanangaona claimed *andriana* status on the basis of their having been "companions" (*namany*) of Andriandranando, which usually means collaterals of some kind but the actual link is not recorded (Callet 1908: 1214–215). There were in fact two groups of *velond-rai-aman-dreny*, one for Antananarivo, one for Ambohimanga, these being the twin capitals

These *velond-rai-amen-dreny* must be carefully distinguished from the *andriana*, which means both "king" and "those descendants of royalty who still partake in royal status." *Andriana* are divided into seven orders, the oldest being, as the principle of horizontal sinking status would dictate, the lowest in rank. According to traditions the rank system was reorganized three times, by three different kings (Ralambo, Andriamasinavalona, Andrianampoinimerina) to add new orders and push the older ones back. Many of the *velond-rai-aman-dreny* insisted they were really *andriana* as well, or had once been, but had been demoted in one of the previous reorganizations.

* * *

So, originally, there would appear to have been a fairly simple opposition between invading stranger-kings and indigenous "owners of the land," with the *andriana* being the most recent descendants of the first. But at some point, however, something happened. The pieces were rearranged. The two Vazimba Queens, Rafohy and Rangita—remembered as local ancestors in the old sacred capital of Alasora—were inserted at the end of the first genealogy, and the three generations after them were framed as a time of great inventions, when the divine spark already manifest in that line from its origins was seen as bursting out in great feats of—often violent—creativity. Stories of stranger-king invaders became stories of technologically superior creator kings routing their enemies. Most of the major institutions of Merina society were said to

---

of the Merina kingdom. We have much better information for the second. The Antananarivo group include the Zanak'Andriampenitra (forest), Antehiroka/ Zanadahy (Vazimba), Zafintsoala (probably same as Trimofoloalina, benefactors), and Tahiamanangaona (possibly Vazimba, former *andriana*); the Ambohimanga group includes the Zanak'Andrianato and Andriamamilaza (forest), Talasora/ Andriamitondra (Vazimba), Tehitany and Zanamarofatsy (benefactors). Callet's sources go into elaborate detail about the different sorts of forest products (eels, hedgehogs, honey, certain species of liana, etc.) brought by the different forest groups, but are mostly vague about how these items were employed. Insofar as there's a clear division of labor, the Vazimba groups appear to carry out the key ritual actions (particularly those involving aggression: killing the sacrificial oxen, performing the circumcision on royal children, laying down the red earth in the tomb and placing the royal bodies in it, etc.), whereas, as noted previously, *andriana* groups do all the acts of creation, fashioning, or construction (ibid.: 15, 163–65, 254, 256–62, 306–9, 316, 390, 401, 407–11, 423–24, 435, 533–35, 589–90, 632, 812–13, 1136–137, 1211–214; Cousins [1876] 1963: 44–45; Domenichini 1978).

have been invented by, or "appeared" under, such kings and their companions during the three generations immediately following Rafohy and Rangita, but kings continued to be seen as at least potential inventors. Even those lines that broke off the royal genealogy that continued to be recognized as *andriana* were those who were identified with (and often continued to maintain monopolies on) particular technological breakthroughs: writing, metallurgy, and so forth. Crucially, this allowed all rulers before Andriamanelo, of any royal line, to be uniformly written off as mere primitives from an earlier historical epoch "when Vazimba ruled the land" (Savaron 1928: 68).

We don't know precisely when this happened, but most likely it was around the time of that Merina monarchs began reclaiming the vast Betsimitatra marshes surrounding Antananarivo (Raison 1972; Cabanes 1974), an enormous project which created thousands of hectares of new land, and, it seems, a reversal of the older system where kings ruled over people, but the indigenous *tompon'tany* or "masters of the land" still owned the soil. Merina kings began referring to themselves as *tompon'tany*, claiming possession of all land in the kingdom, as an extension of the elementary principle of sovereignty,[71] and groups like the Talasora and Antehiroka were stripped of any ritual role in relation to the land they might once have had and reduced to "nurturing" the royal household and maintaining the royal dead (Fugelstad 1982: 65–70).

Whereas in Bali, whose rulers also claim divine origins, kings continually decline from grace, creating a contradiction of vertical and horizontal sinking status, Merina kings in this new version of dynastic history advance—which, if nothing else, means the two principles, ascending status for the kings, descending status for everyone who splits off the royal line, are brought in consonance with one another.

The progressive ideology helps explain the Napoleonic ambitions of nineteenth-century Merina kings, who all aspired to become Enlightenment

---

71. For instance, the *Tantara* observes that insofar as the king is "*tompony'tany*," he has ultimate sovereignty; others may possess specific portions and even sell it, but they may not sell it to anyone who is not the king's subject as it would bring it out from under the king's ultimate control (Callet 1908:365). Sovereignty was conceived not just as the power over life and death but as the power to appropriate and dispose of land or possessions with impunity; thus, it is said that when King Andriamasinavalona granted a benefactor's family permanent immunity from all accusations of crime against persons or property, his advisor Andriamampandry quickly intervened to point out that anyone who had that right effectively would be king, since that is what the essence of sovereignty consists of (Kingdon 1889: 5–6).

philosopher-kings, and how they came to be seen by their subjects above all as playful and obstreperous children. I think it also helps explain how the logic of the royal ancestral cult came to be popularized, culminating in the development of the kind of spectacular mortuary ritual—the landscape dotted everywhere with stone tombs, the periodic festivals which draw even urban professionals to flock to the countryside to exhume the bodies of their ancestors and rewrap them with new silk shrouds—that the highlands are famous for to this day. The problem the Merina sovereigns faced was above all how to hold their own in the face of the ever-burgeoning, and ever more ancient, legions of the ancestral dead. ("Even the dead," one Malagasy proverb goes, "desire to be more numerous.") Even after the magnificent gesture of writing them all off as primitive "Vazimba," local people seem to have maintained the cults of their bygone monarchs' tombs, now mixed up with an older conception of Vazimba spirits of lost spirits of the waters and the wild, as the true "owners of the land" (e.g., Callet 1908: 256). With the collapse of the monarchy after the French invasion of 1895, every local descent group immediately claimed *tompon'tany* status, insisting they were owners of their own ancestral territories. The overwhelming majority also insisted that their founding ancestors, or *razambe*, were themselves of some kind of royal descent.

Such claims are not necessarily fabrications. Since there were so many kings and kingdoms over such a long period, and since cognatic descent allows one to trace through either male or female lines, no doubt virtually anyone in Imerina could make such a claim on some basis or another. What did happen to all the collateral lineages that spun off the ruling dynasty before Andriamanelo (apart from those that were named *velond-rai-aman-dreny*)? We cannot know. The sources are focused almost exclusively on those closest to royalty. But occasionally more obscure groups do come into focus for one reason or another.

In 1895, for instance, shortly after French forces had seized the Malagasy capital, there was an insurrection in the lands surrounding Arivonimamo in which a family of Quaker missionaries were killed. It was spearheaded by a very large descent group called the Zanak'Antitra, and for this reason that group—which is not even mentioned in the 1,243 pages of the *Tantara ny andriana*—came under a degree of sustained attention (Clark 1896; Renel 1920: 39, 128–29; M. Rasamuel 1947, 1948; Peetz 1951a; Danielli 1952). Thus we have some idea what the story of a local ancestor might look like around the time mortuary rituals, as they have come to be practiced today, were taking shape (Larson 2001). The Zanak'Antitra claimed to be descended from a line of *andriana* that split off from the Zanak'Andriampenitra, forest-dwellers of the Ankaratra mountains, far to the south of the Merina heartland—the latter, a group which themselves claimed to have split off from the royal dynasty many generations before (as seen in figure 3 above).[72] Sometime around 1790, they say their ancestor Andriantsihianka and his family were forced to flee their ancestral lands during a disastrous war and asked for refuge from a certain Princess Ravao. She agreed to take them in on condition he renounce his *andriana* status. Later, even when her husband, king Andrianampoinimerina, offered to restore his rank, Andriantsihianka refused, insisting that he preferred not to rule over others.

By the 1990s, this story appears to have become a template. The vast majority of rural people insisted their ancestors were, at some point, *andriana*. Many insisted they still were.[73] In effect, the country is now populated by the descendants of dozens of little stranger-kings—with the result that that same logic of sinking status and the burden of rivalrous, oppressive, and ever-more-numerous ancestors that once haunted the center of power has instead been pushed off onto just about everybody else.[74] We are left with a population struggling with the memories of their own grandparents and great-grandparents through the very tools (adverse sacralization, effacement, etc.) once deployed against kings, in a kind of generalized war against the dead.

---

72. As with all such things, the derivation is contested: Grandidier (1914: 650) accepts it; Dez (1971b: 104) is more skeptical.

73. Where I did my fieldwork around Arivonimamo, the largest descent groups were the Andrianetivola and Zanakantitra, both of whom claimed to have been refugees who gave up their *andriana* status, the Andriamasoandro, who claim descent from a different line of kings, and the Andriatsimihenina, who alone insisted on commoner status, but were otherwise vague about their origins. I myself worked in a community of Andrianamboninolona or Zanak'Ambony, who traced back to the fifth officially ranked order of *andriana*. They kept their rank as they had been placed as military colonists in the region under Andrianampoinimerina (Graeber 2007a: 99–100). Pier Larson has collected numerous local histories from the Vakinankaratra region which begin with refugees willingly abandoning their *andriana* status.

74. I am, of course, simplifying massively. Most people in the very heartland of the old kingdom identify with *hova* ancestries that were closely allied with royalty; matters are also much complicated by the presence of a large population of descendants of slaves who have simultaneously become de facto guardians of the royal ancestors and in certain respects identify with Vazimba.

CONCLUSIONS

This is an essay on the archaeology of sovereignty (sometimes in the literal sense, mostly though metaphoric); it is very much not an essay on the origins of the state. The reader will probably have noticed I barely touch on the subject.

This is intentional. Some of the kingdoms discussed in this essay (Inka, China, et al.) are universally considered to be states; with others (Benin, Natchez, et al.), it depends on one's definition; still others (Shilluk, Jukun, et al.), almost no one would consider to be states. Yet for the specific questions I am investigating here, whether or not a kingdom is a state makes very little difference.

It seems to me that "the state" is itself becoming something of a shopworn concept. Since the mid-twentieth century there have been endless debates, for instance, about "the origins of the state"—in fact, when treating with the sort of material I've been treating with here, it often seems to be considered about the only question really worth asking. Such debates almost always assume that "the state" is just one thing, and that in speaking of the origins of the state one is necessarily also speaking of the origins of urbanization, written literature, law, exploitation, bureaucracy, science, and almost anything else of enduring importance that happened between the dawn of agriculture and the Renaissance, aside, perhaps, from the rise of world religions. From our current vantage, it has become increasingly clear this is simply wrong. "The state" would better be seen as an amalgam of heterogeneous elements often of entirely separate origins that happened to have come together in certain times and places, and now appear to be in the process of drifting apart.

One aim of this collection has been to begin to develop a new set of frameworks, and in this essay, I have been examining the notion of sovereignty—which I think to be embedded in what we call "divine kingship"—in that light. Asking about the origins of sovereignty is very different than asking about the origins of the state. But it is, perhaps, of even greater long-term significance.

* * *

It might be well to clarify what I mean by "sovereignty" before turning to my conclusions. At its simplest, the term refers to the power of command. But the power of command is not itself a simple concept. All human languages we know of have imperative forms, and in any society there will be situations where it is considered appropriate for some individuals to tell others what to do. This need have very little to do with larger power structures. It might even to some degree fly in the face of them. In highland Madagascar, women use imperative forms freely, especially in managing household affairs (Graeber 1996b). It's far more common to see women issuing direct orders to men than the other way around; but such societies can in no sense be considered matriarchies. One of the ways male patriarchs express their authority, in fact, is by their refusal to give direct orders.

Malagasy women, when they send children off on errands, or tell their husband to stop drinking and come and help set the table, have little or no means of compulsion at their disposal. In that sense, they are not really issuing "commands." What I mean by the "power of command" is, instead, the ability to issue orders backed up by the threat of punishment.[75]

Now, those who live in liberal societies are also used to making a sharp distinction between situations where such commands can be issued "arbitrarily," by individuals—say, a dictator, or gangster—and situations where the individual issuing the orders is seen as enforcing a system of rules or laws. This, however, is ultimately a somewhat artificial distinction. First of all, the distinction is blurry at best in practice. Even in the most legalistic order, officials are allowed a degree of "discretion" over when, how, and whether to issue orders or sanctions (when they claim their hands are tied, they're usually being dishonest), and they are almost always protected from any serious consequences if they do break the rules. A judge or employee of the tax office knows he will never be charged with theft or extortion even if it's found he knowingly dunned money on false pretenses, and a policeman or prison guard knows he will never be charged with murder or assault—or even, for that matter, rape—pretty much no matter what he does. As a result, orders given by a dictator, and a traffic cop in a constitutional republic, have far more in common with each other than either do with orders given by someone with no coercive power at all.

---

75. Said punishment may not be immediately physical, but is ultimately physical in nature: firing an employee is not itself violent, but can have effects equivalent to violence in a context where someone without money can expect to be, for instance, physically forced out of from their home for nonpayment of rent. The formulation also assumes a preponderance of means of punishment on one side. A Malagasy woman might have a number of ways to sanction a husband who refuses orders to carry out a task, but the husband has even more. I might note the patriarchal stereotype of housewives as "nags" could be considered the direct result of delegating managerial responsibilities to women without also granting them adequate means of enforcement.

In theory, of course, the traffic cop is different than the dictator because he has been duly appointed within a constitutional order, following correct procedures—even if he may not be following correct procedures when he shoots or arrests someone; but all one is really saying here is that insofar as he can exercise discretion—that is, arbitrary power—it is as an extension of the sovereignty (arbitrary power) of the government itself. That sovereignty, as Carl Schmitt periodically appears, like some embarrassing uncle, to remind us, consists above all in the ability to set the law aside. It is the ghost of divine kingship still hanging over us. The police who regularly get away with murder are simply exercising that small—but lethal—bit of royal power that has been delegated to them by its current holder, an entity we refer to as "the people."

I will return to this point later on. All I want to draw attention to here is that there is a reason the word "order" has the semantic range that it does. Sovereignty, in the sense of the power to stand outside a moral or legal order and as a consequence to be able to create new rules, to embody (at least potential) chaos so as to impose order, and the power of command, the ability to give "orders" in the military sense, invariably draw on and partake of one another. This is what I'm referring to when I speak of the "principle of sovereignty."

Divine kingship simply represents this principle in its purest form. The "monopoly of coercive force" which Weber so famously attributed to the modern state is its secularization.

What I have tried to do in this essay is to develop at least an initial outline, first, of how the principle of sovereignty originally came into being, and, second, of what tends to happen when sovereignty becomes the central organizing principle of political life—as it remains almost everywhere today. I want to emphasize that I don't think there was anything particularly inevitable about this development. One could probably make a case that in any complex human society there are likely to be *some* circumstances in which *some* people can issue arbitrary commands—that is, unless there is a social consensus that powers of command are wrong and inappropriate. Still, there is an enormous difference between a social order in which sovereign powers appear in some limited circumstances, and one where sovereignty is the dominant organizing principle of social life. Historically, the latter is much less common. In most of the earliest civilizations we know about, for instance, sovereignty does not appear to have played this role. Egypt had its divine king, and so it seems did China; but in the Indus Valley, the Tripolye civilization, even early Mesopotamia for the most part, we see no sign of such a figure, or any other human entity claiming to be either the ultimate source or ultimate arbiter of the legitimate use of force—let alone one that stood outside the legal or moral order and thus claimed to constitute it.[76] Even in classical Greece, at least before Alexander, such powers remained firmly in the hands of the gods.[77]

Once the principle of sovereign power takes root, however, it appears to be almost impossible to get rid of. Kings can be killed; kingship abolished; but even then, the principle of sovereignty tends to remain. Therefore, understanding the history of this principle could hardly be more important.

* * *

The first conclusion this exploration reached is that while Hocart's hypothesis of the ritual origins of royal power seems confirmed by—or, at the very least, is perfectly consistent with—the evidence, the devolution of divine powers onto mortal humans, or, perhaps better said, its breaking out of ritual frames, did not follow a single or a simple trajectory. Most hunter-gatherers we know of have plenty of kings, but they studiously avoid allowing sovereign powers to fall into the hands of mortal humans, at least on any sort of ongoing basis, and usually in any form at all. There seems no reason to believe this was not true in the distant past as well. Societies in which powers of command can only be exercised in ritual contexts have certainly been documented. In many, at least—the societies of central California are one example, but there are other very similar examples in Chile and Tierra del Fuego (Loeb 1931)—these powers do take on aspects of what I'm calling sovereignty, in that those giving the orders make a point of breaking ordinary rules and conventions so as to demonstrate that they stand outside the moral order, can act arbitrarily and with impunity, even make up

---

76. In other words, a state according to either Weber's definition, or that of his teacher Jhering—the latter defined the state not, like Weber, as the only entity whose agents had the legitimate right to use coercive force within a territory, but, rather, as the institution which has the exclusive right to judge the legitimacy of any use of coercive force. I might note here that even Egypt tended to swing back and forth between dynastic periods and extremely long interdynastic periods where there was no pharaoh, so even here sovereignty was at the very least episodic.

77. It is even possible that in world-historical terms, kingship only became the predominant mode of political organization relatively recently. The Bronze Age seems to have been dominated by decentralized confederations, either aristocratic or relatively egalitarian. Kingdoms, while they did exist, appear to have often been small. It's only much later that monarchy becomes, as it were, the default mode of political organization.

rules as they go along. But for this reason they are also seen as ridiculous. And the clowns that exercise such powers tend to be the last people who would exercise power of any sort in everyday life.

This opens up a specific trajectory, where sovereign powers, while gradually losing their clownish aspects, are nonetheless contained within a specific ritual season or time or year. The alternate trajectory—the one which can lead to full-fledged divine kings and hence ultimately to (among other things) the modern nation-state, allows sovereign powers to emerge on an ongoing basis. But instead they are confined in space. The actual historical origins of such arrangements remain obscure. Perhaps they always will. The Natchez, the best example of a classic divine kingship we know of in North America, appear at the tail end of a long political history beginning with the peaceful and decentralized Hopewell civilization, based on some kind of ritual amphictyonies, the rise of the vast imperial center of Cahokia, its abandonment and replacement by a number of smaller warring kingdoms, and their collapse and replacement by tribal republics that explicitly rejected the principle of hereditary authority (the Natchez being by the eighteenth century about the only old-fashioned Mississippian divine kingship still extant).

Whatever the background, the Natchez case illustrates structural features which, I think, can be found in any divine kingship. It might be helpful to list them:

1. The sovereign's origins are external to society (stranger-king).
2. The sovereign remains in a fundamental sense external to society, insofar as he is not bound by ordinary morality or law.
3. All insist on the sovereign's absolute power over the life, death, and property of subjects when physically present.
4. The physical presence of the sovereign is carefully circumscribed.
5. Sovereign and people exist in a fundamental constitutive antagonism (war), which is paradoxically seen as key to the sovereign's immortality, and transcendent, metahuman quality.
   a. In life, this manifests itself adverse sacralization: the imposition of elaborate taboos that deny the mortal qualities of the king, cut him off from regular contact with his subjects, and often, imprison him in a carefully bounded physical space (village, compound, palace).
   b. Such acts of adverse sacralization at the same time often make that village, compound, or palace into a kind of miniature paradise where basic

dilemmas of mortal existence can be seen to be at least temporarily or provisionally overcome.

c. Ritual regicide (documented mainly in Africa) is simply the most extreme form of such adverse sacralization.

Consider again the Jewish version of the story of Alexander the Great, where the conqueror almost finds himself trapped forever in the Garden of Eden. It is, in its own way, a perfect expression of the tensions within the concept of sovereignty. In his quest to become a god, the all-conquering king finally attains Eden, and has before him the prospect of finally undoing all the dilemmas of human existence that were a consequence of the Fall—but only on condition he be denied all contact with his subjects. In which case, in what sense is he a sovereign?

This dilemma was perhaps formulated most explicitly in the Greco-Roman world, since the classical gods were so obviously figures of desire: they were not merely metahumans (Platonic representations of the perfect forms of power, wisdom, beauty, or proficiency)—at least in literature, they were always represented as just human enough that worshipers could imagine what it might be like to themselves embody such a principle forever, even if such a dream could only inspire permanent frustration. Hence their notorious envy of human happiness, whose full achievement would mean they would no longer exist. It is significant, I think, that such pantheons were, in both Greece and Rome, largely created in the wake of the collapse of systems of divine kingship. In that sense, the Euhemerists were right: they are gods inspired by humans aspiring to be gods.

Since one cannot actually become a Greek god (as that is the entire point of Greek gods: they are that which it is impossible to become, however much you might like to), and since return to a prelapsarian state is neither possible nor desirable, the absolute victory of kings only creates (or exacerbates) another set of problems: how to deal with the burden of one's own ancestors insofar as those ancestors have succeeded in finding a way to attain at least partial immortality. The second half of this essay—the bulk of it, actually—is an outline of some of the difficulties (e.g., the contradiction of vertical and horizontal sinking status) dynastic monarchs can create, and some of the strategies latter-day monarchs have adopted to deal with such difficulties. (Not all of them: conquest and marriage, for instance, were largely unaddressed.) None of these strategies are completely effective. But they help explain some of the apparently irrational aspects of many early kingdoms, from the frenetic expansiveness of the Inkas, or monument-building of early Egypt, to systematic massacres of royal courtiers that followed so many early sovereigns' deaths.

* * *

What does all this have to say about our situation in the present? As I have said, the principle of sovereignty is still with us; once it becomes the organizing principle of social life, anywhere, it tends to prove extraordinarily difficult to uproot. Few, at this point, seem to be able to imagine what it would meant to uproot it.

This is partly because some of the elements we are discussing here are elementary structures of human social existence that will always be present in human life in one form or another. There will always be a tendency for those who successfully violate norms and conventions, particularly violently, to be seen either as divine, or as buffoons—and sometimes both at the same time, as Achille Mbembe (1992) has argued of African kleptocrats, and one might just as easily say of European heads of state like Silvio Berlusconi or American ones like Donald Trump. The only way we could really make sure such buffoons never gain systematic coercive power over their fellows is to get rid of the apparatus of coercion itself. The logic of sacralization and abstraction, adverse and otherwise, will probably always be with us as well, though for the moment at least elites have done rather well at minimizing its adverse aspects.

Still, sovereignty in the form we have it now is a very specific thing with a very specific history. To take the story down to the present day would, no doubt, require another book—or at the very least another over-long essay. But it might be well to end with at least an outline of what it might be like.

This book, focusing as it does on divine kingship, has had relatively little to say even about Axial Age kingship—that is, the kind that became prevalent in the core regions of Eurasia after, say, about AD 500. The appearance of the great world religions, which, as I've said, emerged largely as a popular reaction to the increasingly cynical, materialist basis of early Axial Age kingship, led to endlessly complicated theological debates about the status of worldly monarchs in China, India, and the Christian and Muslim worlds. Francis Oakley (2006, 2010) has mapped out some of the complexities of Christian thought on the subject, much of it focusing on which person of the Trinity the king or emperor most resembled. These were crucial in negotiating the balance of power between church and temporal authorities in a time and place where sovereignty was, as the saying goes, "parcelized" (Wood 2002)—that is, broken up and distributed in an endless variety of often contradictory and overlapping ways.

Modern nation-states, of course, are based on the principle of "popular sovereignty," that is, that since the Age of Revolutions at the end of the seventeenth century and beginning of the eighteenth, the power once held by kings is now ultimately held by an entity called "the people." Now, on the face of it, this makes very little sense, since who else can sovereign power be exercised on but the people, and what can it possibly mean to exercise a punitive and extralegal power on oneself? One is almost tempted to conclude that the notion of popular sovereignty has come to play the same role that Enlightenment critics and conservative defenders of the church both argued that the Mystery of the Trinity had played in the Middle Ages: the very fact that it made no sense rendered it the perfect expression of authority, since a profession of faith then necessarily meant accepting that there was someone else far wiser than you could ever be. The only difference, in that case, would be that the higher wisdom of archbishops has now been passed to that of constitutional lawyers.[78]

Still, I think, the reality is a bit more complicated. The "people" being referred to in the notion of "popular sovereignty" is a rather different creature than the kind that face off against Shilluk or Malagasy kings. I suspect it is a product more of empires than of kingdoms. I also suspect that empires—the kind that gave birth to the modern notion of the nation-state, anyway—are quite different from the galactic polities described in this book, however much the latter might often superficially resemble them. What I am speaking of here are empires that are not, like so many kingdoms, essentially voluntary arrangements dressed up in antagonistic terms, but arrangements genuinely rooted in military conquest, or converting voluntary arrangements into those ultimately founded in force. No ongoing human relation is ever founded exclusively on force, of course; but still, it was when the Athenian *demos* declared that its allies were no longer free to leave the alliance, lest their cities be attacked, that the Delian League became the Athenian empire.

There is something interesting about such arrangements. They are rarely, if ever, simply a matter of a royal dynasty imposing itself on an ever-greater array

---

78. The notion of popular sovereignty might depart from the logic of transgression so evidenced in other forms of sovereign power, but in fact it does not: the legitimacy of systems of constitutional law is derived from "the people," but the people conveyed that legitimacy through revolution, American, French, etc.—that is, through acts of illegal violence.

of conquered peoples. Many in fact do not begin as kingdoms at all, but as re-publics (like the Athenian, Carthaginian, or Roman empires, or the American more recently), alliances of nomadic clans (like the Goths, Avars, Arabs, and Mongols), and so on.[79] If they congeal around a single emperor, of necessity a stranger to most of those he governs, he may well trace his origins to wan-dering heroes from distant realms, in good stranger-king fashion; but the key structural feature of any true empire is not the emperor, but the existence of a core population that provides the heart of its military, whether Akkadians, Han, Mexica, Romans, Persians, Franks, Tatars, Russians, Athenians, Amhara-Tigre, or French. As a result—and this is crucial I think—a degree of sovereignty is, effectively, vested in the imperial nation itself. These are for this reason the first nations properly so called. This leads to a complex political struggle where conquered peoples increasingly come to define themselves in national terms as well. Thus do empires become the nurseries of nations, and ethnolinguistic groups that see their destiny as bound, in some sense, with a real or imagined apparatus of rule.

This is not a story we can tell here. But it underlines just how much the ap-parently exotic tribulations of bygone monarchs still find their echoes in forms of ultimately arbitrary power that still surround us, like so many bruised and indignant deities, in national politics to this day.

---

79. Empires might begin without a king, or with a relatively weak one, and then congeal around an imperial line over time; alternately, they might begin as kingdoms, like the English, French, or Russian, and then develop some variety of republican form.

Bibliography

Abinal, Antoine, and Victorine Malzac. 1899. *Dictionnaire malgache–français*. Tananarive: Imprimerie de la Mission catholique, Mahamasina

Abler, Thomas S. 2004. "Seneca moieties and hereditary chieftainships: The early-nineteenth-century political organization of an Iroquois nation." *Ethnohistory* 51 (3): 459–88.

Abraham, Roy Clive. 1933. *The Tiv people*. Lagos: Government Printer.

Abubakar, Sa'ad. 1986. "Precolonial government and administration among the Jukun." *Annals of Borno* 3: 1–13.

Acciaioli, Greg. 2009. "Distinguishing hierarchy and precedence: Comparing status distinctions in South Asia and the Austronesian world, with special reference to South Sulawesi." In *Precedence: Social differentiation in the Austronesian world*, edited by Michael P. Vischer, 51–90. Canberra: ANU Press.

Ackerman, M. 1833. *Histoire des révolutions de Madagascar, depuis 1642 jusqu'à nos jours*. Paris: Librairie Gide.

Adelstein, Ludwig. 1967. *The idea of progress in classical antiquity*. Baltimore: Johns Hopkins University Press.

Adler, Alfred. 1977. "Faiseurs de pluie, faiseurs d'ordre." *Libre* 2: 45–68.

———. 1982. *Le mort est le masque du roi: La royauté sacrée des Moundang du Tchad*. Paris: Payot.

———. 1987. "Royauté et sacrifice chez les Moundang du Tchad." In *Sous le masque de l'animal: Essais sur le sacrifice en Afrique noire*, edited by Michel Cartry, 89–130. Paris: Presses Universaires de France.

Afigbo, Adiele. 2005. *Nigerian history, politics and affairs: The collected essays of Adiele Afigbo*. Asmara: Africa World Press.

Afolayan, Funso. 2005 "Benue River peoples: Jukun and Kwarafa." In *Encyclopedia of African history*, Vol. 1, edited by Kevin Shillington, 143–44. New York: Fitzroy-Dearborn.

Alpers, Edward, and Christopher Ehret. 1975. "Eastern Africa." In *The Cambridge history of Africa*, Vol. 4: *From c.1660 to c.1790*, edited by Richard Gray, 469–536. Cambridge: Cambridge University Press.

Andaya, Leonard. 1993. *The World of Maluku: Eastern Indonesia in the early modern period*. Honolulu: University of Hawai'i Press.

———. 2006. "The stranger-king complex in Bugis-Makassar." Paper presented at the KITLV Workshop, "Stranger-kings in Southeast Asia and elsewhere." Jakarta, Indonesia, 5–7 June.

Anderson, Graham. 2012. "The *Alexander Romance* and the pattern of hero-legend." In *The Alexander Romance in Persia and the East*, edited by Richard Stoneman, Kyle Erickson, and Ian Netton, 83–102. Groningen: Bakuis Publishing.

Ando, Clifford. 2013. *Imperial ideology and provincial loyalty in the Roman Empire*. Berkeley: University of California Press.

André, C. 1899. *De l'esclavage à Madagascar*. Paris: Arthur Rousseau.

Andriamanantsiety, Z. J. 1975. *Tantaran' Andrianamboninolona*. Antananarivo: Musée d'Art et d'Archéologie de l'Université de Madagascar.

Andriamifidy, Pasteur. 1950. *Tantaran'Ambohitrarahaba, Karakain'ny Terak'Andriamanarefo*. Antananarivo: Antsiva Ambandia.

Anon. 1879a. "Ny mampanankarena ny olona: Ny lapitaly." *Mpanolo Tsaina* 1 (January): 1–8.

———. 1879b. "Ny mampanankarena ny olona: Ny karama." *Mpanolo Tsaina* 2 (April): 114–22.

———. 1900. "A brief native account of Radama II." *Antananarivo Annual and Madagascar Magazine* 23: 486–88.

———. 1956. "The installation of a new Shilluk king." *Sudan Notes and Records* 37: 99–101.

Apata, Z. O. 1998. "Migrations, changes and conflicts: A study of inter-group relations." *Journal of the Pakistan Historical Society* 2: 79–87.

Arens, William. 1979. "The divine kingship of the Shilluk: A contemporary evaluation." *Ethnos* 44: 167–81.

———. 1983. "A note on Evans-Pritchard and the prophets." *Anthropos* 78: 1–16.

———. 1984. "The demise of kings and the meaning of kingship: Royal funerary ceremony in the contemporary southern Sudan and Renaissance France." *Anthropos* 79: 355–67.

Århem, Kaj. 2016. "Southeast Asian animism in context." In *Animism in Southeast Asia*, edited by Kaj Århem and Guido Sprenger, 3–20. London: Routledge.

Århem, Kaj, and Guido Sprenger, eds. 2016. *Animism in Southeast Asia*. London: Routledge.

Asher-Greve, Julia. 2006. "From 'Semiramis of Babylon' to 'Semiramis of Hammersmith'?" In *Orientalism, Assyriology and the Bible*, edited by Steven Holloway, 323–73. Sheffield: Sheffield Phoenix Press.

Atkinson, Ronald R. 1989. "The evolution of ethnicity among the Acholi of Uganda: The precolonial phase." *Ethnohistory* 36: 19–43.

Augustins, Georges. 1971. "Esquisse d'une histoire de l'Imamo." *Bulletin de Madagascar* 301: 547–58.

Backus, Charles. 1981. *The Nan-Chao kingdom and T'ang Chinese southwestern frontier.* Cambridge: Cambridge University Press.

Baer, Mark David. 2008. *Honored by the glory of Islam: Conversion and conquest in Ottoman Europe*. Oxford: Oxford University Press.

Bakhtin, Mikhail. 1984. *Rabelais and his world*. Translated by Hélène Iswolsky. Bloomington: Indiana University Press.

Balandier, Georges. 1968. *Daily life in the kingdom of Kongo: From the sixteenth to the eighteenth century*. Translated by Helen Weaver. New York: Pantheon Books.

———. 1972. *Political anthropology*. Translated by A. M. Sheridan Smith. Harmondsworth: Penguin.

Balikici, Asen. 1970. *The Netsilik Eskimo*. Garden City, NY: The Natural History Press.

Balvay, Arnaud. 2008. *La Révolte des Natchez*. Paris: Éditions du Félin.

Barbosa, Duarte. (1518) 1918. *The Book of Duarte Barbosa: An account of the countries bordering on the Indian Ocean and their inhabitants.* Translated by Mansel Longworth Dames. London: Hakluyt Society.

Barjamovic, Gojko. 2011. "Pride, pomp and circumstance: Palace, court and household in Assyria 879–612 BCE." In *Royal courts in dynastic states and empires: A global perspective*, edited by Jeroen Duindam, Tülay Artan, and Metin Kunt, 27–62. Leiden: Brill.

Barrett, S. A. 1917. "Ceremonies of the Porno Indians." *University of California Publications in American Archaeology and Ethnology* 12: 397–441.

———. 1919. "The Wintun Hesi ceremony." *University of California Publications in American Archaeology and Ethnology* 14: 437–88.

Bárta, Miroslav. 2005. "The location of the Old Kingdom Pyramids in Egypt." *Cambridge Archaeological Journal* 15 (2): 177–91.

Barth, Fredrik. 1969. *Ethnic groups and boundaries: The social organization of culture difference.* Bergen: Universitetsforlaget.

———. 1975. *Ritual and knowledge among the Baktaman of New Guinea.* New Haven, CT: Yale University Press.

———. 1987. *Cosmologies in the making: A generative approach to cultural variation in inner New Guinea.* Cambridge: Cambridge University Press.

Bascom, William. 1965. "The forms of folklore prose narratives." *The Journal of American Folklore* 78 (307): 3–20.

Bateson, Gregory. 1935. "Cultural contact and schismogenesis." *Man* 35: 178–83.

———. 1958. *Naven.* Second edition. Stanford: Stanford University Press.

Bauer, Brian S. 1998. *The sacred landscape of the Inca: The Cusco Ceque system.* Austin: University of Texas Press.

Beattie, John. 1971. *The Nyoro state.* Oxford: Clarendon Press.

Beidelman, Thomas O. 1966a. "The ox and Nuer sacrifice: Some Freudian hypotheses about Nuer symbolism." *Man* (N.S.) 1: 453–67.

———. 1966b. "Swazi royal ritual." *Africa* 36 (4): 373–405.

———. 1981. "The Nuer concept of *Thek* and the meaning of sin: Explanation, translation, and social structure." *History of Religions* 21 (2): 126–55.

Beltrame, Giovanni. 1881. *Il fiume bianco e i Dénka.* Verona: Mazziana.

Benjamin, Walter. 1978. "Critique of violence." In *Reflections: Essays, aphorisms, autobiographical writings,* 277–300. Edited by Peter Demetz. New York: Harcourt Brace Jovanovich.

Berce, Yves-Marie. 1976. *Fête et révolte.* Paris: Hachette.

Bere, R. M. 1947. "An outline of Acholi history." *The Uganda Journal* 11: 1–8.

Berg, Gerald. 1977. "The myth of racial strife and Merina kinglists: The transformation of texts." *History in Africa* 4: 1–30.

———. 1979. "Royal authority and the protector system in nineteenth-century Imerina." In *Madagascar in history: Essays from the 1970s,* edited by Raymond K. Kent, 102–22. Albany: The Foundation for Malagasy Studies.

———. 1980. "Some words about Merina historical texts." In *The African past speaks: Essays on oral tradition and history,* edited by Joseph Calder Miller, 221–39. London: Dawson.

———. 1988. "Sacred acquisition: Andrianampoinimerina at Ambohimanga, 1777–1790." *Journal of African History* 29 (2): 191–211.

———. 1995. "Writing history: Ranavalona the ancestral bureaucrat." *History in Africa* 22: 73–92.

———. 1996. "*Virtù*, and *fortuna* in Radama's nascent bureaucracy, 1816–1828." *History in Africa* 23: 29–73.

———. 1998. "Radama's smile: Domestic challenges to royal ideology in early nineteenth-century Imerina." *History in Africa* 25: 69–92.

Bernard-Thierry, Solange. 1960. "Les Pélerinages des Hauts-Plateaux Malgaches." In *Les Pélerinages, sources orientales III*, 289–301. Paris: Éditions du Seuil.

Berndt, Ronald M. 1953. *Djaggawul: An Aboriginal religious cult of north-eastern Arnhem Land*. New York: Philosophical Library.

Bierhorst, John. 1992. *History and mythology of the Aztecs: The Codex Chimalpopoca*. Tucson: University of Arizona Press.

Birmingham, David. 1975. "Central Africa from Cameroons to the Zambezi." In *The Cambridge history of Africa*, Vol.4: *From c. 1600 to c. 1790*, edited by Richard Gray, 325–83. Cambridge: Cambridge University Press.

Blitz, John H. 1999. "Mississippian chiefdoms and the fission–fusion process." *American Antiquity* 64 (4): 577–92.

Bloch, Maurice. 1971. *Placing the dead: Tombs, ancestral villages, and kinship organization in Madagascar*. London: Seminar Press.

———. 1977. "The disconnection between power and rank as a process: An outline of the development of kingdoms in Central Madagascar." *European Journal of Sociology* 18: 303–30.

———. 1982. "Death, women and power." In *Death and the regeneration of life*, edited by Maurice Bloch and Jonathan Parry, 211–30. Cambridge: Cambridge University Press.

———. 1985. "Almost eating the ancestors." *Man* (N.S.) 20: 631–46.

———. 1986. *From blessing to violence: History and ideology in the circumcision ritual of the Merina of Madagascar*. Cambridge: Cambridge University Press.

———. 1989. "The ritual of the royal bath in Madagascar: The dissolution of death, birth, and fertility into authority." In *Ritual, history and power: Selected papers in anthropology*, 187–211. London: Athlone Press.

———. 1995. "The symbolism of tombs and houses in Austronesian societies with reference to two Malagasy cases." *Austronesian Studies* August: 1–26.

———. 2008. "Why religion is nothing special but is central." *Philosophical Transactions of the Royal Society B* 363: 2055–61.

Boas, Franz. (1888) 1961. *The Central Eskimo*. Lincoln: University of Nebraska Press.

———. 1890. "Second general report on the Indians of British Columbia." In *Sixth report on the north-western tribes in Canada*, 10–163. London: British Association for the Advancement of Science.

———. 1897. "The social organization and secret societies of the Kwakiutl Indians." *Report of the US National Museum for 1895*, 311–738.

———. 1899. "Fieldwork for the British Association, 1888–1897." In *A Franz Boas reader: The shaping of American anthropology, 1883–1911*, edited by George Stocking, 88–106. Chicago: University of Chicago Press.

———. 1901. "The Eskimo of Baffin Land and Hudson Bay." *Bulletin of the American Museum of Natural History*, Vol. 15.

———. 1921. "Ethnology of the Kwakiutl, based on data collected by George Hunt." *Thirty-fifth annual report of the Bureau of American Ethnology to the Secretary of the Smithsonian Institution, 1913–1914*, Parts 1 and 2. Washington, DC: Government Printing Office.

———. 1925. "Contributions to the ethnology of the Kwakiutl." *Columbia University contributions to anthropology*, Vol. III. New York: Columbia University Press.

———. 1930. "The religion of the Kwakiutl Indians." *Columbia University contributions to anthropology*, Vol. X. New York: Columbia University Press.

———. 1935. "Kwakiutl culture as reflected in mythology." *Memoirs of the American Folk-lore Society*, Vol. 28. New York: G. E. Stechert.

———. 1940. "The social organization of the Kwakiutl." In *Race, language and culture*, 356-69. New York: Free Press.

Bogoras, Waldemar. 1904–9. "The Chukchee." *Memoirs of the American Museum of Natural History*, Vol. XI. Leiden: E. J. Brill.

Bondarenko, Dmitri M. 2005. "A homoarchic alternative to homoarchic state: Benin kingdom of the 13th–19th centuries." *Social Evolution and History* 4 (2): 18–89.

Bondarenko, Dmitri M., and Andrey V. Korotayev. 2003. "'Early state' in cross-cultural perspective: A statistical reanalysis of Henri J. M. Claessen's database." *Cross-Cultural Research* 37 (1): 105–32.

Bostoen, Koen, Odjas Ndonda Tshiyavi, and Gilles-Maurice Schriver. 2013. "On the origin of the royal Kong title ngangula." *Africana Linguistica* 19: 53–83.

Boston, J. S. 1968. *The Igala kingdom*. Ibadan: Oxford University Press.

Bouveignes, Olivier and Msgr. J. Cuvelier. 1951. *Jerome de Montesarchio: Apotre du vieux Congo*. Namur: Collection Lavigerie.

Bradbury, R. E. 1957. "The Benin kingdom and the Edo-speaking peoples of south-western Nigeria." *Ethnographic Survey of Africa, Western Africa*, Part XIII. London: International African Institute.

———. 1967. "Kingdom of Benin." In *West African kingdoms in the nineteenth century*, edited by Daryll Forde and P.M. Kaberry, 1–35. London: Oxford University Press for the International African Institute.

———. 1973. *Benin studies*. Oxford: Oxford University Press.

Brain, Jeffrey. 1971. "The Natchez 'Paradox'." *Ethnology* 10 (2): 215–22.

Bray, Warwick. 1978. "Civilising the Aztecs." In *The evolution of social systems*, edited by Jonathan Friedman and Michael Rowlands, 373–98. Liverpool: Duckworth.

Brennan, Paul W. 1977. *Let sleeping snakes lie: Central Enga traditional religious belief and ritual*. Bedford Park, South Australia: Association for the Study of Religion, Special Studies in Religion no. 1.

Brewer, Jeffrey. 1981. "Bimanese personal names: Meaning and use." *Ethnology* 20 (3): 203–15.

Brightman, Robert. 1999. "Traditions of subversion and the subversion of tradition: Cultural criticism in Maidu clown performances." *American Anthropologist* 101 (2): 272–87.

Brisch, Nicole, ed. 2008. *Religion and power: Divine kingship in the ancient world and beyond*. Oriental Institute Seminars no. 4. Chicago: The Oriental Institute of the University of Chicago.

Brown, C. C. E., ed. 1952. "'The Sejarah Melayu or 'Malay Annals': A translation of Raffles MS 18." *Journal of the Malaya Branch of the Royal Asiatic Society* 25: 7–276.

Brown, Jennifer S., and Robert Brightman. 1988. *"The order of the dreamed": George Nelson on Cree and Northern Ojibwa religion and myth*. St. Paul: Minnesota Historical Society Press.

Brumbaugh, Robert. 1987. "The Rainbow Serpent in the Upper Sepik." *Anthropos* 82: 25–33.

———. 1990. "Afek Sang: The 'Old Woman" myth of the Mountain Ok." In *Children of Afek: Tradition and change among the Mountain Ok of central New Guinea*, edited by Barry Craig and David Hyndman, 54–87. University of Sydney. Oceania Monograph 40.

Brundage, Burr Cartwright. 1979. *Fifth sun: Aztec gods, Aztec world*. Austin: University of Texas Press.

Burton, John W. 1980. "Sacrifice: A polythetic class of Atuot religious thought." *Journal of Religion in Africa* 11 (2): 93–105.

Burton, John W. 1982. "Nilotic women: A diachronic perspective." *Journal of Modern African Studies* 20 (3): 467–91.

Burton, W.F.P. 1961. *Luba religion and magic in custom and belief*. Tervuren, Belgium: Musée Royal de l'Afrique Central, Sciences Humaines no. 35.

Cabanes, Robert. 1972. "Cultes des possession dans la plaine de Tananarive." *Cahiers du Centre d'Étude des Coutumes* 9: 33–66.

———. 1974. "Evolution des formes sociales de la production agricole dans la plaine de Tananarive." *Cahiers du Centre d'Étude des Coutumes* 10: 47–60.

Callet, R. P. 1908. *Tantara ny andriana eto Madagascar*. 2 vols. Tananarive: Académie Malgache.

Calnek, Edward E. 1974. "The Sahagun Texts as a source of sociological information." In *Sixteenth-century Mexico: The work of Sahagun*, edited by M. S. Edmundson, 189–204. Santa Fe, NM: School of American Research.

———. 1982. "Patterns of empire formation in the Valley of Mexico, late postclassic period, 1200–1521." In *The Inca and Aztec states, 1400–1800: Anthropology and history*, edited by Collier George, Renato J. Rosaldo, and John D. Wirth, 43–62. New York: Academic Press.

Camboué, R. P. 1907. "Notes sur quelques mœurs et coutumes malgaches." *Anthropos* 2: 981–89.

———. 1909. "Les Dix premiers ans de l'enfance chez le Malgaches : Circoncision, nom, éducation." *Anthropos* 4: 375–86.

Campbell, Gwyn. 2005. *An economic history of imperial Madagascar, 1750–1895: The rise and fall of an island empire*. Cambridge: Cambridge University Press.

Campbell, Roderick. 2014. "Transformations of violence: On humanity and inhumanity in early China." In *Violence and civilization: Studies of social violence in history and prehistory*, edited by Roderick Campbell, 94–118. Oxford: Oxbow.

Carrasco, David. 2000. *Quetzalcoatl and the irony of empire: Myths and prophecies in the Aztec tradition*. Revised edition. Boulder: University Press of Colorado.

Carrasco, Pedro. 1971. "Social organization of ancient Mexico." In *Archaeology of ancient Mexico, handbook of Middle American Indians*, Vol. 10, edited by Gordon F. Ekholm and Ignacio Bernal, 349–75. Austin: University of Texas Press.

Champlin, Edward. 2003. *Nero*. Cambridge, MA: Harvard University Press.

Chapus, Georges-Sully. and Emmanuel Ratsimba, eds. 1953–1958. *Histoires des rois*, Vol. 4 (French translation of Callet's *Tantara ny andriana*). Tananarive: Académie Malgache.

Charlevoix, Père. 1763. *Letters to the Duchess of Lesdiguieres*. London: R. Goadby.

Chase, Arlen F., and Diane Z. Chase. 1996. "More kin than king: Centralized political structure among the late classical Maya." *Current Anthropology* 37: 803–10.

Chase-Dunn, Christopher, and Kelly M. Mann, 1998. *The Wintu and their neighbors: A very small world system in northern California*. Tucson: University of Arizona Press.

Childe, V. Gordon. 1945. "Directional changes in funerary practices during 50,000 years." *Man* 4: 13–19.

Chimalpahin, Don Domingo de San Auton Munon Chimalpahin Quauhtlehuanitzin. 1997. *Codex Chimalpahin*, Vol. 2. Edited and translated by Arthur J. O. Anderson and Susan Schroeder. Norman: University of Oklahoma Press.

Claessen, Henri J. M. 1984. "The internal dynamics of the early state." *Current Anthropology* 25: 365–70.

———. 1986. "Kingship in the early state." *Bijdragen tot de taal-, land-, en volkenkunde* 142 (28): 113–27.

———. 2015. "Sacred kingship: The African case." *Social Evolution & History* 14 (1): 3–48.

Claessen, Henri J. M., and Peter Skalník. 1978. *The early state.* The Hague: Mouton.

Clark, Henry. 1896. "The Zanak'Antitra tribe: Its origins and peculiarities." *Antananarivo Annual and Madagascar Magazine* 16: 450–56.

Clastres, Hélène. 1995. *The Land-Without-Evil: Tupí-Guaraní prophetism.* Translated by Jacqueline Grenez Brovender. Urbana: University of Illinois Press.

Clastres, Pierre. 1962. "Échange et pouvoir: Philosophie de la chefferie indienne." *L'Homme* II (1): 51–65.

———. 1977. *Society against the state: The leader as servant and the humane uses of power among the Indians of the Americas.* Translated by Robert Hurley. New York: Urizen Books.

Clendinnen, Inga. 1991. *Aztecs: An interpretation.* Cambridge: Cambridge University Press.

Cobo, Bernabe P. (1653) 1979. *History of the Inca empire: An account of the Indians, customs and their origins together with a treatise on Inca legend, history and social institutions.* Translated by Roland Hamilton. Austin: University of Texas.

Codere, Helen. 1950. *Fighting with property: A study of Kwakiutl potlatching and warfare.* Seattle: University of Washington Press.

Coedès, Georges. 1968. *The Indianized states of Southeast Asia.* Canberra: Australian National University Press.

Cohen, Ronald 1976. "The natural history of hierarchy: A case study." In *Power and control: Social structures and their transformations*, edited by Tom R. Burns and Walter Buckley, 185–214. Berkeley Hills, CA: Sage Publications.

———. 1981. "Evolution, fission and the early state." In *The study of the state*, edited by Henri J. M. Claessen and Peter Skalník, 87–115. The Hague: Mouton.

Cole, Jennifer. 2001. *Forget colonialism: Sacrifice and the art of memory in Madagascar.* Berkeley: University of California Press.

Collins, Randall. 1992. "The geopolitical and economic world-systems of kinship-based and agrarian-coercive societies." *Review: Comparing World-Systems* 15 (3): 373–88.

Collins, Robert O., and James M. Burns, 2007. *A history of sub-Saharan Africa.* Cambridge: Cambridge University Press.

Conrad, Geoffrey W. 1981. "Cultural materialism, split inheritance, and the expansion of ancient Peruvian empires." *American Antiquity* 46 (1): 3–26.

Conte, Matthew, and Jangsuk Kim. 2016. "An economy of human sacrifice: The practice of sunjang in an ancient state of Korea." *Journal of Anthropological Archaeology* 44: 14–30.

Cooper, Jerrold. 1983. *The curse of Agade.* Baltimore: Johns Hopkins University Press.

———. 2012. "Divine kingship in Mesopotamia, a fleeting phenomenon." In *Religion and power: Divine kingship in the ancient world and beyond,* edited by Nicole Brisch, 261–66. Oriental Institute Seminars no. 4. Chicago: The Oriental Institute of the University of Chicago.

Copalle, André. (1826) 1970. *Voyage à la capitale du roi Radama, 1825–1826.* Antananarivo, Madagascar: Association Malgache d'Archéologie.

Cortés, Hernando. 1843. *The despatches of Hernando Cortés: The conqueror of Mexico, addressed to Emperor Charles V, written during the conquest, and containing a narrative of its events.* Translated by George Folsom. New York: Wiley & Putnam.

Cousins, William E. 1873. *Malagasy Kabary from the time of Andrianampoinimerina.* Antananarivo: Printed at the Press of the London Missionary Society.

———. (1876) 1963. *Fomba gasy.* Edited by H. Randzavola. Antananarivo: Imarivolanitr`a.

———. 1896. "The abolition of slavery in Madagascar: With some remarks on Malagasy slavery generally." *Antananarivo Annual and Madagascar Magazine* 21: 446–50.

Craig, Barry, and George E. B. Morren, Jr. 1990. "The human ecology of the Mountain-Ok of central New Guinea: A regional and inter-regional approach." In *Children of Afek: Tradition and change among the Mountain-Ok of central New Guinea,* edited by Barry Craig and David Hyndman, 9–26. University of Sydney. Oceania Monograph 40.

Crazzolara, J. P. 1950. *The Lwoo, Part I: Lwoo migrations.* Verona: Missioni Africane.

———. 1951. *The Lwoo, Part II: Lwoo traditions.* Verona: Missioni Africane.

Crocker, Jon Christopher. 1985. *Vital souls: Bororo cosmology, natural symbolism, and shamanism.* Tuscon: University of Arizona Press.

Crumrine, N. Ross. 1969. "Čapakoba, the Mayo Easter ceremonial impersonator: Explanations of ritual clowning." *Journal for the Scientific Study of Religion* 8 (1): 1–22.

Cunnison, Ian G. 1951. *History on the Luapula: An essay on the historical notions of a central African tribe.* Capetown: The Rhodes-Livingstone Institute.

———. 1956. "Perpetual kinship: A political institution of the Luapula peoples." *Rhodes-Livingstone Journal* 20: 28–48.

———. 1957. "History and genealogies in a conquest state." *American Anthropologist* 59: 20–31.

———. 1959. *The Luapula peoples of northern Rhodesia.* Manchester: Manchester University Press for The Rhodes-Livingstone Institute of Northern Rhodesia.

Curtis, Edward S. 1907. *The North American Indian,* Vol. I: *The Jicarillo, Navaho.* New York: Johnson Reprint.

———. 1915. *The North American Indian,* Vol. X: *The Kwakiutl.* New York: Johnson Reprint.

Cuvelier, Joseph. 1946. *L'ancien royaume de Congo: Fondation, découverte, première évangélisation de l'ancien Royaume de Congo, règne du Grand Roi Affonso Mvemba Nzinga.* Brussels: Brouwer.

Cuvelier, Joseph, and Louis Jadin. 1954. "L'ancien Congo, d'après les archives romaines (1518–1640)." *Académie royal des sciences coloniales: Section des sciences morales et politiques. Mémoires* 36 (1)

D'Hertefelte, Marcel. 1964. "Mythes et idéologies dans le Rwanda ancient et contemporain." In *The historian in Tropical Africa,* edited by Jan Vansina, Raymond Mauny, and L. V. Thomas, 219–38. London: Oxford University Press.

Dahle, Lars Nilsen and John Sims. (1887) 1986. *Anganon'ny ntaolo, tantara mampiseho ny fombandrazana sy ny finoana sasany nanganany.* Edited by L. Sims. Antananarivo: Trano Printy Loterana.

Dalley, Stephanie. 1996. "Herodotos and Babylon." *Orientalistische Literaturzeitung* 91: 525–32.

———. 2005. "Semiramis in history and legend: A case study in interpretation of an Assyrian historical tradition, with observations on archetypes in ancient historiography, on euhemerism before Euhemerus, and on the so-called Greek ethnographic style." In *Cultural borrowings and ethnic appropriations in antiquity,* edited by Erich S. Gruen, 12–22. Oriens et Occidens VIII. Stuttgart: Franz Steiner Verlag.

———. 2013a. "The Greek romance of Ninus and Semiramis." In *The romance between Greece and the East,* edited by Tim Whitmarsh and Stuart Thomson, 117–26. Cambridge: Cambridge University Press.

———. 2013b. *The mystery of the Hanging Garden of Babylon: An elusive wonder traced.* Oxford: Oxford University Press.

Danieli, Mary. 1952. "Andriantsihianika and the clan of the Zanak'Antitra." *Folklore* 63 (1): 46–47.

Danowski, Déborah, and Eduardo Viveiros de Castro. 2017. *The ends of the world*. Translated by Rodrigo Guimaraes Nunes. Cambridge: Polity Press.

Dapper, Olfert. (1686) 1970. *Description de l'Afrique*. New York: Johnson Reprint.

Davidson, Andrew. 1867. "Choreomania: An historical sketch, with some account of an epidemic observed in Madagascar." *Edinburgh Medical Journal* August: 124–36.

———. 1889. "The ramanenjana or dancing mania of Madagascar." *The Antananarivo Annual and Madagascar Magazine* 13: 19–27.

Davies, Nigel. 1974. *The Aztecs: A history*. New York: G. P. Putnam's Sons.

———. 1977. *The Toltecs: Until the fall of Tula*. Norman: University of Oklahoma Press.

———. 1980. *The Toltec heritage: From the fall of Tula to the rise of Tenochtitlan*. Norman: University of Oklahoma Press.

———. 1984. "Human sacrifice in the Old World and the New: Some similarities and differences." In *Rituals of human sacrifice in Mesoamerica*, edited by Elizabeth H. Boone, 211–26. Washington, DC: Dumbarton Oaks Research Library.

Davis, Kingsley. 1941. "Intermarriage in caste societies." *American Anthropologist* 43: 376–95.

Dawkins, Richard MacGillivray. 1937. "Alexander and the Water of Life." *Medium Aevum* 6 (3): 173–86.

de Heusch, Luc. 1958. *Essai sur le symbolisme de l'inceste royal en Afrique*. Brussels: Université Libre de Bruxelles.

———. 1962. *Le pouvoir et la sacré*. Annales du Centre d'Étude des Religions 1. Brussels: Institute de Sociologie, Université Libre de Bruxelles.

———. 1966. *Le Rwanda et la civilization interlacustre: Étude d'anthropologie historique et structural*. Brussels: Université de Bruxelles Libre.

———. 1981. "Nouveaux regards sur la royauté sacré." *Anthropologie et Societés* 5 (3): 65–84.

———. 1982a. *The drunken king, or The origin of the state*. Translated by Roy Willis. Bloomington: Indiana University Press.

———. 1982b. *Rois né d'un coeur de vache*. Paris: Gallimard.

———. 1991. "The king comes from elsewhere." In *Body and space: Symbolic models of unity and division in African cosmology and experience*, edited by Anita-Jacobson-Widding, 109–17. Uppsala: Studies in Cultural Anthropology 16.

———. 1997. "The symbolic mechanisms of kingship: Rediscovering Frazer." *Journal of the Royal Anthropological Institute* (N.S.) 3 (2): 313–32.

———. 2000. *Le roi de Kongo et les monstres sacrés*. Paris: Gallimard.

———. 2005a. "Forms of sacralized power in Africa." In *The character of kingship*, edited by Declan Quigley, 25–37. Oxford: Berg.

———. 2005b. "A reply to Lucien Scubla." In *The character of kingship*, edited by Declan Quigley, 63–66. Oxford: Berg.

de Surgey, Albert. 1988. *Le Système religieux des Evhe*. Paris: Harmattan.

———. 1990. "Le prêtre-roi des Evhé du Sud-Togo." In *Systèmes de pensée en Afrique noire*, Vol. 10: *Chefs et rois sacrés*, edited by Luc de Heusch, 93–120. Paris: École Pratique des Hautes Études.

Delivré, Alain. 1974. *L'Histoire des rois d'Imerina: Interprétation d'une tradition orale*. Paris: Klincksieck.

Descola, Philippe. 1996. *In the society of nature: A native ecology in Amazonia*. Translated by Nora Scott. Cambridge: Cambridge University Press.

———. 2013. *Beyond nature and culture*. Translated by Janet Lloyd. Chicago: University of Chicago Press.

Devereux, George, and Edwin M. Loeb. 1943. "Antagonistic acculturation." *American Sociological Review* 8: 133–47.

Dewar, Robert, and Henry Wright. 1993. "The culture history of Madagascar." *Journal of World History* 7 (4): 417–66.

Dez, Jacques. 1971a. "Essai sur le concept de Vazimba." *Bulletin de l'Académie Malagache* 49 (2): 13–20.

———. 1971b. *La légende de l'Ankaratra*. Tananarive: Université de Madagascar, Faculté des lettres et sciences humaines.

Dixon, Roland B. 1902. "Maidu Myths." *Bulletin of the American Museum of Natural History* 17: 33–118.

Dixon, Roland B. 1905. "The Northern Maidu." *Bulletin of the American Museum of Natural History* 27: 121–343.

———. 1907. *The Shasta*. New York: American Museum of Natural History.

Domenichini, Jean-Pierre. 1977. *Les Dieux au service des rois: Histoire des Palladium d'Emyrne*. Paris: Karthala.

———. 1982. "Antehiroka et Vazimba: Contribution à l'histoire de la société du XVIIIe au XIXe siècle." *Bulletin de l'Académie Malgache* 56 (1–2): 11–21.

———. 2004. "Vazimba et esprits *helo*: La profondeur chronologique." *Études Océan Indien* 51–52: 2–19.

———. 2007. "La question Vazimba: Historiographie et politique." Centre d'histoire de l'Université de la Réunion.

Domenichini, Jean-Pierre, and Bakoly Domenichini-Ramiaramanana. 1980. "Regards croisés sur les grands Sycomores, ou l'armée noire des anciens princes d'Imerina." *Asie du Sud Est et Monde Insulindien* XI (1–4): 55–95.

Domenichini-Ramiaramanana, Bakoly. 1982. *Du ohabolana au hainteny: Langue, littérature et politique à Madagascar.* Paris: Karthala.

Donald, Leland. 1997. *Aboriginal slavery on the northwest coast of North America.* Berkeley: University of California Press.

Douglas, Eduardo de J. 2010. *In the palace of Nezahualcoyotl: Painting manuscripts, writing the pre-Hispanic past in early colonial period Tetzcoco.* Austin: University of Texas Press

Douglas, Mary. 1959. "Animals in Lele religious symbolism." *Africa* 27: 46–58.

———. 1980. *Evans-Pritchard.* London: Fontana Books.

Driberg, Jack Herbert. 1932. "The status of women among the Nilotics and Nilo-Hamites." *Africa* 5 (4): 404–21.

Drinkwater, John F. 1978. "The rise and fall of the Gallic Iulli: Aspects of the development of the aristocracy of the Three Gauls under the empire." *Latomus* 37: 817–50.

Drucker, Philip. 1940. "Kwakiutl dancing societies." *University of California Anthropological Records* 2, no. 6: 200–30. Berkeley: University of California Press.

Drucker-Brown, Susan. 1975. *Ritual aspects of the Mamprussi kingship.* Cambridge: African Studies Center.

Du Pratz, La Page. 1774. *History of Louisiana.* London: T. Becket.

Duran, Frey Diego. 1994. *The history of the Indians of New Spain.* Translated by Doris Heiden. Norman: University of Oklahoma Press.

Dutton, George E., Jayne S. Werner, and John K. Whitmore, eds. 2012. *Sources of Vietnamese tradition.* New York: Columbia University Press.

Edland, Sigmund. 2006. *Evangelists or envoys? The role of British missionaries at turning points in Malagasy political history, 1820–1840. Documentary and analysis.* School of Mission and Theology Dissertation series Vol. 3. Stavenger: Misjonshøgskolens forlag.

Edmonds, William J. 1895. "By-gone ornamentation and dress among the Hova Malagasy." *Antananarivo Annual and Madagascar Magazine* 20: 469–77.

———. 1897. "Charms and superstitions in Southeast Imerina." *Antananarivo Annual and Madagascar Magazine* 22: 61-67

Egharevba, Jacob. 1968. *A short history of Benin.* Fourth edition. Ibadan: Ibadan University Press.

Eilers, Wilhem. 1971. *Semiramis. Entstehung und Nachhall einer altorientalischen Saga.* Osterreiche Akadamie der Wissenschaften Philosophisch-historische Klasse, Sitzungsberichte, Vol. 274, Abhandlung 2. Vienna.

Ekholm, Kajsa. 1972. *Power and prestige: The rise and fall of the Kongo kingdom*. Uppsala: Skriv Service AB.

———. 1978 "External exchange and the transformation of central African social systems." In *The evolution of social systems*, edited by Jonathan Friedman and Michael Rowlands, 115–36. Liverpool: Duckworth

———. 1980 "On the limitation of civilization: The structure and dynamics of global systems." *Dialectical Anthropology* 5: 155–66.

———. 1985a. "Sad stories of the death of kings: The involution of divine kingship." *Ethnos* 50: 248–72.

———. 1985b. "Towards a global anthropology," *Critique of Anthropology* 5: 97–119.

———. 1991. *Catastrophe and creation: The transformation of an African culture*. Philadelphia: Harwood Academic Publishers.

Ekholm, Kasja, and Jonathan Friedman. 1979. "'Capital,' imperialism and exploitation in ancient world systems." In *Power and propaganda: A symposium on ancient empires*, edited by Mogens Trollo Larsen, 41–58. Copenhagen: Copenhagen Studies in Assyriology.

Elias, Norbert. (1939) 1978. *The civilizing process I: The history of manners*. Translated by Edmund Jephcott. New York: Pantheon Books.

Elkin, A. P. 1930a. "The Rainbow Serpent myth in North-West Australia." *Oceania* 1: 349–52.

———. 1930b. "Rock paintings of North-West Australia." *Oceania* 1: 257–79.

Ellen, R. F. 1986. "Conundrums about panjandrums: On the use of titles in the relations of political subordination in the Moluccas and along the Papuan coast." *Indonesia* 14: 47–62.

Ellis, Stephen. 1985. *The rising of the red shawls: A revolt in Madagascar, 1895–1899*. Cambridge: Cambridge University Press.

———. 2002. "Witch-hunting in Central Madagascar, 1828–1861." *Past and Present* 175: 90–123

Ellis, William. 1838. *History of Madagascar*. 2 vols. London: Fisher & Son.

———. 1867. *Madagascar revisited, describing the events of a new reign, and the revolution which followed*. London: John Murray.

Elmberg, John-Erik. 1968. *Balance and circulation: Aspects of tradition and change among the Mejprat of Irian-Barat. Stockholm*: The Ethnographical Museum, Monograph Series no. 12.

Ethridge, Robbie. 2010. *From Chicaza to Chickasaw The European Invasion and the Transformation of the Mississippian World, 1540–1715*. Chapel Hill: University of North Carolina Press.

Evans-Pritchard, E. E. 1937. *Witchcraft, oracles and magic among the Azande.* Oxford: Clarendon Press.

Evans-Pritchard, E. E. 1948. *The divine kingship of the Shilluk of the Nilotic Sudan.* The Frazer Lecture for 1948. Cambridge: Cambridge University Press.

———. 1940. *The Nuer: a description of the modes of livelihood and political institutions of a Nilotic people.* Oxford: Clarendon Press

———. 1949. *The Sanusi of Cyrenaica.* Oxford: Clarendon Press.

———. 1951. "Shilluk king-killing." *Man* 51: 116.

——— 1954. "The meaning of sacrifice among the Nuer." *Journal of the Royal Anthropological Institute* 84: 21–33.

———. 1956. *Nuer religion.* Oxford: Clarendon Press.

———. 1957. "The origin of the ruling clan of Azande." *Southwestern Journal of Anthropology* 13: 322–43.

———. 1971. *The Azande: History and political institutions.* Oxford: Clarendon Press.

Evens, T. M. S. 1989. "The Nuer incest prohibition and the nature of kinship: Alterological eeckoning." *Cultural Anthropology* 4 (4): 323–46.

Eyre, Christopher. 2002. *The cannibal hymn: A cultural and literary study.* Liverpool: Liverpool University Press.

Fairley, Nancy J. 1987. "Ideology and state formation: The Ekie of Southern Zaïre." In *The African frontier: The reproduction of traditional African societies*, edited by Igor Kopytoff, 89–100. Bloomington: Indiana University Press.

Fallers, Lloyd. 1965. *Bantu bureaucracy: A century of political evolution among the Basoga of Uganda.* Chicago: University of Chicago Press.

Fausto, Carlos. 2012. "Too many owners: Mastery and ownership in Amazonia." In *Animism in rainforest and tundra: Personhood, animals, plants, and things in contemporary Amazonia and Siberia*, edited by Marc Brightman, Vanessa Elisa Grotti, and Olga Ulturgasheva, 29–47. New York: Berghahn Books.

Feachem, Richard. 1973. "The religious belief and ritual of the Raiapu Enga." *Oceania* 43: 259–85.

Federici, Silvia. 2012. *Revolution at point zero: Housework, reproduction, and feminist struggle.* San Francisco: PM Press.

Feeley-Harnik, Gillian. 1974. "Divine kingship and the meaning of history among the Sakalava of Madagascar." *Man* (N.S.) 13: 402–17.

———. 1982. "The king's men in Madagascar: Slavery, citizenship and Sakalava monarchy." *Africa* 52: 31–50.

———. 1984. "The political economy of death: Communication and change in Malagasy colonial history." *American Ethnologist* 8: 231–54.

————. 1985. "Issues in divine kingship." *Annual Review of Anthropology* 14: 273–313.

————. 1986. "Ritual and work in Madagascar." In *Madagascar: Society and history*, edited by C. P. Kottak, J.-A. Rakotoarisoa, A. Southall, and P. Vérin, 151–74. Durham, NC: Carolina Academic Press.

Feierman, Steven. 1968. "The Shambaa." In *Tanzania before 1900*, edited by Andrew Roberts, 1–15. Nairobi: East African Publishing House

————. 1974. *The Shambaa kingdoms: A history*. Madison: University of Wisconsin Press.

Firaketana.1937. *Firaketana ny fiteny sy ny zavatra Malagasy*, edited by Ravelojaona, Randzavola, and Rajaona. 6 vols. Tananarive. Madagascar: Imprimerie Industrie.

Firth, Raymond. 1971. *History and traditions of Tikopia*. Wellington: The Polynesian Society.

Fischer, J. L. 1964. "Solutions for the Natchez Paradox." *Ethnology* 3: 53–65.

Fisher, H. J. 1975. "The central Sahara and Sudan." In *The Cambridge history of Africa*, Vol.4: *From c. 1600 to c. 1790*, edited by Richard Gray, 58–141. Cambridge: Cambridge University Press.

Folbre, Nancy. 1995. "Holding hands at midnight: The paradox of caring labor." *Feminist Economics* 1 (1): 73–92.

Forge, Anthony. 1990. "The power of culture and the culture of power." In *Sepik heritage: Tradition and change in Papua New Guinea*, edited by Nancy Lutkehaus, 160–70. Durham, NC: Carolina Academic Press.

Formicola, Vincenza. 2007. "From the Sunghir children to the Romito dwarf: Aspects of the Upper Paleolithic funerary landscape." *Current Anthropology* 48: 446–53.

Fortes, Meyer. 1940. "The political system of the Northern Territories of the Gold Coast." In *African political systems*, edited by Meyer Fortes and E. E. Evans-Pritchard, 238–71. London: Oxford University Press.

————. 1945. *The dynamics of clanship among the Tallensi*. London: Oxford University Press for The International African Institute.

————. (1949) 1969. *The web of kinship among the Tallensi*. London: Oxford University Press for The International African Institute.

Fortes, Meyer, and E. E. Evans-Pritchard, eds. 1940. *African political systems*. London: Oxford University Press.

Frankfort, Henri. 1948. *Kingship and the gods: A study of ancient Near Eastern religion as the integration of society and nature*. Chicago: Oriental Institute.

Frankfort, H., and H. A. Frankfort. (1946) 1977. "Introduction." In *The intellectual adventure of ancient man: An essay on speculative thought in the ancient Near East*, H. Frankfort, H. A. Frankfort, John A. Wilson, Thorkild Jacobsen, and William A. Irwin, 1–27. Chicago: University of Chicago Press.

Fraser, Robert. 1990. *The making of The golden bough: The origins and growth of an argument*. New York: St. Martin's Press.

Frazer, James George. 1911a. *The dying god: Part III of The golden bough*. London: Macmillan.

———. 1911b. *The magic art and the evolution of kings: Part I of The golden bough*. London: Macmillan.

———. 1911c. *The scapegoat: Part VI of The golden bough*. London: Macmillan.

———. 1918. *Folklore in the Old Testament: Studies in comparative religion, legend and law*, Vol. 3. London: Macmillan & Co.

———. (1921) 1976. "Introduction." In *Apollodorus: The library*, Vol. 1, ed. James George Frazer, ix–xliii. Loeb Classical Library. Cambridge, MA: Harvard University Press.

Freeman, Joseph John, and David Johns. 1840. *A narrative of the persecution of the Christians in Madagascar*. London: John Snow.

Fried, Morton H. 1967. *The evolution of political society: An essay in political anthropology*. New York: Random House.

———. 1975. *The notion of tribe*. Menlo Park, CA: Cummings.

Friedman, Jonathan. 1992. "General historical and culturally specific properties of global systems." *Review* (Fernand Braudel Center) 15: 335–72.

Friedman, Jonathan, and Michael J. Rowlands. 1978. "Notes toward an epigenetic model of the evolution of 'civilization.'" In *The evolution of social systems*, edited by Jonathan Friedman and Michael J. Rowlands, 201–76. Pittsburgh: University of Pittsburgh Press.

Friedman, Kajsa Ekholm, and Jonathan Friedman 2008. *Historical transformations: The anthropology of global systems*. Lanham, MD: AltaMira Press.

Fromm, Erich. 1973. *The anatomy of human destructiveness*. New York: Holt Rinehart & Winston.

Frost, John. 1974. "A history of the Shilluk of the Southern Sudan." Ph.D. dissertation, University of California, Santa Barbara.

Fugelstad, Finn. 1982. "The Tompon-Tany and Tompon-Drano in the history of Central and Western Madagascar." *History in Africa* 9: 61–76.

Gale, H. P. 1956. "Mutesa I—was he a god? The enigma of Kiganda paganism." *Uganda Journal* 20: 72–87.

Gardener, D. S. 1987. "Spirits and conceptions of agency among the Mianmin of Papua New Guinea." *Oceania* 57: 161–77.

Geertz, Clifford. 1980. *Negara: The theatre state in nineteenth-century Bali*. Princeton, NJ: Princeton University Press.

Geertz, Hildred, and Clifford Geertz. 1964. "Teknonymy in Bali: Parenthood, age-grading and genealogical amnesia." *The Journal of the Royal Anthropological Institute of Great Britain and Ireland* 94 (2): 94–108.

———. 1975. *Kinship in Bali*. Chicago: University of Chicago Press.

Gell, Alfred. 1997. "Exalting the king and obstructing the state: A political interpretation of royal ritual in Bastar District, central India." *Journal of the Royal Anthropological Institute* (N.S.) 3 (3): 433–55.

Gesick, Lorraine. 1983. "Introduction." In *Centers, symbols, and hierarchies: Essays on the classical states of Southeast Asia*, edited by Lorraine Gesick, 1–8. New Haven, CT: Yale University Southeast Asian Studies, Monograph Series no. 23.

Gewertz, Deborah B. 1983. *Sepik River societies: A historical ethnography of Chambri and their neighbors*. New Haven, CT: Yale University Press.

———. 1991. "Symmetrical schismogenesis revisited?" *Oceania* 61: 236–39.

Giersch, C. Patterson. 2006. *Asian borderlands: The transformation of Qing China's Yunnan frontier*. Cambridge, MA: Harvard University Press.

Giesey, R. E. 1967. *The royal funerary ceremony in Renaissance France*. Geneva: Libraire E. Droz.

Gifford, Edward Wilson. 1927. "Southern Maidu religious ceremonies." *American Anthropologist* (N.S.) 29 (3): 214–57.

Gillespie, Susan. 1989. *The Aztec kings: The construction of rulership in Mexica history*. Tucson: University of Arizona Press.

Gilmore, John. 1887. "The origins of the Semiramis legend." *The English Historical Review* 2 (8): 729–34.

Girard, René. 1977. *Violence and the sacred*. Translated by Patrick Gregory. Baltimore: Johns Hopkins University Press.

———. 1989. *The scapegoat*. Translated by Yvonne Freccero. Baltimore: Johns Hopkins University Press.

Girling, F. K. 1960. *The Acholi of Uganda*. Colonial Office: Colonial Research Studies no. 30. London: HM Stationery Office.

Glasse, R. M. 1965. "The Huli of the Southern Highlands." In *Gods, ghosts, and men in Melanesia: Some religions of Australian New Guinea and the New Hebrides*, edited by Peter Lawrence and Mervyn J. Meggitt, 27–49. Melbourne: Oxford University Press.

Goldman, Irving. 1975. *The mouth of heaven: An introduction to Kwakiutl religious thought*. New York: John Wiley & Sons.

Goodenough, Ward H. 1986 "Sky World and this world: The place of Kachaw in Micronesian cosmology," *American Anthropologist* 88: 551–68.

Gose, Peter. 1996a. "Oracles, divine kingship, and political representation in the Inka state." *Ethnohistory* 43 (1): 1–32.

———. 1996b. "The past is a lower moiety: Diarchy, history, and divine kingship in the Inka empire." *History and Anthropology* 9 (4): 383–414.

Graeber, David. 1995. "Dancing with corpses reconsidered: An interpretation of Famadihana in Arivonimamo (Madagascar)." *American Ethnologist* 22 (2): 258–78.

———. 1996a. "Beads and money: Notes toward a theory of wealth and power." *American Ethnologist* 23 (1): 4–24.

———. 1996b. "Love magic and political morality in Central Madagascar, 1875–1990." *Gender and History* 8 (3): 416–39.

———. 1997. "Manners, deference and private property." *Comparative Studies in Society and History* 39 (4): 694–728.

———. 2001. *Toward an anthropological theory of value: The false coin of our own dreams.* New York: Palgrave.

———. 2004. *Fragments of an anarchist anthropology.* Chicago: Prickly Paradigm Press.

———. 2005. "Fetishism and social creativity, or fetishes are gods in process of construction." *Anthropological Theory* 5 (4): 407–38.

———. 2007a. *Lost people: Magic and the legacy of slavery in Madagascar.* Bloomington: Indiana University Press.

———. 2007b. "On the phenomenology of giant puppets: Broken windows, imaginary jars of urine, and the cosmological role of the police in American culture." In *Possibilities: Essays on hierarchy, rebellion, and desire,* 375–418. Oakland, CA: AK Press.

———. 2007c. "Oppression." In *Possibilities: Essays on hierarchy, rebellion and desire,* 255–98. Oakland, CA: AK Press.

———. 2009. *Direct action: An ethnography.* Oakland, CA: AK Press.

———. 2011a. *Debt: The first 5000 years.* Brooklyn, NY: Melville House.

———. 2011b. "The divine kingship of the Shilluk: On violence, utopia and the human condition, or, elements for an archaeology of sovereignty." *HAU: The Journal of Ethnographic Theory* 1 (1): 1–62.

Grandidier, Alfred. 1914. *Histoire physique, naturelle et politique de Madagascar,* Vol. IV, Book 2: *Ethnographie.* Paris: Imprimerie Nationale.

Gray, Robert 1961. *A history of the Southern Sudan, 1839–1889.* Oxford: Oxford University Press.

Grey, Sir George. (1855) 1956. *Polynesian mythology.* New York: Taplinger.

Griffin, Miriam T. 1984. *Nero: The end of a dynasty.* London: Batsford.

Grimal, Nicolas. 1988. *A history of ancient Egypt.* London: Blackwell.

Gumplowicz, Ludwig. 1899. *The outlines of sociology*. Philadelphia: American Academy of Political and Social Science.

Guyer, Jane. 1993. "Wealth in people and self-realization in Equatorial Africa." *Man* (N.S.) 28: 243–65.

Haas, M. R. 1939. "Natchez and Chitimacha clans and kinship terminology." *American Anthropologist* 41: 597–610.

Haile, John. 1891. "Famadihana, a Malagasy burial custom." *Antananarivo Annual and Madagascar Magazine* 16: 406–16.

Hallowell, A. Irving. 1960. "Ojibwas ontology, behavior, and world view." In *Culture in history: Essays in honor of Paul Radin*, edited by Stanley Diamond, 17–49. New York: Columbia University Press.

Halpern, Abraham M. 1988. "Southeastern Pomo ceremonials: The Kuksu Cult and its successors." *University of California Anthropological Records 29*. Berkeley: University of California Press

Hamayon, Roberta N. 1996. "Shamanism in Siberia: From partnership in supernature to counter-power in society." In *Shamanism, history, and the state*, edited by Nicholas Thomas and Carolyn Humphrey, 76–89. Ann Arbor: University of Michigan Press.

Handelman, Don. 1981. "The ritual clown: Attributes and affinities." *Anthropos* 76: 321–70.

Hansen, Thomas Blom, and Finn Stepputat 2005. *Sovereign bodies: Citizens, migrants, and states in the postcolonial world*. Princeton, NJ: Princeton University Press.

———. 2006. "Sovereignty revisited." *Annual Review of Anthropology* 35: 295–315.

Haring, Lee. 1982. *Malagasy tale index*. Folklore Fellows Communications no. 231. Helsinki: Suomalainen Tiedeakatemia.

———. 1992. *The verbal arts in Madagascar: Performance in historical perspective*. Philadelphia: University of Pennsylvania Press.

Harrison, Simon. 1985. "Ritual hierarchy and secular equality in a Sepik River village." *American Ethnologist* 12: 413–26.

———. 1990. *Stealing people's names: History and politics in a Sepik River cosmology*. Cambridge: Cambridge University Press.

Hart, C. W. M. 1943. "A reconsideration of Natchez social structure." *American Anthropologist* 45: 379–86.

Hastie, James. N.d. "Diary of James Hastie." Typescript copy, National Archives, Antananarivo.

Healy, Andrew J., and Neil Malhotra. 2013. "Retrospective voting reconsidered." *Annual Review of Political Science* 16: 285–306.

Healy, Andrew J., Neil Malhotra, and Cecilia Hyunjung Mo. 2010. "Irrelevant events affect voters' evaluations of government performance." *Proceedings of the National Academy of Sciences of the United States of America* 107 (29): 12804–9.

Hébert, Jean-Claude.1958. "La parenté à plaisanterie à Madagascar." *Bulletin de l'Académie Malgache* 142: 175–217; 143: 267–33.

Helms, Mary. 1988. *Ulysses' sail: An ethnographic odyssey of power, knowledge and geographical distance.* Princeton, NJ: Princeton University Press.

———. 1993. *Craft and the kingly ideal: Art, trade, and power.* Austin: University of Texas Press.

———. 1998. *Access to origins: Affines, ancestors, and aristocrats.* Austin: University of Texas Press.

Henderson, Bernard W. 1905. *The life and principate of the Emperor Nero.* London: Methuen.

Herman, John E. 2006. *Amid the clouds and mists: China's colonization of Guizhou, 1200–1700.* Cambridge, MA: Harvard University Press.

Hiatt, L. R. 1996. *Arguments about Aborigines: Australia and the evolution of social anthropology.* Cambridge: Cambridge University Press.

Hieb, Louis. 1972. "Meaning and mismeaning: Toward an understanding of the ritual clown." In *New perspectives on the Pueblos*, edited by Alfonso Ortiz, 163–95. Albuquerque: University of New Mexico Press.

Hilton, Anne. 1985. *The kingdom of Kongo.* Oxford: Clarendon Press.

Hocart, A. M. (1927) 1969. *Kingship.* London: Oxford University Press.

———. 1929 *Lau Islands, Fiji.* Honolulu: Bernice P. Bishop Museum Bulletin 62.

———. 1933. *The progress of man: A short survey of his evolution, his customs and his works.* London: Methuen.

———. (1936) 1970. *Kings and councillors: An essay in the comparative anatomy of human society.* Chicago: University of Chicago Press.

———. (1950) 1968. *Caste: A comparative study.* New York: Russell and Russell.

———. (1952) 1970. *The life-giving myth and other essays.* London: Tavistock and Methuen.

———. 1954 *Social origins.* London: Watts.

Hodgkins, Gael Atherton. 1977. "The sea spirit of the Central Eskimo: Mistress of sea animals and supreme spirit." Ph.D. dissertation, Divinity School, University of Chicago.

Hofmayr, Wilhelm. 1911. "Religion der Shilluk." *Anthropos* 6: 120–31.

———. 1925. *Die Shilluk: Geschichte, Religion, und Leben einze Niloten-Stammes.* Mölding: Verlag der Administration des Anthropos.

Houlder, James A. 1912. *Among the Malagasy: An unconventional record of missionary experience*. London: James Clarke.

———. (1915) 1960. *Ohabolana or Malagasy proverbs: Illustrating the wit and wisdom of the Hova of Madagascar*. Antananarivo: Trano Printy FLM.

Howell, P. P. 1941. "The Shilluk settlement." *Sudan Notes and Records* 24: 47–67.

———. 1944. "The installation of the Shilluk king." *Man* 44: 145–47.

———. 1952a. "The death and burial of reth Dak wad Fadiet of the Shilluk." *Sudan Notes and Records* 33: 156–65.

———. 1952b. "The death of reth Dak wad Fadiet and the installation of his successor: A preliminary note." *Man* 52: 102–4.

———. 1952c. "Observations on the Shilluk of the Upper Nile: The laws of homicide and the legal functions of the Reth." *Africa* 22: 97–119.

———. 1953a. "The election and installation of reth Kur wad Fafiti of the Shilluk." *Sudan Notes and Records* 34: 189–203.

———. 1953b. "Observations on the Shilluk of the Upper Nile: Customary law: Marriage and the violation of rights in women." *Africa* 23: 94–109.

———. N.d. Howell Papers, Archives, University of Durham, SAD 68–69.

Howell, P. P., and W. P. G. Thomson. 1946. "The death of a Reth of the Shilluk and the installation of his successor." *Sudan Notes and Records* 27: 5–85.

Howell, Signe. 1985. "Equality and hierarchy in Chewong classification." In *Contexts and levels: Anthropological essays of hierarchy*, edited by R. H. Barnes, Daniel de Coppet, and R. J. Parkin, 167–80. Oxford: JASO.

———. 1989. *Society and cosmos: Chewong of Peninsular Malaysia*. Chicago: University of Chicago Press.

———. 2012. "Knowledge, morality, and causality, in a 'luckless' society: The case of the Chewong in the Malaysian Rain Forest." *Social Analysis* 56: 133–47.

Hudson, Charles. 1978. *Southeastern Indians*. Knoxville: University of Tennessee Press.

Hughes, Jonathan. 2002. *Arthurian myths and alchemy: The kingship of Edward IV*. Stroud: Sutton Publishing.

Huxley, Francis. 1956. *Affable savages: An anthropologist among the Urubu Indians of Brazil*. London: Rupert Hart-Davis.

Ingham, Kenneth. 1958. *The making of modern Uganda*. London: Allen & Unwin.

Irstam, Tristram. 1944. *The king of Ganda: Studies in the institutions of sacral kingship in Africa*. The Ethnographical Museum of Sweden (N.S.) 8. Stockholm.

Isichei, Elizabeth. 1997. *A history of African societies to 1870*. Cambridge: Cambridge University Press.

Ixtlilxóchitl, Fernando D'Alva. 1840. *Histoire des Chichimeques; ou des anciens rois de Tezcuco*. 2 vols. Paris: Bertrand.

Izard, Michel. 1985. *Gens du pouvior, gens de la terre: Les institutions politiques de l'ancien royaume du Yatenga (Bassin de la Volta Blanche)*. Cambridge: Cambridge University Press.

————— 1990. "De quelques paramètres de la souveraineté." In *Systèmes de pensée en Afrique noire*, Vol. 10: *Chefs et rois sacrés*, edited by Luc de Heusch, 69–91. Paris: École Pratique des Hautes Études.

Izard, Michel, and J. Ki-zerbo, 1992. "From the Niger to the Volta." In *General history of Africa*, Vol. V: *Africa from the sixteenth to eighteenth century*, edited by B. A. Ogot, 327–67. Berkeley: University of California Press for UNESCO.

Jacobsen, Thorkild. (1946) 1977. "Mesopotamia: The cosmos as a state." In *The intellectual adventure of ancient man: An essay on speculative thought in the ancient Near East*, H. Frankfort, H. A. Frankfort, John A. Wilson, Thorkild Jacobsen, and William A. Irwin, 125–84. Chicago: University of Chicago Press.

Janzen, John M. 1982. *Lemba, 1650–1930: A drum of affliction in Africa and the New World*. New York: Garland Press.

Jenkins, David. 2001. "The Inka conical clan." *Journal of Anthropological Research* 57 (2): 167–95.

Johansen, J. Prytz. 1954. *The Maori and his religion in its non-ritualistic aspects*. Copenhagen: Munksgaartd.

Johnson, Rev. Samuel. (1921) 2006. *The history of the Yorubas*. Lagos: CSS Ltd.

Jorgensen, Dan. 1980. "What's in a name: The meaning of meaningless in Telefolmin." *Ethos* 8: 349–66.

—————. 1990a. "Placing the past and moving the present: Myth and contemporary history in Telefolmin." *Culture* 10: 47–56.

—————. 1990b. "Secrecy's turns." *Canberra Anthropology* 13: 40–47.

—————. 1990c. "The Telefolip and the architecture of ethnic identity in the Sepik Headwaters." In *Children of Afek: Tradition and change among the Mountain Ok of Central New Guinea*, edited by Barry Craig and David Hyndman, 151–60. Oceanica Monograph 40.

—————. 1996. "Regional history and ethnic identity in the hub of New Guinea: The emergence of the Min." *Oceania* 66: 189–210.

—————. 1998. "Whose nature? Invading bush spirits, traveling ancestors, and mining in Telefolmin." *Social Analysis* 42: 100–16.

Josselin de Jong, J. P. B. 1928. "The Natchez social system." *Proceedings, 23rd International Congress of Americanists*: 553–62.

Julien, Gustave. 1909. *Institutions politiques et sociales de Madagascar*. 2 vols. Paris: Libraire Orientale et Americaine.

Jully, Antoine.1898. "Notes sur Robin." *Notes, reconaissances et explorations* March: 511–16.

———. 1899a. "Croyances et pratiques superstitieuses chez les Merinas ou Hoves." *Revue de Madagascar* 1 (October): 311–28.

———. 1899b. "Documents historiques: Origine des 'Andriana' ou nobles." *Notes, reconaissances et explorations* 1 (19): 890–98.

Kagwa, Apolo. 1971. *Kings of Buganda*. Nairobi: East Africa Publishing House.

Kantorowicz, E. H. 1957. *The king's two bodies: A study in medieval political theology*. Princeton, NJ: Princeton University Press.

Kaplan, Flora E. 1997. "Iyoba: The queen mother of Benin." In *Queens, queen, others, priestesses, and power: Case studies in African gender*, edited by Flora E. Kaplan, 73–102. Annals of the New York Academy of Sciences, Vol. 810. New York: New York Academy of Sciences.

Kapteijns, Lidwien, and Jay Spaulding. 1982. "Precolonial trade between states in the Eastern Sudan, ca 1700–ca 1900." *African Economic History* 11: 29–62.

Kasanga, Fernand. 1956. *Tantaran' ny Antemoro-Anakara teto Imerina tamin'ny andron' Andrianampoinimerina sy Ilaidama*. Tananarive: Societé Imprimerie Antananarivo.

Kasetsiri, Charnvit. 1976. *The rise of Ayudhya: A history of Siam in the fourteenth and fifteenth century*. Kuala Lumpur: Oxford University Press.

Keesing, Roger. 1982. *Kwaio religion: The living and the dead in a Solomon Islands society*. New York: Columbia University Press.

Kellogg, Susan M. 1986. "Kinship and social organization in early colonial Tenochtitlan." In *Ethnohistory: Supplement to the Handbook of Middle American Indians*, Vol. 4, edited by Ronald Spores, 103–21. Austin: University of Texas Press.

Kenny, Michael. 1988. "Mutesa's crime: Hubris and the control of African kings." *Comparative Studies in Society and History* 30: 595–612.

Kent, Raymond.1970. *Early kingdoms in Madagascar, 1500–1700*. New York: Holt, Rinehart & Winston.

Kingdon, A. 1889. "A Malagasy hero, who offered himself for his king and his country." *Antananarivo Annual and Madagascar Magazine* 8: 1–7.

Kirchhoff, Paul. 1949. "The social and political organization of the Andean peoples." In *Handbook of South American Indians*, Vol. 5, edited by Julian H. Steward, 293–311. Washington, DC: Government Printing Office.

———. 1955. "The principles of clanship in human society." *Davidson Journal of Anthropology* 1: 1–10.

Knight, Vernon James. 1986. "The institutional organization of Mississippian religion." *American Antiquity* 51 (4): 675–87.

———. 1990. "Social organization and the evolution of hierarchy in southeastern chiefdoms." *Journal of Anthropological Research* 46 (1): 1–23.

Kopytoff, Igor. 1989. "The internal African frontier: The making of African political culture." In *The African frontier: The reproduction of traditional African societies*, edited by Igor Kopytoff, 3–84. Bloomington: Indiana University Press.

Kowalewski Stephen A. 1996. "Clout, corn, copper, core–periphery, culture area." In *Pre-Columbian world systems*, edited by Peter N. Peregrine and Gary M. Feinman, 39–50. Madison, WI: Prehistory Press.

Krige, E. Jensen, and J. D. Krige. 1943. *The realm of a rain queen: A study of the pattern of the Lovedu society.* Cape Town: Juta & Company.

Kroeber, Alfred L. 1922. *Elements of culture in native California.* Berkeley: University of California Press.

———. 1925. *Handbook of the Indians of California.* Bureau of American Ethnology Bulletin 78. Washington, DC: Smithsonian Institution.

———. 1932. "The Patwin and their neighbors." *University of California Publications in American Archaeology and Ethnology* 29 (4): 253–423.

———. 1945. "The ancient oikoumene as an historic culture aggregate," *Journal of the Royal Anthropological Institute* 75: 9–20.

———. 1947. *Cultural and natural areas of Native North America.* Berkeley: University of California Press.

———. 1948. *Anthropology: Race, language, culture, psychology, prehistory.* New York: Harcourt, Brace and Company.

Kuhrt, Amelie. 2013. "Semiramis (Sammuramat)." In *The encyclopedia of ancient history*, edited by Roger S. Bagnall, Kai Brodersen, Craige B. Champion, Andrew Erskine, and Sabine R. Huebner, 6133–34. Oxford: Blackwell.

Kunijwok, G. A. W. 1982. "Government and community in a modern state: A case study of the Shilluk and their neighbors." Ph.D. thesis, Oxford, Bodleian Library.

Kurimoto, Eisei. 1992. "An ethnography of 'bitterness': Cucumber and sacrifice reconsidered." *Journal of Religion in Africa* 22 (1): 47–65.

Kus, Susan, and Victor Raharijaona. 2000. "House to palace, village to state: Scaling up architecture and ideology." *American Anthropologist* 102 (1): 98–113.

———. 2001. "'To dare to wear the cloak of another before their very eyes': State co-optation and local re-appropriation in mortuary rituals of Central Madagascar." *Archaeological Papers of the American Anthropological Association* 10 (1): 114–31.

————. 2008. "'Desires of the heart' and laws of the marketplace: Money and poetics, past and present, in Highland Madagascar." *Research in Economic Anthropology* 27: 149–85.

Kwon, Heonik. 2008. *Ghosts of war in Vietnam*. Cambridge: Cambridge University Press.

Lagercrantz, Sture. 1944. "The sacral king in Africa." *Ethnos* 9 (3/4): 118–40.

————. 1950. *Contribution to the ethnography of Africa*. Studia Ethnographica Upsaliensia 1. Uppsala: Uppsala universitet. Institutionen för allmän och jämförande etnografi.

Laman, Karl. E. 1953–68. *The Kongo II*. Studia Ethnographica Upsaliensa. 4 vols. Uppsala: Almqvist & Wiksell.

Lambek, Michael. 2002. *The weight of the past: living with history in Mahajanga, Madagascar*. New York: Palgrave Macmillan.

Lan, David 1985. *Guns and rain: Guerillas and spirit mediums in Zimbabwe*. London: James Currey.

Lancaster, Chet S. 1989. "Political structure and ethnicity in an immigrant society: The Goba of the Zambezi." In *The African frontier: The reproduction of traditional African societies*, edited by Igor Kopytoff, 101–21. Bloomington: Indiana University Press.

Lang, Andrew. (1898) 1968. *The making of religion*. New York: AMS Press.

Larson, Pier. 1995. "Multiple narratives, gendered voices: Remembering the past in Highland Central Madagascar." *The International Journal of African Historical Studies* 28: 295–325.

————. 1996. "Desperately seeking 'the Merina' (Central Madagascar): Reading ethnonyms and their semantic fields in African identity histories." *Journal of Southern African Studies* 22 (4): 541–60.

————. 2000. *History and memory in the age of enslavement: Becoming Merina in Highland Madagascar, 1770–1822*. Portsmouth, NH: Heinemann.

————. 2001. "Austronesian mortuary ritual in history: Transformations of secondary burial (Famadihana) in Highland Madagascar." *Ethnohistory* 48 (1/2): 123–55.

————. 2006. "Review of Gwyn Campbell, *An economic history of imperial Madagascar, 1750–1895: The rise and fall of an island empire*. Cambridge: Cambridge University Press, 2008." *American Historical Review* 111 (5): 1644–45.

Law, Robin. 1985. "Human sacrifice in pre-colonial West Africa." *African Affairs* 84: 53–87.

Lawrence, Peter, and Mervyn J. Meggitt. 1965. "Introduction." In *Gods, ghosts, and men in Melanesia: Some religions of Australian New Guinea and the New Hebrides*, edited by Peter Lawrence and Mervyn J. Meggitt, 1–26. Melbourne: Oxford University Press.

Le Petit, Père Maturin. 1848. "The massacre by the Natchez (1729)." In *The early Jesuit missions in North America*, Vol. 1, edited by William Ingraham, 265–312. New York: Wiley.

Leach, Edmund. 1954. *Political systems of Highland Burma*. Cambridge, MA: Harvard University Press.

———. 1961. *Rethinking anthropology*. London: Cunningham & Sons.

———. 1976. *Culture and communication: The logic by which symbols are connected*. Cambridge: Cambridge University Press.

———. 2011. "Kingship and divinity: The unpublished Frazer Lecture, Oxford, 28 October 1982." *HAU: Journal of Ethnographic Theory* 1: 279–93.

Lehman, F. K. 1967. "Burma: Kayah societies as a function of the Shan–Burma–Karen context." In *Contemporary change in traditional societies*, Vol. II: *Asian rural societies*, edited by Julian H. Steward, 1–104. Urbana: University of Illinois Press.

Lejamble, G. 1972. "Les fondements du pouvoir royal en Imerina." *Bulletin du Madagascar* 311: 349–67.

Levi, Doro. 1944. "The novel of Ninus and Semiramis." *Proceedings of the American Philosophical Society* 87 (5): 420–28.

Levi, Jean. 1977. "Le mythe de l'âge d'or et les théories de l'évolution en Chine ancienne." *L'Homme* 17 (1): 73–103.

Lévi-Strauss, Claude. 1952. *Race and history*. New York: UNESCO.

———. 1966. *The savage mind*. Chicago: University of Chicago Press.

———. 1971. "Rapports de symétrie entre rites et mythes de peuples voisins." In *The translations of culture: Essays for E. E. Evans-Pritchard*, edited by T. O. Beidelman, 161–78. London: Tavistock.

———. 1990. *Mythologiques*, Vol. 4: *The naked man*. Translated by John Weightman and Doreen Weightman. Chicago: University of Chicago Press.

———. 1995. *The story of Lynx*. Translated by Catherine Tihanyi. Chicago: University of Chicago Press.

Lieberman, Victor. 2003. *Strange parallels: Southeast Asia in global context, c.800–1830*, Vol. 1: *Integration on the mainland*. Cambridge: Cambridge University Press.

Lienhardt, R. Godfrey 1952. "The Shilluk of the Upper Nile." In *African worlds*, edited by Daryl Forde, 138–63. Oxford: Oxford University Press.

———. 1953. "Nilotic kings and their mothers' kin." *Africa* 25 (1): 29–42.

———. 1961. *Divinity and experience: The religion of the Dinka*. Oxford: Clarendon Press.

———. 1979. "Getting your own back: Themes in Nilotic myth." In *Studies in social anthropology*, edited by J. H. M. Beattie and R. Godfrey Lienhardt, 213–37. Oxford: Clarendon Press.

Lincoln, Bruce. 2007. *Religion, empire, and torture: The case of Achaemenian Persia, with a postscript on Abu Ghraib*. Chicago: University of Chicago Press.

Liverani, Mario, ed. 1993. *Akkad, the first world empire: Structure, ideology, traditions.* Padua: Sargon srl.

Llewellyn, K. M., and E. Adamson Hoebel. 1941. *The Cheyenne way: Conflict and case law in primitive jurisprudence.* Norman: University of Oklahoma Press.

Loeb, Edwin M. 1926. "Pomo folkways." *University of California Publications in American Archaeology and Ethnology* 19: 149–405.

———. 1931. "The religious organizations of north-central California and Tierra del Fuego." *American Anthropologist* (N.S.) 33 (4): 517–56.

———. 1932. "The Western Kuksu Cult." *University of California Publications in American Archaeology and Ethnology* 31 (1): 1–137.

———. 1933. "The Eastern Kuksu Cult. *University of California Publications in American Archaeology and Ethnology* 33 (2): 139–231.

Lombard, Jacques. 1965. *Structures de type "feodal" en Afrique noire: Étude des dynamismes internes et des relations sociales chez les Bariba du Dahomey.* Paris: Mouton.

Lommel, Andreas. (1952) 1997. *The Unambal: A tribe in Northwest Australia.* Carnarvon Gorge, Queensland: Takarakka Nowam Kas Publications.

Lorenz, Karl G. 1997. "A re-examination of Natchez sociopolitical complexity: A view from the grand village and beyond." *Southeastern Archaeology* 16 (2): 97–112.

———. 2000. "The Natchez of Southwest Mississippi." In *Indians of the Greater Southeast: Historical archaeology and ethnohistory*, edited by Bonnie G. McEwan, 142–77. Gainesville: University Press of Florida.

Lovejoy, Arthur O., and George Boas. 1935. *Primitivism and related ideas in antiquity.* Baltimore: Johns Hopkins University Press.

Lowie, Robert H. 1909. *The Assiniboine.* Anthropological Papers of the American Museum of Natural History IV. New York: The Trustees.

———. 1917. *Notes on the social organization and customs of the Mandan, Hidatsa and Crow Indians.* Anthropological Papers of the American Museum of Natural History XXI (2). New York: The Trustees.

———. 1927. *The origin of the state.* New York: Harcourt, Brace & Company.

———. 1948a. *Social organization.* New York: Rinehart.

———. 1948b. "Some aspects of political organization among the American aborigines." *Journal of the Royal Anthropological Institute of Great Britain and Ireland* 78 (1/2): 11–24.

MacGaffey, Wyatt. 1970. *Custom and government in Lower Congo.* Berkeley: University of California Press.

———. 1974. "Oral tradition in Central Africa." *International Journal of African Historical Studies* 7: 417–26.

———. 1976. "African history, anthropology, and the rationality of natives." *History in Africa* 5: 101–20.

———. 1981. "African ideology and belief: A survey." *African Studies Review* 24: 227–74.

———. 1986. *Religion and society in Central Africa.* Chicago: University of Chicago Press.

———. 2000. *Kongo political culture: The conceptual challenge of the particular.* Bloomington: Indiana University Press.

———. 2003. "Crossing the river: Myth and movement in Central Africa." International Symposium, *Angola on the move: Transport routes, communication, and history*, Berlin, September 24–26. https://www.zmo.de/angola/Papers/MacGaffey_(29-03-04).pdf.

———. 2005. "Changing representations in Central African history." *Journal of African History* 2: 189–207.

MacLeod, William Christie. 1924. "Natchez political evolution." *American Anthropologist* 26: 201–29.

———. 1933. "Mortuary and sacrificial anthropophagy on the Northwest Coast of North America and its culture-historical sources." *Journal de la Société des américanistes* (N.S.) 25 (2): 335–66.

———. 1937. "Police and punishment among Native Americans of the Plains." *Journal of Criminal Law and Criminology* 28 (2): 181–201.

Mair, Lucy. 1934. *An African people in the twentieth century.* London: G. Routledge & Sons.

———. 1977. *African kingdoms.* Oxford: Clarendon Press.

Makarius, Linda. 1970. "Ritual clowns and symbolical behavior." *Diogenes* 69: 45–73.

Malek, Jaromír. 2000. "Old Kingdom rulers as 'local saints' in the Memphite area during the Middle Kingdom." In *Abusir and Saqqara in the year 2000*, edited by Miroslav Bárta and Jaromír Krejčí, 241–58. Prague: Academy of Sciences of the Czech Republic, Oriental Institute.

Malinowski, Bronislaw. 1948. *Magic, science and religion and other essays.* Boston: Beacon Press.

Malkin, Irad. 1998. *The return of Odysseus: Colonization and ethnicity.* Berkeley: University of California Press.

Marsden, William. 1811. *The history of Sumatra.* London: J. McCreery.

Martin, Phyllis. 1972. *The external trade of the Loango Coast, 1576–1870.* Oxford: Oxford University Press.

Mason, Carol. 1964. "Natchez class structure." *Ethnohistory* 11 (2): 120–33.

Mathews. A. B. 1950. "The Kisra legend." *African Studies* 9 (3): 144–47.

Matthews, Thomas Trotter. 1881. *Notes of nine years' mission work in the Province of Voni-zongo, north west Madagascar.* London: Hodder & Stoughton.

Mauss, Marcel. (1925) 2016. *The gift: Expanded edition.* Translated by Jane I. Guyer. Chicago: Hau Books.

Mayeur, Nicolas. (1777) 1913. "Voyage dans le Sud et dans l'intérieure des terres et paticulièrement au pays d'Hancove (janvier à décembre 1777)." *Bulletin de l'Académie Malgache* 12 (1): 139–76.

———. (1793) 1913. "Voyage au pays d'Ancove (1785)." *Bulletin de l'Académie Malgache* 12 (2): 14–49.

Mbembe, Achille. 1992. "The banality of power and the aesthetics of vulgarity in the postcolony." *Public Culture* 4 (2): 1–30.

Meek, Charles Kingsley. 1931. *A Sudanese kingdom: An ethnographical study of the Jukun peoples of Nigeria.* London: Kegan Paul.

Meggitt, Mervyn J. 1965. "The Mae Enga of the Western Highlands." In *Gods, ghosts and men in Melanesia: Some religions of Australian New Guinea and the New Hebrides,* edited by Peter Lawrence and Mervyn J. Meggitt, 105–31. Melbourne: Oxford University Press.

Mercer, Patricia. 1971. "Shilluk trade and politics from the mid-seventeenth century to 1861." *Journal of African History* 12 (3): 407–26.

Merkur, Daniel. 1991. *Powers which we do not know: Gods and spirits of the Inuit.* Moscow: University of Idaho Press.

Milne, George. 2015. *Natchez Country: Indians, colonists, and landscapes of race in French Louisiana.* Athens: University of Georgia Press.

Mogenson, Hanne. 2002. "The resilience of *Juok*: Confronting suffering in Eastern Uganda." *Africa* 72 (2): 420–36.

Molet, Louis. 1976. "Conception, naissance et circoncision à Madagascar." *L'Homme* 16 (1): 33–64.

Moore, Jerry D. 2004. "The social basis of sacred spaces in the Prehispanic Andes: Ritual landscapes of the dead in Chimú and Inka societies." *Journal of Archaeological Method and Theory* 11 (1): 83–124.

Morgan, Lewis H. 1851. *League of the Ho-dé-no-sau-nee, or Iroquois.* New York: Rochester.

Morland-Simpson, H. F. 1888. "Ethnographical museums." *Archaeological Review* 2 (2): 73–90.

Morris, Ellen F. 2007. "Sacrifice for the state: First Dynasty royal funerals and the rites at Macramallah's rectangle." In *Performing death: Social analyses of funerary traditions in the ancient Near East and Mediterranean,* edited by Nicola Laneri, 15–38. Oriental Institute Seminars 3. Chicago: Oriental Institute of the University of Chicago.

―――. 2014. "(Un)dying loyalty: Meditations on retainer sacrifice in ancient Egypt and elsewhere." In *Violence and civilization: Studies of social violence in history and prehistory*, edited by Roderick Campbell, 61–93. Oxford: Oxbow.

Motolinia, Toribo de Benavente. 1951. *Motolinia's history of the Indians of New Spain.* Translated by Francis Borgia Steck. Washington, DC: Academy of American Franciscan History.

Muhs, Brian. 2016. *The ancient Egyptian economy: 3000–30 BCE.* Cambridge: Cambridge University Press.

Muller, Jean-Claude. 1980. *Le Roi bouc émissaire: Pouvoir et rituel chez les Rukuba du Nigéria Centrale.* Paris: L'Harmattan.

―――. 1981. "Divine kingship in chiefdoms and states: A single ideological model." In *The study of the state*, edited by Henri J. M. and Peter Skalník, 239–50. The Hague: Mouton.

―――. 1990. "Transgression, rites de rajeunissement et mort culturelle chez les Jukun et les Rukuba (Nigeria Central)." *Systèmes de pensée en Afrique noire*, Vol. 10: *Chefs et rois sacrés*, edited by Luc de Heusch, 49–67. Paris: École Pratique des Hautes Études.

Mumford, Lewis. 1967. *The myth of the machine, Vol. I: Technics and human development.* New York: Harcourt Brace Janovich.

Munn, Nancy. 1986. *Walbiri ethnography: Graphic representation and cultural symbolism in a Central Australian society.* Chicago: University of Chicago Press.

Munro, P. 1918. "Installation of the ret of the Chol (King of the Shilluks)." In *Pagan tribes of the Nilotic Sudan*, edited by Charles Gabriel Seligman and Brenda Z. Seligman, 541–47. London: Routledge.

Myers, Fred R. 1986. *Pintup Country, Pintup self: Sentiment, place, and politics among Western Desert Aborigines.* Washington, DC: Smithsonian Institution Press.

Nadel, S. F. 1935. "The king's hangman: A judicial organization in Central Nigeria." *Man* 35: 129–132.

―――. 1942. *A black Byzantium: The kingdom of Nupe in Nigeria.* London: Oxford University Press.

Nakano Glenn, Evelyn. 2012. *Forced to care: Coercion and caregiving in America.* Cambridge. MA: Harvard University Press.

Necipoğlu, Gülru. 1991. *Architecture, ceremonial, and power: The Topkapi Palace in the fifteenth and sixteenth centuries.* Cambridge, MA: MIT Press.

Needham, Joseph. 1954. *Science and civilization in China*, Vol. I: *Introductory orientations.* Cambridge: Cambridge University Press.

Neumann, Christopher K. 2006. "Political and diplomatic developments." In *Cambridge history of Turkey*, Vol. III: *The Later Ottoman Empire, 1603–1839*, edited by Suraiya N. Faroqhi, 44–67. Cambridge: Cambridge University Press.

Newman Philip. 1965. *Knowing the Gururumba*. New York: Holt, Reinhart & Winston.

Nichols, Andrew. 2008. "The complete fragments of Ctesias of Cnidus: Translation and commentary with an introduction." Doctoral dissertation, University of Florida.

Nicholson, H. B. 2001. *Topiltzin Quetzalcoatl: The once and future Lord of the Toltecs*. Boulder: University Press of Colorado.

Nimuendaju, Curt. (1939) 1967. *The Apinaye*. Oosterhout: Anthropological Publications.

Nisbet, Robert. 1980. *A history of the idea of progress*. New York: Basic Books.

Norbeck, Edward. 1961. *Religion in primitive society*. New York: Harper & Row.

Nyaba, Peter Adwok. 2006. "The Chollo predicament: The Threat of Physical Extermination and Cultural Extinction of a People." Nairobi: Larjour Consultancy. http://sudaneseonline.com/board/1/msg/THE-CHOLLO-PREDICAMENT-1023007079.html.

Oakley, Francis. 2006. *Kingship: The politics of enchantment*. London: Blackwell.

———. 2010. *Empty bottles of gentilism: Kingship and the divine in late antiquity and the early Middle Ages*. New Haven: Yale University Press.

Obayemi, Ade M. 1992. "The Yoruba- and Edo-speaking peoples and their neighbours." In *History of Africa*, Vol. 1, edited by J. F. A. Ajayi and Michael Crowder, 250–322. Harlow: Longman.

Oberg, K. 1940. "The kingdom of Ankole in Uganda." In *African political systems*, edited by Meyer Fortes and E. E. Evans-Pritchard, 121–64. London: Oxford University Press.

Ogot, B. A. 1961. "The concept of *juok*." *African Studies* 20: 134–40.

———. 1964. "Kingship and statelessness among the Nilotes." In *The historian in Tropical Africa*, edited by Jan Vansina, Raymond Mauny, and L. V. Thomas, 294–99. London: Oxford University Press.

Okpewho, Isidore. 1998. *Once upon a kingdom: Myth, hegemony, and identity*. Bloomington: Indiana University Press.

Oliver, Lieutenant S. P. 1866. *Among the Malagasy: Sketches in the Provinces of Tamatave, Betanimena, and Ankova*. London: Day & Son.

Oliver, Roland. 1955. "The traditional histories of Buganda, Bunyoro, and Nkole." *Journal of the Royal Anthropological Institute* (N.S.) 85: 111–17.

Oosten, J. G. 1976. *The theoretical structure of the religion of the Netsilik and Iglulik*. Groningen: Rijksuniversiteit te Groningen.

Opler, M. E. 1938. "The sacred clowns of the Chiricahua and Mescalero Indians." *El Palacio* 44: 75–79.

Ottino, Paul. 1983. "Les Andriambahoaka malgaches et l'héritage indonésien." In *Les Souverains de Madagascar*, edited by Françoise Raison-Jourde, 71–96. Paris: Karthala.

———. 1986. *L'Étrangère intime: Essai d'anthropologie de la civilisation de l'ancien Madagascar*. Paris: Éditions des Archives Contemporaines.

———. 1993. "The mythology of the Highlands of Madagascar and the political cycle of the Andriambahoaka." In *Mythologies*, Vol. 2: *Asian mythologies*, edited by Yves Bonnefoy and Wendy Doniger, 961–76. Chicago: University of Chicago Press.

Overing, Joanna. 1983–84. "Elementary structures of reciprocity: A comparative note on Guianese, Central Brazilian, and North-West Amazonian socio-political thought." *Anthropologica* 59–62: 331–48.

———. 1989 "The aesthetics of production: The sense of community among the Cubeo and Piaroa." *Dialectical Anthropology* 14: 159–75.

Oyler, D. S. 1918a. "Nikawng and the Shilluk migration." *Sudan Notes and Records* 1: 107–15.

———. 1918b. "Nikawng's place in the Shilluk religion." *Sudan Notes and Records* 1: 283–301.

———. 1919. "The Shilluk's belief in the Evil Eye." *Sudan Notes and Records* 2: 122–37.

———. 1920a. "The Shilluk peace ceremony." *Sudan Notes and Records* 3: 296–99.

———. 1920b. "The Shilluk's belief in the good medicine man." *Sudan Notes and Records* 3: 110–16.

———. 1926. "Shilluk notes." *Sudan Notes and Records* 9: 57–68.

Packard, Randall M. 1981. *Chiefship and cosmology: An historical study of political competition*. Bloomington: Indiana University Press.

Pagels, Elaine. 1988. *Adam, Eve, and the serpent*. New York: Random House.

Paiva Manso, Visconde de. 1877. *Historia de Congo*. Lisbon: Typographie di Academia.

Park, George. 1990. "Making sense of religion by direct observation: An application of frame analysis." In *Beyond Goffman: Studies on communication, institution, and social interaction*, edited by Stephen Harold Riggins, 235–76. Berlin: Mouton de Gruyter.

Parker Pearson, Mike. 1999. *The archaeology of death and burial*. Texas A & M University Anthropology Series 3. College Station: Texas A & M University Press.

Parsons, Elsie Clews. 1929. *The social organization of the Tewa of New Mexico*. Menasha, WI: American Anthropological Association.

———. 1933. "Some Aztec and Pueblo parallels." *American Anthropologist* (N.S.) 35 (4): 611–31.

———. 1939. *Pueblo Indian religion*, Vol. 1. Chicago: University of Chicago Press.

Parsons, Elsie Clews, and Ralph L. Biels. 1939. "The sacred clowns of the Pueblo and Mayo-Yaqui Indians." *American Anthropologist* (N.S.) 36 (4): 491–514.

Paul, A. 1952 "The Mar of the Shilluk." *Sudan Notes and Records* 33: 165–66.

Pearse, John. 1899. "Women in Madagascar: Their social position, employments and influence." *Antananarivo Annual and Madagascar Magazine* 23: 262–76.

Peetz, Edith. 1951a. "Report of a visit to the shrine of Andriantsihanika." *Folklore* 42: 456–58.

———. 1951b. "A visit to Andrianambodilova, Ambohimiarina, Tananarive, on 1st Alakaosy." *Folklore* 42: 453–56.

Peirce, Leslie. 1993. *The imperial harem: Women and sovereignty in the Ottoman Empire.* Oxford: Oxford University Press.

Pelliot, Paul. 1903. "Le Fou-nan." *Bulletin de L'École Francaise de L'Exteme Orient* 3: 248–303.

Pemberton, John, III, and Furso J. Afolayau. 1996. *Yoruba sacred kingship*. Washington, DC: Smithsonian Institution Press.

Peregrine, Peter N. 1996. "Introduction: World systems theory and archaeology." In *Pre-Columbian world systems*, edited by Peter N. Peregrine and Gary M. Feinman, 1–10. Madison, WI: Prehistory Press.

Petri, Helmut. (1954) 2011. *The dying world in Northwest Australia.* Carlisle, Western Australia: Hesperian Press.

Piankoff, Alexandre. 1968. *The Pyramid of Unas*. Egyptian Religious Texts and Representations 5. Bollingen Series XL. Princeton, NJ: Princeton University Press.

Pigafetta, Filipio (1591) 1881. *A report on the kingdom of Congo and the surrounding countries, drawn on the writings and discoveries of the Portuguese, Duarte Lopez.* London: John Murray.

Pollock, Sheldon. 2009. *The language of the gods in the world of men: Sanksrit, culture, and power in premodern India.* Berkeley: University of California Press.

Powers, Stephen. 1877. *Tribes of California*. Berkeley: University of California Press.

Preaux, Jean-G. 1962 "La sacralité du pouvoir royal à Rome." *Le pouvoir et la sacré*, edited by Luc de Heusch. *Annales du Centre d'Étude des Religions* 1: 103–21.

Prou, Michel. 1987. *Malagasy "Un pas de plus": Vers l'histoire du "Royaume de Madagascar" au XIXe siècle*, Vol. I. Paris: Harmattan.

Provinse, John H. 1937. "The underlying sanctions of Plains Indian Culture." In *Social anthropology of North American tribes*, edited by Fred Eggan, 341–76. Chicago: University of Chicago Press.

Prytz-Johansen, Jørgen. 1954. *The Maori and his religion in its non-ritualistic aspects.* Copenhagen: I Kommission Hos, Ejnar Munksgaard.

Puett, Michael J. 2001. *The ambivalence of creation: Debates concerning innovation and artifice in early China*. Stanford: Stanford University Press.

———. 2002. *To become a god: Cosmology, sacrifice, and self-divinization in early China*. Cambridge, MA: Harvard University Press.

———. 2012. "Human and divine kingship in early China: Comparative perspectives." In *Religion and power: Divine kingship in the ancient world and beyond*, edited by Nicole Brisch, 207–20. Oriental Institute Seminars no. 4. Chicago: The Oriental Institute of the University of Chicago.

———. 2013. "Economies of ghosts, gods, and goods: The history and anthropology of Chinese temple networks." In *Radical egalitarianism: Local realities, global relations*, edited by Felicity Aulino, Miriam Goheen, and Stanley J. Tambiah, 91–100. New York: Fordham University Press.

Pumphrey, M. E. C. 1936 "Shilluk 'royal' language conventions." *Sudan Notes and Records* 20: 319–321.

———. 1941. "The Shilluk tribe." *Sudan Notes and Records* 24: 1–46.

Quigley, Declan. 1993. *The interpretation of caste*. Oxford: Clarendon Press.

———. 2000. "Scapegoats: The killing of kings and ordinary people." *Journal of the Royal Anthropological Institute* (N.S.) 6 (2): 237–54.

———. 2005. "Introduction: The character of kingship." In *The character of kingship*, edited by Declan Quigley, 1–23. Oxford: Berg.

Quimby, George. 1946. "Natchez social structure as an instrument of assimiliation." *American Anthropologist* 48: 134–36.

Rabary, Pasitera. 1910.

Rabeson Jacques. 1948. *Tantaran'ny Tsimiamboholahy: Ahitana ny vako-drazana famongatra, izay misy ny levenam-bola fitadidy*. Antananarivo: Imprimerie Tananarivienne.

Radcliffe-Brown, A. R. 1926. "The Rainbow-Serpent myth in South-east Australia." *Journal of the Royal Aanthropological Institute* 56: 19–25.

Radimilahy, C., S. Andriamampianina, S. Blanchy, J.-A. Rakotoarisoa, and S. Razafimahazo. 2006 "Lieux de culte autochtone à Antananarivo." In *Le dieux au service du people*, edited by Sophie Blanchy, Jean-Aimé Rakotoarisoa, Philippe Beaujard, and Chantal Radimilahy, 143–91. Paris: Karthala.

Radin, Paul. 1914. "Religion of the North American Indians." *Journal of American Folklore* 27: 355–73.

Rafamantanantsoa-Zafimahery, G. M. 1966. "La conseil du roi dans l'ancien organisation du royaume de l'Imerina." *Bulletin de l'Académie Malgache* 44: 137–45.

Raison Jean-Pierre. 1972. "Utilisation du sol et organisation de l'espace en Imerina ancienne." *Terre Malgache = Tony Malagasy* 13: 97–121.

————. 1984. *Les Hautes Terres de Madagascar et leurs confins occidentaux: Enracinement et mobilité des sociétés rurales.* 2 vols. Paris: Karthala.

Raison-Jourde, Françoise. 1976. "Les Ramanenjana: Une mise en cause populaire du christianisme en Imerina, 1863." *Asie du sud-est et le monde insulindien* VII (ii–iii): 271–93.

————. 1983a. "De la restauration des talismans royaux au baptême de 1869 en Imerina." In *Les Souverains de Madagascar: L'histoire royale et ses resurgences contemporaines,* edited by Françoise Raison-Jourde, 337–69. Paris: Karthala.

————. 1983b. "Introduction." In *Les Souverains de Madagascar: L'histoire royale et ses resurgences contemporaines,* edited by Françoise Raison-Jourde, 7–68. Paris: Karthala.

————, ed. 1983c. *Les Soverains de Madagascar: L'histoire royale et ses resurgences contemporaines,* pp. 337-69. Paris: Karthala.

————. 1991. *Bible et pouvoir à Madagascar au XIXe siècle: Invention d'une identité chrétienne et construction de l'Etat (1780–1880).* Paris: Karthala.

Rajemisa-Raolison, Régis. 1985. *Rakibolana Malagasy.* Fianarantsoa: Ambozatany.

Rakotomalala. 2011. *A migration from Indonesia to Madagascar: Arya Damar alias Andriantomara.* Alasora.

Rakotomanolo, Seth. 1981. *Ny foko manendy.* Mahitsy: Monastera Ambohimanjakarano.

Ralaimihoatra, Édouard. 1969. *Histoire de Madagascar.* Antananarivo: Hachette.

Ralaimihoatra, Gilbert. 1973. "Les premier rois d'Imerina et la tradition Vazimba." *Bulletin de l'Académie Malgache* 50 (2): 25–32.

————. 1974. "Généalogue des anciens rois Vazimba et Merina (du quatorziéme siècle au milieu du dix-septième siècle)." *Bulletin de l'Académie Malgache* 51 (1): 47–53.

Ralibera, Daniel. 1977. "Recherche sur la conversion de Ranavalona II." *Omaly sy Anio* 5: 302–12.

Ramilison, Emmanuel. 1952. *Ny loharanon'ny andriana Nanjaka teto Imerina: Andriantomaro-Andriamamilaza.* 2 vols. Ambatomitsangana: Imprimerie Ankehitriny.

Ramirez, José Fernando. 1903. *Histoire de l'origine des Indiens qui habitent la Nouvelle Espagne selon leurs traditions.* Paris: Leroux.

Randles, W. G. L. 1968. *L'Ancien royaume du Congo—des origines a la fin du XIXe siècle.* Paris: Mouton.

Randriamarosata, Pasteur. 1959. *Tantaran'Ambohitrimanjaka sy fiakarana.* Antananarivo: Imprimerie Mami.

Randrianja, Solofo, and Stephen Ellis. 2009. *Madagascar: A short history.* London: Hurst.

Raombana. 1980. *Histoires 1: La haute époque Merina, de la legende à l'histoire (des origines à 1870).* Edited by Simon Ayache. Fianarantsoa: Ambozontany.

———. 1994. *Histoires 2: Vers l'unfication de l'ile et la civilization nouvelle (1810–1828).* Edited by Simon Ayache, editor. Antananarivo: Ambozontany.

———. N.d. *Annales.* Manuscript preserved in the archives of the Académie Malgache, Antananarivo.

Rappaport, Roy A. 1967. *Pigs for the ancestors: Ritual in the ecology of a New Guinea people.* New Haven, CT: Yale University Press.

Rasamimanana, Dr. J., and L. Razafindrazaka. 1909. *Fanasoavana ny tantaran' ny Malagasy: Ny andriantompokoindrindra: Araka ny filazana nangonin' i D. J. Rasamimanana sy L. Razafindrazaka.* Ambohimalaza.

Rasamuel, David. 2007. *Fanongoavana: Une capitale princière malgache du XIVe siècle.* Antananarivo: Arguments.

Rasamuel, Maurice. 1947. *Ny tabataba eto Andrefan'ankaratra sy ny Zanak'antitra.* Antananarivo: Trano Printy FJKM Imarivolanitra.

———. 1948. *Ny menalamba tao Andrefan'Ankaratra 1895 sy 1896 sy ny Zanak'Antitra.* 3 vols. Antananarivo: Imprimerie Soarano.

Rasmussen, Knud. 1930. *Intellectual culture of the Hudson Bay Eskimos.* Report of the Fifth Thule Expedition, 1921–22, Vol. VII. Copenhagen: Gyldendalske Boghandel Nordisk Forlag.

———. 1931. *The Netsilik Eskimos: Social life and material culture.* Report of the Fifth Thule Expedition, 1921–22, Vol. VIII. Copenhagen: Gyldendalske Boghandel Nordisk Forlag.

Ratsimba, Antoine. *Tantaran'ny Zanak'Andrianetivola.* Arivonimamo: Family Notebook.

Rattray, R. S. 1932. *The tribes of the Ashanti hinterland.* 2 vols. Oxford: Clarendon Press.

Ravenstein, Enerst George, ed. 1901. *The strange adventures of Andrew Battell of Leigh in Angola and adjoining regions.* London: The Haklyut Society.

Ray, Benjamin C. 1991. *Myth, ritual and kingship in Buganda.* New York: Oxford University Press.

Razafiarison, Aina Andrianavalona. 2014. *Apports des traditions dans les successions royales Merina.* Paris: Harmattan.

Razafintsalama, Adolphe. 1981. *Les Tsimahafotsy d'Ambohimanga: Organisation familiale et sociale en Imerina (Madagascar).* Paris: SELAF.

Reefe, Thomas Q. 1981. *The rainbow and the kings: A history of the Luba Empire to 1891.* Berkeley: University of California Press

Régnon, Henry de. 1863. *Madagascar et le roi Radama II.* Paris: Toinon.

Renel, Charles. 1910. *Contes de Madagascar.* Paris: E. Leroux.

———. 1915. "Les amulettes malgaches: Ody et sampy." *Bulletin de l'Académie Malgache* (N.S.) 2: 31–279).

———. 1920. "Ancêtres et dieux." *Bulletin de l'Académie Malgache* (N.S.) 5: 1–261.

Riad, Mohamed. 1953. "Some observations of a fieldtrip among the Shilluk." *Wiener Volkerkundliche Mitteilungen* 3: 70–78.

———. 1959. "The divine kingship of the Shilluk and its origin." *Archiv für Völkerkunde* 14: 141–284.

Rice, Michael. 2003. *Egypt's making: The origins of ancient Egypt, 4000 BC–2000 BC.* London: Routledge.

Richards, Audrey I. 1940. "The political system of the Bemba tribe: North-Eastern Rhodesia." In *African political systems*, edited by Meyer Fortes and E. E. Evans-Pritchard, 83–120. London: Oxford University Press.

———. 1960. "The interlacustrine Bantu: General characteristics." In *East African chiefs: A study of political development in some Uganda and Tanganyika tribes*, edited by Audrey I. Richards, 27–40. New York: Praeger.

———. 1961. *Land, labour and diet in Northern Rhodesia: An economic study of the Bemba tribe.* London: Oxford University Press.

———. 1964. "Authority patterns in traditional Buganda." In *The king's men*, edited by Lloyd Fallers, 256–93. London: Oxford University Press.

———. 1968. "Keeping the king divine." *Proceedings of the Royal Anthropological Institute*: 23–35.

———. 1969. "General characteristics." In *East African chiefs: A study of political development in some Uganda and Tanganyika tribes*, edited by Audrey I. Richards, 27–40. New York: Praeger.

Richardson, John. 1885. *A new Malagasy–English dictionary.* Antananarivo: London Missionary Society.

Robbins, Joel. 1995. "Dispossessing the spirits: Christian transformations of desire and ecology among the Urapmin of Papua New Guinea." *Ethnology* 34: 211–24.

———. 1999. "This is our money: Modernism, regionalism, and dual currency in Urapmin." In *Money and modernity: State and local currencies in contemporary Melanesia*, edited by David Akins and Joel Robbins, 82–102. Pittsburgh: University of Pittsburgh Press.

———. 2004. *Becoming sinners: Christianity and moral torment in Papua New Guines.* Berkeley: University of California Press.

Roberts, Andrew, ed. 1968. *Tanzania before 1900.* Nairobi: East African Publishing House.

Rock, Joseph. 1947. *The ancient Na-Khu kingdom of Southwest China.* 2 vols. Harvard–Yenching Institute Monograph 8–9. Cambridge, MA: Harvard University Press.

Roscoe, John. 1911. *The Baganda: An account of their native customs and beliefs*. London: Macmillan.

———. 1915. *The Northern Bantu*. Cambridge: Cambridge University Press.

———. 1923a. *The Bakitara of Bunyoro*. Cambridge: Cambridge University Press.

———. 1923b. *The Banyankole*. Cambridge: Cambridge University Press.

Roscoe, John. 1933. *The Bakitara or Bunyoro*. Cambridge: Cambridge University Press.

Rostworowski de Diez Canseco, M. 1998. *History of the Inca realm*. Cambridge: Cambridge University Press.

Roth, H. Ling. 1903. *Great Benin: Its customs, art, and horrors*. Halifax: H. King and Sons.

Rousseau, Jean-Jacques. 1997. *The social contract and other political writings*. Edited by Victor Gourevitch. Cambridge: Cambridge University Press.

Roux, Georges. 1992. "Sémiramis la reine mystérieuse d'Orient." In *Initiation à l'Orient ancien: De Sumer à la Bible*, edited by Jean Bottéro, 194–203. Série Histoire 170. Paris: Éditions du Seuil.

———. 2001. "Semiramis: The builder of Babylon." In *Everyday life in ancient Mesopotamia*, edited by Jean Bottéro, 141–61. Translated by Andrea Nevill. Baltimore: Johns Hopkins University Press.

Rowe, John H. 1967. "What kind of a settlement was Inca Cuzco?" *Ñawpa Pacha* 5: 59–76.

Rowlands, Michael. 1993. "The good and bad death: Ritual killing and historical transformation in a West African kingdom." *Paideuma: Mitteilungen zur Kulturkunde* 39: 291–301.

Rutherford, Danilyn. 1998. "Love, violence, and foreign wealth: Knowledge and history in Biak, Irian Jaya." *Journal of the Royal Anthropological Institute* (N.S.) 4: 258–81.

———. 2003. *Raiding the land of the foreigners*. Princeton, NJ: Princeton University Press.

Ruud, Jørgen. 1960. *Taboo: A study of Malagasy beliefs and customs*. New York: Humanities Press.

Ryder, A. F. C. 1969. *Benin and the Europeans, 1485–1897*. London: Longman.

Sahagún, Bernadino de. 1953–82. *Florentine Codex: General history of the things of New Spain*. 12 vols. Translated by Arthur J. O. Anderson and Charles E. Dibble. School of American Research Monograph 14. Salt Lake City: School of American Research and University of Utah press.

Sahlins, Marshall. 1958. *Social stratification in Polynesia*. Seattle: University of Washington Press

———. 1981a. *Historical metaphors and mythical realities: Structure in the early history of the Sandwich Island Kingdom*. Ann Arbor: University of Michigan Press.

———. 1981b. "The stranger-king or Dumézil among the Fijians." *Journal of Pacific History* 16: 107–32.

———. 1983a. "Other times, other customs: The anthropology of history." *American Anthropologist* 85 (5): 517–44.

———. 1983b. "Raw women, cooked men, and other 'great things' of the Fijian Islands." In *The ethnography of cannibalism*, edited by Paul Brown and Donald Tuzin, 72–93. Washington, DC: Society for Psychological Anthropology.

———. 1985. *Islands of history*. Chicago: University of Chicago Press.

———. 1992. *Anahulu: The anthropology of history in the kingdom of Hawai'i*, Vol 1: *Historical ethnography*. Chicago: University of Chicago Press.

———. 2008. "The stranger-king or, elementary forms of the politics of life." *Indonesia and the Malay World* 36: 177–94.

———. 2010. "The whole is a part: Intercultural politics of order and change." In *Experiments in holism: Theory and practice in contemporary anthropology*, edited by Ton Otto and Nils Bubandt, 102–26. Oxford: Wiley-Blackwell.

———. 2011a. "The alterity of power and vice versa, with reflections on stranger-kings and the real-politics of the marvelous." In *Power in history: From medieval Ireland to the post-modern world*, edited by Anthony McElligot et al., 283–308. Dublin: Irish Academic Press.

———. 2011b. "Twin-born with greatness: The dual kingship of Sparta." *HAU: Journal of Ethnographic Theory* 1: 63–102.

———. 2012a. "Alterity and autochthony: Austronesian cosmographies of the marvelous." *HAU: Journal of Ethnographic Theory* 2: 131–60.

———. 2012b. *Waiting for Foucault, still*. Chicago: Prickly Paradigm Press.

———. 2013. *What kinship is—and is not*. Chicago: University of Chicago Press.

———. 2014 "Stranger-kings in general: The cosmo-logics of power." In *Framing cosmologies: The anthropology of worlds*, edited by Allen Abramson and Martin Holbraad, 137–63. Manchester: Manchester University Press.

Santos-Granero, Fernando. 1993. "From prisoner of the group to darling of the gods: An approach to the issue of power in South America." *L'Homme* XXXIII (2–4): 213–30.

Sather, Clifford. 1996. "'All threads are white': Iban egalitarianism reconsidered." In *Origins, ancestry and alliance: Explorations in Austronesian ethnography*, edited by James J. Fox and Clifford Sather, 73–112. Canberra: Department of Anthropology, The Australian National University.

Savaron, Charles. 1912. "Notes sur le Farihin-dRangita (marais de Rangita), Nord d'Imerimanjaka." *Bulletin de l'Académie Malgache* (N.S.) X: 373–77.

———. 1928. "Contribution à l'histoire de l'Imerina." *Bulletin de l'Académie Malgache* (N.S.) XI: 61–81.

———. 1931. "Notes d'histoire malgache." *Bulletin de l'Académie Malgache* (N.S.) XIV: 55–73.

Sayce, A. H. 1888. "The Legend of Semiramis." *The English Historical Review* 3 (9): 104–113.

Schafer, Edward H. 1963. *The golden peaches of Samarkand: A study of T'ang exotics.* Berkeley: University of California Press.

———. 1967. *The vermillion bird: T'ang images of the south.* Berkeley: University of California Press.

Schiefflin, Edward L. 2005. *The sorrow of the lonely and the burning of the dancers.* Second edition. New York: Palgrave.

Schmitt, Carl. (1922) 2005. *Political theology: Four chapters on the concept of sovereignty.* Translated by George Schwab. Chicago: University of Chicago Press.

Schnepel, Burkhard. 1986. "Five approaches to the theory of divine kingship and the kingship of the Shilluk of the Southern Sudan." Ph.D. thesis, Oxford, Bodleian Library.

———. 1988. "Shilluk royal ceremonies of death and installation." *Anthropos* 83: 433–52.

———. 1990. "Shilluk kingship: Power struggles and the question of succession." *Anthropos* 85: 105–24.

———. 1991. "Continuity despite and through death: Regicide and royal shrines among the Shilluk of Southern Sudan." *Africa* 61 (1): 40–70.

———. 1995. *Twinned beings: Kings and effigies in Southern Sudan, East India and Renaissance France.* Göteborg: Institute for Advanced Studies in Social Anthropology.

Schrauwers, Albert. 2004. "H(h)ouses, E(e)state and class: On the importance of capitals in central Sulawsi." *Bijdragen tot de Taal-, Land- en Volkenkunde* 160 (1): 72–94.

Schwartz, Peter Hammond. 1989. "'His Majesty the baby': Narcissism and royal authority." *Political Theory* 17 (2): 266–90.

———. 1990. "Rejoinder to Springborg." *Political Theory* 18 (4): 686–89.

Scott, James C. 2009. *The art of not being governed: An anarchist history of upland Southeast Asia.* New Haven, CT: Yale University Press.

Scubla, Lucien. 2002. "Hocart and the royal road to anthropological understanding." *Social Anthropology* 10 (3): 359–76.

———. 2003. "Roi sacré, victime sacrificielle et victime émissaire." *Revue du MAUSS* 22: 197–221.

———. 2005. "Sacred king, sacrificial victim, surrogate victim or Frazer, Hocart, Girard." In *The character of kingship*, edited by Declan Quigley, 38–62. Oxford: Berg.

Seligman, Adam, Robert Weller, Michael Puett, and Bennett Simon. 2008. *Ritual and its consequences: An essay on the limits of sincerity.* Oxford: Oxford University Press.

Seligman, Charles Gabriel. 1911. "The cult of Nyakang and the divine kings of the Shilluk." *Fourth Report of the Wellcome Tropical Research Laboratories*, Vol. B, General Science: 216–38.

———. 1931. "The religion of the pagan tribes of the White Nile." *Africa* 4 (1): 1–21.

———. 1934. *Egypt and Negro Africa: A study in divine kingship.* The 1933 Frazer Lecture. London: Routledge.

Seligman, Charles Gabriel, and Brenda Z. Seligman. 1932. "The Shilluk." In *Pagan tribes of the Nilotic Sudan*, edited by Charles Gabriel Seligman and Brenda Z. Seligman, 37–105. London: Routledge.

Sibree, James. 1880. *Madagascar: The great African island.* London: Trübner & Co.

———. 1889. "The oratory, songs, legends, and folktales of the Malagasy Part II." *Antananarivo Annual and Madagascar Magazine* 14: 171–81.

———. 1896. *Madagascar before the conquest: The island, the country, and the people.* London: T. Fisher Unwin.

———. 1897. "The Malagasy custom of 'brotherhood by blood.'" *Antananarivo Annual and Madagascar Magazine* 21: 1–6.

Simmel George. 1950. "The stranger. In *The sociology of Georg Simmel*, edited by Kurt H. Wolff, 402–8. New York: Free Press.

Simonse, Simon. 1992. *Kings of disaster: Dualism, centralism and the scapegoat king in the Southeastern Sudan.* Leiden: Brill.

———. 2005. "Tragedy, ritual and power in Nilotic regicide: The regicidal dramas of the Eastern Nilotes of Sudan in contemporary perspective." In *The character of kinghip*, edited by Declan Quigley, 67–100. Oxford: Berg.

Skeat, Walter William. 1900. *Malay magic.* London: Macmillan.

Skinner, Elliott P. 1964. *The Mossi of the Upper Volta: The political development of a Sudanese people.* Stanford: Stanford University Press.

Slater, Philip Eliot. 1968. *The glory of Hera: Greek mythology and the Greek family.* Boston: Beacon Press.

Smith, W. Robertson. 1887. "Ctesias and the Semiramis legend." *The English Historical Review* 2 (6): 303–17.

Smith, W. Stevenson. 1971. "The Old Kingdom in Egypt and the beginning of the First Intermediate Period." In *The Cambridge ancient History*, third edition, Vol. 1, Part 2: *Early history of the Middle East*, edited by I. E. S. Edwards, C. J. Badd, and N. G. L. Hammond, 145–207. Cambridge: Cambridge University Press.

Soury-Lavergne and de la Devéze (Pères). "La fête de la circoncision en Imerina (Madagascar): Autrefois et aujourd'hui." *Anthropos* 7 (2): 336–71.

———. 1913. "La Fête nationale du Fandroana en Imerina (Madagascar)." *Anthropos* 9 (2/3): 306–24.

Sousa Martins, Rui de. 1999. "Mito e historia no noroeste de Angola." *Arquipelago. Historia* (2nd series) III: 495–550.

Soustelle, Jacques. 1964. *Daily life of the Aztecs*. London: Pelican.

Southall, Aidan. (1956) 2004. *Alur society: A study in processes and types of domination*. Münster: International African Institute/LIT Verlag.

———. 1988. "The segmentary state in Africa and Asia." *Comparative Studies in Society and History* 30: 52–82.

———. 1989. "Power, sanctity and symbolism in the political economy of the Nilotes." In *Creativity of power: Cosmology and action in African society*, edited by William Arens and Ivan Karp, 183–222. Washington, DC: Smithsonian Institution.

Southwold, Martin. 1967. "Was the kingdom sacred?" *Muwazo* I: 17–23.

Speck, Frank. 1977. *Naskapi: The savage hunters of the Labrador Peninsula*. Norman: University of Oklahoma Press.

Spencer, Robert F. 1959. *The North Alaskan Eskimo: A study in ecology and society*. Smithsonian Institution Bureau of American Ethnology Bulletin 171. Washington, DC: Government Printing Office.

Springborg, Patricia. 1990. "'His Majesty is a baby?': A critical response to Peter Hammond Schwartz." *Political Theory* 18 (4): 673–85.

Stallybrass, Peter, and Allon White. 1986. *The politics and poetics of transgression*. Ithaca, NY: Cornell University Press.

Standing, Herbert F. 1887a. *The children of Madagascar*. London: Religious Tract Society.

———. 1887b. "The tribal divisions of the Hova Malagasy." *Antananarivo Annual and Madagascar Magazine* XI: 354–58.

Stanner, W. E. H. 1959–63. *On Aboriginal religion*. University of Sydney. Oceania Monograph no. 11.

Starkey, David. 1977. "Representation through intimacy: A study in the symbolism of monarchy and court office in early modern England." In *Symbols and sentiments: Cross-cultural studies in symbolism*, edited by Ioan Lewis, 187–224. London: Academic Press.

Stevens, Phillips. 1975. "The Kisra legend and the distortion of historical tradition." *Journal of African History* 16 (2): 185–200.

Steward, Julian H. 1931. "The ceremonial buffoon of the American Indian." *Papers of the Michigan Academy of Science, Arts and Letters* 14: 187–207.

Stewart, Marjorie H. 1993. *Borgu and its kingdoms: A reconstruction of a western Sudanese Polity*. Lewiston, NY: Edwin Mellen Press

Stoneman, Richard. 1995. "Oriental Motifs in the Alexander Romance." *Antichthon* 26: 95–113.

———. 2008. *Alexander the Great: A life in legend*. New Haven, CT: Yale University Press.

Strathern, Andrew. 1970. "The female and male cults of Mount Hagen." *Man* (N.S.) 5: 571–85.

———. 1993. "Great-men, leaders, big-men: The link of ritual power." *Journal de la Société des Océanistes* 97: 145–58.

Strathern, Andrew, and Marilyn Strathern. 1968. "Marsupials and magic: A study of spell symbolism among the Mbowamb." In *Dialectic in practical religion*, edited by E. R. Leach, 179–202. Cambridge: Cambridge University Press for the Department of Archaeology and Anthropology.

Strauss, Hermann. (1962) 1990. *The Mi-culture of the Mount Hagen people, Papua New Guinea*. Edited by Gabriele Stürzenhofecker and Andrew Strathern. Translated by Brian Shields. Pittsburgh Ethnology Monographs no. 13. Department of Anthropolgy, University of Pittsburgh.

Stromberg, Peter. 1990. "Elvis alive? The ideology of modern consumerism." *Journal of Popular Culture* 24 (3): 11–19.

Suriano, Matthew J. 2010. *The politics of dead kings: Dynastic ancestors in the Book of Kings and sncient Israel*. Forschungen zum Alten Testament 2. Reihe. Tübingen: Mohr Siebeck.

Swain, Tony. 1993. *A place for strangers: Toward a history of Australian Aboriginal being*. Cambridge: Cambridge University Press.

Swanton, John R. 1911. *Indian Tribes of the Lower Mississippi Valley and adjacent coast of the Gulf of Mexico*. Washington, DC: Smithsonian Museum Bureau of American Ethnology Bulletin 43.

———. 1912. "Sun worship in the southeast." *American Anthropologist* (N.S.) 30 (2): 206–13.

———. 1946. *Indians of the southeastern United States*. Washington, DC: Smithsonian Museum Bureau of American Ethnology Bulletin 147.

Szalc, Walter. 2012. "In search of the Water of Life: The Alexander Romance and Indian mythology." In *The Alexander Romance in Persia and the East*, edited by Richard Stoneman, Kyle Erickson, and Ian Netton, 327–38. Groningen: Bakuis Publishing.

Tambiah, Stanley Jeyaraja. 1976. *World conqueror and world renouncer: A study of Buddhism and polity in Thailand against a historical background*. Cambridge: Cambridge University Press.

———. 1984. *The Buddhist saints of the forest and the cult of amulets.* Cambridge: Cambridge University Press.

———. 1985. *Culture, thought, and social action: An anthropological perspective.* Cambridge MA: Harvard University Press.

———. 1987. *The Buddhist conception of universal king and its manifestations in South and Southeast Asia.* Kuala Lumpur: University of Malaya Press.

Tamuno, T. N. 1965. "Peoples of the Niger–Benue confluence." In *A thousand years of West African history*, edited by J. F. Ade Ajayi and Ian Espie, 201–11. Ibadan: Ibadan University Press.

Tanner, Marie. 1993. *The last descendant of Aeneus: The Hapsburgs and the mythic image of the emperor.* New Haven, CT: Yale University Press.

Tatje, Terrence, and Francis L. K. Hsu. 1969. "Variations in ancestor worship beliefs and their relation to kinship." *Southwestern Journal of Anthropology* 25 (2): 153–72.

Taylor, Keith 1993. "The early kingdoms." In *The Cambridge history of Southeast Asia*, Vol.2, edited by Nicholas Turling, 137–82. Cambridge: Cambridge University Press.

Taylor, Luke. 1990. "The Rainbow Serpent as visual metaphor in Western Arnhem Land." *Oceania* 60: 329–44.

Terray, Emmanuel. 1994. "Le pouvoir, le sang et la mort dans le royaume asante au XIXe siècle." *Cahiers d'études africaines* 34 (136): 549–61.

Tezozomoc, Alvaro. 1853. *Histoire du Mexique.* 2 vols. Paris: Jannet

Theuws, Jacques A. T. 1983. *World and word: Luba thought and literature.* St. Augustin: Verlag des Anthropos-Instituts.

Thompson, Edward J. 1928. *Suttee: A historical and philosophical enquiry into the Hindu rite of widow-burning.* London: George Allen & Unwin.

Thomson, W. P. G. 1948. "Further notes on the death of a reth of the Shilluk (1945)." *Sudan Notes and Records* 29: 151–60.

Thornton, John K. 1983. *The kingdom of Kongo: Civil war and transition, 1641–1718.* Madison University of Wisconsin Press.

———. 2001. "The origin and early history of the kingdom of Kongo, c. 1350–1550." *International Journal of African Historical Studies* 34 (1): 89–120.

Took, Jennifer. 2005. *A native chieftain in Southwest China: Franchising a Tai chieftaincy under the Tusi system of late imperial China.* Leiden: Brill.

Tooker, Elizabeth. 1963. "Natchez social organization: Fact or anthropological folklore?" *Ethnohistory* 10: 358–72.

Townsend, Richard Fraser. 1987. "Coronation at Tenochtitlan." In *The Aztec templo mayor*, edited by Elizabeth Hill Boone, 371–409. Washington, DC: Dumbarton Oaks Pre-Columbian Symposia and Colloquia.

Trigger, Bruce G. 1969. "The social significance of the diadems in the royal tombs at Ballana." *Journal of Near Eastern Studies* 28 (4): 255–61.

Turner, Victor. 1957. *Schism and continuity in an African society: A study in Ndembu village life*. Manchester: Manchester University Press.

———. (1969) 2008. *The ritual process: Structure and anti-structure*. New Brunswick, NJ: Aldine.

Turton, Andrew. 2000. "Introduction." In *Civility and savagery: Social identity in Tai states*, edited by Andrew Turton, 3–31. Richmond, Surrey: Curzon Press.

Tylor, Edward Burnett. 1903. *Primitive culture: Researches into the development of mythology, philosophy, religion, language, art, and custom*. Fourth edition, 2 vols. London: John Murray.

Udal, John O. 1998. *The Nile in darkness: Conquest and exploration, 1504–1862*. Norwich: Michael Russell.

Valentine, C. A. 1965. "The Lalkai of New Britain." In *Gods, ghosts, and men in Melanesia: Some religions of Australia New Guinea and the New Hebrides*, edited by Peter Lawrence and Mervyn J. Meggitt, 162–97. Melbourne: Oxford University Press.

Valeri, Valerio. 2000. *The forest of taboos: Morality, hunting, and identity among the Huaulu of the Moluccas*. Madison: University of Wisconsin Press.

Valette, Jean. 1962. *Études sur le règne de Radama Ier*. Antananarivo: Imprimerie Nationale.

———. 1979. "Radama I, the unification of Madagascar and the modernization of Imerina (1810–1828)." In *Madagascar in history: Essays from the 1970s*, edited by Raymond K. Kent, 168–96. Albany, NY: Foundation for Malagasy Studies.

van Dijk, Jacobus. 2007. "Retainer sacrifice in Egypt and Nubia." In *Studies in history and anthropology of religion*, Vol. 1: *The strange world of human sacrifice*, edited by Jan Bremmer, 135–55. Leuven: Peeters Publishers.

van Everbroeck, Nestor. 1961. *Mbomb'ipoku le seigneur à l'Abime: Histoire, croyances, organisation clanique, politique, judiciaire, vie familiale des Bolia, Séngele et Ntómb'é njálé*. 1961. Tervusen, Belgium: Musee royal de l'Afrique centrale.

van Wing, R. P. J. 1959. *Études Bakongo: Sociologie, religion et magie*. Léopoldville: Brouwer.

Vansina, Jan. 1985. *Oral tradition as history*. Madison: University of Wisconsin Press.

———. 1992. "Population movement and the emergence of new socio-political forms in Africa." In *General history of Africa*, Vol. V: *Africa from the sixteenth to eighteenth century*, edited by B. A. Ogot, 46–73. Berkeley: University of California Press for UNESCO.

Vernant, Jean-Pierre. 2006. *Myth and thought among the Greeks*. New York: Zone Books.

Vicedom, Georg F. 1977. *Myth and legends from Mount Hagen*. Port Moresby: Institute of Papua New Guinea Studies.

Vicedom, Georg F., and Herbert Tischner. 1943–48. *The Mbowamb: The culture of the Mount Hagen tribes in East Central New Guinea*. 3 vols. Translated by F. E. Rheinstein and E. Klestat. Xeroxed manuscript, Australian National University.

———. 1983. *The Mbowamb: The culture of the Mount Hagen tribes in East Central New Guinea*. Translated by Helen M. Groger-Wurm. University of Sydney. Oceania Monograph no. 25.

Viveiros de Castro, Eduardo. 1992. *From the enemy's point of view: Humanity and divinity in Amazonia*. Chicago: University of Chicago Press.

———. 2015. *The relative native: Essays on indigenous conceptual worlds*. Chicago: Hau Books.

von Glahn, Richard. 1987 *The country of streams and grottos: Settlement and civilizing of the Sjchuan frontier in Sung times*. Cambridge, MA: Council on East Asian Studies, Harvard University.

Wagley, Charles. (1947) 1983. *Welcome of tears: The Tapirape Indians of Central Brazil*. Prospect Heights, IL: Waveland Press.

Wagley, Charles, and Edwardo Galvao. (1949) 1969. *The Tenetehara Indians of Brazil: A culture in transition*. New York: AMS Press.

Walens, Stanley. 1981. *Feasting with cannibals: An essay on Kwakiutl cosmology*. Princeton, NJ: Princeton University Press.

Wall, L. Lewis. 1975. "Anuak politics, ecology, and the origins of Shilluk kingship." *Ethnology* 15: 151–62.

Wallerstein, Immanuel. 1976. *The modern world system*. New York: Academic Press.

Warner, W. Lloyd. (1937) 1964. *A black civilization: A social study of an Australian tribe*. New York: Harper Torchbooks.

Webster, J. N., B. A. Ogot, and J. P. Chretien. 1992. "The Great Lakes Region, 1500–1800." In *General history of Africa*, Vol V: *Africa from the sixteenth to the eighteenth century*, edited by B. A, Ogot, 776–827. Berkeley: University of California Press for UNESCO.

Weiner, Margaret. 1995. *Visible and invisible kingdoms: Power, magic and colonial conquest in Bali*. Chicago: University of Chicago Press.

Wengrow, David. 2006. *The archaeology of early Egypt: Social transformations in North-East Africa, 10,000 to 2650 BC*. Cambridge: Cambridge University Press.

Wengrow, David, and David Graeber. 2015. "Farewell to the 'childhood of man': Ritual, seasonality, and the origins of inequality." *Journal of the Royal Anthropological Institute* (N.S.) 21: 597–619.

Westermann, Dietrich. 1912. *Shilluk people: Their language and folklore*. Philadelphia: Board of Foreign Missions of the United Presbyterian Church of North America.

Weyer, Edward Moffat. 1932. *The Eskimos: Their environment and folkways*. New Haven, CT: Yale University Press.

Wheatcroft, Wilson. 1976. "The legacy of Afekan: Cultural symbolic interpretations of religion among the Tifalmin of New Guinea." Ph.D. dissertation, Department of Anthropology, University of Chicago.

White, Douglas R., George P. Murdock, and Richard Scaglion. 1971. "Natchez class and rank reconsidered." *Ethnology* 10 (4): 369–88.

White, John. 1874. *Te rou; Or, The Maori at home*. London: Low, Marston, Low, and Searle.

Whitman, William. 1947. *The Pueblo Indians of San Ildefonso: A Changing Culture* (No. 34). New York: Columbia University Press.

Willis, Roy G. 1968. "The Fipa." In *Tanzania before 1900*, edited by Andrew Roberts, 82–94. Nairobi: East African Publishing House.

———. 1981. *A state in the making: Myth, history and social transformation in pre-colonial Ufipa*. Bloomington: Indiana University Press.

Wilson, John A. (1946) 1977. "Egypt." In *The intellectual adventure of ancient man: An essay on speculative thought in the ancient Near East*, H. Frankfort, H. A. Frankfort, John A. Wilson, Thorkild Jacobsen, and William A. Irwin, 31–124. Chicago: University of Chicago Press.

Wilson, Monica. 1950. "Nyakyusa kinship." In *African systems of kinship and marriage*, edited by A. R. Radcliffe-Brown and Daryll Forde, 111–39. London: Oxford University Press.

———. 1951. *Good company: A study of Nyakyusa Age villages*. London: Oxford University Press.

———. 1959a. *Communal rituals of the Nyakyusa*. London: Oxford University Press.

———. 1959b. *Divine kings and "the breath of men."* The 1959 Frazer Lecture. Cambridge: Cambridge University Press.

Winans, Edgar V. 1962. *Shambala: The constitution of a traditional state*. Berkeley: University of California Press.

Wissler, Clark. 1938. *The American Indian: An introduction to the anthropology of the New World*. Third edition. New York: Oxford University Press.

Wolters, O. W. 1986. *The fall of Srivijaya in Malay history*. Ithaca, NY: Cornell University Press.

———. 1999. *History, culture, and religion in Southeast Asian perspectives*. Ithaca, NY: Southeast Asia Publications, Cornell University.

Wood, Ellen Meiskins. 2002. *The origin of capitalism: A larger view.* London: Verso.

Woolf, Greg. 2002. "Divinity and power in ancient Rome." In *Religion and power: Divine kingship in the ancient world and beyond*, edited by Nicole Brisch, 243–60. Oriental Institute Seminars no. 4. Chicago: The Oriental Institute of the University of Chicago.

Worms, Ernest A., and Helmut Petri, eds. 1994. *Australian Aboriginal religions.* Kensington, NSW: Helen Yubu Missological Series no. 5

Wrigley, Christopher. 1996. *Kingship and state: The Buganda dynasty.* Cambridge: Cambridge University Press.

Yaya, Isabel. 2015. "Sovereign bodies: Ancestor cult and state Legitimacy among the Incas." *History and Anthropology* 26 (5): 639–60.

Young, Michael W. 1966. "The divine kingship of the Jukun: A re-evaluation of some theories." *Africa* 36: 135–56.

Zahan, Dominique. 1961. "Pour une histoire des Mossi du Yatenga." *L'Homme* 1: 5–22.

———. 1967. "The Mossi kingdom." In *West African kingdoms in the nineteenth century*, edited by Daryll Forde and P. M. Kaberry, 152–78. Oxford: Oxford University Press.

Zuidema, Reiner Tom. 1964. *The Ceque system of Cuzco: The social organization of the capital of the Inca.* Leiden: Brill.

———. 1989. "The moieties of Cuzco." In *The attraction of opposites: Thought and society in the dualist mode*, edited by David Maybury-Lewis and Uri Almagor, 255–75. Ann Arbor: Univerity of Michigan Press.

———. 1990. "Dynastic structures in Andean cultures." In *The northern dynasties: Kingship and statecraft in Chimor*, edited by Michael E. Mosely and Alana Cordy-Collins, 489–505. Washington, DC: Dumbarton Oaks Pre-Columbian Symposia and Colloquia.

Subject Index

Name Index

Ethnonym Index

HAU Books is committed to publishing the most distinguished texts in classic and advanced anthropological theory. The titles aim to situate ethnography as the prime heuristic of anthropology, and return it to the forefront of conceptual developments in the discipline. HAU Books is sponsored by some of the world's most distinguished anthropology departments and research institutions, and releases its titles in both print editions and open-access formats.

www.haubooks.com

Supported by

Hau-N. E. T.
Network of Ethnographic Theory

University of Aarhus – EPICENTER (DK)
University of Amsterdam (NL)
Australian National University – Library (AU)
University of Bergen (NO)
Brown University (US)
California Institute of Integral Studies (US)
University of Campinas (BR)
University of Canterbury (NZ)
University College London (UK)
University of Cologne – The Global South Studies Centre (DE)
and City Library of Cologne (DE)
University of Colorado Boulder Libraries (US)
Cornell University (US)
University of Edinburgh (UK)
The Graduate Institute – Geneva Library (CH)
University of Groningen (NL)
Harvard University (US)
The Higher School of Economics in St. Petersburg (RU)
Humboldt University of Berlin (DE)
Indiana University Library (US)
Johns Hopkins University (US)
University of Kent (UK)
Lafayette College Library (US)
London School of Economics and Political Science (UK)
Institute of Social Sciences of the University of Lisbon (PL)
Ludwig Maximilian University of Munich (DE)
University of Manchester (UK)
The University of Manchester Library (UK)
Max-Planck Institute for the Study of Religious and Ethnic
Diversity at Göttingen (DE)
Musée de Quai Branly (FR)
Museu Nacional – UFRJ (BR)
Norwegian Museum of Cultural History (NO)
University of Oslo (NO)
University of Oslo Library (NO)
Princeton University (US)
University of Rochester (US)
SOAS, University of London (UK)
University of Sydney (AU)
University of Toronto Libraries (CA)

www.haujournal.org/haunet